MORE ADVANCED PRAISE FOR
DEFENDING THE WEST

"This is a dazzling masterwork, a tour de force of beauty, scholarship, and passionate clarity. This book documents that nearly every idea—nay almost every sentence—that Edward Said has written is deliberately false. Said is the master of the Big Lie. Ibn Warraq's landmark book successfully challenges the hijacking of the Western academy and intellectual imagination that Said and his followers have perpetrated. Ibn Warraq creates a portrait of the West that is, in turn, a vigorous reminder of who we are and what our values have meant to the entire world. It should be mandatory reading in every university and should find its way onto every citizen's bookshelf, for it provides the best and most bracing self-defense we can muster against the anti-Western diatribes that pass for received wisdom."

—Phyllis Chesler
Emerita professor of psychology and women's studies
City University of New York
Author of thirteen books including the international best seller
Women and Madness, *The New Anti-Semitism*, and *Death of Feminism*

"This is a far braver book than Edward Said's famous Orientalism—and intellectually a more honest one. It deserves at least as much attention and should be required reading for every student of history."

—Charles Allen
Author of *The Buddha and the Sahibs* and *God's Terrorists*

"Ibn Warraq's magisterial critique of Edward Said's malicious and prodigiously mischievous book shows that the late 'professor of terror' was prone to violence in his intellectual as much as in his political pronouncements. But *Defending the West* teaches by example as much as by direct criticism, for its vast erudition and sweet reasonableness represent the condition to which all scholarship should aspire."

—Edward Alexander
Emeritus professor of English, University of Washington

"Edward Said died in 2003. This book buries him. With extraordinary learning and insight, Ibn Warraq utterly destroys Said and the Saidists, taking apart one of the most prevalent and destructive 'intellectual' movements of recent years. This book is primarily not an attack but a defense, a defense of the West against its opponents and haters. As the war for ideas rages, there have been few books as brilliant as this one, and none more important."

—Douglas Murray
Director of the Centre for Social Cohesion in London
Best-selling author of *Bosie: A Biography of Lord Alfred Douglas*

"An impressive, urgently necessary, and delightfully learned guide to rediscovering the West—and saving it, too."

—Diana West
Author of *The Death of the Grown-Up: How America's Arrested Development Is Bringing Down Western Civilization*

"For decades Edward Said enjoyed the best that Western academic life had to offer—international celebrity, plaudits, honors, and fame beyond the wildest dreams of most professors—while constantly bashing the history, values, and policies that have made this privileged existence possible. In *Defending the West*, the eminent intellectual Ibn Warraq exposes with razor-sharp precision the hypocrisy of Said's writings as well as the perverted academic culture that has made his great success possible. With this important new book Ibn Warraq has once and for all dispatched *Orientalism* to the dustbin of history."

—Efraim Karsh
Head of Mediterranean Studies at the University of London
Author of *Empires of the Sand* (with Inari Karsh) and
Islamic Imperialism: A History

Defending the
west

DEFENDING THE *west*

A Critique of Edward Said's *Orientalism*

IBN WARRAQ

Prometheus Books
59 John Glenn Drive
Amherst, New York 14228-2119

Published 2007 by Prometheus Books

Inquiries should be addressed to
Prometheus Books
59 John Glenn Drive
Amherst, New York 14228–2119
VOICE: 716–691–0133, ext. 210
FAX: 716–691–0137
WWW.PROMETHEUSBOOKS.COM

11 10 09 08 07   5 4 3 2 1

Library of Congress Cataloging-in-Publication Data

Ibn Warraq.
Defending the West : a critique of Edward Said's *Orientalism* / Ibn Warraq.
p. cm.
Includes bibliographical references and index.
ISBN 978–1–59102–484–2
1. Said, Edward W. *Orientalism*. 2. Orientalism. 3. Asia—Study and teaching. 4. Middle East—Study and teaching. 5. East and West. I. Title.

DS12.S243I26 2007
950.072—dc22

2007022518

Printed in the United States on acid-free paper

CONTENTS

For E

I'm a hostage. I'm maroonded.
But I'm in Paris with you.

—From *In Paris with You*, James Fenton

Propter studium sapientiae absolutum.[1]

—Roger Bacon (c.1214–94)

It is futile to condemn several centuries of European expansion, absurd to include under the same malediction Christopher Columbus and [Hubert] Lyautey.[2] The era of colonialisms is over, one must just acknowledge it and shoulder the consequences . . . .

It is fitting for a nation long in tradition and with a strong sense of honour to find the courage to denounce its own errors. But it should not forget all the reasons it could still have for self-esteem. In any case it is dangerous to ask it to confess that it alone was guilty, and to doom it to perpetual penitence.

—Albert Camus, *Chroniques Algériennes 1939–1958*[3]

The predicament of Western civilization is that it has ceased to be aware of the values which it is in peril of losing.

—Arthur Koestler

PREFACE

I originally planned the present work to serve as an anthology of both primary sources and articles by scholars who have replied to, taken issue with parts of, and possibly even refuted in their totality the arguments of Edward Said as presented principally in *Orientalism*, but also in *Culture and Imperialism*. The primary sources were to be prefaced with introductions that would have provided the necessary background to the controversies and the arguments engendered by Said's two most influential works.

In the end, I felt that Said's arguments could only be adequately addressed and refuted against the background of a more general presentation of salient aspects of Western civilization. I abandoned the idea of an annotated anthology. Instead I have identified three of the main themes that run through the history of the West. Since I still wished the work to serve as a source book for a general audience, I have retained many of the quotations from primary sources in the main body of my text: Homer and Aeschylus, Plato and Aristotle, Cicero and Marcus Aurelius, Pico della Mirandola and Guillaume Postel, Sir William Jones and Lord Curzon; from the Greeks to the early Christians, from the Renaissance to the Enlightenment and up to the twentieth century. In the chapters on Orientalists in India, I have treated the writings of Indian scholars as primary sources, because they are essential to any argument that shows that Orientalists were motivated primarily by disinterested intellectual curiosity and they made genuine contributions to our knowledge of India that were recognized and appreciated by Indians themselves.

The book begins with an extended essay based on another, originally written nearly a decade ago as a polemical attack minutely attentive to the text of Said's *Orientalism*. To a certain extent, I regret the tone of that earlier essay, but it still provides, I believe, a useful introduction to the errors and inadequacies of Said's work. After much hesitation I decided to leave it almost intact, since it had already acquired a life of its own and had been anthologized more than once. The only change I have allowed myself is the omission of the discussion of Aeschylus, now defended more robustly in part 2 of the present work.

Part 2 is organized chronologically and argues that three of the defining values of the Occident are rationalism, universalism, and self-criticism. Under rationalism, I include the notions of truth, objective knowledge, and intellectual curiosity. Under universalism, I include the idea of the unity of mankind, openness to "the Other" (a phrase I am reluctant to use, for its use implies a certain attitude or acceptance of certain mental clichés, but the realization that there is no easy and succinct way to get around it has led to my temporary verbal surrender): other ideas, other customs, other people; and under self-criticism the willingness to submit all of the West's traditions to rational scrutiny. Under curiosity, I include all those examples of disinterested study.

In part 2 I compare Western civilization with Islamic civilization, contrasting the value each civilization accords to these three themes. Islamic imperialism and Islam's participation in the slave trade, so often neglected, are contrasted with the Western institutions. The attitudes of people in the Far East, which, if exhibited by the white Western world, some might describe as "racist" and thus almost a taboo subject, are also discussed.

I am at pains to underline the constant to and fro of intellectual and artistic exchange between the Occident and Persia and India, and the Occident and Islam. Civilizations do not develop in isolation. The West has always been willing to learn from others. At one early and brief stage of its development, Islam was equally open, especially to Greek and Indian influences, and transmitted much to the West. But Islam closed its mind at a certain moment, and we are still suffering the consequences.

Such a comparative approach to the history of racism, imperialism, and slavery goes some way toward replying to Edward Said's strictures on the West. Said was able to intimidate Western intellectuals and to get away with so much simply because of his unchallenged ahistorical account, according to which only the West stood in the dock.

Since my arguments in part 2 are of a wider import, I do not always connect them to a precise passage in Said's *Orientalism.* I do not constantly come back to Said's text in the way I do in part 1. Nor do I entirely abandon Said, however; I have, for instance, some harsh observations on Said's misuse of the work of Richard W. Southern and Raymond Schwab.

Part 3 looks at Orientalism in Western music, literature, and painting. Only in the section on painting and the visual arts have I tried to give a full account, though still far from exhaustive, of the West's rendering of the Orient and Orientals—organized chronologically, beginning with Gentile Bellini and Vittore Carpaccio and the Venetians, through the Dutch, particularly Rembrandt, and the eighteenth-century Bosphorus school of painters. When seen against this background of the West's depictions of the Orient from the Renaissance onward, one realizes that the concerns of the Orientalist artists of the nineteenth century were neither unusual nor sinister. The nineteenth-century Orientalists were following a long-established tradition of sympathetic portrayal of the East and her people. And if we combine this artistic heritage with the West's more fundamental characteristic of intellectual curiosity and openness to others, nothing, surely, could be more natural than the development of nineteenth-century Orientalist art.

Many Orientalist paintings are vulgar and sentimental. I, however, have picked out Orientalist artists who merit consideration on aesthetic grounds (at least two of whom are recognized painters of genius: Rembrandt and Delacroix), and who at the same time are free from the kind of prejudice attributed indiscriminately to all Orientalists.

As in part 2, I have tried in part 3 to indicate throughout the influence of Eastern art on Western art, and vice versa. Rembrandt and Delacroix were both enchanted by Mogul miniatures. Mogul art was influenced by Mannerist paintings. Persian and Turkish miniatures also benefited from contact with Dutch artists. Western Orientalist painters influenced Turkish artists such as Osman Bey. In these instances, at least, Islam did not entirely close its doors to Western influence.

I use the term "Orientalism" in both the narrow sense as applied to the modern scholarly investigations, requiring a knowledge of Oriental languages and literature from the nineteenth century onward, and the wider sense, as applied to any consciously and seriously collected body of fact intended to increase the West's knowledge of the East. The term "Orientalist," when applied to artists, painters, composers, librettists, and even novelists, designates any artist who has taken the Orient and Orientals as suitable subjects for his works, however superficial or profound the rendering of the Orient or Orientals may eventually turn out. *Orientalism* in italics designates Edward Said's work.

Said and his followers can only cope with a Manichaean worldview—the Evil West versus the Rest, perceived or presented as morally superior, or good. I have tried to show that this is far from the whole truth: the history of the West shows an astonishing openness to "the Other" that is exhibited by no other civilization in history. The civilization that is at least open to "the Other" is Islam, which divides the world between believer and infidel, *Dar al-Islam* against *Dar al-Harb.* Muslims are taught to be indifferent to their own pre-Islamic past, or that of others, as merely an example of dismissible *Jāhiliyya* (ignorance or barbarism).

Said seems to use the term "Orientalist" for one who, on the whole, studies the Middle East, that is, the Muslim populations of the Middle East. The person who studies the Jews, or the Zoroastrians, is not in Edward Said's view an "Orientalist." For Said, the non-Muslims, and even non-Arabs, hardly exist, are occasionally mentioned, are never discussed or acknowledged as Orientals with a history and presence: there are no Copts, no Maronites, no Mandaeans, no Samaritans, no Assyrians, no Greek Orthodox Christians, no Chaldeans, no Berbers, and of course no Jews in the "Orient" for which Said means—must mean—the Middle East and North Africa, peopled with Arabs and Muslims on the one hand and "all the others" on the other hand. All of those others can never be part of "the Other" about whose fate, at the hands of Western Orientalists and imperialists, Said is so concerned.

In the section on Orientalist art, I provide an alternative account that flatly contradicts the one presented by Said and his followers. But Saidists do not deal with Western paintings and sculpture as objects of artistic analysis or connoisseurship, or aesthetic appreciation, but rather as carriers of meaning—political, even sinister meaning—that can be determined merely by looking at the subject matter itself in a rather crude manner. And I, in my refutation, have been forced to deal with works of art in the same reductive way. Unlike Said and others under his insidious influence, I am perfectly aware of how clumsy such a view of works of art is, good or bad. Such a view misses the point of a great work of art. Unfortunately, there is no other way to deal with the kind of charges made by Said and company without engaging in the same kind of reductionist analysis, albeit with different conclusions.

Early versions of this book in manuscript form were read and discussed with me by friends and colleagues and, as a result, I think, much improved. Hugh Fitzgerald, with his unerring sense for spotting sentimentality and my tendency to "gush," as he describes it, helped considerably with both the matter and the manner. He improved both beyond measure. Austin Dacey and Irfan Khawaja, with their philosophical acumen, saved me from shoddy arguments and made many suggestions that I have adopted. Keith Windschuttle gave much-needed encouragement just when I was having serious misgivings about my work. Professor Fred Siegel of Cooper Union for Science and Art in New York made helpful suggestions, and referred me to works that I had overlooked or had never even heard of. Dr. Elisabeth Puin read through part 3 on Orientalist art and provided me much-needed information on various aspects of Turkish and Persian art.

I thank them all for giving so much of their valuable time and advice, and for saving me from embarrassing errors. It is no formality to insist that any errors that do remain are entirely my own responsibility.

PART 1

EDWARD SAID AND THE SAIDISTS

Consider the following observations on the state of affairs in the contemporary Arab world:

> The history of the modern Arab world—with all its political failures, its human rights abuses, its stunning military incompetences, its decreasing production, the fact that alone of all modern peoples, we have receded in democratic and technological and scientific development—is disfigured by a whole series of out-moded and discredited ideas, of which the notion that the Jews never suffered and that the Holocaust is an obfuscatory confection created by the Elders of Zion is one that is acquiring too much—far too much—currency . . .
>
> . . . [T]o support Roger Garaudy, the French writer convicted earlier this year on charges of Holocaust denial, in the name of "freedom of opinion" is a silly ruse that discredits us more than we already are discredited in the world's eyes for our incompetence, our failure to fight a decent battle, our radical misunderstanding of history and the world we live in. Why don't we fight harder for freedom of opinions in our own societies, a freedom, no one needs to be told, that scarcely exists?[1]

It takes courage for an Arab to write self-criticism of this kind; indeed, without the personal pronoun "we," how many would have guessed that an Arab, let alone Edward Said, had written it? And yet, ironically, what makes self-examination for Arabs and Muslims, and especially criticism of Islam in the West, very difficult is the totally pernicious influence of Edward Said's *Orientalism.*[2] The latter work taught an entire generation of Arabs the art of self-pity—"were it not for the wicked imperialists, racists and Zionists, we would be great once more"—encouraged the Islamic fundamentalist generation of the 1980s, bludgeoned into silence any criticism of Islam, and even stopped dead the research of eminent Islamologists who felt their findings might offend Muslim sensibilities and who dared not risk being labeled "Orientalist." The aggressive tone of *Orientalism* is what I have called "intellectual terrorism," since it seeks to convince not by arguments or historical analysis, but by spraying charges of racism, imperialism, and Eurocentrism from a moral high ground; anyone who disagrees with Said has insult heaped upon him. The moral high ground is an essential element in Said's tactics. Since he believes his position is morally unimpeachable, Said obviously thinks he is justified in using any means possible to defend it, including the distortion of the views of eminent scholars, interpreting intellectual and political history in a highly tendentious way—in short, twisting the truth. But in any case, he does not believe in the "truth."

Said attacks not only the entire discipline of Orientalism, which is devoted to the academic study of the Orient and which Said accuses of perpetuating negative racial stereotypes, anti-Arab and anti-Islamic prejudice, and the myth of an unchanging, essential "Orient," but he also accuses Orientalists as being a group complicit with imperial power and holds them responsible for creating the distinction between Western superiority and Oriental inferiority, which they achieve by suppressing the voice of the "Oriental" and by their antihuman tendency to make huge, but vague, generalizations about entire populations that in reality consist of millions of individuals. In other words, much of what was written about the Orient in general, and Islam and Islamic civilization in particular, was false. The Orientalists also stand accused of creating "the Other"—the non-European, always characterized in a negative way, as, for example, passive, weak, and in need of civilizing by the advanced West (contrasting Western strength with Eastern weakness).

But "Orientalism" is also more generally "a style of thought based upon an ontological and epistemological distinction made between 'the Orient' and (most of the time) 'the Occident'" (p. 2). Thus, European writers of fiction, epics, travel, social descriptions, customs, and people are all accused of "Orientalism." In short, Orientalism is seen "as a Western style for dominating, restructuring, and having authority over the Orient." Said makes much of the notion of a discourse derived from Michel Foucault, who argued that supposedly objective and natural structures in society, which privilege some and punish others for nonconformity, are in fact "discourses of power." The putative "objectivity" of a discipline covered up its real nature; disciplines such as Orientalism participated in such discourses. Said continues, "[W]ithout examining Orientalism as a discourse one cannot possibly understand the enormously systematic discipline by which European culture was able to manage—even produce—the Orient politically, sociologically, militarily, ideologically, scientifically, and imaginatively during the post-Enlightenment period" (p. 3).

From Pretentiousness to Meaninglessness

There are, as I shall show, several contradictory theses buried in Said's impenetrable prose, with its endless postmodern jargon ("a universe of representative discourse," "Orientalist discourse" [p. 71]—and some kind editor really ought to have explained to Said the meaning of "literally" [pp. 19, 87, 93, 138, 179, 218, 307] and the difference between scatological and eschatological [p. 68]), and pretentious language that often conceals some banal observation, as when Said talks of "textual attitude" (pp. 92–93), when all he means is "bookish" or "bookishness." Tautologies abound, as in "the freedom of licentious sex" (p. 190).

Or take these comments:

> Thus out of the Napoleonic expedition there issued a whole series of textual children, from Chateaubriand's *Itinéraire* to Lamartine's *Voyage en Orient* to Flaubert's *Salammbô*, and in the same tradition, Lane's *Manners and Customs of the Modern Egyptians* and Richard Burton's *Personal Narrative of a Pilgrimage to al-Madinah and Meccah.* What binds them together is not only their common background in Oriental legend and experience but also their learned reliance on the Orient as a kind of womb out of which they were brought forth. If paradoxically these creations turned out to be highly stylized simulacra, elaborately wrought imitations of what a live Orient might be thought to look like, that by no means detracts from their strength of their imaginative conception or from the strength of European mastery of the Orient, whose prototypes respectively were Cagliostro, the great European impersonator of the Orient, and Napoleon, its first modern conqueror. (pp. 87–88)

What does Said mean by "out of the Napoleonic expedition there issued a whole series of textual children," except that these five very varied works were written *after* 1798? The pretentious language of textual children issuing from the Napoleonic expedition covers up this obvious fact. Perhaps there is a profound thesis hidden in the jargon, that these works were somehow influenced by the Napoleonic expedition, inspired by it, and could not have been written without it. But no such thesis is offered. This arbitrary group consists of three Frenchmen, two Englishmen—one work of romantic historical fiction, three travel books, and one detailed study of modern Egyptians. François-René de Chateaubriand's *Itinéraire* (1811) describes superbly his visit to the Near East; *Voyage en Orient* (1835) is Alphonse de Lamartine's impressions of Palestine, Syria, and Greece; *Salammbô* (1862) is Gustave Flaubert's novel of ancient Carthage; Edward William Lane's *Manners and Customs of the Modern Egyptians* (1836) is a fascinating firsthand account of life in Egypt, particularly Cairo and Luxor, written after years of residence there (first 1825–28, then 1833–35); Richard Burton's account of his audacious visit to Mecca was first published in three volumes between 1855 and 1856. Lane and Burton both had perfect command of Arabic, classical and colloquial, while the others did not, and both, particularly Lane, made contributions to Islamic studies, but not the three Frenchmen.

What do they conceivably have in common? Said tells us that what binds them together is not only "their common background in Oriental legend and experience but also their learned reliance on the Orient as a kind of womb out of which they were brought forth." What is the background of Oriental legend that inspired Burton or Lane? Was Flaubert's vivid imagination stimulated by "Oriental legend," and was this the same legendary material that inspired Burton, Lane, and Lamartine? "Learned reliance on the Orient as a kind of womb" is yet another example of Said's pompous way of saying the obvious, namely, that they were writing about an Orient of which they had some experience and intellectual knowledge.

Why are these disparate works "imitations"? Take Lane's and Burton's works: They are both highly accurate accounts based on personal, firsthand experience. They are not imitations of anything. James Aldridge in his study *Cairo* (1969) called Lane's account "the most truthful and detailed account in English of how Egyptians lived and behaved."[3] Burton's observations are still quoted for their scientific value in such scholarly works as F. E. Peters's *The Hajj*.[4] Said also says of Lane, "For Lane's legacy as a scholar mattered not to the Orient, of course, but to the institutions and agencies of his European society" (p. 164). There is no "of course" about it, Lane's *Arabic Lexicon* (5 vols; 1863–74) is still one of the first lexicons consulted by any Muslim scholars wishing to translate the Koran into English; scholars such as Maulana Muhammad Ali, who began his English translation in 1909 and refers constantly to Lane in his copious footnotes, as does A. Yusuf Ali in his 1934 translation. What is more, the only place where one can still buy a reasonably priced copy of Lane's indispensable work of reference is in Beirut—the edition published by the Librairie du Liban.

What profound mysteries are unraveled by Said's final tortuous sentence? Count Alessandro Cagliostro was a Sicilian charlatan who traveled in Greece, Egypt, Arabia, Persia, Rhodes, and Malta. During his travels he is said to have acquired considerable knowledge of the esoteric sciences, alchemy in particular. On his return to Europe, Cagliostro was involved in many swindles and seems to have been responsible for many forgeries of one kind or another, but he found time to establish many masonic lodges and secret societies. He died in prison in 1795. He did not contribute anything whatsoever to the scientific study of the Near or Middle East, either of its languages or of its history or culture. He was not a distinguished Orientalist in the way Lane was. Indeed, apart from his "Letter to the French People" (1786), I do not think Cagliostro ever wrote anything worthy of being called scientific, or of scholarly value. Cagliostro, according to Said, was the prototype of "[the above five authors'] imaginative conception." Is he suggesting that they, too, fabricated their entire knowledge of the Egypt, the Near East, and Arabia? If that is what Said means, it is false, for reasons discussed above.

For Said, Napoleon was the prototype of the "strength of European mastery of the Orient," since he was the Orient's first modern conqueror. This would be fine as a metaphor—Lane and Burton mastered Arabic in the way Napoleon mastered Egypt—but unfortunately, in the rest of his book Said seems to suggest something far more literal and sinister in the complicity of Orientalists with the imperial powers.

Orientalism is peppered with meaningless sentences. Take, for example, "Truth, in short, becomes a function of learned judgment, not of the material itself, which in time seems to owe its existence to the Orientalist" (p. 67). Said seems to be saying that "truth" is created by the experts or Orientalists, and does not correspond to reality, to what is actually out there. So far, so good. But then "what is out there" is also said to owe its existence to the Orientalist. If that is the case, then the first part of Said's sentence makes no sense, and if the first part is true then the second part makes no sense. Is Said relying on that weasel word "seems" to get him out of the mess? That ruse will not work either, for what would it mean to say that an external reality independent of the Orientalist's judgment also seems to be a creation of the Orientalist? That would be a simple contradiction.

Here is another example: "The Orientalist can imitate the Orient without the opposite being true." (p. 160). Throughout his book, Said is at pains to point out that there is no such thing as "the Orient," which, for him, is merely a meaningless abstraction concocted by Orientalists in the service of imperialists and racists. In which case, what on earth could "The Orient cannot imitate the Orientalist" possibly mean? If we replace "the Orient" by the individual countries—say, those lying between Egypt and India—do we get anything more coherent? No, obviously not: "India, Egypt, and Iran cannot imitate the Orientalists like Renan, Bernard Lewis, Burton, et al." We get nonsense whichever way we try to gloss Said's sentence.

CONTRADICTIONS

At times, Said seems to allow that the Orientalists did attain genuine knowledge of the Orient—its history, culture, languages—as when he calls Lane's work *Manners and Customs of the Modern Egyptians* "a classic of historical and anthropological observation because of its style, its enormously intelligent and brilliant details" (p. 15); or when he talks of "a growing systematic knowledge in Europe about the Orient" (p. 39), since Said does not have sarcastic quotation marks around the word "knowledge," I presume he means there was a growth in genuine knowledge. Further on, Said talks of Orientalism producing "a fair amount of exact positive knowledge about the Orient" (p. 52). Again, I take it Said is not being ironical when he talks of "philological discoveries in comparative grammar made by Jones" (p. 98). At one point, Said mentions Orientalism's "objective discoveries" (p. 203).

Yet these acknowledgments of the discoveries made by Orientalists are contradicted by Said's insistence that there is no such thing as "truth" (p. 271), or when he characterizes Orientalism as "a form of paranoia, knowledge of another kind, say, from ordinary historical knowledge" (p. 73). Or again, "it is finally Western ignorance which becomes more refined and complex, not some body of positive Western knowledge which increases in size and accuracy" (p. 62). At one point Said seems to deny that the Orientalists had acquired any objective knowledge at all (p. 122), and a little later he also writes, "the advances made by a 'science' like Orientalism in its academic form are less objectively true than we often like to think" (p. 202). It is true that the last phrase does leave open the possibility that *some* of the science may be true, though less than we had hitherto thought. Said also wholeheartedly endorses Abdel Malek's strictures against Orientalism and its putatively false "knowledge" of the Orient" (p. 96–97).

In his 1994 afterword, Said insists that he has "no interest in, much less capacity for, showing what the true Orient and Islam really are" (p. 331). And yet he contradicts this outburst of uncharacteristic humility and modesty when he claims that "[the Orientalist's] Orient is not the Orient as it is, but the Orient as it has been Orientalized" (p. 104), for such a formulation assumes Said knows what the real Orient is. Such an assumption is also apparent in his statement that "the present crisis dramatizes the disparity between texts and reality" (p. 109). In order to be able to tell the difference between the two, Said must know what the reality is. This is equally true when Said complains that "[t]o look into Orientalism for a lively sense of an Oriental's human or even social reality . . . is to look in vain" (p. 176).

Historical and Other Howlers

For a work that purports to be a serious work of intellectual history, *Orientalism* is full of historical howlers.[5] According to Said, at the end of the seventeenth century, Britain and France dominated the eastern Mediterranean, when in fact the Levant was still controlled for the next hundred years by the Ottomans. British and French merchants needed the permission of the sultan to land. Egypt is repeatedly described as a British colony when, in fact, Egypt was never more than a protectorate; it was never annexed, as Said claims (p. 35). Real colonies, like Australia or Algeria, were settled by large numbers of Europeans, and this manifestly was not the case with Egypt.[6]

The most egregious error surely is Said's claim that Muslim armies conquered Turkey before they overran North Africa (p. 57). In reality, the Arabs invaded North Africa in the seventh century, and what is now Turkey remained part of the Eastern Roman Empire—and Christian—until it was conquered by the Seljuk Turks in the late eleventh century.[7] Said writes, "Macdonald and Massignon were widely sought after as experts on Islamic matters by colonial administrators from North Africa to Pakistan" (p. 210). But Pakistan was never a colony; it was created in 1947 when the British left India. Said talks oddly about the "unchallenged Western dominance" of the Portuguese in the East Indies, China, and Japan until the nineteenth century (p. 73). But Portugal only dominated the trade, especially in the sixteenth century, and was never, as historian J. M. Roberts points out, "interested in the subjugation or settlement of large areas."[8] In China, Portugal only had the tiny foothold of Macao. The first decades of the seventeenth century witnessed the collapse of much of the Portuguese empire in the East, to be replaced by the Dutch. In the early eighteenth century there was a Dutch supremacy in the Indian Ocean and Indonesia. However, like the Portuguese, the Dutch did not subjugate "the Orient," but worked through diplomacy with native rulers and through a network of trading stations.[9]

Said thinks that Thomas Carlyle and John Henry Newman were "liberal cultural heroes"! It would be more correct to characterize Carlyle's works as the intellectual ancestry of fascism.[10] Newman was a High Church Anglican who converted to Catholicism. Said also seems to think that Ignaz Goldziher was German (p. 18); Goldziher was Hungarian. Said thinks "Muslim" designates a race (p. 99).

INTELLECTUAL DISHONESTY AND TENDENTIOUS REINTERPRETATIONS

Such errors can be put down to ignorance—Said is no historian—but so many gross errors put into doubt Said's competence to write such a book. On the other hand, we can only qualify as intellectual dishonesty the way he deliberately misinterprets a distinguished scholar's work and conclusions. Said quotes with approval and admiration some of the conclusions of R. W. Southern's *Western Views of Islam in the Middle Ages*:

> Most conspicuous to us is the inability of any of these systems of thought [European Christianity] to provide a fully satisfying explanation of the phenomenon they had set out to explain [Islam]—still less to influence the course of practical events in a decisive way. At a practical level, events never turned out either so well or so ill as the most intelligent observers predicted; and it is perhaps worth noticing that they never turned out better than when the best judges confidently expected a happy ending. Was there any progress [in Christian knowledge of Islam]? I must express my conviction that there was. Even if the solution of the problem remained obstinately hidden from sight, the statement of the problem became more complex, more rational, and more related to experience. . . . The scholars who labored at the problem of Islam in the Middle Ages failed to find the solution they sought and desired; but they developed habits of mind and powers of comprehension which, in other men and in other fields, may yet deserve success.[11]

Now here is Said's extraordinary misinterpretation of the quote from Southern: "The best part of Southern's analysis . . . is his demonstration that it is finally Western ignorance which becomes more refined and complex, not some body of positive Western knowledge which increases in size and accuracy" (p. 62). According to Said, Southern says that positive Western knowledge of the Orient did not increase. This is *not* what Southern is saying. Southern asks a question and replies: "Was there any progress [in Christian knowledge of Islam]? I must express my conviction that there was." Yes, I am firmly convinced that Western knowledge *did* progress; that is what Southern states. Southern adds that the medieval scholars' methodology became more and more sophisticated; they were more mature intellectually, since they developed habits of mind and powers of comprehension that would pay dividends later. How Said can speak, with his usual pretentious vocabulary, of "Western ignorance which becomes more refined" is a mystery, but it is in keeping with his method and his goal of painting the West as negatively as possible. Incidentally, the same passage from Southern contradicts one of Said's principal theses, about Oriental studies being a cause of imperialism. All this thinking about the Orient failed, Southern says, "to influence the course of practical events in a decisive way."

Said also seems to reproach Friedrich Schlegel for holding views that are in fact correct: "[Although by] 1808 Schlegel had practically renounced his Orientalism, he still held that Sanskrit and Persian on the one hand and Greek and German on the other had more affinities with each other than with Semitic, Chinese, American, or African languages" (p. 98). One can only conclude that Said does not know that what Schlegel held is indeed the case: Sanskrit, Persian, Greek, and German all belong to the same family, the Indo-European, and have more in common with each other, by definition, than with any other language in another family, such as Semitic.

Said quotes Sir William Jones's famous encomium on Sanskrit and its affinities to Greek and Latin as though it were of some sinister significance, by prefacing the quote with remarks that are silly:

> [Jones's] most famous pronouncement indicates the extent to which modern Orientalism, even in its philosophical beginnings, was a comparative discipline having for its principal goal the grounding of the European languages in a distant, and harmless, Oriental source: "The Sanscrit language, whatever be its antiquity, is of a wonderful structure; more perfect than the Greek, more copious than the Latin, and more exquisitively refined than either, yet bearing to both of them a stronger affinity, both in the roots of verbs and in the forms of grammar, than could possibly have been produced by accident; so strong indeed, that no philologer could examine them all three without believing them to have sprung from some common source." (pp. 78–79)[12]

What does Said mean by saying modern Orientalism had as its goal "the grounding of the European languages in a distant, and harmless, Oriental source?" It is nonsense. Jones was not the first to see that there were remarkable similarities between Sanskrit and Greek and Latin—as early as the sixteenth century Filippo Sassetti and in 1767 P. Coeurdoux had noticed them—but Jones's independent reflections led him to conclude that there was a similarity, and this was a *discovery*, an exciting scientific discovery that has since been amply confirmed. To say that Orientalists wanted to ground the European languages in Oriental sources is absurd. They *discovered* that they were related in some way; they did not concoct some theory to fit their desire to "ground European languages in Oriental sources." What does "a harmless Oriental source" mean, in any case? Greek and Latin do not have their "sources" in Sanskrit. They simply belong to the same genetic family, possibly descended from some common ancestral proto-Indo-European language.

As Professor K. Paddaya of Pune, India, wrote in his appreciation of Sir William Jones, "[I]t was genuine curiosity and admiration which made some of these officers [of the East India Company like Jones] voluntarily take up the study of [India's] past conditions."[13]

Jones's eulogy on Sanskrit is still quoted with pride by many Indian scholars, who honored Jones's memory by holding conferences in Calcutta and Pune in April 1994 to mark the bicentenary of his death. The bicentenary of the establishment of the Asiatic Society, which Jones founded, was celebrated in 1984 in New Delhi and Calcutta.

Said does not come across as a careful reader of Dante and his masterpiece, *The Divine Comedy*. In his trawl through Western literature for filth to besmirch Western civilization, Said comes across Dante's description of Muhammad in hell, and concludes, "Dante's verse at this point spares the reader none of the eschatological [*sic*] detail that so vivid a punishment entails: Muhammad's entrails and his excrement are described with unflinching accuracy" (p. 68). First, Said does not know the difference between scatalogical and eschatological, and second, how does he know that Dante's description is unflinchingly accurate? He simply means that it was highly graphic.

Said makes much of the fact that earlier in the *Inferno*, three Muslims turn up in the company of virtuous heathens like Plato and Aristotle. Said continues, "[B]ut the special anachronisms and anomalies of putting pre-Christian luminaries in the same category of 'heathen' damnation with post-Christian Muslims does not trouble Dante. Even though the Koran specifies Jesus as a prophet, Dante chooses to consider the great Muslim philosophers [Avicenna and Averroës] and king [Saladin] as having been fundamentally ignorant of Christianity." This comment betrays Said's fundamental ignorance of Christian doctrine, even though he himself was raised as a Christian. Although these people of much worth—*gente di molto valore*—had not sinned, according to Christian doctrine, they could not be saved outside the church—that is, without baptism, the first sacrament and thus the "gateway to the faith." The three Muslims were in the outer circle of hell not because they were ignorant of Christianity, but because they had died unbaptized. Since these regions of hell are timeless and their inhabitants are there forever, the question of anachronism does not arise, especially as these historical figures have an allegorical significance. Said was surely aware that Virgil, who died in 19 BCE, was Dante's guide, *il mio Dottore*, and fulfills an allegorical function. Virgil's voice is that of reason or philosophical wisdom. Allegory is central to any understanding of *The Divine Comedy*: *literra gesta docet, quid credas, allegoria*—the literal sense teaches the facts, the allegory what you should believe.

Furthermore, these illustrious Muslims were included precisely because of Dante's reverence for all that was best in the non-Christian world, and their exclusion from salvation, inevitable under Christian doctrine, saddened him and put a great strain on his mind—*gran duol mi prese al cor quando lo 'ntesi*—great grief seized me at heart when I heard this. Dante was even influenced by the Averroistic concept of the "possible intellect." The same generous impulse that made him revere non-Christians like Avicenna and their nobility of character made Dante relegate Muhammad to eternal punishment in the eighth circle of hell, namely, Dante's strong sense of the unity of humanity and of all its spiritual values—*uni-*

versalis civilitas humani generis—the universal community of the human race. He and his contemporaries in the late thirteenth and early fourteenth century had only vague ideas about the history and theology of Islam and its founder. Dante believed that Muhammad and Ali were the initiators of the great schism between Christianity and Islam. Like his contemporaries, Dante thought Muhammad was originally a Christian and a cardinal who wanted to become a pope. Hence, Muhammad was a *divider* of humanity, whereas Dante stood for the unity—the essential organic unity—of humankind. What Said does not see is that Dante perfectly exemplifies Western culture's strong tendency toward universalism.[14]

SELF-PITY, POSTIMPERIALIST VICTIMHOOD, AND IMPERIALISM

In order to achieve his goal of painting the West in general, and the discipline of Orientalism in particular, in as negative a way as possible, Said has recourse to several tactics. One of his preferred moves is to depict the Orient as a perpetual victim of Western imperialism, dominance, and aggression. The Orient is never seen as an actor, an agent with free will or designs or ideas of its own. It is to this propensity that we owe that immature and unattractive quality of so much contemporary Middle Eastern culture, self-pity, and the belief that all its ills are the result of imaginary Western-Zionist conspiracies.[15] Here is an example of Said's own belief in such conspiracies taken from *The Question of Palestine*: "It was perfectly apparent to Western supporters of Zionism like Balfour that the colonization of Palestine was made a goal for the Western powers from the very beginning of Zionist planning: Herzl used the idea, Weizmann used it, every leading Israeli since has used it. Israel was a device for holding Islam—later the Soviet Union, or communism—at bay."[16] So Israel was created to hold Islam at bay!

As for the politics of victimhood, Said has "milked it himself to an indecent degree."[17] Said wrote:

> My own experiences of these matters are in part what made me write this book. The life of an Arab Palestinian in the West, particularly in America, is disheartening. There exists here an almost unanimous consensus that politically he does not exist, and when it is allowed that he does, it is either as a nuisance or as an Oriental. The web of racism, cultural stereotypes, political imperialism, dehumanizing ideology holding in the Arab or the Muslim is very strong indeed, and it is this web which every Palestinian has come to feel as his uniquely punishing destiny. (p. 27)

Such wallowing in self-pity from a tenured and much-feted professor at Columbia University, where he enjoyed privileges that we lesser mortals only dream of (and a decent salary), all the while spewing forth hatred of the country that took him in and heaped honors on him, is nauseating. As Ian Buruma concluded in his review of Said's memoir, *Out of Place*, "The more he dwells on his suffering and his exile status, the more his admirers admire him. On me, however, it has the opposite effect. Of all the attitudes that shape a memoir, self-pity is the least attractive."[18]

The putative conquest of Egypt by Napoleon plays an important symbolic role in Said's scheme of showing all that is evil in Orientalism. For Said, Napoleon conquered, dominated, engulfed, possessed, and oppressed Egypt (see especially pp. 83–88 in *Orientalism*). Egypt is described as the passive victim of Western rapacity. In reality, the French were defeated and had to retreat hastily after fewer than four years: Napoleon arrived in July 1798 and left for good just over a year later, and the French forces stayed until September 1801. But during this brief interlude, the French fleet was destroyed at the Battle of the Nile, and the French failed to capture Murad Bey. Riots broke out when a house tax was introduced in Cairo, and the French general Dominique-Martin Dupuy, lieutenant governor of Cairo, was killed. Further riots broke out among the Muslims in Cairo when the French left to confront the Turks at Mataria, but the chief victims were Christians, many of whom were slaughtered by the Muslims. The French general Jean-Baptiste Kléber was assassinated. Far from seeing the Egyptians as "the Other" and far from denigrating Islam, from 1798 the French were highly sensitive to Muslim opinion, with Napoleon showing an intimate knowledge of the Koran. Perhaps the ultimate irony was that after the assassination of Kléber, the command of the French army passed to Gen. J. F. Baron de Menou, who had converted to Islam and had set about enacting measures to conciliate the Muslims.

Naguib Mahfouz, the Nobel Prize–winning Egyptian novelist, once said it is thanks to Napoleon's campaign in Egypt that his country has emerged out of centuries of obscurantism. Egypt owes all its modernity to Napoleon![19] Another result of the encounter with the West was the discovery of its ancient, pre-Islamic past, thanks to the work and genius of scholars such as Mariette and Champollion. So much for the evils of the "conquest of Egypt."

Had he bothered to pursue the subsequent history of Egypt, Said would have put Western imperialism in perspective, since he would have come across the history of Muhammad Ali, often considered the founder of modern Egypt. It was never in the interest or even the intention of the Western powers to see the dismemberment of the Ottoman Empire, which time and time again sought and received European support for the preservation of its imperial possessions. After the humiliating retreat of the French, the Ottoman's greatest challenger was a Muslim, the able but ambitious governor of Egypt, Muhammad Ali, "who aspired to nothing less than the substitution of his own empire for that of the Ottomans."[20] Inspired by Napoleon, Muhammad Ali modernized many of Egypt's archaic institutions. In his imperial dreams, Ali was thwarted by the Ottomans, who had the help, once again, of the great powers—Britain, Russia, Austria, and Prussia—that did not wish to use the sultan's plight to expand their imperial possessions. A little later, Muhammad Ali's grandson Ismail also dreamed of transforming Egypt into a modern imperial power. By the mid-1870s, "a vast Egyptian empire had come into being, extending from the Mediterranean in the north to Lake Victoria, and from the Indian Ocean in the east to the Libyan desert."[21]

I have dwelled on these historical details to put nineteenth-century imperialism in context, and to show that Middle Eastern history was created in significant part by Middle Eastern actors, who were "not hapless victims of predatory imperial powers but active participants in the restructuring of their region."[22] But this, of course, does not serve Said's purpose at all, which is to show "the Orientals" as passive victims of Western imperialism, unable to control their own destiny. It is Said who is guilty of the sins he accuses the Orientalists of, namely, suppressing the voice of the people of Egypt, the true history of the Near East, which was created by indigenous trends, desires, and actions freely chosen.

In *Orientalism*, Said writes: "Both before and during World War I secret diplomacy was bent on carving up the Near Orient first into spheres of influence, then into mandated (or occupied) territories" (p. 220). This is totally false. Here is how two historians see it:

> [T]he chain of events culminating in the destruction of the Ottoman Empire and the creation of the modern Middle East was set in motion *not* by secret diplomacy bent on carving up the Middle East, but rather by the decision of the Ottoman leadership to throw in its lot with Germany. This was by far the single most important decision in the history of the modern Middle East, and it was anything but inevitable. The Ottoman Empire was neither forced into the war in a last-ditch bid to ensure its survival, nor maneuvered into it by an overbearing German ally and an indifferent or even hostile British policy. Rather, the [Ottoman] empire's willful plunge into the whirlpool reflected a straightforward [Ottoman] imperialist policy of territorial aggrandizement and status acquisition.[23]

Prime Minister Herbert Henry Asquith noted in his diary in March 1915: "[Foreign Secretary Sir Edward Grey and I] both think that in the interests of our own future the best thing would be if at the end of the War we could say that we had taken and gained nothing." Similarly, the Bunsen Committee of April/May 1915 had a clear preference for the maintenance of an independent but decentralized empire comprised of five major provinces: Anatolia, Armenia, Syria, Palestine, and Iraq-Jezirah. Nearly a year after the outbreak of World War I, Britain still did not wish to see the destruction of Turkey—in Asia[24]—whereas it was an Arab, Sharif Hussein of Mecca, who wanted to establish his own empire on the ruins of that of the Ottomans.

Similarly, when referring to T. E. Lawrence, Said writes: "The great drama of Lawrence's work is that it symbolizes the struggle, first, to stimulate the Orient (lifeless, timeless, forceless) into movement; second, to impose upon that movement an essentially Western shape" (p. 241). Again, it is *Said* who is assuming the Arabs were passive and had decisions made for and imposed upon them as though they were children or imbeciles, incapable of having desires and acting freely. Certainly, the forceful personalities of the sharif of Mecca, Hussein ibn Ali, and his son Faisal played the most important part during World War I and were as responsible as the Western powers for what emerged after it.

Said's use of emotive language concerning Western imperialism with all its supposed evils conceals the real overall historical background of the entire region. Where the French presence lasted fewer than four years before they were ignominiously expelled by the British and Turks, the Ottomans had been the masters of Egypt since 1517, a total of 280 years. Even if we count the later British and French protectorates, Egypt was under Western control for sixty-seven years, Syria for twenty-one years, and Iraq for only fifteen—and, of course, Saudi Arabia was never under Western control. Contrast this with southern Spain, which was under the Muslim yoke for 781 years, Greece for 381 years, and the splendid new Christian capital that eclipsed Rome—Byzantium—which is still in Muslim hands.[25] But no Spanish or Greek politics of victimhood apparently exist.

Said's Anti-Westernism

In a disingenuous 1994 afterword, Said denies that he is anti-Western and that the phenomenon of Orientalism is a synecdoche of the entire West. He claims that there is no such stable reality as "the Orient" or "the Occident," that there is no enduring Oriental reality and even less an enduring Western essence, and that he has no interest in, much less capacity for, showing what the true Orient and Islam really are (pp. 330–33).

But a close reading of *Orientalism* is enough to show Said's anti-Westernism. While he does occasionally use inverted commas around "the Orient" and "the Occident," the entire force of Said's polemic comes from the polar opposites and contrasts of the East and the West, the Orient and Europe, Us and the Other, which he himself has crudely set up.

Said wrote, "I doubt that it is controversial, for example, to say that an Englishman in India or Egypt in the later nineteenth century took an interest in those countries that was never far from their status in his mind as British colonies. To say this may seem quite different from saying that all academic knowledge about India and Egypt is somehow tinged and impressed with, violated by, the gross political fact [of imperialism]—and yet *that is what I am saying* in this study of Orientalism" (p. 11; emphasis in original).

Here is Said's characterization of all Europeans: "It is therefore correct that every European, in what he could say about the Orient, was consequently a racist, an imperialist, and almost totally ethnocentric" (p. 204). In other words, not only are all Europeans racist, but they must *necessarily* be so. Said claims he is explicitly antiessentialist, particularly about "the West." But here is Said again: "Consider first the demarcation between Orient and West. It already seems bold by the time of the *Iliad*. Two of the most profoundly influential qualities associated with the East appear in Aeschylus's *The Persians*, the earliest Athenian play extant, and in *The Bacchae* of Euripides, the very last one extant. . . . The two aspects of the Orient that set it off from the West in this pair of plays will remain essential motifs of European imaginative geography. A line is drawn between two continents. Europe is powerful and articulate; Asia is defeated and distant" (pp. 56–57).

As Keith Windschuttle comments on that passage:

> These same motifs persist in Western culture, [Said] claims, right down to the modern period. This is a tradition that accommodates perspectives as divergent as those of Aeschylus, Dante, Victor Hugo, and Karl Marx. However, in describing "the essential motifs" of the European geographic imagination that have persisted since ancient Greece, he is ascribing to the West a coherent self-identity that has produced a specific set of value judgements—"Europe is powerful and articulate: Asia is defeated and distant"—that have remained constant for the past 2,500 years. This is, of course, nothing less than the use of the very notion of "essentialism" that he elsewhere condemns so vigorously. In short, it is his own work that is essentialist and ahistorical. He himself commits the very faults he says are so objectionable in the work of Orientalists.[26]

And here is another example to prove Said's anti-Western essentialism: "The Orient was Orientalized not only because it was discovered to be 'Oriental' in all those ways considered commonplace by an average nineteenth-century European, but also because it could be—that is, submitted to being—*made* Oriental" (p. 6). Here we have Said's reductionistic absurdity: the "average nineteenth-century European."

A part of Said's tactic is to leave out Western writers and scholars who do not conform to his theoretical framework. Since, for Said, all Europeans are a priori racist, he obviously cannot allow himself to quote writers who are not. Indeed, one could write a parallel work to *Orientalism* made up of extracts from Western writers, scholars, and travelers who were attracted by various aspects of non-European cultures, which they praised and contrasted favorably with their own decadence, bigotry, intolerance, and bellicosity.

Had he delved a little deeper into Greek civilization and history (rather than looking at only Aeschylus),[27] and bothered to look at Herodotus's great history, Said would have encountered two features that were also characteristic of Western civilization and that he is at pains to conceal and refuses to admit exist: the seeking after knowledge for its own sake, and the belief in the unity of mankind, or in other words its universalism. The Greek word *historia*, from which we get our "history," means "research" or "inquiry." Herodotus believed his work was the outcome of research: what he had seen, heard, and read, but also supplemented and verified by inquiry. For Herodotus, "historical facts have intrinsic value and rational meaning." He was totally devoid of racial prejudice—indeed, Plutarch later branded him a *philobarbaros*, whose nearest modern equivalent would be "nigger lover"—and his work shows considerable sympathy for Persians and Persian civilization. Herodotus represents Persians as honest—"they consider telling lies more disgraceful than anything else"—brave, dignified, and loyal to their king. As to the religions of the various peoples he studied, Herodotus showed his customary intellectual curiosity but also his reverence for all of them, because "all men know equally about divine things."[28]

Even in the Middle Ages we find figures in the Christian Church ready to make, in the words of French scholar of Islam Maxime Rodinson, an "outstanding effort . . . to gain and to transmit an objectively based scientific knowledge of the Islamic religion." Rodinson is describing the remarkable Peter the Venerable, Abbot of Cluny. Rodinson is convinced that Peter the Venerable was not only motivated for polemical reasons but "was moved by a disinterested curiosity."[29]

A number of thinkers, writers, and scholars in Europe from the sixteenth century onward took up the theme of the noble savage as a vehicle to criticize their own culture and to encourage tolerance of others outside the West. Perhaps the real founder of the sixteenth-century doctrine of the noble savage was Peter

Martyr Anglerius. In his *De Orbe Novo* of 1516, Peter Martyr criticized the Spanish conquistadores for their greed, narrow-mindedness, intolerance, and cruelty, contrasting them with the Indians, "who are happier since they are free from money, laws, treacherous judges, deceiving books and the anxiety of an uncertain future."[30] But it was left to Michel de Montaigne, under the influence of Peter Martyr, to develop the first full-length portrait of the noble savage in his celebrated essay "On Cannibals" (c. 1580), which is also the source of the idea of cultural relativism. Deriving his rather shaky information from a plain, simple fellow, Montaigne describes some of the gruesome customs of the Brazilian Indians and concludes:

> I am not so anxious that we should note the horrible savagery of these acts as concerned that, whilst judging their faults so correctly, we should be so blind to our own. I consider it more barbarous to eat a man alive than to eat him dead; to tear by rack and torture a body still full of feeling, to roast it by degrees, and then give it to be trampled and eaten by dogs and swine—a practice which we have not only read about but seen within recent memory, not between ancient enemies, but between neighbours and fellow-citizens and, what is worse, under the cloak of piety and religion—than to roast and eat a man after he is dead.[31]

Elsewhere in the essay, Montaigne emphasizes their inevitable simplicity, state of purity, and freedom from corruption. Even their "fighting is entirely noble." Like Peter Martyr, Montaigne's rather dubious, secondhand knowledge of these noble savages does not prevent him from criticizing and morally condemning his own culture and civilization: "[We] surpass them in every kind of barbarity."

The seventeenth century saw some truly sympathetic accounts of Islam, such as those of Pierre Jurieu and Pierre Bayle. Here is Jurieu:

> It may be truly said that there is no comparison between the cruelty of the Saracens against the Christians, and that of Popery against the true believers. In the war against the Vaudois, or in the massacres alone on St. Bartholomew's Day, there was more blood spilt upon account of religion, than was spilt by the Saracens in all their persecutions of the Christians. It is expedient to cure men of this prejudice; that Mahometanism is a cruel sect, which was propagated by putting men to their choice of death, or the abjuration of Christianity. This is in no way true; and the conduct of the Saracens was an evangelical meekness in comparison to that of Popery, which exceeded the cruelty of the cannibals.[32]

The import of Jurieu's *Lettres Pastorales* (1686–89) becomes clear only when we realize that Jurieu was a Huguenot pastor, the sworn enemy of

Jacques-Benigne Bossuet, and he was writing from Holland after the revocation of the Edict of Nantes. He is using the supposed tolerance of the Muslims as a way to criticize Roman Catholicism—for him, the Saracens's "evangelical meekness" is a way of contrasting Catholicism's own barbarity as on St. Bartholomew's Day.

Pierre Bayle was much influenced by Jurieu and continued to sing the praise of Islamic tolerance. He contrasts the tolerance of the Turks with the persecutions of brahmins in India by the Portuguese, and the barbarities exercised by the Spaniards in America: "[The Muslims] have always had more humanity for other religions than the Christians."[33] Bayle was a champion of toleration—was he not himself the victim of intolerance and forced to flee to Holland?

For Jurieu and Bayle in the seventeenth century, "Turk" was synonymous with "Muslim," thus Turkish tolerance turned into Muslim tolerance in general. Later, *Letters Written by a Turkish Spy*, published at the end of the seventeenth century, inaugurated the eighteenth-century vogue for the pseudo-foreign letter, such as Montesquieu's *Lettres Persanes* (1721); Madame de Grafigny's *Lettres d' une Peruvienne* (1747); Marquis d'Argens' *Lettres Chinoises* (1750); Voltaire's Asiatic in the *Philosophical Dictionary* (1752); Horace Walpole's *Letter from Xo Ho, a Chinese Philosopher at London, to His Friend Lien-Chi, at Peking* (1757); and Oliver Goldsmith's *Citizen of the World* (1762), in which Lien Chi Altangi makes philosophical and satirical comments on the manners of the English.

Count Henri de Boulainvilliers' apologetic biography of Muhammad appeared posthumously in London in 1730. It is impossible to exaggerate the importance of this book in shaping Europe's view of Islam and its founder, Muhammad; it certainly influenced Voltaire and Edward Gibbon. Boulainvilliers was able to use Muhammad and the origins of Islam as "a vehicle of his own theological prejudices" and as a weapon against Christianity, in general, and the clergy, in particular. He found Islam reasonable: It did not require one to believe in impossibilities—no mysteries, no miracles. Muhammad, though not divine, was presented as an incomparable statesman and a greater legislator than anyone produced by ancient Greece.

George Sale's translation of the Koran (1734) is the first accurate one in English. Like Boulainvilliers, whose biography of Muhammad he had carefully read, Sale firmly believed that the Arabs "seem to have been raised up on purpose by God, to be a scourge to the Christian church, for not living answerably to that most holy religion which they had received."[34]

The attitude of Voltaire can be seen as typical of the entire century. Voltaire seems later to have regretted what he had written of Muhammad in his scurrilous and—to a Muslim—blasphemous play *Mahomet* (1742), where the Prophet is presented as an impostor who enslaved men's souls: "Assuredly, I have made him out to be more evil than he was."[35]

But Voltaire, in his "Essai sur les Moeurs" (1756) and various entries in the *Philosophical Dictionary*, shows himself to be prejudiced in Islam's favor at the expense of Christianity, in general, and Catholicism, in particular.

In his *The Sermon of the Fifty* (1762), Voltaire attacks such Christian mysteries as transubstantiation as being absurd, Christian miracles as incredible, and the Bible as full of contradictions. The God of Christianity was a cruel and hateful tyrant. By contrast, Voltaire finds the dogmas of Islam to be simplicity itself: there is but one God, and Muhammad is his Prophet. For all deists, the supposed rationality of Islam was appealing: no priests, no miracles, no mysteries. To this was added other beliefs, such as the absolute tolerance of other religions, in contrast to Christian intolerance.

Gibbon, like Voltaire, painted Islam in as favorable a light as possible in order to better contrast it to Christianity. He emphasized Muhammad's humanity as a means of indirectly criticizing the Christian doctrine of the divinity of Christ. Gibbon's anticlericalism led him to underline Islam's supposed freedom from that accursed class, the priesthood. His deistic view of Islam as a rational, priest-free religion, with Muhammad as a wise and tolerant lawgiver, enormously influenced the way all Europeans perceived a sister religion for years to come.

The work that exemplifies the Enlightenment's openness to the Other, and its universalism and tolerance, is surely Gotthold Lessing's *Nathan the Wise*, written in 1778–79. The two themes—"it suffices to be a man" and "be my friend"—run through the play and give it its humanity. Preaching friendship among the three monotheistic religions (Saladin, the great Muslim leader who defeated the Christian Crusaders, is one of the three main characters), Lessing recounts the allegory of the father (God) who gives each of his three sons (representing Islam, Christianity, and Judaism) a ring (representing religion):

> If each of you
> Has had a ring presented by his father,
> Let each believe his own the real ring.
> 'Tis possible the father chose no longer
> To tolerate the one ring's tyranny;
> And certainly, as he much loved you all,
> And loved you all alike, it could not please him
> By favouring one to be of two the oppressor.
> Let each feel honoured by this free affection.
> Unwarped of prejudice; let each endeavour
> To vie with both his brothers in displaying

The virtue of his ring; assist its might
With gentleness, benevolence, forbearance,
With inward resignation to the godhead.[36]

One could multiply examples of Said's quite deliberate omissions: there are the writers sympathetic to the Arabs, Turks, and Islam, such as W. S. Blunt, whose travels in Egypt and Arabia "produced in him a violent reaction against British Imperialism, and the second half of his life was spent in publishing a stream of poems, books and pamphlets championing the nationalist cause in Egypt, India, Arabia and Ireland."[37] Or Lady Mary Wortley Montagu, who wrote, "Sir, these people [the Turks] are not so unpolish'd as we represent them. Tis true their magnificence is of a different taste from ours, and perhaps of a better. I am allmost [*sic*] of opinion they have a right notion of Life, while they consume it in Music, Gardens, Wine, and delicate eating, while we are tormenting our brains with some Scheme of Politics or studying some Science to which we can never attain."[38] Or Marmaduke Pickthall, who eventually converted to Islam, translated the Koran, wrote novels of Egypt, and edited the journal *Islamic Culture*. Or E. G. Browne, who wrote the monumental *Literary History of Persia* (1902–24) and who took up the cause of Iranian nationalism.

The important thing to emphasize here is the grossly biased nature of Said's seemingly scholarly selection; one could go through Western literature and find much evidence that contradicts his thesis. Furthermore, such a selection is not of some peripheral figures culled from the margins of Western culture, but the very makers of that culture, central figures such as Montaigne, Bayle, Voltaire, Gibbon, Lessing, and some I have not quoted, such as Montesquieu (*The Persian Letters*, 1721) and Denis Diderot (*Supplément au Voyage de Bougainville*, 1772), the latter two exemplifying the European Enlightenment's appeal to reason, objective truth, and universalist values.

Most of the time one has the impression that Said is resentful of how thorough and scholarly—in short, scientific and successful—the Orientalists were. He is particularly jealous of their mastery of languages. For example, Said grudgingly admits that Barthélemy d'Herbelot read Arabic, Persian, and Turkish, and then he seems to resent the fact that d'Herbelot arranged his *Bibliothèque orientale* alphabetically (p. 65)! Said talks of "specific Orientalist techniques—lexicography, grammar, translation, cultural decoding . . ." as though they were instruments of torture, used to violate, subjugate, and dominate the Orient (p. 121). The same resentment is expressed of "regulatory codes, classifications, specimen cases, periodical reviews, dictionaries, grammars, commentaries, editions, translations," which can only be seen as Said's hatred of science in general, and Western-generated knowledge in particular (p. 166). Western intellectual energy and curiosity, that is, "activity, judgment, will-to-truth, and knowledge," is dismissed as "all aggression" (p. 204).

MISUNDERSTANDING OF WESTERN CIVILIZATION

The golden thread running through Western civilization is rationalism. As Aristotle said, "Man by nature strives to know." This striving for knowledge results in science, which is but the application of reason. Intellectual inquisitiveness is one of the hallmarks of Western civilization. As J. M. Roberts put it,

> The massive indifference of some civilisations and their lack of curiosity about other worlds is a vast subject. Why, until very recently, did Islamic scholars show no wish to translate Latin or western European texts into Arabic? Why, when the English poet Dryden could confidently write a play focused on the succession in Delhi after the death of the Mogul emperor Aurungzebe, is it a safe guess that no Indian writer ever thought of a play about the equally dramatic politics of the English seventeenth-century court? It is clear that an explanation of European inquisitiveness and adventurousness must lie deeper than economics, important though they may have been. It was not just greed which made Europeans feel they could go out and take the world. The love of gain is confined to no particular people or culture. It was shared in the fifteenth century by many an Arab, Gujarati or Chinese merchant. Some Europeans wanted more. They wanted to explore.[39]

Marxists, Freudians, and anti-imperialists, who crudely reduce all human activities to money, sex, and power, respectively, have difficulties in understanding the very notion of disinterested intellectual inquiry. European man, by nature, strives to know. Science undoubtedly owed some of its impetus to finding ways of changing base metal into gold and to attempts to solve practical problems, but surely science owes as much to the desire to know, to get at the truth. This is the reason philosophers like Karl Popper have called it a spiritual achievement. Hence, the desperate attempts by Said to smear every single Orientalist with the lowest of motives are not only reprehensible but also fail to give due weight to this golden thread running through Western civilization.

One should also have reminded Said that it was this desire for knowledge on the part of Europeans that led the people of the Near East to recover and discover their own past and their own identity. In the nineteenth and early twentieth centuries, archaeological excavations in Mesopotamia, ancient Syria, ancient Palestine, and Iran were carried out entirely by Europeans and, later, Americans. The disciplines of Egyptology, Assyriology, and Iranology, all of which restored to mankind a large part of its heritage, were the exclusive creations of inquisitive Europeans and Americans—whereas, for doctrinal reasons, Islam deliberately refused to look at its pre-Islamic past, which was considered a period of ignorance.[40]

It is worth pointing out that often the motives, desires, and prejudices of a scholar have no bearing upon the scientific worth of a scholar's contribution. Marxists, for example, dismiss an opponent's arguments not on any scientific or rational grounds but merely because of the social origins of the scholar concerned. Theodor Nöldeke's bigotry was well known, and indeed a source of acute embarrassment to his colleagues, but no modern scholar of Islam can ignore his *Geschichte des Qorâns*. Similarly, Henri Lammens's hatred for the Prophet Muhammad is notorious, but as Professor F. E. Peters once said, Lammens, who cast doubt on the authenticity of Muslim traditions and the putatively close connection between the Koran and the life of Muhammad, has never been refuted. Conversely, a scholar who manifests sympathy for all aspects of Islam is not necessarily a good scholar. Said, for instance, quotes with approval Norman Daniel. Maxime Rodinson pointed out that Daniel was not an objective historian, but an apologist of Islam: "In this way the anti-colonialist left, whether Christian or not, often goes so far as to sanctify Islam and the contemporary ideologies of the Muslim world. . . . An historian like Norman Daniel has gone so far as to number among the conceptions permeated with medievalism or imperialism, any criticisms of the Prophet's moral attitudes, and to accuse of like tendencies any exposition of Islam and its characteristics by means of the normal mechanisms of human history. Understanding has given way to apologetics pure and simple."[41]

Rather surprisingly, Said also singles out Louis Massignon for lavish praise for his sympathetic understanding of Islam. Massignon's scholarship is not in doubt. His biography of Al-Hallaj, for example, is considered a masterpiece. But Massignon also exemplifies the very qualities that Said himself dismisses in others. The Frenchman is responsible for perpetuating the myth of the spiritual East as against the materialist West. Said praises him for "identifying with the 'vital forces' informing 'Eastern culture' " (p. 265), and yet earlier Said informs us that "[t]he Orient was overvalued for its pantheism, its spirituality, its stability, its longevity, its primitivity, and so forth" (p. 150). Massignon also displays other unattractive traits that Said does not mention, namely, his anti-Semitism, in the sense of virulent anti-Jewish sentiments, something Massignon's biographers acknowledge.[42] Finally, Massignon was far from being the paragon of Christian spirituality that he becomes in Said's eyes, since one of Massignon's interests in the East was to search its cities for male prostitutes, something he dared not do in the "decadent West"! Mircea Eliade recounts in his *Journal*, "This evening I dine with Massignon. We talk for several hours. Terribly voluble! He is, besides, obsessed with pederasty; again and again he brings the conversation around to 'young male prostitutes' and so on."[43] Massignon was quite ready to exploit the East when it suited him.

Maxime Rodinson criticized Massignon and others for taking the idea of seeing the Koran on its own terms too far,

> though their perspective represented a necessary reaction against an understanding of a text in terms that were too often foreign to the text, and a tendency to isolate themes from the religious context to which they belong—tendencies which were characteristic of the nineteenth century. However, the historian must occasionally ask himself if the reaction has not gone too far. Some of the methods of this school of thought [Massignon and others] must be a matter of concern to historians. To study the internal logic of a faith and to show respect are very legitimate objectives. The scholar has a perfect right to attempt to re-experience within himself the "fire" and the exigencies of the religious consciousness under study. However, the elements that comprise a coherent system could indeed have derived from a variety of very different sources and might well have played an entirely different role in other systems. Respect for the faith of sincere believers cannot be allowed either to block or deflect the investigation of the historian. The result derived from examining a particular faith on a personal "mental testing bench" ought to be made the object of a very severe critical examination. One must defend the rights of elementary historical methodology.[44]

SAID'S *ORIENTALISM*

Orientalism reveals at times Said's contempt for the non-European, negative attitudes toward the Orient, far greater than that of some of the imperialists he constantly condemns. Said speaks of "books and journals in Arabic (and doubtless in Japanese, various Indian dialects and other Oriental languages)" (p. 322). As Bernard Lewis notes, this is indeed contemptuous, with its "assumption that what Indians speak and write are not languages but dialects"; even earlier Said talks of "innumerable Indian dialects" (p. 52), despite the fact that in India there are more than fifteen languages, each of which is spoken by more than 40 million people, and each with a long and rich literary tradition. Where Said the anti-Orientalist taketh away, the Orientalist restoreth, for it was during the British period in India that Sir George A. Grierson carried out *Linguistic Survey of India*, which resulted in his monumental study of several thousand pages where he identified and studied 179 Indian languages. All later research is indebted to this magnificent work of scholarship, which, for Grierson, was a token of his love for India. What is more, far from being neglected or reviled, as Said would no doubt have liked, this Orientalist classic is still in print in India, eighty years after its publication in 1927. This work illustrates perfectly the fact that much Orientalist research gave back to, for instance, Indians, their own rich and varied heritage of which they themselves were not aware.

Said also claims that "[n]o Arab, or Islamic scholar can afford to ignore what goes on in scholarly journals, institutes, and universities in the United States and Europe; the converse is not true. For example, there is no major journal of Arab Studies published in the Arab world today" (p. 323). Said simply chooses to ignore such distinguished journals as *Majallat al-Ahfad* (Omdurman), *Alif: Journal of Comparative Poetics* (Cairo), *Al-Majalla al-'Arabiya li-l-'Ulum al-Insaniya* (Kuwait), *Al-Tawasul al-Lisani* (Fez), *Review of the Arab Academy* (Damascus), *al-Abhath* (Beirut), *Review of Maghribi History* (Tunis), and the bulletins of the faculties of arts and of social sciences of Cairo, Alexandria, and Baghdad, to name a few. And why would the fact that no Arab could afford to ignore what goes on in scholarly journals in the West be bad? And does it not contradict Said's thesis that all Orientalist research was worthless? If it were worthless, why keep up with the work published in these journals?

Said, Sex, and Psychoanalysis

If Said can be said to have a bête noire, it must surely be Bernard Lewis. In a review of Lewis's book *What Went Wrong*? in *Harper's*,[45] Said gave vent to his loathing for Lewis, who is characterized as repetitious, having a veneer of English sophistication, his book unrelieved rubbish, an intellectual and moral disaster, the terribly faded rasp of a pretentious academic voice: "One can almost hear him [Lewis] saying over a gin and tonic, 'You know, old chap, those wogs never really got it right, did they?'" Then there is Said's ultimate argument against Lewis: "His jowly presence seems to delight his interlocutors and editors"!

What strikes one most is Said's sentence accusing Lewis of persisting "in such 'philological' tricks as deriving an aspect of the predilection in contemporary Arab Islam for revolutionary violence from Bedouin descriptions of a camel rising." Said, twenty-five years on, still has not forgotten his battle with Lewis on the issue of a camel rising, to which I will now turn. In *Orientalism*, Said quotes from Lewis's essay "Islamic Concepts of Revolution":

> In the Arabic-speaking countries a different word was used for [revolution] *thawra*. The root *th-w-r* in Classical Arabic meant to rise up (e.g. of a camel), to be stirred or excited, and hence, especially in Maghribi usage, to rebel. It is often used in the context of establishing a petty, independent sovereignty; thus, for example, the so-called party kings who ruled in eleventh century Spain after the break-up of the Caliphate of Cordova are called *thuwwar* (sing. *tha'ir*). The noun *thawra* at first means excitement, as in the phrase, cited in the Sihah, a standard medieval Arabic dictionary, *intazir hatta taskun hadhihi 'lthawra*, wait till this excitement dies down—very apt recommendation. The verb is used by al-Iji, in the form of *thawaran* or *itharat fitna*, stirring up sedition, as one of the dangers which should discourage a man from practising the duty of resistance to bad government. *Thawra* is the term used by Arabic writers in the nineteenth century for the French Revolution, and by their successors for the approved revolutions, domestic and foreign, of our own time.[46]

Among Said's conclusions was that

> Lewis's association of *thawra* with a camel rising and generally with excitement (and not with a struggle on behalf of values) hints much more broadly than is usual for him that the Arab is scarcely more than a neurotic sexual being. Each of the words or phrases he uses to describe revolution is tinged with sexuality: *stirred*, *excited*, *rising up*. But for the most part it is a "bad" sexuality he ascribes to the Arab. In the end, since Arabs are really not equipped for serious action, their sexual excitement is no more noble than a camel's rising up. Instead of revolution there is sedition, setting up a petty sovereignty, and more excitement, which is as much as saying that instead of copulation the Arab can only achieve foreplay, masturbation, coitus interruptus. These, I think, are Lewis's implications. (pp. 315–16)

Can any rational person have drawn any conclusion that even remotely resembled that of Edward Said's from Lewis's scholarly discussion of Classical Arabic etymology? Were one to indulge in some prurient psycho-biography, one might be tempted to ask, "What guilty sexual anguish is Said trying to cover up? Just what *did* they do to him at his Cairo English prep school?" Lewis's concise and elegant reply to Said's conclusions is to quote the Duke of Wellington: "If you believe that, you can believe anything."

In *Orientalism*, Said seems to be obssessed with sexual imagery. He finds D. G. Hogarth's account of the exploration of Arabia "aptly titled *The Penetra-*

tion of Arabia (1904)" (p. 224). And yet, Said himself wrote, "[Sir Richard Burton] was able to penetrate to the heart of Islam and disguised as an Indian Muslim doctor accomplish the pilgrimage to Mecca" (p. 195); and also, "For Lamartine a pilgrimage to the Orient has involved not only the penetration of the Orient by an imperious consciousness" (p. 179). Or again, "The point here is that the space of weaker or underdeveloped regions like the Orient was viewed as something inviting French interest, penetration, insemination—in short, colonization. . . . French scholars, administrators, geographers, and commercial agents poured out their exuberant activity onto the fairly supine, feminine Orient" (pp. 219–20). And yet again, "Before Napoleon only two efforts (both by scholars) had been made to invade the Orient by stripping it of its veils" (p. 76). Just what *did* they do to Said at prep school?

Orientalists' Complicity in Imperialism

One of Said's major theses is that Orientalism was not a disinterested, scholarly activity but a political one, with Orientalists preparing the ground for and colluding with imperialists: "To say simply that Orientalism was a rationalization of colonial rule is to ignore the extent to which colonial rule was justified in advance by Orientalism, rather than after the fact" (p. 39). The Orientalist provides the knowledge that keeps the Oriental under control: "Once again, knowledge of subject races or Orientals is what makes their management easy and profitable; knowledge gives power, more power requires more knowledge, and so on in an increasingly profitable dialectic of information and control" (p. 36).

This is combined with Said's thesis, derived from the Coptic socialist thinker Anwar Abdel Malek, that the Orient is always seen by the Orientalists as unchanging, uniform, and peculiar (p. 98), with Orientals reduced to racist stereotypes and seen as ahistorical "objects" of study "stamped with an otherness . . . of an essentialist character" (p. 97, quoting Malek). The Orientalists have provided a false picture of Islam: "Islam has been fundamentally misrepresented in the West" (p. 272). Said adds Foucault to the heady mix; the French guru convinced Said that Orientalist scholarship took place within the ideological framework he called "discourse" and that "the real issue is whether indeed there can be a true representation of anything, or whether any and all representations, because they *are* representations, are embedded first in the language and then in the culture, institutions, and political ambience of the representer. If the latter alternative is the correct one (as I believe it is), then we must be prepared to accept the fact that a representation is *eo ipso* implicated, intertwined, embedded, interwoven with a great many other things besides the 'truth,' which is itself a representation" (p. 272).

It takes little thought to see that there is a contradiction in Said's major thesis.[47] If Orientalists have produced a false picture of the Orient, Orientals, Islam, Arabs, and Arabic society—and, in any case, for Said there is no such thing as "the truth"—then how could this false or pseudoknowledge have helped European imperialists to dominate three-quarters of the globe? "Information and control," wrote Said, but what of "false information and control"?

To argue his case, Said very conveniently leaves out the important contributions of German Orientalists, for their inclusion would destroy—and their exclusion does indeed totally destroy—the central thesis of *Orientalism*, that all Orientalists produced knowledge that generated power, and that they colluded and helped imperialists found empires. As we shall see, German Orientalists were the greatest of all scholars of the Orient, but, of course, Germany was never an imperial power in any of the Oriental countries of North Africa or the Middle East. Lewis wrote, "[A]t no time before or after the imperial age did [the British and French] contribution, in range, depth, or standard, match the achievement of the great centers of Oriental studies in Germany and neighbouring countries. Indeed, any history or theory of Arabic studies in Europe without the Germans makes as much sense as would a history or theory of European music or philosophy with the same omission."[48] Would it have made sense for German Orientalists to produce work that could help only England or France in their empire building?

Those omitted are not peripheral figures but the actual creators of the field of Middle Eastern, Islamic, and Arabic studies: scholars of the standing of Paul Kahle, Georg Kampffmeyer, Rudolf Geyer, F. Giese, Jacob Barth, August Fischer, Emil Gratzl, Hubert Grimme, Friedrich Schulthess, Friedrich Schwally, Anton Baumstark, Gotthelf Bergsträsser; others not discussed include G. Wustenfeld, Alfred Von Kremer, J. Horovitz, A. Sprenger, and Karl Vollers. Though Theodor Nöldeke, Johann Fück, G. Weil, Carl Heinrich Becker, E. Sachau, and Carl Brockelmann are mentioned, their work and significance are not discussed in any detail; Nöldeke, whose *Geschichte des Qorâns* (1860) was to become the foundation of all later Koranic studies, is considered one of the pioneers, along with Goldziher, of Islamic studies in the West.

But German scholars are not the only ones omitted. Russians (e.g., E. A. Belayev, S. P. Tolstov), Italians (e.g., Leone Caetani), and many Jewish scholars who studied Islam with sympathy, considering it a sister religion (e.g., Abraham Geiger, Paul Kraus), do not rate a mention.

To argue that the French and British Orientalists somehow prepared the ground for the imperialists is to seriously distort history. The first chair of Arabic in France was founded in 1538 at the Collège de France, and yet the first French venture into an Arab country was Napoleon's in 1798. In England, the first chair of Arabic was founded in 1633 at Cambridge, and yet the first British incursion into Arab territory was not until the nineteenth century. Where is the complicity between Orientalists and imperialists here? When the first two chairs of Arabic were founded in the West, it was the Muslims who dominated the Mediterranean, while the Balkans were under Turkish rule and the Turkish Siege of Vienna was still to come.[49]

Said quotes at length speeches and essays by such British statesmen as Lord Cromer, Arthur Balfour, and Lord Curzon that mention the work of some Orientalists. But, as Windschuttle points out, "[T]hese quotations come from works written between 1908 and 1912, that is, more than twenty-five years after the peak of Britain's imperial expansion. Rather than expressing the aims and objectives of potential imperial conquests, these speeches are ex post facto justifications, sanctioned by hindsight."[50] Said quotes Curzon as saying, "[O]ur familiarity, not merely with the languages of the people of the East but with their customs, their feelings, their traditions, their history and religion . . . is the sole basis upon which we are likely to be able to maintain in the future the position we have won" (p. 214).

But here Curzon is speaking to the House of Lords in 1909 to support the funding of a new London school of Oriental studies, and, unsurprisingly, "was painting its prospects in the best light he could."[51]

Silvestre de Sacy, Ernest Renan, and Ignaz Goldziher

Lawrence Conrad, in a remarkable book edited by Martin Kramer,[52] has shown with his usual superb scholarship, clarity, and analytical brilliance how Said's account is not just flawed but fundamentally wrong:

> [I]t is difficult to credit the curious linearity that Said postulates for the development of orientalism from Silvestre de Sacy. As is amply attested by the vast oriental collections of such centers of orientalist learning as Leiden and Berlin, where there were no imperial considerations to stimulate interest in the Orient, or at least (in the case of the Netherlands) not in the Middle East, it is a gross error to characterize European orientalist scholarship as dependent upon "imperial Britain and France" for access to texts. The orientalist tradition in the

> Netherlands and Germany was already well-established by the eighteenth century. In Leiden the decisive impetus (if one is to think in terms of contributions of individuals) had been provided by Jacob Golius (1596–1667), and the treasures of the Warnerian Library provided materials for study by an expanding circle of scholars; in Germany a founding father figure may be identified at Leipzig in Johann Jacob Reiske (1716–74), who had been trained at Leiden.[53]

As Conrad points out in a footnote, "The Islamic holdings at the Leiden University Library roughly equal those of the British Library (ca. 23,000), and those of the Deutsche Staatsbibliothek in Berlin and the Bibliothèque Nationale in Paris are again about the same (ca. 12,000)."[54]

Said first exaggerates de Sacy's influence on Ernest Renan, and then compounds his error by further overestimating both of their importance in the history of Orientalism. Renan himself felt he was continuing the work of Bopp, and only makes "a few passing references to Silvestre de Sacy and assigns him no particular importance for his own intellectual or professional development." Renan had little esteem for de Sacy's kind of scholarship, compiling, editing, and translating.[55] As Conrad concludes, "All this speaks decisively against Said's claim [p. 177] that orientalists after Silvestre de Sacy simply copied and rewrote him."[56] The reception of Renan's *Langues sémitiques* in the nineteenth century also demonstrates decisively against Said's essentialist argument that Orientalism became a static system of ideas that did not generate any new ways of conceptualizing the subject of its study and analysis.[57] Or, as Said himself put it, after Silvestre de Sacy and Renan, "[all that] German Oriental scholarship did was to refine and elaborate techniques whose application was to texts, myths, ideas, and languages almost literally gathered from the Orient by imperial Britain and France" (p. 19).

But Renan's theories were attacked by Semiticists, philologists, and Orientalists in general.[58] Scholarly criticism of Orientalist scholarship is going on all the time; academic integrity demands constant criticism of the research and results of colleagues, individual scholars, or whole groups of scholars, ensuring that their discipline is not a static archive of knowledge, never to be disturbed.[59]

One of the most searching critiques of Renan was provided by Ignaz Goldziher, who, as early as 1889, was recognized as the founder of a new field of scholarship—Arabic and Islamic studies. Goldziher, the most important Orientalist of all, is dismissed by Said in three lines, though Henry Kissinger merits three pages in *Orientalism.*

It is impossible to overestimate the influence of Goldziher, and the new paths he opened up in the study of Islam, Islamic history, Islamic theology, the study of hadith, and so on. As Conrad says, Goldziher's *Muhammedanische Stu-*

dien (1888–89) "encompassed the entire vast range of Arab-Islamic literary culture—historical texts, poetry, *adab*, proverb collections, Koranic exegesis, doctrinal works, fiqh, hadith, biographical dictionaries, and so forth—and from them laid out an incredibly rich vista of historical experience that not only had not been known before, but even had not been sought. It would be no exaggeration to say that Goldziher's colleagues were stunned by his work."[60]

Goldziher was not influenced by Silvestre de Sacy, or by Renan or French Orientalism, but rather by Abraham Geiger of the Jewish Enlightenment, the Tübingen school led by Ferdinand Christian Bauer, and by Moses Mendelssohn and Immanuel Kant. Here is Conrad's summary of Goldziher's criticism of Renan:

> [Renan's research on matters "Semitic"] systematically demeaned and deprecated the object of its study, robbed it of historical worth, defined it almost wholly in terms of negative attributes, denied its relevance as anything more than an artifact, and even then insisted that it be judged against the standard of values and norms of another people and another time a priori privileged and protected from the same harsh scrutiny directed at other peoples. Renaniana was a slippery sphere: one could hold it or drop it, but not work with it. Having demonstrated, along with other scholars, how flawed it was in both conception and execution, Goldziher wisely decided to drop it and urged others to do the same.[61]

Goldziher was to remain an objective but always sympathetic observer of the Islamic world.[62] He constantly criticized Westernization and Western influence in the Near East. He particularly despised Christian missionaries and had no sympathy for Zionism. Goldziher subscribed to the Enlightenment values, and felt that his insights into Islam were equally relevant to Jews since his conclusions about a kindred faith had a universal dimension to them. His spiritual empathy for Islam and Muslims resulted in this extraordinary conclusion: "I became inwardly convinced that I myself was a Muslim. [In Cairo, i]n the midst of the thousands of the pious, I rubbed my forehead against the floor of the mosque. Never in my life was I more devout, more truly devout, than on that exalted Friday."[63] Does this sound like Said's Orientalist? Is this why the most important Orientalist of all was given only three lines?

Since Said spends more time on Renan than other Orientalists despite the fact that Renan is not as important a figure as Said imagines, it is worth pointing out that Renan himself also changed his views. Those who would see Renan as a racist would do well to read his celebrated lecture of 1882, "*Qu'est-ce qu'une nation?*" where he implicitly repudiates his earlier views on racial inequality put forward in the *Dialogues*; and he explicitly rejects the attempt to rest the concept of nationhood on race, language, economics, geography, and religion. Shmuel Almog has also argued that Renan was not consciously anti-Semitic, and points to Renan's explicit denunciation of anti-Semitism, his protest against the Tisza-Eszlar blood libel in 1882, his efforts with Victor Hugo to organize relief committees for the Jews of Russia, and so on.[64]

Basing himself on Muslim sources, Renan drew an exceedingly favorable portrait of the Prophet,[65] while recognizing his moral failings. "On the whole, Muhammad seems to us like a gentle man, sensitive, faithful, free from rancour and hatred. His affections were sincere, his character in general was inclined to kindness. . . . Neither ambition nor religious rapture had dried up the personal feelings in him. Not at all akin to this ambitious, heartless and machiavellian fanatic [depicted by Voltaire in his drama *Mahomet*]." Renan is at pains to defend Muhammad from possible criticisms: "As to the features of the life of Muhammad which, to our eyes, would be unpardonable blots on his morality, it would be unjust to criticize them too harshly. . . . It would also be unjust to judge severely and with our own considered ideas, the acts of Muhammad, which in our days would be called swindles." The Prophet was no imposter: "It would be to totally lack a historical sense to suppose that a revolution as profound as Islam could be accomplished merely by some clever scheming, and Muhammad is no more explicable by imposture and trickery than by illuminism and religious fervour." Being a religious humanist, Renan valued Islam and religion in general, "because it manifested what was divine in human nature"[66] and seemed to answer the deepest instincts of human nature, and in particular it answered the needs of seventh-century Arabia, an idea taken up in modern times by William Montgomery Watt.

Second, Renan concludes his essay with the following observation:

> It is superfluous to add that if ever a reformist movement manifests itself in Islam, Europe should only participate in it by the influence of a most general kind. It would be ungracious of her to wish to settle the faith of others. All the while actively pursuing the propagation of her dogma which is civilisation, she ought to leave to the peoples themselves the infinitely delicate task of adjusting their own religious traditions to their new needs; and to respect that most inalienable right of nations as much as of individuals, the right to preside oneself, in the most perfect freedom, over the revolutions of one's conscience.[67]

These are hardly the words of a cultural imperialist. Nor does Renan believe that Islam is unchanging or essentially incapable of changing:

> Symptoms of a more serious nature are appearing, I know, in Egypt and Turkey. There contact with European science and customs has produced freethought sometimes scarcely disguised. Sincere believers who are aware of the danger do not hide their disquiet, and denounce the books of European science as containing deadly errors, and subversive of all religious faith. I nevertheless persist in believing that if the East can surmount its apathy and go beyond the limits that up to now it was unable to as far as rational speculation was concerned, Islam will not pose a serious obstacle to the progress of the modern mind. The lack of theological centralisation has always left a certain degree of religious liberty to Muslim nations.[68]

Orientalists Fight Back

For a number of years now, Islamologists have been aware of the disastrous effect of Said's *Orientalism* on their discipline. Professor Herbert Berg has complained that the latter's influence has resulted in "a fear of asking and answering potentially embarrassing questions—ones which might upset Muslim sensibilities."[69]

Professor Montgomery Watt, one of the most respected Western Islamologists of the last fifty years, takes Said to task for asserting that Sir Hamilton Gibb was wrong in saying that the master science of Islam was law and not theology. This, says Watt, "shows Said's ignorance of Islam." But Watt rather unfairly adds, "since he is from a Christian Arab background."[70] Said is indeed ignorant of Islam, but surely not because he is a Christian, since Watt and Gibb themselves were devout Christians. Watt also decries Said's tendency to ascribe dubious motives to various writers, scholars, and statemen such as Gibb and Lane, with Said committing doctrinal blunders such as not realizing that non-Muslims could not marry Muslim women.[71]

R. Stephen Humphreys found Said's book important in some ways because it showed how some Orientalists were indeed "trapped within a vision that portrayed Islam and the Middle East as in some way essentially different from 'the West.'" Nonetheless, "Edward Said's analysis of Orientalism is overdrawn and misleading in many ways, and purely as [a] piece of intellectual history, *Orientalism* is a seriously flawed book." Even more damning, Said's book actually discouraged, argues Humphreys, the very idea of modernization of Middle Eastern societies. "In an ironic way, it also emboldened the Islamic activists and militants who were then just beginning to enter the political arena. These could use Said to attack their opponents in the Middle East as slavish 'Westernists,' who were out of touch with the authentic culture and values of their own countries. Said's book has had less impact on the study of medieval Islamic history—partly because medievalists know how distorted his account of classical Western Orientalism really is."[72]

Even scholars praised by Said in *Orientalism* do not particularly like his analysis, arguments, or conclusions. Maxime Rodinson judged that "as usual, [Said's] militant stand leads him repeatedly to make excessive statements," due, no doubt, to the fact that Said was "inadequately versed in the practical work of the Orientalists."[73] Rodinson also calls Said's polemic and style "Stalinist,"[74] while P. J. Vatikiotis wrote, "Said introduced McCarthyism into Middle Eastern Studies."[75] Jacques Berque, also praised by Said, wrote that the latter had "done quite a disservice to his countrymen in allowing them to believe in a Western intelligence coalition against them."[76]

For the English historian of India Clive Dewey, Said's book "was, technically, so bad; in every respect, in its use of sources, in its deductions, it lacked rigour and balance. The outcome was a caricature of Western knowledge of the Orient, driven by an overtly political agenda. Yet it clearly touched a deep vein of vulgar prejudice running through American academe."[77]

The most famous modern scholar who not only replied to but who also mopped the floor with Said was, of course, Bernard Lewis. Lewis points to many serious errors of history, interpretation, analysis, and omission. He has never been answered, let alone refuted.

Lewis points out that even among British and French scholars on whom Said concentrates, he does not mention at all Claude Cahen, Evariste Lévi-Provençal, Henri Corbin, Marius Canard, Charles Pellat, William and George Marçais, or William Wright; only mentioned in passing, usually in a long list of names, are scholars like R. A. Nicholson, Guy Le Strange, Sir Thomas Arnold, and E. G. Browne: "Even for those whom he does cite, Mr. Said makes a remarkably arbitrary choice of works. His common practice indeed is to omit their major contributions to scholarship and instead fasten on minor or occasional writings." Said even fabricates lies about eminent scholars: "Thus in speaking of the late-eighteenth early-nineteenth-century French Orientalist Silvestre de Sacy, Mr. Said remarks that 'he ransacked the Oriental archives. . . . What texts he isolated, he then brought back; he doctored them. . . . [p. 127] If these words bear any meaning at all it is that Sacy was somehow at fault in his access to these documents and then committed the crime of tampering with them. This outrageous libel on a great scholar is without a shred of truth."[78]

Another false accusation that Said flings out is that Orientalists never properly discussed the Orient's economic activities until Rodinson's *Islam and Capitalism* (1966). This shows Said's total ignorance of the works of Adam Mez,

J. H. Kramers, W. Björkman, V. Barthold, and Thomas Arnold, all of whom dealt with the economic activities of Muslims. As Rodinson himself points out elsewhere, one of the three scholars who was a pioneer in this very field was Bernard Lewis.[79]

Said writes of Islamic Orientalism being cut off from developments in other fields in the humanities, particularly the economic and the social (p. 261). But this again only reveals Said's ignorance of the works of real Orientalists rather than those of his imagination. As Rodinson writes, the sociology of Islam is an ancient subject, citing the work of R. Lévy. Rodinson then points out that Émile Durkheim's celebrated journal *L'Année sociologique* listed for every year, starting from the first decades of the twentieth century, a certain number of works on Islam.[80]

NEGATIVE ARAB AND ASIAN REACTION TO SAID'S *ORIENTALISM*

It must have been particularly galling for Said to see the hostile reviews of his *Orientalism* written by Arab, Iranian, and Asian intellectuals, some of whom he admired and singled out for praise in many of his works. For example, Nikki Keddie, praised in *Covering Islam*, talked of the disastrous influence of *Orientalism*, even though she admired parts of it:

> I think that there has been a tendency in the Middle East field to adopt the word "orientalism" as a generalized swear-word essentially referring to people who take the "wrong" position on the Arab-Israeli dispute or to people who are judged too "conservative." It has nothing to do with whether they are good or not good in their disciplines. So "orientalism" for many people is a word that substitutes for thought and enables people to dismiss certain scholars and their works. I think that is too bad. It may not have been what Edward Said meant at all, but the term has become a kind of slogan.[81]

Keddie noted that the book "could also be used in a dangerous way because it can encourage people to say, 'You Westerners, you can't do our history right, you can't study it right, you really shouldn't be studying it, we are the only ones who can study our own history properly.' "[82]

Albert Hourani, much admired by Said, made a similar point: "I think all this talk after Edward's book also has a certain danger. There is a certain counter-attack of Muslims, who say nobody understands Islam except themselves."[83]

Hourani went further in his criticism of Said's *Orientalism*: "Orientalism has now become a dirty word. Nevertheless it should be used for a perfectly respected discipline. . . . I think [Said] carries it too far when he says that the orientalists delivered the Orient bound to the imperial powers. . . . Edward totally ignores the German tradition and philosophy of history which was the central tradition of the orientalists. . . . I think Edward's other books are admirable."[84] Similarly, Aijaz Ahmed thought *Orientalism* was a "deeply flawed book," and would be forgotten when the dust settled, whereas he thought Said's books on Palestine would be remembered.[85]

Kanan Makiya, the eminent Iraqi scholar, chronicled Said's disastrous influence, particularly in the Arab world:

> *Orientalism* as an intellectual project influenced a whole generation of young Arab scholars, and it shaped the discipline of modern Middle East studies in the 1980s. The original book was never intended as a critique of contemporary Arab politics, yet it fed into a deeply rooted populist politics of resentment against the West. The distortions it analyzed came from the eighteenth and nineteenth centuries, but these were marshalled by young Arab and "pro-Arab" scholars into an intellectual-political agenda that was out of kilter with the real needs of Arabs who were living in a world characterized by rapidly escalating cruelty, not ever-increasing imperial domination. The trajectory from Said's *Orientalism* to his *Covering Islam* . . . is premised on the morally wrong idea that the West is to be blamed in the here-and-now for its long nefarious history of association with the Middle East. Thus it unwittingly deflected from the real problems of the Middle East at the same time as it contributed more bitterness to the armory of young impressionable Arabs when there was already far too much of that around.[86]

Orientalism, continues Makiya, "makes Arabs feel contented with the way they are, instead of making them rethink fundamental assumptions which so clearly haven't worked. . . . They desperately need to unlearn ideas such as that 'every European' in what he or she has to say about the world is or was a 'racist.' . . . The ironical fact is that the book was given the attention it received in the 'almost totally ethnocentric' West largely because its author was a Palestinian."[87]

Though he finds much to admire in Said's *Orientalism*, the Syrian philosopher Sadiq al-'Azm finds that "the stylist and polemicist in Edward Said very often runs away with the systematic thinker."[88] Al-'Azm also finds Said guilty of the very essentialism that Said ostensibly sets out to criticize, perpetuating the distinction between East and West. Said further renders a great disservice to those who wish to examine the difficult question of how one can study other cultures from a libertarian perspective. Al-'Azm recognizes Said's antiscientific bent and defends certain Orientalist theses from Said's criticism; for example, al-'Azm says:

> I cannot agree with Said that their "Orientalist mentality" blinded them to the realities of Muslim societies and definitively distorted their views of the East in general. For instance: isn't it true, on the whole, that the inhabitants of Damascus and Cairo today feel the presence of the transcendental in their lives more palpably and more actively than Parisians and Londoners? Isn't it true that religion means everything to the contemporary Moroccan, Algerian and Iranian peasant in a manner it cannot mean for the American farmer or the member of a Russian kolkhoz? And isn't it a fact that the belief in the laws of nature is more deeply rooted in the minds of university students in Moscow and New York than among the students of al-Azhar and of Tehran University.[89]

Al-'Azm also criticizes Said's accounts of Karl Marx and his contradictory appraisal of Louis Massignon. What Said finds insufferable is the nineteenth-century European's feeling of superiority, but Sadiq al-'Azm says that indeed, "nineteenth-century Europe was superior to Asia and much of the rest of the world in terms of productive capacities, social organisation, historical ascendancy, military might, and scientific and technological development."[90]

Nadim al-Bitar, a Lebanese Muslim, finds Said's generalizations about all Orientalists hard to accept, and is very skeptical about Said having read more than a handful of Orientalist works. Al-Bitar also accuses Said of essentialism: "[Said] does to [Western] Orientalism what he accuses the latter of doing to the Orient. He dichotomizes it and essentializes it. East is East and West is West and each has its own intrinsic and permanent nature."[91] Al-Saghir, an Iraqi scholar, also takes Said to task for dismissing all Orientalists a priori. For example, al-Saghir looks at Orientalist works on the Koran, and finds them, on the whole, very valuable, "carefully researched and intellectually honest"; their "overall characteristic is purely scholarly."[92]

The most pernicious legacy of Said's *Orientalism* is its implicit support for religious fundamentalism, and on its insistence that "all the ills [of the Arab world] emanate from Orientalism and have nothing to do with the socio-economic, political and ideological makeup of the Arab lands or with the cultural historical backwardness which stands behind it."[93]

Thus ironically, Said, a Christian agnostic, becomes a de facto apologist and protector of Islam, the least Christian religion and certainly the religion least given to self-doubt. Despite his claims that he does not know anything about Islam, and despite the fact that he has never written a single scholarly work devoted to Islam, Said has always assumed the role in the West of an Islamic expert and has never flinched from telling us in unscholarly journalistic articles what the real Islam is. One's reaction is "stop telling us what Islam is, let us Muslims do that, stop talking for the Muslims." Said is a secularist defending Islam, so one wonders how he will be able to argue for a nontheocratic state once Palestine becomes a reality—in a theocratic Islamic Palestine, he would be put in his dhimmi place. If Islam is such a wonderful religion, why does he not convert to it, and why does he not accept it as the basis for any new constitution? At some stage, Said will have to do what he has been avoiding all his adult life—criticize Islam, or at least indirectly the idea of a theocracy.

Said has much to answer for. *Orientalism*, despite its systematic distortions and its limited value as intellectual history, has left Western scholars in fear of asking questions—in other words, it has inhibited their research. Said's work, with its strident anti-Westernism, it has made the goal of modernization of Middle Eastern societies that much more difficult. His work, wherein all the ills of Middle Eastern societies are blamed on the wicked West, has rendered much-needed self-criticism by Muslims, Arab and non-Arab alike, nearly impossible. His work has encouraged Islamic fundamentalists, whose impact on world affairs needs no underlining.

Part 2

THE THREE GOLDEN THREADS AND THE MISAPPREHENSIONS OF EDWARD SAID

1

THREE TUTELARY GUIDING LIGHTS

PREAMBLE

A visit to the Ontario Science Center in Toronto on New Year's Day 2006 was for me a sobering experience. Tucked away in the section titled "Truth" were many untruthful though undoubtedly politically correct statements denigrating Western civilization. In an effort to be fair, one exhibit gave way to unbridled relativism: "Modern Western science puts the Sun at the centre of the solar system. But other points of view are not necessarily wrong or primitive." And yet the same section, without a hint of irony, was proclaiming how "Eurocentric" or "intolerant" the West was! This science museum, which was implicitly a veritable hymn to the achievements of Western thought and ideas, went out of its way to selectively criticize some Western thinkers for "racism," or, as F. R. Leavis and D. H. Lawrence might both have said, "to do dirt on Western life."

But the museum exemplified the defining values of the Occident, or what are the tutelary guiding lights of, or the three golden threads running through, Western civilization—namely, rationalism, universalism, and self-criticism. One could perhaps argue that universalism and self-criticism were the logical outcomes of rationalism, but I think it more useful to view them as separate but interconnected sets of beliefs and principles. Second, Western civilization can, and has been, characterized in several other ways.[1] I think many of the suggested distinguishing characteristics of the West, such as the separation of spiritual and temporal authority, can be said to derive from one or more of the three golden threads. Thus, in the latter case of the separation of church and state, as Marsilius of Padua argued, "It is the state and not the church that guarantees the civil peace, and reason, not revelation, to which appeal must be made in all matters of temporal jurisdiction."[2] Politics involves willing and free participation, discussion: in short, rationalism, dissent, the right to change one's mind, and the right to oppose and disagree—that is, self-criticism—without recourse or appeal to divine commands or holy scriptures. Similarly, another defining feature, the rule of law, the thought that law is central to civilized existence and its continuation, was derived largely from the Romans. Not only is lawmaking a supremely human and rational activity, but Roman law was also conceived as possessing a *universal* jurisdiction.

RATIONALISM: TRUTH, OBJECTIVE KNOWLEDGE, KNOWLEDGE FOR THE SAKE OF KNOWLEDGE

I would rather discover one cause than gain the kingdom of Persia.
—Democritus

Considerate la vostra semenza
fatti non foste a viver come bruti
ma per seguir virtute e canoscenza.

Take thought of the seed from which you spring
You were not born to live as brutes,
But to follow virtue and knowledge
—Dante (1265–1321), *The Divine Comedy*, Inferno Canto 26, line 118

A Clerk ther was of Oxenford also,
That unto logik hadde long y-go.
As lene was his hors as is a rake,
And he nas nat right fat, I undertake,
But loked holwe, and therto soberly.
Ful thredbar was his overest courtepy
For he hadde geten him yet no benefyce,
Ne was so worldly for to have offyce.
For him was lever have at his beddes heed
Twenty bokes, clad in blak or reed,
Of Aristotle and his philosophye,
Than robes riche, or fithele, gay sautrye.
But al be that he was a philosophre,
Yet hadde he but litel gold in cofre;
But al that he mighte of his freendes hente,
On bokes and on lerninge he it spente,
And bisily gan for the soules preye
Of hem that yaf him wherwith ro scoleye.
Of studie took he most cure and most hede.

Noght o word spak he more than was nede,
And that was seyd in forme and reverence,
And short and quil, and ful of hy sentence.
Souninge in moral vertu was his speche,
And gladly wolde he lerne, and gladly teche.
—Geoffrey Chaucer (c.1340–1400), *The Prologue, Canterbury Tales*

Now, and for us, it is a time to Hellenise, and to praise knowing . . .
—Matthew Arnold, *Culture and Anarchy*

[Consider] the simple truth asserted by Aristotle: "all men possess by nature a craving for knowledge." This is no rare endowment scattered sparingly from heaven that falls on a few heads and passes others by: curiosity, the desire to know things as they are, is a craving no less native to the being of man, no less universal through mankind, than the craving for food and drink. . . . The desire of knowledge does not need, nor could it possibly possess, any higher or more authentic sanction than the happiness which attends its gratification. . . .

[P]eople think that the hunger and thirst for knowledge can be neglected with impunity. And yet, though the man does not die altogether, part of him dies, part of him starves to death: as Plato says, he never attains completeness and health, but walks lame to the end of his life and returns imperfect and good for nothing to the world below.

But the desire of knowledge, stifle it though you may, is none the less originally born with every man: and nature does not implant desires in us for nothing, nor endow us with faculties in vain. "Sure," says Hamlet,

Sure, He that made us with such large discourse
Looking before and after, gave us not
That capability and godlike reason
To fust in us unused.

The faculty of learning is ours that we many find in its exercise that delight which arises from the unimpeded activity of any energy in the groove nature meant it to run in. Let a man acquire knowledge not for this or that external and incidental good which may chance to result from it, but for itself; not because it is useful or ornamental, but because it is knowledge, and therefore good for man to acquire.
—A. E. Housman, *Introductory Lecture*, 1892

Science, according to Aristotle, is the quintessentially rational human activity. Aristotle said, "[A]ll men by nature desire to know. . . . [T]he human race lives also by art and reasonings."[3] Aristotle, who had one of the most curious, in the sense of inquiring, minds of anyone who has ever lived, sees science as the natural development of intellectual curiosity that has been submitted to critical thought. Science and critical thinking are something else for which we are beholden to the Ionian Enlightenment, to the Greeks. The Greeks, unlike their Near Eastern neighbors to whom they acknowledged their intellectual, artistic, and religious debts,[4] were able to view knowledge more abstractly, more theoretically, and more generally. The Greeks, on the whole and more so than the peoples' other contemporary civilizations, sought natural rather than supernatural explanations for observable phenomena, whether in nature or human history. But also implicit in Aristotle's famous observation is another characteristic of intellectual life and scientific curiosity, a singularity of Western civilization and many of its institutions, a desire for knowledge for its own sake, not for purposes of sacrifice, ritual, and propitiation, haruspication or divination. Alcmaeon of Croton wrote, "Man differs from other [creatures] in that he alone understands."[5] Bruce Thornton sums up this saving grace of the Greeks in the following way: "Observing and learning are pleasurable because they express and fulfill a core aspect of our humanity. Anaxagoras when asked why a man should prefer being born to nonexistence, answered 'For the sake of viewing the heavens and the whole order of the universe.'"[6] Human life has value because of our ability to learn about and appreciate our surroundings. So Aristotle defended his interest in lowly animals by saying, "If some [animals] have no graces to charm the sense, yet nature, which fashioned them, gives amazing pleasure in their study to all who can trace links of causation, and are inclined to philosophy. . . . Each and all will reveal to us something natural and something beautiful."[7] And again, Aristotle: "Learning, then, is the most valuable activity for a human. The fifth-century philosopher Democritus claimed that he 'would rather discover one cause than gain the kingdom of Persia.' "[8]

Here is Aristotle as preserved by Iamblichus: "To seek from all knowledge a result other than itself and to demand that it must be useful is the act of one completely ignorant of the distance that from the start separates good things from necessary things; for they differ completely. For the things that are loved for the sake of something else and without which life is impossible must be called necessities and joint-causes; but those that are loved for themselves, even if nothing else follows from them, must be called goods in the strict sense; for this is not desirable for the sake of that, and that for the sake of something else, and so *ad infinitum*—there is a stop somewhere."[9]

We may take Cicero's remarks in *On Duties* as representative of an educated Roman's similar attitude toward knowledge. Man is a rational creature, and by virtue of his rationality, man seeks knowledge. "Inquiry into and searching for truth are primary characteristics of mankind. So when we are free from business obligations and other preoccupations, we become eager to see something new, to hear and learn something; we begin to think that knowledge about the mysteries and wonders of the world is necessary to a happy life."[10]

At least in the West, this idea has obstinately kept its ground from age to age, in the words of Cardinal Newman. Newman, in his classic *The Idea of a University*, devotes an entire chapter to defending the idea of knowledge for its own sake. He wrote:

> Knowledge is capable of being its own end. Such is the constitution of the human mind, that any kind of knowledge, if it be really such, is its own reward. . . . Now, when I say that Knowledge is, not merely a means to something beyond it, or the preliminary of certain arts into which it naturally resolves, but an end sufficient to rest in and to pursue for its own sake, surely I am uttering no paradox, for I am stating what is intelligible in itself, and has ever been the common judgment of philosophers and the ordinary feeling of mankind. . . . [I]ndependent of [the practical advantages of knowledge], we are satisfying a direct need of our nature in its very acquisition; and, whereas our nature, unlike that of the inferior creation, does not once reach its perfection, but depends, in order to it, on a number of external aids and appliances, Knowledge, as one of the principle of these, is valuable for what its very presence in us does for us after the manner of a habit, even though it be turned to no further account, nor subserve any direct end.
>
> [Cicero] considers Knowledge the very first object to which we are attracted, after the supply of our physical wants.[11]

And you shall know the truth, and the truth shall make you free.
—John 8:32

Concomitant with the desire to know is the thought that one should, at least, aim at the truth even though we may only approximate it most of the time; in other words, the goal is to eventually acquire *objective* knowledge after a process of trial and error, conjectures and refutations, corroboration and disconfirmation. The attainment of truth is the common end of all the sciences, understood in the broadest sense. Indeed, philosophers have often defined knowledge in terms of truth, knowledge being justified true belief. Continental charlatans—postmodernists and others—have cast doubt on the possibility of objective knowledge, and they have further argued that the very notion of truth is coercive, imperialist, and a part of the discourse of power. To reject the notion of truth—objective knowledge—is to abandon the very possibility of science, rational discourse, and even morality, civil society, and politics—since ethical and political decisions often depend on having access to knowledge, objective knowledge of civilization *tout court*.

Matthew Arnold makes the same point in his *Culture and Anarchy*:

> For as there is a curiosity about intellectual matters which is futile, and merely a disease, so there is certainly a curiosity,—a desire after the things of the mind simply for their own sakes and for the pleasure of seeing them as they are,—which is, in an intelligent being, natural and laudable. Nay, and the very desire to see things as they are implies a balance and regulation of mind which is not often attained without fruitful effort, and which is the very opposite of the blind and diseased impulse of mind which is what we mean to blame when we blame curiosity. Montesquieu says:—"The first motive which ought to impel us to study is the desire to augment the excellence of our nature, and to render an intelligent being yet more intelligent." This is the true ground to assign for the genuine scientific passion, however manifested, and for culture, viewed simply as a fruit of this passion; and it is a worthy ground, even though we let the term curiosity stand to describe it.[12]

In complete contrast, Bernard Lewis shows in *The Muslim Discovery of Europe*, with example after example, that Muslims, with rare exceptions, did not show the Western curiosity for other cultures, languages, or literature, or share the Western pursuit of knowledge for its own sake.

Lewis points out the differences in attitude of the two civilizations, Islamic and European, to alien languages and literature; contempt in Islam as opposed to intellectual curiosity in the Christian West. To learn a foreign language or infidel script would be impious, though occasionally new converts to Islam brought a knowledge of non-Islamic languages. Even after eight centuries of Muslim presence in Spain, we know of only a single document that reveals any Muslim interest in a European language. European literature provided neither aesthetic appeal nor moral guidance for Muslims. As for history, only the Islamic community was considered worthy of study, as it revealed God's purpose for mankind through it. In contrast, Europeans, in a Europe of different nations and cultures, found it necessary to learn languages. Europe, with its intellectual curiosity, eventually developed the necessary scholarly tools to study Arabic, such as a Latin-Arabic glossary, the first of which was prepared in the twelfth century. This led to a European appreciation of Arabic literature, even an attempt to translate parts of the Koran into Latin. By the sixteenth century there were several glossaries and dictionaries, and a treatise on Arabic grammar available to the interested European public.[13] Then, after the great opening up of the intellectual horizons of the West during the sixteenth and seventeenth centuries, Arabic studies flourished in many European universities, resulting in the publication of dictionaries, grammars, and critical editions of Persian, Turkish, and Arabic texts. Scholars such as Jacob Golius in Holland with his important work *Lexicon Arabico-Latinum* and Edward Pococke in England with a *Lexicon heptaglotton* (1669) were laying the foundations of classical Orientalism. But as Lewis points out, "[T]he purpose of these activities was partly practical, related to the needs of commerce and diplomacy, and also partly scholarly, *to gratify the boundless intellectual curiosity* unleashed by the Renaissance." In contrast, Lewis argues, "Of intellectual interest in Western languages and the literatures enshrined in them, there is not the slightest sign. We know of no Muslim scholar or man of letters before the eighteenth century who sought to learn a Western language, still less of any attempt to produce grammars, dictionaries, or other language tools. Translations are few and far between. Those that are known are works chosen for practical purposes and the translations are made by converts or non-Muslims."[14]

Nothing has changed. In the Arab Human Development Report of 2003, published by the United Nations Development Programme, we learn that "the total number of books translated into Arabic in the last 1,000 years is fewer than those translated in Spain in one year. Greece, with a population of fewer than 11 million, translates five times as many books from abroad into Greek annually as the 22 Arab countries combined, with a total population of more than 300 million, translated into Arabic."[15]

By the seventeenth century, European scholars had developed sophisticated techniques of textual criticism when applying them to classical and biblical texts, and which the new Orientalists were now able to draw upon when examining the languages and literatures of the East. As Lewis reminds us, "To all this there was nothing remotely comparable among the Muslims where scholarship, whether philological or other, was confined to the monuments of their own faith, law, and literature."[16] Even in regard to their own faith, law, and literature, Muslims have yet to learn the science of textual criticism, let alone apply it to the Koran.

The situation is similar as regards Muslim indifference to European history. This indifference is shared even by the great thinker Ibn Khaldun.[17]

Conclusions similar to those of Lewis were arrived at by Sir John Chardin in the seventeenth century during his travels in Persia. Chardin contrasted European intellectual curiosity with its lack in Persia about, for example, the origins of tobacco and sugar.[18] As for traveling for the sake of curiosity, it is totally alien to the Persians' understanding and explains their near total ignorance of what passes in Europe.[19]

Little seems to have changed in modern times, as Michael Field, a journalist for the *Financial Times* with twenty-seven years of experience in the Middle East, explained in 1994: "[Arabs] may be well informed on currency movements and the latest chat on the prospects of the Western economies but know surprisingly little about how Western societies and governments operate. Even those who live in the West or visit it frequently on holiday do not have much understanding of it because, in most cases, when they are there they mix with other Arabs, principally their own relations, and take no interest in the culture, history or institutions of the countries they are in."[20]

Field's sentiments are echoed by Muhammad Talbi, a contemporary Tunisian Muslim intellectual much involved in interfaith dialogues, who wrote,

> Today's Islam—I shall not call it "modern"—is a far cry from the courage of her pioneers, far behind *Sharastānī*, the author of *al-Milal wa 'l-niḥal*,[21] and *Ibn Ḥazm*, the author of *Fiṣal.*[22] *Ibn Rushd* [Averröes] was the last Muslim philosopher open to non-Muslim cultures. Sign of the times, his works which exercised a great influence on the Renaissance in the West, come down to us above all in Latin or Hebrew. In the 14th century, even Ibn *Khaldūn*, whose genius is incontrovertible, wrote, "All the pre-Islamic sciences concerned with religious groups are to be discarded, and their discussion is forbidden."[23] Ibn *Khaldūn*, and only on that occasion, was listened to, or rather he was the intermediary of a way of thinking which has prevailed to this day. Few Muslims, wrote Maryam Jameelah,[24] have a really profound knowledge of the West. How many Muslims, for example, have mastered Greek or Latin, and how many are intellectually equipped to study Judaism and Christianity as well as the secular ideologies from a Muslim point of view? While generations of Western Orientalists have studied Islam to the extent of their needs and goals, is it not essential for some Muslim religious scholars [*'ulamā'*] to become Occidentalists?[25]

The scholar F. R. Rosenthal has pointed out that the process of assimilation of the heritage of classical antiquity into Islam between the eighth and tenth centuries can justly be called the renaissance of Islam. It is impossible to believe that Islamic civilization could have developed to the extent it did without that classical heritage.[26]

For many Western scholars, and for many Muslims, the very idea of an "Islamic philosophy" is a contradiction in terms. Orthodox Sunni Islam has never welcomed philosophic thought, with its unfettered use of reason. Traditionists have always been hostile to philosophy, a "foreign science" that led, they claimed, to heresy, doubt, and unbelief. In this, the traditionists' fears were well founded, for many of the philosophers developed views that were far from orthodox, and others, especially those hostile to the emerging Sunnism, committed themselves entirely to the guidance of reason as was understood in Greek philosophy and gave no more than lip service to Islamic religion. Thus the story of Islamic philosophy is, in part, the story of the tension between reason and revelation, with the eventual triumph of the dictates of revelation, a victory for irrationalism, leading to blind obedience of tradition.

Under Islam, orthodoxy has always been suspicious of "knowledge for its own sake." Unfettered intellectual inquiry is deemed dangerous to the faith. Muslims made a distinction between the native or Islamic sciences and foreign sciences; the former consisted of religion (Koranic exegesis, the science of hadith, jurisprudence, and scholastic theology) and language (grammar, lexicography, rhetoric, and literature). The "foreign sciences" or " the sciences of the ancients" were defined as those common to all peoples and religious communities, as opposed to such sciences as had been peculiarly developed by Islam. As G. E. von Grunebaum says, the foreign sciences are primarily the propaedeutic, physical, and metaphysical sciences of the Greeks: the various branches of mathematics, philosophy, natural history (zoology, botany, etc.), medicine, astronomy, music, magic, and alchemy.

But the study of these foreign sciences was always looked upon with suspicion and even animosity, which increased in the later Middle Ages. A part of the hostility can be attributed to the fact that the ancient authorities were non-Muslim and foreign. All foreign sciences endangered the faith.[27] One can contrast the situation in Islam with that in Christianity. One could argue that in rejecting Marcionism, which had tried to cut all links with Christianity's Judaic roots, Saint Irenaeus had kept open Europe's relationship with the past, which, with its twin peaks of Athens and Jerusalem, was to continue to enrich Western civilization throughout its history.[28] Islamic countries, on the other hand, totally rejected their past and all the ancient pre-Islamic glories, from the civilization of the Indus River to the monuments of Mesopotamia and Egypt, as belonging to a period of ignorance and barbarism, *Jāhiliyya*.

The sciences were seen as praiseworthy, blameworthy, or neutral. All sciences are blameworthy that are useless for acting rightly toward God. The Prophet is reputed to have prayed to God to protect him from useless knowledge.

Useful knowledge was that which was necessary or helpful for the practice of religion. Eventually the ancient sciences were to lose out in this perpetual battle between the theological and the philosophical-scientific approach, since they were not required for the realization of the kind of life God had ordained. Thus, despite the contributions of the Muslim scholars and scientists, these sciences were not rooted in the fundamental needs and aspirations of Islamic civilization. Islam considered the main task and aim of man to be to serve God, to which end the native sciences were, of course, essential, to which one may add history and geography. Any effort beyond that, for example, in the study of the natural sciences, is not essential to the central cultural task and hence can be discarded.

Both von Grunebaum and Renan make the point that Islamic science developed for a while despite Islam.[29] Renan wrote:

> Science and philosophy flourished on Musalman soil during the first half of the Middle Ages; but it was not by reason of Islam, it was in spite of Islam. Not a Musalman philosopher or scholar escaped persecution. During the period just specified persecution is less powerful than the instinct of free inquiry, and the rationalist tradition is kept alive, then intolerance and fanaticism win the day. It is true that the Christian Church also cast great difficulties in the way of science in the Middle Ages; but she did not strangle it outright, as did the Musalman theology. To give Islam the credit of Averröes and so many other illustrious thinkers, who passed half their life in prison, in forced hiding, in disgrace, whose books were burned and whose writings almost suppressed by theological authority, is as if one were to ascribe to the Inquisition the discoveries of Galileo, and a whole scientific development which it was not able to prevent.[30]

Not only did orthodoxy stifle the research of the scientists, but it was also obvious "that their researches had nothing to give to their community which this community could accept as an essential enrichment of their lives."[31] For us, looking from the outside, this loss of scientific endeavor is an impoverishment of Islamic civilization, but for the Muslims there was no loss since this science did not serve the Muslim aim of serving God.[32] The idea of knowledge for its own sake was meaningless in the Muslim context; George Sarton, in his history of science, gives the example of Muslim zoology: "One can find in many Arabic and Persian writings speculations on the order of nature as far as the distribution of the three kingdoms is concerned. The Muslims, with but few exceptions, were hardly interested in the scientific aspects of these matters, but rather in their theological implications; they were not thinking so much of evolution from the human or naturalistic point of view as of creation from the divine one."[33]

As Friedrich von Hayek argues in *The Road to Serfdom*, "[T]otalitarian control of opinion extends, however, also to subjects which at first seem to have no political significance. . . . According to the Webbs, the *Journal for Marxist-Leninist Natural Sciences* has the following slogans: 'We stand for Party in Mathematics. We stand for the purity of Marxist-Leninist theory in surgery.' "[34]

As an example of persecution of the scientists that Renan alludes to above, we might cite the case of Ibn al-Haytham (Alhazen),[35] whose works were branded as heretical and then forgotten in the Muslim East: "A disciple of Maimonides, the Jewish philosopher, relates that he was in Baghdad on business, when the library of a certain philosopher (who died in 1214) was burned there. The preacher, who conducted the execution of the sentence, threw into the flames, with his own hands, an astronomical work of Ibn al-Haytham, after he had pointed to a delineation therein given of the sphere of the earth, as an unhappy symbol of impious Atheism."[36]

It is worth pointing out that where Rosenthal is defending a moderate thesis, Renan is defending a radical thesis. For Rosenthal, there is such a thing as "Islamic civilization," but it developed through contact with the Greek classical tradition. Thus, Islam could make further progress by further contact with Greek rationalism. Renan, on the other hand, rejects the very idea that Islam is compatible with civilization as such. For him, there is simply no such thing as "Islamic science" or "Islamic philosophy." The Greek tradition was utterly incompatible with Islam, and further contact with Greek rationalism would destroy Islam.

Hayek pointed out that totalitarian ideologies and states based on them have always condemned knowledge for its own sake:

> It is entirely in keeping with the whole spirit of totalitarianism that it condemns any human activity done for its own sake and without ulterior purpose. Science for science's sake, art for art's sake, are equally abhorrent to the Nazis, our socialist intellectuals, and the communists. Every activity must derive its justification from a conscious social purpose. There must be no spontaneous, unguided activity, because it might produce results which cannot be foreseen and for which the plan does not provide. It might produce something new, undreamed of in the philosophy of the planner. The principle extends even to games and amusements. I leave it to the reader to guess whether it was in Germany or in Russia that chess-players were officially exhorted that "we must finish once and for all with the neutrality of chess. We must condemn once and for all the formula 'chess for the sake of chess' like the formula 'art for art's sake.' "[37]

The pursuit of knowledge, of truth, is enshrined in what was one of the greatest creations of Western civilization, the university, modeled on the Brotherhood of

Pythagoras, the Academy of Plato, and the Lyceum of Aristotle. Most of the non-Western universities have in some way or other copied the principles and structure of Western universities, and are even run by scholars and administrators trained in Western universities. Dr. Charles Malik, philosopher and Lebanese diplomat, explains in his important work *A Christian Critique of the University* how the Greeks created the modern university as a home for reason, free inquiry, unfettered curiosity, and the search for objective knowledge, which was essentially shareable and which underlined the unity of man as man.[38] Aristotle and the Greeks bequeathed to the world the norms of scientific investigation.

E. R. Dodds, in his classic work *The Greeks and the Irrational*, argued that the Greeks in fact were not quite so blind to the importance of nonrational factors in man's experience and behavior as is commonly assumed both by their apologists and by their critics.[39] And, not every Greek was able to rise to the supreme rationality of an Aristotle. Nonetheless, rationality was bequeathed to the West by the Greeks, and it runs throughout Western history and civilization, like a stream occasionally going underground but always reappearing at unexpected moments. Hence, Malik's points remain valid. Malik draws the further important distinction between Western attitudes toward knowledge and those of other cultures:

> It is interesting to ponder why Chinese or Indians or Muslims or Arabs can enter Freiburg University or the Sorbonne or Oxford or Harvard or Chicago University or Toronto University and specialize and earn a universally respected academic degree in their own Chinese or Indian or Muslim or Arab culture, but no German or Frenchman or Englishman or American or Canadian can enter any Chinese or Indian or Muslim or Persian or Arab university and specialize and earn a universally respected academic degree in his own German or French or British or American or Canadian culture. The reason is that these non-Western universities (and therefore their own native cultures which they themselves reflect) have not yet sufficiently caught the insatiable original Greek curiosity about all being; they are interested in others only to a degree; for the most part only utilitarianly, only to use them, only to learn from them. They are not interested in knowing their essence, their being; they are for the most part wrapped up in themselves; the others are perhaps too strange, too forbidding for them; their original, natural, wholesome curiosity is somehow inhibited.[40]

No university in an Islamic country, with perhaps the noble exception of one in Turkey, offers any profound courses on non-Islamic civilizations, certainly nothing of the depth, quality, and comprehensiveness of courses offered in Western universities on every civilization, ancient and modern. No scholar from the Islamic world writing about his own culture and history has reached anywhere near the scholarship of a Carl Brockelmann or a Theodor Nöldeke on Islamic studies. There is certainly no Muslim scholar who has contributed anything significant to the study of Europe, European history, languages, or literature in the way Europeans, from the sixteenth century onward, have done to Islamic civilization. As Malik observed, Western civilization is defined by total fearlessness of and openness to the truth.

Malik, writing at the height of the cold war about how the non-West is gradually overpowering the West, referred to the bogus "universities" of Soviet Russia:

> An inhibition of original curiosity has blunted Soviet universities about, for instance, the knowledge of Christianity. Christianity is cavalierly dismissed as so much nonsense or superstition or untruth or opium in the hands of the exploiters and oppressors. Nothing authentic is known or taught in Soviet universities about Christianity; whereas practically everything is known or taught in Western universities about communist doctrine and practice. And, as we shall see, this blunting, inhibiting virus has infected Western universities themselves with respect to the knowledge of Christianity. The non-West is gradually overpowering the West! The original universal Greek curiosity is gradually becoming overwhelmed![41]

But his strictures now apply with greater force to Islam. The West, in giving in to political correctness and in being corrupted by Saudi and other Arab money, is ceasing to honor the original intent of the university. In recent years, Saudi Arabia and other Islamic countries (e.g., Brunei) have established chairs of Islamic studies in prestigious Western universities, which are then encouraged to present a favorable image of Islam. Scientific research leading to objective truth no longer seems to be the goal. Critical examination of the sources or the Koran is discouraged. Scholars such as Daniel Easterman have even lost their posts for not teaching about Islam in the way approved by Saudi Arabia.[42]

In December 2005, Georgetown and Harvard universities each accepted $20 million from Saudi prince Alwaleed bin Talal for programs in Islamic studies. The Carter Center, founded by former president Jimmy Carter, is funded in part by bin Talal. Such money can only corrupt the original intent of all higher institutions of education, that is, the search for truth. Now, we shall have only "Islamic truth" that is acceptable to the royal Saudi family, a family that has financed terrorism, anti-Westernism, and anti-Semitism for more than thirty years. Previous donations from various Saudi sources have included gifts of $20 million, $5 million, and $2 million to the University of Arkansas, the University of California–Berkeley, and Harvard, respectively.

UNIVERSALISM AND THE UNITY OF MANKIND: OPENNESS TO THE OTHER—OTHER IDEAS, OTHER CUSTOMS, OTHER PEOPLE

Servare modum, finemque tenere
Naturamque sequi—
Nec sibi, sed toti genitum se credere mundo—
In commune bonus.

To preserve measure, to hold fast to the end, and follow nature—
To believe oneself born not for oneself alone but for all the world
—good for the community of mankind
—Lucan (39 CE–65 CE) *Pharsalia* (*De bello civili*) II.380 ff

Western civilization has ever been open, to a greater or lesser extent, to the Other: to other ideas, other customs, and other people. Though the idea of the unity of mankind did not at first play a great part in their thought, it nonetheless originated with the Greeks, gathered momentum, and led to the cosmopolitanism of the Cynics and the Stoics during the Hellenistic period. Not being burdened with either violent nationalism or racism,[43] the Greeks with their keen, inquiring minds were able to rethink their other prejudices when their geographical knowledge increased, and they arrived at fresh theoretical conclusions and finally moved in the direction of the idea of a common fellowship linking all mankind.[44]

The Greeks were equally open to new ideas from the outside. Greek philosophy is said to have been greatly influenced by the Vedic culture of India.[45] But by far the greater influence of course came from the ancient civilizations of the Near East and also Egypt. Walter Burkert, Rudolf Wittkower, and M. L. West have shown the importance of the cultural encounters with the Orient in the formation of the civilization we call Classical.[46] As Burkert wrote,

> The Cyclopes, Homer observes, are savages just because of their isolation: "For the Cyclopes do not have ships . . . as elsewhere men travel to each other by ships across the sea."[47] Hence they live in a kind of natural paradise, without agriculture, viticulture, city, or state, like lawless ogres. Civilization, by contrast, develops through contact with foreigners and distant partners, mainly by way of travel and commerce. Interaction gives people the chance "to see the

cities of many humans, and to learn about their minds," as Homer says in praise of Odysseus right at the start of the Odyssey. Culture, including Greek culture, requires intercultural contact.[48]

We know that skilled craftsmen fleeing the ravages of Assyrian devastation settled in Greece, bringing with them the refined arts of the East such as bronze work, large-scale architecture, ivory carving, and production of terra-cottas from molds.[49] In turn, Greek merchants had settled in Syria by the ninth century, and Greek mercenaries probably joined Assyrian armies.[50] Papyrus was imported from Egypt and became an integral part of Greek civilization, while the alphabet was probably acquired from the Phoenicians. A Platonic author of *Epinomis* proudly records, "And let us note that [987e] whatever Greeks acquire from foreigners is finally turned by them into something nobler."[51] As Burkert hastily explains, "We have perhaps become more hesitant to judge civilizations by criteria of better or worse. But it is the relation of model and imitation that justifies metaphor of higher versus lower culture and objectively shows cultural influence from one source to another. And yet in the process of acculturation something new may arise; and although Greeks had been on the receiving side for a long time, there is no doubt that the result is Greek. It is Greek art and architecture that have become classical, and Greek literature that has become world literature."[52]

By about 500 BCE, the situation was reversed as the current of influence flowed from West to East. King Darius of Persia summoned Greek sculptors to decorate Persepolis, his new capital. The Persian king also introduced coinage in the manner of Lydians and Greeks. As Horace once remarked, "Conquered Greece conquered the uncivilized victor."[53] Red-figure ceramics from Attica circulated throughout the Mediterranean and even found their way to central Germany. Greek craftsmanship and mythological poetry influenced the East, and the whole of the Mediterranean. Greek craftsmen had finally outgrown their Eastern masters.[54]

Two hundred years earlier, the current flowed, as we noted, from the East to West. It should come as no surprise if we detect a possible influence of Mesopotamian literature on Homer, particularly of the epic *Gilgamesh*. Burkert summarizes the similarities, which were also noted by Sir Maurice Bowra in his *Heroic Poetry*,[55] between the two, "In both cases, in Greek as in Akkadian, 'epic' means narrative poetry which employs a long verse repeated indefinitely, without strophic division; the tale is about gods, sons of gods, and great men from the past, all of whom may interact with each other. Main characteristics of style are the standard epithets, the formulaic verses, the repetition of verses, and typical scenes such as the 'assembly of the gods.'"[56] Many are also struck by the similarity between the openings of *Gilgamesh* and the *Odyssey*—we are told of a hero who wandered wide and saw many things—while his name is intentionally withheld. Since the publication in 1969 of the Akkadian epic *Atrahasis*, scholars have also remarked on correspondences between it and the *Iliad.* There is even a passage in Homer that comes close to being a translation of the Akkadian epic, according to Burkert,[57] who concludes,

> Affinities and similarities between oriental epic and Homeric poetry can no longer be ignored in interpreting Homer. This means that certain limits must be set to deriving Homer in his totality either from purely Indo-european stock or from Mycenaean pre-history. Homeric epic is a many-sided phenomenon. The Eastern influence is most marked in scenes of the divine pantheon, where characters, plots, and basic ideas seem to be borrowed. It would be wrong to overemphasize similarities or to overlook the marked differences. But never forget we are dealing with civilizations which were close to each other in time and space and which had continuous demonstrable contact. To insist on completely separate developments and purely coincidental parallels is to beg the question.[58]

Prefigurations of Greek philosophy are also found in ancient Eastern texts, and we also have the evidence of Greek philosophers' familiarity with Eastern thought; Aristotle, Eudemus, and Theopompus all record Iranian cosmological doctrines. There was even a tendency to exaggerate Greek debt to Oriental civilization, particularly Egypt. But this fact in itself also reinforces my thesis. These false attributions underline the respect with which the venerable civilizations of the East, and especially of Egypt, were held by writers such as Herodotus, for whom there was no shame in admitting Orientalizing influences.

In his book of immense scholarship,[59] West, after examining the doctrines of such writers and philosophers as Pherecydes, Anaximander, Anaximenes, and especially Heraclitus, then carefully sifts through the textual, philological, archaeological, and historical evidence to come to the conclusion that there was a period of active Iranian influence in the development of Greek thought from c.550 to c.480 BCE. There was indeed a milder Oriental influence earlier, but afterward none at all.[60] West eulogizes the influence of Oriental thought on the Greek mind. He believes Oriental fancy freed the Greeks from the limitations of what they could see with their own eyes; that God is intelligence; that the cosmos is one living creature; that the material world can be analyzed in terms of a few basic constituents such as fire, water, earth, metal; that there is a world of being beyond perception, beyond time.[61]

But once again, as Burkert points out, philosophy, in the modern sense, was nonetheless a Greek invention, as much as deductive proof in mathematics.[62]

Before coming back to Burkert's important point made above, echoing the

Platonic author of *Epinomis*, "And let us note that whatever Greeks acquire from foreigners is finally turned by them into something nobler," here, in discussing the Near Eastern influence on Greek culture especially in the early Archaic age, it is perhaps appropriate to mention Martin Bernal's *Black Athena*.[63] Bernal's major arguments have been soundly refuted by many scholars in the last ten years.[64] Mary Lefkowitz has shown that there is little or no historical substance to many Afrocentrist claims about the ancient world.[65]

However, Burkert, a scholar of profound learning, in a chapter of analytical brilliance titled "Orpheus and Egypt," conscientiously goes through all the evidence—textual, historical, and archaeological—to come to the conclusion that "Greek Dionysus, as he shows up in funerary contexts, has undergone the spell of Egypt, and that Bacchic mysteries which claim to guarantee otherworldly bliss are influenced by the Osiris cult. . . . Orpheus brings together a host of older Eastern traditions, Akkadian, Hurrite-Hittite, and Egyptian most of all, traditions that are apt to enrich more than to obfuscate our picture of the Greek spirit."[66]

Philhellenes surely have nothing to fear from admitting the evidence of various cross-cultural contacts and influences, which, as noted above, were in both directions: East to West and West to East. For, as Burkert repeatedly points out, what emerges is something entirely distinctive: what we call Greek civilization. The very strength of this civilization lay in its ability to learn from and improve upon the ideas, art, and literature of the Near East, Persia, India, and Egypt. Here is how Burkert sums up the originality of the Greeks in their ability to transform borrowed ideas to reach astonishing heights, hitherto unattained:

> Older cosmogonic speculation, transformed through the medium of Greek language by Parmenides, arrived at a new fundamental, that of "being," which is revealed by rational argument even beyond appearances. Later Plato introduced the basis of mathematics into the argument, the *a priori* concept—and until today we try to understand and to dominate nature by rational thinking with the aid of mathematical formalism. Parmenides insisted that meaningful language was directed toward "being," which also means toward truth in an absolute sense, beyond any personal, social, or political concern. Philosophy has largely tried to follow such an ideal of truth. It threatens to become obsolete, though, with the onset of relativity and deconstruction within the more modern trends in the social sciences and humanities. It is still to be hoped that the Greek heritage will not be totally lost.
>
> There is no reason to isolate the Greeks, but we continue to philosophize and even to think on Greek lines. Is it Eurocentric to insist, with Parmenides, that thinking and speaking should be adequate to "being"?[67]

In an earlier work Burkert had written, "Culture is not a plant sprouting from its seed in isolation; it is a continuous process of learning guided by curiosity along with practical needs and interests. It grows especially through a willingness to learn from what is '*other*,' what is strange and foreign. A revolutionary period such as the orientalizing epoch provided this very opportunity for cultural development."[68]

Rationality, knowledge, intellectual curiosity, the notion of objective truth, openness to the Other—these are the elements that went into creating the Greek miracle.

SELF-CRITICISM: THE REDEMPTIVE GRACE OF WESTERN CIVILIZATION

> *Nullius in verba.*
> (By nobody's word.)
>
> —Motto of Royal Society, 1663

> *Without criticism there'd be nothing but Hosannas. But man cannot live by Hosannas alone, those Hosannas have to be tempered in the crucible of doubt . . .*
>
> —Fyodor Dostoevesky, *The Brothers Karamozov*, 1880

> *Next to the right to create, the right to criticize is the richest gift that liberty of thought and speech can offer.*
>
> —Vladimir Nabokov, *Lectures on Russian Literature*, 1981

Humans are rational beings with powers of reflection, self-reflection, "a perpetually turning feed-back process,"[69] and by this power of reflection are able to correct and change their situation. Instead of passively accepting their lot, with this power of reflection, humans are able to reform, adjust, improve their beliefs, and reinterpret the ever-growing, ever-changing data. Western man developed from the start this capacity to submit even its most cherished beliefs to scrutiny—*nullius in verba.*

Sir Ernst Gombrich argues that it is this very critical attitude to our own venerable traditions that explains the West's success:

> It has become the fashion to level the charge of Eurocentricity at the West for ignoring our debt to the achievements of other civilizations. Yet while fully acknowledging this debt, we must still ask why the West, after the end of the Middle Ages, so rapidly overtook the great civilizations of the East.

> In the venerable civilizations of the East, custom was king and tradition the guiding principle. If change came it was all but imperceptible, for the laws of Heaven existed once and for all and were not to be questioned. That spirit of questioning, the systematic rejection of authority, was the one invention the East may have failed to develop. It originated in ancient Greece. However often authority tried to smother this inconvenient element, its spark was glowing underground. It was that spark, perhaps, that was fanned into flame by the awareness that our ancestors did not have the monopoly of wisdom, and that we may learn to know more than they have if only we do not accept their word unquestioned. As the motto of the Royal Society (dating from 1663) has it, *Nullius in verba*—By nobody's word. In pre-war years, when the Warburg Institute was housed next door to the Imperial Institute of Science, I overheard two students at lunch. "How does he know it is a wave?" I venture to think that this kind of question was not often heard in ancient China or India. It only became possible thanks to the position of science in our culture.[70]

The greatest critics and critiques of the Western tradition are to be found in the West. Modern denunciations of the West by third-world intellectuals such as Frantz Fanon and Edward Said rely on analyses provided by such Western thinkers as Karl Marx, Sigmund Freud, Friedrich Nietzsche, Antonio Gramsci, Jacques Derrida, Michel Foucault, Jacques Lacan, and Jean-Paul Sartre. The method of critical analysis developed in the West and exemplified by philosophers such as Marx testifies, in the words of Arthur Schlesinger Jr., "to the internally redemptive potentialities of the Western tradition."[71]

Europe has been guilty of terrible crimes, but what civilization has not been? Confining ourselves to the twentieth century, the sins of the West are no worse than the crimes and follies of Asia (the Rape of Nanking, when Japanese soldiers killed more than three hundred thousand unarmed civilians;[72] the crimes of Mao, resulting in the deaths of well over 70 million Chinese in peacetime;[73] Pol Pot, who caused the deaths of 1.7 million people—one-fifth of the population—in Cambodia;[74] the massacre of more than a million Muslims of East Pakistan [now Bangladesh] by the Muslims of West Pakistan),[75] or Africa (under Idi Amin's regime in Uganda, an estimated three hundred thousand people were killed;[76] the massacres in Rwanda left eight hundred thousand people dead; 1.8 million killed in the Sudan,[77] including at least three hundred thousand in Darfur)[78] or the Middle East (the killing of more than a million Armenians by the Turks;[79] the crimes of Saddam Hussein;[80] Hafez Assad's 1982 attack on the Syrian town of Hama, in which, according to the Syrian Human Rights Committee, between thirty thousand to forty thousand civilians died or remain missing;[81] the massacre of Palmyra [Tadmur] Prison in Syria;[82] as many as 2 million people have died since 1979 in Iran because of the policies of the Islamic Republic).[83]

And yet there persists a profound difference between the West and the Rest. Western intellectuals, writers, historians, politicians, and leaders have themselves chronicled the follies of the West and have forced Westerners to fundamentally rethink their policies, ideas, and political and social behavior, thereby bringing about change. Profound self-reflection and courageous acts of self-criticism have brought about movements that have led to the abolition of slavery, the dismantlement of empire, and legislation to defend the human rights of women and minorities and to defend freedom of inquiry and expression.[84]

Slavery has existed in every civilization in human history, but it was the West that first took active steps to abolish it. Samuel Johnson pointed out the contradictions of eighteenth-century American society: "Slavery is now no where more patiently endured, than in countries once inhabited by the zealots of liberty."[85] He denounced his own English compatriots: "Of black men the numbers are too great who are now repining under English cruelty."[86] James Boswell, with the aid of Johnson, was to help prepare the brief for the advocate of Joseph Knight, an African-born slave sold in Jamaica seeking to free himself from his Scottish master subsequent to the celebrated decision by the English Chief Justice Lord Mansfield that slavery was contrary to the laws of England. Lord Kames and his fellow judges, following the dictates of reason to assert a basic principle of equity and justice, wrote, "The dominion assumed over the negro, under the law of Jamaica, being unjust, could not be supported in this country [Scotland] to any extent." They pronounced slavery to be against the law in Scotland and set Knight free.[87]

Johnson dictated a long argument against slavery to Boswell.[88]

Leading figures in the British Enlightenment equally condemned slavery. They included writers such as William Cowper and Laurence Sterne, whose sermons expressing pity for slaves touched the heart of Ignatius Sancho, a slave who became the friend of many men of letters in eighteenth-century London. Sterne and Sancho exchanged touching letters: "[B]ut 'tis no uncommon thing, my good Sancho, for one half of the world to use the other half of it like brutes, and then endeavour to make 'em so. For my own part, I never look Westward (when I am in a pensive mood at least) but I think of the burdens which our brothers and sisters are there carrying—& could I ease their shoulders from one ounce of 'em, I declare I would set out this hour upon a pilgrmage to Mecca for their sakes."[89] "Slavery . . . is a crime so monstrous against the human species that all those who practise it deserve to be extirpated from the earth," wrote Thomas Day in the late eighteenth century.[90] Day also wrote an antislavery poem called "The Dying Negro" (1773). Daniel Defoe had castigated the trade in humans in his *Life of Colonel Jacque* (1722). Joseph Priestley argued later that slavery reduced men and women to "mere brutes," "so that they are deprived of every advantage of their rational nature."[91] Jeremy Bentham later called the colonies where slavery flourished "a disgrace and an outrage upon humanity."[92] William Blackstone, in his influential *Commentaries on the Laws of England*, declared that "a slave or negro, the instant he lands in England, becomes a freeman."[93] The playwright and member of Parliament Richard Brinsley Sheridan took the opportunity, when Lord Percy proposed a bill to phase out slavery in the West Indies, to attack slavery in the House of Commons in 1807.[94]

In 1797 Caleb Bingham put together a collection of speeches and dialogues, taken from various periods of Western history in *The Columbian Orator*. The African American abolitionist Frederick Douglass came across the speeches in *The Columbian Orator*. Douglass wrote, "Every opportunity I got I used to read this book. [Their orations] gave tongue to interesting thoughts of my own soul, which had frequently flashed through my mind, and died away for want of utterance. . . . What I got from Sheridan[95] was a bold denunciation of slavery and a powerful vindication of human rights. The reading of these documents enabled me to utter my thoughts." Douglass was particularly affected by the dialogue between slave and master:

> It is unnecessary to say that a dialogue with such an origin and such an end, read by me when every nerve in my being was in revolt at my own condition as a slave, affected me most powerfully. I could not help feeling that the day might yet come when the well-directed answers made by the slave to the master, in this instance, would find their counterpart in my own experience. [All these speeches of Pitt, Lord Chatham, and others] were all choice documents for me, and I read them over and over again, with an interest ever-increasing, because I was ever-gaining in intelligence; for the more I read them, the better I understood them.[96]

There is surely something moving in the spectacle of an African American abolitionist being inspired by the self-criticism of dead white males.

The eighteenth century was the high tide of the Atlantic slave trade, and yet it also gave rise to the ideals of freedom, equality, and human rights, Western principles that had never entirely died out and were to lead to the abolition of that degrading traffic. Similarly, the West produced its own tradition of anti-imperialism and anticolonialism, and surely one of the factors in the eventual hasty and unseemly abandonment of British India, for instance, was the hostile climate created by the critics of empire in the nineteenth century, such as the philosophical radicals like John Stuart Mill, and early twentieth-century critics such as H. G. Wells, George Bernard Shaw, and John Galsworthy.

Many reasons were advanced for Britain to disengage from its colonies or to desist from empire building, from the humanitarian to the economic. Adam Smith in *The Wealth of Nations* gave his own pragmatic views.[97] Fifty years earlier, Jonathan Swift, in that supreme work of self-criticism and the redemptive grace of Western civilization *Gulliver's Travels*, wrote:

> I had conceived a few scruples with relation to the distributive justice of princes upon these occasions. For instance, a crew of pirates are driven by storm they know not whither, at length a boy discovers land from the topmast, they go on shore to rob and plunder, they see an harmless people, are entertained with kindness, they give the country a new name, they take formal possession of it for the king . . . they murder two or three dozen of the natives . . . return home, and get their pardon. . . . Ships are sent with the first opportunity, the natives driven out or destroyed, their princes tortured to discover their gold . . . and this execrable crew of butchers employed in so pious an expedition, is a modern colony sent to convert and civilize an idolatrous and barbarous people.[98]

Even earlier, John Locke had denied any right of conquest. Samuel Johnson grumbled, "I do not much wish well to discoveries for I am always afraid they will end in conquest and robbery," while Bentham advised the French Revolutionaries to "Emancipate your Colonies!"[99]

I shall return to the British critics of the British Empire in India later, but one nineteenth-century attack on the British government on the subcontinent may be offered here. John Malcolm Ludlow, a Christian socialist writing soon after the Great Mutiny of 1857 when the British public was clamoring for some sort of revenge for the deaths of the British during the uprising, had the courage, nonetheless, to paint an unflattering portrait of the principal actors who shaped British policy. Ludlow castigated Robert Clive and Warren Hastings, writing, "To play fast and loose with the plighted word of state, to sell the mercenary sword to whoever might bid high enough for it, to help wrong and fleece the wrong-doer, such was English custom in those days."[100] Ludlow ends, "I have now gone through with you the story of the establishment of English power in India. It is an ugly one. It begins in feebleness and cowardice; it is pervaded by rapacity; it closes with a course of fraud and falsehood, of forgery and treason, as stupendous as ever lay at the foundation of a great empire."[101] But he did not want to make Clive and Hastings into scapegoats, for he held the British Parliament and the British people ultimately responsible for the oppressive fiscal system, the inequalities of the judicial system, and the poor performance of the agricultural, industrial, and mercantile sectors.

Critics such as Edward Said, chronicling the egregious acts of brutality of European colonial empires, contend that such acts were built into the very nature of Western culture, rather than being aberrations. But, as Windschuttle reminds them, these critics are writing within another part of the Western tradition of anti-imperialism: "Many of them write as if they believe the critique of imperialism first emerged among its colonized subjects as a protest at their bondage. The most they concede to the Western side of the equation is that anti-imperialism also arose within Marxism especially Lenin's book *Imperialism: The Highest Stage of Capitalism* (1917). (Marx himself, some are aware, was in favour of British rule in India, which he thought would hasten the world revolution.)" But in fact the merits of imperialism have been debated in the West since the Middle Ages. Even V. I. Lenin was heavily indebted to the English liberal J. A. Hobson's *Imperialism: A Study*, published in 1902.[102]

The whole of Western literature from the Greeks to the present can be seen as a criticism of life, as Matthew Arnold famously expressed it. The rich vein of satire in Western writings runs from classical antiquity, such as the Greek iambics of Archilochus and Hipponax, the comedies of Aristophanes, the hexameters of Lucilius, the *Saturae Menippeae* of Varro, the iambic satires of Persius, the Roman satires of Horace, the picaresque novel of Petronius, and the various invectives and barbs of Lucius Annaeus Seneca, Juvenal, Lucian, and Menippus, all of whom with ridicule, irony, and piercing criticism punctured the pretensions, hypocrisy, and self-complacency of the Philistines, of other contemporaries, and of society as a whole. This vein continues to be mined by Giovanni Boccacio's *Decameron* (1348–1353), Geoffrey Chaucer's *Canterbury Tales* (after 1387), *The Vision of Piers Plowman* of William Langland,[103] François Rabelais' *Gargantua and Pantagruel* (1532), and on to those masterpieces of satire of the eighteenth century, Swift's *Gulliver's Travels* (1726), Voltaire's *Candide* (1759), Diderot's *Le Neveu de Rameau* (written c.1769, published 1805), and so on. These works questioned the very foundation of contemporary beliefs, scrutinizing every system of thought, every idea, whether religious, philosophical, political, social, or scientific. But self-criticism is not just the chance tenor of scattered writings in the Western canon and is not confined to some minor or subliterary genre such as satire; it is the entire warp and woof of Western civilization. Lionel Trilling once argued that the European novel, taking its inspiration from Cervantes' great work *Don Quixote*, has ever since concerned itself with life as it is and how it ought to be—depiction and implicit criticism.[104] Thus, I do not restrict "self-criticism" to crude novels of social realism and strident denunciation, such as Upton Sinclair's

The Jungle, but to something broader and subtler. Indeed Arnold defined culture as the disinterested endeavor after man's perfection, which could be achieved only by self-criticism, education being but a nurturing of the critical spirit: "The whole scope of the essay," wrote Arnold in the preface to *Culture and Anarchy*, "is to recommend culture as the great help out of our present difficulties; culture being a pursuit of our total perfection by means of getting to know, on all the matters which most concern us, the best which has been thought and said in the world; and through this knowledge, turning a stream of fresh and free thought upon our stock notions and habits, which we now follow staunchly but mechanically, vainly imagining that there is a virtue in following them staunchly which makes up for the mischief of following them mechanically. This, and this alone, is the scope of the following essay. And the culture we recommend is, above all, an inward operation."[105] The ability to turn *a stream of fresh and free thought upon our stock notions and habits*—that truly is the distinctive and redemptive grace of Western civilization, and running through it as a *basso ostinato*.

By contrast, self-criticism remains an elusive goal in modern Islamic cultures. David Pryce-Jones, keeping to the Arab Islamic world, argues that the "acquisition of honour, pride, dignity, respect and the converse avoidance of shame, disgrace, and humiliation are keys to Arab motivation, clarifying and illuminating behaviour in the past as well as in the present."[106] The two codes of honor and shame "enforce identity and conformity of behaviour."[107] In such a system of values, it is impossible to admit publicly that one is wrong, for that would bring shame on the individual, the family, the country, or even his religion. Western-style satire would be very difficult in Arabic society, for that would risk humiliation of one's own culture. Taslima Nasrin, the atheist writer and human rights advocate from Bangladesh, once gave a talk in Germany criticizing Islam for its treatment of women and non-Muslim minorities. After her talk, an Arab warned her never to insult their religion in public again; he felt totally humiliated, especially in front of an infidel audience, even though in private he agreed with many of her strictures of his nominal (and her former) religion.[108]

Daniel Pipes shows in *The Hidden Hand* how conspiracy theories are very influential in the whole of the Middle East, "By filtering reality through a distorting prism, [conspiracism] fosters anti-Western, anti-Israeli, anti-democractic, antimoderate, and antimodern actions. At the same time, and almost paradoxically, it infuses the region's peoples with a sense of passivity."[109] This mentality can only lead to a refusal to take responsibility for one's own destiny, to take responsibility for their own economic, cultural, and political backwardness. Everything is the fault of the West. Edward Said fed into this mentality and reinforced a culture of self-pity: "[I]f only the wicked West and those Zionists would leave us alone, we would be great again as in the time of our forefathers when one Muslim could fell ten infidels with one blow of the sword." Needless to say, self-criticism under these circumstances takes great courage and is rather rare in the Middle East. But there are individual intellectuals who have pointed fingers at themselves and have dared to suggest that Muslims themselves were responsible for their backwardness—economic and otherwise.

Another possible reason for the lack of self-criticism in Islamic countries may be conjectured from Czeslaw Milosz's analysis. In *The Captive Mind*, Milosz devotes a chapter to how people in totalitarian societies develop means to cope publicly with all the contradictions of real life. One cannot admit to contradictions openly; officially, they do not exist. Hence people learn to dissimulate their views, emotions, and thoughts, never revealing their true beliefs publicly. Milosz finds a striking analogy of the same phenomenon in Islamic civilization, where it bears the name *ketman,* or *kitman* (the Persian word for concealment). Milosz found its description in Comte de Gobineau's *Religions and Philosophies of Central Asia.* Milosz wrote, quoting Gobineau, "The people of the Mussulman East believe that 'He who is in possession of truth must not expose his person, his relatives or his reputation to the blindness, the folly, the perversity of those whom it has pleased God to place and maintain in error.' One must, therefore, keep silent about one's true convictions if possible." Sometimes silence does not suffice; then one can resort to all sorts of ruses to deceive: "Thus one acquires the multiple satisfactions and merits of having placed oneself and one's relatives under cover, of not having exposed a venerable faith to the horrible contact of the infidel, and finally of having, in cheating the latter and confirming him in his error, imposed on him the shame and spiritual misery that he deserves."[110] Ketman is practiced equally in front of infidels and other Muslims. Gobineau gives the example of Hadzhi-Sheikh-Ahmed, the founder of one sect who even in his books never openly advanced the heretical ideas that were then attributed to him. He practiced ketman publicly, but in private was daring.[111]

Before discussing the work of two courageous intellectuals from the Middle East who advocate first and foremost self-criticism, I should like to point out that there was an emerging liberal class by the very end of the nineteenth and the beginning of the twentieth century, and it seemed for a breathless and magical while that the Islamic world would finally emerge into the modern world. Consider the work of these Egyptians: Qassem Amin advocated the emancipation of women, Taha Hussein advocated free schooling and the use of reason, and Salama Moussa founded the Egyptian Association of Scientific Culture. As Barry Rubin summarizes:

> During the 1920s and 1930s, such thinkers and political figures—especially but not exclusively, in Egypt—declared themselves rationalists, patriots of their own countries rather than pan-Arab nationalists, part of a Mediterranean people whose history was rooted in all those who had lived on that soil and not just the Arabs or Muslims among them. They dreamed of making Egypt a modern state along European lines while at the same time preserving its own traditions. The view of one such man, Tawfiq al-Hakim, could well stand as a contemporary liberal credo: the highest priority was to understand past mistakes to avoid repeating them; the biggest task was to expose truth no matter who was offended or what established ideas were challenged.[112]

And yet something went wrong. From the 1950s onward, liberal ideas of freedom, democracy, and representative government were no longer in evidence, and "the idea of taking responsibility for the ills of one's own society lost out to the ease of blaming everything on evil foreigners."[113] Hence the need for and the importance of intellectuals like al-Afif al-Akhdar and Tarek Heggy.

Al-Afif al-Akhdar, a Tunisian intellectual, wrote a blistering critique of the Arab world, lamenting that while the rest of the world was embracing modernity, knowledge, and globalization, the Arabs were regressing to the Dark Ages. Why was human knowledge growing except in the Arab world, where all one found was illiteracy, ideological fear, and mental paralysis? "Why," wrote Akhdar, "do expressions of tolerance, moderation, rationalism, compromise, and negotiation horrify us, but [when we hear] fervent cries for vengeance, we all dance the war dance? Why have the people of the world managed to mourn their pasts and move on, while we have . . . our gloomy bereavement over a past that does not pass? Why do other people love life, while we love death and violence, slaughter and suicide, and call it heroism and martyrdom?" Arabs suffer from both an inferiority complex, leading to self-hatred and "national humiliation whose shame can be purged only by blood, vengeance, and fire," and a sense of superiority and the belief that they were chosen by God to lead humanity—in which case why would they want to borrow anything from their inferiors? Despite the Koran's description of the Arabs as the best nation in the world, their history was a chronicle of failures in the last two centuries, which, combined with a "deep-culture of tribal vengefulness," led to "a fixated, brooding, vengeful mentality," driving out "far-sighted thought and self-criticism." Arabs should learn from the Japanese, who understood the "vital necessity to emulate the enemy . . . becoming like him in modern knowledge, thought and politics, so as to reshape the traditional personality and adapt it to the requirements of the time."[114]

Tarek Heggy, an Egyptian intellectual who studied law and management and worked for many years for the Shell Oil Company, wrote, "We have dug ourselves into a cave, cut off from the rest of humanity thanks to a static mind-set that ignores the realities of our time and the new balances of power. . . . We remain locked in a fantasy world of our own making . . . a world in which anachronistic slogans are still widely regarded as sacrosanct, immutable constants. This has resulted not only in our growing isolation from the outside world and in alienating our former allies, but in a disastrous internal situation marked by a pattern of lost opportunities and a climate inimical to democracy and development." Arab intellectuals have failed to create "a cultural climate and system of values in keeping with the requirements of the age"; instead we now have "an intellectualy barren and culturally stagnant landscape which has moved Egypt further away from its dream of catching up with the developed world than it was at the beginning of the twentieth century."[115]

Unfortunately such courageous self-criticisms are rare, and liberal Arab intellectuals "are few in number and face determined oppostion from regimes that continue to control the media and other institutions."[116] Arab liberal thought remains "fragmented, advocated by largely isolated individuals and with little systematic expression. . . . As a result, the liberal case is heard by only a tiny portion of Arabs, its small space hedged about with the thorns of its enemies."[117]

2

Classical Antiquity

Although the Logos is common, most men live as though their understanding were only their own. (fr.2)

For to those who are really awake, there is one well-ordered universe common to all, whereas in sleep each man turns away to a world of his own. (fr.89)

—Heraclitus (fl.c. 500 BC)[1]

I have already adumbrated the theme of Greek openness to ideas from non-Greeks, but here I will discuss their openness to others, their attitudes toward blacks and Jews, and their gradual development and slow acceptance of the idea of the unity of mankind. I have leaned heavily on H. C. Baldry's classic, *The Unity of Mankind in Greek Thought.*[2] Baldry observes admiringly, "[I]t remains remarkable that even on a theoretical level the divided and conflict-ridden Greeks moved so far in the direction of the idea of a common fellowship linking all mankind,"[3] his main thesis being "the notion of the unity of mankind was an attitude of mind which existed in some sense from Homer onwards, but was given varying shape and content by different writers as time went on."[4]

Homer's *Iliad* and *Odyssey* implicitly accord to all humans the same dignity: All the peoples who come into his stories are cast in the same mold as the rest of humanity; all are caught in the network of circumstance and destiny. Odysseus encounters Egyptians, but neither race nor color engenders any special antagonism, and he is impresssed by the wealth and elegance of Thebes,[5] while the Abii (or Abioi) of the extreme north are described as the most well-ordered (civilized?) of men or the most righteous and just of all mortals: "Now Zeus, after that he had brought the Trojans and Hector to the ships, left them to their toil and endless labour there, but otherwhere again he turned his shining eyes, and looked upon the land of the Thracian horsebreeders, and the Mysians, fierce fighters hand to hand, and the proud Hippemolgoi that drink mare's milk, and the Abioi, the most righteous of men."[6]

And in the far south there are the "blameless" Ethiopians, "Burnt-Faced-Men" whose color does not prevent them from being favorites of the gods:

But Poseidon was away now, among the Ethiopians,
Those burnished people at the ends of the earth—
Some near the sunset, some near the sunrise—
To receive a grand sacrifice of rams and bulls.
There he sat, enjoying the feast.[7]

Homer describes the common characteristics of all humans, and though there are divisions, they are not racial or geographical but social. Mankind is united in suffering, a notion found not only in Homer but also in so much of Greek poetry:

Of mortal creatures, all that breathe and move,
earth bears none frailer than mankind. What man
believes in woe to come, so long as valor
and tough knees are supplied him by the gods?
But when the gods in bliss bring miseries on,
then willy-nilly, blindly, he endures.
Our minds are as days are, dark or bright,
blown over by the father of gods and men.[8]

As Baldry suggests, the phrase "father of gods and men" (Zeus) is "pregnant with two ideas, kinship with the divine and the brotherhood of man, which emerge to maturity in later centuries."[9] For Homer (*before* 700 BCE), humans have reason—articulate speech—and technical skills that separate them from the beasts; the inevitability of death distinguishes them from gods. But they *are* divided by sex and class, falling into two groups, the best people and the multitude. Hesiod (c. 700 BCE) goes further, suggesting that men are capable of living in peace with one another since they are endowed with *dike*—justice—which distinguishes them from animals. While for Homer the Ethiopians are "blameless," for Hesiod they are "high-souled." The Homeric epithet *amymon* (blameless) referred primarily to bodily beauty and strength but early on acquired the meaning "good" in a moral sense.[10]

By the early sixth century, Greeks had acquired considerable knowledge of Near Eastern peoples through trade and colonization, and from those Greeks who had fought as mercenaries for various Eastern kings. Trade with the Near East had enriched Greece materially and culturally. Far from setting up insurmountable barriers with "Others," Greeks were open to new ideas and had nothing but high regard for Eastern peoples. Robert Drews, in his exhaustive study *The Greek Accounts of Eastern History*, summarizes:

> The splendor and sophistication of the Eastern civilisations impressed the Greeks profoundly. The Phoenician alphabet, Egyptian sculpture, and Lydian coinage are only the most obvious Eastern stimuli to archaic Greek culture [seventh and sixth centuries]. These cultural borrowings are, of course, the clearest evidence of the admiration with which the Greeks regarded their Eastern neighbours. Greek literature provides additional evidence, limited but helpful. . . . Archilochus, Alcman, and Sappho spoke of the Lydians with scarcely masked envy, and Alcman remarked on the glories of "sacred" Babylon.[11] In general, it would seem that the archaic Greeks held their Eastern neighbours in high esteem, while viewing with contempt the barbarous Thracians and Scythians to the north.[12] Greek respect for the Eastern kingdoms was . . . crucial for the origins of Greek historiography.[13]

Intellectual curiosity was a powerful motivating factor, impelling Greeks to ask about the origins of the world and its peoples, as expressed, for example, in Hesiod's *Theogony*. However, for many scholars, Hecataeus of Miletus is the true father of history. The fragments that we possess of his works, "demonstrate a surprising acquaintance with Egypt, Asia Minor, and even the interior of Asia."[14] Hecataeus learned much in his travels in the East and applied some sort of scientific rigor in his investigations, stripping from legends those elements he found ridiculous, presenting instead rationalized versions of the old stories.[15] His skeptical attitude is apparent in his opening remark to the *Genealogies*: "Hecataeus of Miletus speaks thus. I write what seems to me true; for the Greeks have many tales which, as it appears to me, are absurd."[16]

Aeschylus may well have derived his information about faraway places and peoples that he brings into his plays from Hecataeus. His fascination with exotic locales is reflected in *The Persians*, with its descriptions of the splendors of the Persian court: "[W]hile *The Suppliants* presents at Argos the fifty daughters of Danaus in flight from Egypt, un-Hellenic in dress and language, yet seeking asylum on the ground of kinship with the Greeks. The contrast is accentuated by their dark skins: 'You are more like women of Libya,' says the king of Argos, 'not at all like those of our country' (279–80); and their pursuers, when they arrive, are several times described as black. *But it is notable that here, as elsewhere in ancient literature, there is no suggestion of antipathy based specifically on colour: darkness of skin is only one of the elements in the strangeness of the picture as a whole*."[17]

THE FIRST ORIENTALISTS: HECATAEUS AND HERODOTUS

The antique Persians taught three useful things,
To draw the bow, to ride, and speak the truth.
This was the mode of Cyrus, best of Kings . . .

—Byron, *Don Juan* (1821)[18]

While Homer conceived of humanity on a single pattern, Aeschylus and Herodotus, both perhaps drawing on Hecataeus of Miletus, presented a far more complex, varied, and particularized portrait of many different peoples, each with their own ways and customs (*nomoi*), leading to sentiments such as those expressed by Pindar—"Custom is king of all. Different peoples have different customs, and each praise what is right (*dike*) as they see it"[19]—sentiments indicating an attitude of tolerance of different cultures.

One could consider the Greek historians before Herodotus who wrote those works on Persia, later called Persica, to be the first Orientalists. Such works were attributed to Dionysius of Miletus, Hellanicus of Lesbos, and Charon of Lampsacus. Of Hellanicus's *Aegyptiaca* we have seven fragments, which surveyed Egyptian geography, religion, and customs, describing its wondrous monuments, a subject of deep interest for Greeks. It should be borne in mind that the Persians themselves left only a very meager record of their own history,[20] and it was left to the "first Orientalists," the Greek historians, to recover the Persians' past, a pattern that was to be repeated over the centuries, as Western historians, archaeologists, and philologists slowly, patiently, and brilliantly reconstructed Middle Eastern history and culture. As Drews wrote, "Unlike the Greeks, the Eastern peoples had little interest in the great deeds of men and knew little of their own past,"[21] and "[I]n Susa and Babylon, where 'L'Esprit historien' had not yet awakened, the average man had little knowledge of what was happening, or what had happened, in the king's council or on the borders of the great empire. In Babylon, children learned about the deeds and characters of the gods but were not burdened with useless information about the activities of mere men. . . . [Herodotus and his successors] did not realize that not all peoples were fascinated with, and remembered great *erga* [physical monuments and noble deeds]."[22] Martin Braun also showed how little real historical information was available to the people of the East.[23] The Egyptians, for example, had no word for "history," and most of them knew nothing about the subject. Ludlow Bull writes, "There is no ancient Egyptian word known to the writer which closely corresponds to the English word, 'history.'. . . [N]or is there any Egyptian text known to him which can be said to express an 'idea of history.'"[24] Similarly,

Hermann Kees observes that the Egyptians, "so weighted down by their past, had no concept of history."[25]

With Herodotus we come to not simply tolerance of other cultures, but to a much greater admiration: "Much of Herodotus' work, written sometime in the middle of the fifth century B.C., is infused with the same spirit of lively interest in the foreigner and admiration for his achievements. He pays some foreign peoples an almost exaggerated respect, and sometimes makes comparisons to the disadvantage of the Greeks."[26] Herodotus wrote, "The following is an exhibition of the *historie* of Herodotus of Halicarnassus, so that which has been done by men shall not be forgotten in the passage of time, and that the great and wonderful *erga* [physical monuments and noble deeds] exhibited by both Greeks and barbarians shall not be without acclaim—other matters and especially why they went to war with each other."[27]

Herodotus exemplifies that intellectual curiosity, that thirst for knowledge for the sake of knowledge,[28] which I have characterized not just as one of the underlying themes of Western cultural history, but as the defining feature of it. Herodotus's *History* is full of ethnographical, historical, zoological, and geographical information that attests to his range of interests. Much of his information was derived firsthand. His travels also reveal an astonishing breadth: He seems to have made inquiries in the northern Aegean, in southern Italy, around the shores of the Black Sea, in Egypt, traveling as far up the Nile as Elephantine, at Dodona in northwestern Greece, at Cyrene in Libya. He writes of things seen on the Dnieper in southern Russia, in Babylon on the Euphrates, at Tyre in Lebanon; of talking to Carthaginians and to the inhabitants of Delphi. Equally impressive is Herodotus's understanding of and sympathy for an extensive variety of human experience. Herodotus "writes almost always open-mindedly of the differences that distinguish Persians from Scythians, Babylonians, Indians, and Egyptians, as well as from Greeks."[29]

Herodotus extols the maritime and engineering skill of the Phoenicians (vii.23.3, 44, 99.3), the monuments of Egypt and Babylon (i.93.2), the natural products of the ends of the earth (iii.106–14). He derives the Greek alphabet from Phoenicia (v.58), coinage from Lydia (i.94), measurement of time from Babylon (ii.109.3), and handsomely acknowledges the debt of Greece to Africa (iv.180, 189) and to Egypt, perhaps even exaggerating it as when he finds an Egyptian origin for Hercules (ii.43): "If Herodotus recognizes the merits of the enemy, he is equally clear-sighted in refusing to see a hero in every professed patriot."[30] As for the Persians, Herodotus credits them with the virtues of chivalry, emphasizes their truth telling (i.136.2, 138) and devoted loyalty (iii.128.4, 154 f.; viii.118.3), and ascribes their defeat to inferiority in arms and discipline, not to the lack of valor (ix.62.3).[31] And so we turn to the Persians in greater detail.

After describing in full the history of Cyrus and how he became "the bravest and the best-liked man of his generation,"[32] Herodotus describes Persian customs, many of which he finds admirable even when they differ from the Greeks': "It is not one of their customs to construct statues, temples, and altars; in fact, they count those who do so as fools, because (I suppose) they do not anthropomorphize the gods as the Greeks do."[33] Persians regard themselves as by far the best people in the world,[34] he tells us—a point worth pondering: It is a natural sentiment common to many peoples and civilizations, not peculiar to the "evil West" that constructs "the Other." Continues Herodotus,

> Nevertheless, the Persians adopt more foreign customs than anyone else. For example, they wear Median clothes because they consider them to be more attractive than their own, and they wear Egyptian breastplates for fighting. Also, they learn and acquire the habit of all kinds of divertissements from various parts of the world, including the practice of having sex with boys, which they learnt from the Greeks. Every Persian man has a number of wives, but far more concubines.
>
> After bravery in battle, manliness is proved above all by producing plenty of sons, and every year the king rewards the person producing the most; they think that quantity constitutes strength. Their sons are educated from the time they are five years old until they are twenty, but they study only three things: horsemanship, archery, and honesty. Until they are five years old, they are not taken into their fathers' sight, but live with the women. This is to prevent a father being grieved by the death of a son during the period of his early upbringing.
>
> I think this custom of theirs is very good, and I also approve of the fact that no one, not even the king, can execute anyone who has been accused of only a single crime, nor can any other Persian do irreversible harm to any of his house-slaves for committing a single crime. . . . The most disgraceful thing, in their view, is telling lies, and the next most disgraceful thing is being in debt; but the main reason (among many others) for the proscription of debt is that, according to the Persians, someone who owes money is obliged to tell lies as well.[35]

Perhaps the greatest successor to Herodotus was Hecataeus of Abdera, whose enthusiasm for all things Egyptian bordered on "Egyptomania," as F. Jacoby called it.[36] Hecataeus was overwhelmed by the sheer magnificence and majesty of the monuments in Egypt, which, for him, were the surest proof of the grandeur of its kings. There is good evidence that Diodorus Siculus, in his *Bib-*

liotheca, derived almost all his knowledge of Egypt and its kings and customs from Hecataeus. Diodorus's survey of the deeds of Egyptian kings, and his account of Egyptian customs and society, is full of praise for the lawfulness of the kings, the excellent social structure, the prosperous economy, the just laws and judicial processes, the Egyptians' sound educational practices, and their aversion to the exposure of children.[37] Diodorus wrote that "so long as there remained the system of laws just described," the Egyptians surpassed all other peoples in wealth, in power, in the beauty of their cities and the splendor of their *erga*.[38] Hecataeus extended his generous tributes to the Jews, a theme which I shall treat more fully when discussing Jews and blacks in classical antiquity.

In Anaximander and Xenophanes we encounter the idea of humanity as only one among a number of animal species. But surely the most remarkable account of the sixth century BCE of what unites all humans is that of Heraclitus. For Heraclitus, the key to all things was the *Logos*, a Greek word that signifies both the spoken word (in Latin *oratio*, *vox*) and the faculty of reason or thought (in Latin *ratio*): "Heraclitus' central concept is that of *logos*, by which he apparently means his own discourse, connected discourse and thought in general, and the connected order in things that we apprehend. Most people, he holds, go through life like sleepers, experiencing the world with little understanding, each lost in a private vision. Waking up to the shared public order requires inquiry, sense-experience, and self-examination: 'I went in search of myself.'"[39] *Logos* as a universal rational principle or law is common; thought also is common to all, and the universality of the *Logos* lies behind all human laws or customs (*nomoi*): "Those who speak with understanding must rely on what is common to all, as a city relies on its law, and with far greater reliance. For all humans are nourished by one law, the divine law, which has all the power it desires and is enough, and more than enough, for all."[40] For Heraclitus, it is the tragedy of man though that all men are possessed of reason, or, at least, all men are potentially or in principle rational and that a rationality should bring them together, in reality they behave irrationally and go their own divisive ways.

Aeschylus: Dignity of and Sympathy for the Persians

Ye Powers that rule the skies,
Memory recalls our great, our happy fate,
Our well-appointed state,
The scenes of glory opening to our eyes,
When this vast empire o'er

The good Darius, with each virtue bless'd
That forms a monarch's breast,
Shielding his subjects with a father's care,
Invincible in war,
Extended like a god his awful power,
Then spread our arms their glory wide,
Guarding to peace her golden reign:
Each tower'd city saw with pride
Safe from the toils of war her homeward-marching train.
—*The Persians*, Chorus, Strophe I

For Aeschylus, it is also reason that has contributed the most to the growth of human civilization. In Aeschylus's *Prometheus Bound*, the eponymous hero recounts how he helped man by endowing him with a mind and teaching him all the arts:

Hearken to the plight
Of man, in whom, born witless as a babe,
I planted mind and the gift of understanding.
I speak of men with no intent to blame
But to expound my gracious services:
Who first, with eyes to see, did see in vain,
With ears to hear, did hear not, but as shapes
Figured in dreams throughout their mortal span
Confounded all things, knew not how to raise
Brick-woven walls sun-warmed, nor build in wood
But had their dwelling, like the restless ant,
In sunless nooks of subterranean caves.
No token sure they had of winter's cold,
No herald of the flowery spring or season
Of ripening fruit, but laboured without wit
In all their works, till I revealed the obscure
Risings and settings of the stars of heaven.
Yea, and the art of number, arch-device,
I founded, and the craft of written words,
The world's recorder, mother of the Muse.[41]

Here we have Aeschylus's vision of the human race progressing through history thanks entirely to his reason, the use of his intelligence. Since Edward Said makes much of Aeschylus's creation of the Other, this observation must be kept in mind, but it would also be appropriate here to examine Aeschylus's use of the word "barbaros," and his attitude toward foreigners in general.

In *Barbarians in Greek Tragedy*, Helen Bacon tells us that for the Greeks, the barbarians included the Trojans, Persians, Egyptians, Lydians, Taurians, Scythians, and sometimes even Macedonians and Cretans. Bacon goes on to point out that the theme of the conflict of Greek and barbarian in Sophocles, Euripides, and Aeschylus "is not . . . a simple question of superior Greek against inferior barbarian."[42] In Euripides' *Troades*, we have the irony of Andromache cursing the Greeks for "savage evils" (βαρβαρα κακα), yet the savages are not the Trojans but the Greeks! More specifically coming to Aeschylus's *The Persians*, Bacon points out that though in *Agamemnon* 919–20, "Agamemnon disapproves of the servile foreign custom [of spreading 'your monarch's path with tapestry'] there is no implication here, *or anywhere else in Aeschylus*, that barbarians or their customs as such are intrinsically inferior. Darius has all the "Greek" virtues. Cassandra is morally superior to Clytemenestra."[43] Here is Bacon's final assessment of Aeschylus:

> Aeschylus' handling of foreign material is the reverse of orientalizing. The orientalizing style introduces "oriental" motifs for their own sake, regardless of subject matter, to fill and decorate spaces. We have seen that Aeschylus does have some formulaic foreign references, but even these are not always used in this manner. By far the greater number of foreign references occur only where the context demands them. Far from being introduced for decorative purposes, they are essential parts of the story. . . . [T]here is no question of an occasional exotic touch to add variety and interest. A foreign character in Aeschylus is consistently foreign. Foreignness is part of the characterization, and the poet constantly reminds us of it. He builds and maintains a foreign atmosphere by repeated references to speech and dress and manners, to foreign legends and distant places. And there is no vagueness in his foreign representations, but almost always the concrete individual detail. He represents not "the barbarian" of tradition, but *a* Persian, *a* Trojan, *an* Egyptian, and he has clear notions about their differences in language, dress, customs, and appearance, beliefs. His foreign landscapes are not just distant and exotic scenes, but places on a map, with precise, and sometimes accurate, climate and topography.
>
> Aeschylus differentiates among barbarian peoples, and bases his differentiation on detailed information. This takes the emphasis off foreignness as such, and the related idea of the superiority of Greeks to all foreigners. We have seen that this is not an important theme in Aeschylus. For the moment it is enough to point out that it is difficult to maintain the Greek-barbarian antithesis when there is no "barbarian" as such, but instead many different and fascinating varieties of human beings.[44]

In other words, Aeschylus treated foreigners as individuals, not as "Oriental" stereotypes drawn with contempt but rather as particular humans subject to flaws, and hence eminently suitable subjects for tragedy. He was able to achieve this by his extraordinary knowledge, his insatiable intellectual curiosity, which led him to investigate the language, dress, customs, and traditions of the people he wished to write about. His plays are peppered with words from the Persian (αγγαρος, a mounted Persian messenger [*Ag.* 282], of Assyrian origin but borrowed from the Persian; μανδυη, a woolen cloak), Phrygian or Thurian (βαλ(λ)ην, lord), Egyptian (βαρις, boat), Egyptian or Hebrew (καρβαν or καρβανος, for βαρβαρος), Lydian (παλμυς, king; βακκαρις, incense), and so on. He uses the forty-nine names of Persian princes (Pers. 20–58, 302–30, 955–1001). Including the latter names, Aeschylus uses seventy-one foreign words. As for costumes, Aeschylus, for example, distinguishes the hat and shoes of kings "specifically and accurately."[45] Equally, he shows specific knowledge of foreign institutions: "He refers to the Egyptian gods by Greek names, but in such a way that he knows their Egyptian functions and attributes (e.g., *Suppliants.* 210–21). Herodotus (2.156) attests his unique knowledge of Egyptian religion, saying that he alone of the poets knew a certain λογος which caused him to call Artemis the daughter of Demeter."[46]

Even more astonishing, for several of the phrases in Darius's summary of Persian history in *The Persians* (765–81) parallels can be found in the Behistun Inscription and other Persian documents. The king's titles and those of his nobles are all historical.[47]

Looking more closely at *The Persians*, H. D. Broadhead in his edition of the Greek text notes in the introduction that it is an authentic tragedy with all the dignity one associates with this genre: "[T]he *Persae* was intended to be a genuine tragedy, that the dramatist has on the whole been successful in carrying out his intention, and that the comparative absence of patriotic bias is in keeping with the high moral tone of the play, and particularly of the Darius scene, which contains the essence of the poet's own philosophy. If the doctrine is Greek, it takes no account of national differences—it concerns equally both Greek and barbarian."[48]

As in all tragedies, the *The Persians* presents us a tragic figure who through an error and moral lapse and failure passes from prosperity to misfortune. Aeschylus, however, was dealing with an event of the recent past: *The Persians* was produced at Athens in 472 BCE, eight years after the naval battle at Salamis, which the play celebrates—an event that would undoubtedly evoke deep patriotic enthusiasm. While he sticks broadly to the facts, Aeschylus has tried "to raise the historical to the level of the poetic and the philosophic."[49] Aeschylus deviates in two significant ways from the facts, first by idealizing Darius, and then by changing the facts to fit into his theological framework: "This manner of handling the historical facts itself suggests that as a dramatist he has adopted a (for the most part at least) supra-national attitude: he has treated the Persian in much the same way as he would have treated the Greek in similar circumstances; from the particular he has distilled the universal."[50]

As Broadhead shows in lines 302–30, we have a list of the principal captains and chiefs who fell, and the courage of the Persians is underlined: "It would have been easy for Aeschylus to attribute the victory to the skill and prowess of the Greeks—to make the admission come from the lips of a Persian would heighten the effect!—but of this there is not a word. It was a trick that brought the Persian fleet into its fatal position (εν στενω), and that the trick was successful was due to the θεων φθονος [jealousy of gods]. Finally, the flower of the Persian nobles was cut off and destroyed on Psyttaleia, αισχρως δυσκλεεστατω μορω [in infamy, dishonor, and in ugliness]: the contest was not on even terms, and the Persians were at the mercy of the heavily armed Greek troops."[51]

The description of the ensuing naval battle is subdued and brief where we would have expected the dramatist to provide vivid details and give in to some sort of Greek triumphalism. Significantly, no Greek is named, whereas a long roll of Persian leaders is listed. This was consistent with Aeschylus's intention of presenting a Persian tragedy as seen through Persians eyes. There is a justifiable moment of Greek patriotism during the battle song at lines 402–405, since the very freedoms of the Greeks were at stake and had been bravely defended; Aeschylus was a staunch believer in democracy. All in all, as Broadhead asks, "Could we expect a more restrained and impartial account from the pen of a Greek?"[52]

The final scene, when Xerxes appears on stage in rags, is not meant to ridicule the Persian; the play is a tragedy, not a farce, as H. W. Smyth points out: "Contempt or ridicule of a defeated adversary would destroy the very purpose of tragedy."[53] It is finely analyzed by Broadhead:

> This final scene can be understood and appreciated only if we recognize that Xerxes, unsuitable as he was for the role of traditional tragic hero, is nevertheless the mainspring of the tragedy. In all the earlier scenes he has been present to our minds so that his appearance in the flesh is a veritable climax, which must be reserved for the end of the play. Aeschylus, with unerring instinct, made it follow upon the impressive denunciations of Darius [his father], which, no less than the charge to Atossa [widow of Darius and mother of Xerxes] (833–4), prepare the audience for the picture of the broken monarch, utterly overwhelmed by the shame and disgrace he has incurred, confessing his responsiblity for his country's ruin, wishing that he had perished with his army, deeply moved when

> he recalls the trusty comrades he has lost, answering meekly the reproachful enquiries of the Elders, and finally participating in the mournful antiphonal dirge that fittingly completes the picture of the depths of misery to which the once glorious and triumphant Persia is reduced. There is no chauvinism in this εξοδος [the end of a tragedy]. Gilbert Murray is surely right when he remarks, "This lamentation is not only written with great technical skill, but seems to combine an expression of utter defeat and desolation with a certain nobleness and dignity. The conquered oppressor is not mocked."[54]

Aeschylus's characters are, on the whole, convincingly drawn. The Chorus of Trusty Elders, chosen by Xerxes to manage the affairs of state in his absence, is used by the dramatist to emphasize the stark contrast between the wisdom of the father, Darius, and the folly of the son, Xerxes. The Elders "provide a distinctively Persian background and that through them is conveyed to the audience the most lively impression of the effects of the disaster on the Persians and their vast empire."[55] Atossa is depicted as a dignified queen, intensely devoted to, and anxious for, her erring son—again, a sympathetically drawn character. As for Darius, "This imposing, dignified and majestic figure, more than any other in the play, shows how far Aeschylus has risen above the level of a narrow nationalism. . . . Darius is heroic in stature, indeed is regarded almost as a god. His appearance is a kind of theophany. He has the commanding presence of an Olympian deity whose impressive pronouncements are accepted without question, and are like a strong breeze that blows sanity into a disordered world."[56] And finally, "[T]he dramatist has sought to delineate, not with prejudice or malice, but with sympathetic imagination, the Persian tragedy as he conceived it to have affected the Persian people, and, in particular, the ruling class."[57] *The Persians* is indeed a genuine tragedy, where Aeschylus shows remarkable restraint in describing the Greek victory, which is seen not as being the result of Greek superiority but rather of the transgression of divine law, transgression that would bring disaster upon any human being, be he Greek or barbarian. Furthermore, Aeschylus draws his characters with great compassion and sympathy, and he paints the scene from the Persians' point of view.

Aeschylus, far from exulting over a defeated enemy, is able to summon up a profound human sympathy for the Persians and thus lift himself far above the limitations of the here and now and bring out the universal implications of their overweening pride and the nemesis attendant on those guilty of hubris. To conclude the defense of Aeschylus, here is Seth Benardete, the translator of *The Persians*:

> To show sympathetically, *sine ira et studio* [without anger and bias], on the stage at Athens the defeat of her deadliest enemy testifies to the humanity of

> Aeschylus and the Athenians. No other tragedian we know of, of any country, at any time, has ever dared to go so far in sympathizing with his country's foe. It is the more remarkable when we consider that Aeschylus himself and almost all of his audience fought at Salamis or Plataea and that war, moreover, was between freedom and slavery. Here are the Persians, having started an unjust war and suffering a deserved defeat, presented not as criminals but rather as great and noble, dying deaths that are to be as much pitied as the deaths of Athenians. To praise the Athenians at Athens, Socrates remarks, or the Spartans at Sparta is not very difficult; but to praise the Athenians at Sparta or the Spartans at Athens demands great rhetorical skill; and for Aeschylus to praise before their conquerors the Persians, the enemies of all Greece, is without precedent and without imitation.[58]

Sophocles displays the same large humanity in his plays, as in the famous chorus in *Antigone* (332–64) in praise of man's prowess, intelligence, and achievements, seeing mankind as a species with its own characteristics and triumphs. More specifically, Sophocles moves toward denouncing, at least implicitly, the Greek-barbarian divide in his *Ajax*. Agamemnon insults Teucer, son of the Greek Telamon by a foreign slave mother, Hesione.

> Remember who you are
> And bring some other man, a free man here
> To plead your cause instead of you before us.
> I cannot understand you when you speak:
> Barbarian chatter has no meaning for me.

Teucer replies, having the last word:

> Wretch, with what face can you fling forth such taunts?
> Know you not that of old your father's father
> Was Pelops, a barbarian, and a Phrygian?
> . . .
> Being such, do you reproach *me* with my lineage?[59]

There is also a fragment from the *Tereus* of Sophocles that expresses a conciliatory note of the unity of man: "There is one human race. A single day brought us all forth from our father and mother. No man is born superior to another. But one man's fare is a doom of unhappy days, another's is success; and on others the yoke of slavery's hardship falls" (Fr.532).[60]

With Euripides, on the other hand, it is well to bear in mind that his characters may not necessarily express his own views. As for our theme, his plays bear witness to the varied opinions on foreigners that were prevalent in contemporary Athens. Hence, some mock, disparage, and ridicule, while others speak remarkable—even noble—sentiments about the unity of man: "Every quarter of the sky is open to the eagle's flight: every country is fatherland for a man of noble mind" (Fr.1047). Common fatherland means wider kinship, larger sympathies: "Though a wise man live far from my own land, though I never set eyes upon him, I count him as a friend" (Fr.902). As for slavery, Euripides perhaps suggests that it is an artificial institution: "For many slaves the name is their only disgrace; in spirit they are more free than men who are not slaves" (Fr.831), and "One thing alone dishonours slaves—the name. In all else a slave is no worse than free men, if he is honest."[61] In a choral fragment from his play *Alexander*, Euripides gives voice to a form of universalism: "We waste our words, if we praise high birth rate among mortal men. For when first of old we came into being, and Earth, the mother of mortals, gave them life of their own, she created the same form for all. No separate stamp divides us. High-born and low-born are a single stock. It is time, through custom [nomos], that brings pride of birth" (Fr. 52).

By the late fifth century, there was in Athens a "cosmopolitan trend," as attested by the presence of non-Greeks, including dark-skinned Egyptians.[62] Herodotus, in fact, gathered some of his historical material concerning Darius's recovery of Babylon from a knowledgeable Persian exile, Zopyrus, who arrived in Athens around 443 BCE.[63] Already in the sixth century, Theognis of Megara,[64] an elegiac poet and squirearch dispossessed of his estates, complained to his friend Cyrnus,

> Cyrnus, our city is a city still.
> Its folks are changed. Who once outside our walls
> Pastured like deer, with goatskins round their sides,
> And knew not laws or judgments, these today
> Are good men, Cyrnus; and those high before
> Are now sunk low. Who can endure the sight?[65]

And by about 425 or 424 BCE, the "Old Oligarch" was able to write in the *Constitution of the Athenians*, "The slaves and resident foreigners live without restraint." Whereas other Greeks have their own way of life and speaking, that of the Athenians is a veritable mixture drawn "from all the Greeks and barbarians."[66]

Athenians expressed all shades of attitude toward and opinions of the non-Greeks in their midst. Some leading Sophists expressed thoughts that were exemplary in the largeness of their sympathies, extending them to the entire human race in virtue of the common rationality of mankind that marked it off from the animal kingdom. Some humans were yet to exercise fully their rationality, but these differences were a matter of degree, not kind. All humans were essentially alike, barbarian and Greek. For Hippias, we are all members of one family, by nature though not by custom (a thought implicit in Heraclitus also). Antiphon, a native Athenian Sophist, wrote a treatise on truth and also contrasted nature and convention. His thoughts have been reconstructed by Baldry:

> Our prevailing class distinction between those of high and low birth, which goes back to Homer and [is] still with us, has created within our society a division like that conventionally drawn between Greeks and barbarians, so that this gulf which we imagine separates us from foreigners exists in our own midst, and the two sections of our community do not understand each other, any more than we Greeks understand the Egyptians.
>
> Such a cleavage is wrong, whether in our own society or in the wider world. For by nature Greeks and barbarians are all alike, as a study of their essential attributes will show. After all, the operation of breathing, like all our necessary physical processes, is common to the entire human race.[67]

Now such a plea, it could be argued, presupposes that the prevailing atmosphere, toward non-Greeks especially, was hostile. Yet, as I have tried to suggest, if there were such a negative attitude, it could not have been so pervasive and all-embracing, since then we would not have had the sophisticated, tolerant, and essentially humane views set before the Athenian public in such works as Aeschylus's *The Persians*, some of the works of Sophocles—and even some by Euripides, the large number of Persian exiles, and the ever-growing population of non-Greeks that turned Athens into a truly cosmopolitan center in the eastern Mediterranean. As I shall show later, there was certainly no prejudice against foreigners based solely on the color of their skin; surely, this indicates a remarkable state of grace for any civilization, at any time.

For Thucydides there is such a thing as a permanent "nature of man," with groupings such as "Greek" and "barbarian" being only transient variations. Though he is justifiably proud of Athenian culture and disdainful of barbarian customs, Thucydides does not accept the barbarian-Greek divide as being a part of the permanent nature of things. Like the distinguished historian, the medical writers of the same period see mankind as a single species, maintaining man's unity but admitting his contingent diversity.

SOCRATES AND BEYOND

All Countries that the eye of Heaven visits
Are to the wise man ports and happy havens.

—Shakespeare, *Richard II*

For Socrates, the common possession of reason overrode all divisions, between Greek and barbarian, slave and free. A similar attitude seems to be implied by Democritus, "To a wise man every land is open; for the whole world is the native country of a good soul" (Fr. 247). By the fourth century, we even have criticisms of slavery; Alcidamas, the fourth-century rhetorician and Sophist, condemns slavery in his *Messenian Oration*: "God has left all men free; nature has made no man a slave."[68] Trade and commerce must also have made for better relations and the breaking down of hostile cultural barriers. Similarly, one also wonders what the long-term effect of Greek mercenaries fighting for Persians, like Cyrus at the end of the Peloponnesian War (404 BCE) when more than ten thousand Greeks, including Athenians,[69] took part in his campaign against his brother, must have had on their perceptions of "barbarians."

Xenophon, that model mercenary, during his expedition to Persia, acquired a great deal of firsthand experience of "barbarian" and an abiding admiration for the traditions of the Persian aristocracy, and above all for Cyrus, for whom he was fighting. "I consider," he wrote, "that no one, either Greek or barbarian, has ever been more generally beloved."[70] The third edition of *The Oxford Classical Dictionary*, under the influence of Edward Said no doubt,[71] points to Xenophon's view of "Greek superiority over barbarians,"[72] and yet nowhere in its very long article on him is there any mention of Xenophon's admiration for the Persians. As for the barbarians, in the words of T. J. Haarhoff, Xenophon "in most cases, does not go beyond justifiable rejection of what is uncultured."[73] But even more important, as the perceptive and judicious Baldry points out, there was implicit in Xenophon's outlook "some of the main trends of thought about mankind which came to the fore in the fourth century and were brought into the open by others: that wisdom and merit transcended racial divisions, and therefore not race, but some other criterion, provided the important dividing line among men; that civilised standards were not confined to the Greeks, but other peoples had something to contribute to the concept of civilisation; or that if all civilisation was indeed Hellenic, then Hellenism was not a matter of blood."[74]

Isocrates, an Athenian orator of great distinction and importance who seemed to be groping toward a similar outlook, wrote, "The name 'Hellenes' now seems to belong not to a race but to a mental outlook, and is applied to those who share our culture rather than to men who share a common blood."[75] Plato, often unjustly dismissed in such discussions, also envisaged—especially in his later dialogues—the unity of man, and had some conception of mankind as a single species based on the inner character and mentality of men. In *The Statesman*, Plato puts the following argument in the mouth of the Stranger:

> *The Young Socrates*: What sort of mistake do you say we made just now in our division?
>
> *The Stranger*: The kind of mistake a man would make if he were trying to divide humanity into two, and adopted the popular division whereby most people in this part of the world treat the Greeks as a single class separate from all the rest. All other nations, although their number is unknown and they do not intermingle or share any common language, are called by the single term "barbarian," and because of this one term it is supposed that they constitute one class.[76]

In the *Laws*, Plato praises Persia, especially in the days of Cyrus, and the reason for her "excellence is said to be the opportunity given to the policies of the state: 'consequently at that time they enjoyed general progress, as a result of their freedom, amity, and joint participation in reasoned counsel' [694b]. Later Persian history is described as fluctuating according to the training and character of the Great King [694c–d]."[77]

Although he is well known for his view that some men are by nature slaves, Aristotle seems also to have held other, far more humane views, where he sees mankind as a single species distinguished from all others by certain physical features, and above all by the possession of reason. In the *Nicomachean Ethics* (1155a16–22), Aristotle states that there is a bond of affection between all members of the human race. He even recommends that slaves should eventually be emancipated (*Politics*, 1330a33), clearly contradicting his earlier theory. Aristotle himself provided for the immediate liberation of some of his slaves in his will, and the later emancipation of still others: "Nicanor is also to take care of the slave Murmex, so that he is conveyed in a fashion worthy of us to his own people, together with those of his belongings which we received. They are to free Ambracis and to give her on the marriage of my daughter five hundred drachmae and the maidservant which she has. . . . Tacho is to be freed on the marriage of my daughter, as are Philo and Olympius and his child. Do not sell any of the slaves who served me, but employ them; and when they come of age, send them away free men as they deserve."[78]

CYNIC

John Moles has argued in a witty and erudite essay that Cynic cosmopolitanism must be taken seriously as something positive.[79] Hitherto, scholars have maintained that "when Diogenes answered the question 'Where are you from?' with the words 'I am "a citizen of the cosmos" [*kosmopolitēs*, D. L. 6. 63],' and when he wrote, 'The only good government is that in the cosmos' (*monēn . . . nēorthēn politeian tēn en kosmēi*, D. L. 6. 72), he meant only what he expressed elsewhere in tragic verses (D. L. 6. 38): 'Without a city, without a house, without a fatherland,/A beggar, a wanderer with a single day's bread'—namely, that he had no polis and rejected the polis as 'against nature' (*para phusin*)."[80]

Diogenes' thoughts must be evaluated in the context of the sentiments of preceding Greek philosphers and writers, already discussed, such as Heraclitus, Euripides, Antiphon, Hippias, and Alcidamas. If we are justified in seeing in the latter group, as indeed we are, the presence of some sort of a cosmopolitan ideal, then we are equally justified in Diogenes' case. For the Cynic, the state, *politeia*, is a moral state, and since neither the *polis* nor racial distinction mean anything to him, he is able to live anywhere on earth; "the whole earth" is the Cynic's home. Here the Cynic is expressing positive allegiance to the whole earth, and a sense of allegiance to all mankind.[81] There was a kinship between men and animals, even though man is distinguished from them by possessing reason. Cynics recognized the community of the wise that transcends barriers between men and women, and between the races.[82] An integral part of Cynicism seems to be philanthropy (*philanthrōpia*), love of mankind, and benevolence.[83] There is enough evidence to argue that the Cynics recognized a common humanity in, for instance, their habit of appealing to the customs of foreign countries, in the idea that all human beings are endowed with reason, and so on. Here is Moles characterizing the Cynic: "The Cynic proclaims his allegiance to the cosmos. He can live a virtuous life anywhere: the whole earth serves as his home. He maintains a positive attitude toward the natural world and toward the animal world. He is himself godlike. He recognizes his actual kinship with other sages and his potential kinship with human beings in general, whom he seeks to convert. He is a mediator between men and gods, and this mediation is an important part of his pedagogic activity."[84] Diogenes must be credited with inventing the word *kosmopolitōs*, thereby marking an important stage in the history of ideas. And finally, according to Moles, Cynic cosmopolitanism influenced Stoic cosmopolitanism.[85]

ALEXANDER THE GREAT

Bibliographies of modern research on Alexander list more than a thousand items.[86] Disputes over details, motives, and achievements continue to rage, and nonspecialists have to tread lightly. W. W. Tarn sees Alexander as someone who "proclaimed for the first time the unity and brotherhood of mankind. . . . Above all, Alexander inspired Zeno's vision of a world in which all men should be members one of another, citizens of one State without distinction of race or institutions, subject only to and in harmony with the Common Law immanent in the Universe, united in one social life not by compulsion but only by their own willing consent, or (as he put it) by Love."[87] Most sober modern scholars reject Tarn's account as sentimental and unwarranted by a critical and skeptical scrutiny of the sources. Accordingly, I shall not refer further to Tarn, but instead shall have recourse to Robin Lane Fox, who also rejects Tarn's interpretation after judiciously sifting through all the evidence. I have also consulted Baldry's scrupulous account that also takes issue with, and ultimately discards, Tarn's rosy picture.

Nonetheless, it is undeniable that Alexander inaugurated far-reaching changes in large parts of the Near East, Egypt, and India. While he may not have believed in universal brotherhood, Alexander denied the idea of a single *Herrenvolk*, or master race, and was ready "to treat at any rate one 'barbarian' people on the same level with the Macedonians."[88] As Baldry further points out, "Racial exclusiveness was not part of the Macedonian outlook: absorption of other peoples had been a feature of Macedonian development, and fusion with a ruling class so similar as the Persian was to that of Macedon might seem reasonable to a Macedonian, though outrageous to a Greek. Polygamy was probably a traditional practice of the Macedonian royal house, and Philip [father of Alexander] had certainly used marriage with wives from other peoples as an instrument of political conciliation. The founding of cities—it may well be, with mixed populations—also goes back to Philip. Alexander seems to have learned more from his father than from any thoughts inspired by philosophy."[89] In short, Alexander's nonracial policies may well have had the effect, admittedly indirect, of bringing peoples and cultures within, at least, respectful and admiring distance of one another.

Robin Lane Fox summarizes the results of Alexander's conquests: "Greek athletics would come to be performed in the burning heat of the Persian Gulf; the tale of the Trojan horse would be told on the Oxus and among the natives of the Punjab; far from the frog-pond ['We sit round our sea,' Socrates had told his friends, 'like frogs around a frog-pond'], Greeks would practise as Buddhists and Homer would be translated into an Indian language; when a north-west Indian city came to be excavated, the love story of Cupid and Psyche was found to have been carved on ivory and left beside the elephant-goads of a local Indian mahout. Alexander's story does not end with warfare or with the problems of his personality; had he chosen differently, the ground would never have been cleared for a whole new strand in Asia to grow from his army's reaping." And because of the spread of the legendary narrative *Romance of Alexander*, "there are Afghan chieftains who still claim to be descended from his blood. Seventy years ago they would go to war with the red flag they believed to be his banner."[90]

Alexander's childhood was spent in Pella, which, as his father's fortunes rose, became increasingly cosmopolitan. The hustle and bustle of an international atmosphere at Pella is well described by Lane Fox.[91]

At the battle of Granicus (334 BCE), Alexander defeated the Persians, among whom a Greek, Memnon, married to a Persian woman, served as an adviser, and with twenty thousand Greek mercenaries fighting on their side. Significantly, Alexander, out of respect, had those Persian leaders who were killed in the battle buried, a Greek gesture of piety, though perhaps not necessarily appreciated by Persians since they did not all believe in burial for religious reasons. Throughout his campaigns, Alexander was to show similar tact and respect for persons of other cultures and for their religions, as, for instance, at Siwah in North Africa, or in Babylon, where he ordered the rebuilding of temples. Alexander's passage through western Asia led to further intermingling of populations and cultures.[92]

Alexander encouraged the reappointing of Orientals to the satrapies east of Babylon as a part of his policy of partnership. He maintained Persian friends; showed great respect for the dead Darius, whose corpse he wrapped in his own cloak; and himself adopted the Persian custom of wearing the diadem. At his court he now had a large number of Asiatics, all of whom were accorded the highest respect. Among them were a brother of Darius; a son of Artaxerxes Ochus, Darius's second-in-command; a leading statesman, Artabazus; and a commander, Mazaeus. While he called his leading Macedonians friends, Alexander called the Asiatics "Kinsmen" and let then kiss him in the Persian manner.[93]

Alexander pursued a deliberate policy of intermarriage well described by N. G. L. Hammond.[94] Later in 324 at Opis, Alexander staged a banquet of reconciliation for nine thousand guests.[95]

Both Hammond and Lane Fox bring out another side of Alexander's character and explain the motivating force of his push toward India, a side rarely acknowledged. Alexander felt a sense of yearning (*pothos*), and, like his tutor, Aristotle, was possessed of a curious mind for which the strange new world of India was irresistible: "[O]f Alexander's curiosity there can be no doubt. 'His troops,' said a contemporary, well placed to know, 'took a very hasty view of India, but Alexander himself was keen to be more exact and therefore arranged for the land to be described by those who knew it.'"[96] Alexander's ambitions were those of an explorer as much as a conqueror; his desire, wrote his friend Nearchus the Cretan, to do something that was always new or strange triumphed over his fears.[97] Hammond writes of Alexander's scientific aims to explore unknown regions of the world. Alexander sent Aristotle large sums of money to help found a great library of literary texts and to make a collection of specimens for teaching.[98]

Since our larger theme is Orientalist writings, I should like to devote a few pages to what, and in what manner, the Greek historians tell us about India. However, the only connected narratives of Alexander that survive were written many centuries after his death, but these latter do contain summaries of earlier accounts, which have been skillfully reconstructed by Lionel Pearson and on which I depend for the following account.[99]

Onesicritus of Astypalaea is one of our sources for India preserved by Strabo and others. He is criticized by Strabo for being "the chief steersman of fantasy," a reference to Onesicritus's role under Alexander of chief steersman. And yet Strabo does concede that Onesicritus had some things to say that are believable and worthy of mention.[100] In his descriptions of the country of Musicanus, Onesicritus gives perhaps an idealized picture of a kingdom blessed by nature, with laws and traditions that prevent people from being corrupted by the gifts of nature.[101] He also provides a vivid and sympathetic account, to which I will return later, of Alexander's meeting with Hindu sages.

One of Arrian's principal sources was Aristobulus, and even the normally skeptical Strabo seems to find Aristobulus more trustworthy than many others. Aristobulus served as a minor officer with Alexander, and his account of the expedition has a wealth of generally trustworthy ethnographical, geographical, and botanical information on India, a witness to the Greeks' scientific curiosity. We know he had an eye for accurate architectural detail, since he described, for example, the famous tomb of Sardanapalus at Anchiale. As Pearson observes, "He naturally acquired a special interest in old tombs when later on, he was commissioned to repair Cyrus' tomb at Pasargadae. He described Cyrus' tomb with an exactness which has been commended by modern archaeologists, and his description of the tomb at Anchiale is preferable to other extant descriptions."[102] As Pearson further adds, "Aristobulus also recorded Alexander's distress on finding the tomb of Cyrus at Pasargadae broken open and ransacked, Arrian gives his description of the tomb. Since Aristobulus was given the task of restoring the tomb and had been inside it himself, we might expect an accurate description from him, and archaeologists who identify the tomb with the monument known as Mešed mader i Suleiman are well-satisfied with it: 'the lower part of a square structure built of four-foot stone and a covered chamber above, with a small door leading inside, so narrow that a small man could only just get through.' "[103] He describes his work of preservation, in which he took a personal interest. Alexander's magnanimous gesture to restore the monument of a king of Persia—of a people who were but recently his enemies—and his decision to rebuild the great temple of Marduk (Zeus Belos) in Babylon, destroyed by the Persians, looks forward to Lord Curzon's generous efforts to preserve India's monuments, something I shall examine more closely later in this study.

For India, Aristobulus often gives details overlooked by other scientists, such as in his description of the method of growing rice. He adds valuable information about the Indus river floods, and he seems to be the only Greek writer who paid much attention to the fish in the Indus, "comparing the abundant supply with the scarcity of fish in the Nile as a result of the more numerous crocodiles."[104] He gives excellent botanical descriptions, as when he talks about myrrh trees and gilliflowers.[105]

We now come to the famous meeting with the Indian gurus of Taxila. Here is Aristobulus's "excellent and convincing description" of the Western encounter with the Eastern Sophists of India:

> Aristobulus says that he saw two of the sophists of Taxila, both of them Brahmins, that the older one was shaven and the younger one bearded, and both of them had pupils accompanying them. As a general rule they spent the day in the market, where they were honoured as wise councillors, with the privilege of taking free of cost any of the wares on sale they wanted; and any man whom they approached used to pour sesame oil over their heads so that it ran down their eyes; and since there was plenty of honey and sesame available, they would make cakes and feed themselves for nothing. They also used to come up to Alexander's table and take their dinner standing there; and withdrawing to a place near by they would give a lesson in endurance; the elder man used to throw himself on the ground on his back and expose himself to the blazing sun and the rain (the rains had started, as it was now early spring); the other man stood on one leg, holding up a log of wood about three cubits long in both hands, and when his leg grew tired he used to shift over to the other leg, and in this way remain in the same place all day long. The younger man, in fact, showed himself the more perfect in control, because after following the king for

a short time he soon turned back home again, and when Alexander sent for him he told him to come himself if there was anything he wanted; but the older man accompanied Alexander's expedition until the end, changing his costume and altering his manner of living, and associated freely with the king; and when people found fault with him for this, he used to say that he had completed the forty years of ascetic living in accordance with his vow; and Alexander gave a present to his sons.[106]

Onesicritus's interpretation, on the other hand, is filtered through his own Cynic philosophy and Greek preconceptions. He had studied with the founder of the Cynics, Diogenes himself. Onesicritus was asked to take off his clothes and sit down in order to hear their teaching. "But the heat of the sun was so scorching that nobody could have borne to walk barefoot on the ground, especially at midday," wrote the pupil of Diogenes. But he was excused by the oldest guru, called Mandanis, who asked about Socrates, Pythagoras, and Diogenes, remarking that they paid too much attention to conventions and not enough to nature. Three interpreters were necessary for translation and communication. Mandanis said, "Because my interpreters only understand the simplest language, I cannot prove to you why philosophy is useful. It would be like asking pure water to flow through mud."

All authorities agreed about Calanus's suicide.[107] Arrian continues the story:

The story goes that [Calanus's] body grew enfeebled in Persia, though he had never been ill before; yet he would not submit to the regimen of an invalid, but told Alexander that he was glad to make an end as he was, before experiencing any suffering that would force him to change his old regimen. Alexander argued with him at some length; but when he saw that Calanus would not give in, but would depart in another way, if baulked at this point, he ordered that in conformity with his own instructions a pyre should be built for him and that Ptolemy son of Lagus, the bodyguard, should be in charge of it. Some say that he also had a great procession formed, horses and men, some in full armour, others carrying all sorts of incense for the pyre; others again say that they carried gold and silver cups and royal raiment. For Calanus himself a horse was made ready, since he could not walk because of his illness; and yet he could not even mount the horse, but was borne upon a litter, lying down, crowned with garlands in the Indian fashion and chanting in the Indian tongue. The Indians say that these chants were were hymns of praise to gods. It is said that the horse on which he was to have mounted was a royal horse belonging to the Nasaeans, that before he climbed the pyre it was presented to Lysimachus, one of those who attended on him for instruction, and that he distributed among his associates the cups and rugs which Alexander had ordered to be heaped on the pyre in his honour. So

> then according to the story he climbed the pyre and lay down with decorum in the sight of the whole army. Alexander did not approve of the spectacle afforded by a friend, but the rest were astonished to see that Calanus did not move any part of his body in the flames. When the fire was lit by those detailed for the task, the trumpets (says Nearchus) sounded, as Alexander had ordered, and the whole army raised the shout they would raise when entering battle, and the elephants trumpeted their shrill war-cry, in honour of Calanus.[108]

This is one of most moving and sadly enchanting stories of classical antiquity, bestowing dignity on all concerned, a poignant scene of compassion, resolution, and tolerance for human ways: The army, a bunch of rough fighters from several countries, giving voice to their war cries, the trumpets sounding, the elephants adding their own music all to honor a semi-naked fakir from faraway India silently burning in the flames of the pyre, a Sophist who insisted on adhering to his ancestral customs, so unlike those of the Greeks, Macedonians, and Persians.

Lane Fox describes how this meeting of East and West passed into Western literature, lore, and consciousness from the Renaissance to Puritan England.[109]

Megasthenes, Greek historian and diplomat, wrote a description and history of India, Ινδικα, based on firsthand experience, a work that was for centuries the main source of the West's knowledge of that country. Megasthenes was probably the representative of Seleucus Nicator at the court of Sibyrtius, whom Alexander had appointed satrap of Arachosia and Gedrosia. Megasthenes served on several embassies, which included a mission to meet with Chandragupta (Sandracottus), the founding king of the Maurya Empire in North India. He gave a survey of India's peoples and its tribes, their manners and their arts; he described the country, its soil, climate, animals, and plants, and its government and religion, all with a remarkable openness of mind and unprejudiced eye, and with an equally astonishing sympathy and admiration for India's peoples. Though often credulous, and mistaken in his information, Megasthenes recalled a picture of the state of India at a particular moment, wherein lies its importance. Modern Indian scholars are eternally grateful to those Victorians who first realized that the Sandracottus was the historical Chandragupta, and then to Megasthenes for having preserved the memory of that period. As the contemporary Indian scholar R. K. Jain, of the Institute of Bharatalogical Research in Sriganganagar, Rajasthan, observed in his preface to a reissue of *McCrindle's Ancient India: As Described by Megasthenes and Arrian*, Indian historians, when not neglecting this period entirely, are biased, uncritical, and unchronological, whereas the Greek sources were "unprejudiced; [t]heir sources of information, as admitted by themselves, are the Brahmanas, hence they are not anti-Brahmanic; [t]hey are contemporary with the events and their testimony is direct; they are very valuable sources of [Indian] history, for its re-writing and restructuring."[110]

Megasthenes finds the people of proud bearing, well skilled in the arts, since they drink the very finest water.[111] He writes:

> Of several remarkable customs existing among the Indians, there is one prescribed by their ancient philosophers which one may regard as truly admirable: for the law ordains that no one among them shall, under any circumstances, be a slave, but that, enjoying freedom, they shall respect the equal right to it which all possess: for those, they thought, who have learned neither to domineer over nor to cringe to others will attain the life best adapted for all vicissitudes of lot: for it is but fair and reasonable to institute laws which bind all equally, but allow property to be unevenly distributed.[112]
>
> Among the Indians officers are appointed even for foreigners, whose duty is to see that no foreigner is wronged. Should any of them lose his health, they send physicians to attend him, and take care of him otherwise, and if he dies they bury him, and deliver over such property as he leaves to his relatives. The judge also decides cases in which foreigners are concerned, with the greatest care, and come down sharply on those who take unfair advantage of them.[113]

The Lost Legacy of Alexander

There are two historical subjects that are neglected by such scholars as Baldry when one would have thought them central to their thesis of the cultural interaction of cultures, of East and West, the cultural encounters of Greek and non-Greek civilizations: first, an account of the Seleucids, rulers of an empire founded by Seleucus, stretching from Anatolia to Central Asia; and second, the story of the Indo-Greeks, such as Menander.

Seleucids

Alexander's conquest opened the countries of the Middle East to Greek immigration. Alexander had set the pattern of Greek-style cities with Greek civic institutions, and his policy was followed by the Seleucids. All the dynastic foundations received Greek and Macedonian populations. However, as P. Briant says, "[T]he Graeco-Macedonian dominance in the new cities implies neither an enforced Hellenization of the local peoples nor their marginalization. In Babylonia, what is striking, is the continuity and survival of traditional social, political, and religious institutions. Anu-uballit, governor of Uruk in the reign of Seleucus II, is a specially interesting case: he had received permission from the Seleucid king to add to his Babylonian name the Greek 'Nikarchos'; at the same time he continued to watch over and care for the Babylonian sanctuaries of the city."[114]

The Seleucids founded an empire that stretched from Anatolia, via Syria and Babylonia, to Iran and thence to Central Asia. From the outset, the founder Seleucus I adopted a policy of using local languages, local people in administration, and Achaemenid institutions in the army. Seleucus himself was married to "the Bactrian princess Apame, mother of his successor and eldest son, the half-Iranian Antiochus I, a prototype of the dynastic-marriage alliances with non-Greek dynasties that the Seleucids pursued as a continuing policy in their relations with non-Greek peoples in and beyond their realms."[115] There was perhaps also a matrimonial alliance with Chandragupta's royal family, with the Indian king sending Seleucus five hundred elephants and the latter sending a resident, Megasthenes, to the Mauryan court.[116]

Indo-Greeks

One of the most respected historians of the Indo-Greeks is the Indian scholar A. K. Narain, whose classic work *The Indo-Greeks, Revisited and Supplemented* I rely on for what follows.[117] Narain pays a handsome tribute to the Victorian Orientalists and other nineteenth- and early twentieth-century European scholars, archaeologists, historians, and numismatists, and their "arduous research,"[118] Orientalists such as James Prinsep, Christian Lassen, H. H. Wilson, Alexander Cunningham, Percy Gardner, Alfred von Sallet, Hugh George Rawlinson, Charles J. Rodgers, Edward James Rapson, George Macdonald, John Marshall, and John Allan, all scholars despised by Edward Said and his followers. Narain was particularly grateful to his supervisor, another Western Orientalist, the Australian scholar A. L. Basham, much revered in India particularly for his books *The Wonder That Was India* and *A Cultural History of India*,[119] and to Richard Bertram Whitehead, the famous numismatist, who retired to Cambridge, England, after working for many years in the Indian Civil Service—an Orientalist and imperialist being thanked by an Indian! And finally, the greatest inspiration for Narain was Sir William Tarn's *The Greeks in Bactria and India*.[120] Scholars Narain met in England "were kindly and helpful in my investigations."[121] Before arriving in England, Narain had already trained under the archaeologist Sir Mortimer Wheeler.[122]

The settlement of Greeks to the northwest of India existed before Alexander, a fact attested to by Western classical sources. Arrian, for instance, talks of the

Nysaeans as a non-Indian race, "but descendants of those who came into India with Dionysus; perhaps not only of those Greeks who had been disabled for service in the course of the wars which Dionysus waged against the Indians, but perhaps also of natives of the country whom Dionysus, with their consent, had settled along with the Greeks." Dionysus may be mythical, remarks Narain, but Nysa and its Greeks seem to be real.[123] We also have the evidence of the Branchidae, perhaps originally from Ionia, who were transported by Xerxes to a small town in Sogdiana, somewhere between Balkh and Samarkand, where their descendants were found by Alexander: "They were now a bilingual and partially de-hellenized race, but still attached to their tradition and origin."[124] There seem to have been many Greeks exiled by the Persians to the far eastern parts of the Achaemenid Empire. We have enough material remains to indicate that there were Greeks settled in Afghanistan.

The important point to remember is that these Greeks "who were settled in eastern Iran must naturally have intermarried with Iranians and other local elements of the population; hence the hybrid names and coin-types. . . . They were, in our opinion, much mixed with Iranian elements. Although they had not forgotten their traditions, they had probably to some extent identified themselves with local Iranians in social and political life."[125]

Tarn found it difficult to account for the large number of Greeks in Bactria and suggested that the early Seleucids must have encouraged settlements. However, there seems to be no evidence of such settlements on such a scale, and Narain thinks that the Greeks in Bactria were not Hellenistic Greeks, but "mostly the descendants of earlier settlers, preserving their traditions but such much intermixed with the Iranian peoples, and in some measure reinforced by newcomers."[126] Thus there were Greeks who had dwelled in the region for generations before the arrival of Alexander and Seleucus; they "had not ceased to follow the customs of their native land, but they were already bilingual, having gradually degenerated from their original language through the influence of a foreign tongue."[127]

Seleucus had proceeded to reconquer the eastern half of Alexander's empire, but it proved difficult for him to hold on to it since many of the Greeks and the Iranian nobility were not particularly loyal to the Seleucids. Seleucus appointed his son Antiochus I joint king to manage his Eastern affairs, but the inhabitants of Bactria, Parthia, and surrounding regions realized that the Seleucids, overstretched in the West, were not able to enforce payments of tribute. As E. R. Bevan wrote, "the new colonies in this region, being mainly composed of Greeks, had shown themselves impatient of Macedonian rule, and a leader who could play upon this national feeling could make himself very strong. Diodotus, the Satrap [the governor of a formal territorial subdivision known as a satrapy], probably non-Macedonian like his predecessor Stasanor and his successor Euthydemus, abjured alliance to his Seleucid master and declared himself an independent king."[128]

There seem to have been more than forty Greco-Bactrian kings,[129] covering a time span of about two hundred years, and territories extending from Sogdiana to the Punjab. The consolidation of Greco-Bactrian power was due to Euthydemus and his successors. Among the early group of Greco-Bactrian kings was Antimachus Theos, who is interesting for being the first "to strike the Indian type of square or rectangular copper coins with the figure of an elephant on one side and with a thunderbolt, the attribute of Zeus, on the other. Probably he crossed the Hindu Kush and found it necessary to match the Indian money circulating in the region for local needs."[130]

Demetrius II was the first king to issue silver money on the reduced Indian weight standard, with legends in both Greek and Indian Prakrit; he also issued some square copper bilinguals on the Indian model. Demetrius II adopted the epithet of *Aniketos*—unconquerable, unconquered—and he was the first to translate his epithet into an Indian language.[131]

Among the other notable early Greco-Bactrian kings were the brothers Pantaleon and Agathocles, whose coins are important evidence for the interaction and, perhaps, eventual fusion of cultures. Narain writes:

> While both the brothers struck some copper bilinguals with an Indian Yakshi goddess and maneless lion, Agathocles also issued coins with additional types. The most significant of them are not only those which use the Buddhist motif of Chaitya and devices found on the local coins of Taxila, but the rectangular silver bilinguals which represent for the first time the hero-gods Vàsudeva and Samkarshana of the Brahmanical Bhagavat cult to which later Heliodorus, the envoy of Antialcidas of Taxila to Bhagabhadra of Vidisha (near Bhopal), was devoutly affiliated. It is not without significance that the two brothers are the only ones among the Bactrian kings who introduced on their coins the Indian Brahmi script in addition to Kharosthi, which was normally used in the Indo-Greek bilingual coinage. In fact the six coins of Agathocles with legends in Brahmi script which have been found at Ai Khanum are among the earliest examples of this script found outside the Indo-Pakistan sub-continent. Agathocles was the first Yavana [Greek][132] king to possess Taxila and initiate a forward policy of extending patronage to Indian religions and cults, both Buddhist and Brahmanical. He probably opened, or used, more northerly passes and routes than the usually frequented ones in the south to reach Taxila, and thus made cultural contacts easier between north-eastern and eastern Afghanistan on the one hand and north-western Pakistan on the other.[133]

MENANDER

Of the two the novice became the king of the city of Sâgala in India, Milinda by name, learned, eloquent, wise, and able; and a faithful observer, and that at the right time, of all the various acts of devotion and ceremony enjoined by his own sacred hymns concerning things past, present, and to come.

—Questions of King Milinda[134]

Menander was the greatest of the Yavana kings, and certainly the best known in India, since he is remembered in the Buddhist tradition as Milinda. According to the Pali Buddhist work *Milindapanha* (Questions of King Milinda), he was born in a village called Kalasi and assigned to govern the satrapy of either Arachosia or Paropamisadae. He was married to Agathocleia, who was probably a sister or daughter of Agathocles, and ruled over much of Afghanistan and what is today Pakistan, his kingdom extending to Kabul, Taxila, Ghazni, and Sialkot. According to Strabo and Appollodorus, Menander may have got beyond the Hypanis and even as far as the Ganges and Palibothra. From the coins we learn that he ruled for about twenty-five years and died about 130 BCE. From *Questions of King Milinda*:

Master of words and sophistry, clever and wise
Milinda tried to test great Nâgasena's skill.
Leaving him not again and yet again,
He questioned and cross-questioned him, until
His own skill was proved foolishness.
Then he became a student of the Holy Writ.
All night, in secrecy, he pondered o'er
The ninefold Scriptures, and therein he found
Dilemmas hard to solve, and full of snares.
And thus he thought: 'The conquering Buddha's words
Are many-sided, some explanatory,
Some spoken as occasion rose to speak,
Some dealing fully with essential points.
Through ignorance of what, each time, was meant
There will be strife hereafter as to what
The King of Righteousness has thus laid down
In these diverse and subtle utterances.
Let me now gain great Nâgasena's ear,
And putting to him that which seems so strange
And hard—yea contradictory—get him

> To solve it. So in future times, when men
> Begin to doubt, the light of his solutions
> Shall guide them, too, along the path of Truth.'

Menander's patronage of Buddhism is attested to by coins—one of his copper coin types depicts the Buddhist Dharma-chakra, the Wheel of Law. His dialogue with the Buddhist sage Nagasena is recorded in the *Questions of King Milinda* and is a lucid account of early Buddhist doctrine. Narain thinks that proof of Menander's conversion to Buddhism is to be found in Plutarch's description of his funeral: "[At Menander's death] the cities celebrated his funeral as usual in other respects, but in respect of his remains, they put forth rival claims and only with difficulty came to terms, agreeing that they should erect monuments to him in all their cities."[135] For this, Narain maintains, is "unmistakably Buddhist and recalls the similar situation at the time of Buddha's passing away. Menander's connection with Buddhism is preserved also in the Chinese, Indo-Chinese and Tibetan Buddhist traditions of later times."[136]

Narain is convinced that there was a real fusion of cultures in this part of Bactria and northwest India. Here is how he describes this new melting pot of South Asia:

> A long period of interaction with the people and cultures of the region made the Greeks of Bactria and India parts of the local milieu. They had kept their identity as long as they could before they were absorbed in the melting pot of South Asia. They were socially integrated into the caste system of India, they became Buddhists and Hindus, master craftsmen and architects, adopted Indian names and titles, and wrote in Indian script and languages. In this process they not only internalized many ideas and institutions of Iranian and Indian origin but also made abiding contributions to various aspects of the life and culture of South Asia, for example in art and iconography, literature and drama, astronomy and the calendrical system.[137]

For his conclusion, Narain draws on the recent finds at Ai Khanum, in northern Afghanistan, which was founded in the Seleucid period and continued to flourish under the Greco-Bactrians.[138] Ai Khanum revealed impressive architecture, as well as many sculptures, ceramics, jewelry, and other smaller finds. Particularly fascinating were the many ivory objects.

For the Seleucid period at Ai Khanum, Malcolm Colledge has also detailed the fruitful interaction of cultures as evidenced in the architecture, where Greek and Mesopotamian styles merge.[139]

Menander embraced Buddhism.[140] Can there be a more dramatic evidence of the acceptance of "the Other," a breaking down of cultural barriers, than the adoption of his belief system? As F. L. Holt says, Menander was the greatest of Indo-Greek kings who successfully bridged the cultural divide between Greece and India.[141] Thus, at the dawn of Western civilization, you have the ultimate compliment that a Westerner can pay the Other: convert to his way of life, his philosophy, his religion.

Lack of Racism in Classical Antiquity

Blacks

Frank Snowden Jr., a distinguished African American classicist, has very persuasively argued in two major books[142] that "those Greeks who first described and depicted dark or Negroid peoples did so without bias. The early, unbiased approach toward colored peoples adumbrated what was to follow. Long after the Ethiopian was divested of any romanticization stemming from a mythological aura and long after he was well-known to the Greeks and Romans, whether in Africa or in various parts of the classical world, antipathy because of color did not rise. The Graeco-Roman view of blacks was no romantic idealization of distant, unknown peoples but a fundamental rejection of color as a criterion for evaluating man."[143]

Greeks and Romans classified several physical types of dark and black peoples inhabiting different parts of Africa as Ethiopians. However they might be classified by modern physical anthropologists, to the Greeks and Romans they were all Ethiopians, a large part of whom would be described as blacks today.

Far from being caricatures, the early images of blacks in Western art are very sympathetic portraits of real individuals, depicted with remarkable realism and with scrupulous attention to detail, using, for example, in sixth-century vases in the shape of heads of blacks, raised dots to give the effect of tightly coiled hair. Mulattoes or individuals of white-black mixture appear in the art of the mid-fifth century BCE, reflecting anthropological reality. For instance, the Ethiopian soldiers in Xerxes' army were black, but children of Greek women by them would have been mixed, and it was such mulatto types that attracted Greek artists. In general, miscegenation was, to a certain extent, accepted. We have the example of Aristotle referring to a white woman of Elis and another of Sicily to illustrate the transmission of physical characteristics in the descendants of black-white racial mixture: "Further, children are like their more remote ancestors from whom nothing has come; for the resemblances recur at an interval of many generations, as in the case of the woman in Elis who had intercourse with a negro; her daughter was not negroid but the son of that daughter was."[144]

Herodotus offers us fascinating glimpses of Ethiopian kings, whom, once again, as with other peoples such as the Persians and Egyptians, he describes with a sympathetic eye. One of these kings was Sabacos, who ruled Egypt for fifty years and was remarkable for abolishing the death penalty, preferring to sentence every wrongdoer, according to the seriousness of his crime, to build a dike near his native city.[145] Another group of Ethiopians is described as the tallest and most attractive people in the world.[146] We also have a positive account of Ethiopians in the pages of Diodorus Siculus, where they are depicted both as pious and as the originators of many of Egypt's customs. Pliny the Elder, on the other hand, emphasizes the Ethiopians' wisdom, which he attributed to the southern climate. Virgil praises Ethiopians for their assistance to the ancestors of Rome in the Trojan War. Aeneas gazes at the scenes depicted on the outer walls of Dido's temple at Carthage and recognizes his black ally, Memnon: "He saw too the fighting ranks from the Orient, led by black Memnon with his divine arms."[147] The epic poet Quintus of Smyrna recounts the glorious exploits of Memnon and his black soldiers. Snowden emphasizes the positive Greco-Roman view of blacks, with no stereotyping.[148]

It is a remarkable fact that ancient poets and artists often describe and depict in the most natural way possible the interracial amours of black gods and heroes. Zeus was called Ethiopian by the inhabitants of Chios, and "may have been the black or dark-faced stranger in the *Inachus* of Sophocles and may have appeared as a Negro in the dramatist's satyr-play. Epaphus, the child that Io, the daughter of the primeval king of Argos, bore Zeus, was described by Aeschylus as black and was said by Hesiod to have been the ancestor of the Libyans and Ethiopians."[149] In the *Suppliants* of Aeschylus, the daughters of Danaus were black, and in one version of the legend, they were born to Danaus by an Ethiopian woman.[150] In Heliodorus's *Aethiopica* the Greek hero is totally unconcerned about the fact that the girl he loves was the daughter of an Ethiopian king. As Snowden observes, "[T]here is little doubt that many blacks were physically assimilated into the predominantly white population of the Mediterranean world."[151]

Jews

It is significant that some of the most virulently anti-Jewish writings in classical antiquity come, not from Greeks, but from nationalistic Egyptians like Manetho, the first Egyptian to write of his country's past in Greek, who was responsible for creating and popularizing anti-Jewish motifs. Other anti-Jewish Egyptians include Apion.[152]

By contrast, some of the earliest Greeks are philosemitic. Theophrastus, the disciple of Aristotle, in a fragment preserved by Porphyrius, is favorable to the Jews, declaring them to be philosophers who converse about God during the sacrifice of animals and observe the stars. The esteem in which the Jews are held by him goes hand in hand with his admiration for all things Egyptian.[153] Hecataeus of Abdera is one of the earliest Greek authors to write about Jews. The account preserved in Diodorus Siculus of Hecataeus's *Aegyptiaca* talks of the colony founded in Judaea by Moses, who is described as "outstanding both for his wisdom and for his courage. On taking possession of the land he founded, besides other cities, one that is the most renowned of all, called Jerusalem. In addtion he established the temple that they hold in chief veneration, instituted their forms of worship and ritual, drew up their laws and ordered their political institutions. He also divided them into twelve tribes. He had no images whatsoever of the gods made for them, being of the opinion that God is not in human form; rather the Heaven that surrounds the earth is alone divine, and rules the universe."[154]

Hecataeus lived in an age that thought highly of Jews as attested in the works of Theophrastus, Megasthenes, and Clearchus. There are traces of an essentially sympathetic attitude to Jews in the works of Polybius; Diodorus Siculus; Varro, who thought the God of the Jews to be the same as Jupiter; Timagenes, said to be hellenocentric and barbarophile;[55] Nicolaus of Damascus, who defended the interests of the Jewish communities against the claims of the Greek cities in Asia Minor; Strabo, whose evaluation of Moses is outstanding in its sympathy for the Jewish lawgiver. Pseudo-Longinus has an even higher regard than Strabo for Moses: "A similar effect was achieved by the lawgiver of the Jews—no mean genius, for he both understood and gave expression to the power of the divinity as it deserved."[156] During the Roman period, there were some neutral references to the Jews, as in the works of Epictetus, but there were also hostile attitudes, as in the works of Seneca the Philosopher and Quintilian, whose views were colored by their fear of the putative proselytism of the Jews, while others equated the Jewish rituals with superstition and Judaism as a socially divisive Oriental cult, an attitude whose significance I shall discuss later. Some, such as Suetonius, did not make any distinction between Christianity, Judaism, and the Egyptian cults. All were superstition in their eyes, and at play was a cultural aversion rather than racism.

STOICS AND STOIC COSMOPOLITANISM

The Stoics were undoubtedly influenced by Cynic cosmopolitanism, with Ariston of Chios being the earliest Stoic philospher to come close to the position of the Cynics. But it was mankind viewed geographically that was the decisive factor in the development of the idea of the unity of mankind. The polymath Eratosthenes, influenced by Ariston, saw the study of the world and its peoples as a single whole. In his *Geographica*, Eratosthenes estimated the circumference of the globe with remarkable accuracy, and "he measured and mapped the *oikoumene* [the whole world, the inhabited world] from Thule in the north to Somaliland and Ceylon in the south, from the Pillars of Hercules in the west to furthest India in the east."[157] Strabo has preserved Eratosthenes' views:

> Towards the end of his treatise he declares that praise should not be given to those who divide the total number of mankind into two sections, Greeks and barbarians, or to those who advised Alexander to treat the Greeks as friends and the barbarians as enemies; the division should rather be made, [Eratosthenes] says, according to good qualities and bad. For many of the Greeks are bad, and many of the barbarians civilised-Indians and Arians, for example, and also Romans and Carthaginians, who conduct their political affairs so admirably. It was for this reason, he continues, that Alexander ignored his advisers, and welcomed and favoured all men he could of good repute.[158]

"For many Greeks are bad," says Eratosthenes—another instance of Western self-criticism. Eratosthenes proposed instead a distinction between "civilized" and "uncivilized." As Baldry says, "Here for the first time, or at any rate more clearly than ever before, we have the concept of a multi-racial and multi-lingual civilised humanity, put forward by a Greek whose picture of mankind included non-Greek centres of civilisation comparable with his own."[159]

For Polybius, as for Eratosthenes, the *oikoumene* is a basic concept. Polybius took a comprehensive view of the whole world, transcending frontiers and racial distinctions. The human race forms a single unity analogous to the unity of its geographical environment or that of an individual body.

Posidonius was not only a distinguished Stoic philosopher, but a scientist of extraordinary range and a historian who believed that history must be universal—in short, a polymath, and a tireless seeker after knowledge. He places "human unity in perspective within the organic unity of the world, intermediate between the animal and the divine. He saw mankind both as a whole made up of many diverse parts which he knew and described in his writings, and also as itself a part of the complex unity of the universe."[160]

Cicero, like many of the Greek philosophers we have examined, believed that reason is the common distinctive feature of men and gods, that all men are alike in sharing reason (*ratio*) and have the potentiality for wisdom (*sapientia*):

> This creature which we call man, endowed with foresight and sagacity, complex, intelligent, equipped with memory, full of reason and understanding, has been created by the supreme deity with a certain distinctive status: out of all the species and varieties of living creatures he alone has a share in reason and thought, which is lacking in all the rest. And what is more godlike, not only in man, but in all heaven and earth, than reason, which, once it is full grown and brought to perfection, is rightly called wisdom? Since therefore nothing is better than reason and reason exists in both man and god, reason is the first bond of unity between them. But those who have reason in common also have right reason in common; and since right reason is law, this also must be seen as a common tie linking men with the gods. Now those who have the same law must also have the same justice; and those who share law and justice must be regarded as members of the same community much more so, if they obey the same authorities and powers; and they do obey the order of the heavens, the divine mind, and the god of supreme power. Therefore the whole universe must be seen as a single joint community of gods and men.[161]

For Cicero, men are more alike than unlike, and only their weaknesses keep them apart.[162]

As Baldry remarks, Cicero claims to be speaking for the majority of the thinking men of his time—the Old Academy, the Peripatetics, and the Stoics alike.[163] At last we seem to have reached a stage of maturity of classical antiquity where the idea of human brotherhood is regarded as an essential characteristic of every human being worthy of the name.[164]

> *Insatiate for the good their spirits yearn:*
> *Yet seeing see not, neither hearing hear*
> *God's universal law, which those revere,*
> *By reason guided, happiness who win.*
>
> —Cleanthes, from *Hymn to Zeus*

Stoicism was founded by Zeno of Citium, who is said to have arrived in Athens in 313 BCE, studying under others but eventually teaching in his own right in the Stoa Poecile. Cleanthes, Ariston of Chios, and especially Chryssipus of Soli developed the ideas of Stoicism further on three subjects: namely, logic, physics, and ethics. There was in general a constant appeal to nature and reason, whereby humans are exhorted to live in accordance with human nature, which in turn entails living in accordance with human reason, humans being uniquely endowed with reason in contrast to other animals: "Properly used, human reason will enable us to understand the role of reason in the world, thus of the world's nature." Nature and reason are objective notions; to think rationally necessarily leads to harmony with other rational beings, all striving for the truth. There is thus established a community of reason transcending earthly bonds.[165] As Marcus Aurelius wrote, "If our intellectual part is common, the reason also, in respect of which we are rational beings, is common: if this is so, common also is the reason which commands us what to do, and what not to do; if this is so, there is a common law also; if this is so, we are fellow-citizens; if this is so, we are members of some political community; if this is so, the world is in a manner a state. For of what other common political community will any one say that the whole human race are members?"[166]

Finally we have Marcus Aurelius declaring himself, in effect, a citizen of the world: "But if however the gods determine about none of the things which concern us, I am able to determine about myself, and I can inquire about that which is useful; and that is useful to every man which is conformable to his own constitution and nature. But my nature is rational and social; and my city and country, so far as I am Antoninus, is Rome, but I so far as I am a man, it is the world. The things then which are useful to these cities are alone useful to me."[167]

We have Plutarch's account of Zeno's views, writing in *On the Fortune of Alexander*, "The much admired *Republic* of Zeno . . . is aimed at this main point, that our household arrangements should not be based on cities or parishes, each one marked out by its own legal system, but we should regard all men as our fellow citizens and local residents, and there should be one way of life and order, like that of a herd grazing together and nurtured by a common law. Zeno wrote this, picturing as it were, a dream or image of a philosopher's well regulated society."[168]

Epictetus also wrote:

> If these statements of the philosophers are true, that God and men are akin, there is but one course open to men, to do as Socrates did: never to reply to one who asks his country, "I am an Athenian," or "I am a Corinthian," but "I am a citizen of the universe." For why do you say that you are an Athenian, instead of merely a native of the little spot on which your bit of a body was cast forth at birth? Plainly you call yourself Athenian or Corinthian after that more sovereign

> region which includes not only the very spot where you were born, and all your household, but also generally that region from which the race of your forbears has come down to you. When a man therefore has learnt to understand the government of the universe and has realised that there is nothing so great or sovereign or all-inclusive as this frame of things wherein men and God are united, and that from it come the seeds from which are sprung not only my own father and grandfather, but all things that are begotten and that grow upon, and rational creatures in particular—for these alone are by nature fitted to share in the society of God, being connected with Him by the bond of reason—why should he not call himself a citizen of the universe and a son of God?[169]

Another Stoic cosmopolite, Seneca, wrote of the two commonwealths, that of the common state binding together all men and gods, and another state to which we have been assigned by accident of birth.[170]

As Eric Brown has argued, for some Stoics, living as cosmopolites is just a metaphor for living in harmony with the cosmos. But there were other Stoics who believed that living in agreement with the cosmos entailed ethical obligations toward all human beings. Both Cicero (in *De Officiis*) and Seneca tried to articulate a cosmopolitanism that reconciles special obligations to compatriots with general obligations to human beings as such.[171]

Stoic cosmopolitanism fits naturally into the politically cosmopolitan ambience in the Greco-Roman world. Cicero came from provincial Tuscany, Seneca from Cordova in Iberia, Epictetus from Hieropolis in Phrygia, and Plutarch from Greece—following the increased contacts between cities after Alexander's conquests, and, even more, after the rise of the Roman Empire, which united the whole of the Mediterranean under one political power. Stoic cosmopolitanism should be seen as a natural development of philosophical thought that began as early as the times of Homer and Hesiod, the Sophists, Plato, and Alexander and his team of Orientalists.

3

EARLY CHRISTIANITY TO THE SEVENTEENTH CENTURY

Christian Universalism

Early Christians carried forward the spirit of the classical world as regards the unity of mankind, which was a defining aspect of the Christian understanding of history. Acts 17:26–28 tells us that God "hath made of one blood all nations of men for to dwell on all the face of the earth, and hath determined the times before appointed, and the bounds of their habitation; that they should seek the Lord if haply they might feel after him, and find him, though he be not far from every one of us: for in him we live, and move, and have our being; as certain also of your own poets have said, For we are also his off-spring." The author of Colossians 3:11 wrote, "Lie not one to another, seeing that ye have put off the old man with his deeds; and have put on the new man, which is renewed in knowledge after the image of him that created him, where there is neither Greek not Jew, circumcision nor uncircumcision, Barbarian, Scythian, bond nor free: but Christ is all, and in all." The author of Galatians 3:28 expressed similar sentiments: "There is neither Jew nor Greek, there is neither bond nor free, there is neither male nor female: for ye are all one in Christ Jesus." Early Christianity absorbed Stoic ethics, and perhaps under the influence of Stoic cosmopolitanism, both the Romans and the Christians strove against any kind of exclusiveness based on race. Christian doctrine was to inspire international law. We know, for example, that Hugo Grotius, the Dutch jurist, humanist, and devout Christian who wrote *De jure belli ac pacis* (Concerning the Law of War and Peace, 1625),[1] which is usually considered one of the first texts on international law, derived much of its specific content from the Bible and from classical history. However, like Islam, Christianity did not admit salvation outside its own creed.

Over and above the general Christian sense of the unity of mankind, there is the more specific Christian doctrine of *Apocatastasis*, sometimes known as Christian Universalism, which upholds the doctrine that all free moral creatures—*whether Christian or not*—will share in the grace of salvation. It is found in Clement of Alexandria, Origen, Saint Gregory of Nyassa, and even Ambrose and Chrysostom. It is a strand in Christian thought that has persisted to modern times and has influenced modern ecumenical movements, encouraging interfaith dialogues.

THE DARK AGES?

Charles Freeman argues in his lucid account of the European Middle Ages, *The Closing of the Western Mind*, that the tradition of Greek rational thought was stifled in the fourth and fifth centuries by the political and religious forces that made up the highly authoritarian government of the late Roman Empire. Factors behind this closing of the Western mind include the attack on Greek philosophy first by Saint Paul, and later by the formidable Saint Augustine of Hippo, the adoption of Platonism by Christian theologians, and the enforcement of orthodoxy by emperors desperate to keep good order. The need to impose orthodoxy meant the stifling of any kind of independent reasoning or thought. The authority of the scriptures, as interpreted by the church, had to be accepted without doubt or questioning. Intellectual curiosity, secular learning, and the empiricism of Aristotle were discouraged, even fulminated against: "It was not until the sixteenth century that Copernicus . . . set in hand the renewal of the scientific tradition."[2] Freeman ends his study with a chapter on Saint Thomas Aquinas, who through reviving the works of Aristotle brought reason back into theology and championed it alongside faith.

While Freeman's gallop through the early history of the church is well researched, and his thesis is, in the main, plausible, he may underestimate the role of reason during the early Middle Ages. This study will not do as a nuanced account of the history of ideas, since he entirely ignores the history of science during the period 300 CE–1200 CE. A. C. Crombie, in the preface to *Augustine to Galileo: The History of Science A.D. 400–1650*, which does not appear in Freeman's bibliography, wrote, "Especially I have tried to bring out, what I believe to be the most striking result of recent scholarship, *the essential conti-*

nuity of the Western scientific tradition from Greek times to the 17th century and, therefore, to our own day."[3]

Freeman dispenses with Isidore of Seville in two sentences.[4] But Isidore is important as an educational reformer whose influence was far reaching and incalculable. He studied at the cathedral school of Seville, where the *Trivium* and *Quadrivium* were taught, and within a remarkably short period of time he mastered Latin, Greek, and Hebrew. He rose in the church hierarchy, succeeded to the See of Seville, took prominent parts in the councils of Toledo and Seville, and finally, in 633, presided over the Fourth Council of Seville, which, under Isidore's influence, promulgated a decree commanding all bishops to establish seminaries in their cathedral cities, along the lines of the school already existing at Seville, where the study of Greek and Hebrew as well as the liberal arts was prescribed, and a study of law and medicine encouraged. Long before the Arabs, he had introduced Aristotle to his countrymen.[5]

Saint Isidore was probably the first Christian to compile a summa of universal knowledge, a work that epitomized all learning, ancient as well as modern, and so preserved for posterity fragments of classical learning that would have been otherwise lost. The "Etymologiae" was used throughout the Middle Ages in many educational institutions and was often reprinted, even as late as the fifteenth century. Isidore's friend Bishop Braulio divided it into twenty books that deal with, among other subjects, medicine, libraries, law, God, church, languages, etymology, the physical world, agriculture, beasts, birds, and so on. Isidore is indebted to Boethius, Lactantius, Pliny, Solinus, and Suetonius, among others. His other works include the *Synonyma*, which is in the form of a dialogue between Man and Reason, and the *Chronicon*, a universal chronicle.

There is also no mention in Freeman's book of the Carolingian Revival, an intellectual renaissance of a sort, hardly possible without the use of reason, which was inaugurated during the reign of Charlemagne and continued throughout the ninth century. The Carolingian schools were not outstandingly original in thought, but, nonetheless, many maintained a high reputation as educational centers, where editions and copies of the classics, both Christian and pagan, were produced and were the bases of the later Renaissance scholarship.[6] Among the scholars responsible for this renaissance were Alcuin and Theodulf of Orléans, as well as Rabanus Maurus and Irish monks who promoted the study of Greek in the schools.

Theodulf, bishop of Orléans, a refugee from the Islamic invasion of Spain, was a witness to the intellectual concerns of the imperial court of Charlemagne in Aachen. His greatest contribution was his scholarly edition of the Vulgate, drawing on manuscripts from Spain, Italy, and Gaul, and even consulting the original Hebrew.[7] Alcuin wrote on diverse subjects, from grammar to mathematics, testimony to his intellectual curiosity, and collected rare books, which formed the nucleus of the library at York Cathedral, later having some of them transferred to the Abbey of Saint Martin in Tours. His literary production included works of biblical exegesis and elementary works on astronomy, arithmetic, and geometry. His infectious and unbounded enthusiasm for learning made Alcuin an effective teacher. He summed up his own contributions to learning in this way: "In the morning, at the height of my powers, I sowed the seed in Britain, now in the evening when my blood is growing cold I am still sowing in France, hoping both will grow, by the grace of God, giving some the honey of the holy scriptures, making others drunk on the old wine of ancient learning."[8]

Rabanus Maurus studied under Alcuin in Tours then returned to Fulda, where he had taken his vows, to head the monastic school, which soon became under his guidance the most celebrated seat of learning in the Frankish kingdom. He procured many books for the library; erected chapels, churches, and oratories; and generally advanced the intellectual and spiritual welfare of Fulda. But his influence was far wider than that; to him is due the revival of learning in the schools of Solenhofen, Celle, Hirsfeld, Petersburg, and Hirschau. Rabanus's disciple, Lupus Servatus, abbot of Ferrières, was considered one of the great scholars of the ninth century, a humanist in the manner of the fifteenth century. He encouraged the study of the pagan classics. His eloquent letters talk of his early passion for learning, which was to dominate his thoughts as he set about collecting a library of the Latin classics. He sought out codices in order to be able to make comparisons and to arrive at a good final text.[9]

MEETING OF EAST AND WEST: ARABIC SCIENCE AND EUROPE

Wel knew he the olde Esculapius
And Deiscorides. and eek Rufus,
Old Ypocras, Hal, and Galien;
Serapion, Razis, and Avicen;
Averrois, Damascien, and Constantyn;
Bernard, and Gatesden, and Gilbertyn'.

—Chaucer, Prologue, *Canterbury Tales*

Euclide geomètra e Tolomeo
Ipocràte, Avicenna e Galïeno,
Averoìs, che 'l gran comento feo.

—Dante, *Inferno*, IV.142–144

The West received Greco-Arabic science from Spain, southern Italy, and Sicily, beginning in the tenth and eleventh centuries but gathering momentum during the twelfth and thirteenth centuries. Clearly, the West, as always, was receptive to the new ideas, and it is supremely ironic that while the Arab conquests in Spain and Sicily eventually led to fruitful contact with the West, in effect giving back to the West its own Greek heritage, leading to the European twelfth-century scientific renaissance, it was the Arabs' very conquests in the first place that had shattered the Mediterranean unity and had cut the West off from classical heritage. As Henri Pirenne noted, "It was the end of the classic tradition. It was the beginning of the Middle Ages, and it happened at the very moment when Europe was on the way to becoming Byzantinized."[10]

By the ninth century, independent cities such as Venice, Naples, Bari, Amalfi, and a little later Pisa and Genoa, were trading with the Arabs of Sicily and the eastern Mediterranean. Already by the eleventh century, Constantine the African, a Benedictine monk of Monte Cassino, was disseminating knowledge of Arab scientific works, which, in turn, were often translations of Greek works such as those by Galen and Hippocrates. Adelard of Bath, sometimes called the first English scientist, was sent to Tours in 1100, to one of the schools founded by Charlemagne during the Carolingian Revival previously mentioned, where he probably studied the seven liberal arts: the *trivium* (grammar, rhetoric, and dialectic) and the *quadrivium* (arithmetic, geometry, astronomy, and music). He was to travel extensively over the next ten years or so, in Greece, Sicily, Italy, Asia Minor, Spain, and probably North Africa. Adelard made two important translations from the Arabic. The first was Euclid's *Elements of Geometry*. No Latin version had survived; however, two translations had been made from Greek into Arabic in the eighth and ninth centuries. Adelard's translation was used by Roger Bacon in the thirteenth century, and it became the basis of all editions in Europe until 1533. Adelard was also responsible for translating *Liber Ysagogarum Alchorismi* and *Astronomical Tables* of Al-Khwarizmi from the Arabic into Latin.

At the beginning of the thirteenth century, Leonardo Fibonacci of Pisa was in North Africa, where he acquired a knowledge of Arabic mathematics. It was thanks to Fibonacci that the Hindu-Arabic numerals became widely known in the West. The intellectual curiosity and excitement engendered by the new learning is well expressed by Fibonacci himself in the 1228 edition of his famous *Liber Abbaci*:

> After my father's appointment by his homeland as state official in the customs house of Bugia for the Pisan merchants who thronged to it, he took charge; and in view of its future usefulness and convenience, had me in my boyhood come to him and there wanted me to devote myself to and be instructed in the study of calculation for some days. There, following my introduction, as a consequence of marvelous instruction in the art, to the nine digits of the Hindus, the knowledge of the art very much appealed to me before all others, and for it I realized that all its aspects were studied in Egypt, Syria, Greece, Sicily, and Provence, with their varying methods; and at these places thereafter, while on business, I pursued my study in depth and learned the give-and-take of disputation. But all this even, and the algorism, as well as the art of Pythagoras I considered as almost a mistake in respect to the method of the Hindus. Therefore, embracing more stringently that method of the Hindus, and taking stricter pains in its study, while adding certain things from my own understanding and inserting also certain things from the niceties of Euclid's geometric art. I have striven to compose this book in its entirety as understandably as I could, dividing it into fifteen chapters. Almost everything which I have introduced I have displayed with exact proof, in order that those further seeking this knowledge, with its pre-eminent method, might be instructed, and further, in order that the Latin people might not be discovered to be without it, as they have been up to now. If I have perchance omitted anything more or less proper or necessary, I beg indulgence, since there is no one who is blameless and utterly provident in all things.[11]

Other translators included Gerard of Cremona, Robert of Chester, Alfred of Sareshel, Plato of Tivoli, Burgundio of Pisa, James of Pisa, and Michael Scot. In Sicily, the spirit of tolerance fostered by the Norman rulers led Latin, Greek, and Muslim subjects to live together in comparative harmony, in conditions, as Crombie says, "even more favourable than those in Spain for the work of translation."[12]

TWELFTH-CENTURY RENANISSANCE

The roots of the scientific revolution in Europe that we usually date to the sixteenth and seventeenth centuries lie in the twelfth-century Renaissance, which was a result of the changes in Christian theology, Western philosophy, and Western legal conceptions. Only the West seems to have developed the notion that the natural world is a rational and ordered universe, that man is a rational creature who is able to understand, without the aid of revelation, or spiritual agencies, and able to describe that universe and grasp the laws that govern it. The sources of this European confidence in reason and rationality are to be found in religion, philosophy, and law. The notion of laws of nature had Judeo-Christian groundings, but twelfth-century Christian theologians reaquainted themselves with this principle on reading Plato's *Timaeus*, which had an enormous influence on thinkers such as Peter Abelard, Adelard of Bath, William of Conches, and others. Plato's *Timaeus* presented an image of nature as an orderly, integrated whole; the natural world was a rational order of causes and effects, while man, as a part of the rational order of things, was elevated by virtue of his reason. Platonism seems to have affected every area of inquiry, not just the study of nature but also of the scriptures. The Pauline notion of conscience (*synderesis*)[13] also had the consequence of liberating man's reason from external authorities, so that, it was held, man could arrive at moral truth without the aid of scriptures, and the individual conscience became the supreme arbiter of even scriptural truth.

Where Islamic theologians denied the order of the universe in a doctrine called Islamic Occasionalism and stressed the inherent limits of man, Christian theology liberated man, teaching him that the rational faculty is a God-given gift and that all rational activity helps to celebrate the glory of God. Islamic law and theology rejected the very notion of rational agency. Instead, man had to follow tradition and obey traditional authority. The good Muslim was compelled to desist from investigating nature or questioning the Koran or the hadith. The wisdom of God and the consensus of the suitably learned scholars was considered superior to human agency, and the very idea that human reason could be the source of ethics and law was blasphemous. Thinkers such as al-Ghazali, a contemporary of the Western philosophers of the twelfth-century Renaissance, denigrated human reason, and emphasized the priority of faith and the need to bow to the authority of tradition. *The pursuit of knowledge for its own sake was not tolerated, only knowledge that brought you closer to God was worthwhile.* "For the religiously committed Ghazali this means, not only religious knowledge is higher in rank and more worthy of pursuit than all other forms of knowledge, but also that all other forms of knowledge must be subordinated to it."[14] All those who forsake the pure faith of God and his messenger and his Book and embark on research are in danger of going to hell.[15] Ironically, in his *Deliverance from Error*,[16] al-Ghazali explicitly taxes the two Islamic philosphers who exercised such an influence on Western science and philosophy, Avicenna and al-Farabi, with unbelief, accusing them of being in thrall to the "vicious unbelief" of Plato, Socrates, and Aristotle.

Contrast this essentially antihumanist philosophy with the humanism of late eleventh- and twelfth-century thinkers of Western Christendom. Here is the remarkable declaration of Berengar of Tours, where dialectic emerges as a conscious technique of rational thought: "He is ready to state positively that reason and not authority, is the mistress and judge. Dialectic is the art of arts, and it is the sign of an eminent mind that it turns in all things to dialectic. Anyone who does not do so abandons his principal glory, for it is by his reason that man resembles God. He intends, therefore, to have resort to dialectic in all things, because dialectic is the exercise of reason, and reason is incomparably superior to authority when it is a question of ascertaining the truth." He further wrote, "Reason arrives at truth by dialectic, which is superior to all authorities and which was used by Augustine and even by Christ himself. Whatever is illogical, notably, the doctrine of transubstantiation, is necessarily false," and also "[n]ot by decrees of the Church . . . but by reason which is the image of God in man, do we alter the truth."[17]

For John of Salisbury, as for others at this period, man's reason was a special gift from God: "All who possess real insight agree that nature, the most loving mother and wise arranger of all that exists, elevated man by the privilege of reason, and distinguished him by the faculty of speech. . . . While grace fructifies [human] nature, reason looks after the observation and examination of facts, probes the secret depths of nature and estimates all utility and worth."[18]

In Europe, by the mid-eleventh century, there was a greater sense of human dignity, greater confidence in human powers and reason that could help increase knowledge of the world and of humans themselves.[19]

As noted earlier, philosophers like Adelard of Bath, Hugh of Saint Victor, Thierry of Chartres, Peter Abelard, and William of Conches were inspired by *Timaeus* and its insistence on the rationality or orderliness of the universe in its design and function, and its adumbration of the concept of natural causation, to engage in the scientific investigation of the cosmos, for they found in Plato's work an idea of what science should be: "This concept of science involved the development of a methodology, a compact, interconnected constellation of ideas which helped these men to formulate a precise notion of what natural philosophy could be. These ideas were the principle of causality; the association of the idea of process with nature; the doctrine of primal matter; the mathematical structure underlying the elements and their permutations; the empirical basis for scientific inquiry which combines deductive reasoning, induction and the forming of hypotheses; all while remaining receptive to the painful uncertainty that merely probable knowledge entails."[20]

Hugh of Saint Victor refers to the rational principle underlying the universe: "The ordered disposition of things from top to bottom in the network of this universe . . . is so arranged that, among all the things that exist [in nature] nothing is unconnected or separable by nature, or external."[21]

Thierry of Chartres wrote, "The world would seem to have causes for its existence, and also to have come into existence in a predictable sequence in time. This existence and this order can be shown to be rational."[22]

On the nature of the stars, Adelard wrote, "For whatever is in or on these [stars], I consider that they are the product of a rational nature." Adelard, echoing Aristotle, also wrote, "Man is a rational animal and for that reason he is sociable as well; and he is innately fitted thereby for the two operations of deliberation and action." Adelard does not wish to detract from God's power when he expresses his belief in a rational universe: "I do not detract from the power of God, for all that exists does so from him and by means of His power. However, this is not to say that nature itself is chaotic, irrational, or made up of discrete elements. Therefore it is possible for men to achieve an understanding of this rational order inherent in nature, an understanding as complete as the extent that human knowledge [*scientia*] progresses. . . . Consequently, since we do not turn pale before our present state of ignorance about nature, let us return then, to the method of reason."[23]

William of Conches explains the functioning of reason: "These are the different powers of the mind: intelligence, reason and memory. Intelligence is the force of the intellect whereby man perceives the immaterial, after reason has made him certain of the cause of its existence. Reason—that force or function by which the mind is able to compare and contrast that which exists with other existent things. Memory is that function which allows man firmly to retain what he has thus previously understood."[24] As Tina Stiefel says, for William of Conches the deepest motivation for his research was "the need to get at the truth."[25] He wrote, "Anyone who finds himself put off by the dryness of our discourse, would be much less apt to miss rhetorical embellishments if he fully understood our intention; for if he did understand he would more likely to be astonished at how much we have accomplished. But although many demand a display of rhetorical skill from writers, we know of few who require truth from them. Few even recognize it when they see it, and none of the common people [*multitudine*] do; but of those few who actully boast their honesty, we alone, in fact, sweat out the truth [*soli veritati insubabimus*]. And we prefer to present that truth in a naked state rather than clothed in lies."[26] William believed that scientific research is truly a Christian activity, and the more rational one's pursuits, the better a Christian one becomes.[27] It is our duty as Christians to investigate nature, for that is a token of our gratitude for the gift of the universe, a means of celebrating the glory of God's work. It is also a sign of our rational nature.[28]

Where al-Ghazali everywhere extols tradition, these twelfth-century thinkers in the West advocated a critical examination of all tradition. Peter

Abelard wrote, "Authority is inferior to reason because it deals with opinions about the truth rather than with truth itself, while reason concerns the thing itself and can settle the question."[29] Adelard of Bath was even more forthright: "For authority alone cannot create belief in the thought of a philosopher nor even lead one towards such belief, and this is why logicians agree that citing authority does no even necessarily add probability to a given argument. So if you wish to hear more from me, give and take reason. For I am not a man who can satisfy his hunger from a picture of a steak!"[30]

William of Conches fearlessly claims that it is permissible to differ from even the great past thinkers like the Venerable Bede or the Church fathers if they err in any respect, "for even though they were greater men than we are, yet they were men."[31]

And, perhaps the greatest irony of all, Adelard says he learned his critical attitude toward ancient authority from the Arabs! He wrote, "For I was taught by my Arab masters to be led only by reason, whereas you were taught to follow the halter of the captured image of authority."[32]

This critical attitude did not stop at the holy scriptures. Men like Thierry of Chartres can even be called the fathers of biblical criticism, a title usually kept for such seventeenth-century philosophers as Baruch Spinoza. Thierry of Chartres wrote a commentary on Genesis and explained in his introduction, "This is an exegetical study of the first portion of Genesis from the point of view of an investigator of natural processes and of the literal meaning of the text."[33] William of Conches also examines the Bible in a scientific manner, and beseeches fellow Christians not to take the irrational elements in the Holy Book literally.

THE LEGAL REVOLUTION OF THE TWELFTH CENTURY

The twelfth century also saw profound changes in the concept of law that led to a legal revolution, helping the creation of free and autonomous institutions that embodied the ideals of the period and laid the foundations of the rise of modern science. The most important principle to emerge out of the legal revolution was the principle of treating collective actors as a single entity, a corporate body. As Toby Huff put it, "The emergence of corporate actors was unquestionably revolutionary in that the legal theory which made them possible created a variety of new forms and powers of association that were in fact unique to the West, since they were wholly absent in Islamic as well as Chinese law. Furthermore, the legal theory of corporations brings in its train constitutional principles establishing such political ideas as constitutional government, consent in political decision making, the right of political and legal representation, the powers of adjudication and jurisdiction, and even the power of autonomous legislation."[34]

The legal revolution was set in motion by the papal revolution, which withdrew the spiritual authority that emperors, kings, and princes had hitherto claimed. Henceforth the church exercised all the legal functions that we normally associate with the modern state, though normally we think of the modern state as a secular entity. Ultimately, the revolution in effect separated the religious and secular domains, resulting in the church's legal autonomy and creating separate and autonomous legal jurisdictions.[35]

The work known as the *Decretum*, usually attributed to Gratian, an Italian legal scholar credited with founding the science of canon law, is a synthesis of church law, which was used by later popes and became the basis for the *Corpus juris canonici*. Gratian or whoever redacted the *Decretum* argued that custom must yield to natural law, the validity of a custom now depended upon its duration, its universality, its uniformity of application, and, above all, its reasonableness.[36] Man may use his God-given reason and his conscience to weigh the validity of custom, tradition, religious authorities, and even the holy scriptures. This papal revolution was built on the recovery of Roman civil law, and its reinterpretation and refashioning, which resulted in a new canon law that was of universal application.

Members of medieval societies in the West came together on various occasions and for various reasons to form more or less permanent collectives of a religious, economic, communal, educational, or professional character. Canon law recognized these collectives as legitimate legal entities with rights of assembly, ownership, and representation (both internal and external); in other words, they were legal personalities or corporations with rights.[37] This revolution led to the founding in Europe of universities that were corporate bodies with powers to enact statutes and enforce obedience to them. Such was the University of Paris, for example, founded in 1215. Each collectivity passed laws that governed its members, giving rise to new systems of law—urban law, merchant law, and so on. Guilds and various professional associations became lawmaking bodies.[38] The recognition of such corporate bodies led to the reconstruction of the institutional framework of European society and civilization.[39] As Hastings Rashdall put it, "Ideals pass into great historic forces by embodying themselves in institutions. The power of embodying its ideals in institutions was the peculiar genius of the medieval mind."[40]

By contrast, in the Islamic world, the religious colleges known as madrasas were pious endowments under the law of religious and charitable foundations, and they were not legally independent of religious precepts or commitment or autonomous corporations.[41] The universities of Europe, on the other hand, were legally autonomous corporate enterprises with legal rights and privileges, such as the right to own or sell property, to make contracts, to promulgate its own internal rules and regulations. Nor did Islamic law recognize institutions or have the legal notion of similar corporate bodies, with rights. Many European universities grew out of cathedral schools, but some were lay institutions such as the University of Bologna: "As scholarly guilds, they sprang into existence . . . without express authorization of king, pope, prince, or prelate. They were spontaneous products of that instinct of association which swept like a great wave over the towns of Europe in the course of the eleventh and twelfth centuries."[42]

True to its ability to learn from others, its openness to ideas from the outside, Western civilization during the twelfth and thirteenth centuries eagerly sought out the works of Arabic-writing scholars and scientists from the Islamic world. The West was able to institutionalize the study of Euclid, Avicenna, Averröes, al-Khwarizmi, and others by incorporating the investigation of their works into the university curriculum. The developments, previously described, in legal concepts in the twelfth century, particularly the recognition of groups of men as corporate bodies, led to universities becoming independent—even autonomous—institutions, free from outside authorities. This resulted in, if not entirely unfettered scientific inquiry, certainly a more rational approach to the study of the natural world, and a scientific worldview.

When talking of the Middle Ages, or, more exactly, of the tenth century, historians of science or medievalists tend to talk of "the transmission" of Greek and Arabic learning to the West, or about how the West "received" Greco-Arabic science, or how this science "passed" to the West, all painting a passive picture of the process. Westerners with intellectual curiosity came to admire, "sometimes extravagantly," as Southern expressed it, Islamic culture and civilization as manifested in Spain as they came in contact with it. They *actively* sought books and manuscripts, translators, and teachers of Arabic. The West was to learn much from Islamic scholars, philosophers, and scientists like Al-Farabi, Avicenna, and Averröes, and even learned to respect "chivalric heroes like Saladin."[43]

It is worth pondering that there was a period in Islamic civilization when it was open to outside influences in ways similar to the West. Early Islamic civilization derived much from the Greeks, Romans, Indians, and Persians. But crucially, at a certain date, it rejected the "foreign sciences," which led to intellectual stagnation and decay.

European Attitudes toward Islam and the Koran during the Middle Ages

Before passing judgment on the putative "Orientalist" tendencies of all medieval writings on Islam, one should bear in mind not only the first part of this chapter, but also the previous two chapters. The discussion of how Western civilization has always nurtured individuals, some of whom exerted far-reaching influence motivated by a desire for knowledge, by intellectual curiosity, by a scientific attitude that was able to rise above polemics. In the early Middle Ages, the tone was set by Alcuin and others during the Carolingian Revival, when learning was highly prized, something to aspire to and something to add to.

Again, not every critical judgment on Islam or the Koran must be dismissed as "Christian bias." There is after all, as we shall see, justified and acute criticism. In other words, the Christian scholars may well be correct in their judgments; there are after all valid cross-cultural pronouncements, something that our postmodern sensibilities refuse to acknowledge. Here the pioneering work of Thomas Burman needs to be mentioned. Burman has provided examples of the intellectual fascination that even the most devout Christian could show, for example, with the Arabic language. Many during the Carolingian Revival were already coming to grips with Latin, Greek, and Hebrew; hence, Arabic was not such a formidably different intellectual challenge, but rather a source of wonder, something to be explored for its own sake.

While their Eastern brethren were trying to come to terms in both physical and intellectual ways with the rapid, aggressive, even devastating emergence of the new religion of Islam in the seventh and eighth centuries with its founder and its holy book, it is unlikely that the Western Christians of northern Europe had any precise idea of Islam, and before 1100 CE only a few had even heard of Muhammad, such as Abbot Majolus of Cluny, who had been taken captive by Muslim raiders.[44] Northern Europe was, of course, well aware of the existence of the Saracens by the eighth century. We have, for example, the ecclesiastical history of the Venerable Bede, who describes them without polemic or rancor as the descendants of Hagar and her son Ishmael, and he is totally unperturbed by them.[45] It is an entirely different matter in Spain, parts of which were conquered by the Muslims as early as 711. By the middle of ninth century, Spanish Christians were deeply immersed in Arabic culture, studying its theologians, philosophers, and even writing elegant Arabic.[46] The pious ninth-century layman Paul Alvarus lamented, "The Christians love to read the poems and romances of the Arabs; they study the Arab theologians and philosophers, not to refute them but to form a correct and elegant Arabic. Where is the layman who now reads the Latin commentaries on the Holy Scriptures, or who studies the Gospels, prophets or apostles? Alas! all talented young Christians read and study with enthusiasm the Arab books; they gather immense libraries at great expense; they despise the Christian literature as unworthy of attention. They have forgotten their language. For every one who can write a letter in Latin to a friend, there are a thousand who can express themselves in Arabic with elegance, and write better poems in this language than the Arabs themselves."[47]

As a reaction to this Christian laxism, Eulogius, future bishop of Toledo, and his biographer Paul Alvarus, writing during the reigns of the Cordoban caliphs Abd al-Rahman II (822–852) and Muhammad I (852–886), tried to rouse their Christian brethren from spiritual sloth and denounced Islam, viewing the Prophet as the Antichrist foretold in the Christian scriptures. They remained largely ignorant of Islam as a religion and relied on a slim biography of Muhammad by an anonymous Spanish author for the little they did learn. But as Southern reminds us, the majority of Christians were either admiring of Islamic civilization, or in general "counseled moderation" vis-à-vis Islam.[48]

After the First Crusade (1096), the situation began to change slowly. However, the three biographies of Muhammad that we know of in northern Europe by the first half of the twelfth century were all based on oral testimony and are vague and totally unreliable as history. After 1120 everyone in the West had some idea of Islam and its Prophet, much of which was legendary and fantastic. The legends of Muhammad must be seen against the background of similar legends taken to be truthful accounts of what had really taken place in history—Charlemagne, Arthur, the Miracles of the Virgin, the legendary history of Britain—all products of the same period.[49] Yet even at the height of the misrepresentation of Islam, we have the example of William of Malmesbury, who wrote of Muhammad as a monotheist and not as an idolator in about 1120. As Southern points out, "The earliest account of Muhammad and his religion that has any objective value" was by Petrus Alfonsi, a Spanish Jew who converted to Christianity in 1106. However, his work does not seem to have exercised any lasting influence on the course of Islamic studies in the West.[50]

But we know that by the middle of the twelfth century, rational appraisals of Islam were widespread, culminating in the landmark translation of the Koran into Latin by the English scholar Robert of Ketton.

Robert of Ketton and Mark of Toledo

Peter the Venerable, the abbot of Cluny, "was a learned man who recognized frankly that little trustworthy information about Islam yet existed in Latin, and blamed Christian ignorance on the general loss of zeal for the study of languages."[51] Stimulated by his visits to Cluniac abbeys and priories in Spain in 1141 and 1142, Peter planned an ambitious project to translate Arabic texts into Latin. He set about selecting his translators, and one of the first works to be translated was Al-Kindi's *Risala.* Peter picked two translators, Robert of Ketton and Herman of Dalmatia, the latter translating the *Masa'il Abi-al-Harith 'Abdallah ibn Salam* and the *Kitab Nasab al-Rusul* by Said ibn Umar, and the former the Koran and a collection of Judeo-Islamic legends. Peter himself produced a refutation of Islamic doctrine using reason—out of love, it was said—and not out of hatred.[52]

Robert of Ketton had already been translating scientific works from the Arabic in Spain and is known for his Latin translation, *Liber algebrae et Almucabola*, of al-Khwarizmi's manual of algebra, *al-Kitab al-mukhtasar fi hisab al-jabr wa-al-muqabalah.* The translation of the Koran was entirely another matter, but he set about it in a dedicated manner. Robert completed his translation of the Koran in 1143, and was well paid for his pains. Then he went back to his scientific translations. His was the first complete translation of the Koran in a Western language and became a medieval best seller.[53] Its accuracy has been attacked ever since. Juan (or John) of Segovia objected to what he regarded as the cavalier way Robert had translated and to his division of the Koran into more than the standard 114 suras.[54] Futhermore, Robert "had moved what was at the beginning of many Koranic passages to the end, and vice-versa; he had altered the meaning of Koranic terms as he translated them; he had often left out what was explicitly in the text, but incorporated into his Latin version what was only implicit in the Arabic original."[55]

Ludovico Marracci likewise found Robert's effort more of a paraphrase than a faithful translation.[56] In the eighteenth century, George Sale wrote in the preface to his own translation, "[T]he book deserves not the name of a translation; the unaccountable liberties therein taken and the numberless faults, both of omission and commission, leaving scarce any resemblance of the original."[57]

However, Thomas Burman, in a series of lucid and convincing articles, conference papers, and books,[58] has argued that Robert's rendering is worthy of respect in its own right and certainly stands in comparison with, for example, the more literal translation of Mark of Toledo. Burman contends that Robert's version often reflects accurately the Muslim understanding of their own holy book, more so than Mark of Toledo's literal effort. Burman further shows that Mark was also obliged sometimes to turn to Arabic exegetical literature to make sense of that opaque text.[59]

It is interesting to note that Robert rearranged the order of the passages so that what was at the beginning of many Koranic passages he moved to the end, and vice versa. This is the same basic principle employed by Richard Bell, nearly eight hundred years later, in his famous translation of the Koran that came out between 1937 and 1939.[60]

It is undeniable that the Koran is a difficult text, and all translators have had recourse to *tafsirs* or commentaries, not to mention lexicons and manuals of rare and difficult words. Even Sale, who showed nothing but contempt for Robert of Ketton's rendering, was obliged to smuggle in extraneous exegetical matter to complete his own translation. It is another matter, however, to decide if by using these commentaries one is any closer to what the Koran really means. Robert's reading may indeed reflect the Muslims' own understanding of their sacred scripture, but is this understanding a correct understanding? Recently, German scholar Christoph Luxenberg has tried to show that many of the obscurities of the Koran disappear if we read certain words as being Syriac and not Arabic. If Luxenberg's thesis is anywhere near correct, then the answer to my rhetorical question is no. Furthermore, if, as Gerd Puin once said, one-fifth of the Koran makes no sense, and if the Koran is indeed an abstruse allusive scripture that no one has understood, then, surely, a literal translation such as the one by Mark of Toledo, which reflects the obscurities of the original, is also valuable. Mark's version does not pretend to smooth over the difficulties with arbitrary and sometimes far-fetched glosses or commentaries of the Muslims, and thus can teach us more about the language and syntax of the original. Here is what Mark himself wrote about the style of the Koran: "[S]ometimes he [Muhammad] speaks like a crazy man, sometimes however like one who is lifeless, now inveighing against the idolators, now menacing them with death, occasionally indeed promising eternal life to converts, but in *a confused and unconnected style*."[61]

It is interesting to note here that Günter Lüling praises Rudi Paret's German translation of the Koran, completed in the 1960s, for the same reasons as I praise that by Mark of Toledo: "The sincerity of Paret was such, despite his distaste for theology, that he accomplished in his own way a pioneer work. He created a consistently non-assertive translation; that is, he did not provide a one-sided, oversimple translation, but rather one in which an established set of categorical signs and formulaic comments *constantly alert the reader to the ambivalence, distortion, and untranslatability of the traditional Arabic Koranic text as it stands. So his translation has great potential as a guide to discovering those areas in the text of the Koran where a deeper (and dogma-critical) research has to establish the real significance of the text—or even two texts.*"[62]

Roger Bacon

Roger Bacon played such an important role in the history of Western science and scientific method and was fully conversant with much of the philosophical and scientific literature of Islamic culture. For example, in his researches into optics and cognate sciences, besides his master Robert Grosseteste, his chief sources were Aristotle, Euclid, Pseudo-Euclid, Ptolemy, Diocles, and, above all, Al-Hazen, Al-Kindi, Avicenna, and Averröes.[63] In the final section of his *Opus Maius*, Bacon pleads for a more philosophical approach in confronting the challenge of Islam. He rules out miracles and war; only philosophy is left. But Christians have much to learn in this domain from Islam. "Philosophy," he wrote, "is the special province of the unbelievers: we have it all from them."[64] The Christians needed to learn their language before they could hope to understand and reply to the Muslims. Bacon, unlike his predecessors, saw Islam playing a more positive role in history, which is well summarized by Southern: "Bacon (and he is not the only man of his time to see this) had some conception of an upward movement toward unity and articulateness in which Islam had an essential role to play before it withered away. He entirely abandoned the Bible as an instrument for understanding the role of Islam in the world, and relied exclusively on philosophy. For his knowledge of Islam he relied on Moslem philosophers and the experience of travelers, and not on the meager and casual fragments of information which characterized the earlier writers. The philosophers and travelers were less reliable guides than he supposed. He did not know a great deal, and perhaps he did not know the right things, but he tried to know, and he tried to organize his knowledge."[65]

Ricoldo da Monte Croce

Ricoldo[66] was born in 1243 in Florence, joined the Dominican Order at the age of twenty-four, traveled in the Middle East as a missionary, and lived for a while in Baghdad, where he learned Arabic and witnessed the sale of Christian slaves after the Fall of Acre in 1291. On his return to Italy toward the end of the thirteenth century, when he began his great work, the *Contra legem Saracenorum*, a comprehensive refutation of Islam that concentrated on the Koran and its contents, Ricoldo settled back in the Dominican convent of Santa Maria Novella in

Florence. He died there in 1320. *Contra legem Saracenorum* draws heavily on the *Contrarietas alpholica*, an anonymous work of the eleventh and twelfth centuries, possibly by a Muslim convert to Christianity,[67] which was translated into Latin by Mark of Toledo.

Ricoldo recounts the story of the different recensions of the Koran and all the ensuing quarrels among the Muslims. He states there was no Koran at the death of Muhammad—a startlingly modern idea associated with the theories of John Wansbrough—and argues that the Koran was a most haphazard collection of very human documents collected together after the Prophet's death. Ricoldo found the Koran itself irrational, repetitive, and obscene.[68] Like Mark of Toledo, Ricoldo found the Koran extremely disorderly, illogical, shifting from one historical period to another and from one argument to another, and full of contradictions.[69]

Martin Luther translated Ricoldo's book in 1542.[70] He had read it long before, but thought Ricoldo was exaggerating until he read the Koran in Latin translation and realized that Ricoldo had been speaking the truth.[71]

Juan of Segovia

Juan (or John) of Segovia began life as a professor at Salamanca, attended the Council of Basel in 1433—he was later to write its history—and ended his days in retirement in a small monastery in Savoy. He "took up Koran study in a nearly obssesive way after the fall of Constantinople in 1453."[72] His translation and edition of the Koran is now lost but we do have his preface to it. Though profoundly hostile to Islam, Juan was nonetheless "passionately committed to gaining a thorough and correct understanding of the Koran—determined to understand not only what it says, but how it is put together, how the language in which it was written worked, and how Muslims themselves understood what it means . . . , authorities must be consulted . . . ; the Arabic language itself must be embraced, its thoroughly non-Latin structures and its abounding and intricate vocabulary mastered; the conventions of Koranic narration must be considered, the practices of Arabic, and specifically Koranic, orthography thought through."[73]

Juan found one Muslim scholar, Ica (also of Segovia), to translate the Koran into Castilian, and Juan rendered the Castilian version into Latin. Juan also learned Arabic from Ica and took the trouble to look at the Koran in Arabic, discovering that "one Koran manuscript that he possessed, . . . contained far more vowel marks for case endings than did another that he had recently acquired."[74] Juan even suspected that the lack of proper vowel marks was one of the reasons Muslims did not understand their religion. Juan's version of the Koran must have in the end been very literal since he wanted to make the Latin text conform to the Arabic way of speaking: "What began as a tool for converting the worst of heretics became in the end, therefore, a book of supremely philological character, a volume that privileged lexical and grammatical inquiry and brought the reader's attention ever back to the Arabic text in all its Arab-Muslim particularity."[75] Juan also recognized the Christian elements in the Koran, something acknowledged later by Nicholas of Cusa.

Nicholas of Cusa

Nicholas was born at Cues, present-day Bernkastel on the Moselle, probably in 1401. He was educated at the universities of Heidelberg, Padua, Bologna, and Cologne. He studied Latin, Greek, Hebrew, and later, Arabic. He began his public life in 1421 at the Council of Basel, where he became the passionate advocate for the religious and political unity of Christendom. He was made a cardinal by Nicholas V in 1448.

Nicholas's *Cribratio Alkorani* (1460) was written after his visit to Constantinople in order to convert the Muslims. Nicholas's scrutiny of the Koran was based on knowledge of Robert of Ketton's Latin translation and was very influenced by Al-Kindi's *Risala* and Ricoldo da Monte Croce's *Contra legem Saracenorum*. However, Nicholas does manage some acute and original analysis, such as his observation that the Christian elements in the Koran must have come from Christian apocryphal literature: "Now, at the time that Muhammad began, viz. in 624 A.D., during the reign of Emperor Heraclius, there had long since arisen, and condemned by the synods, many heresies vis-à-vis an understanding of the Gospel and of the Old Testament. Therefore, it is likely that there flocked to Muhammad numerous [men] who possessed the purity-of-understanding of the aforesaid writings [in such way that it was] commingled with the novelty of less true opinions. These men mingled the writings of the Testament with stories from the Talmud and mingled the clarity of the Gospel with apocryphal books. And they recounted [these writings to Muhammad as they thought right."[76]

Here Nicholas seems perfectly aware of the sectarian milieu out of which the Koran must have come, not to mention both the Judaic and Christian elements present in the Muslim scripture. Scholars have been debating ever since which elements predominate, the Christian or the Jewish. Interestingly enough, Nicholas seems to suggest that it is Nestorian Christianity that is the predominant influence as far as the Gospels and Christ are concerned. It should be perhaps mentioned here that for Christoph Luxenberg it is Eastern (Nestorian) Syriac that is the predominant influence on the language of the Koran.[77]

KORAN CRITICISM IN MEDIEVAL EUROPE, 1140–1540

European attitudes toward Islam and the Koran, in particular in the period between 1140 and 1540, were far more complex, ambiguous, and subtle than what scholars, such as Norman Daniel,[78] have argued. Thomas Burman shows clearly Latin Christendom's admiration for the Arab-Islamic world, including the Arabic language.[79] Though sometimes scandalized by it, Christians were also intrigued by the Koran and wrestled intellectually with Arabic syntax and usage, often turning to Arab Koran commentaries to make sense of an opaque text. Burman has drawn attention to a number of manuscripts of Latin translations of the Koran that have extensive interlinear or marginal philological notes, the anonymous authors showing a profound knowledge of the Koranic exegetical tradition.

R. W. SOUTHERN ON THE MIDDLE AGES

I have already recounted how Said tries to distort Southern's views in order to make us believe that Southern somehow supports Said's thesis. But like Raymond Schwab's *The Oriental Renaissance*, Southern's *Western Views of Islam in the Middle Ages* is a complete refutation of Said's arguments. First, Southern shows that there were many different attitudes in Europe between the seventh and fifteenth centuries, lumped together as "medieval." For instance, by the middle of the twelfth century, writes Southern, "rational views of Islam were beginning to be fairly widespread, since we can find them casually and independently expressed by authors in England, France, Germany, and Spain. . . . A habit of independent inquiry became established . . . and showed itself in these traces of candid appraisal of Islam." Then again we have the example of Uthred of Boldon, who, in the 1360s, held that "at the moment of death all human beings, whether Christian or Moslem, or of whatever faith, enjoyed the direct vision of God and received their everlasting judgement in the light of their response to this experience." As Southern adds, "Here was a man who belonged to the most conservative of the religious orders, a doctor of divinity whose ways of thought were orthodox, laborious, and unoriginal, putting forward a view which admitted unbelievers outside Christendom to privileges hitherto, in traditional Christian thought, exclusively reserved for Christian believers. The proposition was condemned and withdrawn, but it was significant. The growing concern about the eternal fate of unbelievers—I do not mean simply a desire to convert them, but a desire to find some means, if it were possible, of including them in the scheme of salvation—is one of the most attractive features of the period." The latter generous impulse—Christian Universalism—was a tendency, argues Southern, in Western culture that led to "a blurring of the clear-cut line between the West and its neighbors."[80] Where is the putatively eternal conflict between East and West, between Us and Them, so dear to the Saidists?

Southern concludes his work with the question "Was there any success" in the West's ability to provide a finally satisfying explanation of Islam? "Was there any progress? I must express my conviction that there was. Even if the solution of the problem remained obstinately hidden from sight, the statement of the problem became more complex, more rational, and more related to experience in each of the three stages of controversy which we have examined. The scholars who labored at the problem of Islam in the Middle Ages failed to find the solution they sought and desired; but they developed habits of mind and powers of comprehension which, in other men and in other fields, may yet deserve success."[81] Yes, there was progress in the West's knowledge of Islam.

How, then, can Said possibly claim that Southern demonstrated that "it is finally Western ignorance which becomes more refined and complex, not some body of positive Western knowledge which increases in size and accuracy?" What on earth is refined ignorance (p. 62)?

Renaissance

In her study on Renaissance humanists' attitudes toward the Ottoman Turks and Islam, Nancy Bisaha explicitly takes issue with Said's analysis of Western discourse concerning the East: "Renaissance humanists, however, present some important challenges to Said's model. Where Said focuses on colonialism as a key component in the formation of West-East discourse, the bulk of humanist rhetoric on the Turks and Islam shows a highly developed sense of Europe as the cultural superior to East—precisely at a time when Europe was fighting for its survival. . . . A second problem in applying Said's model is that, just as it fails to address more open-minded views of a large number of orientalists, it does not help explain expressions of relativism among a handful of humanists." There is, in fact, no one monolithic humanist response to the Turks and Islam.[82]

Before examining Bisaha's examples of humanist relativism, I should like to point to her salutary remarks concerning Muslim prejudice, something I shall refer to later in the present study, and something that Edward Said and his epigones refuse to acknowledge:

> My focus on negative views of the Turks should not suggest that cultural chauvinism is the unique province of the West. Muslims too were guilty of cultural and religious biases in their dealings with Christians. The practice of dhimmitude, often portrayed romantically as proof of Muslim tolerance, was a repressive system whereby Jews and Christians were protected but treated unequally in many ways. Cultural perceptions were no better than legal and political practice. A similar discourse of otherness and cultural/religious superiority had long existed in the Muslim East. During and even after the crusading period Muslim writers dismissively labeled Westerners from all over Europe as the "Franj," or the Franks, using harsh stereotypes to describe them. Also, while Europeans wrote often about the world of Islam—regardless of accuracy—Muslims exhibited slight interest in the West, confident that it had little of value to offer.[83]

Coluccio Salutati was born in Stignano, near Buggiano, today's province of Pistoia, Tuscany. In 1375 Coluccio was appointed chancellor of Florence, and thenceforth, played an important part in rallying the people of Florence to defend their traditional liberty and republicanism. The war ended in 1402, leaving Florence in a powerful position in northern Italy. A skilled writer and orator, Coluccio drew largely upon the classical tradition. He collected eight hundred books, a large library by Renaissance standards, and pursued classical manuscripts, making a number of important discoveries—the most important being the lost letters of Cicero—and substantially altering the medieval conception of the Roman statesman, writer, and orator. Coluccio wrote an influential history, tying Florence's origin not to the Roman Empire, but to the Roman Republic. Coluccio played an important part in modifying traditional church hostility to secular learning, frequently engaging in theological debates on the merits of pagan literature with church officials.

In a remarkable letter to Iodoco, margrave of Moravia and a delegate at the Diet of Frankfurt, Salutati, writing eight years after the stunning victory of the Ottomans at the battle of Kosovo in 1389, gives an extraordinary account, linking the Turks to a noble, ancient people regarded as the ancestors of the Romans. Salutati refuses to condemn the practice of *devshirme*, whereby boys between the ages of eight and eighteen were forcibly taken from their Christian families and converted to Islam, eventually joining an elite fighting force called the "janissaries": "Instead, he applauds the success of the Turks, judging them by their effects rather than the methods of their system, regardless of its exploitation of Christians."[84] Salutati praises the Turks for the simplicity of their lifestyle and military discipline, but also admires their agricultural, military, and political organization. The Turks' willingness to die for Islam is commended: "Indeed they are not barbarians to the extent that they do not believe in the existence of

God or a future life and glory; but they consider it a certainty that fighters for the Lord or his perpetual law are received into glory. To the extent that they believe more firmly, they live more simply and less learnedly."[85]

After describing admiringly the Turks' prowess in battle, Salutati ends his letter with this frank and astonishing admission: "[B]elieve me, when I observe the customs, life, and institutions of this race of men, I remember the religious practice and customs of the mighty Romans." In other words, he implies that the Turkish infidels possess more of the ancient Roman spirit than do modern, weak, and squabbling Italians.[86]

By the fifteenth century, philosphers and scientists writing in Arabic, such as Averröes, Avicenna, and Rhazes (Al-Razi), generally were a normal part of intellectual discussion in scientific and court circles. For example, Nicoletto Vernias maintained Averroism in Padua between 1468 and 1499. Later, his pupils Nifo and Fracanciano continued the tradition. Cardinal Contarini, a Venetian statesman, author of philosophical and theological works, and advocate of Roman Catholic Church reform, wrote, "When I was in Padua, in that most celebrated university of all Italy the name and authority of Averröes the Commentator were most esteemed; and all agreed to the positions of this author, and took them as a kind of oracle."[87] Alexander Achillini taught Averroism between 1506 and 1512, at both Bologna and Padua.[88]

Pico della Mirandola was an Italian philosopher from a distinguished family who relinquished his ancestral property to devote himself to study. In his fourteenth year, Pico went to Bologna to study canon law, in order to prepare himself for an ecclesiastical career. Unable to confine his inquisitive mind to law, Pico began his inquiries into philosophy and theology, spending seven years traveling to Italian and French universities, acquiring a knowledge of Greek, Latin, Hebrew, Syriac, and Arabic.

Pico tried to synthesize the various strands of Renaissance and late medieval thinking: Neoplatonism, humanism, Aristotelianism, Averroism, and Kabbalism, what J. A. Symonds once called his Quixotic quest for an accord between pagan, Hebrew, and Christian traditions.[89] For Pico, the dignity of man is to be found in his ability and freedom to be whatever he wants to be, man's ability and freedom to change and express himself in different ways. Humans have the power of self-transformation. One of the freedoms granted to humanity by God is the freedom of inquiry. Pico constantly refers to Zoroaster,[90] and is clearly familiar with the writings of the Arabians, and even quotes with approval Muhammad: "[A]nd Mahomet, . . . was known frequently to say that the man who deserts the divine law becomes a brute. And he was right . . ."[91] Pico was, of course, much influenced by Averröes's doctrine of the unity of intellect, and he was impressed not only by Averröes. Pico writes, "Among the Arabians, there is in Averröes something solid and unshaken, in Avempace, as in al-Farabi, something serious and deeply meditated; in Avicenna something divine and platonic."[92] Pico's Renaissance humanism is nowhere more apparent than in his gratitude toward foreigners—the Other, as Said would no doubt say—for where would Italian philosophy be without the great Arabic-speaking philosophers? "What should have been our plight had only the philosophical thought of the Latin authors, that is, Albert, Thomas, Scotus, Egidus, Francis and Henry, been discussed, while that of the Greeks and the Arabs was passed over, since all the thought of the barbarian nations was inherited by the Greeks and from the Greeks came down to us? For this reason, our thinkers have always been satisfied, in the field of philosophy, to rest on the discoveries of foreigners and simply to perfect the work of others."[93]

Pico's master Marsilio Ficino, who was responsible for strongly advocating philosophy and Platonism within Christianity, believed in the unity and universality of human aspirations. Like many Renaissance philosophers, Ficino was much impressed by Islamic writers such as Avicenna, but also by other non-Christians such as Zoroaster and the Persians.[94]

Guillaume Postel, Arabist, philologist, comparative linguist, visionary, Cabbalist, and universalist, was born at Dolerie in the parish of Barenton in lower Normandy. Postel came from a humble family and worked hard as a laborer to save enough money to go to Paris, where he eventually found employment with the Spanish Aristotelian Juan de Gelida at the Collège de Sainte-Barbe. He showed his facility in languages early, teaching himself Greek and picking up Spanish and Portuguese from fellow students. He taught himself Hebrew from a grammar and a text of the Psalms. Such was his reputation for languages that Postel was chosen to accompany a mission to Constantinople, where he was able to acquire works of Arabic philosophy, medicine, mathematics, and religion. In fact, thanks to his bibliophilia, Postel was able to bring many texts to the learned communities of the West: texts in Greek, Hebrew, Arabic, and Syriac, such as Euclid's *Elements* in the version of the astronomer al-Tusi; astronomical works by al-Tusi and other Arab astronomers; Latin translations of *Zohar*, the *Sefer Yetzirah*, and the *Sefer ha-Bahir*, works of Jewish Kabbalah; the New Testament in Syriac; the history of Abul-Fida; the *Protevangelium*, the infancy gospel of James. While in Constantinople, he started to learn Arabic, but found it difficult to find willing teachers, "since there are few Turks who are able, and fewer still who are willing, to teach, as though they considered Christians profane and unworthy of their language."[95] Postel ended up befriending a Turkish Christian, whose moving personal story opened up to Postel the possibilities of spreading Christianity in the Orient.

On his way back, Postel stopped in Venice, where he collected material for his first book, *Linguarum duodecim characteribus differentium alphabetum introductio*, which came out in Paris in 1538. This work describes the alphabets and grammars of twelve languages, mainly of the Balkans and the Near East, and it earned Postel the title of "father of comparative philology." Postel was later to develop his idea that the learning of languages was important as an instrument of world unity. Postel's 1538 grammar of classical Arabic, *Grammatica arabica*, was the first in Europe.

Postel considered his *De orbis terrae concordia* (1543) to be his most important work. In it he tried to provide a rational justification of Christian doctrine. An indication of where his thinking was headed is *Alcorani seu legis Mahometi et Evangelistarum concordiae liber*, where Postel points out the numerous elements in common between Protestantism and Islam. Indeed, his greater tolerance for other religions was much in evidence in Πανθενωσια: *compostio omnium dissidiorum*, where, astonishingly for the sixteenth century, he argued that Muhammad ought to be esteemed even in Christendom as a genuine prophet. He felt that there were perfectly valid religious insights among Muslims and other Oriental peoples, believing that their knowledge of final truth had come from the Jews by way of Abraham.[96] He admired the Japanese religion, the Brahmans—did not their name indicate their descent from Abraham?—the Zoroastrians, all seen as offshoots of Judaism.[97]

All these ecumenical sentiments were in accord with Postel's overriding philosophy and religious aim, *concordia*, or harmony, religious unity, unity of heart: not merely the unity of mankind, but the unity of the whole of creation. Postel had inherited his religious tolerance and missionary zeal from Raymond Lull, the Christian martyr. Lull always tried to emphasize those elements Judaism and Islam had in common with Christianity, treating both with respect and sympathy.[98] Lull "clearly felt great admiration for the virtues he discerned among both Jews and Saracens; indeed, in his many comparative treatments of the three major faiths, Lull often gives the impression, as Peers has remarked, less of attempting to teach Christian truth than of 'trying to hold the balance.' With his unusual sympathy for the non-Christian world, Lull was able to describe it with such objectivity and detachment that the accuracy of his representations has been generally conceded by scholars ever since. Such attitudes as these must have stimulated in his Renaissance readers like Postel both latitudinarian religious leanings and a tendency to cultural relativism."[99]

Postel's philosophy owed a great debt to Neoplatonism and the Kabbalah, the Jewish offspring of Neoplatonism. On the other hand, Postel's philosophy of man depended on his view that the essential quality of man resided in his reason. Postel's humanism is closely connected with his confidence in the powers of reason; one had to develop man's rational faculties to solve the problems of human nature. His belief in reason meant that the invocation of authority was a form of coercion and inconsistent with the nature and dignity of man, and such a position inevitably led to religious toleration. Postel had a passionate concern for the unity of the human race, believing that God desired the unity of man: "Since the punishment of the Flood, just as at the beginning of the world, God has wished that the whole world should live like one family, under one king, under one law, under one faith, and with one language."[100] Postel also wrote, "It is the purpose and true aim for which the world was created . . . that in fact as in desire there should be only one world under a single God, under a single king and sovereign bishop, under one faith, one law, and a single common consent."[101] With the coming again of Christ all things will again be united, "lower things with each other, lower with higher, spiritual with temporal, the kingdom of Jerusalem and the rule of the universe, charity and empire, possession and privation."[102]

Postel advocated the concord of the world and saw himself in the service of the whole human race, often adding *cosmopolite* to his name. In his most generous tribute to "the Other," his book on the Turks, Postel wrote,

> Since God put men into this world to be social animals, helping one another and taking delight in being assembled together; and since it is impossible, because of the diversity of customs, languages, opinions, and religions, that men should unite together in one community until they first come know each other: certainly the finest, most useful, and most necessary work in this world of accomplishing perfect human reconciliation, can only be truly to give men such knowledge of each other that means of it, recognizing the vice and virtue in persons or peoples previously unknown, and enduring the vice of another while approving the virtue, the world may come to a general accord.[103]

Can there be a more eloquent refutation of Edward Said's thesis? Postel, with his unbounded faith in man's reason, sees the moral obligation of acquiring true and just knowledge of "the Other" in order to bring about tolerance of one another's failings, a just recognition of one another's virtues, to establish harmony in the world—*concordia mundi*, indeed.

Postel's universalist sentiments led him to minimize differences among the peoples of the world: "Let us rejoice, therefore, oh sons, brothers, fathers, daughters, sisters, mothers, in this, that Turks, Jews, Christians, heretics, pagans, and all the peoples of the world believe in God, and all either have Jesus or seek after

Him."[104] In his *Alcorani seu legis Mahometi et Evangelistarum concordiae liber*, Postel pointed out the similarities of Protestantism and Islam, and generally approved of Muslims.[105]

As regards Islam and Muslims, Postel tried to be as objective as possible. In his *De la république des Turcs*, Postel assured the reader that he would not indulge in gratuitous insults to Turks but would give a balanced account of their virtues and vices in order to persuade the Muslims of the fairness of Christians, who should be seen as men eager for the truth and not as prejudiced judges. He hoped that these laudable sentiments would engender similar attitudes in the Turks. One should approach another culture, civilization, and people with an open mind, and to this end, Postel deliberately attempted to emphasize those aspects of Turkish life that would best reveal the high level of Turkish civilization. He praised the Turks' attention to the religious instruction of children, almsgiving, the proscription of usury, hospitality, the quality of goods and products in the market, amiability and fairness in conversation, and the Turkish judicial system. Many of these observations were based on Postel's own direct observations. He saw Muhammad as a genuine prophet, felt that the Koran should be respected, and was eternally grateful to Muslims for the revival of learning in the Christian world.[106]

In his openness to the Other, and by reason of his deep-seated universalism, Postel eventually went so far as to assert the superiority of the East to the West in his work *Merveilles du monde* (Wonders of the World). For Postel, the arts and manufactures of the East continued to be the finest: "All things we hold in the West as of extraordinary artifice are like mere shadows of oriental excellences."[107] Even the human being of the East is superior to Western man; "the oriental understanding is the best in the world." Postel believed in the superiority of human reason in the Orient, an important concession, as he based all his philosophy on the rationality of religious truth. Persians, Indians, Chinese, Caucasians, Cathayans, and Japanese all relied on natural reason to arrive at religious truth.

As William Bouwsma says, the generosity of his conception is astonishing; his striking receptiveness, bordering on humility, to the accomplishments of the non-European world is a witness to his cosmopolitanism, all pointing from the Middle Ages and the Renaissance to the Enlightenment.[108]

SEVENTEENTH-CENTURY ENCOUNTERS

Travelers in the Orient

In keeping with the tradition established by such Greek historians and travelers as Herodotus, Megasthenes, and Hecataeus of Abdera, seventeenth-century Europeans set out to explore the Near East, Persia, and India, and came back with often sympathetic and accurate accounts of the culture and peoples they encountered.

Adam Olearius

Adam Olearius was a German Orientalist born in Aschersleben, near Magdeburg. He studied in Leipzig, became librarian and court mathematician, and in 1633 was appointed as secretary to an ambassador and a merchant sent by Duke Frederick III of Holstein-Gottorp to Muscovy and Persia.[109] On his return, Olearius published the narrative of his travels, which was to introduce Germany and then the rest of Europe to Persian literature and culture. He also translated into German the *Gulistan* of Sa'adi and other works of Persian literature, which were much admired in the eighteenth century by the philosophes, influencing Montesquieu's *Persian Letters* and Goethe's *West-Eastern Divan*, and were instrumental in preparing the way for German Romanticism's admiration for Persian poetry.

Olearius admires the Persian cities:

> But what contributes most to the greatness of this city is the *metschids*, or mosques, the market places, the bazaars, the public baths and the palaces of great lords that have some relation to the court; but especially the fair gardens, whereof there is so great a number that there are many houses that have two or three and hardly any but hath at least one.
>
> All things in their gardens are very delightful but above all their fountains. The basins, or receptacles, of them are very large and most of marble or freestone. There are belonging to them many channels of the same stone which convey the water from one basin to the other and serve to water the garden. Persons of quality, nay indeed many rich merchants, build in their gardens summer houses or a kind of gallery or hall which is enclosed with a row of pillars whereto they add at the four corners of the main structure so many withdrawing rooms, or pavilions where they take the air, according to the wind then reigning. And this they take so much delight in, that many time these summer houses are handsomer built and better furnished than those wherein they ordinarily live.

He is equally admiring of the moral qualities of the Persians:

> [T]he Persians have so great an aversion for theft, as accounting it a base and infamous crime, as it really is, that they permit not thieves, if they do come in, to stay there many days. . . . The Persians are very neat, as well in their rooms and furniture of them, as in their habit; wherein they would not have so much as a spot to be seen: insomuch that those who are of ability to do it, change them as soon as they are ever so little stained, and others, who are not much before hand with the world, have them washed once a week.
>
> The Persians are of a ready wit and sound judgement. They apply themselves to studies and are very excellent in poesy. Their inventions are rich and their fancies subtle and strong. They are so far from being any way vainglorious that they slight no man, but on the contrary they are complaisant, and of taking conversation very civil and obliging among themselves, but especially to strangers. The submissions wherewith they express themselves in their complements, exceed any thing they do in that kind in France. A Persian, to invite his friend to come into his house, and proffer him his service, delivers himself in these terms: "Let me entreat you to make my house noble by your presence; I sacrifice myself to your commands; I lie prostrate at your feet; to serve you, I wish the apple of my eye might help to pave your way," etc., but for the most part these are indeed but compliments. This puts me in mind of a Persian who coming to our physician to acquaint him with a pain he had in his side, told him that if he could cure him he would give him his head; whereupon it being represented to him that he should not be so much troubled at the want of health, who was so prodigal of his life, he made answer that he meant otherwise, but that it was their manner of speaking.

Persians value friendship: "They are very faithful in observing the particular friendships they contract together, and they enter into fraternities among themselves which last as long as they live, nay they are so exact in the improving of these that they present them before all obligations of either blood or birth."

Persians are a cultivated and refined people: "There is no nation in the world more addicted to poetry than the Persians. There you have poets in all the market-places and in all houses of good fellowship where they entertain and make sport for such as frequent them, as the mountebanks and such as show tricks of legerdemain do in Europe. All bear with them, and the great lords think they cannot give their friends a better entertainment than by diverting them while they are at dinner, with the recital of some poem. The king himself and the khans have, among their other menial servants, their poets, whose only business it is to find out somewhat for their diversion by whom they are maintained, and which they are not to communicate to any other, without the consent of their patrons."[110]

Jean Chardin

Jean Chardin, also known as Sir John Chardin, the French jeweler and traveler, was born in Paris into a family of jewel merchants. His father intended him to take over the family business, but Jean Chardin had an insatiable curiosity for other cultures, and so he set off for Persia and India in 1665. He managed to combine business and his thirst for knowledge. He returned in 1670, but set out again in 1671 for Persia, where he spent four years, then moved on to India and returned in 1680.

In 1686 Chardin published the first part of his *Travels*, but it was only in 1711 that his ten-volume *The Travels of Sir John Chardin* appeared. His book is considered one of the finest works of early Western scholarship on Persia, India, and the Near East, admired for its range, depth, accuracy, and well-balanced judgments. Chardin had a good command of Persian, and often gives detailed and sympathetic accounts of people he met and places he visited. He had direct access to the Safavid court, his political assessments and analysis are highly regarded, and he is generally considered a reliable source on Safavid history, government, economics, anthropology, religion, art, and culture.

Though critical of various aspects of Persian culture, Chardin finds much to praise in their demeanor and manners: "The most commendable Property of the Manners of the Persians, is their kindness to Strangers; the Reception and Protection they afford them, and their Universal Hospitality, Toleration, in regard to Religion, except the Clergy of the Country, who, as in all other Places, hate to a furious Degree, all those that differ from their Opinions. The Persians are very civil, and very honest in Matters of Religion."[111] Chardin found Persians to be "the most Civiliz'd People of the East, and the greatest Complimenters in the World. The Polite Men amongst them, are upon a level with the Politest Men of Europe."[112]

The Turk and Orientalism in French Travel Literature, 1520–1660

Clarence Dana Rouillard's erudite and exhaustive study, *The Turk in French History, Thought, and Literature (1520–1660)*, originally published in 1940, does for the sixteenth and seventeenth centuries what Raymond Schwab did for the eighteenth and nineteenth, that is, provide a thorough analysis of Western attitudes toward the Other, the Muslim, and, in Rouillard's case, specifically toward the Turk. Though it may come as a surprise to those brought up on Edward Said's polemics, Rouillard's conclusions are that, "a period of enlightenment definitely began about this time which was to enable a Frenchman to conceive of a Turk as something other than '*l'infidèle.*' "[113]

In a fascinating survey of attitudes to Turks in French literature *before* the date of his main period of study, Rouillard refers to many authors who wrote very positive accounts of the Turks and their customs and manners, authors I have not seen mentioned, let alone discussed, anywhere else. They must be taken into account as an essential corrective to all those summaries that emphasize only the negative responses to the Other. The earliest French traveler to leave any observations on the Turks was Jean Boucicaut, later marshal of France, who must have sailed to Constantinople shortly before 1389. Boucicaut describes the Sultan Murad as a perfect host who received him in a grand manner, with a great banquet. Gilles le Bouvier set out to see the world in 1402 and went on pilgrimage. In Syria he met many Turks, whom he described in his *Le Livre de la description des pays* as frank, honest, and redoubtable, all the more remarkable a description since this was only six years after the unsuccessful crusade and French defeat at Nicopolis in 1396.

Another tolerant and generous traveler of the fifteenth century was Bertrandon de la Broquière. After a tour of the Holy Land, Bertrandon found himself in Damascus just as a huge caravan was returning from Mecca: "Providing himself with a Turkish costume, . . . Bertrandon joined the Turkish section of the caravan and journeyed with it northward and across Asia Minor as far as Bursa, where he left it to press on and visit Adrianople and Constantinople." Bertrandon gives a complete account of the people, the government, and the sultan that is fair and generous. He talks of the justice and moderation of the sultan's rule; of the military superiority of the Turks. He finds the Turks to be very charitable; poor beggars are often invited to share their meals, "something we don't do." Rouillard summarizes Bertrandon's account: "They [the Turks] never fail to give thanks to God aloud before eating. He records striking examples of the honesty, charity, and piety of his [Turkish] companions, and dwells on the kindness shown him by the leader of the caravan, and by a fellow traveller named Mahommet, both Turks. Our traveller, while fulfilling his mission of studying the means for Christianity to crush the power of the Ottoman empire, sees through the screen of religion, sees and respects the man beneath the 'infidel.' "[114]

A Transylvanian theological student was captured by the Turks in Hungary in 1436 and remained a slave for somewhere between fifteen and twenty years. He was to write a treatise in Latin called *De Vita et Moribus Turcarum* (Of the Life and Customs of the Turks), which appeared in Paris in 1509. What impressed the Transylvanian was the modesty and simplicity of the Turks, "from the soldiers in camp to Sultan Murad himself, a man of affable conversation, ripe and indulgent in judgement, generous in alms, benevolent in all his actions, and tolerant enough to go in person to mass in the Franciscan church at Pera."[115]

The most remarkable book published in Paris in the early sixteenth century was *La Genealogie du grant Turc à present regnant* (The Genealogy of the Great Turk to the Reigning Sultan) by Teodoro Spandugino. Spandugino, born in Italy in the middle of the fifteenth century, accompanied his father to Gallipoli in 1465 to arrange for the ransom of prisoners. He had proceeded to Constantinople hoping to help his brother, who had settled there, recover property seized by the Turks during the war with Venice (1499–1502), but instead discovered his brother had died. Unable to do anything about the property seized, Spandugino spent time thoroughly investigating the Ottoman Empire. On his return to Venice, he found he was in disgrace for having befriended the French ambassador. He spent his last years in France, where his book was published in French in 1519.

The first eight chapters of the book trace the Turkish rulers down from the first sultan, Osman, who is described as "very dignified, clement, just, warlike and liberal, so that his fame will endure as long as there are Turks in the world." There is "Mehemet, . . . bold, rough, bellicose, liberal and magnanimous," who captured Constantinople, and who "wept over the [Byzantine] Emperor's body and gave it honourable burial, though he was reported 'cruel like Nero.'"[116] The remaining chapters describe the manners and customs of the Turks.

At the court, Spandugino admired the fact that the possibilities of advancement among the Turks based on merit were unlimited. As Rouillard remarks, "Here was a democratic practice of promotion where it would be least expected, and we shall see later more striking examples of Western admiration of this system whereby a simple page might become grand vizier through sheer ability,—an admiration which frequently overshadows Christian indignation or pity at the heartless levy of tribute children upon which the system is based."[117]

Spandugino describes the military organization and the religious side of the Ottoman state, noting with admiration that the Turks go to worship more often than Christians, and that there is a general respect for religion, even for elements of Christianity. The importance given to charity by the Turks is also much praised. The Turks are far more charitable than Christians, Spandugino observes. Their sense of hospitality is enormous, and extends as much to Christians and Jews as to their coreligionists.

Rouillard concludes his analysis of this important work with the observation that a reader of *La Genealogie du grant Turc*, with its admiring view of an alien culture, would have his imagination stimulated and his curiosity aroused.[118]

Several travelers in the early sixteenth century came back from Ottoman lands to publish their positive impressions of the Turks. Johannes Boemus also remarks on their free almsgiving, and their tolerance of other religions. Christian

Richer's book *On the Customs and Manners of the Turks*, published in 1540, gives "no hint of Christian imprecation of the Infidel, and the unprejudiced observer accumulates examples to support his assertion that the Turks are a scrupulously clean and honest people."[119] Antoine Geuffroy's work *Estat de la court du Grant Turc* was first published in Paris and Antwerp in 1542, and, as Rouillard explains, "[t]here is clear evidence in these pages not only of curiosity concerning the ways of a strange people, but also of respect for the structure of another great nation."[120]

Rouillard discusses many other authors who observe with impartiality and even respect the manners and customs of the Turks; authors such as Jacques Gassot, impressed by Soliman's magnanimity and the architectural wonders of Constantinople; Jean Chesneau; Pierre Belon, who rebuked the French for their feelings of superiority vis-à-vis the Turks; André Thevet; Philippe du Fresne-Canaye, who concludes that "far from lacking artistic refinements as is commonly believed, the Turks excel the West in that respect"; and Pierre Lescalopier, who much appreciated Turkish charity and hospitality.

Ogier Ghislain de Busbecq, of Flemish origin, educated at Louvain, Paris, and Italy, was in Turkey for more than seven years (1554–62) as an ambassador of Emperor Ferdinand, and was to spend his last days in Paris until his death in 1592. His four "Turkish Letters" were published in Latin in 1589 and finally translated into French in 1646. Busbecq's first letter, dated 1555, records his first visit to Constantinople and is full of admiring descriptions of the hospitals "where Turkish charity is freely extended to all, and is freely accepted by rich and poor travelers alike," and equally of the sights of the city. He visits the Grand Vizier, Ahmed, whom he finds majestic. Busbecq finds the dress and costumes of the Turks far more dignified than those of the Europeans, and he is puzzled as to why the West has such bad taste. Like so many others, he is impressed by the fact that a man rises to his high position solely on the basis of merit, regardless of "birth, wealth, favour, or sale of office." The second letter describes the discipline and continence of the soldiers, the superior sense of values that eliminate dueling in Turkey. He admires their system of education.[121]

Anthoine Regnaut wrote an account of his pilgrimage to the Holy Land, which was published in 1573, and which contains, according to Rouillard, surprisingly impartial descriptions of Muslim and Turkish beliefs and practices. He also "notes the honesty and fairness to strangers of merchants, in contrast to Christian merchants who bargain for all they can get, regardless of value."

The *Voyages du Seigneur de Villamont* were first published in Paris in 1595 and went through eighteen re-editions and at least two reprintings in the next twenty years. Villamont finds the Turks far more rugged and disciplined than

Europeans, and spends time castigating Western civilization for its softness and corruption. He also finds the Turks have a superior concept of valor. Finally, Jean Palerne in his *Peregrinations* claims to find Islam of such gentleness and liberty that he understands why so many convert to it.[122]

Le père Pacifique de Provins, a Capuchin friar, wrote such an impartial account of his travels in Turkey in *Relation du voyage de Perse* (An Account of a Persian Voyage), first published in 1631, that many doubted his Christian allegiance. In Constantinople, le père Pacifique puts to rest many misconceptions about the Turks and their practices, such as that no non-Muslim may enter their mosques. He gives a vivid account of his experience of a Friday service in a mosque: "[H]e tells of the reading, responses, prayers, and the music, 'gentle sound of bagpipes . . . like a human voice of organ stops,' to which the worshippers listen for more than a quarter of an hour in meditation or ecstasy, 'all on their heels, and in an admirable silence, truly this song of the instruments is conducive to devotion.' "[123]

Louis Deshayes, baron of Courmenin, was sent to Palestine to safeguard the Franciscan monks in 1621. His experiences resulted in the work *Le Voyage de Levant fait par le commandment du roi l'année 1621* (Travels in the Levant made on the order of the King, in the Year 1621). Deshayes writes enthusiastically of Constantinople and its port and magnificent mosques: "He remarks that at Constantinople a half of the population are Jews and Christians; the Jews live in greater liberty than they could in Christian countries, and the Christians, of which only twenty-eight families, besides merchants and members of the embassy, are Catholics, enjoy as much freedom of conscience as they would in Christian countries."[124]

Louis Gédoyn, known as "The Turk," was to spend five years in Turkey between 1605 and 1610, and then a further two years as a French consul in Aleppo. His journal and correspondence were published only in the twentieth century, edited by Auguste Boppe. "Gédoyn shows no prejudice against the country and the institutions which he discusses."[125] He writes approvingly of many customs, and various aspects of Turkish life, its simplicity, the emphasis on charity, the fine treatment of horses.

Jean Doublan is indignant at the treatment of the Christians in Jerusalem by the pacha of Damascus, but he is eternally grateful to the pacha of Gaza for his courage, generosity, and for his regard for the holy places and the Christians. Vincent Stochove, who traveled in Turkey in 1630 and 1631, is also truly touched by an old man in Tripoli who fed and lodged him and his companions for two days without payment, an example of charity and tolerance rare, thought Stochove, in Christians.

Perhaps the most fascinating and important book published in France before 1660 is *Les Voyages du sieur Du Loir* (Travels of the Honorable Du Loir): "Du Loir was a man of culture and wide curiosity, versed in antiquity and a student of the language as well as the life, government, and religion of Turkey, who accompanied the French ambassador Jean de la Haye to Constantinople in the fall of 1639 and remained there for seventeenth months."[126] His book consists of ten letters addressed to distinguished men in France, and is an objective account of the manners, customs, history and religion of the Turks. When he notes the attempts by the Turks to efface the forbidden faces and figures in the Hagia Sophia, instead of condemning, Du Loir compares it to the superstitious behavior of Christians who drill holes in slabs of marble to collect souvenirs of the place where the Virgin putatively washed the linen of her son. He praises Turkish courts of law, "so superior to the French that it would be more honest, quick, and cheap to take the case from Paris to Constantinople and back than to have it judged at home." Du Loir, like so many of his compatriots, is impressed by the Turks' religious zeal: "He has even seen Turks show greater respect for a Christian procession of the Holy Sacrament than Christians themselves." The Turks are as gentlemanly as we, argues Du Loir, and proceeds to extol their "honesty, sincerity, simplicity, and sobriety, with some telling contrasts to the bargaining, usury, vanity, intemperance, and gambling among Christians."[126] He remarks on the rarity of blasphemy and the zeal of Turkish charity. *Les Voyages du sieur Du Loir* is a remarkable document, free of prejudice, exuding respect for a people quite alien to the author.

In a brilliant synthesis, Rouillard summarizes the way mainly French travelers opened up the mental and moral horizons of the West by their admiring portrayals of Turks and their religion and customs. In general, the travelers admired (1) The Civil and Military Order: attributed to discipline, obedience, the example of the gentlemanly conduct of the sultan, a different conception of valor than that found in Europe, numerous physical advantages of Turkish camps such as better tents; the sobriety, moderation, and simplicity resulting in steadiness and powers of endurance in war and simplicity of life in peace; the administration of justice; and advancement based on merit. (2) Civilization and Culture: with travelers praising Turkish schools, with their strict supervision and wide curricula, which included the art of poetry, astronomy, and philosophy; all travelers remarked on the cleanliness and sanitation maintained, for example, in Turkish camps; the use of ice in the summer was also admired; most travelers recognized that the Turks loved beautiful things and that the arts and crafts were flourishing. (3) Moral Qualities: honesty is often referred to, as are humanity, tolerance, and clemency. (4) Muslim Religion and Practice: particularly the zeal with which their religion is followed as well as acts of charity are held up as good examples for Christians to emulate.

Rouillard has a high regard for the achievements of these late-sixteenth and seventeenth-century travelers, and "the greater knowledge and wider understanding they brought to French readers of a nation of radically different manners and religion." In so doing, they helped open up minds to accept these new facts. Certain elements of Ottoman civilization aroused the admiration of French travelers, and "the repetition of this admiration, frequently accompanied by sharp, direct disapproval of contrasting Western ways . . . served as an important influence in promoting self-criticism at home."[127] At the end of his long but instructive book, Rouillard further underlines the contributions of the seventeenth century to the development of the critical mentality of the eighteenth: "The constant admiration in travel writings, not only of Turkish civil and military discipline but of fine moral qualities underlying it, could not fail to lead intelligent readers to some readjustment of values, especially when such admiration frequently evolved into sharp criticism of French or Christian institutions or practices. Even that last bulwark of superiority of the Christian over the Infidel, was shaken by revelations of a superior zeal in prayer, reverence, fasting, and charity among the Turks. . . . Whether these French observers were moved by mere curiosity or by a genuine sense of relativity, their opinions were significant in the development of that critical mentality which we are accustomed to associate with the eighteenth century."[128]

And in the essays and other writings of such writers as Châteillon, Henri Estienne, Bodin, Montaigne, Charron, Du Vair, and La Mothe le Vayer, passages "reveal the usefulness of a knowledge of the Turks for their demonstration of the diversity of mankind, and of the consequent obligation to cultivate a sense of relativity and an habitual tolerance."[129]

Native Americans and the New World

Who euer heard of th' Indian Peru?
Or who in venturous vessell measured
The Amazons huge riuer now found trew?
Or fruitfullest Virginia who did euer vew?
Yet all these were, when no man did them know.

—Edmund Spenser, *The Faerie Queene*, 1590

In 1555 Richard Eden translated Peter Martyr's *De Orbe Novo* (The New World [1511]) as *The Decades of the New World or West India*, an account of the voyages of Columbus and his followers. Eden's *Decades* contains a remarkably unprejudiced discussion of the varied skin colors of aboriginal races, seeing the diversity as evidence of God's omnipotence and wisdom, creating different races of men in the same way as he created the beauty of the different colors of a bird's feather.

Thomas Hariot, explorer, navigational expert, mathematician, scientist, and astronomer, attempted to colonize Virginia, where he learned the Algonquian language and wrote most sympathetically about the Native Americans in *A briefe and true report of the new found land of Virginia*, published in 1588. He wrote in an objective, unpatronizing, and unsentimental manner, finding the Indians an intelligent people who "had devised a coherent, if primitive, civilization."[130] Hariot wrote, "For although they haue no such tooles, nor any such craftes, sciences and artes as wee; yet in those thinges they doe, they shewe excellencie of wit."[131]

Nicholas Canny has argued that until the Virginia massacre of 1622, or in the case of New England until the late 1630s or 1640s, the observations of most Englishmen who had direct dealings with Native Americans are very sympathetic.[132] William Wood, for example, praised their generosity in sharing communal meals with him,[133] and found that the Indians of New England "in their planting of corn exceed our English husbandmen."[134] Wood admired their skill in hunting, fishing, and making tools. Wood found that the Native Americans showed greater restraint than the English when playing football: "There is no seeking of revenge, no quarreling, no bloody noses, scratched faces, black eyes, broken shins, no bruised members or crushed ribs, the lamentable effects of rage. But the goal being won, the goods on the one side lost, friends they are at the football and friends they must meet at the kettle."[135] These observers corrected the popular misapprehension that that all Native Americans were the same, pointing to the diversity of tribes, languages, cultures, and physical attributes. Each tribe had its own government; Alexander Whitaker, the minister at Henrico in Virginia, wrote in 1613 "that the law of Nature dwelleth in them: for they have a rude kind of common-wealth and rough government wherein they both honour and obey their kings, parents and governors, both greater and less, they observe the limits of their possessions, murder is scarcely heard of, adultery and other offences severely punished."[136] These examples should suffice to indicate that sympathetic attitudes toward Native Americans were frequent, with sensitive observers like Whitaker, Roger Williams, John Eliot, and Edward Winslow solicitous for their spiritual and material welfare.[137]

Simon Ockley

The life, work, and opinions of Simon Ockley also refute Edward Said's dismissal of all Orientalist research as a mere handmaiden to Western imperialism. As one nineteenth-century biographer put it, Ockley, with the diligence of a scholar, the patient suffering of the martyr, and the enthusiasm and fervor of an ancient votary, devoted his life to Oriental studies: "He perhaps was the first who exhibited to us other heroes than those of Greece and Rome; sages as contemplative, and a people more magnificent even than the iron masters of the world."[138] Born in Exeter, Ockley showed early promise in his studies, and was sent to Queen's College, Cambridge, where he was made Hebrew lecturer at the early age of seventeen. He was chosen Arabic professor in 1711. Prior to that, in 1708 Ockley's translation of Ibn Ṭufayl's philosophical novel *Ḥayy b. Yaḳẓān* (The Improvement of Human Reason) appeared, "to give those who might be unacquainted with it, a specimen of the genius of the Arabian philosophers, and to excite young scholars to reading of eastern authors, . . . [also insisting on] the beauty, copiousness, and antiquity, of the Arabic tongue."[139] But Ockley's fame rests on his *The History of the Saracens*, the first volume of which was also published in 1708. He had taken great pains to collect materials from the most authentic Arabic authors, especially manuscripts, not hitherto published in any European language, but which he consulted at the Bodleian Library.

While at Oxford, preparing the history, Ockley sent a letter to his daughter, which is worth quoting at length to show how much he suffered for his calling. He died at the age of forty-two, leaving his widow and many children in dire poverty:

> My condition here is this: one of the most useful and necessary authors I have is written in such a wretched hand, that the very reading of it is perfect deciphering. I am forced sometimes to take three or four lines together, and then pull them all to pieces to find where the words begin and end; for oftentimes it is so written, that a word is divided as if the former part of it was the end of the foregoing word, and the latter part the beginning of another; besides innumerable other difficulties known only to those that understand the language. Add to this the pains of abridging, comparing authors, selecting proper materials, and the like, which in a remote and copious language, abounding with difficulties sometimes insuperable, make it equivalent at least to the performing of six times so much in Greek and Latin. So that if I continue in the same course in which I am engaged at present, that is, from the time I rise in the morning till I can see no longer at night, I cannot pretend once to entertain the least thought of seeing home till Michaelmas. Were it not that there is some satisfaction in answering

> the end of my profession, some in making new discoveries, and some in the hopes of obliging my country with the history of the greatest empire the world ever yet saw, I would sooner do almost anything than submit to the drudgery.
>
> People imagine, that it is only understanding Arabic, and then translating a book out of it, and there is an end of the story: but if ever learning revives among us, posterity will judge better. This work of mine (in another way) is almost of as different a nature from translating out of the Greek or Latin, as translating a poet from one language to another is different from prose. One comfort I have, that the authors I am concerned with are very good in their kind, and afford me plenty of materials, which will clear up a great many mistakes of modern travellers, who, passing through the eastern countries, without the necessary knowledge of the history and ancient customs of the Mohammedans, pick up little pieces of tradition from the present inhabitants, and deliver them as obscurely as they receive them. One thing pleases me much, that we shall give a very particular account of Ali and Hosein, who are reckoned saints by the Persians, and whose names you must have met with both in Herbert and Tavernier; for the sake of whom there remains that implacable and irreconcilable hatred between the Turks and Persians to this very day, which you may look for in vain in all the English books that have hitherto appeared. It would be a great satisfaction to me, if the author I have were complete in all his volumes, that I might bring the history down five or six hundred years: but, alas! of twelve that he wrote, we have but two at Oxford, which are large quartos, and from whence I take the chief of my materials.
>
> I wish that some public spirit would arise among us, and cause those books to be bought in the east for us which we want. I should be very willing to lay out my pains for the service of the public. If we could but procure £500 to be judiciously laid out in the east, in such books as I could mention for the public library at Cambridge, it would be the greatest improvement that could be conceived: but that is a happiness not to be expected in my time. We are all swallowed up in politics; there is no room for letters: and it is to be feared that the next generation will not only inherit but improve the polite ignorance of the present.[140]

In his *Introductio ad Linguas Orientales* (An Introduction to Oriental Languages), Ockley defines the value of Arabic as (1) throwing light on problems of Hebrew lexicography, (2) assisting the study of Jewish philosophy, (3) affording access to the Koran, (4) aiding geographical and historical studies, and (5) bringing new materials, through the translations, for the critical study of Greek texts.[141] No conspiracy or dreams of empire, just a desire to learn. In his inaugural lecture in 1712, Ockley "expatiates with enthusiasm upon the beauty and utility of the Arabic language and literature, and pays tribute to the past labours of Erpenius, Golius, Pococke, and d'Herbelot; but refers sadly to fortune, always '*venefica*' [poisonous], and to the '*mordaces curae*,'[142] which had long embittered his life."[143] Ockley constantly exhorts his students to widen their academic horizons: "Shame on us, a nation famous throughout the world for our pursuit of learning, that we should have so few scholars dedicating themselves earnestly to these studies."[144] His contemporaries were well aware of the practical, commercial, and missionary implications of learning Arabic, but also, as the vice chancellor of Cambridge put it, "[for] the advancement of good Literature by bringing to light much knowledge which as yet is lockt upp in that learned tongue."[145] Thus the language was well worth studying for its own sake, for its grammar was "admirably consistent and its vocabulary of immense richness."[146]

The importance of Ockley's *History of the Saracens*, a work assiduously researched under very difficult circumstances, can hardly be exaggerated. It was solidly based on reliable Arabic sources and influenced countless scholars throughout Europe, including Edward Gibbon, for whom Ockley was "an original in every sense, who had opened his eyes," and "a learned and spirited interpreter of Arabian authorities, whose tales and traditions afford an artless picture of the men and the times."[147] Ockley found Arabians remarkable "both by their arms and learning . . . [they have] had as great men, and performed as considerable actions, as any other nation under heaven."[148]

It would be fitting to end this account of an early Orientalist, Ockley, with another great modern Orientalist, A. J. Arberry, who wrote, "[Ockley] had never travelled outside the narrow borders of his native land, yet his spirit reached across wide seas and travelled back through centuries; so that he became the first interpreter in Europe of the inner meaning of Arab civilization. He built a bridge between East and West, a bridge of greater sympathy based upon better informed understanding. His life was a lamentable tragedy; what he accomplished remains a glorious example."[149]

Here we have an example of the real disinterested scholar selflessly devoting his life to Oriental research because of his love of learning, love of the Arabic language and culture, now being besmirched by the calumnies from a lazy, pretentious, and fashionable intellectual teaching amid the comforts of Columbia University. "Building a bridge between East and West" is seen by A. J. Arberry as Ockley's contribution. Saidians would do well to ponder this not inconsiderable achievement before hurling abuse at all Orientalists.

Ludovico Marracci[150]

By a strange coincidence, just as a certain Iranian jurisconsult named Khatun Abadi was presenting his translation of the four Gospels into Persian to the shah in Isfahan in 1697, Father Ludovico Marracci was preparing in Padua, Italy, his Latin translation of the Koran, which was published in 1698.

Ludovico Marracci was born in 1612 and began his studies at an early age, pursuing them in Rome, where in 1654 he joined a group of scholars responsible for translating the Bible into Arabic.[151] He became a lecturer in Arabic in 1656 at the University of Sapienza in Rome, where he was to stay until his death in 1700. But how did a priest with a classical education come to master Arabic? While still a student, Ludovico came across a page of Arabic that aroused his intellectual curiosity and pushed him to learn the language of the Koran. His first teacher was a Maronite priest living in Rome, and after a long apprenticeship Marracci was able to master the morphology and syntax of Arabic. Rome at the time was undergoing the intellectual ferment of the Counter-Reformation, and this ferment had led to the founding of the discipline of Oriental studies, particularly after the recently inaugurated relations with the Christian communities of the Near East. Marracci was well established in the Congregation of "Propaganda Fide" by 1645, and later became the personal confessor of Pope Innocent XI. This was also the period of the unsuccessful Ottoman Siege of Vienna (1683), and it was in this context of the Islamic peril that Marracci undertook to translate and refute the Koran but not in a sour spirit: "I wanted to challenge them directly, but in a friendly spirit, with fairness and without bitterness, without despising them or their thinkers, otherwise with some jokes and a pinch of salt, but without vinegar, being content with having recourse to reason and to truth."[152]

Though he was the author of countless other works, Marracci's masterpiece remains *Alcorani textus universus* (The Complete Text of the Koran)[153] to which he devoted nearly forty years of his life. The first part contains a life of Muhammad, a discussion of the origins of the Koran, theological arguments to show that Islam was not prophesized in the Christian scriptures (and that unlike Christianity, Islam did not have any miracles to its credit), and how the Christian dogmas are the truth whereas the Muslim ones are not, and presents arguments to show the moral superiority of Christianity compared to the decadence of Islam. The second part of this work comprises a Latin translation and a fully voweled Arabic text of the Koran and quotes from many Muslim commentators. Marracci's decision to go to the original Arabic texts laid the foundation for a scientific examination of Islam in general, and the Koran in particular. He had access to the commentaries of Baydawi, Jalal al-din al-Suyuti, Ibn Abi Zamanyn, al-Thalabi, and al-Zamakhshari. He further consulted the hadith collections of al-Bukhari, and al-Bakri and his *Kitab al-anwar* (The Book of Lights), and al-Qummi and his *A'lam al-huda* (Signs of the Right Way). For his polemics, Marracci referred to Ibn Taymiyya and his *al-Jawab al-sahih li-man baddala din al-Masih* (The Authentic Reply to Those Who Have

Changed the Religion of the Messiah), also to al-Qarafi and his *al-Ajwiba l-fakhira an al-asila l-fajira* (Glorious Answers to Perverse Questions) and *Bab shariat al-islam* (The Gate of Islamic Law), and to al-Raqili and his *Tayid al-Milla* (Confirmation of the Religion). For Islamic jurisprudence, Marracci used the writings of al-Quduri and for history he had recourse to al-Masudi, and Abu l-Fida and his *Mukhtasar fi akhbar al-bashar* (Compendium of Universal History).

Before he undertakes to refute Islam, Marracci reconstructs the religion of Islam and its tenets, all the while treating his subject with respect, critical and appreciative at the same time. He was aware that the Koran was an object of reverence for the Muslims, who saw it as of divine origin even though he was ready to criticize its origins and contents. Marracci reveals an astonishing grasp of even the smallest details of Islamic history, law, and theology, of its rites and rituals, its dogma concerning Jesus and Christianity, of the influence of Talmudic and Rabbinic Judaism on Islamic religious literature. The Arabic text is beautifully printed, and Marracci is meticulous in his translation and commentary, often quoting the Arab commentators in Arabic.

Maurice Borrmans, in his brilliant analysis of Marracci's skills, as a translator finds him far more consistent and coherent than many modern translators, when, for example, Marracci translates the Bismillah as *In nomine Dei Miseratoris Misericordis* (In the name of God, the Compassionate, the Merciful), thus recognizing that we are not dealing with two different concepts in the root word *rahma*. Marracci respects the tenses of the original, (the passive, the present participles) and even the rhythm of the Arabic words.

When it comes to the actual refutation of Islam and the Koran, Marracci is far more aggressive and even offensive. In this, he was very much of his time.

The scientific importance of Ludovico Marracci cannot be overemphasized and has been recognized by many scholars since. He showed the way by learning Arabic, and then by going to the original Arabic and Islamic sources to inform himself of the religion at first hand, a truly scientific attitude. George Sale, in the preface to his own translation of the Koran into English, found Marracci's translation "very exact" but too literal, while his notes are "of great use," and "[t]he work, however, with all its faults, is very valuable, and I should be guilty of ingratitude, did I not acknowledge myself much obliged thereto."[154] Marracci can truly be called the first Islamologist of modern times, who brought both scientific rigor, and intellectual curiosity to the study of the Koran, and whose translation remains the fundamental work to which all later translations are indebted and a witness to the fact that someone of a rival faith could still write with understanding of Islam.[155]

George Sale

P. M. Holt has rightly called the publication of Sale's translation of the Koran, which appeared in 1734, a "landmark in the history of Koranic studies."[156] Sale's translation was the first accurate translation into English directly from the Arabic,[157] and was annotated from Muslim commentators, especially al-Baydawi and al-Suyuti, the whole prefaced with an extensive "Preliminary Discourse" of some eighty thousand words in which Sale describes accurately the beliefs, rites, and rituals of Muslims, and the sects of Islam. Sale on the whole presents the facts objectively and fairly, without polemics. The translation itself is heavily annotated with references to Arab authors. However, Sale does not advance any startlingly new philological theories or observations, being content to repeat what the Muslim commentators had to say about obscure passages.

Sale does seem, on the other hand, to be unusually aware of all the possible influences on the contents of the Koran and its doctrines, whether of pagan Arabia, apocryphal Christianity, Judaism, or Zoroastrianism. For example, the influence of Zoroastrianism—in Sale's terminology, Magian religion—is noted when discussing the Muslim view of Paradise: "[T]he Mohammedans hold that those who are to be admitted into paradise will take the right-hand way, and those who are destined to hell fire will take the left; but both of them must first pass the bridge, called in Arabic al-Sirat. . . . This circumstance Mohammed seems also to have borrowed from the Magians, who teach that on the last day all mankind will be obliged to pass a bridge which they call Pul Chinavad, or Chinavar, that is, the straight bridge, leading directly into the other world."[158]

Apart from Sale, I am not aware of any research on the Zoroastrian elements in the Koran, save for the pioneering essay by Ignaz Goldziher,[159] and the two works by St. Clair Tisdall.

Reflecting on the Muslim belief that Jesus did not die on the Cross, but rather someone else in his place, Sale notes, "It is supposed by several that this story was an original invention of Mohammed's; but they are certainly mistaken; for several sectaries held the same opinion, long before his time.The Basilidians in the very beginning of Christianity, denied that Christ himself suffered, but that Simon the Cyrenean was crucified in his place. The Cerinthians before them, and the Carpocratians next."[160]

Sale was otherwise dependent upon Marracci and Pococke's *Specimen Historiae Arabum* (Examples of Arab History) and did not add anything original. But his importance lies in his enlightened and objective attitude and the accuracy of his well-annotated translation.

4

INDIAN ORIENTALISTS

By the eighteenth century, as can be seen from our survey of universalism in Western culture and history, the philosophes had a long and distinguished tradition to draw upon when advocating a larger worldview, a humane generosity toward and a greater understanding of diverse peoples, cultures, and religions. As Ernst Cassirer put it,

> In the eighteenth century, however, the peoples of the Orient especially attract attention and demand equal recognition for their religious convictions. Leibniz had already called attention to Chinese civilization; and Wolff in a speech on Chinese wisdom had praised Confucius as a prophet of pure morality and ranked him next to Christ. Voltaire takes up this strain and uses it as his main proof that the core of religion and morality depends little on particular points of faith. In Montesquieu's *Persian Letters* the comparison between Orient and Occident by no means favors the latter; the unbiased observation and criticism of the Persian reveals everywhere the arbitrary, conventional, and accidental elements in all those things which in the opinion of the Occident are supposed to be most certain and sacred.[1]

Diderot also argued a larger conception of God, a larger worldview: "Men have banished divinity from their midst; they have relegated it to a sanctuary; the walls of temple are the limits of its view; beyond these walls it does not exist. Madmen that you are, destroy these enclosures which obstruct your horizon; liberate God; see Him everywhere where He actually is, or else say that He does not exist at all."[2] Voltaire felt that Alexander the Great had "changed the face of Asia, Greece and Egypt, and gave a new direction to the world."[3] Voltaire was "a real cosmopolitan,"[4] as Peter Gay says, a universalist who was also perfectly aware and appreciative of cultural differences: "It follows from this survey of history that everything which pertains intimately to human nature is much the same from one end of the world to the other; that everything which depends on custom is different, and it is mere chance if there is any resemblance. The empire of custom is indeed much larger than that of nature. It extends over manners, over all usage;

it spreads variety over the universal scene. Nature spreads unity; it establishes everywhere a small number of invariable principles: thus the foundation is everywhere the same, and culture produces diverse fruits."[5]

Enlightenment philosophers seem to have been very influenced by the Stoics; David Hume, for instance, was convinced that they dedicated themselves to "the interests of mankind and of society."[6] They also looked to humanists such as Montaigne, Erasmus, Francis Bacon, Jean Bodin, Pierre Bayle, and Gottfried Leibniz for inspiration. Montaigne had written, "[N]ot because Socrates said it, but because it is really by feeling, and perhaps excessively so, I consider all men my compatriots, and embrace a Pole as I do a Frenchman, setting this national bond after the universal and common one."[7] Bodin in his *Colloquium Heptaplomeres*[8] "advocated a suprareligious unity of mankind to which belonged the Indians of America as well as the natives of India."[9] Gottfried Leibniz one of the greatest philosophers and intellects of all time, dreamed of unifying the world: "I am indifferent to that which constitutes a German or a Frenchman, because I will only the good of mankind."[10]

While the philosophes of Europe discussed the abstract ideal of cosmopolitanism, which was a persistent and clearly defined thread running through Enlightenment thought, travelers, explorers, and settlers came face to face, in the concrete, as it were, with other peoples, cultures, and customs. But this encounter did not always result in negative, racist, or contemptuous reactions to other societies. The influence of Said has resulted in the deliberate obfuscation or ignoring of the evidence, where the empirical data are forced into the Procrustean bed prepared by historians afraid of seeming to endorse anything smacking of racism, colonialism, and imperialism. Armed with their principle that "[w]e know, *a priori*, that all Europeans were racists," these historians were bound to come to negative conclusions. Fortunately, there are signs that the intellectual tide is turning. In *The Oxford History of the British Empire*, in five volumes, which came out in the late 1990s, Said's arguments are explicitly engaged with at numerous points and found wanting.[11]

Before turning to the works of eighteenth-century Orientalists, principally in India, I should like to dwell on three travelers. Captain James Cook, who made three voyages to the Pacific, tried to counter the sentimental picture drawn of the Polynesians by the French commander Bougainville. According to Cook, the Polynesians, far from being sexually free or promiscuous, practiced a sexual morality not that different from the one found in contemporary England or France. Nor did they lack private property. Different customs and lifestyles did not betoken an inferior civilization. One should not sit in judgment but rather try to understand these peoples within their own terms of reference. Cook contended that it was the Europeans who had corrupted their morals and disturbed their former tranquility and peace. Furthermore, Cook's voyages had had scientific research as a part of their mission, and the observations made by his team of scientists played an important role in the advancement of knowledge in the fields of astronomy, oceanography, meteorology, linguistics, ethnography, and much more.

William Bartram, botanist, naturalist, and explorer, began a journey in 1773 that was to last four years, which covered parts of present-day Florida, Georgia, South Carolina, and North Carolina. Bartram recorded many observations in his personal journal, including vivid accounts of the Seminole (Siminole), Creek, and Cherokee Indians. His narrative became a classic that influenced the romantic writers in Europe, and such writers as James Fenimore Cooper in the United States.

For Bartram, "This world, as a glorious apartment of the boundless palace of the sovereign Creator, is furnished with an infinite variety of animated scenes, inexpressibly beautiful and pleasing, equally free to the inspection and enjoyment of all his creatures."[12] He is overwhelmed at the beauty of the natural world, its plants, birds, bees, deer, bears, insects, and alligators. His scientific curiosity is boundless, for he is forever observing, recording, noting, classifying, ordering, and collecting everything that he can lay his hands on. He asks us to share in his profound inquisitiveness of mind: "Early in the evening, after a pleasant day's voyage, I made a convenient and safe harbour, in a little lagoon, under an elevated bank, on the West shore of the river; where I shall entreat the reader's patience, whilst we behold the closing scene of the short-lived Ephemera, and communicate to each other the reflections which so singular an exhibition might rationally suggest to an inquistive mind. Our place of observation is happily situated under the protecting shade of majestic Live Oaks, glorious Magnolias, and the fragrant shade Orange, open to the view of the great river and still waters of the lagoon just before us."[13]

Bartram, a warm-hearted, gentle, generous soul, approaches the subject of Native Americans in the same sincere, humble, and yet at the same time scientific spirit, without prejudgment or prejudice:

> In the consideration of this important subject it will be necessary to inquire, whether they [Native Americans] were inclined to adopt the European modes of civil society? Whether such a reformation could be obtained, without using coercive or violent means? And lastly, whether such a revolution would be productive of real benefit to them, and consequently beneficial to the public? I was satisfied in discovering that they were desirous of becoming united with us, in civil and religious society.

> It may, therefore, not be foreign to the subject, to point out that the propriety of sending men of ability and virtue, under the authority of government, as friendly visitors, into their towns: let these men be instructed to learn perfectly their languages, and by a liberal and friendly intimacy become acquainted with their customs and usages, religious and civil; their system of legislation and police, as well as their most ancient and present traditions and history. These men thus enlightened and instructed would be qualified to judge equitably, and when returned to us, to make true and just reports, which might assist the legislature of the United States to form, and to offer to them, a judicious plan for their civilization and union with us.
>
> But I presume not to dictate in these high concerns of government, and I am fully convinced that such important matters are far above my ability; the duty and respect we owe to religion and rectitude, the most acceptable incense we offer to the Almighty, as an atonement for our negligence in the care of the present and future well-being of our Indian brethren, induce me to mention this matter, though perhaps of greater concernment than we generally are aware.[14]

Bartram's assessment of Seminole culture and civilization is most movingly offered after an account of the nefarious deeds of a Seminole woman married to a white man, whom she beguiled and drained of all his possessions:

> It is, however, but doing justice to the virtue and moral conduct of the Seminoles, and American aborigines in general, to observe, that the character of this woman is condemned and detested by her own people of both sexes; and if her husband should turn her away, according to the customs and usages of these people, she would not get a husband again, as a divorce seldom takes place but in consequence of a deliberate impartial trial, and public condemnation, and then she would be looked upon as a harlot.
>
> Such is the virtue of these untutored savages: but I am afraid this is a common phrase epithet, having no meaning, or at least improperly applied; for these people are both well tutored and civil; and it is apparent to an impartial observer, who resides but a little time amongst them, that it is from the most delicate sense of the honour and reputation of their tribes and families, that their laws and customs receive their force and energy. This is the divine principle which influences their moral conduct, and solely preserves their constitution and civil government in that purity in which they are found to prevail amongst them.[15]

Finally, here are three observations from Nathaniel Philbrick's account of America's exploring expedition of 1838–42, showing, first, that such explorations were not motivated by imperialism, rather, in part, by the thirst for knowledge; second, that encounters with other cultures and peoples resulted in two reactions by Westerners that are also apparent in the context of India, that of cultural relativism, which nonetheless has something of condescension about it, and the equally defensible attitude of horror at some of the customs they found, since in this case the Westerners were treating the people they encountered as equals. Finally, one finds evidence of the often forgotten fact that the peoples encountered had not always lived in harmony with their environment, as it is so often claimed, until the arrival of the evil white man.

Midshipman William Reynolds was impressed by the scientists accompanying them on their voyage, for the latter were inspired by the thirst for knowledge. "They are leaving," recorded Reynolds in his journal, "their comfortable homes to follow the strong bent of their minds, to garner up strange things of strange lands, which proves that the ruling passion is strong in life. . . . We, the ignoramuses, will no doubt take great interest in learning the origin, nature & history of many things, which we have before regarded with curious and admiring eyes."[16]

Here is Reynolds again in his observations of the manners of the Tahitians: "Who can judge one nation by another? What man can say, this people shall be my standard, by them I will judge all others? [The Tahitians] differ from us widely, but they are unconscious that they are wrong—that, which we could point at, with the finger of Shame & condemn as obscene & sinful, they deem of no harm, but as worthy of commendation & observance."[17]

Orientalists and Imperialists in India in the Eighteenth Century

The sins of the British in India are there for all to see, but the virtues and its positive legacy have been forgotten or derided. The British, both in India itself and back in Britain, were the first to point out those sins. That being the case, it makes no sense to reduce the whole encounter as a clash between East and West, as Said does in his usual reductive and simplistic way. What both Orientalists and the imperial rulers said on the subject of India cannot be isolated from the larger intellectual and cultural developments in Europe and Britain. Tripta Wahi has shown in his Marxist analysis that Said got it entirely wrong.[18] Wahi argues that nineteenth-century British historical writing on medieval India, for example, cannot be divorced from similar writings on European history. A historian such as William Erskine applies what he has learned from Adam Smith, John Millar, and Adam Ferguson about social evolution—that, for instance, society progressed from "rudeness to civilization" through four stages, namely, "hunting, pasturage, farming and commerce"—to both Asian and European societies. All the strength and weaknesses of British historical writing on India are the strengths and weaknesses of British historical writing of the nineteenth century, *tout court*, whether on India or on Europe. The interest in ancient as opposed to medieval India among British scholars parallels their interest in European classical antiquity, Greece and Rome, rather than medieval European history. There is nothing sinister in this phenomenon, no conspiracy to "antiquate India." This merely reflects the classical bias in their education.

Furthermore, as we see in the works of Sir William Jones, research into the philology of Sanskrit was fascinating for British and European scholars because of the light the ancient language of India could throw on the Greek language and Greek mythology. Greater research into Indo-European origins had the further effect of blurring the distinction between East and West, as the possible common ancestor of the two languages and the affinities between the names of various Hindu deities such as Agni and the Latin word for fire, *ignus*, were recognized for the first time. Erskine, for example, had searched for universal laws of social development that could be applied to both Indian and European societies. Historians saw similarities between various developments in India and Europe. Moreover, arguments such as "they were incapable of taking care of themselves" to justify their presence in an alien land were used both in India and Ireland. If there were some British administrators who thought of Indians as, in some way, inferior, the same individuals probably also thought of large parts of the British population as inferior, uncivilized, and superstitious. The Other was created not along a color line, not in terms of East versus West. Indeed, many a viceroy in India from some noble line in Britain felt perfectly at ease, and even more comfortable, in the presence of a maharajah whose noble ancestry was as long if not longer than his, than in the company of some Kiplingesque Tommy. A scholar such as Henry Thomas Colebrooke was more at ease with Indian Sanskrit scholars than in the company of low-brow petty officials in the British club in Calcutta.[19] Any reading of the debates in the British Parliament in the nineteenth century on the extension of the franchise are revealing, as member after member talks of the moral depravity of the class that would get enfranchised; the British working men were deemed ignorant, incompetent, and generally unfit to be given a share in power that demanded the rational faculty of deliberation.[20] The working men's improvidence, drunkenness, and venality are constantly held up before the eyes of Parliament to deny this unfit class any vote. As Wahi points out, this opinion cut across party lines, with even Liberals arguing that educated opinion was against any extension of the franchise.

The famine of 1769–70 in India, under the East India Company, appalled Horace Walpole and made him feel ashamed of his countrymen: "We have outdone the Spaniards in Peru. They were at least butchers on a religious principle, however diabolical their zeal. We have murdered, deposed, plundered, usurped—nay, what you think of the famine in Bengal in which three millions perished being caused by a monopoly of the servants of the East India Company."[21]

But it was left to Edmund Burke, one of the greatest political writers and orators in English, who devoted a full third of his writings to India,[22] to accuse the East India Company at law. Burke's passionate concern for the welfare of the Indian people is truly remarkable. Already by 1780 and 1781, Burke felt that the East India Company was pursuing a criminal policy, with wide abuse of English law. By 1784 he saw the activities of the company as a part of the wider "catastrophic history of the empire itself."[23] One report of a speech made by Burke reads like this:

> [Laying his hand on a volume of reports that lay on the table], I swear, said he, by this book, that the wrongs done to humanity in the eastern world, shall be avenged on those who have inflicted them: They will find, when the measure of their iniquity is full, that Providence was not asleep. The wrath of Heaven would sooner or later fall upon a nation, that suffers, with impunity, its rulers thus to oppress the weak and innocent. We had already lost one empire, perhaps, as a punishment for the cruelties authorized in another. And men might exert their ingenuities in qualifying facts as they pleased, but there was only one standard by which the Judge of all earth would try them. It was not necessary, but whether they coincided with prior interests of humanity, of substantial justice, with those rights which were *paramount to all others*.[24]

We know that Burke's concern for the reform of the East India Company would continue and eventually lead to the impeachment of its governor-general, Warren Hastings. Burke was to spend fourteen years of his life on "this India business." Burke argued with a moral passion that some very fundamental principles were at stake. He had nothing but admiration for the long-suffering people and the ancient civilization of India:

> This multitude of men does not consist of an abject and barbarous populace; much less of gangs of savages, . . . but a people for ages civilized and cultivated; cultivated by all the arts of polished life, whilst we were yet in the woods. There, have been (and still the skeletons remain) princes once of great dignity, authority, and opulence. There, are to be found the chiefs of tribes and nations. There, is to be found an ancient and venerable priesthood, the depository of their laws,

learning, and history, the guides of the people whilst living, and their consolation in death; a nobility of great antiquity and renown; a multitude of cities, not exceeded in population and trade by those of the first class in Europe; merchants and bankers, individual houses of whom have once vied in capital with the bank of England; whose credit had often supported a tottering state, and preserved their governments in the midst of war and desolation; millions of ingenious manufacturers and mechanicks; millions of the most diligent, and not the least intelligent, tillers of the earth. Here are to be found almost all the religions professed by men, the Braminical, the Mussulman, the Eastern and Western Christian. . . .

All this vast mass, composed of so many orders and classes of men, is again infinitely diversified by manners, by religion, by hereditary employment, through all their possible combinations. This renders the handling of India a matter in a high degree critical and delicate. But oh! it has been rudely handled indeed.[25]

Burke is aware of the country's complexities, and ashamed that the British have not dealt with its people nor its rulers or princes in a morally just fashion, instead breaking treaties, betraying trust, corrupting its leaders. One such, Hafiz Rhamet, "the most eminent of their chiefs, one of the bravest men of his time, and as famous throughout the East for the elegance of his literature, and the spirit of his poetical compositions (by which he supported the name Hafiz) as for his courage, was invaded [and slain]."[26]

Hastings should be impeached, argued Burke, for high crimes and misdemeanors, for betraying the parliamentary trust of the Commons of Great Britain, and in the name of the people of India, whose laws, rights, and liberties he has subverted; whose properties he has destroyed, whose country he has laid waste and desolate, in the name of human nature itself, which Hastings has cruelly outraged.[27]

It was Burke's criticism that led to the reform of the practices of the East India Company and eventually to the formation of the incorruptible Indian Civil Service.

WARREN HASTINGS, THE ORIENTALISTS, AND INDIA

The greatest gift of the English, after universal peace and the modernization of society, and indeed the direct result of these two forces—is the Renaissance which marked our 19th century. Modern India owes everything to it.

—Sir Jadunath Sarkar, 1928

Historically, European oriental research rendered a service to Indian and Asiatic nationalism which no native could ever have given. . . . The resuscitation of their past fired the imagination of the Hindus and made them conscious of a heritage of their very own which they could pit not only against the Muslims' but also against that of the more virile English. Psychologically, the Indian people crossed the line which divides primitive peoples from civilized peoples.

—Nirad Chaudhuri

When the loud cry of trampled Hindostan
Arose to heaven in her appeal from man,

—Lord Byron, *Monody on the Death of the Rt. Hon. R. B. Sheridan*

Edmund Burke displayed a considerable knowledge of India in his speeches and reports leading to the impeachment of Hastings. Ironically, it was Hastings himself and his cultural policy that not only transformed East India Company servants from commercial adventurers to dedicated, incorruptible civil servants, but they were also responsible for the further impetus given to research on Indian antiquities, archaeology, philology, and history, to which Burke was so fond of referring. Henceforth, many Indian intellectuals, scholars, and historians themselves acknowledged their gratitude and scholarly debt to the British presence in India for returning their pre-Islamic and non-Islamic history to them, and thus restoring their cultural pride. This intercultural enrichment of the two societies makes nonsense of Said's reductionist view of the British experience in India as solely a conflict between the East and the West. It all began with Hastings, and it would be fitting to quote his modern Indian admirer V. B. Kulkarni, who wrote, "[Hastings] knew that the quickest route to the heart of a people is through the language of the country and had accordingly proficiency in Bengali and Urdu, besides a fair acquaintance with Persian, the language of the Muslim court. Sitting in a remote Bengali town with ample leisure for reflection, Hastings wondered at the vastness of the country, its richness and variety, and above all the antiquity and splendour of its civilization."[28]

In the preface to Charles Wilkins's Bhagavat Gita, Hastings wrote that Indian writings "will survive when the British dominion in India shall have long ceased to exist, and when the sources which it once yielded both of wealth and power are lost to remembrance."[29] This remark reveals that Hastings was not simply thinking of the utilitarian value of Orientalist knowledge but also of its cultural value, of its value as knowledge, *tout court*. And tellingly, Hastings did not think that British rule would last forever.

In 1772 the company's board of directors ordered Hastings to take responsibility for the administration in the Bengal, and from then on, Englishmen were assigned to districts as collectors whose activities were to be overseen by a board of revenue in Calcutta, setting in motion the beginnings of the eventually much-revered British Civil Service. Calcutta evolved from a village of mudhuts, surrounded by jungle, into a great city, the scene of cultural and intellectual exchange that was both to transform India and to imprint it permanently on the British imagination.

Hastings set about creating an efficient British Civil Service elite that would be sensitive to Indians and their culture, institutions, and traditions, and that would be proficient in Indian languages. He inspired a select group of aides with a love of Asian literature: Charles Wilkins, Nathaniel Halhed, and Jonathan Duncan (governor of Bombay, 1794–1810). Sir William Jones arrived a little later in 1783. Since they were in the Bengal, the Bengali language became the first Indian language to be studied scientifically, with Halhed publishing his *Grammar of the Bengali Language* in 1788, a work the distinguished Bengali scholar Sushil Kumar De describes as "one of the earliest and for some time the best introduction to the scientific study of the language."[30] Halhed, apart from his youthful translation with Richard Brinsley Sheridan of Aristaenetus,[31] had already translated from the Persian the Gentoo Code, a legal code first translated from Sanskrit into Persian by Brahmin scholars, between 1774 and 1776. The printing of the grammar itself marked an important era in the history of Bengali literature. As De admits, "It is chiefly to the exertion of the ever memorable Caxton of Bengal, Charles (afterwards Sir Charles) Wilkins, a Bengal civilian and oriental scholar, that we are indebted for the beautiful types which he had himself prepared and in which art he had instructed the Bengali mechanics, thus introducing, as he did, the art of printing into this country. It is impossible to exaggerate the services thus rendered by this philanthropic Englishman, not only to the cause of vernacular literature but also to the general culture of the people, for it is undoubted that without this useful art of printing the general education of the people under modern conditions could not have been possible."[32]

De also pointed out that Wilkins had taken care to teach his art to his Bengali assistant, one Pancanan, who went on to work at Srirampur, better known as Serampore, where another Orientalist, William Carey, would play an important role in the renaissance of Bengali literature.

Hastings "loved the people of India, and respected them to a degree no other British rule has ever equalled,"[33] which did not go unappreciated by the Indians, for his name passed into folklore, legend, and popular verse. His cultural policy obviously benefited a whole generation of British civil servants, but even more important, it led to the revitalization of Indian culture itself. As G. K. Gleig, the editor of Hastings's memoirs, summarized, "He encouraged bodies of learned pundits to settle in Calcutta, and supported them while they translated out of the Sanskrit into the more acceptable dialects, the poems and mythological and moral treatises of their native land. He founded colleges for the instruction of native youths in the laws and usages of their own country. He held out inducements to the study by the natives of English literature and English science. He laboured, in short, to promote not only the political, but the moral and rational improvement of the provinces."[34]

Wilkins wrote, "[My] curiosity was excited by the example of [my] friend Mr. Halhed to commence the study of Sanskrit,"[35] became perhaps the first Englishman to master Sanskrit (a mastery that led him in 1783 to translate the Bhagavat Gita), and later to tirelessly examine inscriptions in that language to reconstruct the history of the Palas of Bengal.[36] Wilkins is now considered the father of Indian epigraphy, having deciphered the Monghyr inscription and having discovered, deciphered, and translated another celebrated inscription on the pillar at Buddal in Dinajpur. The eminent Indian historian Kejariwal writes that Wilkins's own "account shows the apathy with which antiquities were regarded in eighteenth century India, and highlights the zeal of early British scholars to unravel India's past."[37] Wilkins wrote, "Sometime in the month of November, in the year 1780 I discovered, in the vicinity of the town of Buddal, near which the Company have a factory, and which at that time was under my charge, a decapitated monumental column. . . . It stands in a swamp overgrown with weeds. . . . Upon my getting close enough to the monument to examine it, I took its dimensions, and made a drawing of it, and soon after a plate was engraved, from which the accompanying is an impression."[38] Wilkins went on to compile a Sanskrit grammar, publish several translations from the sacred books of the East, and prepare a new edition of John Richardson's *Persian and Arabic Dictionary*.[39] He also cataloged and annotated the manuscripts collected by his colleague and friend Sir William Jones, who always maintained that but for Wilkins's aid, he would never have learned Sanskrit. Wilkins was one of the founding fathers of the Asiatic Society of Bengal. De praised Wilkins for bringing Bengali literature into the era of printing. Wilkins being a "metallurgist, engraver, founder, and printer" of such elaborate and different alphabets as Persian and Bengali has already been noted.

Wilkins's achievements were summed up in 1922 by the Indian scholar Shumbhoo Chander Dey,[40] who highlighted Wilkins's contributions to Indian epigraphy. It must be emphasized that Wilkins was the first European to study Sanskrit inscriptions that had baffled even the Hindu scholars. His introduction of the art of printing to Bengal was also of specific importance, endearing him to thousands of Indians.

Jonathan Duncan, though not a scholar at the level of Jones or Colebrooke, knew Persian, Sanksrit, and Bengali, and contributed learned articles to *Asiatick Researches.* He typified the new breed of civil servant created by Hastings's policy, dedicated to public service, with a love of Hinduism, always proposing programs of social improvement of Indian peoples, helping abolish infanticide, and devising ways of eliminating corruption among English officials. He helped found Hindu College in the Hindu holy city of Banares "for the preservation and cultivation of the Laws, Literature and Religion of that Nation at this Centre of their Faith."[41] This institution was to be a "public university" offering the Hindus new notions of research, a center for emending Sanskrit texts, and a "precious library of the most ancient and valuable learning and tradition."[42] Hindu College was established in 1791 and survives to this day under the name Sanskrit College. Duncan was also behind another very important discovery in 1794. While collecting stones at the ruins of Sarnath for Jagath Singh, the chief minister of Raja Chait Singh of Banares, workmen uncovered a marble urn containing a statue of a Buddha with an inscription at the base, "a few human bones . . . and some decayed pearls, gold leaves and other jewels of no value."[43] Duncan reported the finds in *Asiatick Researches*, but their importance was not recognized until fifty years later and forms a fascinating page in the story of the discovery of the history of Buddhism. It must be remembered that in the late eighteenth century almost nothing was yet known of the history of Buddhism, incredible as it may seem. It was left to the dedication of a group of Western Orientalists to recover this lost religion. How little was known at the time of the discovery of the urns is reflected in the confusion as to the significance of the finds: "The general belief in Banares was that these were the relics of the 'consort of some former rajah or prince.' "[44] Duncan, however, could not understand why anyone should want to have his remains buried rather than scattered upon the sacred River Ganges, especially at the holy city of Banares. Duncan conjectured, "The bones found in these urns must belong to one of the worshippers of Buddha, a set of Indian heretics, who having no reverence for the Ganges, used to deposit their remains in the earth, instead of committing them to that river; a surmise that seems strongly corroborated by the circumstance of a statue or idol of Buddha having been found in the same place under ground."[45]

Duncan represented the first generation of Orientalists, who not only mastered the relevant Oriental languages and developed a cultural empathy—"four and thirty years' residence have Braminised his mind and body"[46]—but also became dedicated public servants, devoted to the good of the people of India and the advancement of their public health and education.[47] Many came as surgeons and doctors, then mastered various Oriental languages and set about translating texts into English, or writing the first grammars of the languages they became partial to. The Edinburgh-trained John Gilchrist mastered Urdu, translated works from Urdu literature, published an Urdu dictionary and grammar in Calcutta in 1796, and finally helped the development of the College of Fort William. William Hunter followed a similar path, mastering Urdu and teaching at the College of Fort William. But perhaps the greatest of the doctor-Orientalists was H. H. Wilson.

Wilson came to India in 1808 as an assistant surgeon in the employ of the East India Company, but he was recruited by Dr. John Leyden to work as his assistant at the Calcutta Mint, becoming assay master on the latter's death in 1816. During his six-month voyage to India, Wilson learned Hindustani from a fellow passenger. But as he himself wrote, "Excited by the example and biography of Sir William Jones, [I] entered on the study of Sanskrit with warm interest, as soon after [my] arrival in India in 1808 as official occupations allowed."[48] He first translated, in 1813, Kalidasa's *Megha Dutt* (Cloud Messenger), a work Wilson favorably compared to European poetry: "I advance an opinion that we have few specimens either in classical or modern poetry of more genuine tenderness or delicate feeling."[49] He next compiled a monumental Sanskrit-English dictionary, completed in 1819, of more than a thousand pages, "comprehending all the radicals of the language, and between 30 and 40,000 derivatives, with their etymological development and characteristic grammatical inflections." As Wilson himself remarked, this work "has . . . mainly contributed to the extended cultivation of Sanskrit literature on the continent of Europe."[50]

In 1811 Wilson became the secretary of the Asiatic Society of Bengal, a post he occupied for twenty-one years. During his tenure, Wilson acquired Sanskrit and other texts, promoted enthusiastically all branches of Indian learning, and encouraged interaction between English Orientalists and Indian scholars in Calcutta, while contributing some very important articles to the journal *Asiatick Researches*. He was also the secretary to the committee of public instruction and visitor to the Sanskrit College of Calcutta. In 1819 he was sent to Banares to inspect and reorganize the Hindu College, a visit that Wilson used to gather material for his great work on Indian drama. Serving on the boards of the School Book Society and Hindu College, Wilson proposed a curriculum integrating Western science and traditional Indian subjects, all to be taught in English. These and other activities testify to Wilson's sense of public duty and responsibility for the promotion of Oriental learning and the education of native young men. Wilson had a profound respect for Hindu culture and believed that contemporary India would be reinvigorated with the help of Orientalists who were revealing her noble past; at the same time, he understood that India had much to learn from the West.

Joseph Boden had founded the chair of Sanskrit at Oxford in 1827, and Wilson was appointed to the first professorship in 1832. He lived in Oxord for three years, and when he succeeded Sir Charles Wilkins as librarian to the East India Company, he moved to London. He became examiner in Indian languages at Haileybury, the company college. He was an original member of the Royal Asiatic Society, of which he served as director for more than twenty years. Wilson was an indefatigible collector of manuscripts, bringing together 540, both Vedic and classical works, now a part of the Sanskrit collection at the Bodleian Library, Oxford. His works include *Select Specimens of the Theatre of the Hindus* (1826–27, 2 vols.), a translation of *Sankhya karika* (1837), a translation of *Vishnupurana* (1840), *Lectures on the Religious and Philosophical Systems of the Hindus* (1840), *Ariana Antiqua: A Descriptive Account of the Antiquities and Coins of Afghanistan* (1841), and *Sketch of the Religious Sects of the Hindus* (1846). Wilson was highly regarded by Hindu scholars and equally by such European scholars as Max Müller and Monier Monier-Williams.

EARLY ORIENTALISTS

John Zephaniah Holwell

John Zephaniah Holwell was one of the survivors of the infamous Black Hole of Calcutta of June 1756. He served as a surgeon for the East India Company, and was a temporary governor of Bengal. Holwell was fascinated by India and her people, eventually writing several books on Indian religion, mythology, and history,[51] which helped to establish the great antiquity of Indian people and their literature, and pleaded for a study of Indian culture without European prejudice and frame of reference.[52] Holwell wrote in his preliminary discourse to the *Religious Tenets of the Gentoos*, "Having studiously perused all that has been written of the empire of Indostan, both as to its ancient as well as more modern state; as also the various accounts transmitted to us, by authors in almost all ages. . . . I venture to pronounce them all very defective, fallacious and unsatisfactory to an inquisitive searcher after truth; and only tending to convey a very imperfect and injurious resemblance of a people, who from the earliest times have been an ornament to the creation if so much can with propriety be said of any known people upon earth."[53]

The only way to acquire a more profound knowledge of a people was, he believed, to learn their language:

> A mere description of the exterior manners and religion of a people, will no more give us a true idea of them than a geographical description of a country can convey a just conception of their laws and government. The traveller must sink deeper in his researches. . . . His telling us such and such a people, in the East or West Indies, worship this stork, or that stone, or monstrous idol; only serves to reduce in our esteem our fellow creatures to the most abject and despicable point of light. Whereas, was he skilled in the language of the people he describes, sufficiently to trace the etymology of their words and phrases, and capable of diving into the mysteries of their theology; he would probably be able to evince to us, that such seemingly preposterous worship, had the most sublime rational source and foundation.[54]

Henry Thomas Colebrooke

> *In the long list of those who have laboured for the cause of Sanskrit learning and Indian research, no name is held with great veneration than that of Henry Thomas Colebrooke succeeding immediately to the work done by that illustrious Orientalist, Sir William Jones. Colebrooke, by his writings and discourses, had placed the Indian public as well as the Government under a deep debt of gratitude.*
>
> *Colebrooke's fame as an Orientalist of the first rank is an abiding and undying one. . . . At a time when, even among English scholars, literary criticism was unknown and when Indians naturally felt shy and refused to be communicative, Colebrooke was able to astonish the European world by his masterly and, what is even now considered, accurate exposition of Indian religious thought and philosophy. Nor the articles collected deal only with one branch of our national activities.*
>
> —Professor M. S. Ramaswami Iyengar[55]

Henry Thomas Colebrooke was a true polymath. His range of interests is an indication of his boundless intellectual curiosity, inherited from his father, a very learned man and antiquarian, and his mother, a woman of equally remarkable intellectual powers. Under a private tutor, Colebrooke mastered early the classical languages, together with French and German, and also developed a passion for mathematics and astronomy. As Colebrooke's son later wrote, "Every branch of natural history attracted him, and he would say that the wonders revealed by the microscope were more interesting than those of the telescope."[56]

Colebrooke began his Indian career working for the East India Company in 1782, becoming assistant collector at Tirhut in 1786, happy to leave the drinking and gambling of the British in Calcutta. He despised what he considered to be the low moral tone of the society of his fellow Englishmen.[57]

Such was his physical and intellectual energy that, despite his heavy official duties, Colebrooke found time to investigate and then write about the state of husbandry and commerce in Bengal, "a masterly survey of the conditions of agriculture in India."[58] Far from being some vast evil conspiracy by the imperial authorities to enslave Indians, Colebrooke's book was published privately, and, in fact, nearly got him dismissed from the service, since it was a plea for free trade and the abolition of the East India Company's monopoly.[59] As Professor M. S. Ramaswami Iyengar says, Colebrooke pleaded eloquently on behalf of the poor:

> To a government enlightened as is that by which British India is administered, it cannot be a trifling consideration to provide employment for the poorest classes. No public provision now exists in these provinces to relieve the wants of the poor and helpless. The only employment in which widows and female orphans incapacitated for field-labour by sickness or by their rank, can earn a subsistence is by spinning and it is the only employment to which the females of a family can apply themselves to maintain the men, if these be disqualified for labour by infirmity or by any other cause. To all it is a resource which, even though it may not be absolutely necessary for the subsistence, contributes at least to relieve the distress of the poor. Their distresses are certainly great and among none greater than among the many decayed families which once enjoyed the comforts of life. These are numerous in India and whether they be entitled to the particular consideration of Government or not, they have certainly a claim on its humanity.[60]

He was transferred to Purneah, where he began his true studies of Oriental languages and especially Sanskrit. Colebrooke's passion for mathematics and astronomy led him to inquire about the state of knowledge in the two sciences among Hindus, while his administrative duties led him to inquire into Hindu law. Despite a lack of grammars and dictionaries, Colebrooke undertook a systematic study of Sanskrit, the very difficulty of the language being an incentive to his "ingenious and exact" mind. In 1795 Colebrooke was appointed to a magistracy near Banares, where he befriended the Hindu scholars of the Sanskrit College and had access to original manuscripts. But it is worth pointing out that Colebrooke's duties were very heavy, and he carried them out conscientiously. He "had to hear from three hundred to five hundred causes a month, record his proceedings at large, with all the pleadings, evidence, &c., in writing, furnish monthly reports of every cause decided, monthly accounts of all moneys passing through the court, and correspond on the business of the police, &c., with the native magistrates under him, with the magistrates of other districts, and with government."[61]

Colebrooke's *Digest of Hindu Law* was published in 1798. It had taken two years of hard labor, but Colebrooke had refused remuneration, having, he wrote, "committed himself to disinterestedness in literary labours."[62] He was later appointed professor of Hindu law at the College of Fort William, a post also without a salary. Colebrooke then prepared a grammar of Sanskrit. Only the first volume came out in 1806, but it "had the merit of placing the results of the native grammarians in their true light for the first time, and vindicating their authority against the scholars who had regarded them as of little value." His further studies "foreshadowed many of the discoveries of the as yet unborn science of comparative philology."[63]

Intellectual energy and curiosity, and the love and admiration of Hindu culture in particular, impelled him to continue his scholarly activity despite the onerous duties of his official life. All his scholarly work testifies to his immense reading, research, and the originality of his robust intellect, even more impressive when we realize that he had to seek answers to all his Sanskrit inquiries in often hard-to-decipher manuscripts. Colebrooke published twenty articles in *Asiatick Researches*, sponsored by the Asiatic Society of Bengal, of which he became the president in 1807. Of one of his most important works, the essay on the Vedas, H. H. Wilson wrote, "It must have been a work of great labour, and could have been executed by no one except himself, as, independently of the knowledge of Sanskrit which it demanded, the possession of the books themselves was not within the reach of any European save one whose position commanded the respect and whose character conciliated the confidence of the Brahmans. This essay is still the only authority available for information respecting the oldest and most important religious writings of the Hindus."[64]

Almost equally important were Colebrooke's writings on the Jains. Professor Iyengar observes, "Colebrooke and Col. Mackenzie were the first to notice, in the pages of the *Asiatick Researches*, the existence and the tenets of the Jains. To their labours enthusiastically assisted later on by Bühler, Jacobi and Hoernle, Jainism owes its rehabilitation as one of the earliest home religions of India. These essays are justly considered as standards of reference on matters to which they relate."[65]

Colebrooke's intellectual honesty and adherence to scientific method led him to write with a certain dryness, but also with precision and truthfulness. To his knowledge of Sanskrit, Colebrooke brought a prior knowledge of science and mathematics, which gave him a unique position to comprehend Hindu writers on the exact sciences. As Max Müller said, without Colebrooke, many ancient texts would probably have been lost; many of these manuscripts are now preserved in the British Library. He also encouraged, especially under Lord Minto's administration, Oriental studies in the widest sense, not only of Sanskrit but also of other Eastern languages.

On his retirement to England, Colebrooke continued his research and his writings appeared in *The Transactions of the Royal Asiatic Society*, which he had helped found. His learned papers also appeared in *The Transactions of the Astronomical Society* and *The Quarterly Journal of Science*. In England, he was to pursue his research into the physical sciences, astronomy, chemistry, and botany. He annotated William Jones's treatise on Indian plants and had a genus of *Didynamia gymnospermia* named after him, *Colebrookia*. His contributions to Sanskrit and Hindu studies earned him honorary membership in the French Institute and in the Imperial Academy of Saint Petersburg. Politically, like William Jones, he was a staunch liberal who dreamed of settling in America, where he thought a freer political climate existed. He was never decorated, unlike Jones and others, and never made any money out of his intellectual pursuits, dying with his finances in a terrible state. He had collected at considerable personal expense some 2,749 manuscripts, which he later donated to the East India Company. These ended up in the British Library.

Colebrooke summed up his own achievements in letter to H. H. Wilson in 1827: "Careless and indifferent as our countrymen are, I think, nevertheless, you and I may derive more complacent feelings from the reflection that, following the footsteps of Sir W. Jones, we have, with so little aid of collaborators, and so little encouragement, opened nearly every avenue, and left it to foreigners, who are taking up the clue we have furnished, to complete the outline of what we have sketched. It is some gratification to natural pride that the opportunity which the English have enjoyed has not been wholly unemployed."[66]

In his address at the first general meeting, in 1823, of the (later Royal) Asiatic Society of Great Britain and Ireland, of which he was made director, Colebrooke expressed his gratitude to India and Asia: "To those countries of Asia, in which civilization may be justly considered to have had its origin, or to have attained its earliest growth, the rest of the civilised world owes a large debt of gratitude, which it cannot but be solicitous to repay."[67] He advocates "an interchange of benefits," since Europe has much to learn from Asia as well: "In progress of such researches, it is not perhaps too much to expect that something may yet be gleaned for the advancement of knowledge and improvement of arts at home [in Britain]. In many recent instances, inventive faculties have been tasked to devise anew, what might have been as readily copied from an Oriental type; or unacknowledged imitation has reproduced in Europe, with an air of novelty, what had been for ages familiar to the East. Nor is that source to be considered as already exhausted. In beauty of fabric, in simplicity of process, there possibly yet remains something to be learnt from China, from Japan, from India, which the refinement of Europe need not disdain."[68]

Institutions such as the Asiatic Society of Great Britain and Ireland are essential for scientific research:

> The course of inquiry into the arts, as into the sciences, of Asia, cannot fail of leading to much which is curious and instructive. The inquiry extends over regions, the most anciently and the most numerously peopled on the globe. The range of research is as wide as those regions are vast; and as various as the people who inhabit them are diversified. It embraces their ancient and modern history; their civil polity; their long-enduring institutions; their manners and their customs; their languages and their literature; their sciences, speculative and practical: in short, the progress of knowledge among them; the pitch which it has attained; and last, but most important, the means of its extension. . . . [I]t is in Asia that recorded and authentic history of mankind commences.

Colebrooke does not believe that India, for example, has remained the same. Rather, it has lived through "momentous events," which have advanced it "in the scale of civilised life."[69] Asia has perhaps stagnated in recent years but the research of the Orientalists can facilitate "ameliorations" of Eastern cultures. In studying Asia, Englishmen are investigating "the discoveries of the wise, the inventions of the ingenious, and the contrivances of the skilful."[70]

The more we study ancient Indian philosophy, "the more intimate will the relation be found between the philosophy of Greece and that of India. Whichever is the type or the copy, whichever has borrowed or has lent, certain it is that the one will serve to elucidate the other. The philosophy of India may be employed for a commentary on that of Greece; and conversely, Grecian philosophy will help to explain Indian. That of Arabia, too, avowedly copied from the Grecian model, has preserved much which else might have been lost. A part has been restored through the medium of translation, and more yet [may] be retrieved from Arabic stores."[71]

Research will also help the new science of comparative grammar: "The ancient language of India, the polished Sanskrit, not unallied to Greek and various other languages of Europe, may yet contribute something to their elucidation, and still more to the not unimportant subject of general grammar."[72]

As ever with the Orientalists, these languages must be studied for the sake of knowledge: "Connected as those highly polished and refined languages [Sanskrit and Arabic] are with other tongues, they deserve to be studied for the sake of the particular dialects and idioms to which they bear relation; for their own sake, that is, for the literature which appertains to them; and for the analysis of language in general, which has been unsuccessfully attempted on too narrow ground, but may be prosecuted, with effect, upon wider induction."[73]

Why have Britons spread all over the globe? "Political transactions, operations of war, relations of commerce, the pursuits of business, the enterprise of curiosity, the desire of scientific acquirements, carry British subjects to the most distant and the most secluded spots."[74] During their sojourn abroad, the British, through such associations as the Asiatic Society of Bengal, have "contributed their efforts for the promotion of knowledge," have accumulated manuscripts which have been preserved "from prompt decay" and are now in libraries in Britain. They will continue their research, once they return home to Britain, thanks to august bodies such as the Royal Asiatic Society of Great Britain and Ireland.[75]

Colebrooke was completely taken with Vedic India, and his research led him to the conclusion that many practices of contemporary Hinduism, such as the caste system or the worship of several gods, were, in fact, a departure from the authentic Vedic traditions. For example, in "On the Vedas, or the Sacred Writings of the Hindus," Colebrooke pointed out, "I have not found in any part of the Vedas, the least trace of such a worship [of Rama and Khrisna]. The real doctrine of the whole Indian scripture is the unity of the deity, in whom the universe is comprehended."[76] Similarly, the contemporary practice of sacrifice to Kali is a departure from the rituals enjoined in the Vedas. Certainly the discovery of the monotheist tradition in Hinduism must be considered a major contribution and shows how modern Hindus had misunderstood their own religious texts.

Sir William Jones

> *His zeal for work was remarkable, his search for virgin soil was rewarded, his tillage of it was scientific and thorough, his love for it was deep and true, and his harvest was golden and abundant and valuable to all men and for all time. It is through men of his type and temperament that the true spirit of fraternity between the West and the East will be born. It is through the co-operative work of scholars and scientists and artists and philosophers and humanitarians that the bridge of friendship can be thrown across the gulf of separation in spirit. Statesmen may proclaim the need of such kinship of feeling. Diplomats may proclaim that it exists already. But statesmen and diplomats and soldiers and civil officials can only keep up a patched-up outer peace often rent asunder by the frequent convulsions of inner estrangement. Sir William Jones was one of those with whom Indian scholars could and did feel that*

We were nursed upon the self same hill,
Fed the same flock by fountain, shade and rill;
Together both, ere the high lawns appeared
Under the opening eyelids of the Morn
We drove a-field.

—K. S. Ramaswami Sastri[77]

Knowledge, knowledge, and more knowledge—such was Jones's unceasing quest.

—A. J. Arberry[78]

Like many Orientalists, William Jones began as a gifted classical scholar, went on to master French and Italian, and acquired the rudiments of Arabic and Hebrew at an early age. He is said to have known thirteen languages well, and twenty-eight fairly well, at the time of his death.

While in service to Lord Spencer's family, Jones mastered Arabic and Persian. His first book appeared in 1770, a translation into French of the Persian life of Nadir Shah, and in the following year came the first of his articles, also in French, *Traité sur la poésie orientale* (Treatise on Oriental Poetry), which was accompanied by a metrical translation of some of the Persian odes of Hafiz. The year 1771 saw the first edition of his *Grammar of the Persian Language*. His first translation from the Arabic, *The Moallakat* [Mu'allaqāt], the seven poems claimed to have been suspended in the Ka'aba at Mecca, was published in 1783.

Jones began his legal career in 1774, when he was called to the bar at the Middle Temple. He published a number of articles on legal subjects. His "Essay on Bailments" is considered a classic. He dabbled in politics, hoping to represent the University of Oxford in the House of Commons, but his liberal views, his opposition to the war in America, and his detestation of slavery, all expressed with fervor, did not endear him to voters.

In 1783 Jones was knighted and appointed to the judgeship at the high court at Calcutta. He arrived in India in December 1783, and was to stay there until his death in 1794. Jones was to transform the intellectual and cultural life of India when he founded the Asiatic Society of Bengal and the associated journal, *Asiatick Researches*, dedicated to the scientific study of the languages, literature, science, history, and philosophy of India. He delivered eleven anniversary discourses to the society as its president and published various articles in the house journal, many of which constitute permanent contributions to our appreciation of India. Jones, with his intellectual curiosity and knowledge of and passion for classical and other languages and literature, brought an enthusiasm to Oriental studies that he tried to communicate to others. Every Oriental subject, from Hindu chronology, music, philology, Arabic pre-Islamic poetry, Persian odes, Sanskrit drama, Indian botany, and zoology, to the mythology and archaeology of India, held interest for him.

Jones mastered Sanskrit and gave to the Western world its first glimpse of the richness of Indian drama with his translation of Kalidasa's *Sakuntala*, published posthumously in 1799. With his desire to be the Justinian of India, Jones began a complete digest of Hindu and Muslim law as practiced in India, by first consulting Hindu scholars and Muslim lawyers. He did not live long enough to finish this ambitious project though he did manage to complete *Institutes of Hindu Law, or the Ordinances of Menu* (Manu), which was published in 1794.

In his third anniversary discourse of 1786, Jones elaborated a theory of the common origins of European languages and those of India, an intuition that marks the beginning of Indo-European comparative grammar and modern comparative-historical linguistics.[79] He writes

> The Sanskrit language, whatever be its antiquity, is of a wonderful structure; more perfect than the Greek, more copious than the Latin, and more exquisitely refined than either, yet bearing to both of them a stronger affinity, both in the roots of verbs and in the forms of grammar, than could possibly have been produced by accident; so strong indeed, that no philologer could examine them all three, without believing them to have sprung from some common source, which, perhaps, no longer exists: there is a similar reason, though not quite so forcible, for supposing that both the Gothic and the Celtic, though blended with a very different idiom, had the same origin with the Sanskrit; and the old Persian might be added to the same family, if this were the place for discussing any question concerning the antiquities of Persia.[80]

As Trautman says, "The modernity of the formulation is remarkable: the grouping of Sanskrit, Greek, Latin, Gothic (Germanic), Celtic, and Old Persian; their mutual resemblance in lexicon and grammar; the conception of their relationship as co-descendants of a lost ancestral language, which we call Proto-Indo-European—these are exactly the views historical linguists hold today."[81]

In this work, Jones is furthermore identifying the kinship of Indians and Britons, not creating some fictitious "Other." For Jones, Indians, along with Greeks, Romans, and Egyptians, all belonged to the family of ancient nations.

Jones had many Indian friends, both Hindu and Muslim. Lord Teignmouth recounts in his *Memoirs of Sir William Jones* how Jones was affectionately regarded by all those who came into contact with him:

> I could dwell with rapture on the affability of his conversation and manners, on his modest, unassuming deportment; nor can I refrain from remarking that he was totally free from pedantry, as well as from that arrogance and self-sufficiency which sometimes accompany and disgrace the greatest abilities; his presence was the delight of every society, which his conversation exhilarated and improved. His intercourse with the Indian natives of character and abilities was extensive: he liberally rewarded those by whom he was served and assisted and his dependents were treated by him as friends. . . . Nor can I resist the impulse which I feel to repeat an anecdote of what occurred after his demise; the [Hindu] pundits who were in the habit of attending him, when I saw them at a public durbar a few days after that melancholy event, could neither restrain their tears for his loss, nor find terms to express their admiration at the wonderful progress which he had made in the sciences which they professed.[82]

Sir William Jones was a true philosophe of the Enlightenment, with its universalism and openness to others, and in numerous articles and discourses devoted much time to broadening the intellectual and cultural horizons of his countrymen and Europeans in general. In *Traité sur la poésie orientale*, which had been appended to his French translation *Histoire de Nader Chah*, Jones everywhere praises the beauties and subtleties of Persian and Arabic language and literature. The Arabic language is expressive, strong, and sonorous, and the most copious of all languages, while Persian is full of gentleness and harmony, adding to its natural stock many words from Arabic. There is no language comparable to Persian for the delicacy of its composite words. What Francis Bacon said of Latin and Greek, Jones says of Arabic and Persian: the former was created for military and civil action, the latter for the cultivation of the arts. Jones expresses the hope that he can help prepare Europeans to get used to Oriental sentiments and expressions, and eventually take them to their hearts. He compares Arabic and Persian poetry to Shakespeare, Spenser, and Pindar. Perhaps European poetry had for too long subsisted on the perpetual repetition of the same images, continuous allusions to the same fables. And as Jones himself put it in a later essay *On the Poetry of the Eastern Nations*, "[I]t has been my endeavour for several years to inculcate this truth, that, if the principal writings of the Asiaticks, which are reposited in our public libraries, were printed with the usual advantage of notes and illustrations, and if the languages of Eastern nations were studied in our great seminaries of learning, where every other branch of useful knowledge is taught to perfection, a new and ample field would be opened for speculation; we should have a more extensive insight into the history of the human mind; we should be furnished with a new set of images and similitudes; and a number of excellent compositions would be brought to light, which future scholars might explain, and future poets might imitate."[83]

In the preface to his *Grammar of the Persian Language* (1771), Jones again feels the need to plead for wider cultural sympathies: "Some men never heard of the Asiatick writings, and others will not be convinced that there is anything valuable in them; some pretend to be busy, and others are really idle; some detest the Persians, because they believe in Mahomed, and others despise their language, because they do not understand it: we all love to excuse, or conceal, our ignorance, and are seldom willing to allow any excellence beyond the limits of our own attainments: like savages, who thought the sun rose and set for them alone, and could not imagine that the waves, which surrounded their island, left coral and pearls upon any other shore."[84]

That *Grammar* was of use to both the colonial administrator and the merchant, but it transcended utility and opened a window onto the glories of Persian literature and civilization, containing, as it did, examples of poets such as Hafiz, Sa'adi, and an unattributed quatrain from a poet later identified as a certain Umar Khayyam. This first glimpse of Eastern poetry, which he had the temerity to compare to Greek, Latin, and European literature, enchanted such writers as Lord Byron, Thomas More, Edward Fitzgerald (future translator of Umar Khayyam), and Alfred Tennyson. Fitzgerald and Tennyson were inspired by Jones's grammar to learn Persian.

For Jones, the learning of languages was an essential part of a liberal and humane education, whose aims included the cultivation of understanding and increasing our knowledge. As he wrote in "An Essay on Education," "[After] fixing the good of ourselves and our fellow-creatures as the primary end proposed by a liberal education; and considering the cultivation of our understanding, and the acquisition of knowledge, as the secondary objects of it: Now, as neither this knowledge can be perfectly obtained, nor the reason completely improved, in the short duration of human life, unless the accumulated experience and wisdom of all ages and all nations, be added to that which we gain by our own researches, it is necessary to understand the *languages* of those people who have been, in any period of the world, distinguished for their superior knowledge. It follows, therefore, that the more immediate object of education is, to learn the languages of celebrated nations both ancient and modern."[85]

Jones was forever emphasizing the similarities between India and Greece, or pointing out Europe's debt to Indian philosophy, or hinting at a common source for the two great civilizations, writing, for instance, in the third anniversary discourse that it was impossible, "to read the Vedanta, or the many fine compositions in illustration of it, without believing that Pythagoras and Plato derived their sublime theories from the same fountain with the sages of India."[86]

Jones made some important contributions to Hindu chronology, and, as

Michael Franklin points out, "It was no part of the Asiatick Society's project to essentialize Asia's timelessness and fixity, and therefore its inferiority to western Europe. Instead, in his discourse '*On Asiatic history, civil and natural*' of 1793, by identifying the Greek name Sandracottus cited in classical histories of Alexander the Great's invasion of north-western India in 326 BCE with Chandragupta, the founder of the Mauryan empire, and further connecting the key site named by the Greeks as Palibothra with Pataliputra, Jones facilitated the accurate correlation of eastern and western history."[87]

With his work on Indian chronology, and having created a solid framework for the understanding of India's past, Jones, in effect, can be considered the father of Indian history.[88]

Jones's translation of *Sacontala* (Shakuntala) had an enormous influence in Europe, inspiring Schiller, Novalis, Schlegel, and Goethe, who used its introductory scene as a model for the "Vorspiel auf dem Theater" of *Faust* (1797).[89] But even more remarkably, the collection, printing, and translations of Sanskrit texts by Jones and other Orientalists made available for the first time to Indians themselves aspects of their own civilization, changing forever their own self-image. Until now, these texts had been only accessible to a narrow coterie of Brahmins.

Jones's own poetry, particularly *The Hymns*, a blend of Pindar and the imagery of Hindu legends, also played a part in the liberal education of Europe, and influenced English romanticism; *The Hymn to Narayena* inspired Shelley's *Hymn to Intellectual Beauty.* But even more broadly, Jones's translations were enormously influential. Robert Southey and Thomas Moore often cite him, but Shelley and Tennyson also borrowed from him in their *Queen Mab* and *Locksley Hall*, respectively. And Jones was responsible for drawing attention to Oriental literature generally, thereby enriching the English tradition.[90] These happy influences on English literature are consonant with his more comprehensive worldview that aspired to break down cultural barriers, that "recognized no frontiers of race or colour," that accorded full respect to both Hinduism and Islam, and that eschewed sectarian bigotry.[91] On occasions he preferred aspects of Hinduism to Christianity of a certain kind; he wrote in letter to Earl Spencer in 1787, "I am no Hindu; but I hold the doctrine of the Hindus concerning a future state to be incomparably more rational, more pious, and more likely to deter men from vice, than the horrid opinions inculcated on punishments *without end.*"[92]

As for Islam, Jones makes these remarkable observations in *Dissertation sur la littérature orientale* (Discourse on Eastern Literature): "It has been shown that literature and the fine arts are held in the highest esteem by the Orientals. To these proofs we should add one even more convincing. This would be the very words of Muhammad that we have chosen as the epigraph to this work: 'Seek knowledge be it as far as China.' The same lawgiver also said, 'Knowledge is permitted to all believers, male and female.' What! you will exclaim, are these the precepts of this vulgar and blood-stained impostor? of Muhammad? Yes; of Muhammad, this eloquent and virtuous hero, for in truth these latter epithets are merited whatever the opinion of Dominican inquisitors." Jones is a committed Christian and cannot allow Islam full equality, or Muhammad the status of a true prophet, but, nonetheless, Jones finds him a virtuous and sagacious man, a lawgiver on the same level as Alexander, Solon, Lycurgus, while, for Jones, the literary style of the Koran places Muhammad on the same plane as the most elegant of poets and the most gifted of rhetoricians.[93]

The distinguished Arabist Alan Jones[94] believes that Sir William Jones's translation of the *Mu'allaqāt* in particular and Persian poetry in general are successful because of the empathy displayed with them: "[G]ood translation often involves delicate balancing, and judgement and feeling can in some instances raise a translation that, on technical gorinds is only moderately competent to a piece that deserves to be taken seriously. That judgement and feeling is in my view present in Jones's translations of both Arabic and Persian poetry." As he points out, Sir William Jones influenced Goethe more by his Persian and Arabic translations than by his translation of *Sacontala*, and thereby changed the course of European literature. Sir William also influenced Friedrich Rückert, German scholar, poet, and professor of Oriental languages, who made very distinguished translations of Arabic, Persian, and Chinese verse.[95]

THE ASIATIC SOCIETY OF BENGAL, THE COLLEGE OF FORT WILLIAM, AND THE BENGAL RENAISSANCE

> *Dr. Kejariwal tells us of the activities of this small band of scholars who were inspired to reveal India's past. Few if any of them derived any material gains from their work, and most of them appear to have met the expenses of their research out of their own pockets. The main motive in most of their minds seems to have been the study of India for its own sake.*
>
> *When Jones translated Sakuntala and thus introduced the Sanskrit drama to the western world, are we to believe that he consciously thought: "I am doing this in order that my country may dominate a subject people"? Could any such motive have been in the mind of James Prinsep, when he deciphered the inscriptions of Asoka? Was Colebrooke inspired in his pioneering work on the Veda chiefly by motives of patriotism? If these*

scholars had worked to serve their country or the Company in their spare time they could surely have found more effective ways of doing so.

In fact, these pioneer Indologists must have been motivated chiefly, in every case, by the desire for knowledge and understanding—knowledge and understanding of a civilization different from their own, which they recognized as possessing uncharted beauties and unplumbed depths. At the back of all good scholarship is burning intellectual curiosity, a determination to understand—and this the pioneers of the Asiatic Society [of Bengal] possessed in full.

—Professor A. L. Basham[96]

I discovered that even Asoka and Kanishka, not to mention their dynasties, were unknown names till the [Asiatic] Society's work brought them to light. I was thrilled by the account of how Sir William Jones identified the Sandracottus of the Greek texts with Chandragupta Maurya, and Prinseps deciphered the Asokan script. It was astonishing to see that many of the other dynasties—the Palas, the Senas, the Maukharies, the Valabhis and many others which constitute the core of ancient Indian history today—were unknown till, primarily through the exertions of the Society's members in the nineteenth century, these genealogies took coherent shape.

—Professor O. P. Kejariwal[97]

Both the Asiatic Society of Bengal, founded in 1784, and the College of Fort William, founded in 1800, were responsible for the revitalization of Indian culture and society, leading to the Bengal Renaissance and helping to lay the foundations of Indian nationalism.

We can better appreciate the achievements of the Orientalists if we take stock of the cultural situation in India at the end of the eighteenth century. Professor O. P. Kejariwal, in magnificent dithyramb to the disinterested contributions of British Orientalists to the Indian Renaissance, provides a lucid historical background to the founding and work of the Asiatic Society of Bengal. As he says, in the field of intellectual activity, the eighteenth century before the British arrived was a stagnant period:

> Sanskrit had lost its vitality even before the advent of Islam. Destruction of the seats of learning and of monastic centers by Islamic conquerors had rendered it practically a dead language. . . .
>
> With the exception of Urdu, the court language, there was little creative vitality of a high order in the major languages. . . . The situation was worse in the field of historical studies. It seems strange that only about two hundred years ago, even learned Indians were unaware of the existence or significance of such names

> as Chandragupta Maurya, Asoka, Samudragupta, Kanishka, Harsha and even Buddha—names which form the core of ancient Indian history. Thus we can say that in the eighteenth century, India had a past but it had no history. The past was preserved in the form of archaeological and architectural remains, inscriptions on buildings, stone and iron pillars, copper-plates, buried sites of ancient cities, and coins, but there was no work of history to highlight their importance. This lack of historical perspective made India apathetic to its historical remains.[98]

Kejariwal's observations are confirmed by other Indian scholars. R. C. Majumdar, for example, wrote, "We have, therefore, to admit that the literary genius of India, so fertile and active in almost all conceivable branches of study, was not applied to chronicling the records of kings and the rise and fall of states and nations. It is difficult to give a rational explanation of this deficiency, but the fact admits of no doubt."[99]

As Kejariwal laments, Indians, unaware of the importance of historical remains, had left them to crumble and decay, a fact attested to by the British Orientalists. Similarly, many manuscripts would have been lost but for the efforts of such scholars as Charles Wilkins and the German Johann Georg Bühler, who salvaged severely damaged manuscripts of the rare Sanskrit historical work *Rajatarangini*. Similarly, Prinsep's tenure in the Asiatic Society "was full of achievements in retrieving, restoring and trying to preserve the ancient historical monuments of the country. Among these were the Sarnath remains and the Allahabad pillar which yielded such significant information about Asoka and Samudragupta—two of the greatest monarchs of India, and in fact, of the world."[100] As for ancient coins, it has been estimated that nearly 15 million must have been lost; whenever they were discovered by the local people they were melted and turned into ornaments and amulets. Fortunately, Western Orientalists such as James Tod, Dr. Swiney, A. Conolly, Alexander Burnes, and Charles Masson collected, studied, and preserved thousands as they employed people to search them out.[101] Kejariwal continues the sorry list: "Similarly, valuable manuscripts were lost, inscriptions effaced, and dwellings or towns built over important historical sites. Marauders raided old structures like stupas for hidden treasures; local *zamindars* [landlords] pulled down ancient buildings merely to collect bricks for their new houses. The remains of Sarnath provide an example. The local Diwan, Jagat Singh, removed the bricks from the Dhamek stupa so that the entire structure, standing for centuries, seemed on the verge of collapse."[102]

Kejariwal's depressing picture is confirmed by such scholars as Sushil Kumar De, who, despite his hostility toward the British in general, is forced to admit time and time again the dismal situation of the Bengal before the arrival of the British, and the beneficial effects of their presence on the life of the Indians. De chronicles "the moral depravity of the period," referring to the "depraved moral influence of the Muhammedan court upon the courts of the noblemen and also upon society in general."[103] He believes that "Hindu society carried within itself the germs of its own decay. However beneficial the institution of caste might have been to the ancient society, of which it formed the universal and natural basis, it cannot be doubted that its exclusiveness, in course of time, gave rise to a monopoly which, like the monopoly of the medieval monks of Europe, proved injurious to intellectual progress beyond a certain stage. Within the small privileged hereditary class to which the spread of knowledge was confined, the arts and sciences, no doubt, were carried to a pitch of perfection, but competition, thus artificially limited, naturally gave no scope to favourable variations in intellectual development. The intellectual capacity of the individual or the class was increased at the cost of general ignorance and inferiority of the race."[104]

There is also the testimony of Nirad Chaudhuri, who wrote, "In the eighteenth century, on the eve of the establishment of British rule, the Hindus had no recollection of their real past, nor any idea of the true character of the classical Sanskritic civilization. Their Hinduism was a broken-up and simplified version of the Hinduism of ancient India. It was unorganized in space and unsupported in time. Its quality was neutral where it was not purely negative."[105]

Against this background of cultural apathy and decline, on January 15, 1784, with Chief Justice Robert Chambers presiding, thirty European gentlemen of Calcutta gathered to hear Sir William Jones propose the permanent establishment of a research institute, an institute of learning devoted to "Man and Nature: whatever is performed by the one, or produced by the other," the objects of inquiry being limited to "the geographical limits of Asia."[106] Given what we have already suggested about the importance of free institutions and associations for the establishment of scientific traditions, the founding of the Asiatic Society was of immense significance. The membership of the society remained at first exclusively European, but Indian members were admitted in 1829, and the first Indian president, Justice Asutosh Mukhopadhyay, was elected in 1907. The transactions of the Asiatic Society were first published under the title of *Asiatick Researches* in 1788, with four further volumes in 1790, 1793, 1795, and 1797. *Asiatick Researches* was an immediate success. A pirated edition of the first volume came out in England in 1798, and later volumes were translated into German and French. The Asiatic Society flourishes to this day, and proudly hosted its bicentenary celebrations in 1984 in the presence of Prime Minister Indira Gandhi. The Asiatic Society was the direct inspiration behind almost all literary and scientific activities in India, its importance was recognized by the government of India, which by an act of Parliament in 1984 declared it as an "institution of national importance." The scientific importance of such an institution is best illustrated by William Chambers's article "Account of the Sculptures and Ruins at Mavalipuram," the first published article of historical interest. Chambers avowed that he had first visited the ruins in 1772 but had not bothered to take scientific measurements of the objects on the site or note any observations. He would have done so, he tells us, "had there then existed in India so powerful an incentive to diligent inquiry, and accurate communication, as the establishment of this Society."[107]

As Kejariwal observes about Chambers's article, "In this first published article on Indian antiquities, though the author deals at length with the difficulties facing the European researcher into India's past, there is not a word about the benefits of such studies to the British Empire. Many of these pioneer scholars were thus evidently motivated by scholarship itself and one need not look for deeper motives underlying their labours."[108]

The range and depth of the scholarship of the articles published in the journal of the Asiatic Society, *Asiatick Researches*, are astonishing.[109]

College of Fort William

> *No doubt, the College of Fort William's greatest achievement in the history of intellectual progress in this country consists in its revival of the ancient culture of the land, with its all-comprehensive orientalism daring far beyond the intrepid dreams of scholars like Sir William Jones, Wilkins, and Colebrooke.*
>
> —Sushil Kumar De[110]

Marquess Wellesley was named governor-general in 1798, and created the College of Fort William in 1800, thereby inaugurating a cultural revolution that changed the life of India. Though the college was primarily meant to "transform inept, self-seeking servants of the East India Company into efficient, devoted civil servants of the British Empire in India,"[111] its true importance lay in the impetus it gave to Bengali learning. As Sir George Barlow said in 1802, "[T]he establishment of the College of Fort William has already excited a general attention to oriental language, literature and knowledge."[112] Sushil Kumar De comments on Sir George's justifiable claim: "We can realise what this means when we bear in mind the general neglect and oblivion to which Bengali literature and Bengali education had hitherto been consigned."[113] Professor De, a scholar with a highly critical mind, freely acknowledges the positive role of this institution.

The college was responsible for the publication in Bengali of prose works that revitalized Bengali literature, which had practically disappeared after the death of the narrative poet Bharatchandra. "The College was the seminary of western learning in an eastern dress; it helped to diffuse western ideas through the medium of the vernacular. At the same time, orientalism was its principal feature, and it turned the attention of students and scholars to the cultivation of oriental languages, both classical and vernacular."[114] This "Oxford of the East" was the meeting place of two cultures, where mutual respect led to enduring friendships across cultural divides, and to works of equally enduring scholarship. "The best scholars and the greatest intellects of the country met here in friendly intercourse; and we shall see how an attractive personality like [William] Carey's drew around it a band of enthusiastic writers, bent upon removing the poverty of their vernacular. At the invitation and inducement of such scholars, literary works were undertaken by the enlightened Bengali community as well as by the Munshis and Pundits of the College, who would possibly have produced nothing but for the stimulus thus given to their literary zeal and the encouragement yielded by the liberality of government which would have never otherwise been so readily called into being."[115]

Wellesley recruited the best Orientalists of the period to staff this Oxford on the Hooghly. Neil Edmonstone headed the Persian department, assisted by John Harrington and Francis Gladwin; for Arabic, Wellesley recruited Lt. John Baillie; for Hindustani language and literature, John Gilchrist, who had already published an Urdu grammar and dictionary; Colebrooke for the Sanskrit department; and finally William Carey, who alone was responsible for the teaching of all of the Hindu popular languages.

William Carey

The career and influence of William Carey, who is honored by Bengalis as "the father of modern Bengali prose," is truly extraordinary. Surely there cannot be any other cases in the history of cultural contacts between the East and the West, where a Westerner acquires an Eastern language, masters it, and writes in it so well that he relaunches an entire Eastern literature. Joseph Conrad, a Pole whose second language was French, wrote some of the most important novels in the English language, and Vladimir Nabokov, born in Russia, wrote dazzling English prose, but neither can be said to have found English language or literature in a state of decay or neglect, or to have relaunched it, whatever their influence on later writers. Before giving Sushil Kumar De's enthusiastic assessment of Carey's importance, I shall offer a brief look at Carey's life.

William Carey came from a modest family in Northamptonshire, where his father, originally a weaver, became a schoolmaster, allowing young William access to books on a wide range of subjects.[116] He was apprenticed to a shoemaker, and began his life in that trade, but he also seems to have experienced a religious calling, which led him to be baptized in the Baptist Church in 1783. He began preaching to the Baptist congregation at Earls Barton, Northampton, studying Greek, Latin, and Hebrew in his spare time, hoping to deepen his knowledge of the scriptures. He was a schoolmaster, shoemaker, and preacher, fascinated by non-European cultures, probably awakened by his reading of the South Sea voyages of Captain James Cook, whose third voyage had only recently ended with Cook's murder in 1779. His biographer, A. H. Oussoren, recounts how as a teacher, Carey constructed a leather globe showing the world, teaching the children "by marking down the population, language, customs and religion" of all the peoples of the world.[117] His activities led him to found what eventually came to be known as the Baptist Missionary Society, the first evangelical missionary society, on whose behalf Carey offered to go to Bengal. The harsh reality of life in India forced Carey to accept work as a manager of an indigo factory. He soon learned the Bengali and Hindi languages, was one of the first persons to preach in the vernacular languages, and also began translating the Bible into Bengali.

In 1800 Carey joined the Danish missionaries settled at Serampore, north of Calcutta, where he began his translation and missionary work in earnest. With the help of Indian scholars, Carey translated the entire Bible into Bengali, Oriya, Sanskrit, Hindi, Marathi, and Assamese—and parts of it into twenty-nine Indian languages. Carey produced grammars of Bengali (1801), Marathi (1805), Sanskrit (1806), Punjabi (1812), Telinga (1814), and Bhotia (1826), and compiled dictionaries of Marathi (1810), Bengali (1815), and Bhotia (1826). He also began translating the *Ramayana* into English.[118]

Already in 1786, Carey had written a tract later published as *Enquiry into the Obligations of Christians to use the Means of Conversion of the Heathen*, in which he had expressed his missionary philosophy, which is surprisingly liberal, cosmopolitan, and tolerant. Christians must not, he argued, impose their own culture upon others but try to make heathens "useful members of their society." One must try to reach the masses in their own language, hence the need to learn them. One must cultivate friendships, and not be offended by the heathens' response or manners.[119]

But for Bengalis, the real contributions of Carey to the Bengal Renaissance are his *Grammar of the Bengalee Language* and the work known as the *Dia-*

logues, or *Kathopakathan*, in which, in the words of De, "Carey's extraordinary command over colloquial Bengali is nowhere better exhibited." Here are parts, or in some cases paraphrases, of Sushil Kumar De's encomium on Carey's unparalleled achievements: "[T]he extent and variety of topics, the different classes of men dealt with . . . show not only a minute and sympathetic observation and familiarity with the daily occupations of the people, their manners, feelings and ideas but also a thorough acquaintance with the resources of the language in its difficult colloquial forms. The book is indeed a rich quarry of the idioms . . . of the spoken dialect of Bengal."[120] His work is a faithful reflection of the social life of both middle and lower classes in Bengal in the early nineteenth century, and the social range of his characters is truly astonishing, from a respectable Bengali gentleman, a merchant, a landlord, and a Brahman priest to the peasant, a low-class woman, a day laborer, a fisherman, and a beggar. Even in the present day, the work has not lost all the force and precision of its realism. But what of Carey's place in Bengali literature? De replies, "To Carey belongs the credit of having raised the language from its debased condition of an unsettled dialect to the character of a regular and permanent form of speech, capable, as in the past, of becoming the refined and comprehensive vehicle of a great literature in the future."[121]

Carey's wider influence and larger sympathies for Bengali culture and people are also praised by De. He encouraged many Bengali scholars, whom he counted as his friends, and with the aid of the Mission Press at the Serampore, Carey devoted himself to printing the first efforts of native literary talent. Many Bengali classics were printed at the mission and were made available to the general public, perhaps for the first time. Thanks to the enthusiasm of Carey, editions of the *Ramayana* and *Annadamangal* of Bharatchandra were published and remained the standard texts for many years.[122] As the celebrated lexicographer and scholar Ram Kamal Sen wrote, "I must acknowledge here that whatever has been done towards the revival of the Bengali language, its improvement, and in fact, the establishment of it as a language, must be attributed to that excellent man, Dr. Carey, and his colleagues, by whose liberality and great exertions, many works have been carried through the press, and the general tone of the language of the province has been greatly raised."[123]

William Carey's empathy for Indians was expressed in a speech before Lord Wellesley at a public disputation of the college:

> I, now an old man, have lived for a long series of years among the Hindoos. I have been in the habit of preaching to multitudes daily, of discoursing with the Brahmans on every subject, and of superintending schools for the instruction of

> the Hindoo youth. Their language is as familiar to me as my own. This close intercourse with the natives for so long a period, and in different parts of our empire, had afforded me opportunities of information not inferior to those which have hitherto been presented to any other person. I may say indeed that their manners, customs, habits, and sentiments are as obvious to me as if I was myself a native.[124]

As noted earlier, a department was established for each major language, and each department had a number of Indian scholars as a part of the college staff. Research and later publications were inaugurated in collaboration with the Mission Press of Serampore and the Asiatic Society of Bengal. Many of the graduates of the college were to distinguish themselves in Orientalist studies, perhaps the most famous being H. T. Prinsep, Holt Mackenzie, James C. C. Sutherland, Graves C. Haughton, and A. Tod, while the most famous of the Indian scholars included Ramram Basu and Bidyalankar. This collaborative effort led to impressive results of Orientalist scholarship. Many of the British students left essays written in Indian languages, showing not only remarkable linguistic ability but equally remarkable empathy for Indian culture and peoples. These students felt that it was the duty of the English to help Indians recover the sources of their ancient and venerable civilizations, to "bring to light their various forms of government with their Institutions, civil and religious; talents, which have hitherto lain smothered under the despondency of neglect now roused into exertion, shall be encouraged to produce to the world its prominent events and distinguished characters, with superior splendor."[125] So wrote an early student of the college, W. B. Martin. Another student, W. P. Eliot, emphasized that England should not ignore the achievements of Asian civilizations: "While the European world were hordes of barbarians, learning and science flourished in higher perfection in the East in some branches, probably to a greater degree of excellence than has ever been since attained."[126] None of these students saw India as immutably and irremediably backward. They all felt progress was possible, with the help of institutions like the College of Fort William, and the recovery of India's glorious past.

EUROPEAN ORIENTALISTS

Up to now I have concentrated on British Orientalists, since they are the ones most open to the charge of collaboration with the imperial powers, but it should not be forgotten that the pioneering efforts of Sir William Jones and the influence of the journal *Asiatick Researches* were responsible for the renewed interest in India, Hinduism, Jainism, and Buddhism among French, German, Danish, Hungarian, and Swedish scholars, all of whom contributed to our knowledge of Indian history, religion, language, and philosophy. Though the French and Portuguese, and for a short while the Dutch, did have an imperial toehold in India, other European nations did not. Some of the greatest Orientalists were German, and since they do not fit into Edward Said's crude scheme of things, they are neglected by him. I shall later look briefly at the life and work of the German Orientalist Max Müller. Before that I shall deal with France. It must not be thought that because the French had imperial ambitions, French Orientalists were busy plotting night and day, devising means to enslave Indians forever. The life of Anquetil-Duperron is a robust refutation of such a supposition, and I shall now turn to his contributions to Orientalist research.

Anquetil-Duperron

Anquetil-Duperron originally intended to enter the church but acquired early on a taste for Oriental languages, and he seems to have applied himself to Hebrew, Arabic, and Persian. He was enthralled when he came across fragments of the *Vendidad*, a part of the *Avesta* that is a collection of the sacred texts of the Zoroastrian religion, and decided to pursue his research and look for further manuscripts in India. He arrived in India in 1755 and stayed for seven years, often under the most difficult conditions. Far from being an accomplice of the imperialists, Anquetil-Duperron denounced the greedy European merchants who were sucking India dry of its riches. Here is a free translation of his romantic and rhetorical address to all Indians, victims of Western exploitation:

> Peaceloving Indians, ancient owners of a fertile land, you harvest in tranquility the fruits that it provides for your needs. Content with little, only the skies, by stopping the rain, could render you unhappy. Your internecine squabbling, and which nation does not have them? your disputes settled, or at least suspended by the arrival of the monsoon, do not leave in your countryside those signs of devastation with which the activity of the conqueror stamps, that is what the dominating character of a people is capable of.
>
> The Muslims annexed a part of your land, the most beautiful provinces of Hindustan, and left you your manners, customs, should I say? your laws. These were the most fanatical followers of the Arab Prophet, whose banners announced submission to the Koran or death; conquered as much by your gentleness as by the climate, one saw them setting aside this pride, this roughness which was the original character of their sect; they chose their ministers among

> your Brahmins, your Banias are their bankers; your Rajputs, their best soldiers: such that an observer has difficulty in distinguishing, by their habits, by the religion, between the province which obeys the Rajas [Hindus], and that which submits to the Nababs [Muslims].
>
> Was it necessary for the rumours of your riches to penetrate through to the climate where artificial needs have no limits? Soon new foreigners approached your frontiers; inconvenient guests, everything that they touched belonged to them: your squabbles maintained, and aggravated, by Agents who are powerful, and what is more, motivated by self-interest, so that your disputes become eternal: it is no matter that they have invaded your market, have tripled the price of basic foodstuffs, and as to merchandise, have altered its quality; manufacturing industry almost annihilated, the workers fleeing to the mountains, the dying son asking his father what he had done to these foreigners who take away rice from his mouth: nothing touches them, or softens their hearts: your gold, one said to the Peruvians, to the Mexicans: here, the revenue of Hindustan, that is what we demand, even at the cost of rivers of blood.
>
> At least, unhappy Indians, perhaps you will learn that in two hundred years, a European who has seen you, who has lived among you, has dared to ask on your behalf, and present to the Tribunal of the Universe, for your wounded rights, denied by a humanity tainted by a vile interest.[127]

The capture of Pondicherry, or Pondichéry, the French settlement in India, forced Anquetil-Duperron to return to Europe. He spent some time in London and Oxford before heading back to Paris in 1762, weighed down with 180 Oriental manuscripts. With the help of Abbé Barthélemy, Anquetil-Duperron got a post at the Royal Library, was elected to the Academy of Inscriptions, and began the publication and translations of the materials he had gathered in India. In 1771 he published his *Zend Avesta* in three volumes, a collection of the religious texts of the Zoroastrians, a life of Zarathustra, and various fragments. In 1778 came his *Legislation Orientale*, reproaching Montesquieu for misrepresenting Oriental systems of government. His *Récherches historiques et géographiques sur l'Inde* (Research into the History and Geography of India) appeared in 1786. Between 1802 and 1804, Anquetil-Duperron published a Latin translation of some *Upanishads* from the Persian, a work that made a lasting impression on Schopenhauer and his philosophy. For Anquetil-Duperron the *Zend* books and the *Upanishads* "present the same truths as the works of the Platonic philosophers, and perhaps these philosophers received them from the oriental philosophers,"[128] and these discoveries led to a spiritual universality.[129] His writings manifest a profound gratitude toward and great concern for the well-being of India.

For Raymond Schwab, 1771—the year *Zend Avesta* was published—was one of great significance in world history, because Anquetil-Duperron opened up the East to Europe; "The 1771 edition of the *Zend Avesta* marks the first approach to an Asian text totally independent of the biblical and classical traditions. The history *of* languages and history *through* languages both begin with this work, which is also, we could say, the beginning of world history."[130] Furthermore, Anquetil-Duperron's translations of the *Avesta* and *Upanishads* mark the beginning of the influence of Oriental on European thought.

Max Müller

Max Müller was a German philologist, Orientalist, Sanskrit scholar, and editor of the Sacred Books of the East series, a fifty-volume set of English translations, many of which have since become the standard works on their respective subjects.

Like many an Orientalist, Müller began by mastering the classical languages and showed an early interest in Eastern ones, such as Arabic, Persian, and Sanskrit. He studied under the great philologist Franz Bopp, one of the founders of comparative philology as a discipline. Müller went to England in 1846 to work on various Sanskrit texts to be found in the libraries of the East India Company and at Oxford, where Müller eventually established an academic career. He was elected to Christ Church, Oxford, in 1851, and attained the chair of professor of comparative philology. He was later appointed Oxford's first professor of comparative theology at All Souls (1868–75). Müller once wrote that in his lectures he strove to "excite an appetite for knowledge, and to show how such knowledge may best be acquired."[131]

Müller devoted much of his time mastering Sanskrit, writing his first book on that language, *A History of Ancient Sanskrit Literature*, in 1859, followed by his scholarly edition of the *Rig Veda*. Müller's complex and subtle attitude toward Indian culture should be seen against the background of German cultural and intellectual history at the end of the eighteenth and the beginning of the nineteenth century. The German interest in India was the product of the romantic movement, which represented both an intellectual and an emotional urge: "For the Germans the knowledge of India was an ingredient in a process of becoming, by the acquisition of which they wanted to make their European personality deeper and fuller. They felt that India had thoughts and feelings which were different as well as complementary to theirs."[132] Müller retained the enthusiasm of the romantics and the intellectual and scientific curiosity of early scholars of Sanskrit, like Jones, Colebrooke, Wilson, and Wilkins. The results of Sanskrit studies would have value for all humanity, according to Müller, and would certainly regenerate the life of Hindus by "bringing their own cultural heritage to their knowledge."[133]

It is clear from his many popular lectures and books that Müller, like many of the Orientalists, saw his research and particularly his philology as a means of bringing cross-cultural understanding; there was no question of "the Other." Language is for Müller the strongest of ties: "I say intellectual kith and kin, because that kinship is far more important than mere kinship of blood. Blood may be thicker than water, but language is thicker than blood, at least to beings who, though for a time identifying themselves with flesh and blood, are themselves very different from mere flesh and blood." And, what is more, "If history is to teach us anything, it must teach us that there is a continuity which binds together the present and the past, the East and the West. And no branch of history teaches that lesson more powerfully than the history of language and the history of religion."[134] Binding together the East and the West, such was the goal of all Müller's scholarly endeavors.

Müller's writings are replete with his admiration and comprehension of, and insights into, Hindu literature, philosophy, and religious thought. Hindu scholars have always been appreciative of his contributions to scholarship about, and empathy for, Indian civilization. K. S. Ramaswami Sastri wrote a brief sympathetic biography of Müller in which he expresses his gratitude to the German scholar for his life's work.[135]

Müller himself wrote sympathetically of Indian reformers and scholars in his *Biographical Essays*, where he once again expressed his wish for East-West reconciliation: "If I live for one purpose it is for this, that I will preach the union of Eastern and Western philosophy, the reconciliation of Europe and Asia. The idea may seem absurd to many in the present age. It may provoke ridicule and angry reviling. But posterity will prove a better judge."[136] He wrote of Rammohun Roy, Keshub Chunder Sen, and Dayananda Sarasvati. In another collection of essays, *Auld Lang Syne*, Second Series, Müller also spoke of his friendships with Dwarkanath Tagore, Debendranath Tagore, Radhakhanta Deva, Nilakantha Goreh, and others.

Swami Vivekananda's extraordinary tribute to the great German scholar testifies to the nature of Müller's openness toward India:

> Although a world-moving scholar and philosopher, his learning and philosophy have only led him higher and higher to the realization of the spirit; his lower knowledge has, indeed, helped him to reach the higher. This is real learning. Knowledge gives rise to humility. Of what use is knowledge if it does not show us the way to the highest?
>
> And what love he bears towards India! I wish I had a hundredth part of that love for my own motherland. An extarordinary and at the same time intensely

active mind has lived and moved in the world of Indian thought for fifty years or more and watched the sharp interchange of light and shade in the interminable forest of Sanskrit literature with keen interest and heart-felt love, till they have all sunk into his whole soul and coloured his whole being.

Max Müller is a Vedantist of Vedantists. He has indeed caught the real soul of the melody of the Vedanta in the midst of all its settings of harmonies or discords—the one light that lightens up the sects and creeds of the world, the Vedanta, the one principle of which all religions are only applications.

His life has been a blessing to the world; may it be many, many years more, before he changes the present plane of his existence.[137]

Discovery of Buddhism and the Archaeological Survey of India

Naught but the Topes[138] *themselves remain to mock*
Time's ceaseless efforts; yet they proudly stand
Silent and lasting upon their parent rock,
And still as cities under magic's wand;
Till curious Saxons, from distant land,
Unlocked the treasures of two thousand years.

—*The Bhilsa Topes* (Anon.), 1854[139]

Then he composed himself reverently to listen to fragments hastily rendered into Urdu. For the first time he heard of the labours of European scholars, who by the help of these and a hundred other documents have identified the Holy Places of Buddhism.

—Rudyard Kipling, *Kim*, 1901

Surprisingly little of scholarly worth was known about Buddhism in the West until the nineteenth century. Megasthenes had mentioned certain ascetics called Sarmanes, and in the second century CE, Clement of Alexandria talked of Buddha, the primary god of the Indians. In early Christianity, the Buddhist notion of a *Bodhisattva* metamorphosed into St. Josaphat. Marco Polo mentioned that Kublai Khan revered a prophet called Sakyamuni Burkhan. The Portuguese in Ceylon in 1560 came into contact with certain Buddhist practices, and the English merchant adventurer Ralph Fitch observed firsthand ceremonies in Burma in 1586–87, as did the Jesuits and other missionaries in China in the seventeenth century. Robert Knox was kept as a prisoner in Ceylon for many years, managing to escape and return to London in 1680, when he began writing about his harrowing experiences, which included an account of Buddhism and its basic tenets that remained the fullest account of that religion in English until the nineteenth century.

India was the birthplace of Buddhism, and yet for many centuries no one had cared to record or preserve the monuments concerned with the life of Gautama. It was a familiar story of neglect, of wanton destruction by Muslim invaders, of doctrinal hostility felt by the Hindu Brahmins toward the precepts of this sister religion. For example, Mr. Stirling, who was responsible for the publication of the findings of the Dauli Buddhist inscriptions, recorded this reaction when he showed them to Brahmins; "The Brahmins refer to the inscription with shuddering and disgust, to the *Budh Ka Amel*, or the time when Buddhist doctrines prevailed, and are reluctant even to speak on the subject."[140] In 1799 Colin Mackenzie had visited the village of Amaravati, where the local rajah had dug up several curious mounds thinking they might contain something of value, but when Walter Elliot returned to the same village in 1845, he found that "every fragment of former excavations" had been "carried away and burnt into lime."[141] During his brief governorship of Java, Stamford Raffles was responsible for ordering the excavations of the spectacular Buddhist site of Borobudur: "From local Muslim records, [Raffles] established that Islam had effectively obliterated Buddhism on the island in the thirteenth century."[142] The Ajanta caves, containing the astonishing Buddhist paintings, had been abandoned for centuries until rediscovered by Lt. James Alexander in 1824, and the same story could be told about other Buddhist sites rediscovered by Europeans.

Then a group of Europeans, with an insatiable thirst for knowledge, scientific curiosity, and energy, slowly and patiently put together the story of Buddhism in India, in the process recovering texts in Tibetan, Sanskrit, and Pali, found on coins, inscriptions, and sculptures. They excavated and restored monuments that are the pride of all Indians, and a source of consolation for Buddhists everywhere. There were the British scholars, soldiers, and administrators, such as Francis Buchanan, Colin Mackenzie, Alexander Cunningham, and Brian Hodgson, who wrote, "my respect for science in general led me cheerfully to avail myself of the opportunity afforded, by my residence in a Bauddha country, for collecting and transmitting to Calcutta the materials for such investigation";[143] James Fergusson, and James Prinsep; Frenchmen such as Joseph Eudelin de Joinville and Eugène Burnouf; a Hungarian, the eccentric Csoma de Koros, who was "like one of the sages of antiquity, and taking no interest in any object around him, except his literary avocations";[144] all played a part in recovering the lost history of one of the great religions in the world.

Both the Asiatic Society of Bengal and the later Asiatic Society of Bombay, and their respective journals, served as essential for the scientific discussion of new discoveries, aided, though rather erratically, by government acts—for example, the Bengal Regulation XIX of 1810, which allowed the authorities to intervene and protect imperiled monuments. In 1861 Lord Canning took up a plan first proposed by Prinsep in 1848 for an Indian archaeological survey. He gave his blessing to such a survey, which would be "an accurate description—illustrated by plans, measurements, drawings or photographs and by copies of inscriptions—of such remains as deserve notice, with the history of them so far as it may be traceable, and a record of the traditions that are retained regarding them."[145] Lord Lawrence preferred the local governments to list the historical buildings under their rule, and hence the survey was abandoned, only to be revived in 1871 with Alexander Cunningham as director general of the archaeological survey, a distinct department of the government. The department was given the task of making "a complete search over the whole country, and a systematic record and description of all architectural and other remains that are either remarkable for their antiquity, or their beauty or their historical interest."[146]

Cunningham and later James Burgess were faced with an enormous responsibility, which they discharged magnificently, and the amount of work they managed to get done is truly staggering. Surveys were conducted in Delhi and Agra in 1871; Rajputana, Bundelkhand, Mathura, Bodh Gaya, and Gaur in 1872; the Punjab in 1873; Central Province, Bundelkhand, and Malwa between 1873 and 1877. Discoveries included monolithic capitals and other remains of Asoka, specimens of architecture of the Gupta and post-Gupta periods; great stupa of Bharhut; identification of ancient cities such as Sankisa, Sravasti, and Kausambi. In 1872 James Burgess founded the journal *Indian Antiquary*, where important inscriptions and their decipherment by such scholars as Johann Georg Bühler, John Faithfull Fleet, and Julius Eggeling were published, while Cunningham brought out a volume of *Corpus Inscriptionum Indicarum.* Cunningham persuaded the government to set up an epigraphical survey to cope with the increasing number of inscriptions in need of translation and deciphering. Burgess founded the journal *Epigraphica Indica* in 1888, edited by distinguished scholars such as Bühler, F. Kielhorn, and Eggeling, and published twenty volumes on archaeological subjects, seven of them forming a part of the monumental *Archaeological Survey of India, New Imperial Series.*[147]

James Prinsep's contribution to Buddhist and archaeological studies deserves special mention. Prinsep arrived in India in 1819 and, being of a democratic temperament, was disappointed to see Calcutta society divided along racial lines. He was determined to win the confidence and respect of Indians. The opportunity to be of public service came when he was appointed assay-master in the Banares mint. Prinsep improved the sanitation of the holy city by draining "the pools and swamps at the back of the city, a source of malarial agues and fevers, by means of a tunnel that ran under part of the city into the river."[148] Indians treated him with reverence henceforth, and Prinsep further endeared himself to them by a subsequent characteristically generous gesture. The Indian community had presented him with the drained ground, now worth a considerable sum, but Prinsep leveled the ground and had a large bazaar built on it. He then gave the land back to the town though he was himself in need. It is no wonder the town treated him as a hero. Prinsep also took apart stone by stone the mosque of Aurangzeb, which had begun to slip into the river. After strengthening the foundation, Prinsep had the mosque reconstructed. He built a bridge of five arches of large span over the Karamnasa, just outside Banares, to the eternal gratitude of pilgrims who, in the past, had had to pay Brahmins to take them across on piggyback.

Everyone who met him was struck by his enthusiasm, desire for learning, and eagerness to communicate scientific knowledge. As a contemporary once said, Prinsep was one of "the most talented and useful Englishmen ever to work in India. Of his intellectual character, the most prominent feature was enthusiasm, a burning, irrepressible enthusiasm, to which nothing could set bounds [which led him] to apply his mind powers to a greater range of subjects than any human mind can master or excel in."[149] He collaborated with Major J. D. Herbert on the journal *Gleanings in Science*, whose object was "to make known in India the discoveries or advances in art and science made in Europe."[150] When Prinsep succeeded Wilson as the secretary of the Asiatic Society of Bengal, he also became the editor of the *Journal of the Asiatic Society*, which absorbed *Gleanings*. During his seven-year editorship of the *Journal*, Prinsep was to make major discoveries, which deserve to be ranked as high as we rank any discovery in the physical sciences. Prinsep was able to decipher the hitherto unreadable scripts of the most ancient of Indian insriptions, thereby helping complete the puzzle of the origins and history of Buddhism. The Brahmi script was used on the pillars at Delhi and Allahabad and on many rock inscriptions in various parts of India, while the Kharosthi script was found on the coins of the northwest: "He demonstrated that the pillar and rock inscriptions were put up by the emperor Asoka Maurya, whose dates could be approximately fixed through his references to contemporary kings of western Asia in the third century BCE. They allowed the first verified correlation of Indian history and archaeology with those of the Western world."[151] The details of the deciphering have been narrated in Charles Allen's *The Buddha and the Sahibs*,[152] an eloquent defense of the Orientalist enterprise.

The Curious Case of Edward Said and Raymond Schwab

On a number of occasions Said quotes Raymond Schwab, both his *La Renaissance Orientale* and his *La Vie d'Anquetil-Duperron*, approvingly, and Said praises him for his convincing arguments (p. 115) and comprehensive analysis (p. 137). Furthermore, the English translation of Schwab's *La Renaissance Orientale* even carries a foreword by the egregious Said. All of this would lead one naturally to think, perhaps, that Schwab somehow had anticipated and endorsed Said's enterprise, since Schwab's *La Renaissance Orientale* was first published in 1950, twenty-eight years before *Orientalism.* Said has already tried to bamboozle readers into thinking that R. W. Southern somehow supported his own arguments: Notice Said's "brilliantly shown" (p. 61), "the best part of Southern's analysis" (p. 62), and "elegantly shown" (p. 55), to seduce the reader into thinking Southern has almost anticipated Said's own conclusions. As I *brilliantly* show, Southern did no such thing. Nor did Schwab.

If I persuade readers to study Schwab's *La Renaissance Orientale*, my efforts will not have been wasted. For Schwab's book is, on every one of its nearly five hundred pages, a direct, erudite refutation of everything that Said argues for in *Orientalism.* Page after page, Schwab *praises* the Orientalists, all those great scholars that Said can only sneer at. Sir William Jones, Colebrooke, Anquetil-Duperron, and so many others that make a fleeting, shameful appearance in *Orientalism* are paraded, trumpeted, hailed in *La Renaissance Orientale* as heroes, humanists, saviors, and valiant knights of knowledge, to be cherished in cultural history for having enriched Western civilization but also for having broken down cultural barriers, for having taken down the fences that Said wants to resurrect between East and West, between Us and Them.

It is difficult to know what exactly Said has against William Jones, who is accused of closing down vistas by his putatively sinister acts of "codifying, tabulating, comparing" (p. 77), whatever that means. Schwab, on the other hand, thinks Jones has altered our ways of thinking,[153] and has transformed the partial humanism of the classics into the integral humanism of today. Jones is everywhere lauded and is considered the epitome of the dedicated Orientalist, the leading light of Schwab's book. Jones is described as "a well-read jurist, affable and brilliant, enthusiastic and spontaneous." Jones's "open-hearted nature and his curiosity, his penetrating intuition, his ardor, and his grace can all be read in his feature."[154]

"It is fitting that [Jones's] name should be given," continues Schwab, "to a formerly mythical tree: *Jonesia asoka.* Jones was interested in everything, uncovering and compiling information in many fields: Indian chronology, literature, music, fauna and flora. He discovered and guided others to the summits of poetry and philosophy."[155] Jones was spirited and fired with enthusiasm, and his "precious insights" later proved correct and fruitful.[156] There are more than seventy references to Jones in Schwab's book, in which Jones's merits, influence, and contributions to science are recounted and extolled.

Schwab deals handsomely with all the other English Orientalists as well. Here he describes Colebrooke's achievements:

> In 1819 he donated his priceless collection of oriental manuscripts to the East India Company library. His precision, patience, insight, and mental poise produced marvellous results in a work that has not become outdated after more than a century of admiration: the *Essays on the Religion and Philosophy of the Hindus*. Written on topics he had studied thoroughly during the first years of his stay in India, Colebrooke allowed his work to ripen thirty years before publishing it. It exerted a decisive influence in European intellectual circles. Like Anquetil, Colebrooke had a respect for human variety. His constant submission to rational truth, both as a scholar and magistrate, led him to work with positive facts, with equivalent components of a whole, with beliefs different from his own. This kind of integrity is a credit to the English school, which exhibited lofty examples of it, and compensates for the political insensitivities of certain men of action and the blindness of a certain kind of faith. Colebrooke must also be credited, again like Anquetil, with the intransigence that led him to denounce bluntly what he considered faulty or criminal in the colonial methods of his nation. As early as 1795, he did just that in a memorandum on commercial dealings in Bengal, and he continued to do so at every opportunity.[157]

Schwab honors *all* the English Orientalists—"credit to the English school"—and their integrity, and, what is more, explicitly disassociates Colebrooke from any complicity with the imperial power. Schwab writes, "The moral character of the first English Indic scholars was discernible in their open struggle against colonial policies."[158] That, surely, rips Said's thesis to shreds.

Schwab also has some words of praise for Hastings, considering him as a great benefactor in the history of Indic studies. It was thanks to Hastings's genuine love of Indian culture and her peoples that Hindu pandits agreed to collaborate with English scholars.[159]

Said makes the outlandish accusation that the great French scholar Silvestre de Sacy "doctored" the texts that he gathered in the East (p. 127), giving no evidence for this slanderous charge. For Schwab, on the other hand, Sacy is another Orientalist hero: a "great architect of the new linguistics,"[160] one of the fathers of Oriental studies.

> [Sacy] patiently explored the manuscripts and meticulously, with flashes of intuition, drew a method from them, as well as material for the first textbooks. As nothing outwitted him, or tired him, his inquiry extended to the limits of philosophy, developing in the process theories of general grammar and perspectives on the life of idioms. He produced a treatise on the philosophy of language, the first to be backed by rigorous experience, which became widely known and ultimately gave rise to the new linguistics. Bopp, understandably, soon hastened from Mainz to enroll in Sacy's courses, from which comparative grammar was to emerge. The entire family of great orientalists was beginning to take notice of Sacy's ideas. His classroom teaching had an even greater impact than his innumerable publications, and his most enduring contribution, like that of many of his successors, was his students, who went on to become masters because of their contact with him.[161]

Raymond Schwab's *La Renaissance Orientale* is even more profoundly anti-Saidian than the examples that I have given above would suggest, for Schwab chronicles how the learning, the intellectual curiosity, the scientific results of the research, and the sheer enthusiasm of the Orientalists deeply transformed the cultural, religious, and intellectual life of the West. Western writers, poets, novelists, essayists, historians, literary critics, and men of letters, far from treating these discoveries of the Orientalists as alien to their interests and tastes, took them to heart, learned from them, meditated on them, and wrote poems, novels, tales, and commentaries revealing a new sensibility, a new openness. Many of the great names in eighteenth- and nineteenth-century Western literature, philosophy, and culture pass through Schwab's rich work: Goethe, Chateaubriand, Lamartine, Victor Hugo, Byron, Hegel, Herder, Heine, Michelet, the Schlegels, Sainte-Beuve, Wagner, Voltaire, and so on.

> *What Professor Said and his many supporters have consistently failed to ask is where we would be without the Orientalists. They . . . were products of the Enlightenment that transformed European thinking in the late eighteenth century, modern men who saw the world differently from their predecessors. As Orientalists they initiated the recovery of South Asia's lost past. The European discovery of Buddhism and the subsequent resurgence of Buddhism in South Asia arose directly out of their activities. They established the methodology upon which the subcontinent's own historians, archaeologists, philologists and students continue to base their studies. What Said and his supporters seem to find objectionable about this process is that these young men were Westerners.*
>
> —Charles Allen, *The Buddha and the Sahibs*[162]

It should be apparent by now that the Orientalists working in and on India were primarily motivated by intellectual curiosity. It is true that many of them did work in the early days for the East India Company and the British administration in India, but they were not given directives from some central command to devise ways to keep the "natives down." It is true that dictionaries and digests of Hindu and Islamic law did help them administer the Indian population under their jurisdiction, but this seems to me eminently rational, that is, to seek means to better discharge their duties and responsibilities in the most humane way possible without disturbing the traditions and mores of the different communities. Instead of imposing alien laws, the British tried to rule in as rational and equitable a manner as possible, by talking to Indians in their own languages and by applying their own laws. In this endeavor, the rulers were aided by the Orientalists. But this only constituted a minute part of their Orientalist research. Many of them were already proficient in Greek and Latin and were fascinated by Oriental languages from a philological point of view, with some begnning their Oriental research before setting foot in India. Jones, for example, published *A Grammar of the Persian Language* in 1771, whereas he only arrived in India in 1783. In fact, had Jones been elected to Parliament, he would never have set foot in India. Jones was aware of the usefulness of his *Grammar* to the rulers, but he had hoped that "the civil and natural history of such mighty empires as India, Persia, Arabia, and Tartary cannot fail of delighting those who love to view the great picture of the universe, or to learn by what degrees the most obscure states have risen to glory, and the most flourishing kingdoms have sunk to decay: the philosopher will consider those works as highly valuable, by which he may trace the human mind in all its various appearances, from the rudest to the most cultivated state: and the man of taste will undoubtedly be pleased to unlock the stores of native genius, and to gather the flowers of unrestrained and luxuriant fancy."[163]

Far from stereotyping Indians, the Orientalists were perfectly aware of the differences and nuances of caste, class, language, and religion. Many of them spoke at least two or three of the vernacular languages, and, far from considering Indians inferior, were convinced they were heirs to a far greater civilization than that of Europe. It was precisely the knowledge they uncovered that made educated Europeans realize that their civilization was not as old as those of the East, and how much was owed to the East. It is true that many Orientalists found the contemporary India in a state of decay and neglect, but that is because it *was* in such a lamentable state, and this has been confirmed by Indian scholars themselves; I have quoted them above. Nor did they think that India was incapable of change; on the contrary, they went about creating ways to improve the education, health, and life of Indians generally, by creating schools, founding scientific journals, teaching of recent discoveries in Europe, and, of course, above all, by teaching them of their own cultural heritage.

Many Orientalists already had mastered the classics, Greek and Latin, and modern European languages. Hence the Indian languages were a challenge to their linguistic abilities and a means of assuaging their linguistic and intellectual curiosity. Orientalists recovered, preserved, saved, edited, deciphered, and translated the primary sources of our knowledge of India: manuscripts, coins, inscriptions and monuments, and archaeological remains. They wrote and compiled tools necessary for the further study of language, literature, and history: dictionaries, grammars, and commentaries. They established learned societies and journals for the objective discussion of modern research. They wrote histories where none existed, they uncovered the history of Buddhism, they deciphered long forgotten scripts. They taught methodology where none had existed, they introduced disciplines that had never existed in India, such numismatics. It is often said that Norman Kemp Smith's English translation of Kant's German classic *The Critique of Pure Reason* made it available to many Germans themselves for the first time. Similarly, it is no exaggeration to say the Orientalists translated Sanskrit works that became accessible to ordinary Indians for the first time.

If one adds the work of non-English Orientalists like the Germans Bühler, Müller, and Deussen; or the French Anquetil-Duperron, Eugène Burnouf, Silvestre de Sacy; or the Danish Rask and Westergaard; or the Norwegian-German Christian Lassen, and so many others, they make Said's arguments even less plausible.

When they returned to England, English Orientalists carried on their research and founded still more learned Asiatic societies and equally learned journals, bearing witness to the fact that India had become their lifelong passion. Many, like Colebrooke, died poor, and certainly none made any financial gains from their intellectual endeavors. Many of them had Indian friends, and many were devoted to ameliorating the conditions and life of Indians generally. All were appreciated by Indian scholars themselves. Nirad Chaudhuri devoted a whole biography to Max Müller, while P. T. Nair is working on a two-volume biography of James Prinsep. There is a fine study of T. W. Rhys Davids, the pioneering scholar of Pali and Buddhism, by Ananda Wickremeratne.[164] The Indian scholar O. P. Kejariwal has written a tribute to the work of the Asiatic Society of Bengal, in which he explicitly takes issue with Edward Said. Kejariwal writes,

> This work [i.e., his own *The Asiatic Society of Bengal, 1784–1838*] hopes to establish, maybe to a limited extent, that the world of scholarship and the world of administration during this period were worlds apart and not necessarily complementary to each other. Although most of the scholars were in civil service,

> they were rarely extended patronage by the administration. Nor is there much evidence that the administration directed in any manner their scholarly efforts. Thus each scholar pursued the subject of his interest. Jones was fascinated by ancient Indian literature, especially poetry and drama; Colebrooke, Davis, Burrow, Edward Strachey and others took up the ancient Indian sciences; Wilson, Paterson, Mackenzie, Hodgson, Csoma and Turnour, the ancient religious and historical texts; and Prinsep, Masson, Mill, Cautley, Conolly, Cunningham, Burt and many others ancient inscriptions, archaeology and numismatics. Each of these, and many other scholars worked independently of the administration and with whatever time and energy their official work left them at the end of the day.[165]

Kejariwal endorses A. L. Rowse's conclusion, "It was one of the long-term ironies of history that it was British rule that led to the renaissance of India, consciousness of her identity and her past, the ultimate emergence of Indian nationalism."[166]

5

WESTERN ARCHAEOLOGISTS

We must not forget that archaeologists were equally Orientalists who also gave back to humankind its prehistory and history, "wresting the facts of history from the material remains of the past."[1] Archaeology was, as Glyn Daniel reminds us, a creation of the Victorians, with the years between 1840 and 1900 as the creative period for discovery and the development of scientific method.[2] But it was a truly European endeavor, emerging out of English antiquarianism, flowering under the research of Danish and Swedish prehistorians such as C. J. Thomsen, J. J. A. Worsae, Sven Nilsson, L. S. Vedel Simonsen, and H. Hildebrand, and coming of scientific age under Heinrich Schliemann, A. H. Lane Fox Pitt-Rivers, and William Matthew Flinders Petrie. Daniel also reinforces our theses that a thirst for knowledge, a natural curiosity, an interest in languages derived from their classical education, which gave them a thorough philological grounding in Greek and Latin, led Western men and women to the study of the past.[3] Daniel wrote, "Four natural curiosities have prompted the study of the prehistoric human past. . . . The first is an interest in the immediate ancestors of known historic peoples. . . . The second is a natural interest in the non-functional aspects of the present landscape, and in the objects belonging to early man which turn up from time to time through ordinary activities such as ploughing, gardening, or digging drains. . . . [Who built these monuments? Who fashioned and used the stone tools?] These are all natural questions, and they have for hundreds of years predisposed curious men to an interest in antiquarian studies." Encounters with non-Mediterranean peoples also prompted questions as to their origins. The fourth natural curiosity is "the natural curiosity as to how man and his culture came into being, the mechanics of cultural origins and change."[4]

Seton Howard Frederick Lloyd wrote of men like Henry Rawlinson, C. J. Rich, W. K. Loftus, W. F. Ainsworth, and A. H. Layard: "Yet whatever the motive which originally brought them to the country, they one and all remained captivated by the increasing fascination of its antiquities, and their purposeful application to archaeology made Assyriology a science."[5]

Until the twentieth century, archaeologists were exclusively Europeans and Americans, with the exception of Christian Rassam and his brother Hormuzd, two Assyrian Christians. However, the Rassams were not archaeological pioneers and were initially only assistants, overseers, and general agents of Austen Layard, who was responsible for their training, particularly of Hormuzd. Taking Mesopotamia as an example, the general population was either totally apathetic to the excavations of the pioneers like Layard or hostile to their activities on religious grounds. Since by Islamic doctrine, everything—from history to material remains—predating the arrival of Islam was considered of no intrinsic worth, any prehistoric sculptures were to be destroyed as signs of idolatry. Lloyd sums up the situation concerning the artifacts of ancient Iraq:

> Mesopotamia in the nineteenth century was a neglected province of a decaying empire, for the most part shamefully administered by corrupt Ottoman officials. The Arab peoples of the country had reached so low an ebb that their rights were in abeyance and their traditions almost forgotten. For all the manly virtues which they inherited from their imperial ancestors, six centuries of oppression had left them backward and ignorant. In the realm of antiquities, derived, after all, from what they had been taught to consider a heretical age [*jahiliyya*, or the time of ignorance], it would have been absurd to expect them to understand the value, intrinsic or otherwise, of these monuments which chance had located within their territory, let alone the necessity for their preservation. The Westerner, therefore, who considered the stones of Assyria a world-heritage could hardly be blamed for preferring to see them installed in a museum within reach of an epigraphist, rather than rotting in a mound where a chance rainstorm might leave them at the mercy of Arab gypsum-burners.
>
> Up to the last years of the century and the appearance of individuals like Hamdi Bey, the Turks also had been equally indifferent to the fate of pre-Islamic monuments. Indeed, they had often enough opposed and obstructed the activities of Western excavators, but for the wrong reasons. Their opposition was almost always actuated by religious prejudice, personal spite or ordinary malice.[6]

To illustrate the above points, I shall briefly look at aspects of the lives of two pioneering archaeologists, Henry Rawlinson and Austen Layard, both active in Mesopotamia from 1840 onward.

Henry Rawlinson had shown considerable courage, physical agility, persistence, and patience in his attempt to copy the great cuneiform inscription carved into the side of a mountain at Behistun (Bisitun) in Persia. His modern biographer tells us, "He not only had the dedication and skill to copy the inscription, but he also possessed the linguistic abilities to tackle the decipherment, impelled by an unquenchable thirst for knowledge of history and ancient geography and a driving ambition to be first in anything he undertook."[7]

Rawlinson himself wrote, "[Ambition] must not be sought in politics, but in letters—and in that line also I am accordingly still at work. I have published my first memoir on Persian Antiquities and . . . shall thus at any rate be handed down to posterity as having contributed a new chapter to the History of the Earth. I hope however to do much more than this." He felt that intellectual curiosity was also essential: "In my own case it is so certainly. I have now a certain pleasure in discovery *for its own sake only*."[8] The thought that he might be able "to add a new chapter to the history of the world, and thus secure the approbation of all lovers of knowledge" also spurred him on.[9] Knowledge, as John Dewey might have put it, is its own excuse. While in Bombay Rawlinson wrote of his passion for reading and books: "I seldom went to bed without being conscious that I had gained some information in the course of the day of which I had been ignorant when I arose—there is something extremely gratifying in being conscious of continual progression in knowledge,"[10] and, "[f]rom this time [1829 onward] dates my passion for books."[11]

Rawlinson was sent to India as a cadet under the East India Company at the age of seventeen. He learned Hindustani, Marathi, and Persian during his six years as subaltern, after which he was sent to Persia to help organize the shah's troops. Like many an Orientalist in India, Rawlinson on his arrival in Persia applied himself "with diligence to the study of the history, geography, literature and antiquities of the country."[12] While based at Tabriz, Rawlinson was able to explore the regions south and southeast of Tabriz, "constantly compiling notes on the antiquities, villages, tribes and countryside."[13] He met Kurdish tribesmen, whom he found "a remarkably fine, active, and athletic race."[14] And like his fellow Orientalists in India, Rawlinson developed an empathy for many of the peoples he encountered, and, given his gift for languages, was soon able to communicate with many remote tribesmen in their own dialects. He much preferred their manners to those of the city dwellers: "I had no reason to complain of want of courtesy, but, I confess, the rough sterling kindness of the tribes has always pleased me far better than the jaunty bearing of the city fashionables."[15]

At the same time, Rawlinson himself during his five years had made a deep impression on the people of Persia as this account, published in the *Times*, confirms:

> [Travelers to that country a few years later] found that one Englishman had left such a name among every class of society that a letter from him would have been a passport throughout the whole of Persia. That gentleman was Major Rawlinson, of Baghdad, who was supposed to be gifted with almost supernatural powers, as he could dispute with the Mollahs of Ispahan, could write and speak the Persian tongue, was deeply skilled in the poetical learning of that country . . . there was no European who had made such an impression on the population of Persia, and that not merely on the learned societies or the higher and polished societies, which had been aptly called "the French of the East," but his influence extended to the wild chiefs of Koordistan, who respected him as the best shot and the boldest rider they had ever seen.[16]

Rawlinson, was appointed political agent in Ottoman Arabia, a post that enabled him to settle in Baghdad, where he could devote time to cuneiform studies. He turned down a far more prestigious and better paid appointment, the Residency of Nepal, preferring, as he put it, "to work at my old friends the Cuneiforms, although the appointment was of inferior rank and pay—and involved complete Isolation." It had become "the ambition of my life to carry on my cuneiform researches."[17]

Rawlinson, when he had seen that there were three different languages on the Behistun rock, had simply called them Class I, Class II, and Class III. Greatly aided by what he learned from scholars such as Christian Lassen and Eugène Burnouf, Rawlinson managed to decipher and translate approximately two hundred lines of the Behistun inscription between April 1838 and January 1839. However, the final manuscript of his labors on Persian cuneiform, Class I, was not finished until 1845, and appeared in three issues of the *Journal of the Royal Asiatic Society* in 1846 and 1847, amounting to 349 pages, the result of eleven years of work. He was now determined to look at the Class III inscription. The Class III language was thought to be Semitic, and, accordingly, Rawlinson set about learning Hebrew and perfecting his Arabic. By 1850 Rawlinson had nearly finished his masterpiece, *Memoir on the Babylonian and Assyrian Inscriptions*, which eventually came out in January 1852. The latter work contained a partial translation into Latin of "the Class III inscription from Behistun, accompanied by a list of 246 Babylonian-Assyrian characters, and more than a hundred pages of discussion of their meaning and pronunciation. The cuneiform text itself was reproduced on seventeen plates."[18]

Rawlinson always inspired affection from the people who worked with him, particularly in Baghdad. Sir Wallis Budge tells this charming ancedote of Rawlinson's standing in Mesopotamia. Budge met a certain Yaqub, a clerk at the

British Residency in Baghdad who had known and adored Rawlinson. When Yaqub discovered that Budge had letters from Rawlinson, the clerk was overcome with emotions and asked eagerly after his revered former master. Budge continues, "In answer to my questions he [Yaqub] told me that he had been employed in the Residency all his life, and that of all the Consuls-General whom he had served he respected and loved and admired Rawlinson most of all. In knowledge and learning he was, he said 'like God,' as a horseman he was like Antar [an Arab hero], as a king he was like Nimrod, and when he spoke at the Majlis [Town Council] of Baghdad the heart of the Wali Pasha melted, and the knees of his councillors gave way under them." By the end such was Rawlinson's power and influence that "had he taken one dog, and put his English hat on his head and sent him to the Serai, all the people of the bazaar would have made way for him, and bowed to him, and the soldiers would have stood still and presented arms to him as he passed, and the officials in the Serai would have embraced him; and if he had sent another dog with another of his hats across the river to Kazimen, the Shiites and the Sunnites would have stopped fighting each other, and would have asked him to drink coffee with them."[19]

Austen Layard recounts how in his childhood, growing up in Florence, he spent his days reading the romances of Sir Walter Scott, being particularly fond of those set in the Near East, *The Betrothed* and *The Talisman*. "But," Layard continues in his autobiography, "the work in which I took the greatest delight was the 'Arabian Nights.' I was accustomed to spend hours stretched upon the floor, under a great gilded Florentine table, poring over this enchanting volume. My imagination became so excited by it that I thought and dreamt of little else but 'jins' and 'ghouls' and fairies and lovely princesses, until I believed in their existence. . . . My admiration for the 'Arabian Nights' has never left me. I can read them even now with almost as much delight as I read them when a boy. They have had no little influence upon on my life and career; for to them I attribute that love of travel and adventure which took me to the East, and led me to the discovery of the ruins of Nineveh. They give the truest, the most lively, and the most interesting picture of manners and customs which still existed amongst Turks, Persians and Arabs when I first mixed with them, but which are now fast passing away before European civilisation and encroachments."[20]

Later at school in England, Layard continued to devour any works, whether novels or books of travel, concerned with the East.[21] He also admired the works of Disraeli, whom he had met frequently through his aunt and uncle, for "I looked upon him, moreover, as a great traveller in Eastern lands, which had a mysterious attraction for me, and with which my earliest dreams were associated."[22]

From a young age, Layard professed political opinions that were "very radical and democratic. I was even accused of preaching sedition and revolution, and of attempting to corrupt my school-fellows, and to incite them to rebellion."[23] Meetings with Polish refugees in London later confirmed him in his radicalism.[24] Layard always admired anyone, like the Polish and Italian patriots who stood for liberty, and felt that detestation of oppression and persecution "must ever exist in the minds of honest men."[25]

Layard also developed an early love of learning, thanks in part to the encouragement of the scholar Henry Crabb Robinson: "Mr. Robinson was a constant contributor of articles on political and literary subjects to Reviews. He frequently employed me in making translations and extracts for him from Italian, French, and Latin works, and 'looking up' subjects upon which he happened to be writing. This occupation increased my thirst for knowledge, and my desire to follow literary pursuits."[26] Layard spent all his money on books, and all of his time reading.

Layard developed a deep respect for the ordinary Muslims, whether Turk, Arab, or Kurd, often preferring them to the corrupt, cruel officials administering Ottoman Arabia. But even among the bureaucrats and diplomats at the court of the sultan, Layard was able to cultivate deep friendships. He treated each person individually, and was never hasty in his judgments, being sensitive to the often difficult situations of his many Turkish and Arab friends, who were constantly trying to ameliorate the lot of ordinary tribesmen or citizens under their jurisdiction. Here is Layard on the civility of the Turks: "[Travelers like Sir Charles Fellows] spoke to us in the highest terms of the Turkish populations—of their honesty, hospitality, and courtesy to strangers, and expressed their conviction that we should run no danger whatever in trusting ourselves amongst them. Our experience in travelling through the European provinces of Turkey . . . fully confirmed their opinions. We had received the greatest attention and civility from the authorities and the people, and during the whole of our journey we had been exposed to no difficulty, and had not suffered the slightest loss. The person and property of travellers appeared to us indeed to be as safe as in England. We had certainly every reason to be well-satisfied with all we had seen of the Turks, and we did not hesitate to trust ourselves amongst them in Asia."[27] Later in a village on the slopes of Mount Olympus, Layard found the owner of the room kept for travelers, a "handsome, honest, dignified Turk, in his wide turban and flowing garments, who bade us welcome. . . . We spent a very pleasant evening . . . I soon came to appreciate and to esteem these honest, simple, and hospitable Turks, and the more I saw them the more I liked them. A finer and more trustworthy population does not exist."[28] On his journey through Asia Minor, Layard praises Muslims and their concern for travelers and criticizes Christians for their selfishness: "In the middle of the day we came to a fountain of sweet, clear water, surrounded by a group of magnificent trees, tenanted by singing birds. It was a perfect oasis in the midst of the desert. . . . The fountain, as an inscription upon it testified, had been erected by some pious Mussulman for the thirsty traveller. These monuments of the charity and thoughtful care for others of devout Mohammedans are everywhere to be met with on the highways throughout the Turkish Empire. Their ruins may yet be seen in the provinces which have passed from the rule of the Osmanli to that of the Christian, who care little for the wants of others, and is solely intent upon improving his own condition, storing wealth, and persecuting those who differ from him in faith."[29]

As he continues on his travels, Layard encounters the Ourouks, a nomadic Turcoman tribe who were also "hospitable and attentive to their guests,"[30] and the Yezidis, who were equally welcoming.[31] In general, "The Turkish population were at all times polite and respectful to strangers, and in no country in the world would a traveller have received greater civility and hospitality than amongst the Osmanli of Asia Minor." But Layard fears that contact with Europeans will change them for the worse![32]

Despite the corruption of many petty officials, pashas, and governors, Layard still managed to meet men of exceptional abilities such as Namik Pasha, the governor of Thessaly in western Turkey, who gave him hope for the future of that country: "I was disposed to look upon him as one of the men who, by their honesty, abilities and enlightenment, might carry out the reforms initiated by Reshid Pasha, and save his country from the fate which even then appeared to menace it." While in Constantinople, Layard "formed an intimate friendship with Ahmed Vefyk," a diplomat who rose to be a grand vizier: "He was a perfect store of information on all manner of subjects, Western and Oriental, and had even then acquired a smattering of scientific knowledge, which he afterwards considerably extended. His remarkable capacity, his great acquirements, and his upright and honourable character, led his friends to believe that he would rise to the highest offices in the State, and he himself would talk as if he were persuaded that he would one day become Grand Vizier. [He did become the grand vizier.] He was the most cheerful, the most merry, and the most entertaining of companions. As he was always ready to impart information, and had none of the scruples and prejudices which prevented Turks from speaking to strangers, and especially to Europeans, of their domestic affairs." Ahmed's father was "a perfect Turkish gentleman, of the most refined manners, and of very dignified appearance."[33]

Layard admired and became friendly with another distinguished Turkish statesman, Fuad Effendi, who was, with the exception of Ahmed Vefyk, "the most informed and most enlightened Turk" that he knew: "He was ready to listen to arguments and reason, and to abandon his views when persuaded that they were erroneous. He had a fine presence, his countenance was handsome and intelligent, and his disposition and bearing were singularly conciliatory and dignified, uniting the refined courtesy of a European gentleman with the simple but high-bred manners of a Turkish statesman of the old school. He possessed much wit and humour, and his conversation was as entertaining and delightful as instructive. His library was extensive and well-selected, comprising a large selection of MSS, in Turkish, Persian, and Arabic languages, and the best editions of the French classics. He was well-read, and intimately acquainted with the history of his own country, as well as with that of Europe."[34]

Layard was forever trying to correct the misconceptions of Europeans concerning life in the Orient: "It was a great mistake to believe—as it was the fashion in Europeans countries to believe—that every Turk had a harem containing a multitude of wives, concubines, and female slaves who served as both. It was indeed an exception to find a Turkish gentleman, except one belonging to the old school, who possessed more than one wife."[35]

Layard, however, was no romantic who painted the Orient only in glowing colors. He was well aware of the persecution, suffering, and massacres of Christians (mainly Nestorians), of Jews, and of the Yezidis at the hands of bigoted Muslims. He was very careful, however, not to accept every story of every alleged massacre uncritically, verifying the evidence when possible.[36] Layard himself was faced with opposition in his archaeological excavations by religious fanaticism,[37] as had many of his predecessors, such as Claudius Rich. Layard recounts this story of Rich, who was a pioneer of field archaeology in Mesopotamia, and British Resident in Baghdad in 1808: "Rich learnt from the inhabitants of Mosul that, some time previous to his visit, a sculpture, representing various forms of men and animals, had been dug up in a mound forming part of the great inclosure. This strange object had been the cause of general wonder, and the whole population had issued from the walls to gaze upon it. The ulema [Muslim religious scholars] having at length pronounced that these figures were idols of the infidels, the Mohammedans, like obedient disciples, so completely destroyed them, that Mr. Rich was unable to obtain even a fragment."[38]

Layard came across similar hostile reactions to his work, and was conscious of the Islamic injunction against "idols of the Giaours" (infidels) as he had seen the Christian ruins of Bin-bir-Klissie, where the figures of Christian saints had their eyes scratched out, "and their faces, in some instances, totally destroyed, probably by fanatical Mussulmans, who had taken them for the idols of the Giaours."[39]

In general, there was incomprehension as to what the Europeans were up to in these excavations.[40] Many were convinced the French or the English were looking for treasure, gold or silver.[41] There was indifference to the historical significance of any of the remains. Many of the ancient sites were pillaged for their bricks to be used to build or repair the tombs of Muslim saints, and even sculptured heads were broken up for building purposes.[42] On some occasions, Arab workmen uncovering some Assyrian sculpture did get caught up in the general excitement, but many were equally frightened of the reactions of the religious scholars. Layard gives us this touching account of the puzzlement of the Arabs as to all the energy and money spent by the infidels on pieces of stone that were to be transported to Europe:

> The Arab Sheikh [Abd-ur-Rahman], his enthusiasm [excitement] once cooled down, gave way to moral reflections. "Wonderful! wonderful! There is surely no God but God, and Mohammed is his Prophet," exclaimed he after a long pause. "In the name of the Most High, tell me, O Bey [Layard], what you are going to do with those stones. So many thousands of purses spent upon such things! Can it be, as you say, that your people learn wisdom from them; or is it, as his reverence the Cadi declares, that they are to go to the palace of your Queen, who, with the rest of the unbelievers, worships these idols? As for wisdom, these figures will not teach you to make any better knives, or scissors, or chintzes; and it is in the making of those things that the English show their wisdom. But God is great! God is great! Here are stones which have been buried ever since the time of the holy Noah,—peace be upon him! Perhaps they were under ground before the deluge. I have lived on these lands for years. My father, and the father of my father, pitched their tents here before me; but they never heard of these figures. For twelve hundred years have the true believers (and, praise be to God! all true wisdom is with them alone) been settled in this country, and none of them heard of a palace under ground. Neither did they who went before them. But lo! here comes a Frank [European] from many days' journey off, and he walks up to the very place, and he takes a stick (illustrating the description at the same time with the point of his spear), and makes a line here, and makes a line there. Here, says he, is the palace; there, says he, is the gate; and he shows us what has been all our lives beneath our feet, without our having known any thing about it. Wonderful! wonderful! Is it by books, is it by magic, is it by your prophets, that you have learnt these things? Speak, O Bey; tell me the secret of wisdom.[43]

The above is a perfect example of the differences that I have been at pains to point out between the West and its attitude toward knowledge, and Islam's incomprehension at the notion of knowledge for the sake of knowledge (will these figures "teach you to make any better knives?"), and the belief that "all true wisdom is with them [Muslims] alone." Layard's response to the sheikh was "to give him a short lecture upon the advantages of civilization and of knowledge."[44]

Austen Layard, like many early Western archaeologists, was full of admiration for the Assyrian civilization that he was helping to unearth. "The inhabitants of Assyria," wrote Layard, "must at that time have exceeded all the nations of the earth in power, riches and luxury. Their knowledge of the Arts is surprising, and greatly superior to that of any contemporary nation. . . . There is much difference between their sculptures and those of Egypt as exists between those of Assyria and Greece. The lions lastly discovered, for instance, are admirably drawn, and the muscles, bones, and veins quite true to nature, and portrayed with great spirit."[45] Even more, Layard feels a debt of gratitude to the East, but also recognizes that the West is redeeming this debt by its archaeological and historical research: "A stranger laying open monuments buried for more than twenty centuries, and thus proving,—to those who dwelt around them,—that much of civilization and knowledge of which we now boast, existed amongst their forefathers when our 'ancestors were yet unborn,' was in a manner, an acknowledgement of the debt which the West owes to the East. It is, indeed, no small matter of wonder, that far distant, and comparatively new nations should have preserved the only records of a people once ruling over nearly half the globe; and should now be able to teach the descendants of that people or those who have taken their place, where their cities and monuments once stood."[46]

Layard's sense of gratitude to East, a gratitude already observed among the British Orientalists in India, was expressed by Henry David Thoreau at almost the same time when he wrote, "*Ex oriente lux* may still be the motto of scholars, for the Western world has not yet derived from the East all the light which it is destined to receive thence."[47] The notion of *ex oriente lux* also became a prominent feature of the debates in late-nineteenth-century archaeological research. The Scandinavian archaeologist Oscar Montelius argued in his *Orient und Europa* (1899) that all European culture was derived from the ancient East. "At a time when the peoples of Europe were, so to speak, without any civilization whatsoever," he wrote, "the Orient and particularly the Euphrates region and the Nile valley were already in enjoyment of a flourishing culture. The civilization which gradually dawned on our continent was for long only a pale reflection of Oriental culture."[48] In fact, as Daniel tells us, "*ex oriente lux* became the motto of a group of German archaeologists at the end of the nineteenth century. It was the title of a series edited by Hugo Winckler, published at Leipzig, and is the text of Fick's *Vorgriechische Ortsnamen* [1905]."[49]

Layard carried on his excavations first at Kuyunjik and Nimrud, near Mosul, and later among the ruins of Babylon and the mounds of southern Mesopotamia, despite appalling physical conditions and constant dangers, problems with his Arab workmen, the periodic raids from Arab tribesmen, the fanaticism of Muslim Qadis, the obstruction from Turkish bureaucrats, and often the stinginess of official British support. He ended his archaeological endeavors with the following hope: "I shall be well satisfied, and my literary labors, as well as those of a more active nature, will be amply rewarded, if I have succeeded in an attempt to add a page to the history of mankind, by restoring a part of the lost annals of Assyria."[50]

The following remarkable statement from him, written in 1858, a year after the Great Mutiny in India, indicates his attitude toward empire and should allay any Saidian doubts about Layard's collusion with the imperialists:

> Thus sauntering along, I have traversed a good part of the Bombay Presidency and of Central India. I have found the country, in general, quiet, though the population is far from well-affected towards us. In fact, I am afraid that the disaffection to our rule is deep and widespread, and that there are very few natives to be found who do not sympathise with those who are in arms against us. . .
>
> It is not difficult to understand the causes of this general hatred of our rule. It is partly deserved, and partly undeserved, but would have existed under almost any circumstance. We differ from the people in everything which might form a bond of sympathy between the conquered people and their rulers; in language, religion, manners, habits, and feelings. We have done nothing to form any other bond of sympathy, or to create mutual interests. The people we govern are treated like a distinct race, inferior to us—more, indeed, as if they were of a lower order of creatures; not always actually unkindly, though in too many instances with brutality, but with that sort of kindness which would be shown to a pet animal. They are excluded from all share of government, they can never rise to anything beyond the most inferior posts. We are endeavouring to force upon them our old worn-out judicial system, with all its technicalities and delays, which we are gradually ridding ourselves of at home, and which is infinitely more odious to them than it could ever be to us. We have Sanitary Commissioners and Boards interfering with all their private and domestic affairs, no doubt, all for their own good, although they won't so understand it. We are meddling with customs which are of no real importance, and yet are clung to with extraordinary tenacity by the people. We are breaking faith in the most scandalous manner with native princes, and annexing their territories. . . . No civilised government has ever done less for its subjects, and the East India Company is doubly to be blamed, as it has been the landlord of every acre of land, and has raised its rents by way of revenue to the utmost farthing. It is but a sorry justification to say that the people have been worse off under some native governments.[51]

According to a recent report in the *Christian Science Monitor*, an Egyptian cleric, Grand Mufti Ali Gomaa, has declared that Egypt's ancient sculptures are forbidden by Islam.[52] Such a declaration can only have sent a shudder through the entire community of Egyptologists, since all archaeologists are aware of cases like the one cited by Layard, and quoted above, where a crowd incited by clerics will destroy the "idols" of the infidels. Hence, one can at least defend the actions of European archaeologists of the mid-nineteenth century who recovered and shipped back to the prestigious museums of Paris, London, and Berlin the ancient treasures of Assyria, Egypt, and Babylon. In this context, the zeal of the French scholar and archaeologist Auguste Mariette to create an Egyptian National Museum is more commendable and remarkable. Soon after his arrival in Egypt in 1851, Mariette established himself as a pioneering archaeologist, and in 1858 the position of director of the Egyptian Service of Antiquities was created for him by Ismail Pasha. Mariette rid the sites of tomb robbers, took control of excavation and research, and above all devoted himself to preventing the exportation of Egyptian antiquities to Europe. After much lobbying, pleading, and political maneuvering in 1859, a special museum was built at Boulak, on the outskirts of Cairo. Daniel recounts how Mariette had to be eternally vigilant over the treasures of his beloved museum:

> The Empress Eugénie [of France, spouse of Napoleon III, emperor of France] was so delighted by the Egyptian jewellery exhibited in the Exposition at Paris in 1867 that she informed the Khedive Ismail that she would be graciously pleased to receive the whole collection as a present. It was a great moment in archaeology when the Khedive, surprised by this request, yet anxious to please France, and short of money, still made his consent conditional on Mariette's agreement. "There is someone at Boulak more powerful than I," he said to the Empress's agent, "and you must address yourself to him." Mariette firmly refused, and the collection of Egyptian antiquities returned safely from Paris to Boulak. What strength of character and fixity of purpose is revealed in that refusal of Mariette, made to the highest in his native land, in the interests of what he thought right for archaeology and Egypt. It cost him the support of France and, for a short while, the favour of the Khedive.[53]

Mariette's legacy included "the creation of the first National Museum in the Near East, the creation of the first National Service of Antiquities, and the birth of a conscience about the expropriation of antiquities."[54]

Bruce Kuklick defends the legacy of the archaeologists against the strictures of Said and his ilk: "Yet the world of Orientalist scholarship has something to recommend it. The learning that did take place was not theoretical, and it came to the fore in an intellectual enterprise that cost some of its purveyors cherished religious ideas. Creating the discipline was not a tea party, as the American campaigns demonstrated. At Nippur, Joesph Mayer died a wretched death on behalf of knowledge. The Orientalists were not arms dealers, nor were they high officials in the foreign service; they had their own concerns that differentiated them from the latter groups. These concerns resulted in the body of informatiom we have about the ancient Near East and the principles of reasoning that have secured this information."[55]

For Kuklick, the work of the Orientalists represented a real advance in our knowledge and exemplified the possibility of objectivity of scholarly pursuits.[56] Decipherments of the ancient scripts were remarkably successful in recovering the beliefs of ancient peoples. Scientific techniques such as stratified digging have given us real knowledge despite charges of bias in interpretation from the anti-Orientalists, who themselves are working from unchallenged premises. It is ironic that the anti-Orientalists applauded the assault on Judeo-Christian verities as liberating, and yet rejected the same kind of reasoning and methodology that only the Orientalists had developed often at great cost to their own religious certainties.[57] Finally, "rather than demonstrating the bankruptcy of Western attempts to understand the human world around it, Orientalism supplied, at the least, the tools even its harshest censurers need to argue against it."[58]

6

EMPIRE AND CURZON

One of the many grave shortcomings of Edward Said's *Orientalism* is the total disregard of the historical context within which various writers—who stand accused by him of racism, imperialism, and other crimes—wrote. Historically, what came before and what came after British rule was never taken into consideration by Said and his epigones. This leads to a further defect, that of a lack of historical comparisons. The European individuals and powers are condemned in absolute, abstract terms. Kant's saying, in Isaiah Berlin's eloquent paraphrase, that nothing straight can be built out of the crooked timber of humanity, seems to be applied only to the Westerner: "Nothing straight can be built out of the crooked timber of the West." Combined with the fallacy of the moral superiority of the victim or the colonized, these methodological flaws lead to a distorted interpretation of history. Even a casual comparison of the rival imperialism of Islam—with its destruction of Hindu and Buddhist temples, sculptures, and art; forced conversions; taxes demanded by Islamic law; reduction of the Hindu population to second-class status and slavery—should provide a corrective to the dismissal of the British Empire as an entirely negative historical force.

The Indian historian R. C. Majumdar contrasts the lack of Hindu cultural advancement under the far longer period of Muslim colonial rule with the greater achievements during the much shorter interval of British rule: "Judged by a similar standard, the patronage and cultivation of Hindu learning by the Muslims, or their contribution to the development of Hindu culture during their rule . . . *pales* into insignificance when compared with the achievements of the British rule. . . . It is only by instituting such comparison that we can make an objective study of the condition of the Hindus under Muslim rule, and view it in its true perspective."[1]

As for the death and destruction of Islamic imperialism, K. S. Lal has ably marshaled the empirical evidence.[2] In his history of Islamic demography, Lal analyzed the data for the period between 1000 and 1525, from Mahmud of Ghazni to the end of the Delhi sultanate, a half millennium of Islamic invasions and rule during which endless jihad campaigns were waged by Muslim leaders such as Qutbuddin Aibak, Alauddin Khalji, Muhammad and Firoz Tughlaq, and, of course, Amir Timur—all of whom were celebrated in Muslim chronicles as "killers of lakhs" (each lakh equals 100,000) of Hindus. Lal estimates that the number of Hindus who perished as a result of these campaigns was approximately 80 million.[3]

Sir Jadunath Sarkar wrote of British rule in these terms: "The greatest gift of the English, after universal peace and the modernization of society, and indeed the direct result of these two forces—is the Renaissance which marked our 19th century. Modern India owes everything to it."[4]

Now contrast the praise bestowed by Sir Jadunath on the British with his lucid analysis of the dreadful consequences of Islamic imperialism for the peoples of India,[5] from the inferior status of non-Muslims, the nature of jihad, the payment of taxes, and the constant humiliation of Hindus and others: "The barrenness of the Hindu intellect and the meanness of spirit of the Hindu upper classes are the greatest condemnation of Muhammadan rule in India. The Islamic political tree, judged by its fruit, was an utter failure."[6]

Sir Jadunath compares the "utter failure" of "the Islamic political tree" with the fecundity of British rule, to which modern India owes, among so many other things, its renaissance. There *was* a period of Mughal tolerance especially under Akbar the Great, who, significantly, did not consider himself a Muslim.[7] But several hundred years of Muslim rule did not result in the splendid institutions that did emerge after two hundred years of British presence.

One of Joseph Conrad's favorite themes was the essential beastliness of man when not constrained by the necessary institutions of civilized societies. Those historians or polemicists like Said who dwell on the iniquities of individuals—their venality, their greed, their arrogance, or even their racism—are missing the point. It is to the institutions inaugurated, installed, and made to function impersonally that we should pay attention. It is to these institutions that the peoples of India should be grateful. After finishing Macaulay's *History of England*, Tocqueville recommended that "[i]t should be read to see how the underlying honesty, common sense, moderation, and virtue which are to be found in a people, and the sound institutions which these qualities have created or allowed to remain, can fight against the vices of those who lead them. I do not think there were in any country statesmen who were more dishonest than those of whom Macaulay speaks in this part of his history, just as there never was a society which was greater than that which finally emerged out of their hands."[8] The Indian man of letters and historian Nirad Chaudhuri observed that Tocqueville's "essays showed that a basically great historical phenomenon could arise out of very corrupt conditions and high-handed or dubious actions. If there was to be any moralizing on the life of Clive [of India] it should have been at this level, accompanied by a forceful and vivid presentation of the realities of politics and history."[9] Chaudhuri also points out the true feelings of educated and thoughtful Indians about British rule before nationalist agitation began in 1905: "These men were not reconciled to subjection, and emotionally they were anti-British, but intellectually not one of them denied that British rule had rescued India from anarchy and brought peace and prosperity to the Indian people."[10]

The sense of gratitude to British rule is expressed movingly by Bholanauth Chunder, an Indian member of the Asiatic Society of Bengal, in his classic *The Travels of a Hindoo*, published in 1869. Dedicating his book to Sir John Laird Mair Lawrence, viceroy and governor-general of India, Chunder wrote, "I have endeavoured in this work to give the impressions produced by a journey from Calcutta, as far as Delhi, upon the mind of one who is indebted for his education to the paternal government of the British in India; and to whom can I with more propriety inscribe the humble fruits of that education than to the illustrious statesman who presides at the head of that government, and from whose eminent talents and wisdom the country has reaped many signal benefits? That the ascendancy of British rule may long subsist in India to improve the condition of its population, and that your Excellency may long continue to exercise an influence over their welfare and happiness."[11]

The Travels of a Hindoo is sprinkled with Chunder's favorable comments on all aspects of British history and presence in India, often at the expense of some aspect of Hindu culture. "No circumstance," he writes, "should render the name of Hooghly so memorable, as its being the place where was first set up, in our country, the Press, which Bulwer emphatically calls 'our second Saviour.' It was put up in 1778 by Messrs Halhed and Wilkins, on the occasion of the publication of a Bengallee [*sic*] Grammar by the first of these two gentlemen. From that year was Hindoo literature emancipated for ever, from the mystification and falsification of the Brahmins. The great event is scarcely remembered, and has not been thought worth taking notice of by any of our historians, though it has done far more for our civilization and well-being than can be hoped for from railroads and telegraphs."[12] He constantly refers to "the civilization and enlightenment which have followed in the train of British rule," or thanks to "the progress and spread of English knowledge. . . . It has ushered in a period of light. . . . It has silently worked a revolution producing deep and lasting effects, and elevating the Sudra [a member of the lowest Hindu caste] from the level of the swine and oxen to which the Brahmin [the upper priestly caste] had degraded him."[13]

At the end of his two-volume work, Chunder concludes that despite the greatness of many aspects of Asian civilizations—in the arts, religion, literature—they have not produced anything like a great constitution such as the British Constitution. Asia is decidedly wanting in the knowledge of the construction of a civil polity.[14]

WHAT CAME BEFORE

The Mughal Empire was moribund by the time the British began acquiring more and more power in India. It had lost most of its *asabiyah*, or group feeling, as Ibn Khaldun would have put it. The Mughal Empire was, as Chaudhuri said, "a military state and nothing else, and it was overwhelmingly dependent on the military ability of the Turks and to a lesser degree of the Persians, all of whom came from outside India."[15] It was in South India that the first intervention of the British in Indian politics took place. But the British were not the first outsiders to interfere in Indian affairs. For, as Chaudhuri reminds us, "No Muslim ruler in South India had any affiliation with the native people of the south—they were all adventurers from the north or officials from the court of Delhi, and their authority rested mainly on Muslim soldiers from north India and even from outside India. Even more than in the north, Muslim rule in the south was military colonialism. So for the natives, the later establishment of British rule was the replacement of one kind of foreign rule by another."[16]

But British power in India was really founded in Bengal, and here, once again, what came before British rule was most unpleasant. The Marathas began raiding and plundering Bengal in the 1740s. Chaudhuri recounts the sufferings of the people: "The soldiers killed, plundered and raped, and in this respect the Marathas established what might be called an all-time record for India. Under their popular name, Bargi, they remained in the memory of the Bengali people as an embodiment of abominable cruelty. The trials of the population of westernmost Bengal during their invasions from 1742 to 1751 were worse than those of their ruler Alivardi Khan. Contemporary Bengali poets referred to their ferocity, lust and cruelty, and there is in the Bengali language a whole poem called the *Maharashtra Purana*, which describes their atrocities."[17] The poet describes in grim detail how the raiders demanded money, and, if not given, cut off noses and ears or even killed with a sword. Women were seized and raped en masse.

Such was the state of the country on the eve of the rise of the British in India.

Institutions and Toleration

It is worth analyzing the reasons why the British in India prevailed. Superiority of arms and military science, military discipline, the leadership qualities of men of rare distinction are some of the causes of British success. But perhaps the civil discipline of the East India Company's servants, who created, in the words of John Strachey, "the least corruptible . . . ablest and . . . most respectable of all the great bureaucracies of the world,"[18] the Indian Civil Service (ICS), was the determining factor. In 1901, when Queen Victoria died, the ICS comprised "just over a thousand men, of whom a fifth were at any time either sick or on leave. Yet they administered directly (in British India) or indirectly (in the princely states) a population of nearly 300 million people spread over the territory of modern India, Pakistan, Burma and Bangladesh."[19]

The civil servants observed certain standards of conduct and possessed a pride of service, an esprit de corps and discipline that made possible the British supremacy of the nineteenth century.[20] But civil discipline alone would not have sufficed if there had not been also "a body of standards and principles whose authority is recognized by all in some degree. Civil discipline must have a moral content as well as an effective legal sanction. In this the Company's servants were strong, for they carried with them English law as well as English commercialism, and English patriotism as well as individualism."[21] Rudyard Kipling extolled the work of the ICS in this way:

> Year by year England sends out fresh drafts for the first fighting-line which is officially called the Indian Civil Service. These die, or kill themselves by overwork, or are worried to death or broken in health and hope in order that the land may be protected from death and sickness, famine and war, and may eventually become capable of standing alone. It will never stand alone, but the idea is a pretty one and men are willing to die for it, and yearly the work of pushing and coaxing and scolding and petting the country into good living goes forward. If an advance be made all credit is given to the native while the Englishmen stand back and wipe their foreheads. If a failure occurs the Englishmen step forward and take the blame.[22]

British civil servants were eulogized by Abbé Dubois, the French missionary who stayed thirty-two years in India, extolling their "uprightness of character, education and ability," while Baron Hübner, "who in 1886 ascribed the 'miracles' of British administration to 'the devotion, intelligence, the courage, the perseverance, and the skill combined with an integrity proof against all temptation, of a handful of officials and magistrates who govern and administer the Indian Empire.'"

As David Gilmour comments,

> The ICS may have had its critics—even within its own ranks—but about its elevated standards there was no argument. N. B. Bonarjee, a member of the Service, but also an Indian nationalist, praised "its rectitude, its sense of justice, its tolerance, its sense of public duty," as well as "its high administrative ability." After independence in 1947, the new nations of Pakistan and India each displayed pride in its traditions. In Karachi, a Government pamphlet proclaimed that the Pakistan Civil Service was the "successor" of the ICS, "the most distinguished Civil Service in the world," and in India the Home Minister, Vallabhbhai Patel, used it as a model for the Indian Administrative Civil Service, a body that played a crucial role in the integration and unification of the new state. Even at the beginning of the twenty-first century retired members of the IAS [Indian Administrative Service] were recalling the exploits of their British predecessors with almost embarrassing effusiveness.[23]

The British were also tolerant, and particularly after the Great Mutiny of 1857, they pursued a policy of "'religious indifferentism,' a policy of not interfering with the customs of a religion unless they conflicted with the principle of religious equality."[24] Queen Victoria herself had insisted in the royal proclamation to her Indian subjects that "firmly relying ourselves on the truth of Christianity . . . we disclaim alike the right & the desire to impose our convictions on any of our subjects . . . all shall alike enjoy the equal & impartial protection of the law."[25] Thus to the Hindu the British were preferable to the Muslim and to the Muslim more acceptable than the Hindu—religious toleration and social noninterference assured the success of the British.[26]

Percival Spear summarizes the British achievement in India:

> The new rulers reorganised the country more efficiently than before; they were self-consciously tolerant; they studied to preserve rather than destroy. But almost in spite of themselves new thoughts, new ideas, and new ways of life came into the country, with results which have proved incalculable in their range and depth. It is here that we can find the significance of the British connexion with India. The British were the harbingers of the West. At times unconsciously, at times with optimistic zeal, and at times with reluctance or dislike, they were the vehicles of western influence in India. That is why their influence in India has proved creative, and why their period will be looked back on as formative for the India that is yet to be. The British provided the bridge for India to pass from the medieval world of the Mughuls to the new age of science and humanism.[27]

The British restored the unity of India, and re-established order. The English language in time became the lingua franca of the subcontinent, acting as a unifying element, and gave Indians access to Western ideas, moral and religious, and to the principles and workings of English law. The British were also able to bring India into the new world economy by the development of its industry, and the establishment of a railway system.

Perhaps the changes inaugurated by the energetic Lord Dalhousie, governor-general between 1848 and 1856, can stand for the positive achievements of the British in India. He oversaw the building of the railways, established the postal and telegraph services, improved the roads and harbors, and was responsible for such major irrigation works as the Ganges Canal, which stretches 350 miles from Hardwar to Cawnpore and contains thousands of miles of distributaries. As Gilmour concludes, "By the beginning of the twentieth century British India had the largest irrigation system in the world, 37,000 miles of metalled roads and 25,000 miles of railways, over half the total in Asia (including Russia east of the Urals). Immense areas had been transformed. At Queen Victoria's accession, Assam had been primarily a jungle: at her death it contained over 4 million acres under cultivation, many of them in tea plantations."[28] The Ganges Canal irrigation schemes led to tangible benefits for the peasantry, who were better fed, housed, and dressed than ever before. The results were similar for the peasantry in the Punjab with its new network of canals.

India's debt to Lord Dalhousie is generously acknowledged by Indian historian V. B. Kulkarni: "Dalhousie can be truly acclaimed as the maker of modern India and the political settlements made by him endured in all their essentials till the country's partition in 1947."[29] Kulkarni approves of Dalhousie's decision ("a wise one") to annex the Punjab after the Punjab War: "The impact of [Dalhousie's] masterful mind was soon felt by the administration of the province which began to be governed so well and wisely that the Mutiny of 1857 found the martial races of the Punjab solidly ranged on the side of their foreign rulers."[30] All the annexations sanctioned by Dalhousie "were fully justified."[31] For Kulkarni, the British governor-general helped emancipate India from her medieval moorings. The revolution in the modes of transport and communication brought about by Dalhousie "strengthened and vitalized the consciousness of the Indian people about their essential oneness. The printing press, which became the means of dispelling illiteracy and of conferring on the masses of the people the power to read and write, the newspapers that purveyed the news of the country and of the world with comments designed to create and educate public opinion, the Western system of education which gave unhindered access to the scientific and other forms of modern knowledge, the spread of trade and commerce, and the intermingling of the people in increasing numbers due to the improved and quick modes of travel, all these served as a powerful unifying force which was eventually transmuted into a strong demand for political rights." In other words, the British unified India, created modern "India."[32]

Dalhousie endorsed Sir Charles Wood's Education Despatch of 1854 that was forwarded to the government of India for "creating a properly articulated system of education, from the primary school to the University." It was a landmark in the history of education in India. It encouraged the teaching of the arts, science, philosophy, and literature of Europe. It affirmed the value of the study of the Indian languages as the means of spreading enlightenment among the masses, but did not neglect the importance of English. It recommended the establishment of universities in Calcutta, Bombay, and Madras; of institutions for training of teachers for all types of schools; of middle schools; and so on. In short, Dalhousie, concludes Kulkarni, "is entitled to our respect."[33]

Another factor in the longevity of British rule in India was the cooperation of millions of ordinary Indians who filled the ranks of its army, police force, and bureaucracy. During the Great Mutiny of 1857, the armies of Bombay and Madras remained fundamentally loyal, and only about a quarter of the sepoys in the army of Bengal joined the revolt. Sikhs and Gurkhas also played a big part in suppressing the revolt.[34] Modern Indians tend to overlook, and are embarrassed by, the existence of this substantial body of their fellow countrymen who actively cooperated with the British, and perhaps the raj could not have lasted as long as it did without them.[35] The many princely states were also loyal to the raj, the Nizam of Hyderabad, for instance, styling himself "The Faithful Ally of the British Government."[36] At all times the raj was acutely aware of its responsibilities and duties to the people of India, and it never created a totalitarian state that could do what it liked when it chose.[37] The raj operated under powerful constraints: "These were the costs of its armed forces and administration, the amount of revenue it could raise and the need to conciliate Indian opinion. Behind the raj's impressive facade lay a mass of compromises and accommodations made by a government which was always well aware that it lacked the manpower and resources to ride roughshod over its subjects' wishes."[38]

But, as I suggested at the beginning of this chapter, the greatest legacies of the raj were the institutions that it introduced and nurtured and whose importance it taught to the Indian people. First, there was the institution of elected parliamentary government. Early in the history of the British presence in India, governors such as Thomas Munro in Madras and Mountstuart Elphinstone in Bombay had believed that it was the duty of the British to rule justly, and to educate their Indian subjects so that they would be able to govern themselves one day. Munro told the directors of the East India Company: "[Y]ou are not here to turn India into England or Scotland. Work through, not in spite of, native systems and native ways, with a prejudice in their favour rather than against them; and when in the fullness of time your subjects can frame and maintain a worthy Government for themselves, get out and take the glory of the achievement and the sense of having done your duty as the chief reward for your exertions."[39] Though few people agreed with Munro at the time, by exposing Indians to the idea of democracy, and eventually handing over power to them, the raj can be said to have fulfilled that duty. Democracy was slowly but profoundly implanted in the political mind of India, and the electoral processes have survived to this day despite the brief episode in 1977, when Indira Gandhi declared a short-lived emergency during which civil rights were severely restricted.

The second institution the raj bequeathed to India was English law, the very idea of the rule of law, and the nature of that law. The constitution that India drafted and decreed after independence was in part derived from the 1935 Government of India Act, and in part from the Bill of Rights of the US Constitution. But underpinning the entire constitution was the ultimate authority of the law. India accepted unaltered the entire legal system that the raj had put in place, which, in turn, was based on Lord Macaulay's "towering structure," the penal code. In the words of Indian historian K. M. Pannikar, "It is the genius of this man, narrow in his Europeanism, self-satisfied in his sense of English greatness, that gives life to modern India as we know it. He was India's new Manu,[40] the spirit of modern law incarnate."[41]

Finally, India inherited at independence an administrative structure that we have already referred to, the Indian Civil Service. By 1947 the composition of the ICS was half British and half Indian, while the much larger provincial service was almost entirely Indian. Consequently, there was no chaos; no period of adjustment was deemed necessary since many Indians had already been doing the job for years. In years to come, the new Indian civil servants were proud of keeping up the reputation of the ICS for its incorruptibility.

The success of the application of the principles enunciated in the Education Despatch of 1854 meant that at independence there were almost one hundred thousand university professors and lecturers, and more than half a million teachers at the primary and secondary level. There were ninety-two thousand registered doctors; there were craftsmen, mechanics, and even engineers, so that India began its independent existence well equipped to cope with the exigencies of modern life.[42]

Post-independence, India's economic performance had nothing to do with the consequences of British imperialism. It is unfortunate that Nehru, an essentially decent man and a democrat at heart, adopted Soviet-style economic policies that condemned the majority of her people to poverty. By contrast, those countries that chose "the Western model such as Japan, South Korea, Taiwan, and Singapore were able to transform their country into a prosperous, modern, liberal democratic nation in as little as two generations. In Japan's case, the model allowed it to rise from the ashes of total defeat to become a world power in less than forty years."[43] Had Nehru and his successors "chosen the Japanese path, it could have been by now a much greater power than China. It is only in the past decade, with partial adoption of the liberal economic policies of the capitalist West, that its fortunes have begun to turn around."[44]

LORD CURZON

Lord Curzon is an example of a British viceroy of India who also wrote an outstanding study of Persia, making him both an Orientalist and an imperialist, and also the subject of Edward Said's incoherent rant in *Orientalism*. He is a figure worth defending.

Lord Curzon was undoubtedly an imperialist, but he saw British rule as a sacred trust, a responsibility toward its Indian subjects. Two currently unfashionable but, for Curzon, deeply moral notions of duty and responsibility constantly appear in his "Addresses, Discourses, and Lectures." India was a "great, noble and sacred responsibility."[45] Curzon wrote of his and Britain's responsibility in India in these terms: "I do not see how any Englishman, contrasting India as it now is with what it was, and would certainly have been under any other conditions than British rule, can fail to see that we came and have stayed here under no blind or capricious impulse, but in obedience to what some (of whom I am one) would call the decree of Providence, others the law of destiny—in any case for the lasting benefit of millions of the human race. We often make great mistakes here: we are sometimes hard, and insolent, and overbearing: we are a good deal strangled with red tape. But none the less, I do firmly believe that there is no Government in the world (and I have seen most) that rests on so secure a moral basis, or that is more freely animated by duty."[46]

India was "the land not only of romance but of obligation." Curzon told members of the Bengal Chamber of Commerce at a dinner in 1903, "If I thought it were all for nothing, and that you and I . . . were simply writing inscriptions on the sand to be washed out by the next tide, if I felt that we were not working here for the good of India in obedience to a higher law and to a nobler aim, then I would see the link that holds England and India together severed without a sigh. But it is because I believe in the future of this country, and in the capacity of our own race to guide it to goals that it has never hitherto attained, that I keep courage and press forward."[47]

Curzon had a deep affection for the people of India and its civilization. He felt that Indian culture was going through a bad phase, but to think that "the West had a monopoly of wisdom, he declared, was arrogant and foolish; the quality of Indian civilization could be deduced from the country's architectural heritage, which he regarded as 'the most wonderful and varied collection of ancient monuments in the world.' He did not want Indians to become brown Englishmen but encouraged them to assimilate Western thought into their own culture. 'Adhere to your own religion,' he exhorted Muslim students, 'which has in it ingredients of great nobility and of profound truth': from its foundations they should 'pluck the fruit of the tree of knowledge, which once grew best in Eastern gardens, but has now shifted its habitat to the West.' "[48]

Curzon, like many Orientalists and administrators, had no sympathy for the Christian missionaries. He refused to meddle with Hindu customs merely to help the missionaries convert Hindus to Christianity. Curzon believed the way to make the raj's administration equitable "was genuine but never exaggerated sympathy with native thought and ideas [and] a bold lead in everything else," and, of course, "righteousness in administration." His purpose in India was "to hold the scales even" between the different races and religions. As Gilmour summarizes, "[Curzon] would not connive at scandals, . . . or wink at fraud or hush up ill-doing in high places, because the British were in India to set an example, and all their actions should be open to inspection. Only by demonstrating 'superior standards of honour and virtue' could they continue to hold the country."[49] Curzon was vehemently opposed to the racism of "the inferior class of Englishmen," and believed in punishing severely any British soldiers who misbehaved toward Indians.

Curzon acted swiftly when the monsoon rains failed to fall in 1899 and led to the worst famine of the century. By the end of the year, 3.5 million people were receiving famine relief. He personally visited every plague hospital in Bombay and Poona, and almost every infected patient. Curzon paid public tribute to officials of the ICS and other services who had risked their lives to relieve the suffering, but was bitterly disappointed that responsible Indians left all the work to British officials: "It was a curious thing, he reflected, that the Hindu could be tender-hearted about saving peacocks and monkeys but was quite callous about the lives of his fellow humans."[50]

During his travels in India, Curzon was shocked at the decay and neglect of her monuments, and was convinced urgent action was necessary to preserve

India's magnificent cultural heritage: "The British were not so rich in originality themselves, he declared, that they could afford 'to allow the memorials of an earlier and superior art or architecture to fall into ruin'; for him the conservation of India's monuments was 'an elementary obligation of government.' The poor conditions of many buildings may have been caused by Indian neglect or by the depredations of Sikh and Muslim conquerors, but that did not excuse either contemporary indifference or the horrors erected by British engineers in the forts of Agra, Gwalior and elsewhere. Curzon believed his country had 'purged itself of the spirit of stupid and unlettered vandalism' which had in earlier days led it to turn disused palaces into barracks, but he was determined to atone for past crimes by a strenuous programme of restoration."[51]

Curzon told the Asiatic Society of Bengal:

> If there be any one who says to me that there is no duty devolving upon a Christian Government to preserve the monuments of a pagan art, or the sanctuaries of an alien faith, I cannot pause to argue with such a man. Art and beauty, and the reverence that is owing to all that has evoked human genius or has inspired human faith, are independent of creeds, and, in so far as they touch the sphere of religion, are embraced by the common religion of all mankind. . . . There is no principle of artistic discrimination between the mausoleum of the despot and the sepulchre of the saint. What is beautiful, what is historic, what tears the mask off the face of the past, and helps us to read its riddles, and to look it in the eyes—these, and not the dogmas of a combative theology, are the principle criteria to which we must look.[52]

Contrast British imperialist Curzon's civilized instincts to preserve India's monuments with Muslim imperialists' urge to destroy the idols of the infidels. "It is partly, no doubt, because of the *furor islamicus* that post-Gupta remains are surprisingly few in Bihar," wrote art historian J. C. Harle.[53] Here is how Vincent Smith describes the extermination of Buddhists, Buddhist art, and Buddhism also in Bihar: "The ashes of the Buddhist sanctuaries at Sarnath near Banares still bear witness to the rage of the image-breakers. Many noble monuments of the ancient civilisation of India were irretrievably wrecked in the course of the early Muslim invasions. Those invasions were fatal to the existence of Buddhism as an organized religion in northern India, where its strength resided chiefly in Bihar and certain adjoining territories. The monks who escaped massacre fled, and were scattered over Nepal, Tibet, and the south."[54] The intolerance of Aurangzeb resulted in the destruction of hundreds of Hindu temples: in the campaigns of 1679–80, 123 were destroyed at Udaipur, 63 at Chitor, and 66 at Jaipur. Here is one quick survey by Sita Ram Goel of the temples razed to the ground by the *furor islamicus*, all the evidence having been gathered from more than eighty histories, entirely Muslim sources:

> So the temples were attacked "all along the way" as the armies of Islam advanced; they were "robbed of their sculptural wealth," "pulled down," "laid waste," "burnt with naptha," "trodden under horse's hoofs," and "destroyed from their very foundations," till "not a trace of them remained." Mahmûd of Ghazni robbed and burnt down 1,000 temples at Mathura, and 10,000 in and around Kanauj. One of his successors, Ibrãhîm, demolished 1,000 temples each in Hindustan (Ganga-Yamuna Doab) and Malwa. Muhammad Ghûrî destroyed another 1,000 at Varanasi. Qutbu'd-Dîn Aibak employed elephants for pulling down 1,000 temples in Delhi. Alî I 'Ãdil Shãh of Bijapur destroyed 200 to 300 temples in Karnataka. A sufi, Qãyim Shãh, destroyed 12 temples at Tiruchirapalli. Such exact or approximate counts, however, are available only in a few cases. Most of the time we are informed that "many strong temples which would have remained unshaken even by the trumpets blown on the Day of Judgment, were levelled with the ground when swept by the wind of Islãm."[55]

Curzon, on the other hand, carried out his preservationist mission with his usual thoroughness, even fervor. The viceroy had the royal palace in Mandalay cleansed of the English club occupying it; finding a post office built into a beautiful Islamic building, he ordered the entire staff to leave; at Ajunta he ordered the bats to be driven out of the caves; cobwebs, insects, bird nests had to be removed; cracked plaster to be repaired: "On discovering that the ancient skill of *pietra dura* inlay had virtually died out, he went to great lengths to acquire a Florentine mosaicist to repair the Red Fort's marble panels that had been damaged in the Mutiny." He lavished his attention on Agra, his favorite spot in India, believing it to house the most beautiful body of architectural remains in the world: the Taj Mahal, the Red Fort, and its environs. Skilled craftsmen were trained to reproduce the original seventeenth-century work in marble, sandstone, and *pietra dura*. Minarets were re-erected with white Makrana marble. Watercourses and fountains were rebuilt, trees planted, scraggy trees uprooted. By the end, Curzon had spent fifty thousand pounds on Agra alone, "an offering of reverence to the past and a gift of recovered beauty to the future."[56]

If one compares the sense of duty and responsibility to the people of India felt by Lord Curzon with the dissolute behavior of her many princes, one grasps the essential nobility of the viceroy's imperialist vision. Queen Victoria spoiled and doted on those princes even though many left unpaid bills at Windsor. One raja spent all his inheritance on women and gambling in Paris, others were inebriates and sots; the maharajah of Bharatpur was an unstable character who had recently killed his servant, and so on. The list is long. The viceroy wrote of the duties of the native chief: "I claim him as my colleague and partner [who must be] the servant as well as master of his people." He must learn that his revenues were "not secured to him for his own selfish gratification, but for the good of his subjects." His princely duty lay with his people.[57] Curzon gently reminded them of their responsibilities: "I have always been a devoted believer in the continued existence of the Native States in India and an ardent well-wisher of the native Princes. But I believe in them not as relics, but as rulers; not as puppets, but as living factors in the administration. I want them to share the responsibilities as well as the glories of British rule. Therefore it is that I have ventured to preach to them the gospel of duty, of common service in the interests of the Empire, of a high and strenuous aim."[58]

Curzon was proud of the work accomplished by the British in India, including his own. He wrote, "For where else in the world has a race gone forth and subdued, not a country or a kingdom, but a continent peopled, not by savage tribes, but by races with traditions and a civilisation older than our own, with a history not inferior to ours in dignity or romance; subduing them not to the law of the sword, but to the rule of justice, bringing peace and order and good government to nearly one-fifth of the entire human race, and holding them with so mild a restraint that the rulers are the merest handful against the ruled, a tiny speck of white foam upon a dark and thunderous ocean?"[59]

Lord Curzon felt his own administration had accomplished much:

> We endeavoured to frame a plague policy which should not do violence to the instincts and sentiments of the native population; a famine policy which should profit by the experience of the past and put us in a position to cope with the next visitation when unhappily it bursts upon us; an education policy which should free the intellectual activities of the Indian people, so keen and restless as they are, from the paralysing clutch of examinations; a railway policy that will provide administratively and financially for the great extension that we believe to lie before us; an irrigation policy that will utilise to the maximum, whether remuneratively or unremuneratively, all the available water resources of India, not merely in canals, . . . but in tanks and reservoirs and wells; a police policy that will raise standard of the only emblem of authority that the majority of the people see, and will free then from petty diurnal tyranny and oppression. . . . [T]he administrator looks rather to the silent and inarticulate masses, and if he can raise, even by a little, the level of material comfort and well-being in their lives, he has earned his reward. . . .
>
> We have endeavoured to render the land revenue more equable in its incidence, to lift the load of usury from the shoulders of the peasant, and to check

that reckless alienation of the soil which in many parts of the country was fast converting him from a free proprietor to a bond slave. We have done our best to encourage industries which little by little will relieve the congested field of agriculture, develop the indigenous resources of India, and make that country more and more self-providing in the future. I would not indulge in any boast, but I dare to think that as a result of these efforts I can point to an India that is more prosperous, more contented, and more hopeful. Wealth is increasing in India. There is no test you can apply which does not demonstrate it. Trade is growing. Evidences of progress and prosperity are multiplying on every side.[60]

Curzon explicitly repudiates the idea that India, or the East, for that matter, is unchanging and unchangeable, as claimed by Said. India is not stationary, writes the viceroy, and goes on to compare British rule favorably to what went before:

India must always remain a constellation rather than a country, a congeries of races rather than a single nation. But we are creating ties of unity among those widely diversified peoples, we are consolidating those vast and outspread territories, and, what is more important, we are going forward instead of backward. It is not a stationary, a retrograde, a downtrodden, or an impoverished India that I have been governing for the past five and a half years. Poverty there is in abundance. I defy any one to show me a great and populous city, where it does not exist. Misery and destitution there are. The question is not whether they exist, but whether they are growing more or growing less. In India, where you deal with so vast a canvas, I daresay the lights and shades of human experience are more vivid and more dramatic than elsewhere. But if you compare the India of today with the India of any previous period of history—the India of Alexander, of Asoka, of Akbar, or of Aurangzeb—you will find greater peace and tranquillity, more widely suffused comfort and contentment, superior justice and humanity, and higher standards of material well-being, than that great dependency has ever previously attained.[61]

In what can be seen to be his farewell address, Curzon wrote, "and to feel that somewhere among these millions you have left a little justice or happiness or prosperity, a sense of manliness or moral dignity, a spring of patriotism, a dawn of intellectual enlightenment, or a stirring of duty, where it did not before exist—that is enough, that is the Englishman's justification in India. It is good enough for his watchword while he is here, for his epitaph when he is gone. I have worked for no other aim. Let India be my judge."[62]

Kulkarni, very hostile in general to Curzon's term in India, nonetheless praises him for his work in preserving India's monuments: "India will continue to respect his name as the greatest preserver and protector of her ancient monuments and as the foremost inspirer of her country's historical research."[63] Writing in the late 1960s, pro-Congress Indian journalist Durga Das is more generous, dubbing Curzon as "one of the principal architects of modern India, [and] the midwife of India's emergence on the world scene," comparing him to Nehru: "'Both were patrician intellectuals endowed with an abundance of gifts . . . two men of destiny' who devoted themselves to the well-being of India."[64]

The rest of Curzon's public life, outside India, is also of relevance, and, given his pro-Arab position during and after World War I, Said's hostility toward him is surprising. Curzon was averse to making large promises to the Arabs, but once he thought they had been made, was adamant that they should be honored. He told his cabinet colleagues in October 1917 that "[Britain] must be very careful that any peace programme did not work to the detriment of the Arabs and the promises [made to them]."[65] Curzon opposed commitments, however, made to other non-Arab peoples in the Sykes-Picot Agreement and the Balfour Declaration. As to the latter, Curzon thought Palestine was totally unsuitable for large-scale Jewish immigration from Europe. "I cannot conceive a worse bondage to which to relegate an advanced and intellectual community than to exile in Palestine," wrote Curzon to his Jewish fellow cabinet member Edwin Montagu, who was also anti-Zionist. There was simply not enough for all the communities: "[One could not] expel the present Moslem population, [nor] turn all the various sects, religions and denominations out of Jerusalem."[66] Curzon saw Britain as godfather to Arab aspirations in Mesopotamia and in other Arab lands conquered from the Turks.[67]

Finally, it is instructive to observe the behavior of Turkey during the negotiations after World War I, in which Curzon, of course, played an important part. This was far from the received idea of the West feeding on the carcass of the Ottoman Empire. Turkey demanded full independence at the Peace Conference in Lausanne, and was active, confident, even militarily strong, neither supine nor passive, as Said always portrays his Orientals. Curzon often took the side of the Turks against Greece. Thus it is not surprising that Curzon earned the gratitude of the Turks. Ismet Pasha, the chief Turkish negotiator at the Lausanne conference, spoke of the "very highest admiration and respect" that he felt for Curzon, and at Curzon's death sent a moving letter of condolence to his family. At the seventieth anniversary of the conference, the Turkish government invited Curzon's grandson Lord Ravensdale to a commemorative celebration.

Such was the man who is reduced by Said to "[t]he cosmopolitanism of geography was, in Curzon's mind, its universal importance to the whole of the West, whose relationship to the rest of the world was one of frank covetousness" (p. 216).

7

EDWARD SAID AND HIS METHODOLOGY

Edward Said's *Orientalism* gave those unable to think for themselves a formula. His work had the attraction of an all-purpose tool his acolytes—eager, intellectually unprepared, aesthetically unsophisticated—could apply to every cultural phenomenon without having to think critically or having to conduct any real archival research requiring mastery of languages, or research in the field requiring the mastery of technique and a rigorous methodology. Said's *Orientalism* displays all the laziness and arrogance of the man of letters who does not have much time for empirical research, or, above all, for making sense of its results. His method derives from the work of fashionable French intellectuals and theorists. Existentialists, structuralists, deconstructionists, and postmodernists all postulate grandiose theories, but, unfortunately, these are based on flimsy historical or empirical foundations. Claude Lévi-Strauss, with just a few years of field work in Brazil, constructed a grand theory about the structures of the human mind. As Edmund Leach put it in his short monograph on Lévi-Strauss, the French anthropologist never bothered to learn the native languages, never spent more than a few weeks in one place; the subsequent model, peppered with Marxist jargon, that he concocted on such meager empirical foundations is "little more than an amalgam" of his "own prejudiced presuppositions." Leach continues, "Lévi-Strauss . . . is insufficiently critical of his source material. He always seems to be able to find just what he is looking for. Any evidence, however dubious, is acceptable so long as it fits with logically calculated expectations; but wherever the data run counter to the theory Lévi-Strauss will either bypass the evidence or marshal the full resources of his powerful invective to have the heresy thrown out of court. . . . [H]e consistently behaves like an advocate defending a cause rather than a scientist searching for ultimate truth."[1] This tradition was carried on by Michel Foucault, surely one of the great charlatans of modern times.

Said, influenced by Foucault, Marx, and the French intellectual tradition, refuses to acknowledge evidence that does not fit into his already prepared Procrustean bed; evidence such as the work of German Orientalists or the evidence of Indian Orientalists who praise the scholarly contribution of their European colleagues. Generally speaking, Said's thinking can be characterized as "ideological."[2] An ideologue is immune to argument; he believes his ideas about man, history, and society to be self-evident, and anyone opposing them to be either stupid or malevolent. He cannot lose since his interpretation has already been determined in advance of observations. His attitude is immune to facts or reality, and no argument will ever disprove him.[3] The ideology is a way of interpreting the world: I can shut out recalcitrant data, I can shut my eyes if necessary.[4] Ideology is a method of substituting sweeping structural explanations for empirical investigation; for the ideologues, all the failings of his target group are the systematic products of its core identity.

In cultures already immune to self-criticism, Said helped Muslims, and particularly Arabs, perfect their already well-developed sense of self-pity. There is a kind of comfort and absolution in being told that none of your problems are of your making, that you do not have to accept any responsibility for the ills besetting your society. It is all the fault of the West, of infidels. There is no need even to take responsibility for self-determination, it is easier to accept money from the Western donors and to treat it as one's rightful due from them, that is, a kind of jizyah. The attraction of Said's thesis for third-world intellectuals is thus easily understandable. But why was it so successful among Western intellectuals? Post–World War II Western intellectuals and leftists were consumed by guilt for the West's colonial past and continuing colonialist present, and they wholeheartedly embraced any theory or ideology that voiced or at least seemed to voice the putatively thwarted aspirations of the peoples of the third world. *Orientalism* came at the precise time when anti-Western rhetoric was at its most shrill and was already being taught at Western universities, and when third-worldism was at its most popular. Jean-Paul Sartre preached that all white men were complicit in the exploitation of the third world, and that violence against Westerners was a legitimate means for colonized men to re-acquire their manhood.[5] Said went further: "It is therefore correct that every European, in what he could say about the Orient, was consequently a racist, an imperialist, and almost totally ethnocentric" (p. 204). Not only, for Said, is every European a racist, but he must *necessarily* be so. As I have argued, Western civilization has been more willing to criticize itself than any other major culture. These self-administered admonishments are a far cry from Said's savage strictures, and yet they found a new generation ready to take them to heart. Berating and blaming the West, a fashionable game in the

1960s and 1970s that impressionable youth took seriously, had the results we now see when the same generation appears unwilling to defend the West against the greatest threat that it has faced since the Nazis.

When shown that Said is indeed a fraud, his friends and supporters in academia sidestep the criticisms and evidence, and pretend, as did several reviewers of Robert Irwin's book on Said, that Said may indeed have got the "footling details" wrong but he was, nonetheless, onto a higher truth. Said's influence, thus, was a result of a conjunction of several intellectual and political trends: post-French Algeria and post-Vietnam *tiers mondisme* (third-worldism); the politicization of increasingly postmodernist English departments that had argued away the very idea of truth, objective truth; and the influence of Foucault. In effect Said played on each of these confidence tricks to create a master fraud that bound American academics and Middle East tyrants in unstated bonds of anti-American complicity.[6]

In Said's works there is no room for historical comparisons. The West alone stands, tried on the basis of a few examples taken out of historical context, judged and condemned as the source of all evil. There was slavery in the West, but, as pointed out above, the West itself took the first steps to actually abolish it. Indeed, abolitionism, as Olivier Pétré-Grenouilleau reminds us in his path-breaking comparative study,[7] was an Occidental concept that did not resonate in either black Africa or the Islamic world. In his study of the slave trade in the Ottoman Empire in the nineteenth century, Ehud R. Toledano wrote, "Accepted by custom, perpetuated by tradition and sanctioned by religion, slavery was an integral part of Ottoman society." He further adds that no abolitionist movement ever emerged in the Ottoman Empire. On the contrary, Ottoman politics can be characterized as a continual resistance of varying intensity to British abolitionist pressure. Slavery was taken for granted and abolitionism was considered a foreign, English idea—barely understood, let alone accepted.[8] Turkish historian Y. H. Erdem confirms Toledano's findings; there was no organized abolitionist movement in the Ottoman Empire, no abolitionist tracts popularizing the subject and bringing home the suffering of the slaves. Moreover, in modern Turkey, continues Erdem, the abolition of slavery is not a part of the educational curriculum, and there is no specific date for abolition that could have been used as a point of departure for such a study.[9]

Both popular and more academic works on slavery so often leave out the role of black Africa in the whole network of black slavery. But as Pétré-Grenouilleau shows, the slave trade could not have developed without the black Africans themselves offering captives, who had been acquired by means of raids and who were considered spoils of war to European slavers.[10] John Fage estimated that more than three-quarters of the captives sold to the Europeans came from raids and war.[11] Black Africa was a full and active partner in the slave trade, and the black captives were "produced" by it, and was responsible for organizing and strictly controlling the sale of the captives. Neither the Europeans nor the Americans succeeded in establishing a monopoly of the black slave trade in West Africa. Their rivalry benefited the African powers who could concentrate on the offer of captives. On the whole, the African powers remained in control of the sale of the slaves as long as the slave trade lasted. The African powers entered into the slave trade entirely of their own accord.[12] Again, Western-style abolitionism had no impact in black Africa, and there was no opposition to slavery in principle.[13] On the contrary, certain African chiefs even sent delegations to the West to protest the abolition of the slave trade that they found so profitable.[14]

The participation of Arabs in the black slave trade is better known, but still not known widely enough. Using the term "Zanj" either for the Bantu-speaking black population of East Africa south of the Ethiopians, or more loosely for black Africans in general, the tenth-century Arab geographer al-Maqdisi wrote, "As for the Zanj, they are people of black color, flat noses, kinky hair, and little understanding." A tenth-century Persian treatise on world geography describes black Africans as "people distant from the standards of humanity." A thirteenth-century Persian writer observes that "the ape is more teachable and more intelligent than the Zanji." The celebrated sociologist Ibn Khaldun wrote, "Therefore, the Negro nations are, as a rule, submissive to slavery, because [Negroes] have little [that is essentially] human and have attributes that are quite similar to those of dumb animals, as we have stated."[15]

The Koran assumes and accepts the existence of slavery and regulates the practice of that institution, and precisely for that reason the abolition of slavery in Islamic lands proved difficult, and even continues to this day in the Sudan, in Mauritania, and even, evidence suggests, in Saudi Arabia.

Pétré-Grenouilleau, relying on the research of such scholars as Raymond Mauny, Tadeusz Lewicki, Ralph Austen, and Paul Bairoch,[16] concludes that the greatest slave traders were the Orientals, not the Westerners![17] A little more than 11 million captives were deported in the Atlantic slave trade, but between the seventh century and the 1920s, the Arab merchants handled more than 17 million black slaves, of which more than 1.5 million died en route, many across the Sahara.[18] J. Azumah, writing in 1999, records that "[t]he anti-slavery measures of European colonial powers were generally viewed by Muslims not only as a threat to their very livelihood but also as an affront to their religion. . . . Muslims therefore resisted all abolition efforts and chattel slavery persists in Muslim countries today."[19] In a report presented by the secretary general to the United Nations in

October 1995, "the abduction and traffic of young boys and girls from Southern Sudan to the northern part of the country for sale as servants and concubines is highlighted in several paragraphs."[20] In northern Nigeria, "people can still be found who are considered slaves. . . . The death of slavery, pronounced by so many observers, has been a protracted one and is still not over."[21] John Eibner noted that "[b]lack women and children in Darfur continue to be enslaved by government-backed janjaweed militiamen, especially for sexual purposes. In the far south, Khartoum's longtime ally, the Lord's Resistance Army, still perpetrates atrocities against civilians, including enslavement. Moreover, tens of thousands of Dinka and Nuer women and children captured before the government made peace with the Sudan People's Liberation Army remain in bondage. Officials at the Committee for the Eradication of the Abduction of Women and Children estimate the presence of at least 40,000 such slaves in northern Sudan, and have documented the names and locations of more than 8,000."[22]

Jan Hogendorn has documented the manufacture and sale of eunuchs, an activity the anthropologist E. B. Tylor named "The Hideous Trade." As Hogendorn explains, "Eunuchs are castrated males, usually slaves operated upon during boyhood. (Boys survived the operation better than did adolescents or adults.) The major demand for slave eunuchs was as supervisors of women, especially in the harems of rulers, nobility, and the wealthy in the Ottoman Empire and its Muslim neighbours and precursors." He confines his study to the Muslim Mediterranean, that is, the Muslim or once-Muslim parts of southern Europe, North Africa, and the Near East, including all of what became the Ottoman Empire at its greatest extent. In these areas, "the maintenance of large harems by the upper classes greatly stimulated demand for males who could be trusted with large numbers of nubile women."[23] Sub-Saharan Africa was the main source of supply for eunuchs until the end of the trade, well into the nineteenth century.

After Africa became the most important source for Mediterranean Islam, most eunuchs sold to the markets underwent total removal of testicles and penis. This operation was dangerous and resulted in very high death rates. There was first the problem of extensive hemorrhaging, with the possibility of almost immediate death; the second danger lay in infection of the urethra, with the formation of pus blocking it and causing death within a few days. Death rates could be as high as 90 percent when castration was carried out in sub-Saharan west and west-central Africa: "Even higher death rates were occasionally reported, unsurprising in tropical areas where the danger of infection of wounds was especially high. At least one contemporary price quotation supports a figure of over 90 percent mortality: Turkish merchants are said to have been willing to pay 250 to 300 (Maria Theresa) dollars each for eunuchs in Borno (north-east Nigeria) at a time when the local price of young male slaves does not seem to have exceeded about 20 dollars."[24] Very high death rates from the operation in eastern Africa are also postulated; 90 percent is the figure for the Sudan and Ethiopia.

WHITE SLAVERY

But to the narrative:—The vessel bound
With slaves to sell off in the capital,
After the usual process, might be found
At anchor under the seraglio wall;
Her cargo, from the plague being safe and sound,
Were landed in the market, one and all,
And there with Georgians, Russians, and Circassians,
Bought up for different purposes and passions.

—Lord Byron, *Don Juan*

Not so well known to the general public is the history of white slavery, that is, the enslavement of Europeans and North Americans by Arabs, especially during the seventeenth and eighteenth centuries. According to Robert C. Davis, between 1530 and 1780, "there were almost certainly a million, and quite possibly as many as a million and a quarter white, European Christians enslaved by the Muslims of the Barbary coast."[25]

Giles Milton gives a vivid and grim account of the sufferings of some English slaves captured by the Muslims. They suffered unspeakable cruelty and indignities. Many died from their maltreatment, from dysentery, or from the plague or forced labor. Flogged by black slave drivers ferociously loyal to the cruel and violent Moulay Ismail, held in noisome underground dungeons—"filthy, stinking and full of vermin"[26]—often forced to sleep in their own excrement, these Christian slaves were frequently tortured and beaten senseless to make them convert. Conversion did not bring them freedom, but further work of up to fifteen hours a day in the fierce sun, building Moulay Ismail's endless palaces. Those falling ill were sometimes simply executed at the whim of Moulay Ismail: "When, in that weak and feeble condition, [he saw] that [the slaves] could not stand on their legs when dragged before him, he instantly killed seven of them, making their resting place a slaughter house," witnessed one English slave.[27] "We were driven like beasts thither and exposed to sale," wrote William Okeley, who was auctioned at Algiers. "Their cruelty is great, but their covetousness exceeds their cruelty."[28]

The utter wanton cruelty and capriciousness of Moulay Ismail terrified the white European slaves. As one French padre observed, "[I]t is one of his common diversions, at one motion, to mount his horse, draw his cimiter and cut off the head of the slave who holds his stirrup."[29] When one of the Spanish slaves walked past him without doffing his hat, Moulay "darted his spear at him," piercing deep into the man's flesh and causing him further horrible pain when the sultan ripped the barbed tip out of his skin.[30] When a mason was found guilty of shoddy work, Moulay ordered his black guard to break fifty bricks over the mason's head; the latter, covered in blood, was then thrown into jail.[31] "He was of so fickle, cruel and sanguine a nature that none could be even for one hour secure of life," wrote Thomas Pellow, one of the English slaves. Moulay Ismail's viciousness was mirrored in the equally cruel black slaves who were appointed to oversee the white captives and their work: "[They] immediately punish the least stop or inadvertency, and often will not allow the poor creatures time to eat their bread," lamented Pellow. Those slaves that were considered to have been slack in their work were beaten with cudgels. The black overseer would strike at the head of the white slaves, "and, when he had broke it, counterfeited the charitable surgeon, applying unslacked lime to stanch the bleeding," wrote Germain Mouette, a French slave.[32] The black slave drivers amused themselves by waking the white slaves at night, beating them, and forcing the already exhausted men to do more hard labor.

It was only in 1816 after a crushing British naval victory, and the total destruction of Algiers, that more than fifteen hundred slaves were freed and that Barbary corsairs ceased to be a menace to European shipping.

Abolition of slavery was very much a Western initiative, as Bernard Lewis has remarked; "[I]t was Europe . . . that first decided to set the slaves free: at home, then in the colonies, and finally in all the world."[33]

Islamic Racism

The situation is similar as regards racism. While the West has taken great steps to legally ban all kinds of discrimination on the basis of race in all aspects of modern Western societies, to the extent of a reverse discrimination against whites, the rest of the world remains vehemently and openly racist. A hatred of Jews is widespread in the Islamic world, often encouraged by the state: as, for instance, in the state funding of the film of *The Protocols of the Elders of Zion*, a forgery taken seriously by all Muslims. This Jew hatred has little to do with the Israeli-Arab conflict, and, like slavery, is deeply ingrained in Islamic culture, sanctioned by the Koran, and encouraged by the example set by Muhammad in his frequent attacks and massacres of Jewish tribes, families, and individuals. *Mein Kampf* is very popular in the Muslim world, and during World War II, the grand mufti of Jerusalem, Haj Amin al-Husseini, met with Adolf Hitler to ask for German help in exterminating the Jews of the Muslim world.

As Kenneth Timmerman notes, "I was stunned to learn the story of Haj Mohammad Amin al-Hussein . . ."[34] "Not only did he meet with Hitler in Berlin in 1941: he became the Arabic voice of Nazi Germany in all their broadcasts to the Arab world, exhorting Muslims to murder Jews and enact Hitler's final solution. Not by coincidence, one of his greatest students is Yasser Arafat, who in moments of weakness claims (wrongly, I believe) that he is Haj Mohammad Amin's nephew."[35] One can scarcely imagine one politician in the West surviving in office if he or she made racist remarks in the way the Malayasian prime minister, Mahathir Muhammad, regularly does. In October 2003 he said to an Islamic conference: "The Europeans killed 6 million Jews out of 12 million, but today the Jews rule the world by proxy. They get others to fight and die for them."[36]

An edition of the official Egyptian daily newspaper *Al-Akhbar* on April 29, 2002, featured a column by Fatma Abdallah Mahmoud, titled "Accursed Forever and Ever." He wrote:

> They [the Jews] are accursed in heaven and on earth. They are accursed from the day the human race was created and from the day their mothers bore them. They are accursed also because they murdered the Prophets. They murdered the Prophet John the Baptist and served up his head on a golden platter to the singer and dancer Salome. Allah also cursed them with a thousand curses when they argued with and resisted his words of truth, deceived the Prophet Moses, and worshiped the golden calf that they created with their own hands!!
>
> These accursed ones are a catastrophe for the human race. They are the virus of the generation, doomed to a life of humiliation and wretchedness until Judgment Day. They are also accursed because they repeatedly tried to murder the Prophet Muhammad. They threw a stone at him, but missed. Another time, they tried to mix poison in his food, but providence saved him from their treachery and their crimes. Allah cursed them when they carried out the criminal massacre of the peaceful Palestinians in Sabra and Shatilla. They are accursed, they, their fathers, and their forefathers . . . until Judgment Day, because they burst into Al-Aqsa Mosque with their defiled, filthy feet and violated its sanctity.
>
> Finally, they are accursed, fundamentally, because they are the plague of the generation and the bacterium of all time. Their history always was and always will be stained with treachery, falseness, and lying. Historical documents prove

> it. Thus, the Jews are accursed—the Jews of our time, those who preceded them and those who will come after them, if any Jews come after them.
>
> With regard to the fraud of the Holocaust . . . Many French studies have proven that this is no more than a fabrication, a lie, and a fraud!! That is, it is a "scenario," the plot of which was carefully tailored, using several faked photos completely unconnected to the truth. Yes, it is a film, no more and no less. Hitler himself, whom they accuse of Nazism, is in my eyes no more than a modest "pupil" in the world of murder and bloodshed. He is completely innocent of the charge of frying them in the hell of his false Holocaust!! The entire matter, as many French and British scientists and researchers have proven, is nothing more than a huge Israeli plot aimed at extorting the German government in particular and the European countries in general. But I, personally and in light of this imaginary tale, complain to Hitler, even saying to him from the bottom of my heart: "If only you had done it, brother, if only it had really happened, so that the world could sigh in relief [without] their evil and sin."
>
> Since their birth, the Jews [have amassed] hatred and hostility towards Islam and the Muslims. They have always laid traps for the Muslims, woven conspiracies and crimes against them, and been biased in favor of their enemies and occupiers. . . . They always try to warp and distort everything fair and beautiful!! Basically, they are a model of moral ugliness, debasement, and degradation. If only Allah would curse them more and more, to the end of all generations. Amen.[37]

One cannot imagine a Western politician or intellectual or Western newspaper writing or publishing such a hateful screed. Sen. Trent Lott was forced to resign in December 2002 as Senate leader for a single remark about segregation, as it happens, not long after the above diatribe against Jews by the Egyptian journalist. There would be an outcry if any Western politician made similar remarks about Arabs, from both inside and outside the West. Such an outcry would be a flagrant case of double standards, but it is also, of course, a compliment to the West. We do not expect such behavior from Western intellectuals and politicians.

Islamic Anti-Semitism

But is Islamic anti-Semitism only a modern phenomenon? What of the so-called golden age of Islamic tolerance, above all as depicted in Islamic Spain? Here the willingness to accept the clichés of the romantics is palpable. And those whom we expect to have done their own research and not merely to accept and pass on these clichés so often disappoint.

Consider the case of Amartya Sen, a celebated economist and winner of the Nobel Prize. Sen has in recent years written on subjects outside his normal area of research. Unfortunately, he seems not to have bothered to check his history, something that would have been easy given the resources available to him.

Let us look at how Amartya Sen treats, for example, the myth of Maimonides. Sen tells us twice in his book *Identity and Violence* that when "the Jewish Philosopher Maimonides was forced to emigrate from an intolerant Europe in the twelfth century, he found a tolerant refuge in the Arab world."[38] I do not know how to characterize this misinterpretation of history—"willful," "grotesque," "dishonest," or "typical"? It is certainly an indication that in the present intellectual climate that one can denigrate Europe any way one wishes, to the point of distorting history, without any of the distinguished scholars who blurbed the book raising an eyebrow. Ironically, the one reviewer who did object to Sen's "potted history," which "is tailored for interfaith dialogues," was Fouad Ajami in the *Washington Post*. Ajami reminded Sen that "this will not do as history. Maimonides, born in 1135, did not flee 'Europe' for the 'Arab world': He fled his native Córdoba in Spain, which was then in the grip of religious-political terror, choking under the yoke of a Berber Muslim dynasty, the Almohades. . . . Maimonides and his family fled the fire of the Muslim city-states in the Iberian Peninsula to Morocco and then to Jerusalem. There was darkness and terror in Morocco as well, and Jerusalem was equally inhospitable in the time of the Crusader Kingdom. Deliverance came only in Cairo—the exception, not the rule, its social peace maintained by the enlightened Saladin."[39]

Moses Maimonides, Jewish rabbi, physician, and philosopher, was fleeing the Muslims, the intolerant Almohades, who conquered Córdoba in 1148. The Almohades persecuted the Jews and offered them the choice of conversion to Islam, death, or exile. Maimonides' family and other Jews chose exile. But this did not bring any peace to the Jews, who had to be on the move constantly to avoid the all-conquering Almohades. After a brief sojourn in Morocco and the Holy Land, Maimonides settled in Fostat, Egypt, where he was physician to the grand vizier Alfadhil, and possibly Saladin, the Kurdish sultan.

Maimonides' *The Epistle to the Jews of Yemen* was written in about 1172 in reply to inquiries by Jacob ben Nathanael al-Fayyūmi, then head of the Jewish community in Yemen.[40] The Jews of Yemen were passing through a crisis, as they were being forced to convert to Islam, a campaign launched in about 1165 by 'Abd-al-Nabī ibn Mahdi. Maimonides provided them with guidance and with what encouragement he could. *The Epistle to the Jews of Yemen* gives a clear view of what Maimonides thought of Muhammad the Prophet, "the Madman," as he calls him, and of Islam generally. This is what Maimonides wrote:

> You write that the rebel leader in Yemen decreed compulsory apostasy for the Jews by forcing the Jewish inhabitants of all the places he had subdued to desert the Jewish religion just as the Berbers had compelled them to do in Maghreb [i.e., Islamic West]. Verily, this news has broken our backs and has astounded and dumbfounded the whole of our community. And rightly so. For these are evil tidings, "and whosoever heareth of them, both his ears tingle" (1 Samuel 3:11). Indeed our hearts are weakened, our minds are confused, and the powers of the body wasted because of the dire misfortunes which brought religious persecutions upon us from the two ends of the world, the East and the West, "so that the enemies were in the midst of Israel, some on this side, and some on that side" (Joshua 8:22).[41]

Maimonides points out that persistent persecutions of the Jews by the Muslims amount to forced conversion: "[T]he continuous persecutions will cause many to drift away from our faith, to have misgivings, or to go astray, because they witnessed our feebleness, and noted the triumph of our adversaries and their dominion over us."[42]

He continues: "After him arose the Madman who emulated his precursor since he paved the way for him. But he added the further objective of procuring rule and submission, and he invented his well known religion."[43] Many medieval Jewish writers commonly referred to Muhammad as *ha-meshugga'*, or "Madman."[44]

Maimonides points to one of the reasons for Muslim hatred of Jews: "Inasmuch as the Muslims could not find a single proof in the entire Bible nor a reference or possible allusion to their prophet which they could utilize, they were compelled to accuse us saying, 'You have altered the text of the Torah, and expunged every trace of the name of Mohammed therefrom.' They could find nothing stronger than this ignominious argument."[45]

He notes the depth of Muslim hatred for the Jews, but he also remarks on the Jewish tendency for denial, a feature that he insists will hasten their destruction:

> Remember, my co-religionists, that on account of the vast number of our sins, God has hurled us in the midst of this people, the Arabs, who have persecuted us severely, and passed baneful and discriminatory legislation against us, as Scripture has forewarned us, "Our enemies themselves shall judge us" (Deuteronomy 32:31). **Never did a nation molest, degrade, debase and hate us as much as they. . . .** Although we were dishonored by them beyond human endurance, and had to put with their fabrications, yet we behaved like him who is depicted by the inspired writer, "But I am as a deaf man, I hear not, and I am as a dumb man that openeth not his mouth" (Psalms 38:14). Similarly our sages instructed us to bear the prevarications and preposterousness of Ishmael in

> silence. They found a cryptic allusion for this attitude in the names of his sons "Mishma, Dumah, and Massa" (Genesis 25:14), which was interpreted to mean, "Listen, be silent, and endure" (Targum Pseudo-Jonathan, ad locum). We have acquiesced, both old and young, to inure ourselves to humiliation, as Isaiah instructed us "I gave my back to the smiters, and my cheeks to them that plucked off the hair" (50:6). All this notwithstanding, we do not escape this continued maltreatment which well nigh crushes us. No matter how much we suffer and elect to remain at peace with them, they stir up strife and sedition, as David predicted, "I am all peace, but when I speak, they are for war" (Psalms 120:7). If, therefore, we start trouble and claim power from them absurdly and preposterously we certainly give ourselves up to destruction.[46]

During the last fifteen years, certain Western scholars have tried to argue that (1) Islamic anti-Semitism, that is, the hatred of Jews, is only a recent phenomenon learned from the Nazis during and after the 1940s, and that (2) Jews lived safely under Muslim rule for centuries, especially during the golden age of Muslim Spain. Both assertions are unsupported by the evidence. Islam 1, that is, the Islam of the texts, as found in the Koran, the hadith (the sayings and deeds of the Prophet and his Companions), and in the Sira (the biography of Muhammad, which obviously overlaps with the hadith); and Islam 2, that is, the Islam developed or elabortated from those texts early on by the Koranic commentators and jurisconsults and then set in stone more than a millennium ago; and even Islam 3, in the sense of Islamic civilization, that is—what Muslims actually did historically do—have all been deeply anti-Semitic. That is, all have been anti-infidel so that Christians too are regarded with disdain and contempt and hatred, but the Jews have been served, or been seen to have merited, a special animus.

Islam 1: Koran, Muhammad, Hadith, and Sunna

Muhammad set the example for anti-Semitism. The oldest extant biography of Muhammad, that by Ibn Ishaq as transmitted by Ibn Hisham, is replete with the Prophet's evident hatred of Jews. He had Jews assassinated if he felt that they had somehow insulted or disobeyed him. When Muhammad gave the command "Kill any Jew that falls into your power,"[47] one of his followers, Ibn Mas'ūd, assassinated Ibn Sunayna, a Jewish merchant. Other followers of Muhammad were happy to obey similar orders from their leader: "Our attack upon God's enemy cast terror among the Jews, and there was no Jew in Medina who did not fear for his life."[48] Other Jews killed included Sallam ibn Abu'l-Huqayq,[49] Ka'b b. al-Ashraf,[50] and al-Yusayr.[51] The Jewish tribe Banu Qurayza, consisting of between six hundred and eight hundred men, were exterminated,[52] while the Jewish tribe of Banu'l-Nadir were attacked, and all who remained alive were banished.[53]

Here are two examples from the hadith of Muhammad's attitude toward Jews; first from *Ibn Sa'd*:

> Then occurred the "sariyyah" [raid] of Salim Ibn Umayr al-Amri against Abu Afak, the Jew, in [the month of] Shawwal in the beginning of the twentieth month from the hijrah [immigration from Mecca to Medina in 622 AD], of the Apostle of Allah. Abu Afak, was from Banu Amr Ibn Awf, and was an old man who had attained the age of one hundred and twenty years. He was a Jew, and used to instigate the people against the Apostle of Allah, and composed (satirical) verses [about Muhammad].
>
> Salim Ibn Umayr who was one of the great weepers and who had participated in Badr, said, "I take a vow that I shall either kill Abu Afak or die before him." He waited for an opportunity until a hot night came, and Abu Afak slept in an open place. Salim Ibn Umayr knew it, so he placed the sword on his liver and pressed it till it reached his bed. The enemy of Allah screamed and the people who were his followers, rushed to him, took him to his house and interred him.[54]

The second example comes from *al-Bukharī*: "Bani An-Nadir and Bani Quraiza fought, so the Prophet (Muhammad) exiled Bani An-Nadir and allowed Bani Quraiza to remain at their places. He then killed their men and distributed their women, children and property among the Muslims, but some of them came to the Prophet and he granted them safety, and they embraced Islam. He exiled all the Jews from Medina. They were the Jews of Bani Qainuqa', the tribe of 'Abdullah bin Salam and the Jews of Bani Haritha and all the other Jews of Medina."[55]

Muhammad's intolerance of other religions is well attested: "I was told that the last injunction the apostle [Muhammad] gave [before his death] was in his words 'Let not two religions be left in the Arabian peninsula.'"[56] Or, as *Abū Dāwūd* put it: "The Apostle of Allah said, 'I will certainly expel the Jews and the Christians from Arabia.'"[57]

After September 11, 2001, many Muslims and apologists of Islam glibly came out with the following Koranic quote to show that Islam and the Koran disapproved of violence and killing: "Whoever killed a human being shall be looked upon as though he had killed all mankind" (Sura V.32). Unfortunately, these wonderful-sounding words, which come from a preexisting Jewish text (*Mishnah*, IV Division),[58] are being quoted out of context. For the very next verse offers quite a different meaning from that of V.32. Here is V.33: "That was why

We laid it down for the Israelites that whoever killed a human being, except as a punishment for murder or other villainy in the land, shall be looked upon as though he had killed all mankind; and that whoever saved a human life shall be regarded as though he had saved all mankind. Our apostles brought them veritable proofs: yet it was not long before many of them committed great evils in the land. Those that make war against God and His apostle and spread disorder shall be put to death or crucified or have their hands and feet cut off on alternate sides, or be banished from the country."

The supposedly noble sentiments of the first verse, taken from a Jewish source, are entirely undercut by the second verse, which has become a murderous menacing by Muhammad of the Jews. Far from abjuring violence, these verses aggressively insist that any who oppose the Prophet will be killed or crucified, mutilated, and banished.

As for the intolerance against Jews and Christians, and their inferior status as dhimmis, we have IX.29–35:

> Fight against such of those to whom the Scriptures were given as believe neither in God nor the Last Day, who do not forbid what God and His apostle have forbidden, and do not embrace the true faith, until they pay tribute out of hand and are utterly subdued.
>
> The Jews say Ezra is the son of God, while the Christians say the Messiah is the son of God. Such are their assertions, by which they imitate the infidels of old. God confound them! How perverse they are!
>
> They make of their clerics and their monks, and of the Messiah, the son of Mary, Lords besides God; though they were ordered to serve one God only. There is no god but Him. Exalted be He above those whom they deify besides Him! . . .
>
> It is He who has sent forth His apostle with guidance and the true Faith to make it triumphant over all religions, howver much the idolaters may dislike it.
>
> O you who believe! Lo! many of the Jewish rabbis and the Christian monks devour the wealth of mankind wantonly and debar men from the way of Allah; they who hoard up gold and silver and spend it not in the way of Allah, unto them give tidings of painful doom.

The moral of all the above is clear: Islam is the only true religion, Jews and Christians are devious and moneygrubbing, are not to be trusted, and even have to pay a tax in the most humiliating way:

> **II.61:** Wretchedness and baseness were stamped upon them [that is, the Jews], and they were visited with wrath from Allah. That was because they disbelieved

in Allah's revelations and slew the prophets wrongfully. That was for their disobedience and transgression.

IV.44–46: Have you not seen those who have received a portion of the Scripture? They purchase error, and they want you to go astray from the path.

But Allah knows best who your enemies are, and it is sufficient to have Allah as a friend. It is sufficient to have Allah as a helper.

Some of the Jews pervert words from their meanings, and say, "We hear and we disobey," and "Hear without hearing," and "Heed us!" twisting with their tongues and slandering religion. If they had said, "We have heard and obey," or "Hear and observe us" it would have been better for them and more upright. But Allah had cursed them for their disbelief, so they believe not, except for a few.

IV.160–61: And for the evildoing of the Jews, We have forbidden them some good things that were previously permitted them, and because of their barring many from Allah's way.

And for their taking usury which was prohibited for them, and because of their consuming people's wealth under false pretense. We have prepared for the unbelievers among them a painful punishment.[59]

Islam 2: Koranic Commentators

Al-Baydawi's *Anwār al-tanzīl wa-asrār al-ta'wil* provided this gloss on Koran II.61: "'[H]umiliation and wretchedness' covered them like a dome, or stuck to them like wet clay to a wall—a metaphor for their denial of the bounty. The Jews are mostly humiliated and wretched either of their own accord, or out of coercion of the fear of having their *jizya* doubled. . . . Either they became deserving of His wrath [or] . . . the affliction of 'humiliation and wretchedness' and the deserving wrath which preceded this."[60]

Ibn Kathir emphasized the Jews' eternal humiliation in accord with Koran II.61: "This ayah indicates that the Children of Israel were plagued with humiliation, and this will continue, meaning it will never cease. They will continue to suffer humiliation at the hands of all who interact with them, along with the disgrace that they feel inwardly."[61]

Islam 3: Islamic Civilization

Here are examples of the persecution of Jews in Islamic lands: the massacre of more than six thousand Jews in Fez (Morocco) in 1033; of the hundreds of Jews killed between 1010 and 1013 near Córdoba and other parts of Muslim Spain; of the entire Jewish community of roughly four thousand in Granada during the Muslim riots of 1066. Referring to the latter massacre, Robert Wistrich writes: "This was a disaster, as serious as that which overtook the Rhineland Jews thirty years later during the First Crusade, yet it has rarely received much scholarly attention." Wistrich continues: "In Kairouan [Tunisia] the Jews were persecuted and forced to leave in 1016, returning later only to be expelled again. In Tunis in 1145 they were forced to convert or to leave, and during the following decade there were fierce anti-Jewish persecutions throughout the country. A similar pattern of events occurred in Morocco after the massacre of Jews in Marrakesh in 1232. Indeed, in the Islamic world from Spain to the Arabian peninsula the looting and killing of Jews, along with punitive taxation, confinement to ghettos, the enforced wearing of distinguishing marks on clothes (an innovation in which Islam preceded medieval Christendom), and other humiliations were rife."[62]

ASIAN RACISM

The racism of the Chinese, Japanese, and Indians of the subcontinent is not frequently discussed, but is amply documented historically and is extant. The visit of US Secretary of State Condoleezza Rice to China in April 2005 led to some repugnant racist attacks on her, as a courageous article by Martin Jacques in the *Guardian*, pointed out.[63] The introduction alone to a pioneering work edited by Frank Dikötter makes for eye-opening reading.[64] This is a necessary corrective to the politically correct posture that deliberately ignores the "racialised identities in East Asia" that have led to discrimination there.[65] Kang Youwei, the celebrated Chinese philosopher of the late nineteenth century, wrote of black Africans who, "with their iron faces, silver teeth, slanting jaws like a pig, front view like an ox, full breasts and long hair, their hands and feet dark black, stupid like sheep and swine," should be whitened by intermarriage—provided, of course, one could persuade a white girl to marry such "a monstrously ugly black." These views have prevailed to this day. As Dikötter writes, "[O]fficial policies endorsing racial discrimination and leading to abuses of human rights can be found in most East Asian states. Myths of origins, ideologies of blood and theories of biological descent have formed a central part in the cultural construction of identity in China and Japan since the nationalist movements of the late nineteenth century. Naturalised as a pure and homogeneous 'Yamato race' in Japan, or as a biological descent group from the 'Yellow Emperor' in China, political territories have been conflated with imaginary biological entities by nationalist writers."[66]

Both Japan and China created "the Other," defined in terms of "civilization" and "barbarism," racialized into binary oppositions between "advanced" and "backward" groups of people. For the Japanese, the Chinese were a different race, while they themselves were culturally and biologically unique. In the context of Japanese colonial expansion to Korea and China, "it was assumed that the differences in economic and political capacities of the peoples of East Asia were the result of natural or biological laws: colonial populations were regularly contrasted with Japanese modernity. 'Spiritual and physical purity' were said to be the attributes which marked the Japanese as the 'leading race' in their divine mission in Asia. In war-time Japan, a sense of unique purity—both moral and genetic—was central to the notion of racial separateness in which other population groups were dehumanised as beasts and ultimately as demons. In both China and Japan, other population groups were also ranked according to their presumed attributes."[67]

The state disseminated these racial theories by means of school textbooks, anthropology exhibitions, and travel literature, and certainly found a popular audience receptive to them. As Dikötter emphasizes, the pseudoscientific theories helped self-definition but also produced the racially excluded Others, notably "Blacks" and "Jews," even though these groups were not heavily represented in China and Japan. Nonetheless, they are central in the racial taxonomies drafted in China and Japan in the twentieth century.[68] Writing in the late 1990s, Dikötter felt that in East Asia, in contrast to other regions, "there is no clear sign that the hierarchies of power maintained through racial discourse are being questioned." Talk of Japanese biological uniqueness and purity seems to dominate discussions. Blacks and blackness have become symbols of the savage Other, and are reflected in such essays as "We Cannot Marry Negroes" by Taisuke Fujishima. An influx of foreign workers has led to fears of racial contamination, and the Japanese government refused to ratify the International Convention on the Elimination of Racial Discrimination. A similar situation prevails in China, where African students on university campuses are periodically attacked since they are imagined as belonging to an inferior species.[69] Theories of racial purity are used to legitimize discrimination against social groups, such as the Tibetans and Uighurs.

Dikötter concludes on a somber note: "In an era of economic globalisation and political depolarisation, racial identities and racial discrimination have increased in East Asia, affecting both the human rights of marginalised groups and collective perceptions of the world order. Official policies endorsing racial discrimination and leading to abuses of human rights can be found in most East Asian states."[70]

Racism in India and Pakistan is also prevalent. Black African students often face overt racism on Indian university campuses, and so do students even from the Northeast of India, as Aparna Pallavi reports:

> As an undergraduate student at Delhi University in the early 1990s, Dr. Renu (Gupta) Naidu took little notice when her friends routinely referred to students from the Northeast as "Chinkies" or hurled obscenities or racial insults at them. "Any Northeastern student entering a college campus earns the epithet 'Chinky' on day one, and has to live with being looked at as, at the very least, an oddity, for the rest of her or his stay," says Naidu. "Students told me about being asked questions like whether they eat rats." This racial hostility comes unbidden from the non-Northeastern student community. Naidu had herself faced discrimination as a 'non-Marathi" student during her post-graduation at Nagpur, and it dawned on her that Northeastern students, with their distinctive "non-plainspeople" epicanthic features, behavior and dress habits, were in all likelihood confronting far more discrimination than she had. In June 2006, Naidu was awarded a PhD for her work on the lives of Northeastern tribal girl students in Delhi, with her research based on interviews with 200 students from 10 colleges in Delhi University's North Campus. The first disturbing fact—statistics compiled from official records of various colleges in the city—that Naidu's study has uncovered is that the dropout rates of Northeastern students touches 50 per cent, with more girls dropping out than boys. The reasons for this trend, according to Naidu, lie in the intense socio-cultural conflict, and the resultant stress, that impact all aspects of the lives of students from the Northeast.[71]

Discrimination against Dalits, formerly referred to as the untouchables, remains strong, and semantic games do not change the fact that it is a kind of racism. The National Campaign on Dalit Human Rights (NCDHR) describes itself as a "part of a wider struggle to abolish 'untouchability' and to 'cast out caste.' 'Untouchability' and caste discrimination continue to be a brutal reality for more than 160 million Dalits living in India today, despite the fact that more than half a century has passed since India was born as a 'democratic' and independent state."[72] Here is an account of a typical attack against Dalits: "Gohana is a small Tehsil, a local administrative unit, in Sonepat District in the State of Haryana. It is situated about 60 kilometers away from the National Capital, New Delhi. It witnessed a caste rivalry between Dalits and the dominant caste 'Jats,' culminating into mass exodus of Dalits and finally burning down of about 55 to 60 Dalit houses with full support of local Police from 27 August 2005 up to 31 August 2005. A violent mob of about 1,500 to 2,000 Jats armed with spears, batons, petrol and kerosene oil went on a maddening spree burning down houses belonging to a particular Dalit caste 'Balmikis,' who are other wise called

'Bhangis,' the manual scavengers."[73] The Delhi Declaration in August 2005 on behalf of the Dalits specified that between 1981 and 2001 about three hundred thousand cases of "untouchability and atrocities were registered with the police."[74] This declaration lists many varieties of the discrimination that Dalits face on a daily basis in modern India.

In a well-documented attack on Gandhi, G. B. Singh points out that at the time of the Zulu Wars in South Africa, the Mahatma was urging Indians to show "their patriotism by killing blacks."[75] Singh argues, "Gandhi is overly eager to see his Indians in a war against blacks. After all, he tells them rather frankly, they too are colonists over blacks and therefore, standing shoulder to shoulder with fellow white colonists is a natural progression."[76] Singh then ends his chapter with a quote from Richard Grenier's 1983 article, which made the same points: "It is something of an anomaly that Gandhi, held in popular myth to be a pure pacifist . . . , was until fifty not ill-disposed to war at all. [I]n three wars, no sooner had the bugles sounded than Gandhi was clamoring for arms. To form new Regiments! To fight! To destroy the enemies of the empire! Regular Indian army units fought in both the Boer War and World War I, but this was not enough for Gandhi. He wanted to raise new troops, even, in the case of the Boer and Kaffir Wars, from a tiny Indian colony in South Africa."[77]

And what of non-Western imperialism? Japanese incursions into Korea and China are still remembered with horror, especially the Rape of Nanking, when Japanese soldiers killed more than three hundred thousand unarmed civilians.[78] Islamic colonialism trampled under foot and permanently destroyed many cultures. In the words of Michael Cook, "The Arab conquests rapidly destroyed one empire, and permanently detached large territories of another. This was, for the states in question, an appalling catastrophe."[79] Or, as Cook and Crone put it, the Muslim conquests were achieved at "extraordinary cultural costs."[80]

Professor Speros Vryonis Jr., in his *The Decline of Medieval Hellenism in Asia Minor and the Process of Islamization from the Eleventh through the Fifteenth Century*, describes how the essentially Hellenic and Christian way of life, with its magnificent monasteries, was destroyed by the Turkish invasions of the eleventh century. Many people fled or were captured, massacred, or enslaved.

After his survey of the conquest of Anatolia, Vryonis writes,

> This . . . survey of Anatolia during the latter part of the eleventh and twelfth century indicates that violence, destruction, and upheaval accompanied the Turkish invasions and occupation of the peninsula. Consequently, the lament of Anna Comnena on the fate of Byzantine Anatolia constitutes something more than an empty rhetorical exercise:

> "And since the succession of Diogenes the barbarians tread upon the boundaries of the empire of the Rhomaioi . . . the barbarian hand was not restricted until the reign of my father. Swords and spears were whetted against the Christians, and also battles, wars, and massacres. Cities were obliterated, lands were plundered, and the whole land of the Rhomaioi was stained by blood of Christians. Some fell piteously [the victims] of arrows and spears, others being driven away from their homes were carried off captives to the cities of Persia. Terror reigned over all and they hastened to hide in the caves, forests, mountains, and hills. Among them some cried aloud in horror at those things which they suffered, being led off to Persia; and others who yet survived (if some did remain within the Rhomaic boundaries), lamenting, cried, the one for his son, the other for his daughter. One bewailed his brother, another his cousin who had died previously, and like women shed hot tears. And there was at that time not one relationship which was without tears and without sadness."[81]

To underline his point Vryonis simply lists, on two pages, all the towns, villages, and provinces that were "pillaged, enslaved, massacred, or besieged"—a total of at least eighty towns and villages, thirty-four environs of towns and villages, and thirteen provinces.

Vryonis quotes the fourteenth-century author Demetrius Cydones on similar consequences of the conquest of Anatolia at a later date: "They took from us all the lands which we enjoyed from the Hellespont eastward to the mountains of Armenia. The cities they razed to the ground, pillaged the religious sanctuaries, broke open the graves, and filled all with blood and corpses. They outraged the souls of the inhabitants, forcing then to deny God and giving to them their own [i.e., the Turks'] defiled mysteries. They [the Turks] abused their [Christians'] souls, alas, with wanton outrage! Denuding them of all property and their freedom, they left the [Christians as] weak images of slaves, exploiting the remaining strength of the wretched ones for their own prosperity."[82]

Vryonis concludes, "The sultans confiscated the vast majority of Christian lands, revenues, and buildings and bestowed them upon their Muslim secular and religious followers. Consequently, mosques, medresses, tekkes, hospitals, and the like spread across Anatolia, often in the very building and on the same lands formerly belonging to the Greek church."[83] By the end of the fifteenth century the destruction of the Byzantine Empire was complete.[84] Contrast this with the presence of the British in India, which led to the Bengal Renaissance!

We can legitimately criticize many aspects of non-Western cultures without being reduced to sullen silence by shouts of "Orientalism" in Said's pejorative sense. Postmodernism and its child, cultural relativism, have discouraged cross-cultural judgments in recent years. As a result, we ignore the suffering and deny the rights of large sections of humankind. The philosopher Bernard Williams wrote, "In the fascinating book by Bernal de Diaz, who went with Cortez to Mexico, there is an account of what they felt when they came upon the sacrificial temples. This morally unpretentious collection of bravos was genuinely horrified by the Aztec practices. It would surely be absurd to regard this reaction as merely parochial or self-righteous. It rather indicated something which their conduct did not indicate, that they regarded the Indians as men rather than as wild animals."[85] Similarly, in India some British administrators were shocked by the Hindu custom of *suttee* (the burning of widows on the funeral pyres of their husbands), and the practice of infanticide. Eventually steps were taken to suppress them, particularly under Lord Bentinck in the 1830s. In India, there were many British Orientalists who were so sympathetic to Indian culture that they were unable to bring themselves to criticize any aspect of it. While it was commendable on their part to see local customs from the perspective of the Indians themselves, such an attitude leads to a relativism, that makes cross-cultural criticism, and hence reform, nigh impossible. Finally, such uncritical acceptance of another's culture smacks of insincerity or even worse, condescension, implying such unpleasant opinions as: "They are not ready for reform"; "We must not judge them by our standards"; and so forth. In this context, the controversial work of Indian scholar Javed Majeed makes sense. Majeed actually defends James Mill's *The History of British India*, which had nothing but contempt for Hindu culture, as a healthy antidote to Orientalist romanticism.[86]

Is it so reprehensible to have cultural and aesthetic preferences? The cultural relativist, of course, cannot object if I choose to opt for my own cultural customs. I am not a racist if I do so. When William Empson says he prefers Western music—"I think it is true to say that European music is a much larger creature than Far Eastern music, it is fresh air"[87]—is he being racist?

I would go further. I endorse the Universal Declaration of Human Rights of 1948, and whatever the historical pedigree or the intellectual origins of the notion of human rights, I believe they are universal and exemplified fully, or at least realizable, only in Western-style democracies with their firm separation of church and state.

I have noted how Said neglected serious discussion of German Orientalists, for that would have destroyed his argument of the complicity of Orientalists with imperialists—Germany did not have colonies in the Middle East.[88] Another group of scholars that obviously does not fit into his simplistic schema is the Jews, and thus they are excluded from his study. But as Martin Kramer in his invaluable collection of essays wrote, "No appreciation of Islamic studies is complete without some appreciation of the special character of the contribution made by Jews."[89] Bernard Lewis, thirty years earlier, had made the same point: "In the development of Islamic studies in European and, later, American universities, Jews, and in particular Jews of Orthodox background and education, play an altogether disproportionate role. . . . The role of these scholars in the development of every aspect of Islamic studies has been immense—not only in the advancement of scholarship but also in the enrichment of the Western view of Oriental religion, literature, and history, by the substitution of knowledge and understanding for prejudice and ignorance."[90] While Goldziher and Weil make fleeting appearances, usually in a long lineup of names that are frequently paraded before us, there is no discussion of their work or of its importance. Other Jewish scholars are simply ignored—scholars such as Abraham Geiger, H. Derenbourg, Josef Horovitz, Max Meyerhof, Ernst Herzfeld, Richard Walzer, Richard Ettinghausen, and Paul Kraus, to name some of the most prominent.

For Said it is the Arabs and "Orientals" who are the victims of European imperialism, but not the Jews. Said does not mention the incovenient fact that the Jews constituted a significant part of the population of the Arab countries, and made great contributions to them, but were chased out or persecuted especially during moments of Arab nationalism or Muslim fervor. A great number of the Sephardic Jews ended up in Israel fleeing from Muslim persecution, so that they now constitute about 50 percent of the Israeli population. It makes no sense to talk of Israel as a European colony, or to reduce everything to the East versus West anti-imperialist struggle, as Said does.

Another curious omission in Said's *Orientalism* is the "Orientals" themselves. By the latter term Said seems to mean only Muslims. He himself complains that Orientals are never given a voice,[91] and he uses Marx's saying "They cannot represent themselves; they must be represented" as an epigraph to his introduction. But Orientals have been representing themselves for centuries: in art, literature, and philosophical and historical writings. They seem to exist for Said only when written about by Orientalists. Surely that is a truly "Orientalist" position, in his pejorative definition. I have given voice to these Orientals—that is, I have quoted Orientals themselves, as Said never does—and the picture that emerges is far different from what Said has "represented" to us. Said has the exasperating habit of telling Orientals what they should think. If they do not, and if they are contemporary Orientals, like the Iraqi Kanan Makiya, Said subjects them to what Christopher Hitchens calls "venomous attacks." In recent years, where Said had editorial influence, he tried to censor any Orientals who disagreed with his thesis.

Second, Said always posits a passive role for Orientals. They are not autonomous individuals, moral subjects with their own desires and in charge of their destiny, but helpless victims of Western conspiracies. That they were actively and politically engaged with the world is denied by Said; such an admission would destroy the main thrust of his arguments. In modern history, as Hitchens pointed out, Said's position or "reverse-Orientalist dogma" cannot explain "the alliance of the Turkish empire with imperial Germany, any more than it can account for the current colonization by post-Ottoman Turkey of Christian and European Cyprus."[92] I have referred to Islamic and Turkish imperialism in some detail. Susan Bayly also argues against the notion of the passive Orient beloved of Said: "Throughout the nineteenth century there was much debate, exchange, and 'resistance' across the realm of culture, rather than any one-sided transfer of values or institutions. Indeed, it was Asians as much as Britons who shaped these developments in faith, knowledge, and perception."[93] As C. A. Bayly noted, also in the *Oxford History of the British Empire*, one of the many unfortunate consequences of Said's influence was the proliferation of histories that denied "Asians, Africans or Polynesians 'agency' in their own histories more thoroughly than had the nineteenth-century Imperial writers. Some even espoused the view that history could only represent the view of the white conqueror; we can never know the mind of the 'native.' "[94]

Critical Misgivings

Though the view from the Ivory Tower is undoubtedly more pleasant and extensive, one would have hoped scholars to show more courage, and at times be willing to join the fray down in the village square. I have met several learned and well-known historians, literary critics, and Islamologists who firmly believe that Said more or less destroyed their disciplines—perhaps not single-handedly, but with the help of his postmodernist friends—and yet who at the same time were unwilling to risk censure, ridicule, or something far more serious by committing themselves in writing. We should, on the other hand, be grateful to those who did stand up to the intellectual bullying of Edward Said. I have drawn attention to many of these courageous souls throughout the present work. I should like now to review the work of more recent scholars critical of Said.

In a 2003 article in the *Atlantic Monthly*, Christopher Hitchens asks why Edward Said, so well placed to explain East to West and West to East, failed to do so. Outwardly, Hitchens keeps a respectful tone—according far too much merit to Said's *Orientalism*, I think—but his article is quite searching and at times biting. Said is one-sided in his criticism, with the West bearing the brunt, and does not allow, for instance, for Muslim or Turkish imperialism; nor does Said allow that direct Western engagement in the Middle East is legitimate. Quoting Said's introduction to the new edition of *Orientalism*, "*That these supreme fictions* ["the Orient" and "the West"] *lend themselves easily to manipulation and the organisation of collective passion has never been more evident than in our time, when mobilizations of fear, hatred, disgust and resurgent self-pride and arrogance—much of it having to do with Islam and the Arabs on one side, 'we' Westerners on the other—are very large-scale enterprises*," Hitchens comments, "This is composed with a certain obliqueness, which may be accidental, but I can't discover that it really means to say that there are delusions on 'both' these ontologically nonexistent sides. A few sentences further on we read of '*the events of September 11 and their aftermath in the wars against Afghanistan and Iraq*.' Again, if criticism of both sides is intended (and I presume that it is), it comes served in highly discrepant portions. There's no quarrel with the view that 'events' occurred on September 11, 2001; but that the military interventions in Afghanistan and Iraq were wars 'against' either country is subject to debate. A professor of English appreciates the distinction, does he not?"[95]

Hitchens then takes Said to task for suggesting that the American forces in Baghdad deliberately set themselves to annihilate Iraq's cultural patrimony, when in reality "by design the museums and libraries of Baghdad survived the earlier precision bombardment without a scratch and splinter; that much of the looting and desecration occurred before coalition forces had complete control of the city; that no looting was committed by U.S. soldiers; and that the substantial reconstitution of the museum's collection has been undertaken by the occupation authorities, and their allies among Iraqi dissidents, with considerable care and scruple." Responsibility for the looting lies with Iraqi officials and Iraqi mobs.

In the subsequent correspondence engendered by his article, Hitchens pointed out that Said accused him of "racism at bottom," and that Said's work had been "undergoing a qualitative degeneration from what was once a very exalted standard."

Philosopher Irfan Khawaja at a conference in 2005 argued

> that Said is committed to an incoherent set of claims about whether or not doctrines have essences. On the one hand, he is committed by the nature of his thesis to the claim that Orientalism has an essence. On the other hand, he indicts Orientalism for the claim that Islam has an essence. The first claim commits Said to the belief that doctrines can *have* essences. The second commits him to the belief that they

> *cannot*. The combination is obviously inconsistent, but both claims are central to his thesis. Given their inconsistency, Said is obliged, logically, to give up one claim. But given the nature of his thesis, he cannot disavow either claim without disavowing the thesis of his book. The book is therefore an obvious intellectual failure. To add insult to injury, Said explicitly admits that he "designed the book to be theoretically inconsistent." It follows that the book is an *avowed* failure. To add yet further insult to injury, Said has the audacity of accusing Orientalists of violating the laws of logic—a criticism that can be described, at best, as a lifelong act of hypocrisy.[96]

Dr. David Armitage in *The Oxford History of the British Empire* takes issue with Said's position in *Culture and Imperialism* of English literature's indebtedness to, and complicity with, the British Empire in the early-modern period. Armitage shows that

> the impress of Empire upon English literature in the early-modern period was minimal, and mostly *critical* where it was discernible at all, while contemporaries understood literature and empire, what Bacon called *res literaria* and *imperium*, in terms far different from those adopted by modern scholars. Post-colonial studies have generated proto-colonial studies, and recent scholarship has found the literature of the sixteenth and seventeenth centuries to be deeply, because necessarily, inflected by the "imperial" experiences of racial difference, irreducible "otherness," assertions of hierarchy, and national self-determination. However, to apply modern models of the relationship between culture and imperialism to early-modern literature and Empire demands indifference to context and inevitably courts anachronism. It is therefore necessary to be as sceptical about post-Imperial dymystifications as it once was about mid-Imperial complacencies.[97]

Along the way, Armitage provides ample evidence for the anti-imperial strain within European humanism: "humanists were among the greatest critics of European overseas activity in the sixteenth century." Armitage cites the work of George Buchanan, who became a fierce critic of "commercial expansion, territorial conquest, and the exploitation of native people by European powers."[98] Buchanan's greatest pupil was Michel de Montaigne. Armitage argues convincingly that Milton's *Paradise Lost* is a humanist epic that criticizes the expansion of England under the Rump Parliament:

> Throughout his epic, Milton expressed his distaste for the expansion of Pandemonium in classical republican terms, as Satan's minions rejected an option of their own,

> *preferring*
> *Hard liberty before the easy yoke*
> *Of servile pomp*
>
> [*PL*, ii.255–57]
>
> in favour of a venture "[i]n search of this new world" [*PL*, ii.403]. The denizens of Pandemonium became creeping serpents, while the first people of Eden (found at first like the
>
> *American so girt*
> *With feathered cincture, naked else and wild*
>
> [*PL*, ix.1116–17]
>
> were condemned to loss of innocence, expulsion from their native country:
>
> *The world . . . all before them, where to choose*
> *Their place of rest, and providence their guide*
>
> [*PL*, xii. 646–47]
>
> The angel Michael recommended
>
> *The paths of righteousnes . . .*
> *And full of peace*
>
> [*PL*, xi. 814–15]
>
> rather than the bloody enterprise of "subduing nations" [*PL*, xi. 192], and this was consonant with the criticisms of Interregnum foreign policy and the republican warnings against the dangers of territorial expansion that Milton had expressed both overtly and covertly for some fifteen years.[99]

In his article "Ireland and the Empire," David Fitzpatrick points out the crudeness of Said's views concerning Ireland: "Said's specification of 'Ireland's colonial status, which it shares with a host of non-European regions: cultural dependence and antagonism together,' is based upon a premiss incapable of historical verification. Said assumes that 'Irish people can never be English any more than Cambodians or Algerians can be French,' finding confirmation in the record of Irish protest against British government. As argued in the next section, the political expression of Irish attitudes towards Empire was far more various and discordant than this allows. Ireland had its rebels, its 'mediators' and 'collaborators' or 'shoneens,' its Imperialists, and its unselfconscious metropolitans. The battlegrounds of Anglo-Irish and intra-Irish conflict are littered with the ghoulish shards of incompatible images representing the Empire, and Ireland's place within it."[100]

Robert E. Frykenberg confirms many of this book's observations regarding Orientalists in India: "The search of knowledge about India and Indian culture, later to become known as 'Orientalism' was never merely a 'colonialist' imposition upon a hapless India. Orientalist enterprises provided careers for hundreds of Indian scholars throughout India. The scholarly tradition so founded continues down to this day. All-India surveys followed: archaeological, epigraphic, numismatic, and geographic."

Frykenberg explains that "the most impressive orientalist explorations were collaborative, unofficial, and voluntary," citing the example of Col. Colin Mackenzie and his privately funded project to collect as many original manuscripts as possible with the help of Maratha Brahman scholars: "Collections so acquired, reflecting the civilization of South India, manuscripts in every language, became a lasting legacy—something still being explored. Privately financed efforts by dedicated and enthusiastic gentry, European and Indian alike, multiplied. Collections of manuscripts in every part of India, such as those of C. P. Brown (Madras) and Walter Elliot (London), Saraswat Mahal (Thanjavur), Saiyidia Library (Madras and Hyderabad), Khuda Bhaksh (Patna), and Salar Jung (Hyderabad) and Inayat Jung (Aligarh), proliferated. Work done by the Asiatic Society of Bengal and by the Madras Literary Society, reflected in their journals, became a fashion. Neither the scorn of James Mill, nor that of Edward Said, has diminished the appeal of this tradition in India."[101]

Frykenberg also points out a growing number of scholars have argued that "the entire corpus of anti-Orientalist 'colonial discourse analysis' is itself a form of neo-colonialist, Eurocentric nihilism—an ideological approach which hoists and impales itself upon its own petard. All in all, the renewed excitement over various aspects of Orientalism has not been damaged nor diminished by the 'attack' led by Edward Said."[102]

Frykenberg ends his essay with a look at the work of Eugene Irschick and a critique of antihistorical history among the historians of the raj. Irschick argues that "Indians have always been in the forefront of historical understandings of events in India. They were engaged in the production of such histories before 1858 and they have always remained so engaged. Ironies persist: some Indians, especially Marxists and those currently attacking constructions of Orientalism, are often Eurocentric in conceptual and theoretical frames of reference; and some Europeans, especially those who have depended upon local peoples of India for their understandings, are often more Indocentric in outlook."[103]

Finally, Frykenberg summarizes his own argument: "[H]istorical understandings of India, never wholly one or the other, always were and still are products of a dialectical process in which both Indians and Westerners have contributed to an evolving synthesis."[104]

D. A. Washbrook, while not unrespectful of Said, points out the essential contradictions in his position: "The reverse side of his 'Orientalism' is an 'Occidentalism' whereby his analysis of the 'the West' follows precisely the same Enlightenment malpractices which he criticizes in the latter's approaches to 'the East.' He represents European culture in ways which essentialize, objectify, demean, de-rationalize, and de-historicize it; and he re-evaluates it negatively in the light of its own standards of Reason and Freedom." Said's position leads to extreme cultural relativism, which can only lead to Said trapping himself "inside a web of solipsism."[105]

Bassam Tibi argues that Said's influence has made it almost impossible to criticize Islam in the West. Said was guilty of essentializing the West, and refused to acknowledge that his book was responsible for it, calling the Syrian philosopher Sadiq al-'Azm "silly" for having dared to suggest it.[106]

Robert Irwin, in a superb recent book that was published when my own was already nearing completion, has characterized Said's *Orientalism* as "a work of malignant charlatanry in which it is hard to distinguish honest mistakes from wilful misrepresentations." Irwin is a distinguished Orientalist who is perfectly placed to answer many of Said's arguments, and correct many of Said's distortions of the views and work of certain scholars of the past. It is Said who set the terms of the debate, and "[o]ne finds oneself having to discuss not what actually happened in the past, but what Said and his partisans think ought to have happened. Once one has entered the labyrinth of false turns, *trompe-l'oeil* perspectives and cul-de-sacs, it is quite difficult to think one's way out again and reflect rationally and dispassionately about the subject. The distortion of the subject matter of *Orientalism* is so fundamental that to accept its broad framework as something to work with and correct would be merely to waste one's time."[107]

8

THE PATHOLOGICAL NICENESS OF LIBERALS, ANTIMONIES, PARADOXES, AND WESTERN VALUES

It could be argued that the three defining characteristics of the West—rationalism, universalism (with its underlying or implied liberalism), and self-criticism—can lead to their opposites, or to other undesirable consequences. A number of thinkers have remarked on the paradox of democracy: A character in G. K. Chesterton's *The Napoleon of Notting Hill* observes, "The situation invites paradox. We [England] are, in a sense, the purest democracy. We have become a despotism. Have you not noticed how continually in history democracy becomes despotism. People call it the decay of democracy. It is simply its fulfilment."[1] James Burnham, another conservative thinker, also underlined the contradictions inherent in liberalism, with its overwhelming sense of guilt, that could lead to the suicide of the West.[2] It is argued that rationalism can lead to scientism, with its adulation of science and technology at the expense of human values, or the undermining of national myths; that universalism can lead to cosmopolitanism, which tends to deprive one's sense of belonging and loyalty to one's own country or culture; and limitless self-criticism leads to self-hatred, as witnessed in the buffooneries of Michael Moore, the exaggerations of Robert Fisk, and the fanaticism of Noam Chomsky. The anti-racism of Western liberalism turns into the racism of multiculturalism; multiculturalism that, inadvertently perhaps, in effect forced individuals back into cultural ghettoes from which earlier generations had tried to escape, and forced an identity onto individuals, whether the latter welcomed it or not. Multiculturalism offered group equality at the expense of bondage for those individuals who differ, but it was the freedom for those who differ that made the West what it is today.

Legitimate self-criticism of a culture or country of which one is proud, made with a view to making it better still, must be distinguished from the irrational self-hatred as evidenced in the works of certain liberals. As Winston Churchill wrote in 1933: "The worst difficulties from which we suffer do not come from without. They come from within. They do not come from the cottages of the wage-earners. They come from a peculiar type of brainy people always found in our country, who, if they add something to its culture, take much from its strength. Our difficulties come from the mood of unwarrantable self-abasement into which we have been cast by a powerful section of our own intellectuals. They come from the acceptance of defeatist doctrines by a large proportion of our politicians. . . . Nothing can save England if she will not save herself. If we lose faith in ourselves, in our capacity to guide and govern, if we lose our will to live, then indeed our story is told."[3]

"The United States had it coming" is essentially the response to the horror and barbarity of 9/11 of some liberals and intellectuals on the Left. Despite abundant evidence to the contrary, such intellectuals insist that 9/11 was a Bush administration conspiracy. Other liberals fall into the root-cause fallacy: poverty, US foreign policy, Israel, and even the Crusades are the usual suspects in their minds. But the root cause of Islamic terrorism is the foreign policy of . . . bin Laden. The root cause of Islamic fundamentalism is Islam.

Poverty is not the root cause of Islamic fundamentalism.[4] The research of sociologists such as the Egyptian Saad Eddin Ibrahim and the economist Galal A. Amin, and the observations of journalists like the Palestinian Arab Kahild M. Amayreh and the Algerian Berber political leader Saad Saadi, all lead to the same conclusion: modern Islamists are young men from the middle or lower middle class who are highly motivated, upwardly mobile, and well educated, often with science or engineering degrees.[5]

Equally, those who back militant Islamic organizations are also the well-off. They are more often the urban rich rather than the poor from the countryside. Neither wealth nor a flourishing economy is a guarantee against the rise of militant Islam. Kuwaitis enjoy high incomes but Islamists usually win the largest bloc of seats in Parliament. Many modern militant Islamic movements increased their influence in the 1970s, just as oil-exporting states enjoyed very strong growth rates.

In general, Westerners attribute too many of the Arab world's problems, observes David Wurmser of the American Enterprise Institute, "to specific material issues" such as land and wealth.[6] Islamists themselves rarely talk about poverty. As Ayatollah Khomeini put it, "We did not create a revolution to lower the price of melon."[7] Islamists need the money to buy weapons and to fund propaganda. Wealth is merely a means, not an end.

Poverty as an explanation for all creeds has always been proferred by the liberals, as Burnham noted in *Suicide of the West*: "Communism, dictatorship, Mau Mau[8] and other political badnesses are explained as the results of hunger and poverty. Foreign aid plus democratic reforms . . . will bring a rise in the standard of living, which will in turn do away with the tendencies toward tyranny, aggression and war. . . . The yearly programs of Americans for Democratic Action are at pains to protest that our real 'enemies' are not wicked people or nations or creeds, and certainly not the Soviet Union or communism, but hunger and racial discrimination; the real war is the 'war against want.'"[9] As Burnham also said, "Of course men do not act rationally, generally speaking. They don't even consider food the matter of highest priority, whatever ideologues may imagine."[10]

Nor is the existence of Israel the cause of Islamic terrorism. As Benjamin Netanyahu put it, "The soldiers of militant Islam do not hate the West because of Israel, they hate Israel because of the West."[11] As early as 1995, Netanyahu warned,

> [I]t is impossible to understand just how inimical—and how deadly—to the United States and to Europe this rising tide of militant Islam is without taking a look at the roots of Arab-Islamic hatred of the West. Because of the media's fascination with Israel, many today are under the impression that the intense hostility prevalent in the Arab and Islamic world toward the United States is a contemporary phenomenon, the result of Western support for the Jewish state, and that such hostility would end if an Arab-Israeli was eventually reached. But nothing could be more removed from the truth. The enmity toward the West goes back many centuries, remaining to this day a driving force at the core of militant Arab-Islamic political culture. And this would be the case even if Israel had never been born.[12]

Or, as Wagdi Ghuniem, a militant Islamic cleric from Egypt, said, "[S]uppose the Jews said 'Palestine—you [Muslims] can take it.' Would it then be ok? What would we tell them? No! The problem is belief, it is not a problem of land."[13] Christopher Hitchens wrote: "Does anyone suppose that an Israeli withdrawal from Gaza would have forestalled the slaughter in Manhattan? It would take a moral cretin to suggest anything of the sort; the cadres of the new jihad make it very apparent that their quarrel is with Judaism and secularism on principle, not with (or not just with) Zionism."[14]

More recently, Bernard Lewis is reported to have said, "[T]he only real solution to defeating radical Islam is to bring freedom to the Middle East. Either 'we free them or they destroy us.'"[15] But what of the born-free Muslims in the West who are Islamists, such as the four London bombers of July 7? Freedom did nothing for them.[16]

Nor is American foreign policy the cause. US foreign policy toward the Arab and the Muslim world has been one of accommodation rather than antagonism. During the Cold War, the United States always supported Muslims against Communists. Recent United States military action in the Middle East has been on behalf of Muslims, rather than against them. The United States protected Saudi Arabia and Kuwait from Iraq, Afghanistan from the Soviets, Bosnia and Kosovo from Yugoslavia, and Somalia from warlord Muhammad Farah Aidid. US foreign policy has nothing to do with the deaths of 150,000 Algerians at the hands of Islamist fanatics.

The root cause of Islamic fundamentalism is Islam. American foreign policy has nothing to do with the stoning to death of a woman for adultery in Nigeria. It has everything to do with Islam, and Islamic law. The theory and practice of jihad—bin Laden's foreign policy—was not concocted in the Pentagon; it is directly derived from the Koran and the hadith, Islamic tradition. But Western liberals and humanists find it hard to admit or accept or believe this. They simply lack the imagination to do so. Liberalism, with its good intentions, can too readily become dogmatic. The trouble with Western liberals and all humanists is that they are nice—they are pathologically, terminally nice. They think everyone thinks like them, they think all people, including the Islamic fundamentalists, desire the same things, have the same goals in life. For liberals, the terrorists are but frustrated angels forever thwarted by the Great Anarch, the United States of America. Humanists are so nice that they even invite terrorists to their conferences. At the Mexico Humanist Conference in 1996, several speakers represented the Iranian group called the Mujahaddin. Last year, this group was put on President George W. Bush's list of terrorist groups. In February 2003 they offered themselves as the personal bodyguards of Saddam Hussein. At the humanist conference in Holland in July 2002, one of the keynote speakers, who had already been honored with a humanist award, was a smooth-talking charmer and Abdullah an Naim. His real goal could not be hidden for long: sharia.

Western liberals are used to searching for *external* explanations for behavior that they cannot comprehend; Hitler's behavior cannot be explained as a reaction to the Treaty of Versailles,[17] or the economic situation in the 1920s or 1930s. Evil is its own excuse. The Islamic fundamentalists are utopic visionaries who wish to replace Western-style liberal democracies with an Islamic theocracy, a fascist system of thought that aims to control every act of every individual. Joseph Conrad described such people: "Visionaries work everlasting evil on earth. Their Utopias inspire in the mass of mediocre minds a disgust of reality and a contempt for the secular logic of human development."[18] French philosopher Christian Godin recently pointed out that Islamic totalitarianism is potentially far more dangerous than either the Nazi or Communist variety, since the latter, despite their exterminating follies, presupposed their own preservation. For the Nazi, the inferior race does not deserve to exist; for the Stalinist, the enemy of the people does not merit to continue living—but for the Islamist, it is the world *itself* that does not deserve to exist.[19]

The number of people who have written about 9/11 without once mentioning Islam is extraordinary. We must take seriously what the Islamists say to understand their motivations, to understand 9/11. The four greatest influences on the modern rise of militant Islam have been the Egyptian Hasan al-Banna, the founder of Muslim Brethren; Sayyid Qutb; the Indo-Pakistani Maududi; and the Iranian Ayatollah Khomeini. They all repeat the same message, derived from classical writers like Ibn Taymiyyah, and ultimately from the Koran and the hadith: namely, it is the divinely ordained duty of all Muslims to fight non-Muslims in the literal sense until man-made law has been replaced by God's law, the sharia, and Islam has conquered the entire world. Here is Maududi in his own words:

> In reality Islam is a revolutionary ideology and programme which seeks to alter the social order of the whole world and rebuild it in conformity with its own tenets and ideals. "Muslim" is the title of that International Revolutionary Party organized by Islam to carry into effect its revolutionary programme. And "Jihad" refers to that revolutionary struggle and utmost exertion which the Islamic Party brings into play to achieve this objective. . . .
>
> Islam wishes to destroy all States and Governments anywhere on the face of the earth which are opposed to the ideology and programme of Islam regardless of the country or the Nation which rules it. The purpose of Islam is to set up a State on the basis of its own ideology and programme, regardless of which Nation assumes the role of the standard bearer of Islam or the rule of which nation is undermined in the process of the establishment of an ideological Islamic State.[20]

One survivor of the Holocaust, asked what lesson he had learned from his experience of the 1940s in Germany, replied, "If someone tells you that he intends to kill you, believe him."[21] Unfortunately, many liberals, leftists, and humanists, even after 9/11, have yet to learn this lesson. One may note here that many leftists are not just self-critical, they are inverted nationalists. They identify with their nations' enemies: just as Whig radicals empathized with Napoleon, Kim Philby and his cohorts made the Soviet Union their adopted homeland, and the hard left Israeli academic Ilan Pappe identifies with Hezbollah.

When not criticizing the West for its failings, Western intellectuals have had the tendency to exaggerate the virtues of nonwhite cultures, often in the most comical fashion possible. In *The Handbook of North American Indians* (1911), Franz Boas provided four Eskimo words for snow, noting the distinct roots of *aput* (snow on the ground) and *gana* (falling snow). Later in an article called "Science and Linguistics" in the MIT journal *Technology Review* in 1940, Benjamin Lee Whorf expanded on the idea, proposing at least seven distinct words for snow. From then on, the number of words in popular accounts steadily grew to almost four hundred. One could perhaps find fourteen words in an Eskimo language to describe different kinds of snow or conditions. But one could find even a greater number in English: avalanche, sleet, blizzard, slush, dusting, snowbank, flurry, snow cornice, frost, snow fort, hail, snow house, hardpack, snowman, ice lens, snowball, snowflake, snowstorm, powder, spindrift, ice, icicle, iceshockle, ice floe, iceberg, berg, growler, calf, serac, nieve, glacier, firn, slob (slob ice), graupel, rime, hoar, permafrost, snow melt, and meltwater, not to mention the countless more compound words we can create with snow- and ice-.[22]

We are told of the ecological and environmental wisdom of Native Americans or primitive cultures before the arrival of the white man. Unfortunately, the reality is more sobering.[23] The Noble Savage was not always particularly noble or in possession of primordial wisdom. In any case, the limitations of life in the South Seas, evoking Karl Marx and Friedrich Engel's "the idiocy of rural life,"[24] were well described by Herman Melville, particularly in *Omoo*.

One could devote an entire monograph to the myth of Eastern spirituality or Eastern spiritual wisdom, which probably began as early as Herodotus, and the historians who followed Alexander the Great to India. Westerners, on the whole, are totally ignorant of the atheistic tradition in Indian history and culture. For example, the Carvakas (Charvakas) represented the materialist school of Indian thought in the sixth century BCE. Carvaka philosophy found no room for a deity, immortality, soul, or karma, and regarded the universe as subject to perpetual evolution.[25] Dale Riepe concludes his study of the naturalistic tradition in India with these observations: "Our examination of the early schools of Indian philosophy has led us to conclude (1) that the views of Uddalaka, Carvaka, and early Vaisesika are clearly naturalistic; and (2) that the views of the Ajivikas, Jains,

Samkhya, and Theravada and Vaibhasika Buddhism are certainly strong in some naturalistic elements. Carvaka is naturalistic on all three counts of theory of knowledge, metaphysics, and ethics; to a lesser degree this is also true of Uddalaka's philosophy . . . Theravada and Vaibhasika Buddhism and Jainism find no teleological principle in the world; they find no deity. They are, consequently, humanistic systems in which the individual man achieves the highest ethical goals without nonhuman aid."[26]

Since independence, Riepe adds, naturalism has again raised its ancient and honorable standard in the new India.

There is also a flourishing Atheist Centre in South India. But are not the majority of the people of India believers? Yes, undoubtedly, but they are no more spiritual, however defined, than the average Christian in the United States. The majority of Indians are struggling to survive physically and materially, and are trying to acquire all the materialist benefits that Westerners take for granted. They are not indifferent to materialism. Rather, they despair of ever acquiring the worldly comforts that are flaunted in their faces in the cinema, and in the richer parts of their cities, and understandably find solace in religion.

What of Eastern mysticism? First, Islamic mysticism, that is, Sufism, was almost entirely derived from Gnosticism and Oriental Christian mysticism, which itself had absorbed the Neoplatonic ideas of Plotinus, Pseudo-Dionysus, and others.[27] The West itself has a long tradition of mystical writings that rival anything from Buddhism and Hinduism: Blessed Angela of Foligno, Saint Anselm, Saint Bernard of Clairvaux, Jacob Boehme, St. Bonaventura, Saint Catherine of Sienna, Meister Eckhart, Saint François de Sales, Walter Hilton, Saint John of the Cross, Julian of Norwich, Margery Kempe, Raymond Lull, Jan van Ruysbroeck, Saint Theresa, and Thomas à Kempis among them.[28] But it always seems more fulfilling to those disillusioned with "Western materialism" to find mystical experience in a tradition remote from Christianity—*ex oriente lux*. Heaven forbid that they admit that religious ecstasy of the mystical kind was equally available in the elegant verses of Saint John of the Cross.

Can one take the Islamic afterlife seriously as "spiritual" when it offers only a crass materialism of the sexual kind, with promises of the delights of a celestial bordello? Rachid Boudjedra, the Algerian novelist, essayist, and playwright, makes some scathing remarks about religion in Algeria, and assails the hypocrisy of the majority—80 percent of the so-called believers is his figure—who pray or pretend to pray only in the month of Ramadan, the holy month of fasting; who go on pilgrimage for the social prestige; who drink wine and fornicate and still claim to be good Muslims.[29] Many Muslims are impelled by a fear of hell, and out of a desire to reserve a place for themselves in heaven they pray now and then; the rest of their lives are no more "spiritual" than anyone else who lives for the creature comforts of this world.

"Spiritual" has become a hopelessly vague term for a hopelessly vague outpouring of emotions when in the presence of the sentimental object of one's choosing. But if we take it to mean "relating to spirit, the mind, the higher faculties; highly refined in thought and feeling, habitually or naturally looking to things of the spirit,"[30] then I suggest that the person who saves up money to make his pilgrimage to northern Bavaria to listen to Wagner's operas at the Bayreuth Festspielhaus is probably more spiritual than the average "believer" of whatever faith who makes a pilgrimage to absolve his worldly sins, or to have his or her material body cured of some biological ill. In the West, the promotion, playing, and appreciation of Western classical music are spiritual activities. Even the smallest of French villages, for example, takes pride in its annual music festivals. The appreciation of the visual arts, the pride in and preservation of ancient monuments, the activities of the New York Historical Society, the meetings of the Poetry Society at Barnes and Noble, a visit to the Fra Angelico exhibition at the Metropolitan Museum of Art, a night at the opera—all are spiritual endeavors. They indicate an interest in the higher faculties, in things of the spirit and mind. The West does take an interest in the spiritual in the more conventional sense: going to church, for example. But the West also reveals its interest in, and encouragement of, the life of the mind in many more varied ways than are available to the rest of the world.

EAST VERSUS WEST

God has made the Orient!
God has made the Occident!
North and South his hands are holding,
All the lands in peace enfolding.

—Goethe, *West–östlicher Divan*

We are all familiar with Kipling's lines,

> Oh, East is East and West is West, and never the twain shall meet,
> Till Earth and Sky stand presently at God's great Judgment seat;

which seem to imply, as one of Kipling's biographers says, "that the peoples on opposite sides of the globe are so different that they will never understand each other until the Day of Judgement."[31] But perhaps less familiar are the two following lines, which assert that class, race, nation, and continent are irrelevant when two men of equal courage face each other:

> But there is neither East nor West, Border, nor Breed, nor Birth,
> When two strong men stand face to face, tho' they come from the ends of the earth.

Talking of India, John Strachey once wittily said, "To know a no ball from a googly and a point of order from a supplementary question is genuinely to have something in common."[32] India is a democracy with a constitution, inspired by Western models, that protects human rights. For the educated Indian at least there is no clash of civilizations. Christians,[33] Hindus, Buddhists, or Jains of Indian origin tend to prosper in the West in all fields, as economists, entrepreneurs, artists, and scientists. They have no problems integrating into Western societies and are happy to practice their faith in private and enjoy the intellectual freedoms and economic opportunities. They also contribute much to the intellectual and artistic life of the West.

The ancient Indian ruler Asoka promulgated on rock edicts and cave inscriptions principles that foreshadow the modern notion of human rights. The fourteen rock edicts that probably date from sometime soon after 257 or 256 BCE can with some justification be read as one of the first bills of human and animal rights. Religious tolerance, for example, is extolled in Rock Edict 12:

> Beloved-of-the-Gods, King Piyadasi, [King Asoka] honours both ascetics and the house-holders of all religions, and he honours them with gifts and honours of various kinds. But Beloved-of-the-Gods, King Piyadasi, does not value gifts and honours as much as he values this: there should be growth in the essentials of all religions. Growth in essentials can be done in different ways, but all of them have as their root restraint in speech, that is, not praising one's own religion or condemning the religion of others without good cause. And if there is cause for criticism, it should be done in a mild way. But it is better to honour other religions for this reason. By so doing, one's own religion benefits and so do other religions while doing otherwise harms one's own religion and the religions of others. Whoever praises his own religion due to excessive devotion and condemns others with the thought "Let me glorify my own religion" only harms his own religion. Therefore, contact [between religions] is good. One should listen to and respect the doctrines professed by others. Beloved-of-the-Gods, King Piyadasi, desires that all should be well-learned in the good doctrines of other religions. Those who are content with their own religion should be told this: Beloved-of-the-Gods, King Piyadasi, does not value gifts and honours as

> much as he values that there should be growth in the essentials of all religions. And to this end many are working—Dhamma Mahamatras, Mahamatras in charge of the women's quarters, officers in charge of outlying areas and other such officers. And the fruit of this is that one's own religion grows, and the Dhamma is illuminated also.[34]

Thus the human rights declaration of 1948, though historically derived from Western philosophers, charters, and constitutions—such as John Locke, Montesquieu, the Magna Carta, the Glorious Revolution of 1688, the Bill of Rights of the US Constitution—finds an echo in the ancient cultures of India. In the late 1990s the Asian Human Rights Commission issued an Asian Human Rights Charter that fully endorsed the Universal Declaration of Human Rights, the International Covenant on Economic, Social and Cultural Rights, the International Covenant on Civil and Political Rights, and other international instruments for the protection of rights and freedoms.[35]

Thus, there is no reason to think that there are inherent cultural, historical, or psychological barriers to Asians accepting the principles of the human rights declaration of 1948. One must be skeptical of Asian leaders who justify tyranny by appealing to "Asian values." As Janadas Devan argued,

> Crucially, the claim of differential cultural identities also enables Asian establishments to reject the democratic ethos already present in modern Asian history—from the May Fourth movement in China to the nationalist, anti-colonial struggles in India, Indonesia, and elsewhere—as an aberrant foreign importation. Such erasures of recent Asian history are especially useful in Singapore because the state there is itself the agent of a democratizing process—involving social and economic enfranchisement as well as the ballot box—that it also wishes to contain. The very success of Singapore's modernity has led the state to formulate a sanitized cultural inheritance to restrain its citizens from demanding rights and responsibilities beyond those already granted to achieve modernity. By misrepresenting, thus, political possibilities *within* Asian modernity as a choice *between* Eastern and Western cultural identities, the state can contain the threats to its power that its own success has generated.

Devan concluded, "Is it too much to claim, really, that Asian nationals have agency? that when they seek a more democratic future for themselves it is because democracy is as much a part of *their* modernity as it is of the West's?"[36]

In the United States today there are an estimated 1.5 million Iranians, a large percentage of whom are said to be secularists, who believe in a firm separation of church and state. There is also a large number of organizations in the West that are fighting for human rights in Iran, that is, recording the daily violations of the rights of Iranian women and men.[37]

There are, of course, also many courageous Iranian individuals working in the West to bring about human rights in their country. There is no clash of civilizations for them, they are fighting for rights taken for granted by Westerners. I have addressed Iranians in Paris, Stockholm, Washington, DC, Chicago, and Los Angeles, and I can attest that they were all ferociously anti-Khomeini, pro-democracy, and largely secular. My first book, *Why I Am Not a Muslim*, was translated into Persian soon after its publication the United States. Iranians can also look to their heritage to find early adumbrations of human rights as in the Proclamation of Cyrus. Hirad Abtahi, a legal adviser at the International Criminal Court at the Hague, argues for the universality of human rights, and finds that Cyrus's proclamation of 538 BCE is a pioneering document that contains "theoretical principles which foreshadow the core principles of present days [*sic*] human rights, that is: freedom of thought, conscience and religion, protection of civilians, protection of property, and more generally, the idea of peace."[38] Abtahi quotes Plato's encomium on the Persia of Cyrus: "[T]he Persians, under Cyrus, maintained the due balance between slavery and freedom, they became, first of all, free themselves, and after that, masters of many others. For when the rulers gave a share of freedom to their subjects and advanced them to a position of equality, the soldiers were more friendly towards their officers[. . .]; and if there was any wise man amongst them, able to give counsel, since the king was not jealous but allowed free speech and respected those who could help at all by their counsel, such a man had the opportunity of contributing to the common stock the fruit of his wisdom. Consequently, at that time all their efforts made progress, owing to their freedom, friendliness and mutual interchange of reason."[39]

Here, there is no crude Saidian East versus West. Instead, history offers an Athenian praising a Persian, a European extolling an Oriental. On September 12, 2001, there was a spontaneous candlelight vigil and march of two hundred thousand Iranians in Tehran as a show of solidarity with the United States and the families of the victims of the World Trade Center tragedy.

Can we legitimately speak of a clash of civilizations? The situation is evidently more complex than a conflict of West versus East. But it will not do to pretend in a rush of ecumenical sentimentality that we all have the same values. Islam poses the greatest challenge to Western values. Islam does not accept the West's core principles of religious tolerance; freedom of conscience, belief, and expression; the separation of church and state; equality before the law; and notions of citizenship and loyalty to the state.

It is important to bear in mind the distinction between theory and practice, the distinction between what Muslims ought to do and what they in fact do; what they should have believed as opposed to what they actually believed and did. We might distinguish three Islams: Islam 1, Islam 2, and Islam 3. Islam 1 is what the Prophet taught, that is, his teachings as contained in the Koran; Islam 2 is the religion as expounded, interpreted, and developed through the Traditions (hadith) by the theologians and jurists, and includes the sharia, Islamic law, and the corpus of dogmatic theology; Islam 3 is what Muslims actually did do and achieved, that is to say, Islamic civilization, as known to us in history, roughly equivalent to Christendom.[40]

When I speak of Islam as being incompatible with several articles of the Universal Human Rights Declaration of 1948, I am speaking of Islam 1 and Islam 2. Sometimes Islam 3, that is, Islamic civilization, has been more tolerant than allowed by Islams 1 and 2, and vice versa. For example, Islams 1 and 2 quite clearly condemn homosexuality, and yet until recently, Islam 3 tolerated it far more than Christendom; conversely, Islams 1 and 2 are quite relaxed about circumcision, for it is not mentioned in the Koran. Many jurists recommend it, but without exception all male Muslim children are circumcised. In this case, Islam 3, Islamic civilization, follows a practice that is not made obligatory by Islams 1 and 2.

By stating that Islam 1 and Islam 2 constitute a certain set of fixed, timeless principles, precepts, and prescriptions, am I not guilty of essentialism? Who decides what Islams 1 and 2 are? Is Islam doomed to remained fixed in its medieval mind-set? Can Islams 1 and 2 change?

We can establish what, for instance, the four Sunni schools of law say on apostasy. But to say what the situation is today, and what it was a hundred years ago, requires empirical and historical research, respectively. We would need serious sociological inquiry into the beliefs of, say, Moroccans, about what they understand, for example, of the theory of jihad. The results of such an inquiry would differ considerably according to the country, class, education, and even ethnicity of the person questioned. We all tend to be rather casual and careless in the way we describe a certain belief as Islamic, without ever specifying whether we mean Islam 1, 2, or 3. Like many a Christian, who, for example, may confuse the Virgin Birth with the Immaculate Conception, there are many Muslims who simply do not know what the Islamic doctrine is on any given point. The majority of Muslims in the world are not Arabs and do not know Arabic, and many have never read the entire Koran. How many Christians have read the entire Bible?

Quite clearly, the attitude of Muslims toward Islam 1 and Islam 2 can change. Clearly, many Muslims are not even aware of many Islamic doctrines that could affect their behavior. Many Muslims ignore Islams 1 and 2, and yet others try to reinterpret Islams 1 and 2 to conform to what they believe should be the case. For example, many Muslim feminists try to reinterpret or ignore Koranic passages in order to improve the lives of Muslim women. Only time will tell if such strategies will work. It is up to Muslims themselves to discuss these issues openly rather than pretend that there are no problems, or that these problems have nothing to do with Islam.

On June 22, 2006, the Pew Research Center published the findings of the Pew Global Attitudes Project. The center's Web site published the results of other polls conducted in several Islamic and Western countries of Muslim and non-Muslim attitudes toward terrorism, citizenship, democracy, Jews, women, causes of poverty, and so on. Unfortunately, several methodological worries spring to mind and put the validity or usefulness of the results into doubt. We are never sure of the level of education of the interviewees, or in which language and by whom the interviews were conducted, or precisely where they were conducted—factors that could influence the responses of the interviewees. One question was "Can democracy work well in your country?" Seventy-four percent of the Jordanians interviewed responded yes. But one's pleasure is immediately dampened after a little reflection: Do the Jordanians mean the same thing as Europeans or Americans by "democracy"? Would there be a Bill of Rights in Jordanian democracy? Would apostasy be tolerated? Would women or Jews be allowed to run for parliament? Did fear play any factor in their responses? Would few Muslims in Muslim countries reply according to the prevailing opinion, for fear of getting into trouble?

If one takes the polls at face value, without worrying about the methodology, one could indeed find results that would cheer up some—and results that would profoundly depress others. In Jordan, Pakistan, and Indonesia, there has been a decline in support for terrorism. And yet 15 percent of British Muslims believe that violence against civilian targets in order to defend Islam is justified. Muslims living in the West express, on the whole, very favorable opinions of Christians, and yet many Muslims living in the West have no desire to integrate since their primary allegiance is to Islam, not to their host country; 81 percent of British Muslims were willing to declare that they saw themselves as Muslims first and foremost.

There seems to be an irreconcilable clash of values, priorities, and loyalties—in brief, a clash of civilization between Muslims and the rest of the world. And yet there are many courageous individuals in Islamic countries who are fighting for human rights, such as Asma Jahangir in Pakistan, Ahmad al-Jarallah in Kuwait, Tarek Heggy in Egypt (who defended democracy as "the finest achievement of humanity"), and al-Afif al-Akhdar in Tunisia. A group of Arab intellectuals produced the Arab Human Development Report in 2002, which "warned that the lack of progress in the Arab world was due to such internal barriers as the lack of political freedom, the absence of civil liberties, and the low status of women."[41] They are undoubtedly in a minority, but as long as there are courageous intellectuals fighting for the same human rights we take for granted in the West, we cannot talk simplistically of a clash of civilizations.

Since September 11, 2001, journalists have noted that in Islam there is no separation between mosque and state. Indeed, in classical Arabic there is no pair of words corresponding to "lay" and "ecclesiastical," "spiritual" and "temporal," "secular" and "religious." But what these same journalists fail to add is that the doctrinal lack of a separation of mosque and state did not mean that Islamic history was a chronicle of a series of relentless Muslim theocracies. On the contrary, as L. Carl Brown demonstrated recently, Muslim history has been often marked by a de facto separation of state and religious community.[42]

Many of the modern leaders of culturally Islamic countries were secular—though not necessarily democratic—in their outlook and in their approach to the problems of modern industrializing societies: leaders such Muhammad Ali Jinnah of Pakistan, Nasser of Egypt, Sukarno of Indonesia, and Bourguiba of Tunisia. Unfortunately, corruption, nepotism, incompetence, pandering to the mullahs, obscurantist religious scholars, the need to assert a non-Western cultural identity, and above all economic failure in Islamic countries led to the rising influence—though these factors are not the cause—of the Islamic fundamentalists, who, sensing that their time had come, demanded ever more Islam in public life.

DEFENDING THE WEST

A Look at the Worst

"that if way to the Better there be, it exacts a full look at the Worst"
—T. Hardy, *In Tenebris II*

The excesses of Western popular culture make one cringe and render our efforts to defend Western civilization much harder. The self-indulgence and mindlessness of popular entertainment are the apparent price we pay for our freedoms. But the openness of Western societies means that our ills and squalor are exposed publicly, while the worst in Islamic societies is hidden from infidels. In those societies notions of shame and honor forbid the public display of one's own shortcomings. In the last five years, Asian political leaders and the media have openly acknowledged the problems of drug abuse, HIV infection, child abuse, child labor, forced prostitution, and the plight of women. Nonetheless, the West perhaps remains ignorant of the extent of the problem in Islamic societies, which remain most secretive and unreliable in their data.

Consider, for example, the following report from Agence France-Presse published on June 26, 2000. A United Nations Drug Control Programme (UNDCP) representative, Bernard Frahi, said Pakistan had to be congratulated on its poppy eradication efforts over the past twenty-five years. Seizures of opium had risen 212 percent in the last year. But, he said, "drug abuse remains a major concern. . . . With an estimated four million drug users, *Pakistan has probably the highest number of drug addicts in the world*. . . . A particular problem (is) the rising number of injecting heroin abusers."[43] Saleem Azam, whose non-government organization Pakistan Society runs rehabilitation centers in Karachi, said the number of heroin addicts for the past three years had been growing at an "alarming rate" of one hundred thousand per year. He said the addicts were directly or indirectly affecting nearly 20 million dependents or family members with emotional, social, and financial repercussions. In 2000 it was Pakistan, not a Western country, that had the greatest number of drug users. And yet drug abuse is the first accusation hurled at the West by self-righteous Muslims, as though such a problem could not exist in a land where Islam predominates.

Similarly, child abuse, child pornography, and prostitution are also major causes for concern in the West—but again, these are also problems outside the West. An Iranian filmmaker has won several international awards for her courageous clandestine documentary showing the plight of young prostitutes and the growing problem of drug abuse in contemporary Iran. Nahid Persson earned high honors at the recent Créteil International Women's Film Festival for *Prostitution behind the Veil*, her chronicle of two young women on the streets of Tehran:

> Fariba and Minna are close friends who provide each other with support. Persson describes their lives: "Their life was about finding clients and getting money so that they could buy an egg or some food for their children. And because of their addiction, they had to buy heroin. They didn't have a normal life. When one becomes addicted to drugs, one forgets about [real] life." Drug addiction is a major problem in Iran, especially among young men. But the number of female drug users is said to be growing. Iranian newspapers estimate that there are currently about 300,000 women working the streets. Many are runaways who have fled abusive families. Others sell their bodies out of simple poverty. Persson says both women acquired their heroin addictions through drug-addicted husbands.[44]

By 2005 Iran was considered to harbor the greatest number of drug addicts in the world. A report by the United Nations found that Iran had the highest drug addiction rate in the world—2.8 percent of the population over age fifteen: "With a population of about 70 million and some government agencies putting the number of regular users close to 4 million, Iran has no real competition as world leader in per capita addiction to opiates, including heroin."[45] The director of the Iranian National Centre for Addiction Studies estimated that 20 percent of Iran's adult population was "somehow involved in drug abuse." Earlier estimates had put the total number of illegal drug users in Iran at more than 7 million. On April 7, 2005, Akbar Alami, a member of Iran's *Majlis* (parliament) from Tabriz, northwest Iran, revealed publicly that the actual number of drug users in Iran was closer to 11 million. Drug addiction is also the main cause for the spread of HIV/AIDS in Iran.

An unemployment rate of about 20 percent and a lack of social freedoms are among the main causes for drug use among Iran's young population, according to some analysts. Eurasianet.org cited twenty-year-old Amir from Tehran as saying that for many of his friends, using drugs is a way to escape: "We don't have entertainment here, and drugs are very cheap and easy to get. Whatever you get from the supermarket, for the same price you can buy drugs in your neighborhood. Because of this lack of entertainment, whenever young people get together, the only thing they think about is getting and using drugs because it makes them happy. And also because of the problems they have, they want to get rid of these problems for some time. They have no hope in the future. They think there is no future for them in Iran."[46]

It is a lack of social freedoms that is one of the main causes of drug abuse. Iran is an Islamic republic, an Islamic theocracy, with forced dosages of religion—but clearly Islam is not enough.

The sexual abuse of children is also widespread in the Muslim East, where the fact that girls as young as nine can be married off to middle-aged men adds to the problem. The United Nations Children's Fund (UNICEF) reported in 2005 the following situation in Pakistan

- The net enrollment rate among adolescents (11–19 years) is less than 30 percent.
- Many of them end up working in the streets, in farms, brick kilns, and carpet weaving industries or as domestic workers and industrial labourers.
- An estimated 3.6 million children under the age of 14 are working in exploitative and hazardous labour.
- Only a third of all Pakistani children under the age of five are registered at birth. Children without official identity are more vulnerable to abuse and exploitation and the existing laws do not protect them.

- The current age of criminal responsibility is seven. Children are sometimes detained in jail together with adults and are physically and sexually abused.
- Violence against girls, boys and women, including murder, rape, honour killings, police torture, burning and corporal punishment are reported in local newspapers every day. More than 17,000 cases of child abuse were reported in the media from 2000 to 2004.[47]

Women, along with non-Muslim minorities, are the ones who suffer most in Islamic societies. For instance, the limitations of their rights are enshrined in the constitution of the Islamic Republic of Iran, which explicitly reduces women to second-class citizens. A segregated healthcare system means that many women receive inadequate attention as there are not enough well-trained women doctors and nurses. A raped woman is liable to be executed or stoned to death for fornication. Here are some gruesome facts and figures from the Web site Women's Forum Against Fundamentalism in Iran (WFAFI).[48]

Since 1979, when the mullahs took power, thousands of women have been executed in Iran on political grounds for their opposition to the policies of the ruling government. Among those executed were dozens of pregnant women. Women who oppose the regime are imprisoned and tortured. Most are repeatedly raped or have body parts amputated. Courageously, women played a very active role in the demonstration of forty thousand teachers outside the Majlis [parliament] on January 12, 2002, and some women were arrested and imprisoned for just participating in a demonstration.

At least twenty-two women were sentenced to stoning or stoned to death during President Khatami's tenure (August 2, 1997 to August 2, 2005). Girls ages ten to seventeen are the prime victims of sexual slavery in Iran. Ninety percent of runaway girls end up in prostitution or are sold in the Persian Gulf human traffic market. Women and girls bear the brunt of Iran's poor economic conditions. Seven hundred thousand children, aged ten to fourteen, work in the black labor market in Iran. Statistics released by Iran's Organization of Management and Planning itself show that 51 percent of the country's population lives below the poverty line. Iran's deputy health minister, Ali Akbar Sayari, admits that 20 percent of Iranians go hungry daily. Sixty-seven percent of the students deprived of education are girls between the ages of eleven and sixteen. Only 11 percent of Iranian women are employed. The rate of mental illness is very high among women, leading to a high rate of suicide. In a western province of Iran, Heyran Pournajaf, a spokesman on women's affairs, reports, "About 70% of those who commit suicide in Ilam are women." The director general of social affairs of the governor reported that "90% of these women were between 17 and 35 years old.

The real number of suicides is much higher than what we have." The World Health Organization considers Iran as one of three countries in the world with the highest rate of suicide.

In January 2006 the Women's Forum Against Fundamentalism in Iran issued this press release: "In recent days, Iranian women have seen a new wave of nationwide suppression, attacks and violence sponsored by Ahmadinejad's regime. Alarmed by ongoing protests and strikes throughout the country, Mahmoud Ahmadinejad and his government are once again targeting and escalating violence against women to instill fear in society. While there must be a concerted effort to politically criticize the misogynous regime in Tehran, WFAFI urges the rights advocates, women's groups and international NGOs to launch a campaign in support of Iranian women."[49]

The hypocrisy of the Islamic Republic of Iran should now be apparent. The West does not need lectures on the superior virtue of societies in which women are kept in subjection, endure clitoridectomies, are stoned to death for alleged adultery, have acid thrown on their faces, are married off against their will at the age of nine, or where the human rights of those considered to belong to lower castes are denied.[50]

Relativism

Moral relativism, and the attendant consequences of multiculturalism, political correctness, and moral equivalence, along with an overriding sense of guilt, have left Western intellectuals ill prepared, unable, or unwilling to defend the West. Marianne Talbot, lecturer in philosophy at Oxford University's Department of Continuing Education, notes the debilitating effects of relativism on the young:

> [M]any of the young have been taught to think their opinion is no better than anyone else's, that there is no *truth*, only truth-for-me . . . to question it amounts in the eyes of the young, to the belief that it is permissible to impose *your* views on others.
>
> The young have been taught, or so it seems, that they should never think of the views of others as false, but only as *different*. They have been taught that to suggest someone else is wrong is at best rude and at worst immoral: the truth that one should always be alive to the possibility that one is wrong has become the falsehood that one should never be so arrogant as to believe that one is right.[51]

This tendency toward relativism and its corrosive accompanying moral equivalence and selective indignation was noted by George Orwell in the 1940s and James Burnham in the 1960s.[52] The sense of guilt also leads to self-hatred, as Burnham noted, "When the Western liberal's feeling of guilt and his associated feeling of moral vulnerability before the sorrows and demands of the wretched become obsessive, he often develops a generalized hatred of Western civilization and of his own country as part of the West"—sentiments summed up in Robert Frost's famous saying that a liberal is one who won't even take his own side in a quarrel.[53]

Western Values: A System That Does Not Affront Our Reason and Humanity[54]

In contrast to the mind-numbing certainties and rules of Islam, Western civilization offers what Bertrand Russell once called liberating doubt, which leads to the methodological principle of scientific skepticism.[55] Politics as much as science proceeds by tentative steps of trial and error, open discussion, criticism, and self-correction.[56] Political decisions are a result of rational inquiry, compromise, and free exchange of ideas. One could characterize the difference between the West and the Rest as a difference in epistemological principles. Western institutions such as universities, research institutes, and libraries are, at least ideally, independent academies that enshrine these epistemological norms, and where the pursuit of truth is conducted in a spirit of disinterested inquiry, free from political pressures. The humanities as much as the hard sciences are bound by the rules and rigors of logic and scientific inference, and are committed to the testing, verifiability, falsifiability, and refutability of hypotheses. The possibility of alternatives is freely discussed in scientific journals. In other words, behind the success of modern Western societies, with their science and technology and their open institutions, lies a distinct way of looking at the world, and interpreting it, and the recognition and rectifying of the problems besetting them. Problems are lifted out of the religious sphere and treated as empirical problems whose solutions lie in rational procedures, open to rational intersubjective criticism, not in an appeal to revelation. The whole edifice of modern science and its methodology is one of Western humanity's greatest gifts to the world.[57]

The political principle embodied in the apothegm "reason not revelation" is the separation of church and state, or the separation of religious and secular authority. It is customary to begin arguments in favor of a separation of church and state with Jesus's own words: "Render therefore to Caesar the things that are Caesar's; and unto God the things that are God's" (Matt. 22:21). Philosopher

Roger Scruton takes the debate further back to the Greeks, arguing that the tension between religion and politics is present in the tragedies of Sophocles and Aeschylus. In Sophocles' *Antigone*, as G. W. F. Hegel describes it,

> the public law of the state is set in conflict over against inner family love and [religious] duty to a brother; the woman, Antigone, has the family interest as her "*pathos*" [passion, affection, "loyalty"], Creon, the man, has the welfare of the community as his. Polynices, at war with his native city, had fallen before the gates of Thebes, and Creon, the ruler, in a publicly proclaimed law threatened with death anyone who gave this enemy of the city the honour of burial. But this command, which concerned only the public weal, Antigone could not accept; as sister, in the piety of her love for her brother, she fulfils the holy duty of burial. In doing so she appeals to the law of the gods; but the gods whom she worships are the underworld gods of Hades (Sophocles, *Antigone*, 451), the inner gods of feeling, love, and kinship, not the daylight gods of free self-conscious national and political life.[58]

Creon is concerned for the safety of the *polis*, the city-state, and wishes to restore and maintain order. For him loyalty to the city takes precedence over any private loyalty to friend or family.[59] It is man's ingenuity and rationality that has conquered nature and established man-made laws in cities:

> And speech and thought, quick as the wind
> and the mood and mind for law that rules the city—
> all these he has taught himself.[60]

As Scruton argues, a similar conflict informs Aeschylus's *Oresteia*: "In the political order, we are led to understand, justice replaces vengeance, and negotiated solutions abolish absolute commands. The message of the *Oresteia* resounds down the centuries of Western civilization: it is through politics, not religion, that peace is secured. Vengeance is mine, saith the Lord; but justice, says the city, is mine."[61]

The Christian approach to the separation of religious and secular authority was developed by Saint Augustine in *The City of God*, where human history is seen as a struggle between two cities, a heavenly city of God and an earthly city of the world. The ecclesiastical order is not charged with temporal affairs, though it is considered prior to the civil order. *The Pastoral Rule* of Saint Gregory imposed the duty of civil obedience on the clergy.[62] Pope Gelasius I, in a famous letter to Emperor Anastasius, in his Fourth Tractate, and in other works, formulated the "doctrine of the two powers," according to which "this world" is governed by two sovereignties, the sacred authority of the priests (*auctoritas sacrata pontificum*) and the royal power of kings and emperors (*regalis potestas*).

Milton Anastos describes Gelasius's achievement:

> Each of these [Gelasius] defined as independent and supreme in its own sphere, but subordinate to the other in that of the other. The emperor, as the sovereign ordained by God, was entitled to obedience from the clergy in the temporal realm. But he had no priestly functions, and was required to bow in submission to the priests, and especially to the bishop of Rome, who was the highest among them, in all ecclesiastical matters. "Hearken to my admonitions in this life, I beg you," Gelasius warned the Emperor, "rather than hear me make accusations against you, heaven forbid, at the divine judgment." Ignoring the papal authorities who had not refused to ascribe priestly qualities to the emperors, Gelasius declared that it was Christ, the last ruler to have been both Priest and King, who separated the functions of the two powers, so that the Christian emperors would need assistance from the priests to attain eternal life, and the priests would depend upon the emperors for the conduct of temporal affairs. Many clerics had protested against imperial infringements upon the freedom of the Church in language much like that used by Gelasius. But he was the first to state formally as a juridical principle that the two powers had equal standing, were jointly responsible for the administration of human society, and imposed limitations upon each other.[63]

In the wake of the religious wars in Europe between 1540 and 1650, many seventeenth-century thinkers such as Baruch Spinoza, John Milton, John Locke, and dissident minority Protestants such as the Baptists and Anabaptists called for a separation of civil and ecclesiastical powers.[64] A number of different arguments were evoked by these distinguished philosophers and writers to advocate the separation. For Locke, as for certain Church Fathers such as Tertullian, sincere religious belief can only be adopted freely, and the state promotion of religion inevitably leads to the use of coercive force. Locke wrote, "And such is the nature of the understanding, that it cannot be compelled to the belief of any thing by outward force. Confiscation of estate, imprisonment, torments, nothing of that nature can have any such efficacy as to make men change the inward judgment that they have framed of things."[65]

Many Anabaptists, who had suffered persecution under Protestant and Catholic authorities, argued that the state should not interfere in religious affairs, and vice versa. The Anabaptist Leonard Busher pleaded to King James of England for a separation of church and state in *Religious Peace: or, a Plea for Liberty of Conscience*, "as kings and bishops cannot command the wind, so they cannot command faith."[66]

Freedom of conscience is a fundamental principle of Western-style democracies, and, as Roger Scruton expressed it, "[f]reedom of conscience requires secular government."[67] Thomas Paine once made the brilliantly simple observation that supposing, for the sake of argument, "that something has been revealed to a certain person, and not revealed to any other person, it is revelation to that person only. [It is] hearsay to every other, and consequently they are not obliged to believe it."[68] Thomas Nagel fleshes out the subtle philosophical arguments behind Paine's simple formulation, arguing that reasons given for political decisions must meet a certain standard of "higher-order impartiality" or objectivity since they must appeal to all members of society, to all citizens who participate in the process of government. One should be prepared "to submit one's reasons to the criticism of others, and to find that the exercise of a common critical rationality and consideration of evidence that can be shared will reveal that one is mistaken. This means that it must be possible to present to others the basis of your own beliefs, so that once you have done so, they have what you have, and can arrive at a judgment on the same basis."[69]

However, the standard of impartiality is not met when "part of the source of your conviction is personal faith or revelation—because to report your faith or revelation to someone else is not to give him what you have, as you do when you show him your evidence or give him your arguments." If political reasons fall short of objectivity, political debate degenerates into a mere "clash between irreconcilable subjective convictions" rather than a disagreement in "the common, public domain."[70]

Freedom of conscience requires secular government, and secular law is made legitimate by the consent of those who must obey it.[71] Citizens participate in government, in the making and enacting of the law. In an Islamic theocracy, sovereignty belongs to God. One has but to obey unquestioningly the dictates of those who interpret the Holy Book. In a democracy, sovereignty rests with the people; freedom is the cardinal principle. As Scruton summarizes, "Without freedom there cannot be government by consent; and it is the freedom to participate in the process of government, and to protest against, dissent from, and oppose the decisions that are made in my name, that confer on me the dignity of citizenship. Put very briefly, the difference between the West and the rest is that Western societies are governed by politics; the rest are ruled by power."[72]

Freedom of thought demands freedom of expression, and freedom of expression is important in a democracy to enable citizens to criticize the government, to offer alternatives, and to find ways to improve their political lot. But it was freedom of expression and thought that also bore Western civilization its spiritual fruits, in which may be included scientific discoveries as well as the literary, artistic, musical, and philosophical creations of astonishing diversity, power, beauty, profundity, and truth. The same freedom of thought, intellectual curiosity, rationality, and leaps of imagination that produced the theories of Kepler and Tycho Brahe, Copernicus and Galileo, Newton and Einstein, Darwin and Crick, produced the works of Chaucer and Dante, Shakespeare and Racine, Goethe and Samuel Johnson; the paintings of Giotto and Cimabue, Raphael and Michelangelo; the architecture of Alberti and Palladio, Wren and Hawksmoor; the music of Bach and Palestrina, Haydn and Mozart, Wagner and Verdi.

Rationalism has given us the wonderful edifice of modern science, an understanding of the universe, a deeper comprehension of our own origins, bequeathing us a grand vision, or, as Darwin says, "There is grandeur in this view of life, with its several powers, having been originally breathed by the Creator into a few forms or into one; and that, whilst this planet has gone cycling on according to the fixed law of gravity, from so simple a beginning endless forms most beautiful and most wonderful have been, and are being evolved."[73] But it is its artistic creations that constitute Western civilization's spiritual heritage, and which, in place of explanation, give us meaning. Western civilization has strived for objective truth, and at the same time, provided meaning that is not entirely imposed by some medieval text but is something richer, taking into consideration our sense of self, our sense of personhood, treating us as adults with personal responsibility and intentionality.

Law in the Western tradition is "a means to resolve conflicts by discovering the solution to them." For example, the English common law is "founded on the idea that the legal process involves searching for the just solution to conflict, or the just punishment for a crime." Even though it may have been influenced by Christian ideas of God's commandments, the law is a very human construction, a "human attempt to resolve our own conflicts by treating each party to them as a responsible individual individual, acting freely for himself. The common law consists of freedoms won by the citizen from the state, which the state must then uphold."[74] Scruton argues that this conception of law owes much to the Christian notion of forgiveness, which "underlines our conception of citizenship, as founded in consent."[75]

By contrast, the notion of an individual—a moral person—who is capable of taking rational decisions and accepting moral responsibility for his free acts is lacking in Islam. Ethics is reduced to obeying orders. Of course, there is the notion of an individual who has legal obligations, but not in the sense of an individual who may freely set the goals and contents of his life, of the individual who may decide what meaning he wants to give to his life. Under Islam it is God and the Holy Law that set limits as to the possible contents of your life.

It is worth emphasizing that the US Bill of Rights, or its equivalent, is essential for safeguarding the civil and political rights of an individual against the government. As Thomas Jefferson put it: "A bill of rights is what the people are entitled to against every government on earth, general or particular, and what no just government should refuse, or rest on inferences."[76] Individuals have rights that no mythical or mystical collective goal or will can justifiably deny. Hayek wrote that "individual freedom cannot be reconciled with the supremacy of one single purpose to which the whole society must be entirely and permanently subordinated."[77] The first ten amendments, and the Fourteenth Amendment of the US Constitution, limit the power of both the federal and the state governments, protecting individuals' rights of freedom of religion, speech, press, petition, and peaceful assembly, and the rights of persons accused of crimes against government abuses. They prevent the government from depriving anyone of civil liberties.

Liberal democracy extends the sphere of individual freedom, attaching great value to each man or woman. Individualism is not a recognizable feature of Islam. Instead, the collective will of the Muslim people is constantly emphasized; there is certainly no notion of individual rights that developed only in the West, especially during the eighteenth century. The constant injunction to obey the caliph, who is God's shadow on earth, is hardly inducive to creating a rights-based individualist philosophy.

While all humans, every Hottentot and Eskimo, Semite and Indo-European, Polynesian and Native American, belong to the same species, *Homo sapiens*, they do not live under the same cultural conditions or institutions. The distinguishing institutions, with their inherited wisdom, of the West are its chief glory even though Westerners have not always lived up to them. The African American abolitionist Frederick Douglass was able to read the Declaration of Independence and the US Constitution in order to point out the universal values embedded or implicit in them, and then he used them to advocate the abolition of slavery: "[T]he constitution of the United States—inaugurated 'to form a more perfect union, establish justice, insure domestic tranquillity, provide for the common defense, promote the general welfare, and secure the blessings of liberty'—could not well have been designed at the same time to maintain and perpetuate a system of rapine and murder like slavery. Especially, as not one word can be found in the constitution to authorize such a belief. . . . [T]he constitution of our country is our warrant for the abolition of slavery in every state in the American Union."[78]

Only within the framework of certain institutions can humankind hope to realize its humanity, that we discard our hard-won institutions at our own peril, the veneer of civilization of most people disappears outside their civilizing confines.

PART 3

ORIENTALISM IN PAINTING AND SCULPTURE, MUSIC AND LITERATURE

But the criticisms offered of Western culture are really confirmations of its claim to favor. It is thanks to the Enlightenment and its universal view of human values that racial and sexual equality have such a commonsense appeal to us. It is the universalist vision of man that makes us demand so much of Western art and literature—more than we should ever demand of the art and literature of Java, Borneo, or China. It is the very attempt to embrace other cultures—an attempt that has no parallel in the traditional art of Arabia, India, or Africa—that makes Western art a hostage to Said's caviling strictures. And it is only a very narrow view of our artistic tradition that does not discover in it a multicultural approach that is far more imaginative than anything now taught under that name. Our culture invokes an historical community of sentiment, while celebrating universal human values. It is rooted in the Christian experience but draws from that source a wealth of human feeling that it spreads impartially over imagined worlds. From Ariosto's Orlando Furioso *to Byron's* Don Juan, *from Monteverdi's* Poppea *to Longfellow's* Hiawatha, *from* The Winter's Tale *to* Madame Butterfly, *our culture has continuously ventured into spiritual territory that has no place on the Christian map.*

—Roger Scruton, "What Ever Happened to Reason?"[1]

INTRODUCTION

Stephen Schwartz once wrote, "[Bernard Lewis] has, it is true, been brutally attacked—most notably by the charlatan Edward Said. Said's *Orientalism*, a ridiculous imposture from its first page to its last, is now a standard text in Anglo-American universities, but reads like the product of a rather dense college student who has just discovered Marxism; there can be no more telling condemnation of the present state of the American academy than the ascendancy of Said."[2] I would be inclined to argue that the inherent dishonesty, charlatanry, and imposture of Said's *Orientalism* begins with the cover: a reproduction of Jean-Léon Gérôme's *The Snake Charmer*.[3] The painting was chosen presumably because it was striking, a suitable subject, and would help sell the book. If so, the choice is hypocritical, since Gérôme is often singled out as the quintessential "Orientalist" painter who, putatively, held nothing but contempt for his "Oriental" subjects. However, authors do not always get to pick their cover illustrations, or cannot even be bothered to do so; often it is the art department of the publisher that decides. But the author can always object. Why did Said not object? A growing number of publishers in recent years have discovered beautiful "Orientalist" paintings with which to illustrate their book covers, such as Assia Djebar's *Femmes d'Alger dans leur appartement* (Women of Algiers at Home),[4] with Eugène Delacroix's eponymous masterpiece on the cover, as well as the series devoted to short monographs on various world cities or regions by famous writers of the nineteenth and early twentieth centuries, published by Magellan in collaboration with the French geographical journal *Geo*. The elegantly produced titles include *Tanger*, with Georges Clairin's *L'entrée à la mosquée du chérif Ouassane* (Sherif Oussane's entry into the Mosque [1875]) on the cover; *Fès,* with Robert Burns's *L'Heure Dorée* (The Golden Hour [1920]); and *Le Rif* (The Rif), with Eugène Girardet's *Camp Bédouin dans les Dunes* (Bedouin Camp in the Dunes [1895]). The paperback edition of Francis Steegmuller's *Flaubert in Egypt* also reproduces Delacroix's *Femmes d'Alger dans leur appartement*,[5] and Sarga Moussa's *Le Voyage en Égypte* (Travels in Egypt),[6] an anthology of European travel writings on Egypt, carries Alois Stoff's *Devant les pyramides* (In front of the Pyramids [1906]).

Sumptuously produced and lavishly illustrated works devoted to Orientalist paintings may be a sign that the baneful influence of Edward Said is at last on the wane. One hopes that hitherto fearful curators who hid Orientalist paintings in the storage rooms of their museums will now dust them off and proudly present them for what some of them are: masterpieces of eighteenth-, nineteenth-, and early-twentieth-century European art.[7]

9

ORIENTALS AS COLLECTORS

In an article in *Art+Auction*,[1] John Dorfman reported that "[g]iven that 'Orientalism' is a cultural curse word these days, it's noteworthy that so-called Orientalist painting is basking in the warm glow of the art-market's favor." Works once dismissed—thanks largely to Edward Said's poisonous influence—as "imperialist" and "examples of subtle and persistent Eurocentric prejudice against Arab-Islamic peoples and their culture" now fetch large sums at international auctions.[2] The top price for this once-despised genre is $4.5 million, paid in June 2005 for John Frederick Lewis's *The Midday Meal, Cairo*, at Christie's New York. Christie's New York also sold Ludwig Deutsch's *Palace Guard* in April 2006 for $1.6 million, while Jean-Léon Gérôme's *La Mosquée Bleue* fetched $1.8 million at Christie's London on June 14, 2006.

Dorfman defends Orientalist art: "Although there is a strong fantasy element in Orientalist art, there's more to it than harems, slave auctions and snake charmers. The artists traveled to Arab lands in the wake of invasions, and in many cases, their work was strictly reportorial." He quotes the specialist dealer Brian MacDermot of Mathaf Gallery in London, who remarks, "They were travelers who tended to paint what they saw, and a lot of the painting was extraordinarily accurate." We can witness this accuracy in David Roberts's depictions of ancient Egyptian monuments, where the hieroglyphic inscriptions can be read even today by Egyptologists, even though Roberts himself did not know the language. Deborah Coy, an expert with Christie's, points out that the Orientalist paintings are "the only record we have of these things," because Islamic custom strongly discouraged local artists from depicting the products of a pre-Islamic infidel civilization.[3]

However, the final irony is reserved by Dorfman for his last paragraph: "That may help explain the popularity of such works among modern-day Arabs, especially in the Gulf States and Saudi Arabia. Far from spurning these 19th-century crowd-pleasers, Middle Eastern collectors see them as pieces of their past worth bringing back home."[4] Evidently, rich, cultivated Arabs did not heed Said—even if they had heard of him—and found nothing contemptuous in the Occidental representations of Oriental life and culture.

Of course, Gulf Arabs or Saudis are not the first Muslim collectors, as Francis Haskell reminds us in his fine article on Khalil Bey, who built up a great collection of pictures in Paris in the second half of the nineteenth century.[5] Khalil Bey was attracted to the erotic paintings of Courbet and Ingres, some of which he managed to buy or even commission. He owned several Orientalist paintings by such artists as Delacroix, Théodore Chassériau (such as his magnificent *Combat de cavaliers arabes* [The Combat of Arab Horsemen] now in the Fogg Art Museum in Cambridge, Massachusetts), Prosper Marilhat (*Une rue du Caire* [A Street in Cairo]; Khalil Bey was born nearby in the same year that Marilhat visited the city), Jean-Léon Gérôme (the bête noire of anti-Orientalist polemic), Théodore Rousseau, Jean-Baptiste-Camille Corot, Constant Troyon, Charles François Daubigny, Jean-Louis-Ernest Meissonier, and also Dutch genre paintings of Gerard ter Borch (such as *Officer Dictating a Letter while a Trumpeter Waits*, now in the National Gallery in London). He was proud of his acquisition of Jean August Dominique Ingres's *Bain Turc*, and was in no way offended by a Westerner's fantasy of the erotic Orient.

Modern Turkish collectors also seek out the works of the Bosphorus Painters, who recorded so faithfully their beloved capital. Recently two such collectors, Suna and İnan Kiraç, created a foundation to house their collection and open it to the public. The Pera Museum in Istanbul makes their family collection available to a wider audience. In the foreword to the catalog of their first exhibition, *Portraits from the Empire*, they wrote, "The works of art [in the exhibition, and which are the main part of the permanent collection] can be considered, in general terms, 'orientalist' in nature, bringing us face to face with images of the Ottoman world and its people, their portraits and portrayals, sometimes very familiar and sometimes remote, even nearly foreign, in their physiognomies. These paintings, most of them created before the eye of the camera replaced the human eye, in the times when observing, studying, interpreting and depicting the world was the priority of painters, present the lost faces of an era long past with amazing reality and vividness. *Portraits from the Empire* is a *Tale of East and West*, face to face."[6] Represented painters include Jean-Baptiste Vanmour, Antoine de Favray, Pierre Désiré Guillemet, Adolph Diedrich Kindermann, and Jules Joseph Lefebvre.

Philippe Julian noted in the 1970s that "[r]ich Levantines and Egyptian princes simply adored the Orientalists," and added a little later, "Now, when money is flowing into the Middle East, dealers manage too repatriate them, for the oil magnates have a high regard for works that recall a former Islamic civilization or hark back to a picturesque and legendary past. . . . The large sales of Orientalists held in London recently were extremely successful and attracted buyers from the Middle East."[7]

A number of distinguished Orientals own other works by John Frederick Lewis; the crown prince of Jordan owns the Lewis watercolor of *Arab with his Camels*,[8] while the art collection of Sayaji Rao III Gaekwad, Maharaja of Baroda, contains Lewis's *In the Bey's Garden, Asia Minor*; whereas *A Cairo Bazaar, the Della'l* remains in a private Middle Eastern collection.[9]

A certain number of works by Orientalist sculptor Charles Cordier (1827–1905) of blacks and Arabs are owned by Oriental collectors, or are in museums open to the public in Cairo and elsewhere. Zulfikar and Shelina Jetha own *Negress of the Colonies*; the bronze bust of Ismail Pacha is in a private collection in Morocco; the marble bust of Ismail Pacha is in the Museum of the Palace of Manial, Cairo; and the bronze equestrian statue of Ismail Pacha is in the military museum in the Citadel, Cairo. Another bronze equestrian statue of Ismail Pacha stands in a public place—Opera Square, Cairo.

Mohammed Mahmoud Khalil studied law in France and married a Frenchwoman, Emilienne Hector Louis, in 1903. In 1924 Khalil founded the Societé des Amateurs des Beaux-Arts with Prince Youssef Kamal. Khalil put together a magnificent collection of works of art, including Orientalist painters such as Alexandre-Gabriel Decamps, Diaz de la Pena, Delacroix, Chassériau, Félix Ziem, and the sculptor Charles Cordier. They are all housed in his former art nouveau palace in Cairo, now the Mohammed Mahmoud Khalil Museum.

We may also note the private collection of Orientalist art of the Algerian tycoon Djillali Mehri, whose collection was exhibited in Paris in late 2003. It includes works by Étienne Dinet, the one Orientalist who converted to Islam. Publishers in North Africa have recently brought out works celebrating Orientalist art, such as Éditions Tell, based in Blida, Algeria. If the feverish activity on the Internet is any indication, then lovers of art have simply disregarded the hateful creed of the ideologues that relegated Orientalists to obscurity in museum basements, and they are enjoying the paintings by Delacroix,[10] Chassériau,[11] Fausto Zonaro,[12] and hundreds of others.[13] There are also encouraging signs in exhibitions devoted to Orientalist painters such as Chassériau, who was celebrated in a magnificent manner in Paris in February 2002, and New York in October 2002–January 2003. The lavishly produced, thorough, and very scholarly catalog is free of any references to Said or any of his slavish art history followers such as Linda Nochlin.[14]

A museum of Orientalist arts, close to the National Museum, is scheduled to open in 2007 in the Middle Eastern Emirate, Qatar. It will house nearly five hundred works by Orientalist artists such as Eugène Fromentin and Jean-Léon Gérôme, both of whom will be discussed and defended. Gérôme is, of course, the target of a calumnious article by Linda Nochlin and is often held to be the archetypical "Orientalist" painter.

10

PAINTING AND SCULPTURE

Greeks and Orientals

Western civilization was ever open to new ideas, and that includes the world of art. In a series of lectures, Rudolf Wittkower has shown the non-European influences on European art and the process of "assimilation and adaptation of non-European import ware."[1] He has argued that "this process went on throughout the entire history of Western art."[2] He distinguishes six major waves of penetration in the course of two thousand years, and begins his lectures with Near Eastern influences on the West:

> The first wave of oriental art inundated the young Greek art of the seventh century BC. Oriental monsters and oriental compositional principles made their entry then, reaching the Greek mainland, as archaeologists have shown, from Assyria to Phoenicia and on by way of Cyprus and Crete. . . .
>
> The second period of oriental penetration resulted from Sassanian power and Roman weakness. The Roman Empire was wide open to the influence of Eastern mystery religions and in the third century Mithraism had spread far and wide and seemed to emerge as the victorious religion. Roman institutions became increasingly orientalized and Constantine's predecessor Diocletian, who ruled the eastern part of the divided Empire, remodeled it into a centralized bureaucracy along oriental lines. He even introduced the ceremonial Persian dress at his court.
>
> Not unexpectedly, Roman art became receptive to oriental representational principles.[3]

Wittkower then moves on to the Greek East: "But though Byzantium remained the custodian of Hellenistic culture, the character of the rising empire was largely formed by its contact with the East. Runciman has rightly said that the history of the 'Byzantine Empire is the history of the infiltration of Oriental ideas to tinge the Graeco-Roman traditions.' The new synthesis was immensely effective in the arts."[4]

The Scythians constitute the fourth wave of Orientalism: "The Scyths transformed the semirealistic heraldic oriental animal style into one of extreme decorative ornamentation, a style that maintained its expressive energy for no less than fifteen hundred years in spite of many important modifications and that can be found over the whole north of Asia and Europe from the Pacific to Ireland."[5]

The fifth wave of Eastern penetration came from the southern trade routes and the influence of Islamic civilization from Spain and Sicily: "Moreover, the Mediterranean always was an inland waterway that pulled peoples together rather than kept them apart. Although its shores were held by three deeply divided parties—Catholic, Orthodox, and Islamic—trade along ancient and new routes flourished. At an early period the old ports of Amalfi, Salerno, and Naples were wide open to oriental commerce, and so was Marseilles. Venice's oriental trade began in the tenth century and Genoa's in the eleventh."[6]

Genoa and Venice went even further in their commercial rivalry. Rather than cooperate with Venice, Genoa preferred to make a treaty with Sultan Saladin of Egypt in 1177, while "in the thirteenth century Venetian interests were entirely cosmopolitan: They extended by way of Constantinople to the shores of the Black Sea, to Armenia, and beyond."[7]

The deepest impact of the fifth penetration was felt mainly—though not exclusively—in the decorative arts; Romanesque and Venetian Gothic architecture also show distinct traces of Near Eastern and Islamic influence. Rosamond E. Mack sums up the Oriental influences on Italian art by arguing "(1) that Oriental trade and travel contributed to artistic development in Italy and made a permanent impression on Italian taste; (2) that the influential models varied according to what was admired at critical stages in the development of Italy's craft industries; (3) that Oriental art objects acquired an elite status in Italy that increased their influence there; and (4) that East-West trade, travel, and industrial competition continued to foster cosmopolitan taste and artistic exchange in the Mediterranean."[8]

The sixth and last penetration occurred when Babylonian astrology entered the European consciousness: "While astronomical manuscripts down to the eleventh century are firmly rooted in the Western, Graeco-Roman tradition, the imagery of astrological manuscripts after this period shows that the Greek celestial sphere was orientalized under Arab influence."[9]

However, like Walter Burkert, Wittkower emphasizes the originality of

Western civilization, despite the strong influences of and borrowings from the Orient: "The impact of foreign civilizations never had the power to deprive Europe, after its consolidation, of its typically occidental mode of expression, a mode of expression that the Greeks created about twenty-five centuries ago. It is one of the miracles of the Western mind that so many and often discordant non-European influences were assimilated, and that in the long run they spurred original, typically Western creation rather than impeded it. In fact, the uninterrupted contact of Europe with non-European civilization helped intensify the unbelievable variety of European art."[10]

These reflections on the influence of Oriental art and culture should be borne in mind in my survey of the beginnings of "Orientalism" in Western art. Given my arguments that Western civilization was open to the world, it should not surprise if painters and sculptors also empathized with Oriental or non-European subjects. Greeks were not racists, and evidence for this comes from Greek art as well as literature.

In *The Negro in Greek and Roman Civilization: A Study of the Ethiopian Type*, Grace Hadley Beardsley notes, "The negro . . . was rendered with the utmost fidelity to the racial type during the most restrained and idealistic period of Greek art."[11] From the evidence of frescoes in the palace of Minos, we can deduce that Cretans showed some knowledge of blacks.[12] In the art of mainland Greece, the first appearance of blacks is on a series of vases in the form of heads, some single and some janiform, dated to the latter part of the sixth century BCE. There are a number of fine terra-cottas of blacks, but the masterpiece of Greek representation of a black must be the famous Hellenistic bronze in the Bibliothèque Nationale in Paris. Beardsley describes this masterpiece as the finest statuette of a black from antiquity, dwelling on its grace, the dreamy sadness of the expression, the attitude, hair, and so on.[13] Many such figurines in Greek art show some pathos for the Ethiopian, or the black's lot.[14]

Fourteenth and Fifteenth Centuries: Orientals in Renaissance Painting

In two pioneering articles in the *Burlington* magazine, Hermann Goetz has drawn our attention to the presence of Orientals in Italian, German, and Netherlandish art, particularly from the late thirteenth century on. Goetz argues that the Orientals portrayed are carefully observed, not stereotypes, with particular fidelity being paid to their dress.[15]

It is generally accepted that the earliest realistic Italian representations of non-Europeans were painted by Giotto di Bondone: "the first artist to individualize his figures' appearance and actions to make his narratives more vivid,"[16] as in *The Mocking of Christ* in the Arena Chapel, Padua. Slaves may have been used for the individualized Muslims in *St. Francis Proposing the Trial by Fire to the Sultan*, in the Bardi Chapel in Santa Croce, Florence, dating from sometime between 1310 and 1326. The Muslims "are described in considerable naturalistic detail. The sultan is characterized by his rich garments and a turban surmounted by a crown, a fantastic creation but appropriate from an Italian perpsective. The two advisers closest to the sultan have quite different physiognomies and headdresses. Furthermore, the exceptionally large, originally sumptuous Spanish-style textile in the background of the painting establishes a plausible setting in a luxurious Islamic court."[17]

In the paintings of Gentile da Fabriano and Benozzo Gozzoli, we find Christian types from the East, derived (in the case of Gozzoli), from observing Byzantines, especially at the time of the visit of John VIII Palaeologus, who led a Byzantine delegation to the Council of Ferrara-Florence in 1438–39. As Goetz says, in their paintings we find Eastern Christians as well as real Muslims, some of whom

> still wear the older costume distinguished by a large-patterned jāmah (coat) with a tight-fitting turban—the latter being an intermediate form between the fashions seen in the works of the older masters and the pagri (turban) still generally worn in India today, while others are dressed in the new fashions from the Timurid kingdom of Turkestan: the tight-fitting, long coat, fastened across the breast, or the short riding-jacket (jubba—in Byzantine, zūpa), and the Timurid turban, a cap, often vertically fluted, and wound round to two-thirds of its height with a shawl. Towards the end of the century a later Timurid fashion predominated in western art, when the little turban-cap disappeared almost entirely in a shawl which had expanded into a broad, solid pad from which, however, a loose end was permitted to hang down on to the neck.[18]

Pisanello (Antonio di Puccio Pisano) was the next great artist to depict Orientals based on personal observations of foreign delegations to Italy. There is a remarkable study of a Central Asian holding a bow and arrow, "probably after a groom belonging either to the retinue King Sigismund of Hungary brought to Rome in 1432–1433 or to the Eastern delegation to the Council of Eastern and Western Churches, which convened in Ferrara in March 1438. Sometime in the 1430s Pisanello used the figure as a picturesque accessory, lost amid Western imagery, in his *Saint George and the Princess* in the Church of Sant' Anastasia, Verona."[19]

The exotic aspects of the Byzantine emperor John VII Palaeologus's delegation fascinated Pisanello. He was particularly intrigued by the emperor's costume and horse, the various Eastern Christians—representing different communities such as Armenians, Russians, Abyssinians, Copts, and Jacobites from Mesopotamia—and their headgear. The drawings, now in the Louvre, show the emperor in two outfits: "He wears hunting gear, a sword, and a Tatar-style hat with a pointed top, turned-up brim, and long pointed visor." What is even more interesting is the fact that Pisanello, rather like Delacroix in the nineteenth century, noted their colors as if he were preparing a painted portrait: "The hat of the emperor should be white on top and red underneath, the profile black all around. The doublet of green damask and the mantle on top crimson. . . . The boots of pale yellow leather; the sheath of the bow brown and grained, and also that of the quiver and scimitar."[20] Pisanello's annotations remind us that often an artist's primary concern is aesthetic, and he is anxious to solve a technical problem of faithfully translating onto canvas his direct observations as recorded in his drawings.

By the end of the fifteenth century, as Goetz says, a new tradition sprang up that was based on firsthand studies in Turkey as well as on observations of Turkish prisoners, refugees (such as Prince Cem [or Djem] at Rome, a pretender to the Ottoman throne in the fifteenth century), and ambassadors (sent to Venice and, in 1562, to France).[21]

Fifteenth and Sixteenth Centuries: Venetians and the Love of Color

What F. Gilles de la Tourette says of the fifteenth-century Venetians and their love of color, the picturesque, and the quest for beauty, in fact applies as well to describe what the nineteenth-century Orientalists were searching for, and what we find so attractive in their tableaux in North Africa, Egypt, the eastern Mediterranean, and Ottoman Turkey. The canvases of Gentile Bellini and Vittore Carpaccio regale us with the play of light, topographical details, and the colorful costumes and manners of Orientals.[22]

The Orientalists' artistic curiosity—an analogue of intellectual curiosity so characteristic of Western civilization—enabled them to portray the vivid colors, the warmth, the passion, and the festivities of the Mediterranean; to record and celebrate other ways of living; and to extend the horizons of beauty to other lands.

At the time of the Byzantines, Venetians were already living in their city of lagoons amid color, "of colour in all its pure violence, magnificent like the gold of a polished nugget or the violent heat of a red ruby simply bevelled."[23] By the fifteenth century, it was the Muslim presence that was creating a new ambience for the Venetian sensibility. Commercial contacts led to artistic ones, with mutual admiration for each other's cultural accomplishments.

The fall of Constantinople in 1453 did not deter Venice from trading with the Turks. Continued commercial ties with the Turkish Empire made it possible for great European artists to record Turks for the Western world.

In August 1479 the Venetian Senate received a letter from Sultan Mehmet II, beseeching the republic to send him a painter well versed in the art of portraiture. A European ambassador to Turkey had taken with him several portraits that had occasioned such delight and astonishment that the sultan immediately requested to meet the painters themselves. The Senate resolved to send Gentile Bellini, who embarked, in the company of the sculptor Bartolomeo, that September for Constantinople. We have an eyewitness account of Bellini's work for the sultan; Giovanni Mario Angiolello, a native of Vicenza, was in the employ of the sultan's elder son, Mustapha. At Mustapha's death, Angiolello came to live at the court of the sultan in Constantinople and got to know Bellini, about whose activities he reported in his *History*.[24]

Sultan Mehmet II first asked for a view of Venice, and then a portrait of himself. The sultan even requested a self-portrait from the artist, who then painted the costumes and dress of different Oriental countries, as well as a portrait of his favorite sultana. Bellini worked assiduously for Mehmet II, who employed Bellini to decorate his apartments with erotic paintings and to portray members of the court. Thus the sultan must have owned, at the end of a year, a large number of the Venetian's work, which included a remarkable painting depicting a dervish "with haggard eyes."[25] The sultan liked to compare Bellini's portraits with the "originals."

Gentile Bellini apparently made numerous sketches for his own amusement of the most famous sights. These included monuments and costumes of Oriental nations that he saw for himself, noting the gestures, graceful attitudes, and facial expressions of the Turks, whose compatriots he had already encountered in the cosmopolitan streets of Venice. Given his predilection for vivid colors, processions, movements, and costumes, Bellini must have been overcome with his first encounter with the Orient.

The portrait of Mehmet II by Bellini remains one of the most important Venetian paintings of the fifteenth century, not simply for its beauty but also because of its psychological penetration. Bellini was innovative in painting the sultan not in profile, as had been the custom hitherto in Italian painting, following the techniques of medals, but in three-quarters view, probably under the influence of Antonello de Messina, a recent arrival in Venice. One immediately recognizes the sultan's subtlety and the sharpness of his cunning, indicative of his renowned art of diplomacy.[26] He is dressed in a simple caftan with a large collar of fur. In front of him is a magnificent piece of brocade, suggesting his passion for works of art.

Bellini painted several portraits of the sultan; all of them are now lost. But Paolo Giovio, bishop of Como, must have acquired one, since his famous history *Vitae virorum illustrium* (Lives of Illustrious Men [1549–57]) contains an engraving of one such portrait. A bronze medallion of the sultan was also cast by Bellini and is now housed in the National Gallery of Art in Washington, DC. Other works include "two particularly handsome Turkish portraits of a man and a woman."[27]

Otherwise, we have examples of Bellini's Orientalism in his *La predica di S. Marco ad Alessandria* (St. Mark Preaching in Alexandria), housed in the Pinacoteca di Brera, Milan, most likely portraying Egyptians and Christian Indians of Cairo. Though the painting contains an extraordinary number of figures, Bellini manages to give many of them individualized features. For example, to the extreme right foreground, two Cairenes with large turbans and long silk scarves are in deep discussion. An Egyptian to the viewer's left is depicted with a noble but wizened face and a long, hoary beard, running his long, elegant fingers through the white scarf; his compatriot is in a long, faded burgundy robe and stands with a hand on his hips. The overall impression is of elegance, dignity, even nobility. The figures with long black-and-white stripes and distinct hats are Indians of Cairo; that they were accurately depicted is something we learn from the fascinating book of engravings by Cesare Vecellio, another Venetian Orientalist to be discussed later.

The Isabella Gardner Museum in Boston holds a pen-and-gouache portrait of a Turkish boy in a "flat patterned style similar to that of the Turkish miniatures that influenced such later works as his 'Portrait of Doge Giovanni Mocenigo' (1478–85)."[28] While generally attributed to Gentile Bellini, this miniature may, in fact, have been the work of Costanzo da Ferrara (see below).

Pisanello made a commemorative medal relief portrait of John VIII (1438), emperor of Constantinople, and such was his reputation that Mehmet II of the Ottoman Empire wanted to be commemorated in the same way. Another medalist, Costanzo da Ferrara, was invited to Constantinople by the sultan to paint his portrait and create a medal for him. Ferrara finished his medal in 1481, the year Mehmet II died. According to Rosamond E. Mack, Costanzo's contributions have been undervalued. He is now

> considered the most likely author of a group of exceptionally objective detailed images of persons seen at court or on the streets of Istanbul that have traditionally been attributed to Gentile [Bellini]. At least one, a miniature of a seated scribe [now in the Isabella Gardner Museum in Boston, see p. 311], long remained in the royal collection in Istanbul and was often copied by Turkish and Persian artists at the court. The miniaturist's fascination with the scribe's facial features and his taj and belted robe—a dolman made from an Italian-style brocade—distinguishes a series of seven forthright studies of men and women in different ethnic and official costumes that accurately record the mixed population of Istanbul. Five of these drawings are considered close European copies after Costanzo, indicating that his images circulated.[29]

Vittore Carpaccio, who studied under Gentile Bellini, was also taken with the Orient, as is evident in the *The Sermon of St. Stephen in Jerusalem*, now in the Louvre, but originally created for the upper hall of the Scuola di Santo Stefano in Venice between 1511 and 1520. In the foreground we find a group of Eastern women sitting cross-legged on the ground, enraptured by the sermon; mingling with them are Oriental men in turbans, Greeks—recognizable by their high hats—on the far left, and Westerners, all witness to the universality of the saint's message: "The temple behind, a symbol of Judaism, is depicted as a 'tempio' of the Italian Renaissance. On the hill of Jerusalem one can make out the church of the Holy Sepulchre. The city—which some historians have identified as Damascus—is rendered as a conglomerate of ancient buildings and minarets of a mineral-like austerity. . . . The work makes evident Carpaccio's fondness for rendering materials—crimson velvets and brocade (on the saint's chasuble)—as well as a fascination for the Orient, which he shared with the other Venetian painters. The cycle of paintings is based on the theme of historical continuity between Judaism and Christianity."[30]

Similar interest in Oriental costumes and figures are evident in *St. George Baptizing the Gentiles*, in the Scuola di San Giorgio degli Schiavoni in Venice. Elegant blacks dressed in the Venetian manner also make appearances in Carpaccio's paintings, as in the detail of the painting of the *Miracle of the Holy Cross* in the Gallerie dell'Accademia, Venice, which shows a graceful black gondolier.

Goetz insists that Carpaccio

> must have been in Palestine, especially at Jerusalem, for his *Scenes from the Life of St. Ursula* in the Accademia at Venice, the St. George with the slain Dragon, and the other scenes from the legend of this saint in S. Giorgio de Schiavoni, as well as the Sermon of St. Stephen, etc., are reminiscent of life in Palestine, and of the Haram-ash-Sharif with the mosque of Omar at Jerusalem. His orientals

> are Syrians, Arabians and Nubians of the later Mameluke Empire; his Mamelukes use the same queer indented turbans as that on the head of Sultan Kansuwah Ghuri, and his oriental ladies wear the ancient cylindrical Syrian mitra which, but little altered, may be seen today worn by the women of Bethlehem. The theory of Molmenti that Carpaccio was never in the East and derived his inspiration from Breydenbach's *Iter in terram sanctam* seems to me untenable. There may be some influence from this side; but Carpaccio's knowledge of Eastern life is too extensive and well-founded to be drawn from such an insufficient source.[31]

Goetz's theory that Carpaccio actually visited the East is not generally accepted.

Bellini and Carpaccio greatly influenced the "Orientalist" taste of the period. Artists such as Andrea Mantegna, Antonio Pollaiuolo, and Bernadino Pintoricchio came under their sway. Pintoricchio painted a magnificent series of frescoes in the Borgia Appartments of the Palazzi Pontifici in Vatican. In one of the frescoes, the *Disputation of S. Catherine*, Sultan Mehmet II's son, Cem (or Djem), is shown as a majestic figure astride an impressive white horse. Other elegant, handsome, and realistic Oriental figures in turbans—including a black man—also grace the composition.[32] As Rosamond E. Mack has shown, Pintoricchio was also much influenced by Costanzo da Ferrara's studies of the varied ethnic population of Istanbul.[33] Meanwhile, Mantegna depicted Oriental figures in several paintings of *Adoration of the Magi*, as in the splendid piece in the Getty Museum in Los Angeles, where "[t]hree kings pay homage to the Christ Child, who in turn makes a sign of blessing. Jesus Christ, his mother the Virgin Mary, and Mary's husband Joseph have haloes and wear simple garments, while the Magi are dressed in exotic clothing and jewels and bear exquisite gifts. Caspar, bearded and bareheaded, presents the Christ Child with a rare Chinese cup, made of delicate porcelain and filled with gold coins. Melchior, the younger, bearded king behind Caspar, holds a Turkish censer for perfuming the air with incense; on the right, Balthasar the Moor carries a covered cup made of agate."[34]

Cesare Vecellio, a relative of Titian's, was an author, painter, wood engraver, and well-known author of two early printed works on costume and invaluable ethnographical details: *De gli habiti antichi et moderni di diverse parti del mondo* (Of Ancient and Modern Costumes of Diverse Parts of the World [1590]) and an enlarged edition, *Habiti antichi et moderni di tutto il Mondo* (Ancient and Modern Costumes of the Entire World [1598]), and a collection of lace pattern illustrations *Gioiella della Corona per nobili et virtuose donne* (literally, The Jewel in the Crown for Noble and Virtuous Women [1591]).[35]

Margaret Rosenthal, a professor of Italian now translating Vecellio's 1590 work, has described the Venetian's fascination with and admiration for the Orient, its people, and their costumes.[36]

Mack discusses a group of Venetian paintings dating from about the mid-1490s to the early 1520s that she describes as Orientalist, since Syrian, Palestinian, and Egyptian costumes and settings play an important role in them. They mark a shift from Ottoman to Mamluk imagery; the Mamluks, former military slaves, established a dynasty in Egypt, Syria, and Iraq that lasted from 1250 to 1517. The Mamluk iconography first appears in a "new cycle of the story of Saint Mark in the chapel of the silk weavers' guild in Santa Maria dei Crociferi that postdates 1495. A Mamluk context was geographically appropriate for events in the Venetian legend of Saint Mark, set principally in Alexandria. Furthermore, because of their long and close commercial and diplomatic relationship with the Mamluk empire, which was tightly woven into Venice's history and fame, many Venetians could recognize and appreciate this foreign context. The recent arrival of authentic images of Syria and the Holy Land enabled painters to represent stories of Saint Mark—and soon other Eastern Mediterranean saints—in the style Venetian patrons expected."[37]

The most important painted source was *The Reception of the Ambassadors in Damascus*, now in the Louvre and executed sometime between 1488 and 1495 by someone familiar with the contemporary Venetian style. The painting contains so much precise topographical detail—such as the three minarets of the Great Mosque of Damascus, the market, bathhouse, and walled garden—that it must have been painted in situ or based on drawings made from direct observation. Giovanni Mansuetti drew upon it for his *Arrest and Trial of Saint Mark* (1499), now in a private collection in Liechtenstein.[38]

Goetz argues that after the pioneering works of the fifteenth century, by the sixteenth century "the Turk had become a common and extraordinarily correctly depicted figure in Italian art."[39]

SIXTEENTH AND SEVENTEENTH CENTURIES: THE NETHERLANDS—REMBRANDT AND THE JEWS

Between Rembrandt and Melchoir Lorch is the Flemish artist, Pierre Coeck d'Alost (sometimes written Pieter Coecke van Aelst), who lived in Turkey in 1533. He always claimed that he was paid with precious stones by the sultan.[40] Coeck brought back with him a series of cartoons that was probably meant for tapestry designs but after his death appeared as a series of woodcuts, and was published as *Moeurs et Fachons des Turcs* in 1553 by his widow.[41]

At the time of Coeck's sojourn in Turkey, Europe was living in fear of an invasion. The defeat of the Hungarians in 1526 at the Battle of Mohacz by Suleiman the Magnificent terrified the rest of Europe, and yet—as Georges Marlier, author of a monograph on Coeck, notes—fear was mingled with curiosity and even respect. In Jan Swart van Groningen's engravings, published the same year as the disaster at Mohacz, the Turks are depicted as certainly "formidable but never as contemptible: we see a triumphal procession behind Suleiman, who is on horseback."[42] We do not know where Swart van Groningen acquired his knowledge; he certainly never set foot in the Levant. Marlier conjectures that he probably worked in Coeck's atelier, where he imbibed his Orientalism.

Coeck's woodcuts, "although framed by caryatids, classicistic in pose in accordance with the taste of the time, and idealizing human types and composition . . . yet give us an extraordinarily living picture of Muhammedan [Muslim] and Levantine court, military and, above all, private life."[43] As Marlier says, the woodcuts are a veritable "reportage" in images of what the artist witnessed during his sojourn and travels. The woodcuts are presented as seven great compositions "engraved on wood," forming a long, continuous frieze, four and half meters in length and forty-four centimeters in height. The seven compartments are separated by caryatids, figures that are alternatively masculine and feminine and are clothed in the Turkish fashion: (1) A Military Encampment in Slavonia, (2) The Passage of a Caravan, (3) Turkish Soldiers Relaxing (showing how Turks pray, eat, sit on the ground, greet or salute or pay respect to one another, urinate, and so on), (4) Feast of the New Moon, (5) A Turkish Burial, (6) Feast of Circumcision before Constantinople, (7) The Procession of Suleiman and his guards in the Hippodrome Square: view of the city, mosques, and other monuments.[44] All in all, it is a remarkable achievement, depicting the life, manners, customs, and costumes of people with impressive realism, and peopled with elegant but masculine and firm figures.

Pieter Bruegel the Elder may at one point have been apprenticed to Coeck. Even Rembrandt was influened by Coeck's real pictures of Oriental life.

The most important Dutch painter to show a more than superficial interest in Oriental dress and customs, and to paint with sympathy and sensitivity the life and culture of Jews—the closest Other—was Rembrandt. Wittkower takes Rembrandt's biographer, Jakob Rosenberg, to task for omitting any reference to the Dutch master's interest in Turkish manners: "[Rembrandt] grew up in an ambience in which people were virtually saturated with Turkish things."[45] Jan Lieven's *Esther Accusing Haman* and Pieter Lastman's *Massacre of the Inno-*

cents both made lasting impressions on Rembrandt.[46] He greatly admired "the simple presence" of Persian and Mughal miniatures, owning a set of the latter himself. "In Rembrandt's drawing of the emperor Timur (c.1655) portrayed enthroned under a baldachin, the artist obviously copied directly from a miniature. In his *Abraham Entertaining Angels* [1656], Rembrandt reflects the spirit of a simple, silent presence that he derived from Persian miniatures, but he has transformed that spirit into something quite personal.[47] His drawing of a Moghul horseman in the British Museum in London is directly inspired by Persian miniatures and shows the influence that these miniatures had on his so-called Polish Rider of 1655. This painting dates from a period in which his interest in Moghul miniatures was particularly keen, an influence that has been greatly underestimated by scholars."[48] Drawings of the time of Jahangir (1605–28) were the source on which Rembrandt drew for the Indian features of some figures appearing in several of his paintings, such as the *Marriage of Samson*, *Susanna and the Elders*, and *Portrait of an Oriental*.[49]

Melchior Lorch, an engraver of Danish and German descent, spent four years in Constantinople and worked on his book *On the Costumes and Manners of Turks*, which appeared in 1626, several years after his death, and which contained 124 woodcuts of Oriental views and people. These seemed to have exerted an influence on Rembrandt. Rembrandt's own Orientalism, in turn, exerted an influence on Italian artists, such as Giambattista Tiepolo.

Rembrandt is well known as a painter of Jews and Jewish scripture. Moses Gans, a Dutch-Jewish historian, wrote that Holland's greatest painter expressed deep empathy for Jews, who owed him "an enormous debt of gratitude, [for] there has never been another non-Jewish artist—sculptor, painter, or writer—to depict this rejected group of people who, in his own eyes, despite everything, remained God's people in exile, as truthfully as did Rembrandt."[50] Although there would seem to be an element of romanticization in such appreciations of Rembrandt as a philo-Semite, smitten by the Jewish culture around him in Amsterdam, Steven Nadler has shown that such a view is not unmerited: "Rembrandt did paint, etch, and draw Jews and Jewish settings. There is nothing legendary about this. The faces in some, and maybe many, of his portraits and history and genre works are Jewish; several of the tableaux that he captures on canvas and paper derive from what he saw in the streets of his neighbourhood [in Amsterdam]. Wonderfully, few of his contemporaries found this remarkable."[51] And of course, they do reveal a special sympathy for Jews, and Rembrandt's Old Testament scenes are moving and deeply felt portraits. Since the Jews were seen as an Eastern people, works depicting their life and customs, such as those of Rembrandt, can be regarded as Orientalist.

Nadler goes on to show that Rembrandt was not alone in seventeenth-century Holland in such sympathetic portrayals of Jews and their milieu. Nadler dicusses the work of Romeyn de Hooghe, who worked in a wide variety of media. It is through de Hooghe's etchings and drawings that we learn so much about the daily life of seventeenth-century Jews of Amsterdam: "their clothes, their homes, their means of conveyance, their neighbourhood, even their ancient history and contemporary rituals,"[52] and their synagogues. "De Hooghe depicted the Jews at prayer and at business, enjoying the pleasures of leisure and weeping in moments of grief. They are seen attending the community's school, walking to the *mikvah*, or ritual bath, and unloading their dead from barges after the five-mile trip up river to the cemetery at Ouderkerk. De Hooghe shows them filing into the synagogue for worship, and he memorializes their blind old rabbi, Isaac Aboab, as he is being led by the hand to the pulpit to conduct services," all rendered with remarkable artistry and expressiveness.[53]

As Gerald Ackerman and others have pointed out, we need to set the Orientalist paintings of the nineteenth century firmly within the history of Western art, particularly in seventeenth-century Dutch genre paintings, from which the Orientalists gathered much of their iconographical vocabulary. Hence, what Nadler says of Dutch art of the period of Rembrandt and de Hooghe is of particular interest and importance. Dutch genre painting celebrates the everyday, the humdrum, the ordinary, and constitutes its very strength: "There is a uniformity in the depiction of all walks of life. Ugliness and deformity are there, but they represent the common sins and foibles of all humankind. The taverns of Jan Steen and the brothels of Gerard ter Borch have their share of caricature and lowlife. But there is no special iconography reserved for the Jew. The depictions of Jews and their activities are generically no different from those of wealthy regents, middle-class merchants, and indigent laborers. The naturalistic renderings, the settings of everyday life, and the easy integration in their dress, architecture, and habits into Dutch culture make the Jews in the art of Holland's golden age perfectly ordinary."[54] It is clear to Nadler that the intention of all the Dutch artists depicting Jewish ritual, manner, and style is "to ennoble a religion and a culture in the toleration of which the Dutch may take pride."[55]

Rembrandt lived in Breestraat, in the Jewish quarter of Amsterdam, Vlooienburg, and there he "painted, etched, and drew his Sephardic and Ashkenazic neighbors, sometimes for the sake of their biblical potential. Yet even when his compositions have their source and inspiration more in his literary imagination than in Breestraat, the faces are drawn from familiar acquaintance, not prejudice."[56] But, as Nadler reminds us, de Hooghe and Rembrandt were two of many seventeenth-century Dutch painters and draftsmen "who found these 'foreign residents of the Republic of the Netherlands' a source of artistic and even spiritual stimulation."[57] Other Dutch artists similarly inspired include Bartholomeus Molenaer, Jan Lievens, Govaert Flinck, Pieter van Gunst, Aernout Nagtegaal, Jan Luttichuys, and Jan Luyken.

What Nadler writes of Emanuel de Witte is of great interest in the context of any discussion of Orientalist art, with its many depictions of the interiors of mosques. De Witte achieved fame as a painter of church interiors before he painted the interior of a synagogue: "His respectful portrayals of the Jewish congregation and the architectural achievement of which it was so proud pays homage not only to the particularities of a foreign religion and its customs but also to its local representatives' social and cultural integration, as well as to the toleration that made that integration possible. The objectivity and neutrality of de Witte's depiction, his refusal to make a judgment in a painting that shows two groups of people making judgments of each other, the ordinariness of a work that despite its rare subject is instantly recognizable as belonging to a certain genre of Dutch art, does more to elevate this building and its occupants than any celebratory print of the synagogue could possibly do."[58]

But Rembrandt and his circle also painted other Oriental subjects, especially Persian and Turkish. The presence at the Persian Court of Dutch painters such as Jan Lukaszon van Hasselt (or Hasveldt), Philippe Angel, C. Le Brun, and Jean the Dutchman, as well as the presence of the Dutch Embassy under Joan Cunaeus to the court of Shah Abbas II, helped to keep interest alive in things Persian.[59] Goetz points to Rembrandt's own works as examples, such as the *Presentation of Christ*, the *Young Samson,* the *Portrait of His Father*, *David and Absolom*, the *Prodigal Son* in Leningrad, *Christ and the Woman Taken in Adultery* in London, and the *"Mene Tekel" or Belshazzar's Feast*. "Among his pupils the influence of these studies may be discerned in some works by B. Fabritius, G. Flinck, N. Maes, J. de Wet, and especially in those by G. van den Eeckhout (*Boas and Ruth*; *Eleazar at the Well*). . . . Aert de Gelder, however, occupies an exceptional position not only as the last, but also as one of the most distinguished orientalists of the Dutch school, and even of the whole realm of European painting."[60]

The Flemish Baroque painter Peter Paul Rubens, one of the great masters, made a series of sketches of blacks. *The Four Studies of the Head of a Negro*, painted sometime between 1613 and 1615 and now in the Musées Royaux des Beaux-Arts, Brussels, is a moving study of a particular individual: smiling, sad, pensive, even melancholic. No one would call these studies "caricatures." They are well-observed portraits by a master. *The Head of a Negro* painted between 1618 and 1620 and now in the Hyde Collection at Glen Falls, New York, is one of Rubens's neglected masterpieces. The sitter is the same man as in the *Four Studies*, but painted a few years later. Such is Rubens's genius that we can see a subtle evolution in the face: Here the sitter is much sadder and bowed down, his heavy-hearted expression endowing the portrait with great pathos.

In his celebrated work on Dutch and Flemish painting, Eugène Fromentin remarked that Rubens's portraits were often hackneyed, but particularly so when he was painting Europeans. Fromentin argues that in Rubens's *Adoration of the Kings* in the Antwerp Museum, the only successful figure is the Ethiopian, or black: "The Ethiopian . . . of the greyish negro type, with his livid, high-cheeked, flat-nosed face, lit up by two shining flashes, the glitter of the eyes and the glistening of the teeth, is without doubt a masterpiece of observation and nature; for he is a portrait, and a portrait of the same model without any alteration."[61]

In his visits to study the masterworks of Western art at the Cleveland Museum of Art, the distinguished African American artist Hughie Lee-Smith first encountered the works of Rubens. The decisive influence was Rubens's studies of blacks, which he came upon in an art book. He was inspired to take up painting as a vocation by them. In particular, he remembers "[Rubens's] painting of heads of Negroes, their beautiful quality."[62]

Eighteenth Century: Dr. Justus on Exotic Hunt Scenes

Yet another example of art refusing to reflect Saidian theories is offered by Dr. Kevin Justus. In a study of the nine paintings of exotic hunts by Jean-Baptiste Pater, Nicolas Lancret, Jean François de Troy, Charles Parrocel, Carle Van Loo, and François Boucher, executed between 1734 and 1738 and now at the Petite Galerie of Louis XV at Versailles, Justus refutes Said's thesis: "By using far off people and places to educate the young Louis in his role and responsibilities as a good monarch, [Cardinal] Fleury and the artists chose not an exotic that was mined, exploited, enslaved and controlled as Edward Said would interpret, but as the visual evidence attests, an exotic that, as fantastic as it was, represented an exotic based on an openness and respect to the foreign, a curiosity about the unusual, and an understanding about the associative power of the symbols chosen to communicate an idea or message. In many ways, these paintings call into question the now standard tropes of Saidian orientalism."[63]

For Justus, "The hunts in Louis XV's galerie counter many of the conclusions of Said, which not only gives the paintings a louder voice in understanding the first half of Louis XV's reign, but brings into high relief the problems with the Saidian approach." Said's "broad generalisations misrepresent and mislead our understanding of the ever changing 18th century. . . . [T]hese elements of the foreign in the hunt paintings were not viewed as part of a conquering colonialist agenda but an actual appreciation and curiosity about the foreign and non-European. Louis's interest in the 'Orient' was well-known. Louis XV's appreciation of the royal gifts of numerous Turkish books and objects from the Porte and the remarkable success of the visit of Mehemet Effendi to Paris and Versailles is more evidence of mutual respect and understanding."[64]

EIGHTEENTH CENTURY: ORIENTALISTS IN CONSTANTINOPLE

The European with the Asian shore
Sprinkled with palaces; the Ocean stream
Here and there studded with a seventy-four;
Sophia's cupola with golden gleam;
The cypress groves; Olympus high and hoar,
The twelve isles, and the more than I could dream,
Far less describe, present the very view
Which charm'd the charming Mary Montagu.

—Lord Byron, *Don Juan*

In the eighteenth century, greater political and trade relations brought many merchants and diplomats to Constantinople. The diplomats in turn brought with them many artists. Under their influence, Western-style portraiture became increasingly popular in Ottoman court circles. From the time of Selim III, who was the sultan of the Ottoman Empire from 1789 to 1807, local artists made portraits using Western techniques, while Selim's nephew Mahmud II had his own portraits painted in oil.

Before the rise of Orientalism proper in European art, many European artists, drawn by their first intimations of the East and by the fashion for *turquerie* that was a result of the new relations, worked intensively in the lands of the empire and depicted the Ottoman world. Their work was without prejudice but with the vivid realism of reportage, and imbued with respect, affection, and wide-eyed wonder. Some of these artists working in Ottoman Turkey became known collectively as the Bosphorus Painters. Auguste Boppe, in his groundbreaking study, lists some twenty-seven Western artists of the eighteenth century who worked in the eastern Mediterranean and Turkey and the lands of the

Ottoman Empire, artists who had firsthand experience of the Orient.[65] There was nothing imaginary about their knowledge. These artists—painters in oil, portraitists in pastels, draughtsmen in pen and ink—pose an enormous ideological problem for Saidists. These eighteenth-century Orientalists were working in an independent Muslim country and the lands of its empire, and thus they could not be accused of bringing to Turkey attitudes of colonial superiority or imperialism. Their work itself refutes any such charges. Hence, the Bosphorus Painters are never discussed by Said or his followers. Furthermore, these artists were often employed by Turks—including the sultan himself, those at his court, and the nobility—because the Turks *liked* the work of the Orientalists. Finally, these Orientalists were themselves in awe of Islamic civilization, overwhelmed by the color, costumes, manners, refinement, the magnificence of the imperial court, the army of the Janissaries, and the scenes of everyday life, as hundreds of Orientals gathered together in the capital from all parts of the Islamic world. The Orientalists paid homage to it in painting after painting, portrait after portrait.

One of the subjects most commonly painted by European artists in Constantinople employed in diplomatic circles was the audience ceremonies at the Ottoman palace; while in Europe, audience ceremonies for Ottoman ambassadors were also painted.

Distinctive costumes of different groups of people in the empire were depicted with great care, as were portraits of foreign ambassadors, interpreters, and—increasingly—Ottoman dignitaries. In addition to several audience scenes and pictures of Istanbul, Jean-Baptiste Vanmour painted state officials in their traditional costumes. These were published in Marquis de Ferriol's *Recueil de cent estampes représentant différentes nations du Levant* (A collection of a hundred engravings representing different nations of the Levant) in 1714,[66] a work depicting a great variety of manners and costumes.[67]

As Philip Mansel pointed out, "*Recueil de cent estampes* was the main source for those images of turqueries, by artists such as Boucher and Guardi, so popular in eighteenth-century Europe; it was immediately translated into English, German, Spanish and Italian. Vanmour had single-handedly brought the Ottoman Empire into the visual repertory of Europe."[68]

Thus Vanmour, sometimes written Van Mour, was well received in the homes of Turks themselves, not only at the imperial court. His atelier became the fashionable rendezvous of elegant society of Constantinople. More important, as Boppe tells us, his long sojourn in the Orient gave Vanmour access to places and subjects normally off limits to Europeans, such as Turkish women at their toilette or at the baths.[69] Vanmour also painted the whirling dervishes.

Another European artist working in Istanbul in the eighteenth century was

Antoine de Favray. While working in Rome, de Favray made a favorable impression on representatives of the Order of Malta, was invited to join them in Malta in 1744, and was nominated a Knight of the Order. In Malta he painted several canvases evoking the manners and dress of Maltese women; these portraits gained him entry to l'Académie des Beaux-Arts in Paris. As soon as he was elected, de Favray set off for Constantinople in 1762, where he was employed by the French ambassadors Comte de Vergennes and Comte de St. Priest until 1771. His portraits of Vergennes and his wife depict the couple in Turkish costume seated in the Oriental style. De Favray also painted the view of Constantinople from the sea with great patience and great topographical accuracy.

Jean-Étienne Liotard, known in his native city as "the Turkish painter" and eighty-seven of whose works—pastels, oil paintings, drawings, miniatures, and enamels—are now to be found in the Musée d'Art et d'Histoire of Geneva, can be seen as yet another Orientalist who shared many of the characteristics of his nineteenth-century successors. Liotard imposed a sober style, bare and realist, giving his portraits an almost photographic precision and earning him the title "painter of truth." Liotard was a cosmopolitan, open to the outside world, having traveled in the Orient as much as Europe, and eager to embrace and paint those of the East or West, in all walks of life. Intellectually curious, Liotard worked in Paris, then traveled by way of Italy to Constantinople, where he stayed from 1738 to 1743. Contrary to the painters who stayed in Europe and painted "Turkish fantasies," Liotard painted an Orient far more objective, well observed, precise, and relentlessly sober.

As Claire Stoullig, who organized the Liotard exhibition in Geneva (2002), said, "Liotard's Orient is particularly touching, where the Swiss painter, far from being just a visitor, had the generosity to live like the Orientals. The artist showed a tenderness, an attachment for the Oriental way of life. Sensitive to the interdependence of cultures, and like a true man of the Enlightenment, Liotard was open to other worlds."[70]

Little is known about the life of Jean-Baptiste Hilair, sometimes written Hilaire, but as Boppe says, on the evidence of his work as draughtsman or painter, he came under the influence of the Orient early. No one else, wrote Boppe, knew how to render the softness of the light in the Bosphorus or to present the interior of Muslim and Christian houses, mosque courtyards, the narrow streets of the bazaar, the thousand or so people in colorful costumes, so precisely depicted as to gest and attitude. No detail of the life of the Levant escaped his watchful eye. One of Hilair's drawings was worth a full page of the *Memoirs of Baron de Tott*.[71] Hilair added much by his drawings to the value of the *Tableau de l'Empire Ottoman* (A Picture of the Ottoman Empire) of Mouradja d'Ohsson that was published in 1787.[72] He also contributed to Choiseul-Gouffier's *Voyage pittoresque de la Grèce* (A Colorful Voyage through Greece).

Louis-François Cassas spent seven years traveling in Italy, Sicily, and Dalmatia before embarking for Constantinople in 1784 with Count Choiseul-Gouffier. From there, Cassas set sail for Egypt, but the situation in Egypt was too dangerous for him to be able to get to Cairo, so he set off for Cyprus, Syria, and Palestine. He came back to Constantinople in 1786 with nearly three hundred drawings and sketches. Only a part of his work was ever published, including the first volume of his *Voyage pittoresque de la Syrie, de la Phénicie, de la Palestine et de la Basse-Égypte* (A Colorful Voyage through Syria, Phoenicia, Palestine and Lower Egypt) in 1799.

Antoine Ignace Melling studied under his father, Joseph, who, in turn, had trained under Carle Van Loo. Melling traveled widely in Italy, Egypt, and Anatolia before settling down at Constantinople, where he became the official designer, draughtsman, and architect to Sultana Hadidge (Princess Hatice). As one contemporary European visitor observed, Melling, "architect, painter, decorator and gardener, demolished, rebuilt, destroyed and recreated unceasingly."[73] When Selim III, who was sultan of the Ottoman Empire from 1789 to 1807, wanted a garden at the palace he had just been given by his sister Bekhan that would resemble that of Hadidge, he asked Melling to design it. Melling spent long hours at the Tower of Leandre, or the Tower of Galata, or on the terraces of the embassies at Pera, sketching and painting the views of Constantinople. But it is his views of the shores of the Bosphorus—that strait of about thirty kilometers that connects the Mediterranean and Sea of Marmara in the south to the Black Sea in the north—that have established Melling's reputation. Thanks to his powers of sympathetic observation and artistic skills, the quays of the Bosphorus come alive: the crowds of valets pushing, under the command of eunuchs, at the gates of a palace; sitting in the shadow of the plane trees are Muslim women keeping a watchful eye on their children fishing. A little farther on, a Greek in a long cylindrical hat sells amulets near a fountain whose waters have apparently worked miracles; an ambassador's carriage passes by; gypsies make a bear and two monkeys dance and, for a brief moment, the reveries of an Armenian or Greek at his window waiting for a pleasant breeze from the Black Sea are interrupted; and so on.[74]

Melling left for Paris in 1802, where he spent the next seventeen years preparing his book on the Bosphorus and Constantinople for publication. *Voyage pittoresque de Constantinople et des rives du Bosphore* (Colorful voyage through Constantinople and the banks of the Bosphorus), containing a volume of text and an album of forty-eight engravings taken from his drawings by various engravers such as Schroder, Le Rouge, and Pillement fils, came out in 1819.[75]

Appreciation of Melling's work in modern times comes from the Turkish novelist Orhan Pamuk, who devotes a rapturous chapter to Istanbul as depicted in the *Voyages pittoresque*. "Of all the western artists who painted the Bosphorus, it's Melling I find the most nuanced and convincing," wrote Pamuk in his *Istanbul*. Pamuk admires Melling's attention to humanizing details and his precision, finding his views paradoxically at once sad and consoling. Even his depiction of the scene inside the harem, Pamuk judges to be full of dignity, elegance, and seriousness: "[I]t is his poetic vision that makes him a painter who speaks to modern-day *Istanbullus*." Pamuk scrutinizes Melling's views with a magnifying glass: "I'll look at the watermelon sellers on the left and observe with pleasure that today's watermelon sellers display their wares in just the same way. . . . Melling's city, like ours, teems with peddlers hawking clothes and food who display their wares on three-legged tables." For Pamuk, Melling is an insider; the Westerner painted the city with Western techniques, but saw the city as an *Istanbullu* at a time when the latter were not capable of painting themselves or their city.[76]

The catalog of the Pera Museum exhibition in Istanbul tells us, "[T]his tradition of painting, particularly portraiture, introduced by western artists, gradually spread from court and diplomatic circles to broader sectors of society; first to high-ranking state officials and then to leading Ottoman families, whose members increasingly commissioned portraits of themselves. Even more importantly, this tradition of oil painting influenced local artists, one of the most renowned being Osman Hamdi Bey, who did many works that place him among the artists of the orientalist movement."[77]

While they had no access to Ottoman harem life, Western artists were able to observe women from afar, "when they were travelling from place to place, shopping in the company of eunuchs, or enjoying country outings. . . . Pleasing scenes of women in gauzy yashmaks and colourful outer robes promenading in their carriages, strolling in meadows, or being rowed along in graceful caiques, lacy sunshades in hand, were a favourite topic for western painters."[78]

Western painters were not permitted to portray Ottoman—that is, Muslim—women in indoor attire from life, so they instead turned to Greek, Armenian, Jewish, and Levantine women in such scenes. Ottoman palace women and those of the upper classes were always eager to have their portraits painted, and Western female painters such as Henriette Brown and Mary Walker were in constant demand. When these portraits of them in European clothing of the latest fashion were completed, they had to be concealed in cupboards or by a curtain so that the male servants of the household could not see them.[79]

NINETEENTH CENTURY: THOMAS HOPE

Most books on Orientalism understandably leave out Thomas Hope; his drawings were found only recently. In 1977, during a reorganization of the library of the Benaki Museum in Athens, "five folio-size volumes of about 350 unsigned drawings were discovered, bound in contemporary gilt-tooled Russia leather. Two are inscribed along the spine 'Drawings by T. Hope.' "[80] They have never been published in their entirety, but some were reproduced in 1993–94 in *Cornucopia*, a journal published three times a year in Istanbul. They are exquisite drawings, many in pen and sepia, so finely executed that they were initially cataloged as engravings. Before discussing them, I should like to say something about Hope's life and ideas, which are so important for our theme, and he leads us most naturally from the eighteenth to the nineteenth century.

Thomas Hope (1769–1831) was a designer, a collector of great eccentricity. Having inherited a great fortune, Hope took the grand tour between 1787 and 1795, covering much of Europe and the Near East, and recording it in a series of 350 superb drawings, now in the Benaki Museum. Like many a later Orientalist, Hope recorded "the architecture, ornament, landscape and costume in Hungary and the Balkans, Turkey, Greece and Egypt." Another happy result of his grand tour was a long novel in three volumes, *Anastasius* (1819), "a descriptive account of life, manners, politics and architecture in the Old Ottoman Empire."[81] Hope was eminently qualified to write such an account, for, as he himself explained, "I resided nearly a twelve month in Constantinople; visited the arsenal and bagnio frequently; witnessed the festival of St. George; saw Rhodes, was in Egypt, in Syria, and every other place which I have attempted to describe minutely in Anastasius . . . and had at one time an Albanian in my service."[82]

Exotic clothes sent Hope into raptures, and his novel is full of admiring descriptions of costumes encountered in the Ottoman Empire. In 1809 Hope was to publish *Costume of the Ancients* in two volumes, and in 1812 *Designs of Modern Costume*, his attempt to reform modern dress. Hope commissioned a full-length portrait of himself in Turkish costume from Sir William Beechey; it was hung in his London mansion in Duchess Street. That mansion was designed as a museum to express Hope's love of Oriental art and to display his collection of Persian carpets and ornaments of gold, in a room decorated in the "Saracenic" or "Moorish" taste. As David Watkin explains, "In such rooms Hope showed himself to be a key creator of the Regency style, anticipating John Nash's orientalised interiors of 1815–23 for the Prince Regent in the Royal Pavilion at Brighton. Hope specially commissioned the three large Indian pictures in the Blue Room from Thomas Daniell in 1799–1800. In order to suggest parity between Eastern and Western civilisations, these impressive topographical views were framed identically with a fourth painting of Panini of the Forum in Rome."[83]

Hope's desire to dissolve the boundaries between Eastern and Western cultures is reflected in his book *Household Furniture and Interior Decoration Executed from Designs by Thomas Hope* (1807). The title page of the book was framed by an elaborate Islamic border, which, Hope explained, was "copied from the frame of a picture, representing a Turkish personage." Watkin sums up what Hope was trying to achieve:

> [Hope] believed that its "congelations and stalactites" were derived from the "Grecian architects of the lower empire" and were "remarkable for the play, or rather the flicker, of light and shade." He pointed out that in Istanbul this singular ornament adorns the capitals, the entablatures, the niches and the gateways of "most of the Greek churches and Mohammedan mosques, designed by Grecian builders." It attracted Hope as a universal form which appeared "throughout Europe, Asia and Africa . . . in almost all the splendid Saracenic monuments of Arabia, Egypt and Persia," in the Moorish buildings of Spain and India, and even in the zigzag carvings round the doorways of Norman churches in England. Hope wanted to make a synthesis of all styles, and this chevron ornament seemed a symbol of the dissolution of the boundaries commonly supposed to exist between Eastern and Western cultures.[84]

Hope may have been influenced by Giambattista Piranesi's *Diverse Maniere d'Adornare i Cammini* (Diverse Manners of Ornamenting Chimneys [1769]), which expressed a similar desire for a fruitful combination of diverse styles, in Piranesi's case, of Grecian, Tuscan, and Egyptian.

One of the illustrations to David Watkin's article in *Cornucopia* is Hope's exquisite watercolor-and-sepia drawing of the octagonal Türbe of Valide Gülnus Emetullah in Üsküdar. Ahmet III built this tomb for his mother. As Watkin says, "The play of Western and Eastern themes in the Turkish Rococo of the eighteenth-century Tulip period seems to have been Hope's idea of Perfection."[85]

The West's striving for universalism is reflected in art, as in literature. Hope is one exemplar.

11

OCCIDENTAL INFLUENCE ON EASTERN ART

Roman and Byzantine Influence

The influence of the East on the West in art has a corollary: Islamic art owes a great deal to Greco-Roman and Byzantine influences. Islamic art and architecture owes an enormous debt to the rich and ancient traditions of the Near East, with which the Arabs came into contact after the rapid conquests of the seventh century. As K. A. C. Creswell, the scholar of Islamic architecture, put it rather bluntly, "Arabia, at the rise of Islam, does not appear to have possessed anything worthy of the name of architecture."[1] Oleg Grabar and Richard Ettinghausen also point out that "the conquering Arabs, with few artistic traditions of their own and a limited doctrine on art, penetrated a world which was not only immensely rich in artistic themes and forms yet universal in its vocabulary, but also, at this particular juncture of its history, had charged its forms with unusual intensity."[2]

The Dome of the Rock (691 CE) in Jerusalem, one of the earliest Islamic monuments, was obviously influenced by the centrally planned buildings known as "martyria" and bears a close relationship to the Christian sanctuaries of the Ascension and the Anastasis. The interior equally owes a great deal to the Christian art of Syria, Palestine, and Byzantine. As for the minaret, Creswell has shown that it was derived architecturally from Syrian church towers.[3] In his classic work on Arab painting, Ettinghausen in a chapter pointedly titled "Byzantine Art in Islamic Garb" writes: "[D]uring the Umayyad period the two major elements of Arab painting were classical and Iranian; these elements existed side by side and, apart from a deliberate choice of subject matter, showed no Islamic slant. In the subsequent Abbasid period the Iranian [i.e., non-Islamic or pre-Islamic Iran] element became prevalent. At the end of the 12th century, the classical element again predominates, this time by way of Byzantine inspiration."[4]

WESTERN INFLUENCE IN IRAN

As for Iran, we know of a Portuguese painter in Shiraz at the time of Ismail I, and under Abbas I there were several Dutch artists, such as Jan Lukaszon van Hasselt, who worked as a court painter and was later made ambassador to Holland.[5] We tend to think of Persian miniatures as quintessentially Oriental and sui generis, but we now know that starting at least with Abbas I's reign, there were Italian pictures for sale in Isfahan, and that they exerted an influence on Persian art. Don Garcia de Silva Figueroa, sent by Philip III of Spain as ambassador to the shah in 1617, described a royal pavilion he visited: "[T]here were fine pictures incomparably better made than those which one usually sees in Persia . . . we learned that the painter . . . was called Jules, that he was born in Greece and brought up in Italy where he had learned his art. . . . It was quite easy to see that this was the work of a European, because one recognized the Italian manner." Abbas II invited Italian and Dutch painters, such as Philippe Angel from the East India Company of Holland, to Isfahan, where they also influenced the development of the art of miniatures; the shah himself took lessons from two Dutch artists.[6]

Increasing contact between Europe and Iran, and the number of Western artists actually living in Iran, led to a greater appreciation of Western art and to its further influence on Persian art, particularly on mural paintings in royal palaces and on miniatures.[7] In the latter works we see a new realism; stereotyped figures give way to portraits of real individuals. Several European painters worked and resided in Iran, some working directly for the shah: "Even more remarkable is the action of Abbas II in sending a Persian artist to Italy for further training. He is known as Muhammad Zaman and stayed in Rome, where he studied modern techniques. He is said to have adopted the Catholic religion and is sometimes mentioned as Muhammad Paolo Zaman. Several other Persian painters of the time show evidence of European influence and perhaps even training—if not in Europe then at least by European artists in Iran."[8]

WESTERN INFLUENCE ON TURKISH ARTISTS

Islamic artists sometimes adopted Western techniques, as in the portraits of Ottoman ruler Mehmet II. One watercolor on paper painted around 1480, now in the Topkapi Palace, is believed to be by Shiblizade Ahmed, a pupil of the Ottoman artist Sinan Bey of Bursa, to whom the painting was previously attributed. Western techniques are evident in the painter's use of color tones in rendering the folds of the sitter's clothes and his handkerchief, suggesting mass and volume. Ottoman painter Sinan Bey, not to be confused with the famous architect, was said to have studied under a Venetian master called Paoli.

By the eighteenth century, the Western influence on Turkish art was more and more evident. We know of several Western artists who were employed by the Ottoman court or by those close to it: artists such as a Pole called Mecti, who converted to Islam, and an Armenian called Raphael, who worked at the palace between 1781 and 1785. "By the end of the eighteenth century, the old artistic tradition was virtually dead, and even book illustrations to Turkish literary works were predominantly Western in style."[9] Abduljelil Çelebi, known as Levni, "began as an illuminator, and even in this traditional area his surviving work reveals Western rococo influences."[10]

Western Influence on Mughal Art

Mughal art in India also came under Western influence. We know that European prints started to come into India from the 1540s onward with the arrival of Francis Xavier, who was sent to India in 1542. He was followed by fifty Jesuit colleagues in 1555. Gregory Minissale conjectures that "[s]ome of these mid-sixteenth century prints were probably acquired by the Mughal embassy to Goa in 1575. The second wave, dating from the latter part of the century, must have arrived at the Mughal court with the three Jesuit missions, the first in 1580, the second in 1591, and the third in 1595."[11] Minissale, however, tries to show that Mughal India acquired European prints of nonreligious subjects and topographical materials through other channels as well: "Individual travellers and merchants took engravings of classical nudes and mythical subjects to the East; this would explain the presence in Mughal albums of prints of nude, mythological and classical subjects, and motifs from maps in background landscapes."[12] Minissale finds evidence of Flemish, Dutch, and German influence—artists such as Jacob Golzious, Simon Bening, and Gottfried von Kempen—on the art of Mughal India, in particular in the illustrated *Khamsa* of Nizami in the British Library, dating from 1593–95.

One wonders at the similarities between Carlo Crivelli's *The Annunciation with St. Emidius* in the National Gallery, London, dating from 1486, and Basawan's *The Foppish Dervish Rebuked*, a miniature from the *Baharistan* of Jami, painted in 1595 and now in the Bodleian Library at Oxford.[13] Both artists place their figures within an architectural framework, both show peacocks on the upper-right-hand side of the building, while on the upper-left-hand side, slightly further in the mid-distance, both depict two figures conversing on top of the arch as birds fly around above them. The Mughal artist has made a concerted effort at rendering perspective in the European manner.

Carlo Crivelli, *The Annunciation with Saint Emidius*, 1486. National Gallery, London.

Basawan, *The Foppish Dervish Rebuked*, 1595. Illustration to Jami's *Baharistan* (Spring Garden). Bodleian Library, Oxford.

12

NINETEENTH-CENTURY ORIENTALIST ART

Linda Nochlin and "The Imaginary Orient"

In the guest book at the Dahesh Museum on Madison Avenue in New York City, there is an entry by a tourist, possibly German, who enthuses about the Orientalist paintings in the collection, saying how much she admired and enjoyed them. Then, almost as an afterthought—as though she has only just remembered to put on her ideological spectacles—she adds words to the effect that "of course, they were Orientalist works, hence imperialist and reprehensible." Apparently, she felt guilty for having enjoyed and appreciated Orientalist art. How many other ordinary lovers of paintings, sculpture, drawings, watercolors, and engravings have had their natural inclination to enjoy works of Orientalist art damaged or even destroyed by the influence of Edward Said and his followers? How many people have had their enjoyment of Jane Austen spoiled by Said's insidious claim that Austen was condoning slavery?

Nowadays, when discussing Orientalist art, one often begins with Linda Nochlin's article "The Imaginary Orient," a work obviously influenced by Said's *Orientalism.*[1] Nochlin's article can hardly be called art criticism. It is purely polemic, and at times quite hysterical. For her, the important element in any analysis of such art must be "the particular power structure in which these works came into being. For instance, the degree of realism (or lack of it) in individual Orientalist images can hardly be discussed without some attempt to clarify *whose* reality we are talking about." We are immediately in the fantasy world of relativism and parallel universes—"whose reality?" indeed. Nochlin assumes that the Orientalist artist must in every case be a symbol of the prevailing political reality, in other words, in the grip of blind historical forces against which he is helpless, that he must have an imperialistic agenda and must be a racist. The thought that the artist may indeed be an individual, with his own personal aesthetic reasons for being in a foreign land, that he possesses free will, that the artist may actually love the country and its people that he paints, never seems to have occurred to her. For her, he represents the Occident, out to rape the submissive and backward Orient.

It is unfortunate for her ideological argument that she begins with Gérôme's *Snake Charmer*, which she claims is "a visual document of nineteenth-century colonialist ideology." It was *placed* in Constantinople, capital of the Ottoman Empire and seat of the Caliphate—and, of course, was not a European colony. The fact that so many Orientalist artists were working in parts of the Ottoman Empire—in Turkey itself, or Syria and Palestine and the Holy Land—is a simple refutation of this nonstop nonsense about "colonialist ideology." Egypt was conquered by the Ottomans in 1517 and remained a Turkish colony until 1798, when the French expedition under Bonaparte arrived with the intention of reinstating the authority of the Ottomans. The French interlude lasted barely three years. In 1801 a joint British-Ottoman expedition ended the French adventure. Between 1801 and 1882 Egypt was not occupied by a European power, and it was certainly not a European colony; indeed, in a strict sense, it was *never* a European colony. It was an Ottoman colony for nearly three hundred years. David Roberts, who painted many magnificent scenes of Egypt and its monuments, died in 1864, and so could not have known that country under European occupation. Algeria was under French rule for 132 years, but, as we shall see, those artists who went there—such as Eugène Fromentin—developed an affection for and commitment to it. Morocco and Tunisia were under French rule for a brief period, roughly forty years each, only in the twentieth century.

Nochlin continues: "[T]he watchers huddled against the ferociously detailed tiled wall in the background of Gérôme's painting are resolutely alienated from us, as is the act they watch with such childish, trancelike concentration. Our gaze is meant to include both the spectacle and its spectators as objects of picturesque delectation."[2] "Ferociously detailed tiled wall"? What exactly is her complaint? The wall is very skillfully rendered, and Gérôme, like many other Orientalist painters, delighted in depicting sensuous, colorful detail of materials, cloths, carpets, costumes, and ceramics and marble. "Childish, trancelike concentration": apart from the condescension implicit in "childish," Nochlin finds their gaze "trancelike"; I would describe it rather as "interested," especially the black figure on the left who leans forward in eager anticipation, with a slight smile on his face.

"Clearly, these black and brown folk are mystified—but then again, so are we. Indeed, the defining mood of the painting is mystery, and it is created by a specific pictorial device. We are permitted only a beguiling rear view of the boy holding the snake. A full frontal view, which would reveal unambiguously both his sex and the fullness of his dangerous performance, is denied us. And the insistent, sexually charged mystery at the center of this painting signifies a more general one: the mystery of the East itself, a standard *topos* of the Orientalist ideology."[3]

Notice Nochlin's own mystification suddenly, by a sleight of hand, becomes the Orientalists' topos of "the mystery of the East." What is the mystery? We cannot see the boy's genitals, in which case, how does she know he is a he? She finds his buttocks "beguiling," and apparently is disappointed that she cannot see more. She hates being left in an "ambiguous" state. And why are the spectators—condescendingly described by Nochlin as "black and brown folk"!—mystified, since *they do* have a full-frontal view of his sex and hence of his performance? Sexually charged mystery indeed! In what way would a full-frontal view reveal to us a "dangerous performance" that is not obvious from the dorsal view? Perhaps the performance is dangerous simply because it involves a snake, but we do not need a front view to figure that out; any angle will do. It is Nochlin herself who leaps from one canvas to generalize about all the Orient. It is Nochlin herself who is guilty of the very reductionistic, essentialist Orientalist generalization of which she accuses this artist. How can one go from one scene depicting a snake charmer to the claim that this represents the entire East? Perhaps it does for Nochlin; it certainly does not for me or thousands of others.

Nochlin claims that the watchers in the painting are "huddled" against a wall, but huddled implies discomfort. They do not look at all uncomfortable. It is Nochlin who is uncomfortable looking at them. She claims that they are "alienated" from "us," but the "us" is really an elliptical expression for herself, for Linda Nochlin. Some of the watchers are looking at the boy with the snake, but some appear to be watching an unrendered event behind the flutist. This further undermines Nochlin's analysis.

"Gérôme suggests that this Oriental world is a world without change."[4] Gérôme, claims Nochlin, avoids the French presence. But there was no French colonial presence in Turkey where this painting is placed. "The absence of a sense of history, of temporal change, in Gérôme's painting is intimately related to another striking absence in the work: that of the telltale presence of Western man. There are never any Europeans in 'picturesque' views of the Orient like these."[5] But here Gérôme is not painting a historical subject or scene. All that Nochlin's extraordinary criticism amounts to is a demand that he paint another picture altogether, whose subject matter is to be dictated by her. Gérôme did indeed paint historical subjects, such as his impressive *Napoléon and His General Staff* in 1867, now in a private collection. Of this painting, Lisa Small of the Dahesh Museum wrote, "This particular image combines Gérôme's two great themes, Orientalism and history, depicting a somber Napoléon retreating from

Acre. As [Earl] Shinn [editor of one hundred photogravures of Gérôme's paintings in ten volumes] describes it, the emperor, mounted on his ungainly beast of burden, in this burning and dreary march . . . with his discontented and defeated army around . . . experiences, for the first time, the bitterness of disappointed ambition."[6]

Several points need to be made. First, history was one of Gérôme's important themes. Second, the subject is Napoléon's defeat; there is no colonial or imperialistic triumphalism. Many Orientalist painters tackled historical subjects, especially the presence of the French in the Near East and North Africa, though Nochlin insists that the French are always "absent." Philippe Julian's excellent survey defines Orientalism as "a form of Romanticism just as it is a new way of painting history, with which it is often closely linked. The artists found fresh inspiration in political events. Between 1820 and 1830, the independence of Egypt, the liberation of Greece, and the conquest of Algeria brought the Near East and the Middle East into the mainstream of European affairs."[7] The painting of history is a part of the definition of Orientalism, hence Nochlin's claim is jejune. Historical works placed in the Orient include: Gérôme's *Oedipe ou le général Bonaparte en Égypte*; Anne-Louis Girodet de Roussy-Trioson's *Revolt in Cairo* (1810); Alexandre Bida's *Massacre des Mamelouks*; and Antoine-Jean Gros's *Charge de cavalerie exécutée par général Murat à la bataille d'Aboukir*, and his *Battle of Aboukir* (1806). Many Orientalists painted Napoléon in the Orient, among them Jean Charles Tardieu, Pierre Narcisse Guérin, Henry Lévy, and Leon Cogniet.[8]

"Indeed," continues Nochlin, "it might be said that one of the defining features of Orientalist painting is its dependence for its very existence on a presence that is always an absence: the Western colonial or touristic presence."[9]

If you have ever visited the Taj Mahal, the seventeenth-century Mughal masterpiece in Agra, you have not resisted the temptation to take a photograph of it. If you have taken a photograph, you were anxious not to include some fat Western tourist, in shorts, hat, and sunglasses with a camera slung around his neck, in the frame. You waited until there were no tourists near to spoil the view; such tourists would have looked out of place and as inappropriate as their dress. Orientalist paintings were often commissioned by Europeans or Americans back home, and the latter certainly did not want to buy views that showed tourists. Evidence of this comes from the books of two very gifted modern Indian photographers, Rai and Raghubir Singh. No Western tourists disfigure their photos. In Raghu Rai's photo portrait of Calcutta, there are sixty-three black-and-white photos of Calcutta and its inhabitants in the 1980s.[10] Some are of busy city scenes, others are almost rural, still others are portraits of individuals of the city.

Not one single photo shows a Westerner. Indeed, many of them have the genre quality we associate with Orientalist paintings: women and Kali along the Ganges River, a Marwari takes a rickshaw to work, workers carrying a wooden beam into a sawmill, transporting potatoes to the vegetable market, monsoon rains flood the streets, and so on. There are no Western tourists in sight.

Rai's book of photographs of the Taj Mahal is pure Orientalism, using this term in a nonpejorative sense. Taken in the 1980s, his photos have a remarkable affinity to the work of the Orientalist painters of the nineteenth century. One shows what may be a camel skeleton lying in a river bed, bearing an uncanny resemblance to Gustave Guillaumet's *Le Sahara* in the Musée d'Orsay. There are striking images of decaying monuments, Indian women in colorful traditional costumes, naked children playing on dirt roads, and women carrying copper or metal vessels on their heads.[11]

Similarly, Singh shows us a Rajasthan circa 1980,[12] a place still nonindustrial, made up of hundreds of villages, with few modern comforts, and nary a *rastaquouère*[13] in sight.

One can imagine what Nochlin's criticism of an Orientalist work that *did* show a European would be: "Of course, Gérôme would have to put in a European to remind us that it is really the European who is the master; there is no space that belongs to the Oriental, it has all been usurped by the colonialist. The Oriental cannot be left alone even in his own home."

Nochlin complains of Gérôme's technique: It is too smooth; she thinks he is trying to hide his art. But Gérôme is famous precisely for his meticulous finish; it is a style of painting shared by other great painters, such as Jean Auguste Dominique Ingres, with his superb draughtsmanship and precise neoclassical linear style, and without thick impasto. As Delacroix put it, "[T]he sight of a few Ruysdaels, especially a snow effect and a very simple marine where one sees no more than the sea in dull weather, with one or two boats, appeared to me the climax of art, *because the art in it is completely concealed*. That astounding simplicity."[14] Second, there is the naive assumption that if we can see the broad brush strokes and bright daubs of color, we can somehow better understand the technique, and this, according to Nochlin, is a good thing. A far more sympathetic analysis of Gérôme is offered by Gerald Ackerman. He seems to be answering Nochlin when he writes,

> [Gérôme's] compositions are models of effective simplicity. In the famous histories, our eyes are led through the narrative as if this were the natural way to observe. In work after work resonances of shapes and colors occur, almost unsuspected under the objective exactitude of his realism, as in the delicate, *First Kiss*

> *of the Sun*. The brilliance of his coloring is always within a controlled harmony. Each canvas seems to have its own particular color scheme; he does not always bang at the same chromatic chords. But above all Gérôme loved the act of painting, the exercise of his skill. It was not a task for him, even though, as a true academician, he believed that the conception of the idea was the real creative act and that the rest was "execution." He nevertheless did the "execution" energetically and cheerfully. He never tired out at the corners, and only in old age did he allow pictures of a lesser finish to leave his studio. Most of his paintings are meticulously finished with labor that only love could sustain. Gérôme worked with a limited palette, but he knew his pigments profoundly, even using some colors that seemed harsh but which he knew would eventually tone down in harmony with the colors around them. His objectivity may have produced a surface that some find offensive because they think it conceals art—a skill always admired in actors—but it is one of the self-effacing traits of his realism; he was matching the objectivity of his technique to that of his observation.[15]

In any case, Gérôme's technique was not followed or copied by all Orientalists. Some were even close to the impressionists in their style, such as Félix Ziem; some impressionists, in the strict sense, such as Degas, Renoir, and Manet, also painted scenes from the Orient.

Nochlin complains about "a plethora of authenticating details," especially the "unnecessary ones." Orientalists are accused of painting an imaginary Orient, and then also accused of insisting on "authenticating details." One cannot have it both ways. Should they have left out the authenticating details? Would that have improved the paintings? And would not these details help dispel the mystery that seems to vex Nochlin? Surely it is the artist's prerogative to decide which details are necessary and which are not.

"Neglected, ill-repaired architecture functions, in nineteenth-century Orientalist art, as a standard topos for commenting on the corruption of contemporary Islamic society." Has Nochlin ever been to the Orient? It is *her* Orient that seems to be imaginary. Even now, one of the most distressing sights, at least for me, as someone originally from India, is the physical decay of so many beautiful historical palaces and monuments in contemporary India. It was even worse in the nineteenth century, until a British viceroy, Lord Curzon, did something about it (see part 2, chap. 6). The situation was—and is—similar in North Africa, Syria, Egypt, and other Islamic lands. The Orientalists painted what they saw. It is true that ruins do attract the romantic mind, and have been popular at least since the ruins of ancient Rome were painted by Hubert Robert. But delight in ruins is an aesthetic attitude, not a political statement.

New York Times journalist Alan Cowell wrote in 1989 that Cairo "oozes decay."[16] As for Istanbul or Constantinople, Orhan Pamuk's entire book on the city is about decay, ruin, neglect, and poverty. He grieves for "a city that has been in decline for a hundred and fifty years"; he finds melancholic joy "in the crumbling fountains that haven't worked for centuries; the poor quarters with their forgotten mosques, . . . the dilapidated little neighbourhood shops packed with despondent unemployed men; the crumbling city walls like so many upended cobblestone streets."[17] It is ironic and amusing that Edward Said was himself accused of "Orientalism" in the pejorative sense when he complained of the decay in modern-day Cairo.[18]

And, it is well-attested that tiles in Turkish mosques often fell off simply because of the poor quality of the glue used.[19] To capture that dilapidation in paint is not part of the "project of imperialism." Is not Nochlin's claim that Orientalists always paint a timeless Orient, "a world without change," contradicted by her other claim that Orientalists were always painting decay? Decay is a sign of mutability, that things are no longer what they were. Nochlin wants to have it both ways.

Nochlin complains that there are too many lazy natives in Orientalist paintings, not enough people doing their jobs, not enough activity. But she cannot have looked carefully. There is a rich-toned work by Rudolf Ernst in the Dahesh Museum of two men in their workshop, beating copper objects into shape; Charles Wilda's *A Coppersmith, Cairo* (1884); E. Aubry Hunt's *The Farrier, Tangiers*; Edwin Lord Weeks and Eugène Girardet painted tailors at work; and there are any number of paintings of the bazaar bustling with activity, such as Germain-Fabius Brest's *View of Constantinople* of 1870, now in the museum in Nantes; Albert Pasini's *Bazaar at Constantinople*; Amadeo Preziosi's *Market Scene in Cairo*; Fausto Zonaro's *Barbers Working in a Square in Constantinople*. Then there are busy port scenes in numerous paintings such as Carlo Bossoli's *Oriental Port*. Dervishes are often portrayed, and they are hardly inactive. There are also paintings of hunting with falcons, guns, on horseback, and so on, as in the works of Eugène Fromentin. And what of the exhilarating sense of movement in Giulio Rosati's *Successful Raiding Expedition*?[20]

The absence of certain activities in a painter's oeuvre cannot possibly be taken to mean that he, the artist, thought the natives were "a lazy bunch of layabouts." In such a shallow interpretation, from the Dutch and Flemish genre paintings of the seventeenth century, one would get the impression that the Dutch spent their entire time in taverns, brothels, and merrymaking. There are few paintings of people engaged in any work or craft; exceptions include Gariel Metsu's *Interior of a Smithy* and Quirijn van Brekelenkam's *Interior of a Tailor's Shop*. Yet we know that seventeenth-century Netherlands was a hive of commercial activity, and was extraordinarily successful economically. As the art historian Wayne Franits notes, there are also few paintings of commercial activities in Dutch ports, but we know how busy the ports were.[21]

Nochlin contemptuously dismisses Delacroix, who, she claims, was said to have read Herodotus for descriptions of Oriental debauchery. There are no such descriptions in Herodotus. He gives a sober, not a prurient, account of the well-known institute of temple prostitution, and a sympathetic account of the manners and customs of Orientals.

Nochlin lets fly one baseless charge after another. One wonders if she has bothered to really look at, let alone enjoy, a work of Orientalist art. Here are her final thoughts on Orientalist art: "Works like Gérôme's, and that of other Orientalists of his ilk, are valuable and well worth investigating not because they share the esthetic values of great art on a slightly lower level, but because as visual imagery they anticipate and predict the qualities of incipient mass culture. As such, their strategies of concealment lend themselves admirably to the critical methodologies, the deconstructive techniques now employed by the best film historians, or by sociologists of advertising imagery or analysis of visual propaganda, rather than those of mainstream art history."[22] Evidently, for Nochlin and her ilk, Orientalist art, as John MacKenzie pointed out, "exists on an entirely different plane from that considered by 'mainstream art history.'"[23] In his brilliant demolition, so far from the fashionable nonsense of "deconstruction" offered by Said and his ilk, MacKenzie takes them to task for their imprecision, especially the cavalier way they talk about "imperialism." MacKenzie insists, "It will not do to pick and mix artists from different points in the nineteenth century and portray them as locked into a set of racial and imperialist assumptions. The durability of the oriental obsession, from the late eighteenth to the early twentieth centuries must raise doubts that its 'deconstruction' can be anything other than highly complex, producing different results at varying periods, as well as opposing dualities among artists and even within the single artist's work."[24]

Orientalist art must be seen as a continuation of those aesthetic impulses that began at the dawn of Western painting. Many Orientalist painters and sculptors were motivated by the same artistic desires as those of the Renaissance. Gentile Bellini, Carpaccio, and other Venetians, but also Rembrandt and the Flemish Pierre Coeck d'Alost, have been mentioned. Nochlin seems irritated by Gérôme's Arabic calligraphy, but in fact, a little "mainstream art history" would reveal that from the late thirteenth century onward, Western artists were fascinated by Oriental script and used it in many of their works. Many artists, not knowing Oriental languages or scripts, invented pseudoscripts for decorative purposes and used them on textiles, gilt halos, and frames for religious images:

artists such as Duccio, Giotto, Fra Angelico, Andrea Mantegna, Gentile da Fabriano, and so on.[25] The one exception was Pisanello, who copied almost exactly the Arabic script that says "al-Muayyad Abu Nasr Shaykh" in his *Studies of Costume Worn by the Emperor John VIII Palaeologus and Eastern Delegates at the Council of Eastern and Western Churches in Ferrara* (1438), a drawing now in the Louvre. Rosamond Mack points out that "Italians admired the aesthetic qualities of Islamic calligraphy" and used it in patterned textiles. Early Italian painters were confused about Arabic writing, but Mack writes, "the misapprehension was driven by Western veneration of Christianity's Eastern roots and the desire to possess and preserve that sacred heritage."[26]

Artistic concerns were paramount: "Artistic concerns also played an important role in the various adaptations of Arabic writing and the Islamic objects on which such writing appeared. Giotto and his contemporaries developed an immediately recognizable version of the Eastern honorific garment to make their representations more vivid and, in their view, more accurate. The imitation writing on halos and frames was ornamentally sophisticated, consistent with the Eastern garments, and perhaps also emphasized that these were images of a universal faith."[27] Aesthetic concerns, along with the ubiquitous Western desire for universalism, were the main impelling forces.

Gérôme and other Orientalists were more successful in rendering Arabic script; they also admired the aesthetic qualities of Arabic calligraphy. Referring to the Arabic inscriptions in Gérôme's *Snake Charmer*, Nochlin quotes Richard Ettinghausen, a great scholar and expert on Islamic art, as saying that they could "be easily read." Then Nochlin adds a contradictory footnote: "Edward Said has pointed out to me in conversation that most of the so-called writing on the back wall of the Snake Charmer is in fact unreadable." *Pace* Said, the large frieze at the top of the painting, running from right to left, is perfectly legible. It is the famous verse 256 from Surah II, *al-Baqara*, The Cow, written in *thuluth* script. It reads,

> *lā ' ikrāha fi-d-dīni qat-tabayyana–r-rušdu mina-l-ghayyi famay-yakfur biṭ-ṭāghūti wa yu'mim bi-l-lâhi faqadi-s-tamsaqa bil-' urwati-l-wuṯqā la-nfiṣāma lahā w-al-lāhu sami' un* [*'alīm*]. . .[28]

Unfortunately, the inscription thereafter is truncated, so that the upper part is lost, but even then one can make out parts of it, probably not a Koranic verse but rather a dedication to a caliph; the name *Uthman* is just visible, and possibly the word *sultan*. The Turkish artists and architects often added a dedication in mosques, and even on coats of arms, such inscriptions as "The ruler of the

Ottoman Empire, Sultan Abdülhamit who puts his trust in God." Or was Gérôme simply copying faithfully a real wall with those very verses? Since writing the above lines, I have learned from Professor Ackerman that Gérôme executed the painting in his Paris studio, copying a photo from the Topkapi Palace published by Abdullah Frères, the Istanbul photography firm. This discovery makes Nochlin's remarks even further off the mark.

Many copper vessels, plates, and weapons decorated with silver and gold and produced in Egypt, Turkey, or Morocco—both contemporary and those manufactured a hundred years ago—show what purport to be Arabic scripts or inscriptions, but in fact are gibberish, since the artisan producing such objects is often illiterate, certainly ignorant of classical Arabic and the complex rules of Arabic calligraphy.[29]

Let me summarize: Does the frieze represent actual writing? The answer is yes. Is the writing in any sense legible? Here again, the answer is yes. It is not easily legible, but neither are all the stylized inscriptions in, for instance, the Dome of the Rock. It is simply a feature of Islamic calligraphic art, and in this case Gérôme was not inventing the writing. But even if Gérôme had invented the inscriptions, what conclusion would follow? Only that Gérôme did not know Arabic. But neither does Nochlin. If Gérôme's ignorance of Arabic is an obstacle to painting about the Orient, why isn't Nochlin's ignorance of Arabic (or Turkish) an obstacle to writing about Orientalism in art?

There were at least four hundred Orientalist artists of stature, British, American, French, Italian, and German, producing thousands of works of quality and artistic merit.[30] It does not do to generalize about artists from so many varied backgrounds, each with his cultural, and above all, aesthetic perspectives, in the calumniating fashion that Nochlin does. It is Nochlin who sees the entire Orient defamed in one painting. It is her generalizations and tendentious readings that are offensive. It is she who is degrading the Orient by such claims, not the artists she misreads and exploits for tendentious ends. These artists often portrayed the essential dignity of that non-European Other, the Oriental.

EUGÈNE DELACROIX

As Victor Hugo wrote in the preface to *Les Orientales* (1829), "There is more interest in the East nowadays than there has ever been. Never before have Eastern studies made such progress. In the age of Louis XIV everyone was a Hellenist, now they are all Orientalists. Never have so many fine minds, at one and the same time, delved into the abyss that is Asia. . . . Everywhere the East has come to preoccupy the mind and imagination. . . . Everything there is large, rich, and fertile. The whole continent is leaning towards the East."[31]

One could argue that Orientalism was a reaction to the cold severities of neo-classicism and satisfied the romantic feeling for the picturesque and for local color. Many painters who have left us their written testimonies talk of color when describing their firsthand experiences of North Africa, the eastern Mediterranean, and the Levant. As Phillipe Julian says, Eugène Delacroix "found in Morocco the colour he sought and an inexhaustible source of inspiration."[32] Delacroix's first and only visit to Morocco in 1832 was a sort of awakening as to what the real, as opposed to the imaginary, Orient had to offer. He wrote to a friend, "The white draperies, the half-naked riders. . . . [A]ntiquity has nothing more beautiful."[33] And in his journal, he wrote, "Some of their ancient customs on solemn occasions have a dignity that is lacking in ours. For instance, the custom for the women to visit the graves every Friday with branches, which they buy in the marketplace. The betrothal ceremonies with music; the presents borne behind the parents, couscous, sacks of corn carried on donkeys and mules, an ox, materials on cushions, etc. . . . In many ways they are closer to nature than we—their clothes, for instance and the shape of their shoes. Hence there is beauty in everything they do. But we, with our corsets, narrow shoes and tabular clothing, are lamentable objects. We have gained science at the cost of grace."[34]

Delacroix finds beautiful the minaret of a mosque at Meknes, admires fine paneling on a window, is struck by the beauty of the landscapes. He cannot help but look with the eyes of a gifted observer—the eyes, above all, of a painter: "As we were coming home, superb landscapes on the right, the Spanish mountains in the softest possible tones; the sea, a dark blue-green, the colour of a fig. The hedges, yellow on top because of the bamboos, green at the bottom because of the aloes." Describing his first glimpse of the king of Morocco, Delacroix writes,

> Strong resemblance to Louis-Philippe but younger; thick beard, moderately dark complexion, *Burnous* [voluminous hooded cloak worn on desert journeys] of fine cloth, almost closed in front. The *haik* beneath it, worn over the upper part of the chest and almost entirely covering the thighs and legs. A string of white beads threaded on blue silk round the right arm, of which we could see very little. Silver stirrups. Yellow heelless slippers. Saddle and harness, gold and rose-coloured. Grey horse with a hogged mane. Parasol with unpainted wooden handle and a small gold ball on top; red outside, red and green divisions underneath. . . . The carriage which appeared after him was covered in green cloth and drawn by a mule caparisoned with red; the wheels were gilded. Men fanning it with white handkerchiefs as long as turban cloths.[35]

Elsewhere, Delacroix observed of Morocco that "[t]he picturesque abounds here, at each step there are twenty paintings that would assure the glory and fortune of twenty generations of painters."[36] Everything awakens his artistic curiosity; he is fascinated by the people and country; he enthuses about the light and landscape: "All of Goya palpitates around me." Tangiers is, for Delacroix, "a place made for painters . . . beauty abounds here, not the 'beauty' so praised in the fashionable canvases." In every street he encounters "the living sublime." He discovers living classical antiquity around him: "It is beautiful, like at the time of Homer. . . . The Romans and Greeks are there, at my gate." The Orient is a manifestation of a modern Classicism.[37] Delacroix's fascination for Morocco and Algiers is evident in the seven large notebooks of sketches and drawings, and in a large album of eighteen watercolors that he offered to Count de Mornay at the end of the voyage.[38]

On the way back he stopped at Algiers, and then back in Paris, Delacroix wrote, "Paris bores me to death; since my journey I have seen things and people in a different light," obviously recalling the natural physical intensity of Moroccan life as opposed to the artificial expressions of the romantic attitude in Parisian society.[39]

The result of his stay in Algiers was *Women of Algiers* (1834), which Julian calls "a masterpiece of genuinely experienced Orientalism,"[40] rather than the imagined one conjured up by his reading of Byron that led to such paintings as the *Death of Sardanapalus* of 1827. Delacroix had made watercolor sketches of women during his sojourn, and in the same notebook had recorded with great care the details of the clothes they wore: "Pearly blue-black crayon—blue silk (or white?)—green-white stripe—blue and rose (red?)—show."[41]

In *Jewish Wedding* (1837–41), Delacroix again recaptures all the immediacy of the watercolors done during his brief journey. No wonder that Théophile Gautier wrote, "Morocco belongs to Delacroix who discovered and conquered it: it is his own picturesque *pashaliq*."[42] With *Jewish Wedding*, *Jewish Musicians of Mogador* (1847), and *Arabs Playing Chess* (1847–48), Delacroix re-creates, or reinvigorates the genre paintings of Dutch and Flemish sixteenth- and seventeenth-century art. But where, for example, in Pieter Bruegel the Elder's *The Peasant Wedding Dance* (c. 1566), now in the Detroit Institute of Arts, the subjects appear flat and caricatured, Delacroix's figures are well-observed individuals, solid and dignified, nothing of the buffoonery present in the Flemish work. The subject of chess players has attracted many artists since at least Lucas van Leyden, Hans Muelich, Anthonis Mor, Cornelis de Man, Francois Boucher, Jean Hubert, and Delacroix's contemporary Honoré Daumier. It inspired several nineteenth-century Orientalists as well, such as

Gérôme, Alma-Tadema, Ludwig Deutsch, Ernst Rudolph, Frederick Arthur Bridgman, and Edwin Lord Weeks.[43] Assorted Nochlins and Saids insist that depictions of Orientals playing games show that the Orientalist painters are suggesting that Orientals are immature. This is grotesque. Ackerman sees Gérôme's *The Chess Players* as "the glorification of an honest recreation,"[44] and one that requires great concentration and mental power. And we know that Delacroix himself was a passionate chess player. Delacroix's 1845 portrait of Abd al-Rahman, Sultan of Morocco (now in the Musée des Augustins, Toulouse) was described by Charles Baudelaire as a "grande coquetterie musicale," and more precisely thus: "In spite of the splendour of its tones, this painting is so harmonious that it is grey-grey as in a summer's atmosphere, when the sun spreads out on each object an aura of trembling dust."[45] There is a grace, even grandeur, in the pose of the sultan astride his horse, possibly inspired by the etching of the Turkish emperor Selim III in Melling's *Voyage pittoresque*.

Alexandre Gabriel Decamps

With Alexandre Gabriel Decamps, the world of Dutch genre painting has truly been displaced to the Orient. And unsurprisingly, Decamps was much influenced by Rembrandt and Bartolomé Murillo, the latter a Spanish painter known for his sentimental pictures of urchins in city streets. Decamps made his way to Constantinople and eventually set up a studio in Smyrna (today's Izmir, Turkey) in 1828. Later, he was to travel further, in Italy, Greece, and Egypt. Decamps' personal contact with the Orient impelled him to produce a book of lithographs on his return to France in 1829, of such subjects such as Turkish children and the old merchant. He later painted *Turkish Bodyguard on the Road to Magnésie du Méandre* (1833), *Turkish Children Playing with a Turtle* (1836), *Turkish Children Near a Fountain* (1846), all in the Musée Condé, Chantilly. Other unpretentious paintings of daily life include the charming *Turkish Children Rushing Out from a School*, in the Louvre, the modeling of the figures recalling the *Peasants Drinking and Making Music in a Barn* (c. 1635) by Adriaen van Ostade. Children "represented with or without their parents, gradually developed into an enormously popular subject in Dutch Seventeenth-Century painting."[46]As Julian says, "Above all, the Orientalist picture is a genre painting."[47] Decamps had disciples in G.-Fabius Brest, and L.-Amable Crapelet.

13

PAINTERS AS WRITERS

The actual writings of the artists themselves—in the form of journals, travel notes, diaries, and letters home—reveal their fascination, admiration, respect, enthusiasm, reverence, and even love of the places and people of the Orient, which effectively refutes the obloquy heaped on them as "Orientalists."

Léon Belly

Léon Belly painted what many would consider the masterpiece of nineteenth-century Orientalism, *Pèlerins allant à la Mecque* (1861), now in the Musée d'Orsay, Paris. In a sensitive appreciation of the painting, Jane Munro wrote, "The initial idea for this painting came during Belly's second trip to Egypt in 1855–56. In a letter of 1 June 1856, he recorded his intention to paint a desert scene with Arabs and dromedaries, and to reproduce, like Courbet, 'the truly beautiful and interesting features of the everyday life of our fellow men.' "[1]

After a brilliant formal analysis of technique and composition, Munro continues: "En route to Syria in 1850, Belly had noted the emotional sobriety of mural painting in Padua and Milan, and the calm rationality of Greek religious architecture. It was this grandeur of effect that he recaptured in the present painting creating a sense of respect and admiration for what he considered to be a very humane religion. For Belly, the occasion represented more than mere ethnographical curiosity, as his comments on the advanced intelligence of the Egyptians reveal: 'In what way are we superior to this people who precede us by three thousand years?' In this he reflected the concern of painters in the latter half of the century to describe not only the picturesque qualities, but the full realities of Oriental life."[2]

Belly's letters to his mother, Madame Nicolas Belly, are worth quoting further. On October 27, 1855, Belly wrote,

> The closer one gets to the Nile, the more the landscape becomes marvellous: superb trees, the roots swimming in these immense lakes, are reflected perfectly in the calm waters while thousands of birds of all kinds swirl around, landing or flying in all directions; the sky of serene purity, of a blue, of such a tenderness! In a word, the gentlest of harmonies with the most sparkling of lights. There is a kind of music in this light. Among all the painters of landscapes, it is surely [Théodore] Rousseau who has succeeded the most in rendering the impression created by the physiognomy of this country. . . . The Nile seems immense, undoubtedly because all the islets of sand which were visible when I took my first voyage have disappeared in the rise in the water level. One took ourselves to be in the middle of a lake; the small elevation of the banks increases further this illusion, above all when we did not see either trees or villages.

In February 1856, Belly enthused about the minarets, the hills of Mokattam "in the luminous haze of the evening, the long caravans of the Bedouin heading towards the arid plain," and "a street in Cairo with its prodigious movements of figures and the magic of the sunlight and large reflected shadows."

A little later, he justified his prolonged sojourn in the Orient:

> Only duties to myself can keep me here. I wish to consecrate five months to learning to paint men in a way we do not at home, to studying beautiful well-proportioned bodies, real movements, and not what I could do in Paris by taking some models who are the most vulgar and devoid of all beauty. What I would learn here would be to reproduce admirably beautiful things which reveal themselves at every instant without effort, and in the everyday life of these peasants, these sailors, these Arabs of the desert. . . . Do not imagine, however, that I want to paint only scenes of this country—no, but I study here a beauty which a painting cannot ignore, which is the basis of all the works of the Italians and which is called grace, right proportion, appropriateness of movement, nature at its most natural.

Light, the dazzling light, "this cascade of light," but also the shadows cast by that light are the elements that he feels must be the basis of any painting. As for the people, "The Arabs seem truly sensitive to the beauties of nature, and their physiognomy becomes beautiful and intelligent when one speaks of it to them." On June 1, 1856, Belly explained the problems any sensitive artist must encounter, thereby reminding us that he was, above all, trying to solve problems of an aesthetic kind. Often the aesthetic impulse was the primary motivating force:

> This scene of women, drawing water from the waters of the Nile is extremely interesting to render, that will teach me to really draw. It is not enough to accept

> the first pose that comes along when it is graceful; one has to find its quintessence and study in agitated nature the simple and right movement, then choose between that which expresses the action in the simplest way and that which brings out the beauty the most—to study the same movement in the different natures of women, in the different effects of light! The relationship of the figures to the landscape is yet another study that needs to be done. . . . Every evening at four o'clock, we walk on the banks of the river at Gizeh to study the movements of the women drawing water: the air is fresh and delicious, and the landscape is, at this hour, of a marvellous beauty.

Belly reads Champollion and historians of ancient Egypt so that he is able to understand the monuments that he is going to encounter:

> I was amazed at the advanced and intelligent state of the Egyptians in comparison with other nations at that time; how their religion, despite this appearance of idolatry was only the external form of their worship, was humane; what subtle harmony between the civil laws which governed the nation and the divine laws instituted by the priests! It is difficult to believe in progress however, when one sees the nations in times past having reached almost the limits of wisdom and art disappearing suddenly almost without leaving a trace. In what way are we superior to this people who precede us by three thousand years? What have we invented which goes beyond the knowledge of the ancients? Undoubtedly the exact sciences have made great progress because they are based on a long series of successive works; but the arts, the principles of morals, the good and wise administration of a Nation, philosophy? The Egyptians knew at least as much as we, and do we know if in two thousand years traces of us will be as visible in history as theirs will be then?[3]

Alfred Dehodencq

Alfred Dehodencq was much taken in his childhood with *A Thousand and One Nights*, and by Bernardin de Saint-Pierre's 1787 novel, *Paul et Virginie*, set in Mauritius. He was greatly influenced by the romanticism of Chateaubriand and Lord Byron. In a letter written between 1845 and 1846, Dehodencq recounts how he used to fly away in his imagination to "the beautiful countries of the Orient, where the sky is always pure, trees always in flower conveying a soft serenity to the soul."[4] He sets off for Spain, which for so many Orientalists was but a foretaste or a stepping stone to the Orient of the Maghreb. Spain furnished similar scenes of genre that delighted the Orientalists in Egypt or Algeria—the gypsies, the Moorish architecture of al-Andalus, the intensity and brightness of the light, the festive atmosphere, and the life in the streets. Once there, he is not disappointed, but delighted, even overwhelmed by the charm and warmth of the people, by Diego Velázquez, by the constant to and fro of the crowds, by the sky, by the costumes.

Thus prepared psychologically, Dehodencq arrives in Tangiers in 1853 and writes of the admirable view that greets him: "In the foreground, white houses glistening in the sunlight, and outlined against the sea, a ravishing mosque, here and there clumps of fig-trees, in the background fading away on the right the coast of Africa, and to crown it all, the blue mountains of Spain and the Rock of Gibraltar. . . . I must make some serious studies of this people I hardly saw during my first and too rapid voyage."[5]

Even after his return to France, Dehodencq still has in his nostrils "this odor, this perfume for me of old hay, of butter and dust, which seizes you, which impregnates you the first time you set foot on Moroccan soil."[6] As his biographer, Gabriel Séailles, says, Dehodencq liked the Moroccans because he understood them; a fraternal sympathy helps him participate in their lives.[7] Séailles makes clear that Orientalism was not born out of a capricious impulse of the nomadic painter, looking for novelty at any cost. Orientalism was not an error, an unfortunate consequence of the conquest of Algeria. No, it has its own aesthetics, it has its raison d'être in human sensibility, which can find poetry in the simplest of human situations. For Chardin, the corner of a table sufficed. In Morocco, for Dehodencq there were plenty of occasions to find poetry in the peoples and their traditions, in the Arabs, Berbers, Jews,[8] and the Africans of the Sudan, in their costumes, in the light. He wanted to show them in their true milieu.

GUSTAVE GUILLAUMET

Gustave Guillaumet, sometimes called the Oriental Millet, was a realist painter who threw himself wholeheartedly into the life of an Algerian oasis, where he sojourned at least ten times. His paintings reveal the artist's keen attention to ordinary scenes of daily life. He felt that the character of the country was changing under the impact of the French, and was, at times, outraged: "In order to extend a street, they pulled down a mysterious passage vaulted like an arch of a cloister into which people taking a walk used to disappear and at the end of which we used to see them re-appear in a shaft of sunlight, like in a blaze of glory."[9]

Henri Regnault

Henri Regnault first discovered the Orient in Andalusia, and then in Morocco in 1869. He settled in Tangiers in a house that he decorated with Oriental motifs and that he described in this way: "Each time we go up on our rooftop terrace, we are dazzled by the brilliance of this town of snow, which descends to the sea, like a great staircase of white marble or a flock of white seagulls. On a neighbouring terrace, some black women spread out carpets to give them some air, or some Moorish women hang their haiks and laundry out to dry on lines, caftans of yellow cloth with silver brocades, rose or soft green coloured silk, scarves of gold, etc. Our eyes, in short, see the Orient."[10]

Eugène Fromentin

Eugène Fromentin was not only a great Orientalist painter but also a gifted novelist, art critic, and travel writer. Fromentin's encounter with Algeria is described by his biographers as "visual ecstasy," as he tries to come to terms with his profoundly moving experiences. He is struck by the beauty of the people, "[t]hose who, in the interests of local colour, try to illustrate the Bible by using Arab costume, are imbeciles who do not know how to put it to good use. I challenge anyone to show me someone of Antiquity better cloaked, better proportioned, more thoroughly beautiful than the Bedouin taken in any situation whatsoever, whether in the market, in the cafe, in the street. Unfortunately, it is very diffcult to draw them as they pass by since they do not wish to pose; their religious Code forbids it."[11]

Fromentin is equally impressed by "the Arab horseman in all his beauty, and ardour and the horse in all its swiftness, the very beautiful costumes, the sharp gunshots, the strange wailing of the women each time the cavalier reaches the end of the hippodrome." His second visit to Algeria resulted in a series of remarkable drawings of Arabs, where the full individuality and personality of each figure is scrupulously respected.[12] On leaving Algeria, he was very heavy-hearted in abandoning this "prodigious country."[13]

It is clear from Fromentin's later travel writings that his first two voyages to Algeria were of profound significance for his intellectual, spiritual, and of course, artistic development. He expresses his deep gratitude to the land and people of Algeria, in the moving accounts set down in *Un été dans le Sahara* (A Summer in the Sahara) and *Une anneé dans le Sahel* (A Year in the Sahel). His soul responds to every undulation of the landscape, to every turn in the road, to every nuance in the scene, to every color that strikes his eye. Fromentin is equally moved by the people, who he believes have much to teach Europeans. After describing the handsome face of his host, Fromentin describes the obligatory ceremonies and etiquette of the *diffa*, the meal of hospitality, and the dignity with which the host discharges his duty of devoting his entire attention to looking after his guest. In so doing, the host "was giving a great and beautiful lesson to those of us from the North."[14] In *Une anneé dans le Sahel*, Fromentin is happy to meet again those with whom he had formed sincere friendships. There is Si-Brahim el-Tounsi, an embroiderer by trade, who impresses Fromentin by "the serenity of someone at peace with all men and his own conscience." There is Sid-Abdallah, the shopkeeper, always "amiable, courteous . . . full of the goodnaturedness of a happy man." Fromentin is also struck by the "perfect dignity" of Sid-Abdallah's manner,[15] and is impressed by many Algerians: "Up to now, I have only provided you with a general portrait of the Algerians. I have talked about the gravity, discretion, and the natural dignity in their bearing, in their language, in their habits, wishing to indicate the overall features that strike you on your first arrival fresh off the boat from a European country where these very qualities are the most rare."[16]

The colors, always the colors, attract him, whether of the evenings just before and just after sunset—"the glowing twilight"—or of the costumes of the women during a festival, or gathering, displaying "the countless splendors of colour": "Women wrapped in red, of a vivid redness without nuance, without any softening or toning down, the pure red scarcely expressible by the [artist's] palette, further enflamed by the sun, all pushed to a passionate extreme by all kinds of irritations. This vast display of flamboyant fabrics was spread out on a carpet of Spring grass, of the most vivid green, and stood out against the sea of a blueness of the fiercest kind, for there was a little wind, and the sea was rippling. From a distance, what one noticed first was the verdant mound, crimsonly sprinkled with poppies."[17]

Fromentin's compassionate understanding and celebration of everyday life, and of ordinary people, translated into equally sympathetic paintings of Arab horsemen, Arab children, or portraits of dignified, even majestic sheikhs.

THÉODORE CHASSÉRIAU

Théodore Chassériau's great-grandmother and grandmother were native West Indians, born into Creole families of tradespeople or planters, a fact of family history that is often used to explain his fascination with the East. As Raymond Escholier wrote, "Chassériau did not have to discover the Orient. He carried it within him"[18]—that is, if we take the liberty of letting the West Indies stand for the East. However, more solidly we can assert that he had studied under Ingres, the painter of *Bather of Valpinçon* and *Grande Odalisque*; he admired Delacroix, who led the discovery of a classical and poetic Orient; and he was a friend of Prosper Marilhat, a great Orientalist landscape painter.[19]

On his arrival in Algeria, Chassériau fell in love with the "country . . . very beautiful and very new." During the next few months, his credo was, "I work and I look." As Vincent Pomarède says, "[T]he aesthetic discoveries of that Algerian trip—light, colors, and atmosphere—coincided with his artistic convictions at the time, which celebrated fidelity to the representation of nature. Did he not assert that 'nothing shines more than nature, nothing is more radiant'? He amassed souvenirs of the Orient likely to enrich his future compositions and applied to his search for motifs the precepts he set down in his private notebooks: 'Render what is in your soul in a visible, true, and refined manner, since nature alone possesses freshness and mordancy.' "[20]

In many of his preparatory drawings of cavalry charges, Chassériau is more interested in solving the compositional and formal problems that all artists have to face than in depicting visual reality. Pomarède analyzes in his work, "the sophisticated linear play of the bodies plunged in mortal combat and the optimal description of soldiers in action."[21] Chassériau was also able to draw upon a long Western artistic tradition of hunt and battle scenes, from Raphael and Rubens to such near contemporaries as Horace Vernet and Delacroix. And yet, Pomarède insists, "[I]t would be a mistake to think that he was indifferent to the political situation. Surely, he favored the architectural transformations of the city of Algiers in the wake of colonization, but he regretted [in a letter to his brother] that Constantine was 'the only truly Arabian city left in this country' and that 'this beautiful and unique land [is] so close to losing its originality and becoming thoroughly French.' "[22]

"He was," continues Pomarède, "in fact, fascinated by Algerian customs and civilization and deplored the fact that its colonization was being effected by the sword. In the *Arab Horsemen Removing Their Dead* [1852, Louvre], he proved that his preoccupations were both artistic and political, and that this painting was not merely a pretext for depicting an aesthetic and emotional theme. Unlike Eugène Delacroix, he saw in the streets of Algiers more than just latter-day descendants of Brutus and Cato, or a 'living Antiquity.' He was also interested in modern-day Algeria and, having seen human suffering, he wanted to record it in his paintings, not hesitating to elevate this suffering to the status of History."[23]

EDWIN LORD WEEKS

Edwin Lord Weeks was not only a superb Orientalist painter, but a great writer on art and travel, and his *From the Black Sea through Persia and India* must surely be one of the neglected masterpieces of travel writing, illustrated with 130 or so of his own drawings, yet to be republished in its entirety.[24]

Weeks's parents were merchants of tea and spices in Newton, Massachusetts, near Boston. They did not seem to mind their son's decision to pursue a career in art. Weeks first set off to the Key Islands in Florida, then Suriname in South America, the first of many voyages that confirmed him later as a painter of the Orient. For many years, Weeks traveled back and forth from America to Paris, the Near East, and North Africa, "specializing in picturesque figure subjects and desert landscapes."[25] It is uncertain if Weeks ever studied under Gérôme in his studio at the École des Beaux-Arts in Paris; it is more probable that he enrolled in Léon Bonnat's classes, where Weeks learned the dual principles of absolute realism and love of color. Bonnat was a Basque by birth and Spanish by training, having studied in Madrid under Federico Madrazo. Bonnat was influenced, in turn, by Mariano Fortuny, known for his "audacious colors and dashing brushwork."[26] Weeks seems to have felt both Bonnat's and Fortuny's influence.

Weeks undertook the first of his many journeys to the Orient in 1872, traveling to Egypt, Syria, Lebanon, and Palestine. In the spring of 1875 Weeks journeyed to Cairo and in the following autumn to Morocco, returning to Paris the next summer. In 1878 Weeks, based in Tangiers, decided to record Muslim culture "in parts of Morocco where few, if any, foreigners ventured, an audacity heightened by his determination to bring along his attractive wife. When Weeks journeyed in 1878 to Rabat and the neighbouring city of Salé on the coast of Morocco, he called it 'the most notable campaign in a hostile country that I have indulged in as yet,' and underscored its dangers by observing, 'we got out of it by the skin of our teeth.'"[27] Even as they landed in Rabat, they were surrounded by a menacing mob, obviously unused to seeing Westerners in their midst, and they had to be escorted by armed soldiers. Weeks wrote later, "Evidently they were not pleased to see us. Upon entering [Salé], which is the Mecca of the Moors, although we had a soldier to precede us, we were actually pursued by a mob, who finally gave us a shower of stones." Famine in the area allowed him to pay the local people to pose for him. Weeks wrote, "There are magnificent types here, grand looking old men. . . . Arab girls with faces like African madonnas and such lustrous eyes; strange types from far off provinces . . . such as Gérôme has never rendered."[28] He was equally fascinated by the hitherto unexplored and unpainted landscape with its Roman baths and Arab gateway, often in a state of ruin. Weeks journeyed once more to Morocco in 1880, when he visited Marrakesh for the first time.

Before Weeks's departure for India, his friend the art critic S. G. W. Benjamin appraised his achievements: "The art qualities in which Mr. Weeks excels are light and color. He has a passion for brilliant effects but renders them so skillfully that his pictures do not seem either crude or sensational. He has less feeling for form, but by careful, industrious effort and study, he is overcoming his feebleness in this respect. His style is broad and his method of laying on color massive. He is in such direct sympathy with the oriental subjects he loves, that one would not imagine on looking at his pictures, that they were painted by one who was born and brought up under the cold skies, and amid the rigid social customs of New England."[29]

It was not until 1882 that Weeks succeeded in reaching India, a place he had dreamed of for years. In fact, Weeks eventually made three extended voyages to India: 1882–83, 1886–87, and 1892–93, each lasting six to eight months. His literary masterpiece, *From the Black Sea through Persia and India*, as Ulrich Hiesinger points out, "purports to be a continuous narrative, [although] the section dealing with India actually summarizes his experiences over an entire decade of intermittent travels there."[30] It is precisely his love of, and direct sympathy with, Oriental subjects that makes Weeks's narrative such a delight. He is patient, observant, appreciative, and deeply moved by the places and people of India, all delicately rendered in accompanying drawings and pictures.

On his long journey across Turkey, Weeks observes the drivers and muleteers at Baiburt "mending their multicolored rags, and the great brass samovars" steaming over the fireplaces; "the picture has the rich and bituminous tone of a Teniers."[31] On leaving Kurdish territory, he finds that though previous Europeans were somewhat wary, even afraid of the Kurds, Weeks found them friendly and "not bad fellows."[32] He is struck by the beauty of Lake Urumiyah, "the delicate and ethereal beauty of its coloring, strangely impressive in its sun-steeped desolation."[33] In Tehran, Persia, Weeks paints a word picture of a scene that is pure "genre": "This street [Boulevard des Ambassadeurs] is an amusing combination of semi-European and Persian life; the little shops have plate-glass windows half-filled with meagre but varied assortment of under-clothing, kerosene-lamps and gas-fixtures, hardware, violins, and sheets of music; there is also a well-furnished barber's shop, with a fine assortment of cosmetics, kept by an Armenian hailing from Stamboul or Pera. There are many high-walled gardens, a hospital, guard-houses for the municipal police, and little Persian cafés or tea shops have placed inviting benches in front of their doors, usually filled by loungers with 'kalyans' or water-pipes."[34]

One of his characteristic drawings shows studies of six heads, each of which is a distinct individual. Outside Isfahan, Weeks describes "[t]he broad and stony but dry bed of the stream was carpeted for a great distance with the stamped cotton prints, fresh from the dyers' vats along the banks, which are now so familiar in our own markets. They are spread out to dry in the sun and to the highly colored landscape they add a foreground of vivid and startling color, of which rich Venetian red is the key-note."[35] In Shiraz, Weeks comes across this example of decay and crumbling tiles: "In the city there are many picturesque nooks and corners, and a few elaborately built and imposing bazaars. One cannot convey in words an idea of the beauty, both in color and 'motif,' of the crumbling panels of tiled mosaic which adorn the outer walls of the old 'Madrasseh' and of some of the mosques."[36]

On the ship to "Kurrachee" (Karachi), Weeks meets an educated Hindu who seems to come straight out of Kipling's *Kim*, which, incidentally, Weeks illustrated when it came out in 1901. Where Kipling satirizes, Weeks is gently amused and clearly admires:

> He has a round jovial face, is constantly laughing and displaying a fine set of teeth, and looks about twenty-five years of age. . . . This gentleman is a welcome addition to our circle, and without apparent effort gives a spurt of renewed life to the after-dinner talk. . . . [O]ur Hindoo friend ranges joyously from one topic to another, expressing himself in sonorous and correct English, rolling his R's, and prefixing each statement with "you see, sir," which contrasts finely with the Scotch and Irish accent of the others. I think we began with Edison's latest inventions and what is being done by rival electricians; but just now he is reading Darwin and Herbert Spencer, and from these points of departure, in an airy, optimistic, half-mocking vein, he flutters lightly on like a butterfly in a garden, through the realms of speculative science: from Emerson, Carlyle, Professor Fiske, by easy transitions, to Bellamy's socialistic millennium, Buddhism, Theosophy, Longfellow, and we are let down at last to the hard present with the Presidential election, Gladstone, Parnell, Home Rule, and the Chicago exhibition. Having touched upon Indian art and the Art idea in general, he became inspired with the beauty of the tropic night, the wake of fire streaming behind us, and 'larger constellations burning' overhead.[37]

Weeks, like many Orientalists, is impressed by Muslim devotion and the beautiful mosques.[38] Here is his description of Vazir Khan Mosque in Lahore, a place where he makes the effort to find out what the inscriptions say:

> The mosque is almost purely Persian, but for the two jutting windows on each side of the tall and deep recess above the entrance. The entire front of the

> gateway is a brilliant mosaic of the kind known as "kashi-work," and the four massive towers, as well as the façade of the inner court, repeat the same scheme of blue and yellow and faded green. Age has but mellowed the tone of the whole edifice, and the great Persian letters of the inscription over the main entrance are still resplendent in vivid turquoise blue. ["Remove thy heart from the gardens of the world, and know that this building is the true abode of man."] The frescoed walls within the niche, of which the ornamentation above is less deeply indented than in the Persian examples of similar work, have taken rich bituminous and smoky tone like an old painting; and the dado above the square platform on each side of the steps, which is of marble, once white, threaded with slender black lines forming interlaced stars and hexagons, has been toned by age and the contact of many garments to a golden brown.[39]

He is, however, not impressed by the mendicants who hang about its precincts. Nonetheless, he finds Islam as practiced in India "broadly democratic," and the stranger is welcome in its mosques, unlike elsewhere in the Islamic world.[40]

Indeed, anyone wanting a documentary background to Kipling's *Kim* would do well to read Weeks's wonderfully evocative and vivid descriptions of Lahore, where Kipling's novel begins. Weeks was writing in late 1892, the year that Kipling started *Kim*:

> The dark brick wall of the mosque, relieved by brilliant panels of unglazed tiles, and pierced by a window here and there, shadows for some distance the street, which expands beyond into a little square, littered in the afternoon with baskets of small hucksters, and the sunny wall of the house which rises across the way is a thing to study and to enjoy. Its oriel-windows are delightfully irregular in size and shape, and the intervening spaces, from the eaves down to the ragged little shop roofs and tattered awnings, once gaudily painted with intermingled combinations of arabesque designs, gods, and animals, have been toned to a mellow golden hue by the sun; dilapidated cane mats hang at some of the windows, and the shadow of a great tree flickers on the wall in the afternoon.
>
> A few steps farther on and the wealth of old woodwork becomes fairly prodigal; the side streets, as well as this main artery, give one the impression that each householder has vied to outdo his neighbour in throwing out these crowded ranks of beautiful windows, and in covering every inch of wall with decoration and with color. Where the windows do not project they are made interesting by complicated stucco mouldings, by panels of painted flowers, by courses of glazed red and blue bricks, and they usually open upon a long wooden balcony, high enough for one to sit and look down through the interstices of the wooden gratings. Even under the sides overhanging the street, the brackets are richly painted, and often mirrors are inserted in the centers of elaborate rosettes. Pea-

> cocks of tinted stucco perch on the white domes of the windows, and peacocks of painted wood, twisted into the shape of brackets, uphold the rows of great square "moussarabies." At one end of this marvellous street there is a perspective of golden domes, and at the other end tower the lofty minars of Vazir Khan. Beyond the group of gilded domes, and near the extreme end of the street there is a house front most lavishly decorated by the painters' brush.[41]

But as Weeks writes, "chapters might be devoted to description which, after all would convey to the reader's mind but an inadequate idea of this decayed splendor."[42]

It was not only Islam and mosques that impressed Weeks. He has equally long, rapturous, and eloquent descriptions of the Golden Temple of the Sikhs in Amritsar, a place that enchanted him.[43] "There is much which is impressive in the ritualism of the Sikhs," wrote Weeks.[44] Weeks's *The Golden Temple, Amritsar* (1890), now at Brown University, is his homage to Sikhism, and captures perfectly the atmosphere of stillness and serenity that one finds at any gurdwara.

Weeks's travels in Rajasthan are described with his artist's eye, proving his accomplishments as a literary Orientalist: Jaipur, Amber, Udaipur, Bikaner, and all their cultural splendor are paraded before us. The people he encounters move him greatly by their natural dignity, exquisite manners, and grace, reflective of an ancient civilization and tradition. "As I remember the resplendent personages," reminisces Weeks, "who came to make brief visits of ceremony or to pay their respects to some passing notability of official or diplomatic rank, the glittering bravery of attire and the elaborate trappings of their horses, the inimitable twist of their blue-black beards, and the deferential grace of their 'salaams,' carefully graded to correct degree, the melancholy truth is borne in upon me that the 'dude' of Western descent is after all, but a crude and unfinished production—in fact, he is 'not in it at all.' "[45]

For Weeks, as for James Fergusson, the British author of *History of Indian and Eastern Architecture*, "the high-caste Hindoo is almost incapable of bad taste."[47] Weeks proceeds to give examples of Hindu and Muslim good taste in a superb account of Indian art. Weeks made good use of Orientalist scholars like Fergusson and Louis Rousselet. The former "pioneered the use of photographs to record and transmit views of architectural monuments. In 1876 [Fergusson] published his classic study, *History of Indian and Eastern Architecture*, which served as the standard reference for Weeks in his study of Indian architecture and which he often quoted in his writings."[47] Weeks was to follow suit in using photography to document his travels and help his work.

Weeks was also influenced by Louis Rousselet, who spent four years traveling in India and published in 1875 a monumental travel book of "more than eight hundred pages containing over three hundred illustrations and maps, newly documenting abandoned temples, monumental palaces, and eminent personages throughout the land," under the title *L'Inde des Rajahs: Voyage dans l'Inde centrale et dans les présidences de Bombay et du Bengale*."[48] An English translation appeared a year later. Weeks mentions Rousselet in his travel writings.

Weeks's love of Indian art and architecture is evident in all his Indian paintings, where he pays so much attention to architectural detail, rendered with astonishing accuracy. His tribute to Hinduism is seen in *The Last Voyage—A Souvenir of the Ganges* (1885), now in a private collection. It tells the story of two fakirs; one is dying, and the other is striving to cross the Ganges so that his companion can die on the holy shore. In a letter, Weeks explained the scene: "Some bodies are floating in the water, being those of people too poor to pay the burning expenses. . . . The background is absolutely as I found it, and I saw the incident of the dying man being carried across, as they believe that if one dies on the other side, he is changed into some lower animal, and does not attain to full glory."[49] It is surely a poignant painting, capturing the special atmosphere of Banares by a skillful use of the effects of light on the sacred water, and on the emotionally charged Hindu temples on the shore; a touching scene sensitively handled.

14

JOHN FREDERICK LEWIS

John Frederick Lewis was born in London into an artistic family. His father, Frederick Christian Lewis, was a distinguished engraver who made his son start etching at an early age. J. F. Lewis copied the etchings of Adriaen van Ostade and other Dutch masters, but his heart was set on painting. He exhibited early and started working for Sir Thomas Lawrence, for whom he drew a great deal, sketching in animals and backgrounds to Sir Thomas's portrait pictures.[1] In 1824 Lewis turned his attention to sporting subjects, producing several works illustrating the hunting life at Windsor for George IV. Animal studies seemed to dominate his output during this period.

Between 1827 and 1832 Lewis traveled within Britain and to Belgium, Italy, and Switzerland. By 1829 Lewis seems to have devoted himself entirely to watercolors, becoming a member of the Old Water-Colour Society. In 1832 Lewis traveled to Spain, where he stayed for two years, producing work of the genre and earning himself the epithet "Spanish Lewis." He was briefly in Tangiers in 1833. While in Madrid, Lewis made watercolor copies of the Old Masters in the Prado, including Velázquez, but also such lesser artists as Murillo with his beggar boys. We know that Lewis had closely studied the Dutch and Flemish masters, not only from his own engravings, but also because there were seventy-five engravings after Cuyp, Rembrandt, Frans Snyders, Rubens, Frans Hals, and van Ostade in his possession at his death in 1876. Velázquez's *Las Meninas* (1656) had a lasting influence on him: "the figure silhouetted in a background doorway or arch appears over and over again in Lewis's eastern interiors and street scenes."[2] He was especially moved by the Alhambra, and produced a series of architectural drawings of great beauty. Indeed, Lewis's prolonged study of decorative Islamic details and the architectural forms of Muslim culture affected him for the rest of his life.[3]

From his sketches made during his sojourn, Lewis produced two volumes of lithographs, each containing twenty-five plates and a vignette on the title page: in 1835 *Lewis's Sketches and Drawings of the Alhambra*, and in 1836 *Lewis's Sketches of Spain and Spanish Character.*

Lewis spent one year in and around Istanbul (Constantinople) before sailing in 1841 for Egypt, where he was to remain for ten years. He lived in Cairo, but made many excursions to the Desert of Sinai, to Suez, and up the Nile to Nubia. On his way to Cairo, Lewis had made sketches in the Levant of soldiers, gypsies, Circassians, Levantine ladies, Turkish girls, even a dervish. He was taken with Islamic architecture and fascinated by mosques. At his death, Lewis left thirty-four studies of mosques around Constantinople. His nephew, Major-General Michael Lewis, noted that in all there is a sense of great space and dignity.[4] The draftsmanship is always powerful and precise; Lewis was moved by the manifestations of ordinary piety, and the atmosphere of calm was re-created at a later time in *Interior of a Mosque, Afternoon Prayer, 1857* (now in a private collection), reproduced in Ackerman.[5]

One painting of his last period is *The Hhareem* (1849), a watercolor now in the Victoria and Albert Museum. One early critic described it thus: "This was the first of the drawings of his last or 'oriental' period, in which he developed a new style of manipulation, very minute in touch, but extremely broad in effect, and with extreme elaboration of detail and a brilliant complexity of light and shade, retaining all his mastery of draughtsmanship and fine feeling for colour. The novelty of the first drawings in this style was emphasized by the new spirit in which his subjects were treated—the spirit, not of a traveller in search of the picturesque, but one who by a long sojourn in a strange country had become intimate with the character of the inhabitants and familiar with their mode of life."[6] It was indeed a long sojourn of ten years in Egypt, during which Lewis lived in harmony with his surroundings. Despite the inevitability of the subject of the "harem," Lewis treats it in his own way, and the result is restrained; three women languorously grace the foreground clad in gorgeous silks and brocades, all bathed in "patterned meshes of light striking through latticed-windows (one is of stained glass) onto walls and fabrics."[7] We are witnesses to a serene world that Lewis had learned to admire.

There are several harem pictures by Lewis: *Harem* (1876), in the Birmingham (UK) Art Gallery; *Hhareem Life*, *Constantinople* (1858), Laing Art Gallery, Newcastle (UK); and *Life in the Harem, Cairo*, (1858), in the Victoria and Albert Museum. In each there is that feeling of calm and soothing light with figures in a rich and elegant room; in the latter two pictures the room is uncluttered. The two earlier works also reveal a complex geometrical composition made up of rectangles, that of the mirror, the elaborately depicted tiles, and the frame in front of which we stand, all lending harmony and balance. In the Birmingham picture, we have the latticed windows that gently spread their light and patterns on fabrics, and the recession into the private depths through archways.[8]

There is also a seductive oil painting of *The Reception* (1873), now in the Paul Mellon Collection,[9] with the characteristic lattice windows and the play of light on various surfaces, impeccably rendered and finished. At the center of the room is a pool of water scintillating with reflections, the high ceiling creating a feeling of space and lightness, and the calm far from the madding crowd. We know that this was Lewis's room in his house in Cairo.

All four pictures mentioned above and all his other reception subjects display what Lawrence Gowing, talking of Vermeer, calls "the purity of the household light."[10]

Dutch influence on the Orientalist painters as a whole—and what Lawrence Gowing says about Dutch genre painting—is highly relevant for our study.

John Ruskin, the great English social critic, art critic, poet, artist, and reformer who believed passionately in the moral significance of great art, was an early admirer of Lewis's art, and later its passionate advocate. Lewis's work played an important part in the life of both Ruskin and his father. Ruskin wrote, "To this task, [Lewis] has brought not only intense perception of the kind of character, but powers of artistical composition like those of the great Venetians, displaying, at the same time, a refinement of drawing almost miraculous; and appreciable only, as the minutiae of nature itself are appreciable, by the help of the microscope. The value, therefore, of his works, as records of the aspect of the scenery and inhabitants of the south of Spain and of the East, in the earlier part of the nineteenth century, is quite above all estimate."[11] Ruskin was to shower lavish praise on Lewis's masterpiece *A Frank Encampment in the Desert of Mount Sinai, 1842—The Convent of St. Catherine in the Distance* (1856), a watercolor now in the Paul Mellon Collection.

The scene represents the meeting of two cultures, and the composition subtly mingles, compares, and contrasts them. The work was commissioned by Lord Castlereagh, who recorded his Near Eastern travels in his *Diary of a Journey to Damascus* (1847). Castlereagh set off from Cairo to Damascus across the Sinai desert in mid-May 1842, spending five days encamped at Mount Sinai. Castlereagh's entourage included Count von Pahlen, A. Schranz (his artist), Mr. Tardew (his physician), Sheikh Hussein (his guide), and Mahmoud (his dragoman).[12]

As Caroline Bugler summarizes, "It represents a meeting between East and West, with Shaykh Hussein, whose homeland was Mount Sinai, standing on the left with camels, and Castlereagh dressed in Eastern clothes, recumbent amidst the Western refinements of books, furniture, a newspaper, a map and a bottle of Harvey's sherry on the right. The dead game represents the outcome of a day's shooting, a popular pastime among Western tourists. In the background is the monastery of St. Catherine, whose monks frequently extended their hospitality to travellers; the Christian shrines of the Chapel of the Burning Bush and the Tomb of St. Catherine were housed in the monastery, which stood alongside a mosque."[13]

Lewis told William Makepeace Thackeray, as the novelist passed through Cairo, that "even this life at Cairo was too civilised for him: Englishmen passed through; old acquaintances would call; the great pleasure of pleasures was life in the desert-under the tents, with still more nothing to do than in Cairo; now smoking, now cantering on Arab [horses], and no crowd to jostle you; solemn contemplations of the stars at night, as the camels were picketed, and the fires and pipes were lighted."[14] Lewis was attracted to the life outside Cairo, to the desert, to the encampment so minutely re-created in his watercolor. The tall, dignified figure of Sheikh Hussein looks on, with perhaps a slightly disdainful expression, as Castlereagh, despite all the accoutrements and encumbrances of civilization, seems exhausted, and is totally dependent on the sheikh and his unencumbered, patient cameleers. The Convent of St. Catherine, where M. Tischendorf discovered the copy of the Bible known as the "Codex Sinaiticus," in an ecumenical gesture, also came to house a mosque near the Church of the Transfiguration. It stands exactly in the middle of the composition, though in the background, and aids perfectly the passage from the West to the East.

15

HEGEL AND THE MEANING, SIGNIFICANCE, AND INFLUENCE OF DUTCH GENRE PAINTING

Eugène Fromentin, an Orientalist painter—that is, a painter of North African, Middle Eastern, and Turkish scenes and people—in his celebrated work on the Old Masters of Belgium and Holland, characterizes the Dutch school in this manner:

> Dutch painting . . . was and could be only the portrait of Holland, its exterior image, faithful, exact, complete, and like, with no embellishment. Portraits of men and places, citizen habits, squares, streets, country places, the sea and sky—such was to be, reduced to its primitive elements, the programme followed by the Dutch School, and such it was from its first day to the day of its decline. In appearance nothing can be more simple than the discovery of this art of earthly aim; but until they tried to paint it, nothing had been imagined equally vast and more novel.
>
> The moment had come for thinking less, for aiming less high, for more closely examining, for observing better, and for painting as well, but differently. It was painting [of] the crowd, consisting of the citizen, the working-man, the upstart, and the first comer, entirely made for them and made of them. It was necessary to become humble for humble things, little for little things, subtle for

> subtleties; to welcome all without omission or disdain; to enter into their intimacy familiarly, and affectionately into their habits; it was a matter of sympathy, of attentive curiosity, and patience. Henceforth genius was to consist of lack of prejudice, of not knowing what one knows, of letting the model be a surprise, and only asking him how he wished to be represented.[1]

An analogous set of principles applies to Orientalist art: no disdain, but rather sympathy, patience, attentive curiosity, and the surprise of discovery.

Fromentin continues: "Add to these the towns and their exteriors, existence within doors and without, the fairs, intemperance and debauchery, good-breeding and elegance; the distresses of poverty, the horrors of winter, the disarray of taverns with tobacco, pots of beer, and laughing waiting-maids, trades and suspicious places on every floor—on one side the security of home, the benefits of labour, abundance in fertile fields, the charm of living out of doors, with business affairs, cavalcades, siestas, and hunts. Add to these public life, civic ceremonies, and civic banquets, and you will have the elements of a wholly new art with subjects as old as the world."[2]

Fromentin painted those Orientalist hunts and cavalcades, as did so many other painters attracted to the Orient, and John Frederick Lewis precisely captured the "security of home," the langourousness of siestas," and the bustle of markets and "fairs," subjects prefigured in Dutch seventeenth-century art.

The Dutch in the seventeenth century divided subject matter into various groups: *geselschapje*, or merry company scenes; a *buitenpartij*, or outdoor scene; a *bordeeltjen*, or brothel scene. Modern critics, in addition, talk of barrack room scenes (*kortegarden*), scenes from peasant life, domestic interiors, and so on.[3] An Amsterdam city surgeon and connoisseur, Jan Sysmus, in the 1670s used the terms *jonkertjes* and *juffertjes* (dandies and damsels), to describe the subjects painted by Vermeer and Ter Borch.[4] A precursor of the golden age of seventeenth-century Dutch painting is Pieter Bruegel the Elder, who painted peasant life, kermesses, and weddings.

Christopher Brown argues that the peasant scenes of Brueghel—and, by extension, those of the Fleming Adriaen Brouwer, the Dutchmen Adriaen van Ostade and Jan Steen, and their followers—can be read on three different levels: first, "ethnographically, that is, as an accurate description of country customs, which reflects a new interest in peasant life, in folk customs and in proverbs";[5] second, as moral sermons; and third, simply as comic scenes. At least the first of these traits is shared by many Orientalist artists. Many of the Orientalists, on their way to Egypt, the Holy Land, or the Maghreb, passed through either the European provinces of the Ottoman Empire, where they encountered, sketched, and painted Greeks, Albanians, Armenians, and other Levantines in their traditional costumes, or Spain, where they equally recorded their fiestas, customs, costumes, and dances, all of ethnographical interest.

In contrast to the life of peasants painted by van Ostade and others, there was another school of genre painting based at Leiden, known as the *fijnschilder* because of the meticulous finish of the pictures. These paintings dealt, especially after 1650, with what Lawrence Gowing calls "prosperous and leisurely domesticity."[6] The founder was Gerard (or Gerrit) Dou, who worked in Rembrandt's Leiden studio. John Evelyn saw Dou's *Young Mother*, and in his diary described it as "painted . . . so finely as hardly to be distinguish'd from enamail [enamel]."[7] Dou's style, with its meticulous finish, was imitated and developed by his pupils Frans van Mieris the Elder and Pieter van Slingelandt. In some of his paintings, Gabriel Metsu also turned to the *fijnschilders* for inspiration. All *fijnschilder* painters took a delight in, and were able to meticulously render, diverse textures and surfaces: silk or satin fabrics, Persian carpets, feathers, upholstery on chairs, softness of a girl's skin, marble floors, gilt moldings, wine glasses, and so on.

The fascination with texture and its realistic and impeccable rendition is also evident in the Orientalists, exemplified by Gérôme's paintings of carpets, ceramic tiles, and marble floors. Ludwig Deutsch is another painter who reflects the same interests. The work of J. F. Lewis shows both a coarse period of genre paintings set in Spain in the style of Jan Steen's peasant scenes with their robust humor, and a *fijnschilder* period of prosperous domestic interiors. Lewis, like the Dutch masters, was creating an ideal world—but created out of elements that he had experienced, a world he had inhabited for ten years. The world Lewis depicted was a personal vision that he brought back from the Orient, and the world he wished to evoke was one of elegance, stillness, and quiet. It was Lewis's homage to, and a token of gratitude for, a culture that he had immersed himself in and that had given him so much spiritual sustenance. Lewis's iconography can often be traced to the Dutch masters. Lewis had a love of perspective with a view through into a far room, as in his *Life in the Harem, Cairo*; *An Eastern Girl Carrying a Tray*; *Interior of a School*; *An Intercepted Correspondence, Cairo*; and *And the Prayer of Faith Shall Heal the Sick*. *The Harem*, which is prefigured in Nicolaes Maes's *A Sleeping Servant and Her Maid*, painted in 1655 and now at the National Gallery, London, "is the earliest known genre painting with a view through into a far room,"[8] and was thereafter a favorite motif in Dutch painting. Furthermore, the pose of the servant girl, sleeping on her left arm that is resting on her knee, recalls the pose of the tired or bored girl, scarcely listening as the Mullah reads from the Koran in Lewis's *And the Prayer of Faith Shall Heal the Sick*, now in the Paul Mellon Collection. This was, of course, a very conventional attitude used in many Dutch paintings. Indeed, Vermeer's *Christ in the House of Martha and Mary* (1664–65, now in Edinburgh), where Mary rests her head on her right hand as in Lewis's work, is, in many ways, closer to the Orientalist's work. Then there is Lewis's sumptuous *The Midday Meal, Cairo*, which owes something to the Dutch tradition of alfresco garden parties of David Vinckboons, Esias van de Velde, and Willem Buytewech: the elegance, the architectural setting, the attention to detail, the love of perspective.

Gowing speaks of the "warmth and liberality which the influence of Rembrandt spread through the genre school."[9] Elsewhere he notes the humane and descriptive tendencies of the Dutch genre school, a quality best expressed by Hegel in his *Lectures on Aesthetics*, where the transforming power of art is held up as its redeeming feature:

> In this way Dutch painting, for example, has recreated, in thousands and thousands of effects, the existent and fleeting appearance of nature as something generated afresh by man. Velvet, metallic lustre, light, horses, servants, old women, peasants blowing smoke from cutty pipes, the glitter of wine in a transparent glass, chaps in dirty jackets playing with old cards—these and hundreds of other things are brought before our eyes in these pictures, things that we scarcely bother about in our daily life, for even if we play cards, drink wine, and chat about this and that, we are still engrossed by quite different interests. But what at once claims our attention in matters of this kind, when art displays it to us, is precisely this pure shining and appearing of objects as something produced by the *spirit* which transforms in its inmost being the external and sensuous side of all this material.[10]

The human spirit is able to create out of the recalcitrant material provided by nature, by means of art, an "ideality," lying somewhere between purely objective indigent existence and purely inner ideas. Art "furnishes us," continues Hegel,

> with the things themselves, but out of the inner life of mind; it does not provide them for some use or other but confines interest to the abstraction of the ideal appearance for purely contemplative inspection. Now, consequently, through this ideality, art at the same time exalts these otherwise worthless objects which, despite their insignificant content, it fixes and makes ends in themselves; it directs our attention to what otherwise we would pass by without any notice. The same result art achieves in respect of time, and here too is ideal. What in nature slips past, art ties down to permanence: a quickly vanishing smile, sudden roguish expression in the mouth, a glance, a fleeting ray of light, as well as spiritual traits in human life, incidents and events that come and go, are there

and are then forgotten—anything and everything art wrests from momentary existence, and in this respect too conquers nature.[11]

Art fixes the transitory and holds up for our contemplation all that is permanent even in the most banal of objects, inherent in the most ordinary of human activities, as described with such fidelity by the Dutch masters. It exalts the familiar, makes us look anew at what we had taken for granted. The humaneness of Dutch genre painting exists in the way the Dutch turn to "joy in the world as such, to natural objects and their detailed appearance, to domestic life in its decency, cheerfulness, and quiet seclusion, as well as to national celebrations, festivals, and processions, to country dances and the jollities and boisterousness of wakes-week."[12] Art is an end itself, not for some other end or use; if we can talk of an end, that end is only contemplation. The Orientalists essentially approach their novel subject matter in the same humane manner, drawing upon a rich tradition in Western art, literature, and philosophy; depicting the everyday realities of unfamiliar climes, landscapes, and cities in a vivid, enthusiastic spirit that enables us to look at the humdrum in a fresh way and that helps extend our sympathies.

16

CHARLES CORDIER

ORIENTALIST SCULPTOR

Charles Cordier studied drawing at a young age and then modeling at sculptor Louis-Victor Bougron's studio in Lille. In 1844 Cordier arrived in Paris, where his career as a sculptor truly took shape. He eventually ended up, in 1846, in the studio of the sculptor François Rude, and it was in that studio that Cordier encountered a freed black slave, Seid Enkess, who worked professionally as a model. This was a meeting that proved decisive for Cordier's aesthetic direction—and life. Cordier made a portrait of Enkess that was exhibited at the Salon in 1848, and his work as an ethnographic sculptor began in earnest. Significantly, 1848 was the year that slavery was completely abolished in all French colonies and possessions, and the principle that a slave is liberated when he sets foot on French soil was to be applied to the colonies and possessions of the republic. In his *Memoirs*, Cordier noted the importance of the date for him: "My art incorporated the reality of a whole new subject, the revolt against slavery and the birth of anthropology."[1]

Working for the anthropological section of the National Museum of Natural History, Cordier set off for Egypt in 1865 to study human diversity before it all disappeared into a uniform grey mass. He spelled out his intentions in sailing up the Nile: "to choose Copts, or Abyssinians with their true beauty—now that is what has not yet been done; artists have produced mere suggestions. I wish to present the race just as it is, in its own beauty, absolutely true to life, with its passions, its fatalism, in its quiet pride and conceit, in its fallen grandeur, but the principles of which have remained since antiquity."[2]

"Because," Cordier insisted, "beauty is not province of a privileged race, I give to the world of art the idea of the universality of beauty. Every race has its beauty, which differs from that of other races. The most beautiful Negro is not the one who looks most like us, nor the one who presents the most pronounced characteristics associated with his race. It is the individual in whom are united such forms and traits, and a face that reflects with harmony and balance the essential moral and intellectual character of the Ethiopian race."[3]

When visiting Algiers, Cordier preferred to live among the Algerians: "I lived in a native quarter, in the Casbah; I got on well with everyone, and as my door was always open, pretty soon I entertained quite a crowd of visitors." Ms. de Margerie shows Cordier's total lack of racism, as "it was an Arab of El-Aghouat whom he chose to represent the white race when he sculpted the heads symbolizing 'the three principal types of human beings,' works that he offered to the Society of Anthropology." Cordier's neutral, scientific, and ethnographical approach is evident in the fact that he "included French regional types in his ethnographic gallery, exhibited in 1860."[4]

Despite his scientific focus, Cordier never reduced his models to types; they were always tokens, specific portraits of individuals, such as his *Said Abdullah*, exhibited at the Salon of 1848.[5] His success in sculpting non-Europeans led one critic to comment that Cordier was moved "less by the charms of the Greek Venus than by those of the African Venus."[6] Ten years after his mission to Algeria, Cordier recounted his fascination with the Orient: "Irresistibly attracted, I set out for this new sphere with all the curiosity with which one would open, for the first time, A Thousand and One Nights. . . . The objective of my thought was a prism through which I could produce works that were entirely new. Also, when I sailed for the first time along the coast of Africa, at Algiers, sparkling white Algiers . . . such joy! Immediately upon landing I rented a small house in an indigenous quarter. The marble courtyard was upheld in four corners by columns that supported four arcades."[7] Cordier himself had three Moorish houses built, two in Paris and one in Nice. He died in Algiers at the age of seventy-eight in 1905.

Cordier devoted much of his energy to representing human diversity: Abyssinian, Egyptian, French, Greek, Indian, Italian, Maltese, Nubian, Sudanese, and Turkish people. The expressiveness, dignity, and even majesty of the three polychrome portraits of Africans, in bronze and onyx-marble, make them "three of the most popular sculptures at the Musée d'Orsay." With another sculpture, dated 1867, in white, black, and antique yellow marble, whose present whereabouts is unknown, Cordier represented two children embracing each other; one is black and the other white. Cordier gave it the title *Aimez-vous les uns les autres*—Love one another. As the organizers of the splendid exhibition in 2004–2005 of the works of Charles Cordier say in their foreword, "Through his art, Cordier forever engenders respect for the Other."[8] That should hardly be the criterion of artistic value, but at least it is a defense of Cordier, if such were needed, against the malevolence of the Saidists.

17

RELIGION, PIETY, AND PORTRAITS

There sleeps as true an Osmanlie
As e'er at Mecca bent the knee;
As ever scorn'd forbidden wine,
Or prayed with face towards the shrine,
In orisons resumed anew
At solemn sound of "Alla Hu!"

—Lord Byron, *The Giaour*

"Alla Hu!" the concluding words of the Muezzin's call to prayer from the highest gallery on the exterior of the minaret. On a still evening, when the Muezzin has a fine voice, which is frequently the case, the effect is solemn and beautiful beyond all the bells in Christendom.

—Lord Byron, Notes to *The Giaour*

Orientalists painted not only many different communities living in the Near East, North Africa, and India—Jews, Christians, Muslims, Hindus, and Sikhs—but also depicted with delicacy and respect these same communities in prayer, in churches, in front of the Wailing Wall in Jerusalem, in front of temples, gurdwaras, and, of course, in mosques.[1] There is nothing sinister in Gérôme painting the interiors of mosques—it is surely perverse and shows the lasting damage of Edward Said's work and influence, for anti-Orientalists to extract something negative out of these paintings that show nothing but respect for the unostentatious piety of Muslims. The Orientalists were observant and noticed the way that all Muslim men were equal in prayer, and accordingly depicted worshippers of different social classes praying together, side by side. Given the essential sympathy that many of the Orientalists evidently felt for the Orient and its peoples, why would the same Orientalists suddenly display hostility toward them when depicting them in their moments of devotion? The painter Frédéric Goupil-Fesquet traveled with his uncle, the Orientalist Horace Vernet, to Egypt in 1839 and 1840, and left us a vivid account of their experience. When he encountered Muslims praying, Goupil-Fesquet wrote, "A holy respect comes over the spectator in the presence of this silent gathering. The expression of humility and veneration imprinted on every face, which no distraction can alter, gives their features a stately grandeur that seems to harmonise with the building itself. Prayer makes all men equal: the half-naked fellah next to the rich man in his silk quftan and gold-embroidered turban, his ornate weapons removed for the moment, both believing in the same God, both come to worship with the same fervour."[2]

Ackerman and MacKenzie have put up a spirited defense of the maligned Orientalists. The latter, referring in particular to Ludwig Deutsch's *At Prayer*, which graces the cover of the new edition of his pioneering book, *Orientalism: History, Theory and the Arts*, and challenging the generalizations of Said and his followers, wrote, "Mosques, prayer and devotions were a common subject for Orientalist painters. It is hard to see such paintings as denigrating their originals, however idealised the images may be. On the contrary, the figure [in *At Prayer*] has a handsome and pious dignity, in which the centrality of religion amidst the fine detail of oriental design is intended to convey a sense of a reverential world the West has lost."[3] In the meantime Ackerman, author of a monograph on Gérôme, argued that "the pious Muslims who say their daily prayers in their mosques, or on their rugs in the desert or even on shipboard in the paintings of our Orientalists are presented with dignity and with obvious admiration for their unabashed public piety."[4] I have looked through currently available books on Orientalism and have gone through all their reproductions of Muslims, Jews, Hindus, Sikhs, and Christians; I cannot find any that denigrate any religion or worshipper depicted. (See chap. 8, n7.)

I have pointed out how Dutch artists such as Romeyn de Hooghe and Emanuel de Witte depicted Jews and synagogues with respect and reverence. The Orientalists of the late nineteenth century were drawing upon a humane tradition established 250 years earlier.

MacKenzie finds Rana Kabbani's and Linda Nochlin's claims that Orientals or blacks are always portrayed as ugly or loathsome in Orientalist paintings "grotesque." To my examples of the essential dignity, handsomeness, or even majesty of the figures painted by Orientalists, here are still others offered by MacKenzie: "There is a handsome, muscular splendour about *The Nubian Guard* of Ludwig Deutsch [1855–1935], a haughty pride to the *North African Man in Travelling Costume* by William Collins [1862–1951], a gorgeous elegance with finely rendered skin and features to Gérôme's *Black Bash-Bazouk*, and an idealised winsome beauty to *A Nubian Girl Standing beside the First Cataract of the Nile* by Prisse d'Avennes [1807–79]."[5] As for Jews, Martin Kramer rightly points out that "[t]he romantic representations of Jews in the work of the Orientalist painters were almost wholly sympathetic and admiring." Kramer finds nothing offensive toward Jews in the works of Delacroix, Dehondencq, or Chassériau, for example.[6] Perhaps I could add a few random examples from easily available books: the regal bearing of *The Dignitary* of Rudolf Ernst, the bravado and authority of the *Black Palace Guard* of Georges Clairin, the good-humored charm of *Heart's Springtime* by Étienne Dinet, and the dandyish pride of *Amer, the Bedouin* by Carl Haag.[7]

18

ORIENTAL AND AFRICAN AMERICAN ORIENTALISTS

The existence of Muslim and African American Orientalists helps to refute any crude belief that Orientalism was a way for the West to control and denigrate the East, or still more absurdly part of an ideological struggle between the whites and blacks.

Osman Hamdi Bey, the man responsible for the founding of the School of Fine Arts in Istanbul in 1883, was an archaeologist, diplomat, and a distinguished Orientalist painter who learned his trade in Paris in the studios of Gustave Boulanger and Paul Baudry. A great portraitist, Bey greatly influenced the course of Turkish painting by such works of realism as *Woman with Mimosas* (1906) and *Profile of a Young Woman* (1886). He also painted the traditional Orientalist subjects: *The Gate of the Mosque* and *Turkish Women at the Entrance of the Ahmed-Djami Mosque*.

Other Turkish artists who first studied in France include Cheker Ahmet Pacha, who worked in Gérôme's studio, and Abdulmecit, son of Sultan Abdulaziz, who captured the splendor of the court in its dying days.

In his memoir, *De Pontoise à Stamboul*, Edmond About recounts this encounter: "Our guide is an aide-de-camp of the Sultan, a junior officer called Ahmed who finished his studies in Paris not in the Military Academy as one would expect but in the atelier of Gérôme. He was a painter, good enough in fact so as to prompt Courbet to ask him for one of his landscapes and the jury of the Salon awarded him 'an honourable mention.' "[1]

There is one Orientalist American painter who deserves special mention. Henry Ossawa Tanner, son of an African American bishop of the African Methodist Church, was born in Pittsburgh, Pennsylvania. Determined to pursue a career as a painter from an early age, Tanner first studied under Henry Price in Atlantic City, and then, between 1879 and 1885, under Thomas Eakins at the Pennsylvania Academy of Fine Arts. Eakins, now recognized as one of the greatest American painters, learned his style of teaching at the École des Beaux-Arts in Paris. Eakins's encouragement, teaching, and art had a great influence on Tanner.

After a first exhibition of his works in Cincinnati, Ohio, Tanner was subsidized so that he might travel to Europe. He never got farther than Paris, where he enrolled at the Académie Julien, whose faculty members at the time included the Orientalist painter Jean-Joseph Benjamin-Constant and Jean-Paul Laurens. Benjamin-Constant recognized Tanner's gifts and encouraged him, eventually giving Tanner his photograph and inscribing it, "To my pupil Tanner, his master and friend, always confident of his final success."[2]

Tanner's early works include such genre paintings as *Banjo Lesson* and *The Young Sabotmaker*. Tanner had always admired Rembrandt and the Dutch masters for being "down to—and close to—earth. . . . One must recognize," Tanner told a visitor, "that the Dutch had a sense of order, structure, and organisation in which they believed their art should operate, but they brought to this also the important elements of humanity and feeling."[3]

Banjo Lesson was accepted by the Paris Salon of 1894, winning high praise from Benjamin-Constant. Tanner submitted *Daniel in the Lions' Den* to the Salon of 1896. At the suggestion of a celebrated French master, the painting was moved from its original place to one where the jurors could better appreciate its qualities; the painting won an honorable mention.[4] His *Raising of Lazarus* was presented to the Salon of 1897, where it won a medal, and the French government offered to buy it for its museum in Luxembourg.

In early 1897 Tanner traveled in Egypt and the Holy Land, visiting Jerusalem, the river Jordan, the Dead Sea, and Jericho. He was to revisit Jerusalem the following year, along with North Africa. Tanner's profound respect for religious emotions is expressed in his *Jews at the Jerusalem Wailing Wall*, probably painted soon after his first visit to the Holy Land. After his return, Tanner worked on many religious pictures, such as *The Flight into Egypt*, *The Good Shepherd*, and *Christ and His Disciples on the Road to Bethany*.

A visit to North Africa in 1910 led Tanner to use more brilliant color, in the manner of Delacroix. He traveled to the city of Tetuan in Morocco, outside the usual tourist circuit. This visit gave him a chance to execute some oil sketches of local scenes, many of which he used in his later religious paintings.[5] In North Africa between 1908 and 1912, Tanner produced such paintings as *Entrance to the Casbah*, showing his richer use of color under the influence of the bright colors found in Morocco.

Tanner's work was gradually forgotten until its revival in the 1960s. Tanner's teacher and the great influence on his life, the painter Thomas Eakins, had studied under Jean-Léon Gérôme. The painter who did more than anyone else to bring Tanner to the attention of the jury at the Paris Salon was Jean-Léon Gérôme. Many roads lead back to Gérôme.

19

ORIENTALISM AND MUSIC

MOZART

Western art has, in the words of Roger Scruton, "continuously ventured into spiritual territory that has no place on the Christian map,"[1] and has done so with generosity, tolerance, affection, and a noble vision of universal humanity. Literature and music, as much as painting and architecture, has acknowledged other civilizations and other peoples, embraced them as equals, and sometimes treated them as superior souls from whom the West could learn. In her biography of Mozart as a dramatist, Brigid Brophy includes a dazzling chapter on the exotic in eighteenth-century art, reminding us of Western humankind's ventures "to unpath'd waters, undreamed shores": China, Turkey, Persia, Babylon, Egypt, Abyssinia, South America, India, and even outer space.[2]

Brophy sings the virtues of Mozart's *Die Entführung aus dem Serail* (*Il Seraglio*) and *Die Zauberflöte*, and places them firmly within the Enlightenment's cosmopolitanism and its educative program: "To admire and copy foreign countries inside Europe was scarcely less obligatory than to admire, collect and copy the exotic products of other continents."[3] In *Il Seraglio*, when Pasha Selim is introduced, he is the "raw material of nobility, aristocratic and imposing, but uninstructed," but "is allowed to develop a good deal more character than a mere exotic touch." By the end, the pasha becomes a new man, who "shews himself a nobler pagan than Belmonte's father has been a Christian—for, by one of those dénouements of identity which are set off like catherine wheels by rococo plot-making, Belmonte has turned out to be the son of an ancient enemy who used the Pasha ill. The moral purpose of the exotic vein is pointed when the ostensibly barbarian Pasha stigmatises Belmonte's father as 'dieser Barbar.'"[4]

Brophy continues:

> This bloody and unjust man is, of course, a Christian of the deepest Catholic dye—a Spanish grandee [As his son, Belmonte, admits, being prepared to die without complaint in recompense of *'das Unrecht'* done by his father to the Pasha (Act III, dialogue before No. 21).] Frederick the Great's opera [*Montezuma*] had indicted the atrocities of the Spaniards against the Mexicans in order to shew that it was Christianity which was the "barbarie." [In Bernardin de Saint-Pierre's *Paul et Virginie*, Paul uses the same verbal paradox when, in the primitive bliss of Mauritius, he speaks of Europe as 'ce pays barbare.'] *Il Seraglio* exposes a Spaniard's vindictive treatment of a Turk, and shews that it is the Turk who is capable of learning the lesson of non-vengeance. The Pasha does not take the opportunity to avenge himself on the father through the son—because he disdains to follow the Christian barbarian's example. "I hold your father in too much detestation," he tells Belmonte, "to be able to tread in his footsteps." Pedrillo's narrative ballad has evoked the Crusades to the advantage not of Christian chivalry but of Selim's historical precursor in nobility, Saladin.

Thus the pasha frees Belmonte, for revenge would only damage the revenger's moral nature, and Constanze, because neither force nor kindness on his part can alter the fact that she does not love him. The pasha "reforms his government, to the extent of giving a brisk warning to his corrupt officer, Osmin."[5]

Die Zauberflöte has the same emotional subject matter as *Il Seraglio*, namely, the testing of love against the fear of death. But the former also has familiar themes of the Enlightenment: the triumph of light over dark, but seen through Freemasonry's allegorical symbolism. As Brophy reminds us, "Mozart, at least when he was young, grieving and writing to his worried and conservative father, disliked Voltaire, but six years after Voltaire's death, joined the Freemasons—who adulated Voltaire, practised the Enlightenment's morality (including toleration) and were, for that reason, condemned (twice, during the eighteenth century) by papal bull. Catholicism declined to return Masonry's compliment of toleration because Masonry, as a 'universal' system of morality, seemed to imply that the church was not necessary to morals and because Masonry insisted (from 1723 onwards) on extending the tolerance it offered its Christian members equally to Jews and Deists."[6]

Brophy argues that "Masonry's central allegory, the triumph of light over dark, is shared with the very metaphor of the Enlightenment, with everyday speech (which says 'I see' in the sense of 'I understand') and with the cult of Osiris (the sun) and Isis (the moon, which can illuminate even the night). In pursuit of the allegory, a first-degree initiant into Masonry is blindfolded and presented as 'a poor Candidate in a state of darkness'. . . . The candidates in the opera undergo the Masonic darkness by being at various times, veiled, subjected to ordeal-by-darkness and aware of spiritual darkness (Tamino's 'everlasting night'); their spiritual enlightenment at the initiation coincides with Sarastro's victory, in which 'the sun's rays expel night.'"[7]

Sarastro is clearly an allusion to Zoroaster, and Brophy wonders if the librettists—Mozart himself may have had a hand in writing the libretto—acquired their knowledge of Zoroaster from Lucian, the Voltaire of the ancient world, who took the Cynic Menippos as a hero of his romance: "Menippos says that when he had made up his mind to visit the Underworld he decided 'to go to Babylon and ask a favour of one of the Magi, the disciples and successors of Zoroaster (τινος των μαγων των Ζωροαστρου μαθητων και διαδοχων).'"[8] One modern biographer of Mozart, Maynard Solomon, thinks that "Mozart's attraction to a Zoroastrian orientalism is in the tradition of the Masonic lodges and reading societies, which were hotbeds of interest in the exotic, the oriental, and the miraculous."[9] Solomon is also convinced that Mozart's attachment to Freemasonry was deep:

> There was a powerful appeal in Freemasonry's idealism, its undogmatic approach to religion, its teachings on self-development and spiritual uplift. It surely exercised a powerful ideological pull upon Mozart that stemmed from its humanitarian and enlightened aspirations, its ideals of equality, liberty, tolerance, and fraternity, and its vision of salvation through love and reason. . . . Freemasonry . . . touched his religious yearnings through its fusion of contemporary enlightened teachings with ancient traditions, and through its polytheistic eclecticism, which combined Christian, classical, and exotic religions into a heady blend—witness the opening lines of Mozart's cantata, K.619, with its undogmatic acceptance of every deity:
>
> You who revere the
> Creator of the boundless universe,
> call him Jehova or God,
> call him Fu, or Brahma.
> Hark! Hark to the words
> of the Almighty's trumpet call!
> Ringing out through earth, moon, sun,
> its sound is everlasting.[10]

Freemasonry clearly answered to many of Mozart's longings: attraction to mystery and illumination, search for knowledge and quest for beauty, fantasy and brotherhood. The Masons believed in the possibility of social transformation "and the return of humanity from a state of innocence and grace." As Solomon concludes his chapter on Mozart's deep commitment to Freemasonry: "A young composer's fascination with *The Arabian Nights*, with Fénelon's rationalist utopian novel, *Les Aventures de Télémaque*, and with every variety of literary and musical orientalism converge in the Masonic Temple, creating in its consecrated premises a miniature simulacrum of a fantastic illuminated city, casting an anticipatory beam of light from a desired future into a shadowed present. We are left without certainty, but perhaps with some room for mystery and the miraculous."[11]

The Arabian Nights, Brahma, Zoroaster, Turkish Pasha: Where did Mozart imbibe his Orientalism? The first European version of *The Arabian Nights* was a translation into French begun in 1704 by French Orientalist Antoine Galland; in 1771 Anquetil-Duperron published his *Zend Avesta* (3 vols.), containing collections from the sacred writings of the Zoroastrians, a life of Zoroaster, and fragments of works ascribed to Zoroaster. Barthélemy d'Herbelot's *Bibliothèque Orientale, ou Dictionnaire universal . . . des Peuples de l'Orient* (1697), completed after d'Herbelot's death in 1695, contained an entry on *Brahma*. As for Turkey, any number of travelers reported back on their impressions of the Ottomans, such as Johann (Hans) Schiltberger; Ogier Ghiselin de Busbecq, who was Ferdinand I of Austria's ambassador to the Ottoman Empire under the rule of Suleiman the Magnificent; and Lady Mary Wortley Montagu; while the theme of the generous and compassionate Turk, as we shall see in discussing Christoph Willibald Gluck, was quite common in theater, opera, and ballet in mid-eighteenth-century Vienna and Paris. It is far more likely that Mozart made his acquaintance of Zoroaster through the influence of Anquetil-Duperron's translations than through reading Lucian. For we know that as soon as the French version of the *Avesta* appeared, Johann Friedrich Kleuker, professor of theology in the University of Riga, published a German translation of it in Leipzig and Riga between 1776 and 1777, and also, importantly, of Anquetil-Duperron's historical dissertations. Anquetil-Duperron had tried to show, in a memoir on Plutarch, that the data of the *Avesta* fully agree with the account of the Magian religion given in the treatise "Isis and Osiris." Kleuker enlarged the circle of comparison to the whole of ancient literature.[12] Given the importance of the figure of Isis and Osiris in the symbolism of Freemasonry and, as Brophy argues, for Mozart's *Die Zauberflöte*, it seems possible that Anquetil-Duperron and Kleuker remain the major source for both Freemasonry and Mozart's knowledge of Zoroaster. Lucian would surely have been too cynical for Mozart, who would have been offended by Lucian's antireligious satire in the same way that Mozart disliked Voltaire.

The Orientalists and their indefatigable intellectual curiosity, scholarship, and translations had incalculable consequences for the development of art, philosophy, and politics in Europe, an influence passionately chronicled by Raymond Schwab in *The Oriental Renaissance*. Orientalists changed forever the intellectual and spiritual landscape of Europe, and allowed artists, writers, and composers to enter imaginatively and sympathetically into civilizations hitherto unfamiliar to Westerners, to accord the Orient dignity and respect, and to people European works with Orientals, seen as equals. It was in this intellectual and spiritual milieu that Mozart created some of his most sublime music. Perhaps *Die Zauberflöte*, *Il Seraglio*, and cantata K.619 can be seen as reflections in art of Orientalist research.

Christoph Willibald Gluck and Jean-Philippe Rameau

Christoph Willibald Gluck, the Bohemian composer, may well have had a hand in writing music for the Turkish-themed opera *La finta schiava* (The Feigned Slave Girl). Orientalist subjects figure in several of his operas. The Assyrian queen Semiramis is the heroine of Metastasio's *La Semiramide riconosciuta* (Semiramis Recognized), for which Gluck wrote the score in 1748, while Metastasio's comedy *Le cinesi* (The Chinese), a parody of French manners and music, figured Chinese women as the main characters; Gluck finished the music for it by 1754. The crystal and transparent decor was designed in a Chinese style by Giovanni Maria Quaglio. Gluck's next *opéra comique*, *Le Cadi dupé* (The Qadi Duped), was also a "Turkish" genre piece, performed in December 1761 in Vienna. His most famous *opéra comique* is perhaps *La Rencontre imprévue, ou les Pèlerins de la Mecque* (The Unforeseen Encounter, or The Pilgrims to Mecca), first performed in Vienna's Burgtheater in January 1764. It was based on a 1726 French play by Alain René Le Sage and Jacques-Philippe D'Orneval, who may, in turn, have derived their inspiration from Boccaccio. The French fairground theaters played many pieces with exotic themes in the eighteenth century. Louis Fuzelier and Jean-Philippe Rameau's opéra-ballet *Les Indes galantes* (The Amorous Indies [1735]) introduced the character of the compassionate and "Generous Turk," inspiring imitations such as those by Charles Simon Favart, the foremost *opéra comique* librettist of the century.

Rameau's *Les Indes galantes*—opéra-ballet in a prologue and four entrées (*Le Turc généreux* [The generous Turk]; *Les Incas du Pérou* [The Incas of Peru]; *Les Fleurs-fête persane* [Persian Flower Festival]; *Les Sauvages* [The Savages]; 1735), with a libretto by Louis Fuzelier—sings the virtues of exotic countries that France had just lost, such as India. While the prologue despairs of Europe, the four entrées lead us to more exotic locales. The first entrée is set on an island in the Indian Ocean. Emilie, a Christian woman abducted by pirates, is made a slave to Pasha Osman, who is in love with her. But Emilie resists his advances, since her heart is devoted to Valère, who is still searching for her since their separation. While in the garden of Osman, a violent storm washes a ship ashore with its surviving sailors, among whom is Valère. The sultan Osman appears, and the lovers fear the worst, but against all expectations he sets the young lovers free. The sultan recognizes Valère as someone who had once been his master, but had rendered the Turk his freedom. They sing each other's praises, and the first entrée ends amid much rejoicing and dance. The librettist Fuzelier always claimed the Turk Osman was based on a contemporary grand vizier.

Les Sauvages seems to have been inspired by Rameau witnessing in Paris the dancing of two American Indians ten years earlier. It ends with the heroine choosing the noble savage rather than competing Europeans from France and Spain.[13]

Le Turc généreux inspired the Viennese choreographer Franz Hilverding to create a ballet with music by Joseph Starzer. It was witnessed by the sultan's envoy to the Viennese court, who was impressed by its accuracy, and probably also by the flattering portrait of the title character.

Gluck composed several "Turkish" pieces in addition to the *opéra comique Le Cadi dupé*, including at least three ballets: *Les Turcs* (The Turks) and *Les Corsaires* (The Pirates) of 1759 and *Les Pèlerins* (The Pilgrims) of 1762. Viennese spectators were able to judge the accuracy of the music of these pieces, as authentic Janissary bands were on hand for comparison. On July 15, 1763, just as Gluck must have been composing his opera, the theatergoer and diarist Carl von Zinzendorf reported, "Yesterday at Schönbrunn I heard the Turkish music of Harsch's regiment, which makes the most beautiful effect on earth."[14]

The French theater in Vienna recruited Count Giacomo Durazzo, an Italian diplomat, as theater intendant. It was at the count's insistence that Gluck agreed to set *Les Pèlerins de la Mecque* (The Meccan Pilgrims). The count's father, in his youth, had been abducted by Muslim pirates, perhaps the reason the subject appealed to the count. The story has strong affinities to Rameau's *Les Indes galantes* and Mozart's *Il Seraglio*: Ali and Rezia, through many adventures, and despite the temptations of other girls and the courtship of the sultan, remain true to one another. The sultan pardons and frees the lovers, and forgives the dervish who betrayed them.

The Battle of Vienna took place on September 11 and September 12, 1683, after Vienna had been besieged by Turks for two months. This was surely one of the most significant battles in Western history. As early as fifty years later (Lesage and D'Orneval's play came out in 1726), Western artists, instead of demonizing the Turks, were depicting them as generous, noble, and compassionate figures. Then we also have the remarkable spectacle of Franz Hilverding's *Le Turc généreux* (The generous Turk) of 1758 (with music by Joseph Starzer) being witnessed by the sultan's envoy to the Viennese court, and impressing him by its accuracy and generous treatment of the Turkish sultan. And yet strident anti-Orientalist hysteria insists that Western artists, writers, and musicians were wicked and painted a racist picture of what they like to call "the Other."

The Nineteenth Century

The nineteenth century, like the eighteenth of Mozart, Gluck, and André Ernest Modeste Grétry, celebrated the East in music, with François-Adrien Boieldieu's one-act opera *Le Calife de Baghdad* (The Caliph of Baghdad [1800]) starting off the century. It is quite extraordinary the number of distinguished composers who set their operas in the East: Gioacchino Rossini, Carl Maria Weber, Giacomo Meyerbeer, Jacques Halévy, Georg Joseph Vogler, Georges Bizet, and Félicien David, among others. Félicien David was one of the rare composers who actually traveled, between 1832 and 1835, to the East, visiting Constantinople, Smyrna, Jaffa, Jerusalem, and Cairo, where he lived for two years. On his return to France, David wrote a sequence of *Mélodies orientales*, containing, as he claimed, genuinely Oriental melodies. In 1844 David achieved great success with his "ode-symphonie" *Le Désert*, described by MacKenzie as "a three-movement symphonic ode for spoken voice, choir, and orchestra." Its various sections included "a prayer to Allah" and "the muezzin's call."[15]

20

LITERATURE AND ORIENTALISM

SEVENTEENTH CENTURY: MADELEINE DE SCUDÉRY

Madeleine de Scudéry, sometimes called Mademoiselle de Scudéry, was an extraordinarily successful novelist, read by some of the greatest figures of the French seventeenth century—from Corneille to Madame de Lafayette, Pascal to Madame de Sévigné—but has been largely neglected ever since.

Two of her novels are of particular interest for our study: *Ibrahim ou l'illustre Bassa* (Ibrahim or the Illustrious Pasha [1641]) and *Artamène ou le Grand Cyrus* (Artamène or Cyrus the Great [1649–53]).

Artamène ou le Grand Cyrus was published in ten volumes and was an immediate success. It is set in the Orient of Cyrus the Great, who became the king of the small kingdom of Anshan in Persia in about 557 BCE, and who conquered Media, Sardis, Lydia, Babylonia, and the neo-Babylonian Empire in 539 BCE.[1] It is the longest novel in the French language, running to more than thirteen thousand pages in the original edition. De Scudéry had read the classical sources, Herodotus and Xenophon's essentially sympathetic account, and also Plutarch, Justin, Polyaenus, Pliny the Elder, Ovid, Strabo, even the Bible, before embarking upon her literary work. The novel recounts Cyrus the Great's love for Princess Mandane, and his military conquests. Cyrus is the infallible hero, and along with his heroism, his religious tolerance is emphasized. He is described as a man of noble bearing, with eyes "filled with vivacity, sweetness, and majesty." He is always gallant and respectful of Mandane. De Scudéry is able to enter into her characters with sympathy and obviously won over her audience, given the success of her novel. De Scudéry was also able to draw upon one of the three threads running through Western civilization: respect and admiration of the Other, in this case a legacy from Herodotus and Xenophon.

Her earlier novel, *Ibrahim ou l'illustre Bassa*, is even more significant for our theme. Like her later novel on Cyrus, *Ibrahim* is well researched, based on works such as the *History of the Decline of the Greek Empire and the Establishment of that of the Turks* by Laonicus Chalcondyle (Nicolas Chalcondylas), a Greek historian of the fifteenth century; and the histories of the Italian Paolo Giovio, whose two treatises on the Turks were published in France in 1538 and 1544. As Clarence Dana Rouillard says, the four volumes of her "generous novel" *Ibrahim* contain the most ambitious use of Turkish history and description in French literature before 1660.[2] The main plot relates the story of the rise and fall of the Christian Ibrahim as a pacha at the court of Sultan Soliman (Suleyman), the whole story ending happily with a magnanimous gesture on the part of Soliman.

De Scudéry gives us local color, describing the triumph of the Great Soliman in the Hippodrome, Ibrahim's palace, and the portrait gallery of the sultans, military campaigns, the meeting of the Divan, the reception of an ambassador, and a host of other incidental details about dress, decorative objects, meals, and the Turkish passion for flowers. Finally, as Rouillard adds, "Mlle. de Scudéry must have seen a copy of a letter from a Sultan, for the introduction and conclusion to Soliman's letter to the Senate of Genoa have all the proper formulae."[3]

It was Marie-Christine Pioffet in 1996 who dug deeper into de Scudéry's philosophy.[4] In an elegant essay blissfully devoid of anti-Orientalist jargon—Edward Said is not mentioned once—Pioffet begins by noting de Scudéry's desire to record human diversity by being faithful to the local color for which she had studied: "the manners, costumes, laws, religions, and the inclinations of peoples." But de Scudéry also has a moral purpose. She desires a synthesis between the two worlds—between the East and the West—and this is evident in the choice of her hero, the Greek Justinian disguised as a Muslim, and it is for this reason that we find the Turkey of de Scudéry so "heteroclite." Ibrahim decides to have his palace built by Italians, but in its ornamentation and furnishing it can be considered a mix of several cultures. The library is full of books, all that is best in both Oriental and European languages; even the collection of arms are equally from "all the Nations of the world." This cosmopolitanism is reflected in the town of Chio, "inhabited by all kinds of nations," and the island on which it is situated is "one of the most agreeable for its freedom and conversation." De Scudéry is attracted to the idea of the mixing of peoples, answering to the Baroque ideal of diversity. Genoa is described as owing its charm to the Franco-Italian interpenetration: "[T]here liberty was much greater than in the rest of Italy; the nearness of France allowed the passage of her customs [into Genoa]." No less appreciated is the marriage of Moorish and Hispanic cultures, which will eventually render the court of Abdalla the equal of that of the Louvre.

The novel of de Scudéry, Pioffet continues, is hardly a faithful representation of the Ottomans, but an amalgam or juxtaposition of disparate cultural elements. The organization of the narrative framework itself, born out of the fusion of two stories originally quite distinct—that of the grand vizier of Soliman and that of Auguste Mascardi—satisfies an aesthetic need. The eastern Mediterranean world is seen in the novel not as something antithetical to the Occident, but rather as a kind of double in which we look for an echo of our own interests—something universal even. In de Scudéry, conflicts between cultures are, it seems, not inevitable.

Justinian is at ease in both worlds, ready to don Muslim garb when required. Beyond the cultural diversity it depicts and celebrates, the novel tries to bring about a symbiosis between Turkish and European elements. Pioffet argues that de Scudéry rejects the cleavage between the Orient and the Occident. It is in this quest for universality that one can make sense of the words of the French marquis in the novel, who observed that "all men were so different from one another that often there was a greater difference between individual Italians than between the entire country and the peoples such as Persians and Tartars";[5] this complex viewpoint manages however to acknowledge both human diversity and universality. Even though their outward behavior may be different, the sentiments of the Turks are not. In *Ibrahim*, the passage from the Other to the Universal is all the easier, since Otherness is not perceived as being intrinsic to nature, but only an exterior covering.

Jane Austen and Slavery

Edward Said's most egregious misreading of a literary work concerns Jane Austen's *Mansfield Park* (1814). Even before mangling Austen, Said was responsible for having created an atmosphere of hostility and prejudice against the West and Western culture—from painting to literature. In such an atmosphere, Austen is unlikely to get a fair trial. This is important, since the pusillanimous have accepted without question or qualm the terms of debate set by Said.

There are several references to Antigua and Sir Thomas's plantation in *Mansfield Park*, but only a single explicit reference to the slave trade. From such flimsy textual evidence it is unwise to deduce authorial intent. Certainly one cannot conclude that Austen condoned slavery. But Said, realizing that there is little textual justification, brings other novels written later—in some cases a hundred years later—to bear upon *Mansfield Park*:

> We must first take stock of *Mansfield Park*'s prefigurations of a later English history as registered in fiction. The Bertrams' usable colony in *Mansfield Park* can be read as pointing forward to Charles Gould's San Tomé mine in *Nostromo*, or to the Wilcoxes' Imperial and West African Rubber company in Forster's *Howards End* [1910], or to any of these distant but convenient treasure spots in *Great Expectations*, Jean Rhys's *Wide Sargasso Sea* [1966], *Heart of Darkness*—resources to be visited, talked about, described, or appreciated for domestic reasons, for local metropolitan benefit. If we think ahead to these other novels, Sir Thomas's Antigua readily acquires a slightly greater density than the discrete, reticent appearances it makes in the pages of *Mansfield Park*.[6]

So Austen's "discrete" reticence must be filled out by reading ahead a hundred years. In other words, there is nothing that would justify describing Austen as condoning slavery, but we must look to works written by others, not Austen herself, and written a hundred years later to do so!

Said covers his tracks, using a common ploy laid bare by Alan Sokal and Jean Bricmont in *Fashionable Nonsense*. Intellectual impostors often, in willfully vague language, try to have it both ways: "Indeed, they offer a great advantage in intellectual battles: the radical interpretation can serve to attract relatively inexperienced listeners or readers; and if the absurdity of this version is exposed, the author can always defend himself by claiming to have been misunderstood, and retreat to the innocuous interpretation."[7] Here is how Said does it, denying his own thesis: "All the evidence says that even the most routine aspects of holding slaves on a West Indian sugar plantation were cruel stuff. And everything we know about Jane Austen and her values is at odds with the cruelty of slavery. Fanny Price reminds her cousin that after asking Sir Thomas about the slave trade, 'there was such a dead silence' as to suggest that one world could not be connected with the other since there simply is no common language for both. That is true."[8]

In a recent article, Susan Fraiman takes to task Said's lazy and unwarranted reading of Austen:

> Yet had Said placed Sir Thomas Bertram, for example, in line with the deficient fathers who run unrelentingly from *Northanger Abbey* through *Persuasion*, he might perhaps have paused before assuming that Austen legitimates the master of Mansfield Park. If truth be told, Said's attention even to his chosen text is cursory: Austen's references to Antigua (and India) are mentioned without actually being read, though Said stresses elsewhere the importance of close, specific analysis. Maria Bertram is mistakenly referred to as "Lydia" [p. 104]—con-

> fused, presumably, with Lydia Bennett of *Pride and Prejudice*. And these are just a few of the signs that *Mansfield Park*'s particular complexity—including what I see as its moral complexity—has been sacrificed here, so ready is Said to offer Austen as "Exhibit A" in the case for culture's endorsement of empire.[9]

Gabrielle White devotes an entire book to defending Jane Austen from Edward Said. She examines Austen's last three novels, and sets them in the context of the world of the abolitionists. White writes, "The last three novels, the so-called Chawton novels [*Mansfield Park*, *Emma*, and *Persuasion*], were written in the decade after the 1807 Abolition. Amongst Jane Austen's favourite writers were people who were passionately anti-slavery, such as William Cowper, Doctor Johnson and Thomas Clarkson. One of her naval brothers was known to be abolitionist. I use the term 'abolition' in connection with both the slave trade and slavery. Cowper's tirade against slavery in lines 37–39 of Book Two of his epic poem *The Task* is severe, and leads up to the question: 'We have no slaves at home—then why abroad?' Jane Austen would have been aware of the popular campaign for abolition."[10]

For White, *Mansfield Park*

> challenged the pro-slavery lobby amongst readers in a context after slave trading had been made a felony; it gave succour to the anti-slavery campaigners; and it told the story of a young girl that could retain readers' interest once the hopes of abolition and emancipation would be achieved. It is only after change that the author is prepared to have done with everything else and restore all to "tolerable comfort." The narrator stipulates a change for the better "for ever" in the eldest son and heir, Tom, who is reformed. The fictional world of *Mansfield Park* in the context of abolition warrants portraying the novel as a subversive view of English society and as undermining the status quo of slavery. The upshot of *Mansfield Park* is relative to the abolitionist climate in which it was written. That a tone is set and an agenda bruited by references to Antigua and the West Indies becomes apparent as the plot unfolds.[11]

In the novel, Fanny Price recounts a conversation she had with her uncle, Sir Thomas Bertram: "'Did you not hear me ask him about the slave trade last night?' she asks her cousin Edmund, and then adds: '—but there was such dead silence!'" Not only Sir Thomas, but his children sat in the room "without speaking a word." Brian Southam has argued that Sir Thomas's silence indicates that he was unable to answer her satisfactorily, and that by simply daring to raise the question at all, Fanny was able to make her abolitionist sympathies clear—she was indeed "a friend of the abolition."[12] Fanny Price also approves of anyone who speaks up for the oppressed: "To be the friend of the poor and oppressed! Nothing could be more grateful to her . . ."[13]

The dialogue on the slave trade in *Emma* (vol. 2, chap. 17) also leads to an abolitionist reading. Jane Fairfax, in talking of agencies through which one can hire governesses, says, "There are places in town, offices, where inquiry would soon produce something—Offices for the sale—not quite of human flesh—but of human intellect." To which Mrs. Elton, obviously horrified, replies, "Oh! my dear, human flesh! You quite shock me; if you mean a fling at the slave-trade, I assure you Mr. Suckling was always rather a friend to the abolition." It is evident from the context and Mrs. Elton's reply that all present were clearly against the slave trade; otherwise, why would Mrs. Elton so hastily rush to make it clear that no acquaintance of hers could possibly be for slavery?

In *Persuasion*, Austen celebrates the Royal Navy and "by implication its impending work to enforce in law over slave trading."[14] We know Jane was very proud of her brothers in the Royal Navy, which played its part in the suppression of the slave trade. Her brother Frank wrote home condemning slavery after a visit to Antigua in 1806.[15] Fanny Austen, Jane's niece, kept a diary for 1809 that contains an antislavery story, further evidence that women in Jane Austen's family and circle were in favor of abolition.[16] White also suggests that the title *Mansfield Park* is itself a reference to Lord Mansfield and his famous verdict of 1772 that ruled that a black defendant, James Somersett, could not be taken against his will back out of England and returned to slavery in the colony of Virginia, already quoted but which bears requoting: "The state of slavery . . . is so odious. . . . Whatever inconvenience, therefore, may follow from the decision, I cannot say this case is allowed or approved by the law of England; and therefore, the black must be discharged."[17]

As White says, Edward Said was "way off the mark," since he is insensitive to the satire present in Austen. Said was not known for his sense of humor. He was even less sensitive to irony; as R. S. Rajan put it, "Said's reading [of *Mansfield Park*] is not without problems, both as a matter of interpretation of Austen's style (he overlooks, for example, the operation and effects of irony), as well as in historical understanding (of her position on abolition, for instance)."[18] Finally, White notes, "Jane Austen's untimely death in 1817 meant she would not live to see further outcome of the popular resolve for abolition during the reappraisal of early years, both in her undermining the status quo of chattel slavery, and in celebrating the abolition of the British slave trade."[19]

Did Edward Said even have a coherent thesis in his section on Jane Austen and empire in *Culture and Imperialism*? He tells us that "[t]he first thing to be done now is more or less to jettison simple causality in thinking through the relationship between Europe and the non-European world, and lessening the hold on our thought of the equally simple temporal sequence."[20] He cannot even manage to tell us straightforwardly to jettison these two things; we are "more or less" to do so.

If we are to jettison simple causality, does he mean we ought to adopt complex causality—or rather, causality as such? No answer is forthcoming. A few lines above, Said informs us that European culture did not "cause" imperialism. Does he mean "cause" simply or complexly? If there is neither a causal nor a temporal relation, what relation does he have in mind? He evades the latter question by introducing the metaphor of "counterpoint." But counterpoint is a concept drawn from music. How can it apply here? No answer is given. In the same paragraph, we are told incoherently that "[t]he inherent mode for this counterpoint is not temporal but spatial." Does he mean "simple spatiality" or "complex spatiality"? How can there be space without time or causality?

If we now ask the question, "What is the relationship between a European novel and European imperialism?" we find that Said has not even pretended to tell us. Said does recognize that this is a fundamental issue, but evades it by introducing irrelevant and obfuscating side issues and metaphors. Without an answer to that question, Said does not have a coherent thesis.[21]

George Eliot and *Daniel Deronda*

Christopher Hitchens defended George Eliot's *Daniel Deronda* from Edward Said and two others, concluding his contribution to the series *Art of Criticism* with the following remark: "This counterpoint—between the rising incense and the dying cadence, the triumphant and the modest, the prophetic and the quotidian—is nowhere more boldly confronted than in the chapters of *Daniel Deronda*, which have already easily outlived the distinctly earthbound, confining objections made to them."[22]

Said complains of "the total absence of any thought about the actual inhabitants of the East, Palestine in particular."[23] Hitchens points out that Said is looking "through a retrospective optic."[24] Said accuses Eliot of being callous: "The few references to the East in *Daniel Deronda* are always to England's Indian colonies, for whose people—as people having wishes, values, aspirations—Eliot expresses the complete indifference of absolute silence."[25] To this argument from silence, Hitchens had already replied earlier in the lecture by quoting a letter that George Eliot had written to Harriet Beecher Stowe:

> As to the Jewish element in "Deronda," I expected from the first to last in writing it, that it would create much stronger resistance and even repulsion than it has actually met with. But precisely because I felt that the usual attitude of Christians towards Jews is—I hardly know whether to say more impious or more stupid—in the light of their professed principles, I therefore felt urged to treat Jews with such sympathy and understanding as my nature and knowledge could attain to. *Moreover, not only towards all oriental peoples with whom we English come in contact, a spirit of arrogance and contemptuous dictatorialness is observable which has become a national disgrace to us.*[26]

"There is nothing I should care more to do," she continued, "if it were possible, than to rouse the imagination of men and women to a vision of human claims in those races of their fellow men who must differ from them in customs and beliefs."

Hitchens denies that Eliot "could not care less about the colonial subjects of the British Crown," by quoting her:

> We do not call ourselves a dispersed and a punished people; we are a colonising people and it is we who have punished others.[27]

> Are we to adopt the exclusiveness for which we have punished the Chinese?[28]

> He [Mixtus] continues his early habit of regarding the spread of Christianity as a great result of our commercial intercourse with black, brown and yellow populations; but this is an idea not spoken of in the sort of fashionable society that Scintilla collects around her husband's table; and Mixtus now philosophically reflects that the cause must come before the effect, and that the thing to be striven for is the commercial intercourse—not excluding a little war if that also should prove needful as a pioneer of Christianity.[29]

> [T]he Irish, also a servile race, who have rejected Protestantism though it has been repeatedly urged on them by fire and sword and penal laws, and whose place in the moral scale may be judged by our advertisements, where the clause "No Irish need apply" parallels the sentence which for many polite persons sums up the question of Judaism—"I never *did* like the Jews."[30]

This, as Hitchens notes, "scarcely supports a finding of indifference towards the colonized."[31]

Though Eliot in her generosity sees the establishment of a new nation in the East as "a halting-place of enmities," a reconciliation of the East with the West, Said refuses to acknowledge that Jews are Easterners or Orientals at all. That would spoil his vision of the establishment of Israel as a Western conspiracy, his Manichaean view of the world as a battle between the East and the West. Said is silent about Jews of Arab lands, even though there were Jewish communities at the time of the Romans in Egypt, North Africa, Morocco, the eastern Mediterranean, and Persia, long before the Arab conquests of the seventh century. For George Eliot, the purpose of the novel was to extend our moral sympathies; Edward Said remained unwilling to extend his sympathies to Eastern Jews.

RUDYARD KIPLING AND INDIA

Was Rudyard Kipling a racist, as Edward Said claims? Consider this poem:

> WE AND THEY
>
> All good people agree,
>
> And all good people say,
> All nice people, like Us, are We
>
> And every one else is They:
> But if you cross over the sea,
>
> Instead of over the way,
> You may end by (think of it!) looking on We
>
> As only a sort of They![32]

Relativism, like cholesterol, comes in two forms: good and bad. Kipling's poem reminds us that the good type of relativism was originally only a way of preaching tolerance of others—the Other. And yet Edward Said wants us to believe that Kipling's views of Orientals in *Kim* are "stereotypical," that Kipling considers all Indians as inferior, and that he posits a colonial divide that could not be bridged.[33] Said gets much of the import and tenor of Kipling's novel flatly wrong. Said also has the irritating habit of claiming to know how the "Indian reader" will react to the novel.[34] I am an Indian reader, and do not read it as Said's ideal Indian reader does, and I shall quote other Indian readers who do not either.

Craig Raine, in a splendid article in the *Kipling Journal*, defends Kipling from charges of racism. He quotes two letters, revealing "the private man in the secrecy of his correspondence," written between late 1885 and early 1886, to Margaret Burne-Jones, when Kipling was working at the *Civil and Military Gazette*. In one, Kipling attacks the very notion of the stereotypical "native": "When you write 'native, ' who do you mean? The Mahommedan who hates the Hindu; the Hindu who hates the Mahommedan; the Sikh who loathes both; or the semi-anglicised product of our Indian colleges who is hated and despised by Sikh, Hindu and Mahommedan." As Raine remarks, "Kipling recorded these distinctions. He didn't invent them. And they still exist. In the aftermath of the recent race riots in Oldham, the Today Programme had an interview in which a Hindu woman complained about the blanket label 'Asians'—and blamed the riots on sections of the Moslem community."[35]

The second letter talks of "the immeasurable gulf that lies between the races in all things, you would see how it comes to pass that the Englishman is prone to despise the natives—(I must use that misleading term for brevity's sake)—and how, except in the matter of trade, to have little or nothing in common with him. . . . Now this is a wholly wrong attitude of mind but it's one that a Briton who washes, and don't take bribes, and who thinks of other things besides intrigue and seduction most naturally falls into. When he does, goodbye to his chances of attempting to understand the people of the land."

As Raine informs us, Kipling then describes his novel *Mother Maturin* as an attempt to penetrate the authentic native life, which remained unaffected by British rule: "The result has been to interest me immensely and keenly in the people and to show me how little an Englishman can hope to understand 'em." Of this life, Kipling avers that "our rule, so long as no one steals too flagrantly or murders too openly, affects it in no way whatever." The letter continues with a remark often quoted against him: that the Indians are a cross between children and men, "touchy as children, obstinate as men." But Kipling goes on: "[T]he proper way to handle 'em is not by looking on 'em 'as excitable masses of barbarism' (I speak for the Punjab only) or the 'down trodden millions of Ind groaning under the heel of an alien and unsympathetic despotism,' but as men with a language of their own which it is your business to understand; and proverbs which it is your business to quote (this is a land of proverbs) and bye-words and allusions which it is your business to master; and feelings which it is your business to enter into and sympathise with."[36]

Craig Raine quotes a letter from Kipling criticizing a clergyman for his insensitivity: "[16 October 1895]: it is my fortune to have been born and to a large extent brought up among those whom white men call 'heathen'; and while I recognise the paramount duty of every white man to follow the teachings of his creed and conscience as 'a debtor to do the whole law,' it seems to me cruel that white men, whose governments are armed with the most murderous weapons known to science, should amaze and confound their fellow creatures with a doctrine of salvation imperfectly understood by themselves and a code of ethics foreign to the climate and instincts of those races whose most cherished customs they outrage and whose gods they insult."[37] Kipling is equally shocked by Americans (*From Sea to Sea* vol. 2, p. 61): "Very many Americans have an offensive habit of referring to natives as 'heathen.' Mahommedans and Hindus are heathen alike in their eyes."

These are hardly the words of a racist. Kipling was a far more complex man than assumed by Said in everything he writes of him. Ambiguity and complexity always pose a problem to anyone who has a Manichaean view of the world in the way Said does.

Raine offers an ingenious interpretation of Kipling's famous poem "White Man's Burden," addressed to the people of the United States:

> The poem "The White Man's Burden" has been widely misread. In effect, critics have stopped, affronted, at the first stanza: "Your new-caught, sullen peoples,/Half-devil and half child." It is the imputation of childishness that lodges in the throat—and, alas, in the brain. Has anyone, I wonder, read to the end of the poem and understood it? The reward for taking up the White Man's Burden is stated in the last line: "The judgment of your peers!" Who are those "peers," those equals? Since the poem is addressed to the USA, you might think that "peers" refers to British imperialists. But you would be wrong. The "peers" in question are the "new-caught, sullen peoples"—raised to equality. As the previous three stanzas make clear.
>
> Take up the White Man's burden—
>
> And reap his old reward:
> The blame of those ye better,
>
> The hate of those ye guard—
> The cry of hosts ye humour
>
> (Ah, slowly!) toward the light:—
> "Why brought ye us from bondage,
>
> Our loved Egyptian night?"
>
> Take up the White Man's burden—

> Ye dare not stoop to less—
> Nor call too loud on Freedom
>
> To cloak your weariness;
> By all ye cry or whisper,
>
> By all ye leave or do,
> The silent, sullen peoples
>
> Shall weigh your Gods and you.
>
> Take up the White Man's burden—
>
> Have done with childish days—
> The lightly proffered laurel,
>
> The easy, ungrudged praise.
> Comes now, to search your manhood
>
> Through all the thankless years,
> Cold-edged with dear-bought wisdom,
>
> The judgment of your peers!
>
> In this account, the imperialist aim, which mustn't be rushed, is eventual independence: "Nor call too loud on Freedom/To cloak your weariness.' In other words, grant freedom at the proper juncture, when the moment is ripe—and not because fatigue makes you want to rest. Kipling's penultimate stanza ends explicitly with the judgment of the colonised on the colonisers: "The silent, sullen peoples/Shall weigh your Gods and you." But Kipling waits until the last line of the poem to spring his surprise—a surprise marked by an exclamation mark. There he makes it clear that, in the end, the judgment of the colonised on the colonisers will be the judgment of equals, "the judgment of your peers." The aim, then, is not subjection and exploitation in perpetuity, but "Freedom" with a capital "F" and elevation to equality.[38]

If correct, Raine's interpretation would be one refutation of Said's critique of Kipling. Under this interpretation there is neither a permanent racial divide nor a permanent empire.

Kipling laments the lack of a bard of the Eurasians: "[W]e know nothing about their life which touches so intimately the White on the one hand and the Black on the other. . . . Wanted, therefore, a writer from among the Eurasians, who shall write so that men shall be pleased to read a story of Eurasian life; then outsiders will be interested in the People of India, and will admit that the race has possibilities."[39] Kipling saw a racial mixture as inevitable in the United States: "Wait till the Anglo-American-German-Jew—the Man of the Future—is properly equipped. He'll have the least little kink in his hair now and again; he'll carry the English lungs above the Teuton feet that can walk for ever; and he will wave long, thin, bony Yankee hands with the big blue veins on the wrist, from one end of the earth to the other. He'll be the finest writer, poet, dramatist, 'specially dramatist, that the world as it recollects itself has ever seen. By virtue of his Jew blood—just a little, little drop—he'll be a musician and a painter too."[40]

Other evidence outside *Kim* for Kipling's lack of racism is his membership of a Masonic lodge where he met "men of different religions on an equal footing: his 'brethren' there included members of the Islamic, Sikh, Christian and Jewish religions." Though he rarely attended their meetings, "he appreciated Freemasonry for its sense of brotherhood and egalitarian attitude to diverse faiths and classes."[41]

In *Kim*, Creighton tells Kim, "There is a good spirit in thee. Do not let it be blunted at St. Xavier's. There are many boys there who despise the black men. . . . [D]o not at any time be led to contemn the black men." A little later, Kim tells Mahbub, " 'They say at Nucklao [Lucknow] that no Sahib must tell a black man that he has made a fault.' Mahbub's hand shot into his bosom, for to call a Pathan a 'black man' [*kala admi*] is a blood-insult. Then he remembered and laughed, 'Speak, Sahib. Thy black man hears.' " Not only is this a reminder that political correctness is as old as Simla, but that racism between Indians—the lighter-skinned Aryans despising the darker Dravidians in the south—was also a reality that Kipling was perfectly aware of. In chapter 13, Kipling refers to some Indian coolies who are "used to comprehensive ill-treatment from their own colour."

In reading Kipling, it is always advisable not to take everything he says literally, and to remember the philosopher W. V. O. Quine's remark that it does not matter what you believe as long as you are insincere. Time and again we come across Kipling expressing the most bigoted views imaginable, and then retracting or contradicting them as his prejudice is countered by his experience of individuals and more intimate contact with other peoples and cultures: Chinese, Japanese, and Jew.[42]

Coming back to Said's more specific charges about *Kim*, as Mark Kinkead-Weekes has written, *Kim* was "the answer to nine-tenths of the charges levelled against Kipling and the refutation of most of the generalisations about him."[43] Let us take the charges one by one.

Said claims that Kipling's India has "essential and unchanging qualities."[44] Kipling talks of "a large manufacturing city, and the crowded tram-car," hardly signs of an unchanging, primitive country. But more decisively, Kipling writes in chapter 4, "Nowadays, well-educated natives are of opinion that when their womenfolk travel—and they visit a good deal—it is better to take them quickly by rail in a properly screened compartment; and that custom is spreading. But there are always those of the old rock who hold by the use of their fore-fathers." Times are changing. "Nowadays"—in other words, it was not always like that. Then we have, in chapter 1, the decisive "The Curator smiled at the mixture of old-world piety and modern progress that is the note of India to-day."

According to Said, "Kipling is less interested in religion for its own sake."[45] This is a gross misreading of the whole novel and Kipling's attitude toward religion in general. Here is what Lionel Trilling, a far more subtle literary critic, said: "[*Kim*] suggested not only a multitude of different ways of life but even different modes of thought. Thus, whatever one might come to feel personally about religion, a reading of Kim could not fail to establish religion's factual reality, not as a piety, which was the apparent extent of its existence in the West, but as something at the very root of life."[46]

Nirad Chaudhuri considers *Kim* to be "the finest novel in the English language with an Indian theme, but also one of the greatest of English novels in spite of the theme. . . . *Kim* is great by any standards that ever obtained in any age of English literature." He also makes it clear that religion is one of the four major themes in *Kim*, and that anyone who gets that wrong has not "quite understood what *Kim* is about."[47]

Kipling understood Buddhist philosophy, had evidently taken the time and trouble to read extensively on it, and was proud of his own countrymen's rediscovery of Buddhism: "For the first time he heard of the labours of European scholars, who by the help of these and a hundred other documents have identified the Holy Places of Buddhism."[48]

The novel slowly unfolds the symbiotic relationship of the Lama and Kim, each on his particular quest, for the "River that washes away all sin," and for Kim a search for his identity; the Wheel and the Way, the illusion and the reality, the beginning and the end.[49] The Lama realizes that his way of life depends on the freedom and protection guaranteed by the raj, which defends "weaponless dreamers" like him. But Kim, too, changes, grows spiritually: "I was made wise by thee, Holy One," said Kim . . . forgetting St. Xavier's; forgetting his white blood; forgetting even the Great Game as he stooped, Mohammedan fashion, to touch his master's feet in the dust of the Jain temple. "My teaching I owe to thee. I have eaten thy bread three years. My time is finished. I am loosed from the schools. I come to thee."

Throughout the novel, Kipling contrasts the Christian Bennett and his intolerance with the deep natural piety, and to a certain extent the superstitions of the people of India, and their natural veneration of the Lama despite the doctrinal differences:

> [The Lama] began in Urdu the tale of the Lord Buddha, but, borne by his own thoughts, slid into Tibetan and the long-droned texts from a Chinese book of the Buddha's life. The gentle, tolerant folk looked on reverently.

> The family priest, an old tolerant Sarsut Brahmin, dropped in later, and naturally started a theological argument to impress the family. By creed, of course, they were all on the priest's side, but the lama was the guest and the novelty. His gentle kindliness, and his impressive Chinese quotations, that sounded like spells, delighted them hugely; and in this sympathetic, simple air, he expanded like the Bodhisat's own lotus, speaking of his life in the great hills of Such-zen, before he said, "I rose up to seek enlightenment."

> "How thinkest thou of this one [the Lama]?" said the cultivator aside to the priest.
>
> "A holy man—a holy man indeed. His Gods are not the Gods, but his feet are upon the way," was the answer. "And his methods of nativities, though that is beyond thee, are wise and sure."

> These merry-makers stepped slowly, calling one to the other and stopping to haggle with sweetmeat-sellers, or to make a prayer before one of the wayside shrines—sometimes Hindu, sometimes Mussalman—which the low-caste of both creeds share with beautiful impartiality.

> [The Lama] was prepared to spend serene years in his quest; having nothing of the white man's impatience, but a great faith.

Contrast the above with the following: "Bennett looked at him with the triple-ringed uninterest of the creed that lumps nine-tenths of the world under the title of 'heathen.'"

Said devotes several pages to the Great Mutiny—pages full of tendentious reading of Indian history. He writes, "For the Indians, the Mutiny was a nationalist uprising against British rule." It is Said himself who takes it to be so:

> In such a situation of nationalist and self-justifying inflammation, to be Indian [*sic!*] would have meant to feel natural solidarity with the victims of British reprisal. To be British meant to feel repugnance and injury—to say nothing of

> righteous vindication—given the terrible displays of cruelty by "natives," who fulfilled the roles of savages cast for them. For an Indian, *not* to have had those feelings would have been to belong to a very small minority. It is therefore highly significant that Kipling's choice of an Indian to speak about the Mutiny is a loyalist soldier who views his countrymen's revolt as an act of madness. Not surprisingly, this man is respected by British "Deputy Commissioners" who, Kipling tells us, "turned aside from the main road to visit him." What Kipling eliminates is the likelihood that his compatriots regard him as (at very least) a traitor to his people.[50]

Much of this is gobbledygook. The mutiny has been analyzed in a masterly fashion by Geoffrey Moorhouse, an author quoted favorably on another issue by Edward Said. Moorhouse concluded, "What the whole episode *never remotely* resembled was a national struggle for independence."[51] Here is what really happened. First, "it was restricted to a comparatively small area of the sub-continent. There were uprisings in Bombay, Hyderabad, and Indore, all swiftly put down by military force before they got out of hand. Otherwise the country outside northern India never made a move, and even there the rebellion was localized. Neither the Sikhs nor the Gurkhas, the Rajputs nor the Marathas raised a hand against the British. Few of the native princes allowed themselves to become involved, and some put their resources at the Government's disposal. Thousands of Indian troops remained loyal to their officers while others were butchering anyone associated with the white regime."[52] The loyalist soldier in *Kim* is not an isolated Benedict Arnold but one of many thousands who remained loyal to the raj. In fact the mutineers were decidedly in the minority, since only about a quarter of the sepoys in the army of Bengal joined the revolt![53] Kipling did not eliminate a likelihood; it is Said who introduced an improbability.

Second, "the insurgence," continues Moorhouse, "consisted of varied elements and grievances. There was a largely high-caste army of sepoys in the Bengal Army, inflamed by what they saw as a religious threat, which included their gradual displacement by lower castes in the military structure and on the land. There was a rural rebellion of peasants against social displacement caused by land reforms, which had them more than ever the prey of moneylenders; yet the toughest peasant rebels were those who had resisted social upheaval and had complaints about taxation." Thus it was not a simple rebellion against colonial rule.

Third, "[m]any Indians, too, shared this nightmare, for the disorder of the Mutiny became a great excuse for the settling of old scores, and plenty of natives perished because they were suspected of casting spells or had given offence in some quite trifling way."[55] Indians suffered from the violence of other Indians, and were glad when the nightmare was over. Thus they would have thanked the loyalist soldier, not treated him as a traitor.

Then there is the old "Orientalist" charge laid against Creighton: "Everything about India interests Creighton, because everything in it is significant for his rule."[56] The thought that Creighton might actually have interests, and a passion for Indian things for the sake of knowledge, never enters Said's head. Here is how Kipling characterizes that aspect of Creighton that has nothing to do with subduing recalcitrant natives:

> No money and no preferment would have drawn Creighton from his work on the Indian Survey, but deep in his heart also lay the ambition to write "F.R.S." after his name. Honours of a sort he knew could be obtained by ingenuity and the help of friends, but, to the best of his belief, nothing save work-papers representing a life of it-took a man into the Society which he had bombarded for years with monographs on strange Asiatic cults and unknown customs. Nine out of ten would flee from a Royal Society soirée in extremity of boredom; but Creighton was the tenth, and at times his soul yearned for the crowded rooms in easy London where silver-haired, bald-headed gentlemen who know nothing of the Army move among spectroscopic experiments, the lesser plants of the frozen tundras, electric flight-measuring machines, and apparatus for slicing into fractional millimetres the left eye of the female mosquito. By all right and reason, it was the Royal Geographical that should have appealed to him, but men are as chancy as children in their choice of playthings.

That is an explicit, and a decisive refutation of Said, and a summary of one of the main theses of this book: the intellectual curiosity of Western man.

Kipling ends the paragraph by observing, "So Creighton smiled, and thought the better of Hurree Babu, moved by like desire." Kipling finally and touchingly concedes that people like Hurree Babu, though sometimes slightly absurd figures who seem to have swallowed an English dictionary whole, are not simply aping the white man, but are motivated by a *like desire* to acquire knowledge, and are intellectually overwhelmed even by the whole new world of the mind opened up by their contact with Western learning. For Said, Babu remains a "grimacing stereotype of the ontologically funny native, hopelessly trying to be like 'us.'"[57] But Babu is, like Creighton, eager for knowledge. Babu is not trying to be like white men but being true to himself, as someone enamored of learning. Toward the end of chapter 12, Kipling presents a respectful portrait of Hurree Babu as a changed man influenced by the Lama: "but, as he was ever first to acknowledge, there lay a wisdom behind earthly wisdom—the high and lonely lore of meditation. Kim looked on with envy. The Hurree Babu of his knowledge—oily, effusive, and nervous—was gone; gone, too was the brazen drug-vendor of overnight. There remained—polished, polite, attentive—a sober, learned son of experience and adversity, gathering wisdom from lama's lips." Not only India, but her people also can change.

Conclusion

It should be evident that one cannot reduce the colorful and gifted individuals known as Orientalists and their works to as yet another expression of colonialism and imperialism. Many of these artists worked in Turkey and the Ottoman Empire, which were not parts of any Western colonial empire. Others worked in Egypt and Morocco, neither of which were strictly speaking colonies in the mid-nineteenth century; the latter of which only became a French protectorate in 1912, and the former came under dual French and British control in 1879. Algeria did come under French rule in 1830, but Orientalists such as Eugène Fromentin sympathized with the Algerian people, and others like Charles Cordier actually settled there. Many Orientalists were opposed to Western interference in the Orient, both for political reasons—they were democratic in their sympathies—and for aesthetic ones—they did not want to see too rapid a change in the lands they had come to love. They had come to the Orient to escape industrialization. The Orientalists had their own individual reasons for exploring artistically foreign climes, customs, people, and costumes. Many passed through either Asia Minor, Greece and Albania, or Spain. In all cases our Orientalist painters were enthralled by the descriptive, genre possibilities of the peoples and their colorful traditions. They did not see the Spanish in any different manner from how they saw the Algerians or Moroccans; there was no racism on their part. On the contrary, they painted Arabs, Spanish gypsies, Algerians, Albanians, Berbers, Greeks, and Armenians in the same fashion, according all their subjects dignity, humanity, and individuality. In this, they were influenced by, and followed the tradition of, the great Dutch masters, whom they explicitly acknowledged as their teachers.

The nineteenth-century Orientalists, just as such artistic ancestors as Gentile Bellini, Carpaccio, and Pisanello, were struck by—overwhelmed by—this new world of bright skies and vivid colors. Delacroix's painting was modified immediately with "his contact with the Orient, and the intensification of color so afforded is passed on to the whole line of successors."[1]

Indeed, the Orientalists must be seen not only against the background of Venetian colorists and the Dutch masters but also against the entire background of Western civilization, with its intellectual and artistic curiosity and the very often essentially sympathetic attitudes to the Other that I have described throughout this book, from the ancient Greeks, by way of liberal-minded European and American travelers, all the way to the Orientalist scholars writing about India, Persia, and the Near East in the eighteenth and nineteenth centuries.

The Orientalists began as realists, but their styles changed, and even became impressionistic, the style of their artistic rivals. They recorded, observed, and rendered homage to a world and people they had sought out, sometimes risking their lives—as, for example, Edwin Lord Weeks, did in Morocco—to do so. They returned again and again—some settling for ten years (J. F. Lewis), others passing their last days there (Charles Cordier).

But as Delacroix famously said, "The first virtue of a painting is to be a feast for the eyes";[2] paintings are to be enjoyed, and surely the Orientalist works provide that feast for the eyes, with their sumptuous interiors, glorious colors, and dramatic skies. One wonders if the anti-Orientalists ever look at paintings as paintings, if they ever enjoy them—or do they see them as merely objects to be grimly introduced into evidence? One group of people who do actually enjoy them are Orientals, the very people the Orientalists are supposed to have vilified and denigrated. Museums in Cairo, in Istanbul, in India, and private collectors throughout North Africa and the Near and Middle East are the proud possessors of works by Orientalists. These Orientals love the Orientalists painters, were inspired by them, and even, like Osman Hamid Bey in Paris and elsewhere, tried to study with them.

"Art's greatest benefit to men," wrote George Eliot, "is to widen their sympathies."[3]

Who has done more than the great Western artists—from Aeschylus to Jane Austen, George Eliot, and Rudyard Kipling, and painters from Pieter Coeck, Rembrandt, and Bellini to Decamps, Weeks, J. F. Lewis, and Gérôme, as well as a whole host of others I have not had time to discuss, from Herman Melville to Longfellow, from Jules Robert Auguste to Felix Ziem—to widen our sympathies, to open our eyes, to reevaluate our preconceptions, to extend the bounds of dignity?

APPENDIX

LETTER TO THE *WALL STREET JOURNAL*

Soon after Edward Said died, I wrote an article about him for the *Wall Street Journal.* The short article elicited an angry letter defending Said. I wrote the following letter in reply:

EDWARD SAID INSULTED COURAGEOUS AUTHORS

In an Oct. 7 [2003] letter attacking my criticism of the late Edward Said ("Orientalism," editorial page, Sept. 29), Hutham S. Olayan assures us that "[w]ere he still with us, [Said] would shred Ibn Warraq's flimsy pronouncements in the full light of day." However, my 17,000-word critique of Edward Said's works has been accessible for more than a year. Said never bothered to reply; perhaps his shredder was out of order. We are also told that Said tried "to enoble rather than belittle individuals and whole peoples." On the contrary, Said stooped to name-calling and personal insults when he met anyone who dared criticize or disagree with him; he called the courageous Iraqi Kanan Makiya, author of *Cruelty and Silence*, a "native informer," and Fouad Ajami, author of *The Arab Predicament*, a "Western stooge," hardly enobling descriptions. Here is Said's characterization of all Europeans: "It is therefore correct that every European, in what he could say about the Orient, was consequently a racist, an imperialist, and almost totally ethnocentric." ("Orientalism," p. 204.) In other words, not only is every European a racist, but he must necessarily be so. "All Europeans," as Damon Runyon would say, is a whole lot of people.

Finally, my pseudonym "Ibn Warraq" does not mean "son of paper"—it means "son of a stationer, book-seller, paper-seller."

Ibn Warraq
Paris

NOTES

Notes to Epigraphs

1. For the unfettered study of knowledge.

2. Hubert Lyautey (1854–1934), the very able colonial administrator in Morocco between 1912 and 1925.

3. Albert Camus, *Chroniques Algériennes 1939–1958*. Paris: Folio Essais, 1958, pp. 22–22. Cf. Pascal Bruckner's *La Tyrannie de la Penitence. Essai sur le masochisme occidental* (Paris: Grasset, 2006).

Part 1: Edward Said and the Saidists

1. Edward Said, "Israel-Palestine: A Third Way," *Le Monde Diplomatique* (September 1998).

2. Edward Said, *Orientalism* (New York: Vintage, 1994).

3. Quote of J. M. White in his introduction to Lane's *Modern Egyptians* (New York: Dover, 1973), p. v.

4. F. E. Peters, *The Hajj* (Princeton, NJ: Princeton University Press, 1994); references to and quotes from Burton are to be found on pp. 72, 100, 128–29, 175–77, 187–88, 215–18, 225–26, 242, 255–56, 257–58, 265, 289, 338, 350.

5. Keith Windschuttle, "Edward Said's 'Orientalism' Revisited," *New Criterion* 17, no. 5 (January 1999).

6. Ibid.

7. Ibid.

8. J. M. Roberts, *History of the World* (New York: Oxford University Press, 1993), p. 503.

9. Ibid., p. 504.

10. Bertrand Russell, *In Praise of Idleness* (London: Allen & Unwin, 1935), pp. 82–108.

11. R. W. Southern, *Western Views of Islam in the Middle Ages* (Cambridge, MA: Harvard University Press, 1962), pp. 91–92, 108–109.

12. Jones's quote comes from *Collected Works*, ed. Garland Cannon (New York: Curzon, 1993), vol. 3, pp. 34–35.

13. K. Paddaya, ed., *Bulletin of the Deccan College Post-graduate Research Institute* 54, no. 55 (1994/1995). Special numbers devoted to Jones.

14. See Keith Windschuttle, "The Ethnocentrism of Clifford Geertz," *New Criterion* 21, no. 2 (October 2, 2002).

15. See Daniel Pipes, *The Hidden Hand: Middle East Fears of Conspiracy* (New York: St. Martin's Griffin, 1998).

16. Edward Said, *The Question of Palestine* (New York: Vintage, 1980), p. 29.

17. Windschuttle, "Edward Said's 'Orientalism' Revisited."

18. Ian Buruma, review of *Out of Place: A Memoir* by Edward Said, *New York Times Book Review*, October 3, 1999.

19. Quoted in *Courrier International* 395, May 28, 1998.

20. Efraim Karsh and Inari Karsh, *Empires of the Sand: The Struggle for Mastery in the Middle East, 1789–1923* (Cambridge, MA: Harvard University Press, 2001), p. 27.

21. Ibid., p. 45.

22. Ibid., p. 2.

23. Ibid., p. 3; emphasis in the original.

24. Ibid., p. 203.

25. Howard Bloom, *The Lucifer Principle: A Scientific Expedition into the Forces of History* (New York: Atlantic Monthly Press, 1995), p. 231.

26. Windschuttle, "Edward Said's 'Orientalism' Revisited."

27. Original section on Aeschylus omitted here; instead, readers are advised to read the extended study of Aeschylus's *The Persians* in part 2, chapter 2.

28. Herodotus, *The Histories*, book II.3, quoted by J. L. Myers, "Herodotus," in *The Oxford Classical Dictionary* (Oxford: Oxford University Press, 1978). Much of this paragraph is indebted to J. L. Myers.

29. Maxime Rodinson, "The Western Image and Western Studies of Islam," in *The Legacy of Islam*, ed. Joseph Schacht and C. E. Bosworth (Oxford: Oxford University Press, 1974), pp. 15–16.

30. William Brandon, *New Worlds for Old: Reports from the New World and Their Effect on the Development of Social Thought in Europe, 1500–1800* (1986: Ohio University Press, 1986), p. 6.

31. Michel de Montaigne, *Des Cannibales* in *Oeuvres completes*, ed. Albert Thibaudet and Maurice Rat (Paris: Gallimard, 1962).

32. Pierre Bayle, "Mahomet and Nestorius," in *Dictionnarie historique et critique* (*A General Dictionary*), 5th ed., 10 vols., trans. J. P Bernard, T. Birch, and J. Lockman (London: n.d.) 1734/41.

33. Ibid.

34. Ockley, Prideaux and Sale, "The Treatment of Arab History" in *Historians of the Middle East*, ed. Bernard Lewis (New York: Oxford University Press, 1962), p. 302.

35. G. H. Bousquet, "Voltaire et Islam," *Studia Islamica* 38 (1968).

36. Gotthold Ephraim Lessing, *Nathan the Wise*, trans. William Taylor of Norwich (London, 1830).

37. P. J. Keating, "W. S. Blunt," in *The Penguin Companion to Literature*, vol. 1 (Harmondsworth, UK: Penguin, 1971), p. 55.

38. Quoted in Bernard Lewis, *Islam and the West* (New York: Oxford University Press, 1993), pp. 83–84.

39. J. M. Roberts, *The Triumph of the West* (London: B. B. C. Publications, 1985), p. 176.

40. Bernard Lewis, "La carte du Proche-Orient," in *Islam et Politique au Proche-Orient aujourd'hui* (Paris: Gallimard, 1991), pp. 162–63.

41. Rodinson, "The Western Image and Western Studies of Islam," p. 59.

42. C. Destremau and Jean Moncelon, *Louis Massignon* (Paris: Plon, 1994), p. 258.

43. Mircea Eliade, *Journal I, 1945–1955*, trans. Mac Linscott Ricketts (Chicago: University of Chicago Press, 1990).

44. Maxime Rodinson, "A Critical Survey of Modern Studies on Muhammad," in *Studies on Islam*, ed. Merlin L. Swartz (New York: Oxford University Press, 1981), p. 57.

45. Edward Said, "Impossible Histories: Why the Many Islams Cannot Be Simplified," reviewing Bernard Lewis, *What Went Wrong? Western Impact and Middle Eastern Response*, *Harper's* (July 2002).

46. Quoted from Bernard Lewis, "Islamic Concepts of Revolution," in *Revolution in the Middle East, and Other Case Studies: Proceedings of a Seminar*, ed. P. J. Vatikiotis (London: Allen & Unwin, 1972), pp. 33, 38–39.

47. Windschuttle, "Edward Said's 'Orientalism' Revisited."

48. Lewis, *Islam and the West*, p. 108.

49. Ibid., p. 126.

50. Windschuttle, "Edward Said's 'Orientalism' Revisited."

51. Ibid.

52. Lawrence I. Conrad, "Ignaz Goldziher on Ernest Renan: From Orientalist Philology to the Study of Islam," in *The Jewish Discovery of Islam*, ed M. Kramer (Tel Aviv: Moshe Dayan Center for Middle Eastern and African Studies, 1999), pp. 137–80.

53. Ibid., p. 140.

54. Ibid., p. 170, n18. The rest of the footnote reads: "See Geoffrey, ed., *World Survey of Islamic Manuscripts,* (London: Al-Furqân Islamic Heritage Foundation, 1992–94), 1:275–90 (Paris), 320–29 (Berlin); 2:365–76 (Leiden); 3:471–90 (London)."

55. Ibid., p. 142.

56. Ibid.

57. Ibid., p. 139.

58. See ibid., nn30–34 for the full references.

59. Lewis, *Islam and the West*, p. 118.

60. Conrad, "Ignaz Goldziher on Ernest Renan," p. 162–63.

61. Ibid., p. 161.

62. Ibid., p. 164.

63. Raphael Patai, *Ignaz Goldziher and His Oriental Diary* (Detroit: Wayne State University Press, 1987), p. 28.

64. Shmuel Almog, "The Racial Motif in Renan's Attitude to Jews and Judaism," in *Antisemitism through the Ages*, ed. Shmuel Almog (Oxford: Pergamon, 1988), pp. 255–78. Referred to by Conrad, "Ignaz Goldhizer on Ernest Renan," p. 156.

65. Ernest Renan, "Muhammad and the Origins of Islam" in *The Quest for the Historical Muhammad*, ed. Ibn Warraq (Amherst, NY: Prometheus Books, 2000), pp. 127–66.

66. H. W. Wardman, *Ernest Renan: A Critical Biography* (London: University of London Athlone Press, 1964), p. 89

67. Renan, "Muhammad and the Origins of Islam," pp. 163–64.

68. Ibid., p. 163.

69. Herbert Berg, "The Methods and Theories of John Wansbrough," in *The Quest for the Historical Muhammad*, ed. Ibn Warraq (Amherst, NY: Prometheus Books, 2000), p. 502.

70. William Montgomery Watt, *Muslim-Christian Encounters* (London: Routledge, 1991), p. 110.

71. Ibid.

72. R. Stephen Humphreys, *Tradition and Innovation in the Study of Islamic History: The Evolution of North American Scholarship since 1960* (lecture presented at the Institute of Oriental Culture, University of Tokyo, October 21, 1997). R. Stephen Humphreys is King Abdul Aziz Ibn Saud Professor of Islamic Studies at the University of California, Santa Barbara.

73. Maxime Rodinson, *Europe and the Mystique of Islam*, trans. Roger Veinus (Seattle: University of Washington Press, 1987), p. 131 n3; quoted by M. Kramer, *Ivory Towers on Sand* (Washington, DC: Washington Institute for Near East Policy, 2001), p. 30.

74. Interview with Rodinson in *Approaches to the History of the Middle East*, ed. Nancy Elizabeth Gallagher (London: Ithaca Press, 1994), p. 124; quoted by Kramer, *Ivory Towers on Sand*, p. 38.

75. P. J. Vatikiotis, *Among Arabs and Jews: A Personal Experience, 1936–1990* (London: Weidenfeld and Nicolson, 1991), p. 105; quoted by Kramer, *Ivory Towers on Sand*, p. 38.

76. Jacques Berque, "Au-delà de l'Orientalisme; Entretien avec Jacques Berque," in *Qantara* 13 (October/November/December 1994): 27–28; quoted by Kramer, *Ivory Towers on Sand*, p. 30.

77. Clive Dewey, "How the Raj Played Kim's Game," *Times Literary Supplement*, April 17, 1998, p. 10; quoted by Kramer, *Ivory Towers on Sand*, p. 31.

78. Lewis, *Islam and the West*, p. 112.

79. Maxime Rodinson, *La Fascination de l'Islam* (Paris: Editions La Découverte, 1978), p. 97 n132. The other two scholars are Jean Sauvaget and Claude Cahen.

80. Ibid., p. 123.

81. Interview with Nikki Keddie in *Approaches to the History of the Middle East*, ed. Nancy Elizabeth Gallagher (London: Ithaca Press, 1994), pp. 144–45; quoted by Kramer, *Ivory Towers on Sand*, p. 37.

82. Quoted by Kramer, *Ivory Towers on Sand*, p. 38.

83. Interview with Albert Hourani in *Approaches to the History of the Middle East*, ed. Nancy Elizabeth Gallagher (London: Ithaca Press, 1994), p. 41; quoted by Kramer, *Ivory Towers on Sand*, p. 38.

84. Ibid., p. 30.

85. Aijaz Ahmed, *In Theory: Classes, Nations, Literatures* (London: Verso, 1992), pp. 160–61.

86. Kanan Makiya, *Cruelty and Silence* (New York: Norton, 1993), pp. 317–18.

87. Ibid., p. 319.

88. Sadiq al-'Azm, "Orientalism and Orientalism in Reverse," *Forbidden Agendas: Intolerance and Defiance in the Middle East*, ed. Jon Rothschild (London: Al Saqi Books, 1984), p. 350.

89. Sadiq al-'Azm, *Orientalism and Orientalism in Reverse* [in Arabic] (Beirut, 1981), p. 18, quoted in Emmanuel Sivan, *Interpretations of Islam: Past and Present* (Princeton, NJ: Darwin Press, 1985), p. 144.

90. Al-'Azm, "Orientalism and Orientalism in Reverse," p. 363.

91. Quoted in Sivan, *Interpretations of Islam*, p. 136.

92. Ibid., p. 139.

93. Ibid., p. 151.

Part 2: The Three Golden Threads and the Misapprehensions of Edward Said

Chapter 1: Three Tutelary Guiding Lights

1. See, for example, William H. McNeill, *Rise of the West: A History of the Human Community* (Chicago: University of Chicago Press, 1963); Immanuel Wallerstein, *Geopolitics and Geoculture: Essays on the Changing World-System* (Cambridge: Cambridge University Press, 1991); Karl Deutsch, "On Nationalism, World Regions, and the Nature of the West," in *Mobilization, Center-Periphery Structures and Nation-Building: A Volume in Commemoration of Stein Rokkan*, ed. Per Torsvik (Bergen: Universitetsforlaget; Irvington-on-Hudson, NY: Columbia University Press, 1981); Roger Scruton, *The West and the Rest: Globalization and the Terrorist Threat* (New York: Continuum, ISI Books, 2002); F. A. von Hayek, *The Road to Serfdom* (London: Routledge, 1944; reprint, Chicago: University of Chicago Press, 1976).

2. Scruton, *The West and the Rest*, pp. 4–5.

3. Aristotle, *Metaphysics*, 980a, book I, part 1, trans. W. D. Ross in *Complete Works*, ed. Jonathan Barnes (Princeton, NJ: Princeton University Press, 1985), vol. 2, p. 1552.

4. All discussed below.

5. Alcmaeon Fr.1a Diels, trans. Freeman, quoted in Bruce Thornton, *Greek Ways: How the Greeks Created Western Civilization* (San Francisco: Encounter Books, 2000), p. 144.

6. In Aristotle, *Eudemian Ethics*, 1216a, book I, part 5, trans. J. Solomon, in *Complete Works*; quoted in Thornton, *Greek Ways*, p. 145.

7. Aristotle, *Parts of Animals*, 645a, Book I, Part 5, trans. W. Ogle, in *Complete Works*; quoted in Thornton, *Greek Ways*, p. 145.

8. Democritus Fr.118 Diels, trans. Freeman; quoted in Thornton, *Greek Ways*, p. 145.

9. Aristotle, *Fragments*, F 58 R 3 (*Iamblichus*, Protrepticus 52.16–54.5 *Pistelli*), in *Complete Works*, vol. 2, p. 2408.

10. Cicero, *De Officiis*, trans. Harry G. Edinger (Indianapolis: Bobbs-Merrill, 1974), bk. 1, sec. 13, p. 9.

11. John Henry Cardinal Newman, *The Idea of a University* (San Francisco: Rinehart Press, 1960), pp. 77–79.

> Hence it is that Cicero, in enumerating the various heads of mental excellence, lays down the pursuit of Knowledge for its own sake, as the first of them. "This pertains most of all to human nature," he says, "for we are all of us drawn to the pursuit of Knowledge; in which to excel we consider excellent, whereas to mistake, to err, to be ignorant, to be deceived, is both an evil and a disgrace." And he considers Knowledge the very first object to which we are attracted, after the supply of our physical wants. After the calls and duties of our animal existence, as they may be termed, as regards ourselves, our family, and our neighbours, follows, he tells us, the search after truth. Accordingly, as soon as we escape from the necessary cares, forthwith we desire to see, to hear, and to learn; and consider the knowledge of what is hidden or is wonderful a condition of our happiness.

12. Matthew Arnold, *Culture and Anarchy: An Essay in Political and Social Criticism* (London, 1869), chap. 1, p. 7. See also Matthew Arnold. "The Function of Criticism at the Present Time," in *Essays in Criticism* (London and Cambridge: Macmillan, 1865).

13. Bernard Lewis, *The Muslim Discovery of Europe* (London: Phoenix, 1994), p. 75.

14. Ibid., p. 73.

> And Muslims used the Arabic script to the exclusion of all others. For Muslims to learn an infidel script would involve an element of, so to speak, impiety, even of pollution, and few, indeed, were Muslims who ever attempted to learn a foreign language. Non-Islamic languages were unknown except for previous knowledge brought into the fold by new converts to Islam. This situation is in striking contrast with that prevailing in Europe, split into many countries and nations, each with its own language. Europeans found it necessary, at an early age, to learn languages other than their own and to prepare tools for this purpose. In the Islamic world grammar and lexicography were for long limited to Arabic, for the religious task of enabling non-Arab converts to Islam to read and understand the sacred scriptures. . . . From the whole eight centuries of the Muslim presence in Spain only one document has survived that indicates any kind of interest in a European language.

15. *Arab Human Development Report 2003: Building a Knowledge Society* (New York: United Nations Development Programme, Regional Bureau for Arab States, 2003), p. 82.

16. Lewis, *The Muslim Discovery of Europe*, p. 137.

17. Ibid., p. 151.

18. Sir John Chardin, *Travels in Persia 1673–1677* (New York: Dover, 1988), pp. 143–44.

> I remember to have heard it made a Point of Debate among some knowing Persons in Europe, whether Tobacco and Sugar were Originals of the New World, or whether they always grew in the Eastern Countries. I have endeavoured to find the Truth of this upon the Spot. But you would scarce believe how little Curiosity the Eastern People have in such Remarks and Observations. There's scarce a Person among their Learned Men, who keeps a Register of the Discoveries that are made in the Arts and Sciences. As for Tobacco, I could not learn in Persia, whether it was originally the growth of that Country, or brought thither from Foreign Parts; and I found my Enquiries all in vain.

19. Ibid., pp. 193–95.

> As for what relates to travelling, those Journeys that are made out of pure Curiosity, are still more inconceivable to the Persians, than walking Abroad [i.e., going for a walk]. They have no Taste of the Pleasure we enjoy in seeing different Manners from ours, and hearing of a Language which we do not Understand. When the French Company in the East-Indies sent Deputies to the King of Persia, the King of France sent two likewise, but without any Character, Nam'd Lalain, and Boullaye; and the Credential Letter imported, *That these Gentlemen having an Inclination to Travel, and joining with these French Merchants, who are Deputies, in order to see the World; the King made use of this Opportunity to write to his* Persian *Majesty to recommend this Company of* French Merchants to him. . . . [The Persian Ministers] hung mightily upon those words, *Gentlemen who have a mind to travel*, which could not be put into their language, without an Air of Absurdity, being a thing not practis'd, or even so much as known. They ask'd me if it was possible that should be such People amongst us, who would travel two or three thousand Leagues with so much Danger, and Inconveniency, only to see *how they were made, and what they did in Persia, and upon no other Design*. . . . It is from this Spirit of theirs no doubt, that the Persians are so grossly Ignorant of the present State of other Nations of the World, and that they do not so much as understand Geography, and have no Maps; which comes from this, that having no Curiosity to see other countries, they never mind the Distance, nor Roads, by which they might go thither. They have no such thing among 'em as Accounts of Foreign Countries, neither *Gazettes, News A-la-main,* nor *Offices* of *Intelligence*. . . . The Ministers of State generally Speaking, know no more what passes in *Europe*, than in the World of the Moon. The greatest Part, even have but a confus'd Idea of Europe, which

> they look upon to be some little Island in the *North* Seas, where there is nothing to be found that is either Good or Handsome.

20. Michael Field, *Inside the Arab World* (Cambridge, MA: Harvard University Press, 1994), p. 165; quoted by Daniel Pipes, *The Hidden Hand: Middle East Fears of Conspiracy* (New York: St. Martin's Griffin, 1998), pp. 235–36.

21. al-Shahrastānī in his monumental work *al-Milal wa 'l-niḥal* (ed. W. Cureton, 2 vols., London, 1842–46), "aspired to present the doctrinal opinions of all the world's people, that is to reveal the entirety of religions and philosophies, past and present" (E. I., 2 ed. s.v. *al-Shahrastānī*). It contains studies of among others Jews, Mazdaeans, Manichaeans, Sabians, and disciples of ancient Arab cults and of Hindi sects. According to the E. I. 2nd ed., these studies "represent the high point of Muslim histories of religion."

22. Ibn Ḥazm, *Kitāb al-Fiṣal* is an encyclopedia of religious knowledge concerning all the religions that had any connection with Islam. It is, on the whole, comprehensive and accurate, even recording changes in doctrines of various religions over time.

23. Ibn Khaldūn, *The Muqaddimah*, trans. Franz Rosenthal, 2nd ed. (1967; reprint, Princeton, NJ: Princeton University Press, 1980), vol. 2, p. 438.

24. "Review of Seyyed Hossein Nasr, *A Young Muslim's Guide to the Modern World*," *Muslim World Book Review* 14, no. 4 (1994): 16. Since I have not consulted the original article in English by Maryam Jameelah, I have resisted the temptation to put quotation marks around my translation of Talbi's translation.

25. Muhammad Talbi, Interreligious Dialogue for Convergence [Dialogue interreligieux ou conflireligieux pour Dialogue de Témoignage, d'Emulation et de Convergence], http://www.unesco.org/webworld/peace_library/tunisia/andalous/french1.htm. Originally published in *Revue d'Etudes Anadalouses*, Tunisia.

26. F. R. Rosenthal, *The Classical Heritage of Islam* (London: Routledge, 1975), pp. 13–14.

> Islamic rational scholarship, which we have mainly in mind when we speak of the greatness of Muslim civilisation, depends in its entirety on classical antiquity, down to such fundamental factors as the elementary principles of scholarly and scientific research. More than that, the intellectual life of Islam in its most intimate expressions bowed to the Greek spirit. . . . However, in Islam as in every civilisation, what is really important is not the individual elements but the synthesis that combines them into a living organism of its own. . . . The indisputable fact remains, though, that Islamic civilisation as we know it would simply not have existed without the Greek heritage.

27. G. E. von Grunebaum, *Islam: Essays in the Nature and Growth of a Cultural Tradition* (London: Routledge and Kegan Paul, 1955), p. 15.

28. Remi Brague, *Eccentric Culture: A Theory of Western Civilization* (South Bend, IN: St. Augustine's Press, 2002).

29. Von Grunebaum, *Islam*, p. 114: "Those accomplishments of Islamic mathematical and medical science which continue to compel our admiration were developed in areas and in periods where the elites were willing to go beyond and possibly against the basic strains of orthodox thought and feeling."

30. Ernest Renan, *Islamisme et la science*, lecture presented at the Sorbonne, Basel, Bernheim, March 29, 1883.

31. Von Grunebaum, *Islam*, p. 114.

32. Cf. Steven Weinberg, Nobel Prize–winning scientist, who recently wrote:

> Much of the weakening of religious certitude in the Christian West can be laid at the door of science; even people whose religion might incline them to hostility to the pretensions of science generally understand that they have to rely on science rather than religion to get things done. But this has not happened to anything like the same extent in the world of Islam. One finds in Islamic countries not only religious opposition to specific scientific theories, as occasionally in the West, but a widespread religious hostility to science itself. My late friend, the distinguished Pakistani physicist Abdus Salam, tried to convince the rulers of the oil-rich states of the Persian Gulf to invest in scientific education and research, but he found that though they were enthusiastic about technology, they felt that pure science presented too great a challenge to faith. In 1981, the Muslim Brotherhood of Egypt called for an end to scientific education. In the areas of science I know best, though there are talented scientists of Muslim origin working productively in the West, for forty years I have not seen a single paper by a physicist or astronomer working in a Muslim country that was worth reading. This is despite the fact that in the ninth century, when science barely existed in Europe, the greatest centre of scientific research in the world was the House of Wisdom in Baghdad.
>
> Alas, Islam turned against science in the twelfth century. The most influential figure was the philosopher Abu Hamid al-Ghazzali, who argued in *The Incoherence of the Philosophers* against the very idea of laws of nature, on the ground that any such laws would put God's hands in chains. According to al-Ghazzali, a piece of cotton placed in a flame does not darken and smoulder because of the heat, but because God wants it to darken and smoulder. After al-Ghazzali, there was no more science worth mentioning in Islamic countries.

See Steven Weinberg, "A Deadly Certitude," *Times Literary Supplement*, January 17, 2007.

33. Quoted in von Grunebaum, *Islam*, p. 123.

34. Hayek, *The Road to Serfdom*, p. 162.

35. Ibn al-Haytham, great mathematician and physicist, whose works were translated into Latin and were influential in the Middle Ages.

36. T. J. De Boer, *The History of Philosophy in Islam* (London, 1933; reprint, New York: Dover, 1967), p. 153.

37. Hayek, *The Road to Serfdom*, p. 162.

38. Charles Habib Malik, *A Christian Critique of the University* (1982; reprint, Waterloo, ON: North Waterloo Academic Press, 1990). Available online at http://www .leaderu.com/real/ri9902 /malik.html (accessed May 2007).

39. E. R. Dodds, *The Greeks and the Irrational* (Berkeley and Los Angeles: University of California Press, 1962), p. 136.

40. Malik, *A Chiristian Critique of the University.*

41. Ibid.

42. D. Easterman, *New Jerusalems* (London: Grafton, 1992), pp. 92–93.

43. H. C. Baldry, *The Unity of Mankind in Greek Thought* (Cambridge: Cambridge University Press, 1965), p. 4. The lack of color prejudice of the Greeks is discussed below in detail.

44. Ibid., p. 5

45. For example, by German scholar Max Müller, a pioneer in the study of Sanskrit scriptures such as the *Rig Veda.*

46. Walter Burkert, *The Orientalizing Revolution: Near Eastern Influence on Greek Culture in the Early Archaic Age* (Cambridge, MA: Harvard University Press, 1992); *Babylon, Memphis, Persepolis: Eastern Contexts of Greek Culture* (Cambridge, MA: Harvard University Press, 2004). Rudolf Wittkower, *Selected Lectures of Rudolf Wittkower: The Impact of Non-European Civilizations on the Art of the West*, ed. Donald Martin Reynolds (Cambridge: Cambridge University Press, 1989); *Allegory and the Migration of Symbols* (Boulder, CO: Westview Press, 1977). I discuss Wittkower further in chapter 10. M. L. West, *Early Greek Philosophy and the Orient* (Oxford: Clarendon, 1971).

47. Homer, *Odyssey*, 9.125–29.

48. Burkert, *Babylon, Memphis, Persepolis*, p. 1.

49. Ibid., p. 8.

50. Ibid., p. 9.

51. Ibid., p. 12.

52. Ibid.

53. Ibid., p. 99, quoting Horace, *Epodes*, 2.1.156.

54. Ibid., pp. 12–13.

55. C. M. Bowra, *Heroic Poetry* (London: Macmillan, 1952).

56. Burkert, *Babylon, Memphis, Persepolis*, p. 24.

57. Ibid., p. 37.

58. Ibid., p. 47.

59. Dedicated to Walter Burkert.

60. West, *Early Greek Philosophy and the Orient*, p. 239.

> But what invaded Greek speculation in the mid-sixth century was no mere convolvulus that withered away when its season was past, leaving the sturdy stems

of Hellenic rationalism to grow unimpeded as they had always meant to. It was an ambrosia plant that produced a permanent enlargement where it touched. In some ways one might say that it was the very extravagance of oriental fancy that freed the Greeks from the limitations of what they could see with their own eyes: led them to think of ten-thousand-year cycles instead of human generations, of an infinity beyond the visible sky and below the foundations of the earth, of a life not bounded by womb and tomb but renewed in different bodies aeon after aeon. It was now that they learned to think that good men and bad have different destinations after death; that the fortunate soul ascends to the luminaries of heaven; that God is intelligence; that the cosmos is one living creature; that the material world can be analysed in terms of a few basic constituents such as fire, water, earth, metal; that there is a world of Being beyond perception, beyond time. These were conceptions of enduring importance for ancient philosophy. This was the gift of the Magi.

61. Ibid., pp. 241–42.

62. Burkert, *Babylon, Memphis, Persepolis*, p. 69: "[I]t was nowhere else but in Greece that philosophy in the form we know came into being. It may be to the point to recall the different social situation of the Greeks—no kings, no powerful priests, and no houses of tablets, which meant more mobility, more freedom, and more risk for mind and letters. In mathematics too the Greeks developed a new form of deductive proof in restructuring geometry."

63. Martin Bernal, *Black Athena: The Afroasiatic Roots of Classical Civilization*, vol. 1: *The Fabrication of Ancient Greece, 1785–1985* (New Brunswick, NJ: Rutgers University Press, 1987).

64. See especially Mary Lefkowitz, *Not Out of Africa: How Afrocentrism Became an Excuse to Teach Myth as History* (New York: Basic Books, 1996). Lefkowitz has a full bibliography on the controversy generated by *Black Athena*. See also the journal *Arethusa* special issue/Fall 1989: *The Challenge of "Black Athena*," published by the Department of Classics, State University of New York at Buffalo.

65. Lefkowitz, *Not Out of Africa*, p. 157: "There is no evidence that Socrates, Hannibal, and Cleopatra had African ancestors. There is no archaeological data to support the notion that Egyptians migrated to Greece during the second millennium B.C. (or before that). There is no reason to think that Greek religious practices originated in Egypt."

66. Burkert, *Babylon, Memphis, Persepolis*, pp. 88, 98.

67. Ibid., p. 70.

68. Burkert, *The Orientalizing Revolution*, p. 129.

69. S. Hampshire, *Freedom of Mind and Other Essays* (Oxford: Clarendon, 1972), p. 227.

70. E. Gombrich, "Eastern Inventions and Western Response" *Daedalus* 127 (Winter 1998): 193–205.

71. Arthur M. Schlesinger Jr., *The Disuniting of America: Reflections on a Multicultural Society* (New York: Norton, 1992), p. 124.

72. Iris Chang, *The Rape of Nanking: The Forgotten Holocaust* (New York: Basic Books, 1997).

73. Jung Chang and Jon Halliday, *Mao: The Unknown Story* (New York: Knopf, 2005).

74. Ben Kiernan, *The Pol Pot Regime: Race, Power, and Genocide in Cambodia under the Khmer Rouge, 1975–79*, 2nd ed. New Haven, CT: Yale University Press, 2002.

75. S. K. Bhattacharyya, *Genocide in East Pakistan/Bangladesh: A Horror Story* (Houston, TX: A. Ghosh, 1988); also Anthony Mascarenhas, *The Rape of Bangladesh* (Delhi: Vikas, 1971).

76. James Barter, *Idi Amin* (Chicago: Lucent, 2004).

77. Human Rights Watch has many articles on the situation in the Sudan at http://www.hrw.org/. For the period up to 1993, see Millard Burr, *A Working Document: Quantifying Genocide in the Southern Sudan 1983–1993* (Washington, DC: US Committee for Refugees, 1993).

78. Nicholas Thompson, "Adopt a Peacekeeper," *Boston Globe*, March 6, 2005.

79. V. N. Dadrian, *The History of the Armenian Genocide: Ethnic Conflict from the Balkans to Anatolia to the Caucasus* (Oxford: Berghahn Books, 1995); Ara Sarafian, ed., *United States Official Documents on the Armenian Genocide*, 4 vols. (Watertown, MA: Armenian Review, 1995).

80. Kanan Makiya, *The Republic of Fear* (Berkeley and Los Angeles: University of California Press, 1998).

81. Syrian Human Rights Committee, BCM Box 2789, London WC1N 3XX, UK; http://www.shrc.org.uk/default.aspx.

82. Syrian Human Rights Committee, BCM Box 2789, London WC1N 3XX, UK; http://www.shrc.org.uk/data/aspx/d3/1813.aspx; see also Marius Deeb, *Syria's Terrorist War on Lebanon and the Peace Process* (New York: Palgrave Macmillan, 2003).

83. This figure includes the number of Iranians killed in the Iran/Iraq war. See especially www.abfiran.org, which has just begun the grim task of documenting all the assassinations, executions, and murders of Iranian civilians, and Amnesty International, *Iran Violations of Human Rights: Documents Sent by Amnesty International to the Government of the Islamic Republic of Iran* (London: Amnesty International Publications, 1987).

84. Schlesinger, *The Disuniting of America*.

85. Samuel Johnson, *Idler* #11, June 24, 1758.

86. Samuel Johnson, *Idler* # 87, December 15, 1759.

87. Arthur Herman, *How the Scots Invented the Modern World* (New York: Three Rivers Press, 2001), pp. 104–105.

88. James Boswell, *The Life of Johnson*, ed. R. W. Chapman (1904; reprint, Oxford: Oxford University Press, 1983), pp. 876–78:

> [Johnson] had always been very zealous against slavery in every form. . . . Upon one occasion, when in company with some very grave men at Oxford, his toast was, "Here's to the next insurrection of the negroes in the West Indies." His vio-

lent prejudice against our West Indian and American settlers appeared whenever there was an opportunity. Towards the conclusion of "How is it that we hear the loudest *yelps* for liberty among the drivers of negroes?" . . . The argument dictated by Dr. Johnson was as follows. It must be agreed that in most ages many countries have had part of their inhabitants in a state of slavery; yet it may be doubted whether slavery can ever be supposed the natural condition of man. It is impossible not to conceive that men in their original state were equal; and very difficult to imagine how one would be subjected to another but by violent compulsion. An individual may, indeed, forfeit his liberty by a crime; but he cannot by that crime forfeit the liberty of his children. What is true of a criminal seems true likewise of a captive. A man may accept life from a conquering enemy on condition of perpetual servitude; but it is very doubtful whether he can entail that servitude on his descendants; for no man can stipulate without commission for another. The condition which he himself accepts, his son or grandson would have rejected. If we should admit, what perhaps with more reason be denied, that there are certain relations between man and man which may make slavery necessary and just, yet it can never be proved that he who is now suing for his freedom ever stood in any of those relations. He is certainly subject by no law, but that of violence, to his present master; who pretends no claim to his obedience, but that he bought him from a merchant of slaves, whose right to sell him never was examined. It is said that, according to the constitutions of Jamaica, he was legally enslaved; these constitutions are merely positive; and apparently injurious to the rights of mankind, because whoever is exposed to sale is condemned to slavery without appeal; by whatever fraud or violence he might have been originally brought into the merchant's power. In our own time Princes have been sold, by wretches to whose care they were entrusted, that they might have a European education; but when once they were brought to a market in the plantations, little would avail either their dignity or their wrongs. The laws of Jamaica afford a Negro no redress. His colour is considered as sufficient testimony against him. It is to be lamented that moral right should ever give way to political convenience. But if temptations of interest are sometimes too strong for human virtue, let us at least retain a virtue where there is no temptation to quit it. In the present case there is apparent right on one side, and no convenience on the other. Inhabitants of this island can neither gain riches nor power by taking away the liberty of any part of the human species. The sum of the argument is this:—No man is by nature the property of another: The defendant is, therefore, by nature free: The rights of nature must be some way forfeited before they can be justly taken away: That the defendant has by any act forfeited the rights of nature we require to be proved; and if no proof of such forfeiture can be given, we doubt not but the justice of the court will declare him free.

89. Laurence Sterne, "Reply to Sancho. July 27, 1766," quoted in *The Norton Anthology of English Literature: The Restoration and the Eighteenth Century* (New York: Norton, 2000), p. 2808.

90. Quoted in Vincent Carretta, ed., *Unchained Voices* (Lexington: University Press of Kentucky, 1996), p. 6, and in turn quoted in Roy Porter, *Enlightenment: Britain and the Creation of the Modern World* (London: Penguin, 2001), p. 360.

91. Priestly quoted in Porter, *Enlightenment*, p. 360.

92. Priestley and Bentham, quoted in ibid.

93. Quoted in Carretta, *Unchained Voices*, p. 5, and quoted in Porter, *Enlightenment*, p. 360.

94. R. B. Sheridan, "On the Abolition of Slavery: House of Commons, 17th March 1807," in *The Speeches of the Right Honourable Richard Brinsley Sheridan. With a Sketch of His Life. Edited by a Constitutional Friend*, 3 vols. (London, 1842). This "Constitutional Friend" reports the speeches in the third person, though the first-person pronoun is still occasionally used, as if the oration were unmediated. This method does cause some slight confusion, and the reader should thus be aware that "he" is often Sheridan himself:

> Mr. Sheridan having anxiously expected that the bill passed the preceding night was the preamble of the ultimate measure of emancipation, thought that he should be guilty of the grossest inconsistency in giving a silent vote on the present question. With these sentiments he need scarcely say, that the noble earl had his thanks for having directed the attention of the house to this important subject, even at that early period. The noble earl's statement had been misrepresented. He had never proposed to enfranchise the living negroes; his measure, as he understood him, was to commence with infants born after a period, which would remain a matter of future parliamentary discussion. The planters were entitled to fair dealing on this subject. If the house meant to say, that by abolishing the slave trade they had done all that duty demanded, and that they would leave the emancipation of the slaves to the hazard of fortuitous circumstances, let them be explicit, and say so; but if there lurked in any man's mind a secret desire to proceed in that business, a secret conviction that more ought to be done than had been done, it was unmanly, it was dishonourable, not to speak out. For one he would boldly declare that he had further views; he hoped that the young nobleman who had done his feelings so much credit, by the proposition which he had that evening made, would stand to his ground. If he persevered in the pursuit of his object with the same zeal as his right honourable friend opposite had done, he had no doubt that he would meet with the same success. An honourable baronet had talked of a cloven foot; he pleaded guilty to the cloven foot, but he would say that of the man who expressed pleasure at the hope of seeing so large a portion of the human race freed from the shackles of tyranny; it ought rather to be said, that he had displayed the pennon of an angel than the cloven foot of a demon. It was true no immediate connection existed between the abo-

lition of the slave trade and the abolition of slavery, but the same feelings must be roused by the consideration of both questions; and he who detested the one practice must also detest the other. He did not like to hear the term property applied to the subjects of a free country. Could man become the property of man? A colony emancipating from the free constitution of England must carry with it the principles of that constitution, and could no more shake off its well known allegiance to the constitution than it could shake off its allegiance to its sovereign. He trusted that the planters might be induced to lead the way on the subject of emancipation; but he cautioned the house against being too sanguine on the subject. Were the planters themselves always resident on the islands, he should have greater hopes; but it was not probable that because cargoes of human misery were no longer to be landed on their shores, that because their eyes were to be no longer glutted with the sight of human suffering, or their ears pierced with the cries of human distraction in any further importation of negroes, that the slave-drivers would soon forget their fixed habits of brutality, and learn to treat the unhappy wretches in their charge with clemency and compassion. Slavery would not wear itself out; it would become more rigid, unless the legislature became more vigilant, and reminded the planters of the new duty that had fallen upon them, of rearing the young slaves in such a manner, that they might be worthy of freedom. Adverting to the quotation from Gibbon, he contended, that the slavery of the West Indies was unlike any other slavery; it was peculiarly unlike the slavery of ancient days, when the slaves frequently attained to the highest dignities; Aesop, Terence, and Seneca were slaves. Was there a possibility that any of the unfortunate negroes now in the West Indies should emulate such men? It might be dangerous to give freedom to the slaves in a mass, but that it was not dangerous to give it to them in detail, was sufficiently proved by a little pamphlet that had been put into his hands the preceding night, in which it was stated, that a Mr. David Barclay, to his eternal honour be it spoken, who had himself been a slave-owner in Jamaica, and who, regretting that he had been so, on a bequest of slaves being made to him, emancipated them, caused them to be conveyed to Pennsylvania, where they were properly instructed, and where their subsequent exemplary conduct was the general theme of admiration. With this fact before him, should he be told that he must give up all hope of abolishing slavery! No, he would never give it up. He would exclaim with the poet, in the words of the motto of the pamphlet which he had mentioned,

"I would not have a slave to till my ground,
"To fan me while I sleep, and tremble when
"I wake, for all that human sinews bought
"And sold, have ever earn'd."

95. Douglass could have been confused on this point since Sheridan's speech in *The Columbian Orator* does not mention slavery at all. He must have read Sheridan's celebrated antislavery speech elsewhere; quoted above.

96. Quoted in Caleb Bingham, ed., *The Columbian Orator*, rev. Val J. Halamandaris (1979; reprint, Washington, DC: Caring Publishing, 1997), p. ix.

97. Adam Smith, *An Inquiry into the Nature and Causes of the Wealth of Nations*, ed. Edwin Cannan, 5th ed. (London: Methuen, 1904), bk. 4, chap. 7, *Of Colonies*, paragraph 152 (quoted by Keith Windschuttle, "Liberalism and Imperialism," in *The Betrayal of Liberalism*, ed. Hilton Kramer and Roger Kimball [Chicago: Ivan R. Dee, 1999], p. 71):

> To propose that Great Britain should voluntarily give up all authority over her colonies, and leave them to elect their own magistrates, to enact their own laws, and to make peace and war as they might think proper, would be to propose such a measure as never was, and never will be adopted, by any nation in the world. . . . If it was adopted, however, Great Britain would not only be immediately freed from the whole annual expense of the peace establishment of the colonies, but might settle with them such a treaty of commerce as could effectually secure to her a free trade, more advantageous to the great body of the people, though less so to the merchants, than the monopoly which she at present enjoys. . . . [I]nstead of turbulent and factious subjects, [they would] become our most faithful, affectionate, and generous allies; and the same sort of parental affection on the one side, and filial respect on the other, might revive between Great Britain and her colonies, which used to subsist between those of ancient Greece and the mother city from which they descended.

98. Jonathan Swift, *Gulliver's Travels* (London, 1726; reprint, Harmondsworth, UK: Penguin, 1985), p. 243.

99. George Birkbeck Hill, *Boswell's Life of Johnson* (Oxford: Clarendon,1934–50), vol. 1, p. 308; Jeremy Bentham, "Emancipate Your Colonies," in *The Works of Jeremy Bentham*, ed. John Bowring (1843; reprint, Bristol: Thoemmes Press, 1995), vol. 4, p. 407; quoted in Porter, *Enlightenment*, p. 355.

100. John Malcolm Ludlow, *British India, Its Races, and Its History, Considered with Reference to the Mutinies of 1857: A Series of Lectures Addressed to the Students of the Workingmen's College*, 2 vols. (Cambridge: Macmillan, 1858), vol. 1, p. 172.

101. Ibid., p. 198.

102. Windschuttle, "Liberalism and Imperialism," pp. 73–74:

> Many of them write as if they believe the critique of imperialism first emerged among its colonized subjects as a protest at their bondage. The most they concede to the Western side of the equation is that anti-imperialism also arose within Marxism, especially Lenin's book *Imperialism: The Highest Stage of Capitalism* (1917). (Marx himself, some are aware, was in favour of British rule

in India, which he thought would hasten the world revolution.)

The reality, however, is quite different. Since the Middle Ages, the merits of imperialism have been the subject of an extensive debate within Western culture. Much of this debate has been sharply polarized and there have been few times and places in which a favorable policy has been unequivocally endorsed. For most of the past millennium, argument has focused on the political consequences of empire, but since the seventeenth century it has also been a matter of sustained debate about economic policy. Over the last two hundred years, the intellectual tradition that has raised the most objections to imperialism has been not Marxism but liberalism. Indeed, Lenin's work on the subject is no more than a thinly modified expropriation of the book *Imperialism: A Study* published in 1902 by the English liberal writer J. A. Hobson. One of the ironies of the debate in the 1990s is that the author [Mark Crocker] of *Rivers of Blood, Rivers of Gold* [which argues that its imperial record has cost Europe its claim to being civilized] is a journalist on *The Guardian* newspaper in England, which in the nineteenth century and for most of the twentieth was known as *The Manchester Guardian*. Under this name, it was a liberal, anti-imperialist journal whose record provides an effective counterexample to the one-dimensional, ahistorical caricature of the story told by writers like Said, Bhabha, Spivak, and Mark Crocker himself.

103. David Alfred, ed., *The Norton Anthology of English Literature: The Middle Ages* (New York: Norton, 2000), p. 317, describes *Piers Plowman* in this manner: "The poet describes fourteenth-century English society in terms of its failure to represent an ideal society living in accord with Christian principles; hence the satirical poetry for which Langland is noted. Society's failure, of course, is attributable in part to the corruption of the church and ecclesiastics, and whenever he considers clerical corruption, he pours out savagely indignant satire. But he is equally angry with the failure of the wealthy laity—untaught by the church to practice charity—to alleviate the sufferings of the poor."

104. Lionel Trilling, *The Liberal Imagination* (Garden City, NY: Doubleday, 1950).

105. Arnold, *Culture and Anarchy*, preface.

106. David Pryce-Jones, *The Closed Circle: An Interpretation of the Arabs* (London: Paladin Grafton, 1990), p. 34.

107. Ibid., p. 35.

108. Personal communication with the author, 1998.

109. Pipes, *The Hidden Hand*, p. 26.

110. Czeslaw Milosz, *The Captive Mind* (New York: Vintage, 1959), pp. 54–55.

111. I owe this reference to Professor Fred Siegel of the Cooper Union for Science and Art in New York.

112. Barry Rubin, *The Long War for Freedom: The Arab Struggle for Democracy in the Middle East* (Hoboken, NJ: Wiley, 2006), p. 16.

113. Ibid., p. 17.

114. Ibid., pp. 80–81. Rubin is quoting from the following works of Al-Afif al-Akhdar: "How Our Narcissistic Wound and Religious Narcissism Combine to Destroy Our Future"; "Why Religious Narcissism is the Golden Collar [Obstructing] Our Assimilation into the Modern Age"; "Irrational Religious Education is the Obstacle to the [Arabs'] Joining the Modern Age," http://www.elaph.com.:9090/elaph/arabic (June 15, 16, and 23, 2003) translation in MEMRI, no. 576, http://www.memri.org/bin/articles.cgi?Page=archives&ID=SP57603 (September 21, 2003).

115. Rubin, *The Long War for Freedom*, pp. 85, quoting Tarek Heggy, "Comments on the Required Change in Egypt," *Watani*, December 22 and 29, 2002. (*Watani* is an Egyptian weekly Sunday newspaper published in Cairo.)

116. Ibid., p. 26.

117. Ibid., pp. 41–42.

Chapter 2: Classical Antiquity

1. Charles H. Kahn, *The Art and Thought of Heraclitus* (Cambridge: Cambridge University Press, 1979), pp. 29.III and 31.VI. Kahn has his own numbering for the fragments, indicated in Roman numerals.

2. H. C. Baldry, *The Unity of Mankind in Greek Thought* (Cambridge: Cambridge University Press, 1965).

3. Ibid., p. 5.

4. Ibid., p. 122.

5. Homer, *Odyssey*, trans. Stanley Lombardo (Indianapolis: Hackett, 2000), IV.125–132.

6. Homer, *Iliad*, XIII.6.

7. Homer, *Odyssey*, I.22–24; see also *Odyssey*, V.282.

8. Homer, *Odyssey*, trans. Robert Fitzgerald (New York: Doubleday Anchor, 1963), bk. 18, lnn. 129–137, p. 340.

9. Baldry, *The Unity of Mankind in Greek Thought*, p. 12.

10. A. A. Parry, "Blameless Aegisthus: A Study of AMYMON and other Homeric Epithets," in *Mnemosyne*, supp. 26 (Leiden: Brill, 1973), pp. 156–57; referred to by Frank Snowden Jr., *Before Color Prejudice: The Ancient View of Blacks* (Cambridge, MA: Harvard University Press, 1983), p. 125, n49.

11. Robert Drews, *The Greek Accounts of Eastern History* (Cambridge, MA: Harvard University Press, 1973); Drews's footnote: High regard for Lydia: Alcman, no. 24, and Sappho, no. 85 (ed. Bergck); and Archilocus, no. 22 (this and subsequent citations of the lyric poets, unless otherwise noted, follow the edition of Ernst Diehl, *Anthologia Lyrica Graeca*, vols. 1 and 2 [Leipzig, 1924–25]. Alcaeus's brother, Antimenidas, fought at Babylon as a mercenary (Alcaeus, no. 50; cf. Strabo XIII 2,3).

12. Drews's footnote: This is well documented and discussed by Hans Schwabl, "Das Bild der fremden Welt bei den frühen Griechen," in *Grecs et Barbares* (Vandoeuvres: Fondation Hardt, 1962), pp. 18–23. It may seem somewhat strange that the Greeks

should have used one word to describe both their primitive neighbours to the north and highly civilized Eastern neighbours. See Julius Jüthner, *Hellenen und Barbaren* (Leipzig, 1923).

13. Drews, *The Greek Accounts of Eastern History*, p. 5.

14. Ibid., p. 15.

15. Ibid., p. 16.

16. Ibid.

17. Baldry, *The Unity of Mankind in Greek Thought*, p. 18; emphasis mine.

18. Byron, *Don Juan*, canto 16, lines 1–5, is alluding to Herodotus, book I.136: "Their sons are educated from the time they are five years old until they are twenty, but they study only three things: horsemanship, archery, and honesty."

19. Fragments 169, 215 Bergk. Cf. fr. 43, quoted in Baldry, *The Unity of Mankind in Greek Thought*, p. 19.

20. Drews, *The Greek Accounts of Eastern History*, p. 31.

21. Ibid., p. 79.

22. Ibid., p. 107.

23. Martin Braun, *History and Romance in Graeco-Oriental Literature* (Oxford: Oxford University Press, 1938), referred to by Drews, *The Greek Accounts of Eastern History*, p. 179, n115.

24. Ludlow Bull, "Ancient Egypt," in *The Idea of History in the Ancient Near East*, ed. R. Dentan (New Haven, CT: Yale University Press, 1955), p. 3; quoted in Drews, *The Greek Accounts of Eastern History*, p. 187, n137.

25. Hermann Kees, *Kulturgeschichte des alten Orients: Agypten* (Munich: Beck, 1933), pp. 285–89; referred to by Drews, *The Greek Accounts of Eastern History*, p. 187, n137.

26. Baldry, *The Unity of Mankind in Greek Thought*, p. 21.

27. Drews, *The Greek Accounts of Eastern History*, pp. 86–87.

28. Ibid., p. 64.

29. Herodotus's travels summarized by J. P. A. Gould in *The Oxford Classical Dictionary*, ed. Simon Hornblower and Antony Spawforth (Oxford: Oxford University Press, 1999), p. 697.

30. W. W. How and J. Wells, *A Commentary on Herodotus* (1912; reprint, Oxford: Oxford University Press, 1964), vol. 1, p. 38.

31. All summarized in ibid., pp. 37–38.

32. Herodotus, *The Histories*, i.123, trans. Robin Waterfield (Oxford: Oxford University Press, 1998), p. 57.

33. Ibid., p. 60.

34. Ibid., p. 62.

35. Ibid., pp. 62–63.

36. F. Jacoby, *Fragmente der griechischen Historiker*, 15 vols. (Berlin, 1923–50; reprint, Brill Academic Publishers, 2005).

37. Drews, *The Greek Accounts of Eastern History*, p. 126.

38. Ibid., p. 126, quoting Diodorus Siculus, I 71, 5.

39. Martha Nussbaum, "Heraclitus," in *The Oxford Classical Dictionary*, 3rd ed., ed. Simon Hornblower and Antony Spawforth (Oxford: Oxford University Press, 1999), p. 687.

40. Fragment 114, in Diels-Kranz, *Die Fragmente der Vorsokratiker*, 6th ed. (1951; reprint, Zurich: Weidmann, 1985).

41. Aeschylus, *Prometheus Bound*, trans. George Thomson (Mineola, NY: Dover, 1995), p. 20.

42. Helen H. Bacon, *Barbarians in Greek Tragedy* (New Haven, CT: Yale University Press, 1961), p. 4.

43. Ibid., p. 12.

44. Ibid., pp. 62–63.

45. Ibid., p. 28.

46. Ibid., p. 34.

47. Ibid., pp. 39–40.

48. H. D. Broadhead, *The Persae of Aeschylus. With Introduction, Critical Notes and Commentary* (Cambridge: Cambridge University Press, 1960), p. xvi.

49. Ibid., p. xvii.

50. Ibid., pp. xvii–xviii:

> It is an idealised Darius that Aeschylus has portrayed: the blameless father is a foil to his erring son, and the mouthpiece of the philosopher-poet. We might almost say that the facts have been altered so as to fit into the dramatist's theological framework. Xerxes too has been changed, though to a much smaller extent. We know from Herodotus that in preparing the expedition against Greece he was only carrying out his father's express design; yet Darius in the play censures his son for his rashness and impious daring. . . . This manner of handling the historical facts itself suggests that as a dramatist he has adopted a (for the most part at least) supra-national attitude: he has treated the Persian in much the same way as he would have treated the Greek in similar circumstances; from the particular he has distilled the universal.

51. Ibid., p. xviii:

> [T]here is no suggestion that the Persians were not gallant and courageous fighters. On the contrary, it is a reasonable inference from the tribute paid to Syennesis (326–8) that there were many brave warriors who caused great havoc to their foes. In 337f. we learn that in respect of numbers the Persians had an enormous superiority, and had every reason to expect victory; but it is constantly stressed that the gods were against them [345, 354, 362, 373].

52. Ibid., p. xix.

53. H. W. Smyth, *Aeschylean Tragedy* (Berkeley: University of California Press, 1924), p. 70.

54. Broadhead, p. xxiii, quoting Aeschylus, *The Persians*, trans. G. Murray (Oxford: Oxford University Press, 1939), p. 92.

55. Broadhead, *The Persae of Aeschylus*, p. xxv.

56. Ibid., p. xxviii.

57. Ibid., pp. xxix–xxxii.

58. Aeschylus, *The Suppliant Maidens: The Persians*, trans. and intro. Seth G. Benardete (Chicago: University of Chicago Press, 1956), pp. 44–45.

59. Sophocles, *Ajax*, trans. R. C. Trevelyan, in *Complete Greek Drama*, ed. W. J. Oates and Eugene O'Neill Jr., vol.1 (New York: Random House, 1938), ln. 1290–99, p. 356.

60. Baldry, *The Unity of Mankind in Greek Thought*, p. 37.

61. Ibid.

62. Ibid., p. 33.

63. Drews, *The Greek Accounts of Eastern History*, p. 83; referring to J. Wells, *Studies in Herodotus* (Oxford: Basil Blackwell, 1923), pp. 95–111.

64. Baldry, *The Unity of Mankind in Greek Thought*, p. 34, quoting ln. 53–58.

65. Ibid., p. 34.

66. Ibid., p. 35.

67. Ibid., p. 44.

68. Ibid., p. 60.

69. "Mercenaries," in *The Oxford Classical Dictionary*, 3rd ed., ed. Simon Hornblower and Antony Spawforth (Oxford: Oxford University Press, 1999), p. 961.

70. Xenophon, Anabasis, I.9.28, quoted in Baldry, *The Unity of Mankind in Greek Thought*, p. 65.

71. In the article on Xenophon in *The Oxford Classical Dictionary*, there is a cross-reference to an article on Orientalism.

72. Simon Hornblower and Antony Spawforth, eds., *The Oxford Classical Dictionary*, 3rd ed. (Oxford: Oxford University Press, 1999), p. 1629.

73. T. J. Haarhoff, *The Stranger at the Gate* (Oxford: Basil Blackwell, 1948), p. 58.

74. Baldry, *The Unity of Mankind in Greek Thought*, p. 66.

75. Isocrates, *Panegyricus*, 50, quoted in Baldry, *The Unity of Mankind in Greek Thought*, p. 69.

76. Plato, *The Statesman*, 262c–d, quoted in Baldry, *The Unity of Mankind in Greek Thought*, p. 82.

77. Baldry, *The Unity of Mankind in Greek Thought*, p. 83.

78. "Aristotle's Will," in *Complete Works*, ed. Jonathan Barnes (Princeton, NJ: Princeton University Press, 1985), vol. 2, p. 2464.

79. John Moles, "Cynic Cosmopolitanism," in *The Cynics: The Cynic Movement in Antiquity and Its Legacy*, ed. R. Bracht Branham and Marie-Odile Goulet-Cazé (Berkeley and Los Angeles: University of California Press, 1996), pp. 105–20.

80. Ibid., p. 107.

81. Ibid., p. 111.
82. Ibid., p. 113.
83. Ibid., p. 115.
84. Ibid., p. 118.
85. Ibid., p. 119.
86. E.g., Nancy J. Burich, *Alexander the Great: A Bibliography* (Kent, OH: Kent State University Press, 1970).
87. W. W. Tarn, *Alexander the Great*, 2nd ed. (Boston: Beacon Press 1956), pp. 147–48.
88. Baldry, *The Unity of Mankind in Greek Thought*, pp. 120–21.
89. Ibid., p. 127.
90. Robin Lane Fox, *Alexander the Great* (New York: Penguin, 2004), pp. 25–26.
91. Ibid., p. 50:

> From the newly conquered gold mines on his eastern border, there was a sudden flood of gold to attract Greek artists, secretaries, doctors of the Hippocratic school, philosophers, musicians and engineers in the best tradition of the Macedonian monarchy. They came from all over the Aegean world, a secretary from the Hellespont, painters from Asia Minor, a prophet, even, from distant Lycia, who wrote a book on the proper interpretation of omens; there were also, as befitted him, the court fools. . . . As Alexander grew up, he could talk with a man who had lived in Egypt or with a sophist and secretary from Greek towns on the Dardanelles: in the late 350s, the exiled Persian satrap Artabazus brought his family to Pella from Hellespontine Asia and here Alexander would have met his beautiful daughter Barsine for the first time. Some ten years older than Alexander she could never have guessed that after two marriages to Greek brothers in Persian service, she would return to this boy among the spoils of a Persian victory and be honoured as his mistress, while her father Artabazus would later surrender near the Caspian Sea and be rewarded with Iranian satrapies in Alexander's empire. Barsine's visit had started a very strange trail for the future. No contact was more useful than this bilingual family of Persian generals whom Alexander finally took back on to his staff in Asia.

92. Ibid., pp. 141–42:

> In the Caicus valley, for example, the colonists from distant Hyrcania, who had fought with their satrap at the Granicus, lived on in the land called the Hyrcanian Plain, where Cyrus had settled them two centuries earlier but over the years their villages would be merged into a town and mixed with Macedonians. Their traditional fire-worship continued, but when they appear in Roman history, it is as citizens dressed and armed in the style of Macedonian westerners. . . . It was thus among Iranians of the former empire that this mood of Alexander's passing

> made itself most felt. Repeatedly in the next hundred years, Iranians who lived on in Asia Minor are known to have joined the councils and magistracies of the Greek cities whose future Alexander had underwritten, a life of civic duty which contrasted with baronial isolation of their past. Only their religion remained as a solid landmark in a changed world. The worship of the water goddess Anahita was continued by the magi who met to read their sacred texts among assemblies of the Iranian faithful in the hinterland of Greek Asia. An Iranian could no longer be sure of his country tower, but he could still find a place in his goddess's worship; an Iranian eunuch was left to run the temple affairs of Artemis at Ephesus, and in a small Carian town in Alexander's lifetime two Iranians became honorary citizens in order to serve as priests of Anahita, whom the Greeks saw as Artemis, a job for which their background suited them and which they passed from father to son for another three generations.

93. N. G. L. Hammond, *The Genius of Alexander the Great* (Chapel Hill: University of North Carolina Press, 1997), pp. 123–25.

94. Ibid., p. 188:

> Alexander's chivalry towards the Persian Queen Mother and towards the Sogdian princess, Roxane, whom he did not rape but married, made a great impression on the Asian aristocracy. In 324 at Susa he arranged the weddings of more than eighty Persian, Median and Bactrian aristocrats to the leading Macedonians. A daughter of Darius and a daughter of his predecessor, Artaxerxes Ochus, were taken in marriage by Alexander. The weddings were conducted in the Persian manner, in which the bridegroom kissed the bride. Also at Susa Alexander converted into official marriages the liasions which some 10,000 Macedonian soldiers had formed with Asian women; and he gave them wedding presents. It was known that many Macedonians owed money to Asian traders, who had little hope of recovering it. Alexander paid the money *in toto* without requiring the soldiers in debt to reveal their identity. In all these ways Alexander was treating his Macedonians and his Asians as equals in status and in obligation.

95. Ibid., p. 190:

> The Macedonians sat with him; and next to them were the Persians and representatives of the other races in Asia. The Greek diviners and the Persian Magi pronounced the omens favourable. Alexander "prayed especially for concord and for the sharing of the rule between Macedonians and Persians." All who were present poured the same libation and sang the victory song. It was the triumph of Alexander's Asian policy. Macedonians and Asians were to share as equals in the administration of the Kingdom of Asia.

96. Lane Fox, *Alexander the Great*, p. 333.

97. Ibid., p. 386.

98. Hammond, *The Genius of Alexander the Great*, p. 128:

> Scientific exploration was also a part of Alexander's plans. He was already in a part of the world which was largely unknown to Greek scientists. Thus he had been able to investigate the strange behaviour of the river Stiboetes (now Chesmeh-i-Ali) which flowed in and out of underground channels in Hyrcania and to send back to Greece a report, of which a summary is preserved in accounts by Diodorus and Curtius. There is no doubt that he and his scientists and surveyors were in regular correspondence with Aristotle. It was probably in 330 that Alexander sent to him the huge sum of 800 talents, with which Aristotle was able to found in Athens for the first time in history a great library of literary texts on papyrus and to make the first collection of specimens for teaching (especially in the field of zoology). The advance eastwards was to provide a wealth of new discoveries.

99. Lionel Pearson, *The Lost Histories of Alexander the Great* (Oxford: Basil Blackwell, 1960), p. v.

100. Ibid., p. 86.

101. Ibid., p. 102.

102. Ibid., p. 160.

103. Ibid., p. 180.

104. Ibid., p. 175.

105. Ibid., p. 177.

106. Ibid., p. 176.

107. Ibid., pp. 3, 176.

108. Arrian, *Anabasis Alexandri*, trans. P. A. Brunt (Cambridge, MA: Harvard University Press, 1976), vol. 1, pp. 207–11.

109. Lane Fox, *Alexander the Great*, pp. 349–50:

> Legend could hardly leave this meeting between East and West as it had happened. The theme was embellished with variations and for two thousand years, the name of the Gymnosophists, or Naked Philosophers, remained part of the common culture of lettered men. In India their meetings with Alexander passed through his Romance into the Sayings of Milinda, a classic Buddhist text; in the Mediterranean, they were prominent in the works and poems of scholars in Renaissance Florence; in England, after the death of Cromwell, Puritan gentlemen still pinned their revolutionary fervour on the Gymnosophists' ideal, praising the Indians in pamphlets for being Puritans before their time, and denouncing Alexander as the type of a monarch like Charles II. The Gymnosophists' fame had spread far beyond their town by the Murree hills, and all

because a pupil of Aristotle had crossed the Hindu Kush in search of the eastern Ocean and a pupil of Diogenes had left the boats on his native island of Cos, joined the expedition and agreed, in India, to go out in the midday sun.

110. J. W. McCrindle, *McCrindle's Ancient India: As Described by Megasthenes and Arrian*, ed. Ramchandra Jain (1877; reprint, New Delhi: Today and Tomorrow's Printers & Publishers, 1972), pp. v–vi.

111. Ibid., p. 31.

112. Ibid., p. 40.

113. Ibid., pp. 44–45.

114. P. Briant, "Colonization, Hellenistic," in *The Oxford Classical Dictionary*, 3rd ed., ed. Simon Hornblower and Antony Spawforth (Oxford: Oxford University Press, 1999), p. 363.

115. S. Sherwin-White and G. T. Griffith, "Seleucus I," in *The Oxford Classical Dictionary*, 3rd ed., ed. Simon Hornblower and Antony Spawforth (Oxford: Oxford University Press, 1999), p. 1381.

116. A. K. Narain and Romila Thapar, "Sandracottus," in *The Oxford Classical Dictionary*, 3rd ed., ed. Simon Hornblower and Antony Spawforth (Oxford: Oxford University Press, 1999), pp. 1353–54.

117. A. K. Narain, *The Indo-Greeks: Revisited and Supplemented* (Delhi: B. R. Publishing, 2003).

118. Ibid., p. 3.

119. A. L. Basham, *The Wonder That Was India* (New York: Grove Press, 1964); *A Cultural History of India* (Oxford: Oxford University Press, 1975).

120. W. W. Tarn, *The Greeks in Bactria and India*, 2nd ed. (Cambridge: Cambridge University Press, 1951).

121. Narain, *The Indo-Greeks*, p. 483.

122. Ibid., p. 484.

123. Ibid., p. 10.

124. Ibid.

125. Ibid., p. 12.

126. Ibid., p. 13.

127. Diodorus Siculus, xvii.110.4–5; Curtius vii.5–29, quoted in Narain, *The Indo-Greeks*, p. 250.

128. E. R. Bevan, *The House of Seleucus*, 2 vols. (London, Edward Arnold: 1902), p. 287, quoted in Narain, *The Indo-Greeks*, p. 15.

129. Narain, *The Indo-Greeks*, p. 253.

130. Ibid., p. 260.

131. Ibid.

132. Since the Ionians were either the first or the most dominant group among the Greeks with whom the Persians came into contact, they called them *Yauna*, and the Indians referred to them as *Yona* and *Yavana*. For Panini, the Grammarian of Gandhara,

in the fifth century BCE, their script was *Yavanani.*

133. Narain, *The Indo-Greeks*, pp. 264–65.

134. *Questions of King Milinda*, trans. T. W. Rhys Davids, vol. 35 of *The Sacred Books of the East* (Oxford: Clarendon, 1890):

> Of the two the novice became the king of the city of Sâgala in India, Milinda by name, learned, eloquent, wise, and able; and a faithful observer, and that at the right time, of all the various acts of devotion and ceremony enjoined by his own sacred hymns concerning things past, present, and to come. Many were the arts and sciences he knew—holy tradition and secular law; the Sânkhya, Yoga, Nyâya, and Vaiseshika systems of philosophy; arithmetic; music; medicine; the four Vedas, the Purânas, and the Itihâsas; astronomy, magic, causation, and spells; the art of war; poetry; conveyancing in a word, the whole nineteen. As a disputant he was hard to equal, harder still to overcome; the acknowledged superior of all the founders of the various schools of thought. And as in wisdom so in strength of body, swiftness, and valour there was found none equal to Milinda in all India. He was rich too, mighty in wealth and prosperity, and the number of his armed hosts knew no end.

135. Plutarch, *Moralia* 821 D–F.

136. Narain, *The Indo-Greeks*, pp. 269–70.

137. Ibid., p. 276.

138. P. Bernard, *Fouilles d'Aï Khanoum I.* Campagnes 1965, 1966, 1967, 1968, 2 vols., MDAFA XXI (Paris, 1973); H.-P. Francfort, *Fouilles d'Aï Khanoum*, MDAFA XXVII (Paris, 1984); C. Rapin, *La Trésorie du Palais Hellenistique d'Aï Khanoum* (Paris, 1992). Since the mid-1960s, excavations at Aï Khanum have been conducted by the French Archaeological Delegation under the direction first of D. Schlumberger, and since 1965 under Paul Bernard. Excavations continued until the late 1970s when the political situation made archaeological research impossible.

139. Malcolm Colledge, "Greek and Non-Greek Interaction in the Art and Architecture of the Hellenistic East," in *Hellenism in the East: The Interaction of Greek and Non-Greek Civilizations from Syria to Central Asia after Alexander*, ed. Amélie Kuhrt and Susan Sherwin-White (London: Duckworth, 1987), p. 144:

> The occurrence at the Greek settlement at Ai Khanum of Mesopotamian temple architecture is very remarkable and deserves to be fully stressed. Here, in a sanctuary on the main north-south street inside the city stood an almost square temple, the earliest phase of which (phase V) belongs to the late fourth or early third century BCE. It had thick walls, a simple plan, with a vestibule (antecella) and hall (cella) each occupying the full width of the structure and entered through the middle of one long side; it stood on a raised podium which itself was set on a platform. This is an example of the ancient Mesopotamian 'broad

room' temple type, current already in later fourth millennium BCE and to remain popular in western Asia from the third century BCE for about five hundred years; from its later ornamentation it is known as the indented temple. . . . But why here? Various suggestions have been made such as that it was the result of the influence of Mesopotamian colonists among the settlers, or that it may be an Iranian development which was adopted. The local production of figurines and pottery continued, indicating perhaps the mixed character of the population of the city. Apart from the Greek and Mesopotamian styles, a "mixed" style is represented most notably in a grand administrative complex, doubtless the governor's palace. To the early period belong an imposing colonnaded court, corridors and rooms. The peristyle court, and much architectural decoration are Greek in origin. But there are non-Greek features: the use of the court as a passageway, of flat roofing, of Persian-type limestone column bases, whose orthogonal planning and associated corridors recall Assyrian and Persian palace designs, and particularly the so-called Harem of Xerxes at Persepolis. . . . Its scale, and reminiscences of Persian predecessors, . . . illuminate hellenistic royal ideology: its blending of Greek and Achaemenid imperial styles symbolised both the change wrought by conquest and the political traditions to which it was heir. . . . To sum up, the same kinds of artistic production continued under and were encouraged by Seleucus: selected Greek, Mesopotamian and Achaemenid elements and the development of the new style which combined Greek and a variety of local artistic traditions. The juxtaposition of Greek and Achaemenid elements is exemplified in the Ai Khanum palace, while an interchange of styles appears in the darics; and actual blending occurs in the Ai Khanum palace layout and the lion stater coins.

140. F. L. Holt, "Menander 'Soter,'" in *The Oxford Classical Dictionary*, 3rd ed., ed. Simon Hornblower and Antony Spawforth (Oxford: Oxford University Press, 1999), p. 957.

141. Ibid.

142. Frank Snowden Jr., *Blacks in Antiquity* (Cambridge, MA: Harvard University Press, 1970); *Before Color Prejudice*.

143. Snowden, *Blacks in Antiquity*, p. 216.

144. Snowden, *Before Color Prejudice*, p. 15, referring to Aristotle, *De generatione animalium*, 1.18.722a; *Historia animalium*, 7.6.585b.

145. Herodotus, II.137.

146. Herodotus, III.20.

147. Virgil, *Aeneid*, bk. 1.488–489, trans. W. F. Jackson Knight (Harmondsworth, UK: Penguin, 1958), p. 42.

148. Snowden, *Before Color Prejudice*, pp. 58–59: "It is important to emphasize that the overall, but especially more detailed Graeco-Roman view of blacks was highly positive. Initial, favorable impressions were not altered, in spite of later accounts of wild tribes

in the far south and even after encounters with blacks had become more frequent. There was clear-cut respect among Mediterranean peoples for Ethiopians and their way of life. And, above all, the ancients did not stereotype all blacks as primitives defective in religion and culture."

149. Ibid., p. 94.

150. Danaus was the son of Belus, the brother of Aegyptus, eponym of the Egyptians, and brother-in-law of Phoenix, eponym of the Phoenicians. Danaus himself is the eponym of the Danaians, used by Homer and other poets to mean the Greeks.

151. Snowden, *Before Color Prejudice*, p. 97.

152. Menahem Stern, *Greek and Latin Authors on Jews and Judaism* (Jerusalem: Israel Academy of Sciences and Humanities, 1974–1984), vol. 1, p. 62.

153. Ibid., p. 8.

154. Hecataeus, *Aegyptica*, apud: Diodorus Siculus, Bibliotheca Historica, XL, 3, quoted in Stern, *Greek and Latin Authors on Jews and Judaism*, vol. 1, pp. 27–28.

155. M. Sordi in *Aufsteig und Niedergang Der Römischen Welt*, ed. Hildegard Temporini and Wolfgang Haase (Berlin and New York: Walter De Gruyter, 1975–) 2.30.1, 1982.

156. Pseudo-Longinus, quoted in Stern, *Greek and Latin Authors on Jews and Judaism*, vol. 1, p. 364.

157. Baldry, *The Unity of Mankind in Greek Thought*, p. 169.

158. Ibid., p. 169, quoting Strabo, I.4.9.

159. Ibid., p. 171.

160. Ibid., p. 188.

161. Cicero, *De legibus*, I. 22–39.

162. Ibid., I. 195–98:

> That justice is based upon nature will be evident, if you fully realise man's fellowship and unity with his fellow men. No two things are so closely and exactly alike as all of us are to each other. If degeneration of habits and false opinions did not prevent the weakness of our minds and turn it aside in whatever direction it begins to stray, no one would be so like himself as all would be like all. Hence, however man is to be defined, one definition is true of all men—proof enough that there is no difference within the species, for if there were, a single definition would not cover all its members. And indeed reason, our sole ground of superiority to the beasts, whereby we are able to form opinions, to prove or disprove, to discuss a point and settle it and draw conclusions—reason is certainly common to all men, variable in what it learns but equal for all in its power to learn. For the same objects are perceived by all men's senses, and the things that affect our senses do so in the same way in every man; the beginnings of understanding are imprinted on all minds alike, and speech, the interpreter of the mind, expresses the same thoughts though the words may differ. There is indeed no one of any race who, given a guide, cannot make his way to virtue.

163. Baldry, *The Unity of Mankind in Greek Thought*, p. 198.

164. Ibid., p. 203.

165. Julia Annas, "Stoicism," in *The Oxford Classical Dictionary* (Oxford: Oxford University Press, 1999), p. 1446.

166. Marcus Aurelius, "Meditations," bk. 4, chap. 4, in *The Stoic and Epicurean Philosophers*, ed. Whitney J. Oates (New York: Random House, 1940), p. 509.

167. Ibid., p. 533.

168. A. A. Long and D. Sedley, *The Hellenistic Philosophers* (Cambridge: Cambridge University Press, 1987), vol. 1, p. 67A.

169. Epictetus, "Discourses," bk. 1, chap. 9, in *The Stoic and Epicurean Philosophers*, ed. Whitney J. Oates (New York: Random House, 1940), pp. 239–40.

170. Lucius Annaeus Seneca, *Moral Essays*, trans. John W. Basore, Loeb Classical Library (London: W. Heinemann, 1928–35), vol. 2, *On Leisure*. bk. IV.1–V.2:

> Let us grasp the idea that there are two commonwealths—the one, a vast and truly common state, which embraces alike gods and men, in which we look neither to this corner of earth nor to that, but measure, the bounds of our citizenship by the path of the sun; the other, the one to which we have been assigned by the accident of birth. This will be the commonwealth of the Athenians or of the Carthaginians, or of any other city that belongs, not to all, but to some particular race of men. Some yield service to both commonwealths at the same time to the greater and to the lesser—some only to the lesser, some only to the greater. This greater commonwealth we are able to serve even in leisure-nay, I am inclined to think, even better in leisure-so that we may inquire what virtue is, and whether it is one or many; whether it is nature or art that makes men good; whether this world, which embraces seas and lands and the things that are contained in the sea and land, is a solitary creation (a) or whether God has strewn about many systems (b) of the same sort; whether all the matter from which everything is formed is continuous and compact (c) or whether it is disjunctive and a void is intermingled with the solid; what God is—whether he idly gazes upon his handiwork, or directs it; whether he encompasses it without, or pervades the whole of it; whether the world is eternal, or is to be counted among the things that perish and are born only for a time. And what service does he who ponders these things render unto god? He keeps the mighty works of God from being without a witness! We are fond of saying that the highest good is to live according to Nature. Nature has begotten us for both purposes—for contemplation and for action. Let me now prove the first statement. But why anything more? Will not this be proved if each one of us shall take counsel simply of himself, and ponder how great is his desire to gain knowledge of the unknown, and how this desire is stirred by tales of every sort?

171. Eric Brown, *Stoic Cosmopolitanism* (Cambridge: Cambridge University Press, forthcoming), but summarized at http://www.artsci.wustl.edu/~eabrown/abstracts.html#cosmo.

Chapter 3: Early Christianity to the Seventeenth Century

1. Hugo Grotius, *The Rights of War and Peace*, Natural Law and Enlightenment Classics (Indianapolis: Liberty Fund, 2005).

2. Charles Freeman, *The Closing of the Western Mind* (New York: Vintage, 2005), p. xix.

3. A. C. Crombie, *Medieval and Early Modern Science: Augustine to Galileo: The History of Science A.D. 400–1650* (New York: Doubleday Anchor, 1959), p. xii.

4. Freeman, *The Closing of the Western Mind*, p. 317.

5. "St. Isidore of Seville," in *Catholic Encyclopaedia*, http://www.newadvent.org/cathen/08186a.htm.

6. "Carolingian Schools," in *The Oxford Dictionary of the Christian Church*, 3rd ed., ed. F. L. Cross and E. A. Livingstone (Oxford: Oxford University Press, 1997), pp. 290–91.

7. "Theodulf," in *The Oxford Dictionary of the Christian Church*, 3rd ed., ed. F. L. Cross and E. A. Livingstone (Oxford: Oxford University Press, 1997), p. 1603.

8. "Alcuin of York," http://www-history.mcs.st-andrews.ac.uk/Biographies/Alcuin.html.

9. "Carolingian Schools," "Alcuin," "Blessed Maurus Magentius Rabanus," and "Theodulf," in *Catholic Encyclopaedia*, http://www.newadvent.org/cathen/index.html.

10. Henri Pirenne, *Mohammed and Charlemagne* (1939; reprint, New York: Barnes & Noble Books, 1961), p. 164.

11. R. E. Grimm, "The Autobiography of Leonardo Pisano," *Fibonacci Quarterly* 11, no. 1 (February 1973): 99–104.

12. Crombie, *Medieval and Early Modern Science*, p. 35.

13. Perhaps more correctly *syneidesis*. *Synderesis* or *synteresis* was not used by Paul, as it was not a Greek word at the time; it became current in Scholastic philosophy after Saint Jerome derived it from what is now thought to have been a transcription error. See "Synteresis," in *The Oxford Dictionary of the Christian Church*, 3rd ed., ed. F. L. Cross and E. A. Livingstone (Oxford: Oxford University Press, 1997), p. 1570.

14. A. I. Sabra, quoted in Toby Huff, *The Rise of Early Modern Science: Islam, China, and the West* (Cambridge: Cambridge University Press, 1993), p. 86.

15. Huff, *The Rise of Early Modern Science*, p. 144.

16. Al-Ghazali, *Deliverance from Error*, trans. and ed. R. J. McCarthy (Louisville, KY: Fons Vitae, 2004), pp. 62–63.

17. Quoted in Tina Stiefel, *The Intellectual Revolution in Twelfth-Century Europe* (New York: St. Martin's Press, 1985), p. 38.

18. Ibid., p. 36.

19. Ibid., p. 35.

20. Ibid., p. 16.

21. Ibid., p. 41.

22. Ibid.

23. Stiefel, *The Intellectual Revolution in Twelfth-Century Europe*, p. 45.

24. All the quotes of the twelfth-century thinkers come from Stiefel, *The Intellectual Revolution in Twelfth Century Europe*, pp. 36–45.

25. Ibid., p. 52.

26. Ibid.

27. Ibid., p. 53.

28. Ibid., p. 55.

29. Ibid., p. 78.

30. Ibid.

31. Ibid., p. 79.

32. Ibid., p. 80.

33. Ibid., pp. 82–83.

34. Huff, *The Rise of Early Modern Science*, p. 120.

35. Ibid., pp. 125–26.

36. Ibid., p. 128.

37. Ibid., pp. 134–35.

38. Ibid., p. 137.

39. Ibid., p. 138.

40. Quoted in ibid., p. 64, n59.

41. Ibid., p. 161.

42. Ibid.

43. R. W. Southern, *Western Views of Islam in the Middle Ages* (Cambridge, MA: Harvard University Press, 1978), p. 7.

44. Ibid., pp. 15 and 28, n28, where the capture of the abbot in 972 by the Saracens is described.

45. Ibid., p. 18.

46. So lamented Paul Alvarus, a ninth-century biographer of Eulogius, bishop of Toledo. Quoted by Southern in *Western Views of Islam in the Middle Ages*, p. 21.

47. Quoted in ibid.

48. Ibid., p. 22.

49. Ibid., p. 29.

50. Ibid., p. 35, and n2 on the same page.

51. James Kritzeck, "Robert of Ketton's Translation of the Qur'an," *Islamic Quarterly* 2 (1955): 309–12.

52. Ibid., p. 311.

53. Thomas E. Burman, "Tafsir and Translation: Traditional Qur'an Exegesis and the Latin Qur'ans of Robert of Ketton and Mark of Toledo," *Speculum* 73 (1998): 703–32; see also *Juan de Segovia and Quran Reading in Europe, 1140–1560*, www.cishsydney2005.org/images/Burman_paper.doc; "Polemic, Philology, and Ambivalence: Reading the Quran in Latin Christendom," *Journal of Islamic Studies* 15 (2004): 181–209.

54. Burman, "Tafsir and Translation," p. 705.

55. Ibid., p. 705. Burman has this footnote on the same page: "These criticisms

appear in the remarkable preface to his now-lost Latin translation of the Quran (made from the Castilian version of Yca de Segovia): *Prefatio Johannis de Segobia . . . in translationem noviter ex Arabico in Latinum vulgareque Hyspanum libri Alchorani . . .* , ed. D. Cabanelas Rodriguez in *Juan de Segovia y el problema islamico* (Madrid, 1952), pp. 279–302, esp. pp. 288, 293, 295–96. On these criticisms generally, see Cabanelas Rodriquez, *Juan de Segovia*, pp. 131–36, and "Juan de Segovia y el primer Alcoran trilingue," *Al-Andalus* 14 (1949): 157–61.

56. L. Marracci, *Refutatio Alcorani in qua ad Mahumetanicae superstitionis radicem securis apponitur; et Mahumetus ipse gladio suo jugulator*, 2. Padua, 1698, p. 3.

57. George Sale, trans., *The Koran* (1734; reprint, London: Frederick Warne, 1915), p. vii.

58. See note 53 above, and Burman's Web page at the University of Tennessee: http://web.utk.edu/~history/f-burman.htm.

59. Burman, "Tafsir and Translation," p. 707.

60. Richard Bell, ed. and trans., *The Quran*, 2 vols. (Edinburgh: T. & T. Clark, 1937–39).

61. Quoted by Norman Daniel, *Islam and the West: The Making of an Image* (Edinburgh: The University Press, 1962), p. 59; emphasis mine.

62. Günter Lüling, "Preconditions for the Scholarly Criticism of the Koran and Islam, with Some Autobiographical Remarks," *Journal of Higher Criticism*, vol. 3 (Spring 1996): 84; emphasis mine.

63. A. C. Crombie, *Robert Grosseteste and the Origins of Experimental Science, 1100–1700* (Oxford: Clarendon Press, 1953), p. 148.

64. Quoted in Southern, *Western Views of Islam in the Middle Ages*, p. 59.

65. Ibid., p. 61.

66. Sometimes spelled Riccoldo.

67. Norman Daniel doubts the traditional idea that this text was written by an ex-Muslim, preferring to attribute it to a Christian, Mozarab. Daniel, *Islam and the West*, p. 6.

68. Ibid., p. 58.

69. Ibid., pp. 58–59.

70. Martin Luther, *Verlegung des Alcoran*, trans. Ricoldo da Montecroce (Wittenberg: H. Lufft, 1542).

71. Southern, *Western Views of Islam in the Middle Ages*, p. 105, n57.

72. Burman, *Juan de Segovia and Quran Reading*, summarizing his research to be published in *Reading the Quran in Latin Christendom, 1140–1560.*

73. Ibid., p. 5.

74. Ibid., p. 9.

75. Ibid., p. 13.

76. Nicholas of Cusa, *De Pace Fidei and Cribratio Alkorani*, trans. Jasper Hopkins (Minneapolis: Arthur J. Banning Press, 1994), p. 30; in Ludwig Hagemann's edition *Nicolai de Cusa Opera Omnia, Vol. VIII: Cribratio Alkorani* (Hamburg: Felix Meiner Verlag, 1986), p. 980.

77. Christoph Luxenberg, *Die Syro-Aramäische Lesart des Koran. Ein Beitrage zur Entschlüsselung der Koransprache* (Berlin: Verlag Hans Schiler, 2004).

78. Daniel, *Islam and the West.* Maxime Rodinson has criticized Daniel for being an apologist of Islam, which would explain why Daniel often dismisses any criticism of the Koran as invalid since it arose in a polemical context and came from a Christian.

79. Burman, "Polemic, Philology, and Ambivalence," pp. 181–209.

80. Southern, *Western Views of Islam in the Middle Ages*, pp. 76, 77.

81. Ibid., pp. 108–109.

82. Nancy Bisaha, *Creating East and West: Renaissance Humanists and the Ottoman Turks* (Philadelphia: University of Pennsylvania Press, 2004), p. 6.

83. Ibid., p. 11.

84. Ibid., p. 57.

85. Ibid., quoting Francesco Novati, ed., *Epistolario di Coluccio Salutati* (Rome: Forzani E. C. Tipografi del Senato, 1896), vol. 3, p. 209.

86. Bisaha, *Creating East and West*, p. 57, quoting Novati, *Epistolario di Coluccio Salutati*, vol. 3, p. 209.

87. E. Cassirer, P. O. Kristeller, and H. H. Randall Jr., eds., *The Renaissance Philosophy of Man* (1948; reprint, Chicago: University of Chicago Press, 1971), p. 265, quoting Gasparis Contarini Cardinalis, *Opera* (Paris, 1571), p. 179.

88. Cassirer, Kristeller, and Randall, *The Renaissance Philosophy of Man*, pp. 264–69.

89. Quoted in Russell Kirk's introduction to Giovanni Pico della Mirandola, *Oration on the Dignity of Man*, trans. A. Robert Caponigri (Chicago: Regnery, 1967), p. xi.

90. Ibid., pp. 28, 31, 32, 55, 66.

91. Ibid., p. 10.

92. Ibid., p. 45.

93. Ibid., p. 47.

94. Cassirer, Kristeller, and Randall, *The Renaissance Philosophy of Man*, pp. 187, 201, 209.

95. William J. Bouwsma, *Concordia Mundi: The Career and Thought of Guillaume Postel (1510–1581)* (Cambridge, MA: Harvard University Press, 1957), p. 6.

96. Ibid., p. 61.

97. Ibid.

98. Ibid., p. 92.

99. Ibid., p. 93.

100. Ibid., p. 129, quoting *Loy Salique*, 67–68.

101. Bouwsma, *Concordia Mundi*, p. 129, quoting *Raisons de la Monarchie*, ix–x.

102. Bouwsma, *Concordia Mundi*, p. 129, quoting *Πανθενωσια*, p. 120.

103. Bouwsma, *Concordia Mundi*, p. 130, quoting *Histoire et consideration de l'origine, loy, et coustume des . . . Turcs* (Poitiers, 1560), p. 3.

104. Bouwsma, *Concordia Mundi*, p. 194, quoting *Πανθενωσια*, p. 10.

105. Bouwsma, *Concordia Mundi*, p. 196.

106. Ibid., pp. 204–205.

107. Ibid., p. 209.

108. Ibid., p. 296.

109. I have seen three different dates for his birth in the various reference works consulted, namely, 1599, 1600, 1603.

110. Adam Olearius, *The Voyages and Travels of the Ambassadors*, trans. John Davies (1662), http://depts.washington.edu/uwch/silkroad/texts/olearius/travels.html.

111. Sir John Chardin, *Travels in Persia 1673–1677* (New York: Dover, 1988), p. 185.

112. Ibid., p. 189.

113. Clarence Dana Rouillard, *The Turk in French History, Thought, and Literature (1520–1660)* (Paris: Boivin & Cie, 1940; reprint, New York: Ams Press, 1973), p. 8.

114. Ibid., p. 42.

115. Ibid., pp. 47–48.

116. Ibid., p. 171.

117. Ibid., p. 173.

118. Rouillard, *The Turk in French History, Thought, and Literature*, pp. 178–79:

> Such a book is *La Genealogie du grant Turc*, and its contribution to the knowledge of French readers in the early sixteenth century is manifest. A picture has been painted of a people whose government, court, army, religion, and habits of living are vastly different from those of western Europe. Aside from the value as knowledge per se, two further effects stand out. First, these peculiarities are never held up to ridicule. On the contrary, much is described with admiration, even with some criticism, direct or implied, of inferior Christian ways, and another step is taken toward tolerance. Second, for all its wealth of factual detail, there is no attendant loss of glamour. Contrary to the assumption sometimes made that Turkey became just another European nation in the sixteenth century, and so no longer exotic, I think it may safely be asserted that a reader of this little book, or many others . . . would have his imagination stimulated more than repressed, his curiosity aroused more than satisfied.

119. Ibid., pp. 183–85.

120. Ibid., p. 187.

121. Ibid., pp. 220–25.

122. Ibid., pp. 230–33.

123. Ibid., p. 242.

124. Rouillard, *The Turk in French History, Thought, and Literature*, pp. 243–48.

125. Ibid., p. 249.

126. Ibid., pp. 263–67.

127. Ibid., pp. 289–90.

128. Ibid., p. 643.

129. Ibid., p. 644.

130. Nicholas Canny, "England's New World and the Old," in *The Oxford History of the British Empire*, vol. 1: *The Origins of Empire*, ed. Nicholas Canny (Oxford: Oxford University Press, 1998), p. 152.

131. T. Harriot, *A briefe and true report of the new found land of Virginia* (1588), part 3, http://xroads.virginia.edu/%7ehyper/hariot/1590–3.html.

132. Canny, "England's New World and the Old," p. 152

133. Ibid., p. 153.

134. Ibid., p. 154.

135. Ibid., quoting William Wood, *New England's Prospect*, ed. Alden Vaughan (1634; reprint, Amherst: University of Massachusetts, 1977), p. 113.

136. Canny, "England's New World and the Old," p. 156.

137. Ibid., p. 164.

138. Simon Ockley, *The History of the Saracens*, 6th ed. (London: Henry G. Bohn, 1857), p. vii.

139. Ibid., p. x.

140. Ibid., p. xi.

141. A. J. Arberry, *The Cambridge School of Arabic* (Cambridge: Cambridge University Press, 1948), pp. 14–15, quoting *Introductio ad Linguas Orientales*, pp. 115, 123.

142. Latin: Biting worries or cares, cf. *Vino diffugiunt mordaces curae*. By wine biting cares are put to flight. Horace, *Odes*, I, xviii, 4.

143. Arberry, *The Cambridge School of Arabic*, p. 15, quoting *Dictionary of National Biography*.

144. A. J. Arberry, *Oriental Essays: Portraits of Seven Scholars* (London: George Allen & Unwin, 1960), p. 14.

145. Ibid., p. 12.

146. Ibid., p. 15.

147. Arberry, *The Cambridge School of Arabic*, p. 16.

148. Arberry, *Oriental Essays*, p. 28.

149. Ibid., p. 47.

150. I have leaned heavily on Maurice Borrmans's excellent article, "Ludovico Marracci et sa traduction latine du Coran," *Pontificio Istitutio di Studi Arabi e d' Islamistica: Islamochristiana* 28 (2002): 73–86.

151. This was achieved in 1650, but since a particular edition of the Bible had not been followed rigorously as had been asked, the translators were asked to redo it, with Marracci in charge. It was eventually published by Propaganda Fide, in Rome in 1671, in three volumes with the title *Biblia Sacra Arabica Sacrae Congregationis de Propaganda Fide iussu edita ad usum ecclesiarum orientalium additis e regione Biblis latinis vulgatis.*

152. Borrmans, "Ludovico Marracci," p. 75, quoting from Marracci's opuscule *L'ebreo preso per le buone*.

153. Full Title: Alcorani textus universus, ex correctioribus Arabum exemplaribus summa fide, atque pulcherrimis characteribus descriptus, eademque fide, ac pari diligentia

ex Arabico idiomate in latinum translatus. Appositis unicuique capiti notis, atque refutatione: His omnibus praemissus est Prodromus Totum priorem Tomum implens, In quo contenta indicantur pagina sequenti, Auctore Ludovico Marraccio E Congregatione Clericorum Regularium Matris Dei, Innocentii XI. Gloriosissimae memoriae olim Confessario. (Patavi, MDCXCVIII) (Padua: Typographia Seminarii, 1698).

154. Sale, *The Koran*, p. x.

155. Cf. G. Gabrieli, "Gli studi orientali e gli ordini religiosi in Italia," *Il pensiero missionario* 3 (1931): 297–313, 304, quoted by Borrmans, "Ludovico Marracci," p. 83.

156. P. M. Holt, "The Treatment of Arab History in Prideaux, Ockley and Sale," in *Historians of the Middle East*, ed. B. Lewis and P. M. Holt (London: Oxford University Press, 1962), pp. 290–302.

157. Alexander Ross's version was a shoddy translation from the French of du Ryer in 1649.

158. Sale, *The Koran*, p. 71.

159. I. Goldziher, "Islam et Parsisme," in *Actes du premier Congres International d'Histoire des religions*, vol. 1 (Paris, 1900), 119ff.; Rev. W. St. Clair-Tisdall, *The Sources of Islam: A Persian Treatise*, trans. and abr. Sir William Muir (Edinburgh: T. & T. Clark, 1901); St. Clair-Tisdall, *The Original Sources of the Qur'an* (London: Society for Promoting Christian Knowledge, 1905).

160. Sale, *The Koran*, p. 39.

Chapter 4: Indian Orientalists

1. Ernst Cassirer, *The Philosophy of the Enlightenment* (Boston: Beacon Press, 1960), p. 166.

2. Diderot, "Pensées Philosophiques," sec. 26, pp. 24–25, in *Oeuvres Philosophiques*, ed. Paul Vernière (Paris: Garnier Frères, 1964), quoted in Cassirer, *The Philosophy of the Enlightenment*, p. 166.

3. Voltaire, "Alexandre," in *Questions sur l'Encyclopédie, par des amateurs* (1773), vol. 1, p. 145–50, quoted in Thomas J. Schlereth, *The Cosmopolitan Ideal in Enlightenment Thought: Its Form and Function in the Ideas of Franklin, Hume, and Voltaire* (South Bend, IN: University of Notre Dame Press, 1977), p. xviii.

4. P. Gay, "The Subversive Anthropologist," in *The Party of Humanity* (New York: Knopf, 1964), p. 50.

5. Voltaire, *Essai sur les moeurs et l'esprit des nations*, quoted in W. Ferguson, *The Renaissance in Historical Thought* (New York: Houghton Mifflin, 1948), pp. 81–82.

6. David Hume, "The Stoic," in *Essays, Moral, Political, Literary*, ed. T. H. Green and T. H. Grosse (London: Longmans, 1875), vol. 1, p. 207, quoted in Schlereth, *The Cosmopolitan Ideal*, p. xviii.

7. Montaigne, "On Vanity," in *The Complete Works of Montaigne*, ed. Donald Frame (Stanford, CA: Stanford University Press, 1948), p. 743.

8. Jean Bodin, *Colloquium of the Seven about Secrets of the Sublime* (Colloquium

Heptaplomeres de Rerum Sublimium Arcanis Abditis), trans. and ed. Marion Leathers Daniels Kuntz (Princeton, NJ: Princeton University Press,1976).

9. Schlereth, *The Cosmopolitan Ideal*, p. xxiii.

10. Ibid., pp. xxiv–xxv.

11. Nicholas Canny, ed., *The Origins of Empire*, vol. 1 of *The Oxford History of the British Empire* (Oxford: Oxford University Press, 1998); P. J. Marshall and Alaine Low, eds., *The Eighteenth Century*, vol. 2 (1998); Andrew Porter and Alaine Low, eds., *The Nineteenth Century*, vol. 3 (1999); Judith M. Brown and W. Roger Louis, eds., *The Twentieth Century*, vol. 4 (1999); Robin W. Winks and Alaine Low, eds., *Historiography*, vol. 5 (1999).

12. W. Bartram, *Travels and Other Writings* (New York: Library of America, 1996), p. 13.

13. Ibid., p. 87.

14. Bartram, *Travels and Other Writings*, pp. 24–25.

15. Ibid., p. 110.

16. Nathaniel Philbrick, *Sea of Glory: America's Voyage of Discovery, the U.S. Exploring Expedition, 1838–1842* (New York: Penguin, 2003), p. 57.

17. Ibid., p. 133.

18. Tripta Wahi, "Orientalism: A Critique," *Revolutionary Democracy* 2, no. 1 (April 1996), http://revolutionarydemocracy.org/rdv2n1/orient.htm. I am indebted to Wahi's article for many of the ideas in the next page and a quarter.

19. The two examples—Viceroy and Sanskrit scholar—are mine, rather than Wahi's.

20. Wahi, "Orientalism," p. 8.

21. Quoted in C. A. Bayly, Gordon Johnson, and John F. Richards, eds., *Cambridge History of India* (Cambridge: Cambridge University Press, 1929), vol. 5, p. 187.

22. Edmund Burke, *On Empire, Liberty, and Reform: Speeches and Letters*, ed. David Bromwich (New Haven, CT: Yale University Press, 2000), p. 14.

23. Ibid.

24. Ibid.

25. Ibid., pp. 295–96.

26. Ibid., p. 299.

27. Ibid., pp. 399–400.

28. V. B. Kulkarni, *British Statesmen in India* (Bombay: Orient Longmans, 1961), pp. 28–29, quoted in David Kopf, *British Orientalism and the Bengal Renaissance: The Dynamics of Indian Modernization 1773–1835* (Berkeley and Los Angeles: University of California Press, 1969), p. 15.

29. Quoted in "Jones, William," in H. C. G. Matthew and Brian Harrison, eds., *The Oxford Dictionary of National Biography* [henceforth *DNB*] (Oxford: Oxford University Press, 2004), p. 670.

30. S. K. De, *Bengali Literature in the Nineteenth Century, 1757–1857* (Calcutta: Firma K. L. Mukhopadhay, 1962), p. 72.

31. Greek epistolographer, fl. fifth or sixth century CE.

32. De, *Bengali Literature*, p. 73.

33. G. T. Garrett and E. Thompson, *Rise and Fulfillment of British Rule in India* (1935; reprint, Allahabad: Central Book Depot, 1962), p. 124, quoted in Kopf, *British Orientalism*, p. 21.

34. G. K. Gleig, ed., *Memoirs of the Life of Right Honorable Warren Hastings* (London: Richard Bentley, 1841), pp. 156–57, quoted in Kopf, *British Orientalism*, p. 21.

35. Quoted in *DNB*, "Wilkins, Sir Charles," p. 259.

36. C. Wilkins, "A Royal Charter of Land, Engraved on a Copper Plate," *Asiatick Researches* 1 (1788): 123–28.

37. O. J. Kejariwal, *The Asiatic Society of Bengal and the Discovery of India's Past, 1784–1838* (Delhi: Oxford University Press, 1988), p. 44.

38. C. Wilkins, "Inscription on a Pillar near Buddal, Translated from the Sanskrit," *Asiatick Researches* 1 (1788): 131, quoted in Kejariwal. *The Asiatic Society of Bengal*, p. 44.

39. Wilkins's unabridged version of Richardson's work was published in 1806. The abridged version came out in 1810: "This vocabulary is intended for the use of Gentlemen in the Army, in the service of the Honorable East India Company, and others, going out to India, who may think Richardson's Dictionary [of Persian, Arabic and English, Oxon. 1777–80] too bulky or expensive" (from the advertisement).

40. Shumbhoo Chander Dey, "Sir Charles Wilkins," in *Eminent Orientalists: Indian, European American* (1922; reprint, Madras: Asian Educational Services, 1991), pp. 45–46:

> Sir Charles Wilkins occupies a very high place in the domain of Oriental learning. True it is, there have since appeared brighter names in it; but in point of priority none can approach him. He might be called the Morning Star of Oriental lore. Sanskrit was all but unknown to Europeans, and it was Wilkins who, for the first time, opened the rich inexhaustible mines of its untold treasures before their wondering eyes. He knew many Indian languages and had a thorough mastery over some of them. As for his knowledge of Sanskrit, it was simply wonderful at least for the time in which he flourished. He was justly esteemed (as may be seen in extant correspondence) by Sir William Jones, who, as he himself said, owed him "a debt immense of endless gratitude." In Indian epigraphy he was specially the pioneer, being the first European to study Sanskrit Inscriptions, which were unintelligible to the [Hindu] Pundits of his time. Of the five articles by him—in the earlier volumes of the Asiatic Researches—four are on this subject, one of primary importance to the real history of Bengal which has to be written. But the act for which his memory is fondly cherished, and his name regarded with a respect almost bordering on affection, is his introduction of the art of printing in this country [India]. By this noble act he has built for himself a temple in the Indian heart, where he receives daily worship in the shape of prayer and praise from thousands, and will, it is to be hoped, continue to receive it for times unnumbered and through ages without end.

41. Quoted in Kopf, *British Orientalism*, p. 30.

42. Quoted in ibid.

43. Charles Allen, *The Buddha and the Sahibs: The Men Who Discovered India's Lost Religion* (London: John Murray, 2002), p. 94.

44. Ibid.

45. Ibid., p. 94.

46. Comment by Sir James Mackintosh in *Memoirs of the Life of the Right Honourable Sir James Mackintosh*, ed. R. J. Mackintosh, 2 vols. (1835), quoted "Duncan, Jonathan," *DNB*, vol. 16, p. 243.

47. Kopf, *British Orientalism*, p. 31.

48. Kejariwal, *The Asiatic Society of Bengal*, p. 118.

49. Quoted in ibid., p. 255, n8.

50. Ibid., p. 119.

51. John Z. Holwell, *Interesting Historical Events, Relative to the Provinces of Bengal, and the Empire of Indostan With a seasonable hint and persuasive to the honourable court of directors of the East India Company. As also the mythology and cosmogony, fasts and festivals of the Gentoo's, followers of the Shastah. And a dissertation on the metempsychosis, commonly, though erroneously, called the Pythagorean doctrine*, 3 vols. (London, 1765–1771).

52. Kejariwal, *The Asiatic Society of Bengal*, pp. 18–19.

53. Ibid., p. 19.

54. Ibid.

55. M. S. Ramaswami Iyengar, "Henry T. Colebrooke," in *Eminent Orientalists: Indian, European American* (1922; reprint, Madras: Asian Educational Services, 1991), p. 47.

56. "Colebrooke, Henry Thomas," *DNB*, vol. 12, p. 540.

57. Ibid., vol. 4, p. 738.

58. Ibid., vol. 4, p. 739.

59. Ibid., vol. 12, p. 540.

60. Iyengar, "Henry T. Colebrooke," pp. 50–51.

61. "Colebrooke, Henry Thomas," *DNB*, vol. 4, p. 738, which is quoting some other account not credited but very probably Colebrooke's own words published in the life of Colebrooke by his son.

62. Ibid., vol. 4, p. 740.

63. Ibid.

64. Ibid.

65. Iyengar, "Henry T. Colebrooke," p. 57.

66. "Colebrooke, Henry Thomas," *DNB*, vol. 12, p. 540.

67. Reprinted in H. T. Colebrooke, *Miscellaneous Essays, with the Life of the Author by His Son Sir T. E.Colebrooke* (London: Trübner & Co., 1873), vol. 1, pp. 1–7.

68. Ibid.

69. Ibid.

70. Colebrooke, *Miscellaneous Essays*, vol. 1, p. 2.

71. Ibid.

72. Ibid., p. 4.

73. Ibid., p. 5.

74. Ibid., p. 6.

75. Ibid., p. 7.

76. Ibid., p. 100.

77. K. S. Ramaswami Sastri, "Sir William Jones," in *Eminent Orientalists: Indian, European American* (1922; reprint, Madras: Asian Educational Services, 1991), pp. 1–2.

78. A. J. Arberry, *Oriental Essays: Portraits of Seven Scholars* (London: George Allen & Unwin, 1960), p. 66.

79. "Jones, William," *DNB*, p. 671.

80. William Jones, *The Works of Sir William Jones*, ed. A. M. Jones (London, 1807; reprint, 1993 in *Collected Works*, ed. Garland Cannon [New York: New York University Press, 1993]), vol. 3, p. 34.

81. Thomas R. Trautman, "The Lives of Sir William Jones," in *Sir William Jones, 1746–1794: A Commemoration*, ed. Alexander Murray (Oxford: Oxford University Press, 1998), p. 105.

82. Lord Teignmouth, *Memoirs of Sir William Jones* (London, 1807), vol. 2, pp. 306–307.

83. William Jones, *The Works of Sir William Jones*, introduction by Robert D. Richardson Jr., vol. 1 (New York: Garland, 1984), p. 359.

84. William Jones, "Preface to *A Grammar of the Persian Language*," reprinted in *Sir William Jones: A Reader*, ed. Satya S. Pachori (Delhi: Oxford University Press, 1993), p. 158.

85. A. J. Arberry, *Asiatic Jones* (London: Longmans, Green, 1946), p. 33.

86. Jones, *The Works of Sir William Jones*, vol. 3, p. 37, quoted in "Jones, William," *DNB*, p. 671.

87. "Jones, William," *DNB*, p. 671.

88. Trautman, "The Lives of Sir William Jones," p. 105.

89. "Jones, William," *DNB*, p. 672.

90. Arberry, *Oriental Essays*, p. 82.

91. Ibid., p. 83.

92. Ibid.

93. William Jones, "Dissertation Sur La Littérature Orientale," in *The Works of Sir William Jones*, ed. Burton Feldman and Robert D. Richardson Jr. (New York: Garland, 1984), vol. 1, pp. 298–99.

94. No relation.

95. Alan Jones, "Sir William Jones as an Arabist," in *Sir William Jones, 1746–1794: A Commemoration*, ed. Alexander Murray (Oxford: Oxford University Press, 1998), p. 75.

96. A. L. Basham, "Foreword" in O. J. Kejariwal, *The Asiatic Society of Bengal and the Discovery of India's Past, 1784–1838* (Delhi: Oxford University Press, 1988), pp. ix–x.

97. Kejariwal, *The Asiatic Society of Bengal*, pp. xi–xii.
98. Ibid., pp. 3, 5–6.
99. Quoted in ibid., p. 7.
100. Ibid.
101. Ibid., pp. 7–9.
102. Ibid., p. 8.
103. De, *Bengali Literature in the Nineteenth Century*, p. 25.
104. Ibid., p. 28.
105. Quoted in Kopf, *British Orientalism*, p. 66.
106. Kejariwal, *The Asiatic Society of Bengal*, p. 35.
107. Quoted in ibid., p. 38.
108. Ibid., p. 39.
109. From Sir William Jones, *Third Annual Discourse of 1788* on Indo-European Languages and Culture; Charles Wilkins, *A Royal Grant of Land on a Copper Plate* in 1788; S. Davis, *On Astronomical Calculations of the Hindus* in 1795; H. T. Colebrooke, *On the Duties of a Faithful Hindu Widow* in 1795; Jonathan Duncan, *Discovery of Two Urns in the Vicinity of Banares* in 1797; E. Strachey, *On Early History of Algebra* in 1816. These were followed by books, monographs, monthly bulletins, memorial lectures, memoirs, and so on.
110. Quoted in Kopf, *British Orientalism*, p. 66.
111. Ibid., p. 47.
112. Quoted in De, *Bengali Literature in the Nineteenth Century*, p. 107.
113. Ibid., p. 107.
114. Ibid., pp. 106–107.
115. Ibid., p. 107.
116. "William Carey," *DNB*, p. 90.
117. Kopf, *British Orientalism*, p. 53.
118. "William Carey," *DNB*, p. 91.
119. Kopf, *British Orientalism*, p. 53.
120. De, *Bengali Literature in the Nineteenth Century*, pp. 123–25.
121. Ibid., p. 141.
122. Ibid., p. 142.
123. Quoted by De in *Bengali Literature in the Nineteenth Century*, pp. 142–43.
124. Quoted in ibid., p. 125.
125. Kopf, *British Orientalism*, p. 97.
126. Ibid., pp. 99–100.
127. Quoted in Guy Deleury, *Le Voyage en Inde. Anthologie Des Voyageurs Français (1750–1820)* (Paris: Robert Laffont, 1991), pp. xv–xvi.
128. Raymond Schwab, *The Oriental Renaissance: Europe's Rediscovery of India and the East, 1680–1880*, trans. G. Patterson-Black and Victor Reinking (New York: Columbia University Press, 1984), p. 159.
129. Ibid., p. 159.

130. Ibid., p. 17.

131. Quoted in K. S. Ramaswami Sastri, "Max Müller," in *Eminent Orientalists: Indian, European American* (1992; reprint, Madras: Asian Educational Services, 1991), p. 165.

132. Nirad Chaudhuri, *Scholar Extraordinary: The Life of Professor the Rt. Hon. Friedrich Max Müller, P.C.* (Delhi: Oxford University Press, 1974), p. 125.

133. Ibid., p. 134.

134. Quoted in Sastri, "Max Müller," p. 168.

135. Ibid., pp. 167–75:

> Sastri tells us that "Max Müller's luminous conception of and his devotion to the science of language are among his greatest qualities. . . . [His] depth and range of vision in regard to the panorama of human development are equally remarkable. . . . [He] had a keen intellectual apprehension of the Hindu conception of God as revealed in the Vedas. . . . He had also a clear and correct view in regard to the misunderstood doctrine of the noumenon and the phenomenon in the Vedanta philosophy. . . . [He showed] deep insight into Hindu customs . . . [and] had a wonderful insight into the real and distinctive treasure of thought and emotion contained in Sanskrit poetry proper.

136. Max Müller, *Biographical Essays* (Kila, MT: Kessinger, 2005), p. 143.

137. Quoted in Sastri, "Max Müller," p. 204.

138. Tope: from the Pali word *Thupo*, in Sanskrit, *Stupa*, defined as a reliquary containing the ashes of a Buddhist saint.

139. Quoted in Allen, *The Buddha and the Sahibs*, p. v. The Bhilsa Tope is now known as the Great Stupa of Sanchi.

140. Quoted in ibid., p. 123.

141. Ibid., p. 121.

142. Ibid., p. 119.

143. Ibid., p. 106.

144. Quoted in ibid., p. 111.

145. Quoted on the Web page of the Archaeological Survey of India, http://asi.nic.in/index2.asp?sublinkid=28.

146. Ibid.

147. Ibid.

148. Allen, *The Buddha and the Sahibs*, p. 143.

149. Quoted in "Prinsep, James," *DNB*, vol. 40, p. 411.

150. Ibid., p. 395.

151. Ibid., p. 411.

152. Allen, *The Buddha and the Sahibs*.

153. Schwab, *Le Renaissance Orientale*, p. xxiii.

154. Ibid., p. 35–36.

155. Ibid., p. 36.
156. Ibid., p. 38.
157. Ibid., p. 37.
158. Ibid., p. 87.
159. Ibid., p. 35.
160. Ibid., p. 5.
161. Ibid., p. 65.
162. Allen, *The Buddha and the Sahibs*, p. 5.
163. William Jones, *A Grammar of the Persian Language* (1771; reprint, Menston, UK: Scholar Press, 1969), p. xxiv.
164. Ananda Wickremeratne, *The Genesis of an Orientalist: Thomas William Rhys Davids and Buddhism in Sri Lanka* (Columbia, MO: South Asia Books, 1985).
165. Kejariwal, *The Asiatic Society of Bengal*, pp. 226–27.
166. Quoted in ibid., p. 233.

Chapter 5: Western Archaeologists

1. Glyn Daniel, *A Hundred and Fifty Years of Archaeology* (Cambridge, MA: Harvard University Press, 1976), p. 7.
2. Ibid., p. 10.
3. Female archaeologists include Miss Caton-Thompson and Miss E. W. Gardner, working in Egypt in 1920s; Elise J. Baumgärtel also digging in Egypt in 1940s; and Miss Winifred Lamb in Asia Minor in 1928.
4. Daniel, *A Hundred and Fifty Years of Archaeology*, pp. 13–14.
5. Seton Lloyd, *Foundations in the Dust* (Harmondsworth, UK: Pelican Books, 1955), p. 15.
6. Ibid., pp. 211–12.
7. Lesley Adkins, *Empires of the Plain: Henry Rawlinson and the Lost Languages of Babylon* (New York: St. Martin's Press, 2004), p. xxiii.
8. Quoted in ibid., p. 241; emphasis mine.
9. Quoted in ibid., p. 287.
10. Quoted in ibid., p. 25.
11. Quoted in ibid., p. 27.
12. Quoted in ibid., p. 90.
13. Ibid., p. 95.
14. Quoted in ibid., p. 96.
15. Quoted in ibid., p. 99.
16. Quoted in ibid., p. 101.
17. Quoted in ibid., p. 130.
18. Robert Silverberg, *To the Rock of Darius: The Story of Henry Rawlinson* (New York: Holt, Rinehart and Winston, 1966), p. 123.
19. Quoted in Leslie Adkins, *Empires of the Plain*, p. 363.

20. Sir Austen Layard, *Autobiography and Letters* (New York: Charles Scribner's Sons, 1903), vol. 1, pp. 26–27.

21. Ibid., pp. 40–41.

22. Ibid., p. 50.

23. Ibid., pp. 39–40.

24. Ibid., p. 60.

25. Ibid., p. 88.

26. Ibid., p. 57.

27. Ibid., p. 157.

28. Ibid., p. 164.

29. Ibid., p. 168.

30. Ibid., p. 173.

31. Ibid., p. 284.

32. Ibid., pp. 179–80, 193.

33. Ibid., vol. 2, pp. 49–50.

34. Ibid., pp. 92–93.

35. Ibid., p. 95.

36. Ibid., p. 128.

37. Austen Layard, *Nineveh and Its Remains* (New York: George Putnam, 1853), vol. 1, p. 65, where Layard talks of the resentment of the Qadi of Mosul.

38. Ibid., p. 15.

39. Layard, *Autobiography and Letters*, vol. 1, p. 187.

40. Layard, *Nineveh and Its Remains*, vol. 1, pp. 32, 44.

41. Ibid., pp. 47, 49.

42. Ibid., p. 46.

43. Ibid., vol. 2, pp. 70–71.

44. Ibid., p. 72.

45. Layard, *Autobiography and Letters*, vol. 2, p. 167.

46. Layard, *Nineveh and Its Remains*, vol. 2, pp. 71–72.

47. H. D. Thoreau, *The Writings of Henry David Thoreau* (New York: Houghton Mifflin, 1906), vol. 1, pp. 149–50.

48. Quoted in Daniel, *A Hundred and Fifty Years of Archaeology*, p. 180.

49. Ibid., p. 181, n1.

50. Layard, *Nineveh and Its Remains*, vol. 2, p. 364.

51. Layard, *Autobiography and Letters*, vol. 2, pp. 217–18.

52. Ursula Lindsey, "Egypt's Grand Mufti Issues *Fatwa*: No Sculpture," *Christian Science Monitor*, April 18, 2006, http://www.csmonitor.com/2006/0418/p01s02wome.html.

53. Daniel, *A Hundred and Fifty Years of Archaeology*, pp. 163–64.

54. Ibid., p. 164.

55. Bruce Kuklick, *Puritans in Babylon: The Ancient Near East and American Intellectual Life, 1880–1930* (Princeton, NJ: Princeton University Press, 1996), p. 200.

56. Ibid.
57. Ibid., p. 201.
58. Ibid.

Chapter 6: Empire and Curzon

1. R. C. Majumdar and A. D. Pusalkar, eds., *The History and Culture of the Indian People* (London: G. Allen & Unwin, 1952), vol. 6, p. 623.

2. K. S. Lal, *Growth of Muslim Population in Medieval India, A.D. 1000–1800* (Delhi: Research Publications in Social Sciences, 1973), pp. 77–85, 433–61, 631–53.

3. Ibid.

4. Quoted in David Kopf, *British Orientalism and the Bengal Renaissance: The Dynamics of Indian Modernization 1773–1835* (Berkeley and Los Angeles: University of California Press, 1969), p. 1.

5. Sir Jadunath Sarkar, *History of Aurangzib*, 5 vols. (Calcutta: Sarkar & Sons, 1912–1924):

> Islamic theology, therefore tells the true believer that his highest duty is to make "exertion (jihad) in the path of God," by waging war against infidel lands (dar-ul-harb) till they become part of the realm of Islam (dar-ul-Islam) and their populations are converted into true believers. After conquest the entire infidel population becomes theoretically reduced to the status of slaves of the conquering army. The men taken with arms are to be slain or sold into slavery and their wives and children reduced to servitude. As for the non-combatants among the vanquished, if they are not massacred outright,—as the canon lawyer Shaf'i declares to be the Qur'anic injunction,—it is only to give them a respite till they are so wisely guided as to accept the true faith.

> The conversion of the entire population to Islam and the extinction of every form of dissent is the ideal of the Muslim State. If any infidel is suffered to exist in the community, it is as a necessary evil, and for a transitional period only. Political and social disabilities must be imposed on him, and bribes offered to him from the public funds, to hasten the day of his spiritual enlightenment and the addition of his name to the roll of true believers. . . . A non-Muslim therefore cannot be a citizen of the State; he is a member of a depressed class; his status is a modified form of slavery. He lives under a contract (zimma, or "dhimma") with the State: for the life and property grudgingly spared to him by the commander of the faithful he must undergo political and social disabilities, and pay a commutation money. In short, his continued existence in the State after the conquest of his country by the Muslims is conditional upon his person and property made subservient to the cause of Islam. He must pay a tax for his land (kharaj), from which the early Muslims were exempt; he must pay other

exactions for the maintenance of the army, in which he cannot enlist even if he offers to render personal service instead of paying the poll-tax; and he must show by humility of dress and behavior that he belongs to a subject class. No non-Muslim can wear fine dresses, ride on horseback or carry arms; he must behave respectfully and submissively to every member of the dominant sect.

The zimmi is under certain legal disabilities with regard to testimony in law courts, protection under criminal law, and in marriage . . . he cannot erect new temples, and has to avoid any offensive publicity in the exercise of his worship. . . . Every device short of massacre in cold blood was resorted to in order to convert heathen subjects. In addition to the poll-tax and public degradation in dress and demeanor imposed on them, the non-Muslims were subjected to various hopes and fears. Rewards in the form of money and public employment were offered to apostates from Hinduism. The leaders of Hindu religion and society were systematically repressed, to deprive the sect of spiritual instruction, and their religious gatherings and processions were forbidden in order to prevent the growth of solidarity and sense of communal strength among them. No new temple was allowed to be built nor any old one to be repaired, so that the total disappearance of Hindu worship was to be merely a question of time. But even this delay, this slow operation of Time, was intolerable to many of the more fiery spirits of Islam, who tried to hasten the abolition of "infidelity" by anticipating the destructive hand of Time and forcibly pulling down temples. When a class are publicly depressed and harassed by law and executive caprice alike, they merely content themselves with dragging on an animal existence. With every generous instinct of the soul crushed out of them, the intellectual culture merely adding a keen edge to their sense of humiliation, the Hindus could not be expected to produce the utmost of which they were capable; their lot was to be hewers of wood and drawers of water to their masters, to bring grist to the fiscal mill, to develop a low cunning and flattery as the only means of saving what they could of their own labor. Amidst such social conditions, the human hand and the human spirit cannot achieve their best; the human soul cannot soar to its highest pitch. The barrenness of the Hindu intellect and the meanness of spirit of the Hindu upper classes are the greatest condemnation of Muhammadan rule in India. The Islamic political tree, judged by its fruit, was an utter failure.

6. Ibid., p. 297.

7. V. A. Smith and P. Spear, eds., *The Oxford History of India*, 4th ed. (Delhi: Oxford University Press, 1985), p. 350.

8. Quoted in Nirad Chaudhuri, *Clive of India: A Political and Psychological Essay* (London: Barrie & Jenkins, 1975), p. 8. I think Chaudhuri is quoting from Alexis de Tocqueville, *Oeuvres Complètes*, ed. J. P. Mayer and André Jardin (Paris: Gallimard, 1962), pp. 441–553.

9. Chaudhuri, *Clive of India*, p. 9.

10. Ibid., p. 11.

11. Bholanauth Chunder, *The Travels of a Hindoo to Various Parts of Bengal and Upper India* (London: N. Trübner, 1869), vol. 1, p. v.

12. Ibid., p. 14.

13. Ibid., pp. 24, 40.

14. Ibid., vol. 2, pp. 407–409:

> The religion, the laws, the literature, and the arts of Asia, may all be fairly contrasted with those of Europe without suffering much damage or depreciation by the result. But no comparison can hold between the respective forms of government which the two portions of the old world exhibit. The British constitution is undoubtedly the best of all human political contrivances. Nothing approaching to it has ever been known in India or the East. The Oriental mind has produced the religion of the Vedas and of Buddha—that of the Guebers, of the Koran, and of Christianity itself, which is the principal basis of the civilization of Europe. It had framed such copious and refined languages as the Sanscrit and the Arabic. It has furnished the world with codes and jurisprudence, that Lycurgus and Solon adopted for their guide. It has produced songs and poetry scarcely inferior to the effusions of Homer. It has originated arts and inventions that minister yet to the necessities and comforts of mankind. In all these respects, it has an evident right to originality, and may claim an equality, if not a superiority, to the European mind. But it is decidedly wanting in the knowledge of the construction of a civil polity. It has never known, nor attempted to know, any other form of government than despotism. Political science and political reform appear, like the oak and elm, to be the plants of the soil of Europe. Never has any effort been made for their introduction in the plains of Persia, or the valley of the Ganges. Though the most important of all branches of human knowledge, politics have never engaged the attention of the people of the East. They have never studied the theory and practice of a constitutional government. They have never conceived anything like republicanism. They have never understood emancipation from political servitude. They have never known what is a covenant between subject and the sovereign. They have never had any patriotism or philanthropy—any common spirit and unity of feeling for the public weal. Now that it is in contemplation to teach native rulers the art of government, they should improve their tastes and habits, acquire those sterling qualities of the mind which inspire attachment and loyalty, get over the pride and prejudices which are a bar to progress, and be educated in those sound principles of administration, which conduce to the preservation of order, and the physical and moral well-being of the people. They should know the progress that the world has made in humanity—a humanity that is extended even to the inferior animals. They should learn to govern for the good, not of the fewest, but the greatest number.

15. Chaudhuri, *Clive of India*, p. 21.

16. Ibid., p. 23.

17. Ibid., p. 35.

18. Quoted in David Gilmour, *The Ruling Caste: Imperial Lives in the Victorian Raj* (New York: Farrar, Straus and Giroux, 2005), p. xiv.

19. Ibid., p. xiii.

20. Vincent A. Smith and Percival Spear, eds., *The Oxford History of India* (1911; reprint, Delhi: Oxford University Press, 1981), p. 448.

21. Ibid., p. 449.

22. David Gilmour, *The Long Recessional: The Imperial Life of Rudyard Kipling* (New York: Farrar, Straus and Giroux, 2002), p. 40.

23. Gilmour, *The Ruling Caste*, pp. xiii–xiv.

24. Ibid., p. 18.

25. Quoted in ibid., p. 3.

26. Smith and Spear, *The Oxford History of India* (1981), p. 450.

27. Ibid., p. 451.

28. Gilmour, *The Ruling Caste*, p. 9.

29. V. B. Kulkarni, *British Statesmen in India* (Bombay: Orient Longmans, 1961), p. 152.

30. Ibid., p. 153.

31. Ibid., p. 154.

32. Ibid., pp. 163–64.

33. Ibid., p. 166.

34. Denis Judd, *Empire* (London: Fontana Press, 1997), p. 72.

35. Lawrence James, *Raj: The Making and Unmaking of British India* (New York: St. Martin's Griffin, 1997), p. 645.

36. Geoffrey Moorhouse, *India Britannica* (London: Paladin Books, 1986), p. 179.

37. James, *Raj*, p. 645.

38. Ibid.

39. Quoted in Gilmour, *The Ruling Caste*, p. 12.

40. In Indian mythology Manu is the first man and the legendary author of the important Sanskrit code of law, *Manu Samhita*, which dates, in fact, from around 200 CE.

41. Quoted in Moorhouse, *India Britannica*, p. 197.

42. Ibid., p. 198.

43. Keith Windschuttle, "The Cultural War on Western Civilization," in *The Survival of Culture: Permanent Values in a Virtual Age*, ed. Hilton Kramer and Roger Kimball (Chicago: Iven R. Dee, 2002), p. 108.

44. Ibid.

45. David Gilmour, *Curzon* (New York: Farrar, Straus and Giroux, 2003), p. 93.

46. Quoted in ibid., p. 166.

47. Quoted in ibid.

48. Ibid., p. 170.

49. Ibid., p. 171.
50. Ibid., p. 173.
51. Ibid., p. 178.
52. Quoted in ibid., p. 179.
53. J. C. Harle, *The Art and Architecture of the Indian Subcontinent* (London: Penguin, 1986), p. 199.
54. Smith and Spear, *The Oxford History of India* (1985), pp. 235–36.
55. Sita Ram Goel, *Hindu Temples: What Happened to Them, Islamic Evidence* (New Delhi: Voice of India, 1993), sec. 3, chap. 8.
56. Gilmour, *Curzon*, pp. 179–81.
57. Ibid., pp. 185–86.
58. Sir Thomas Raleigh, ed., *Lord Curzon in India, Being a Selection from His Speeches as Viceroy & Governor-General of India, 1895–1905* (London: Macmillan, 1906), p. 42.
59. Ibid., p. 35.
60. Ibid., pp. 39–40.
61. Ibid., p. 58.
62. Quoted in Gilmour, *Curzon*, p. 343.
63. Kulkarni, *British Statesmen in India*, p. 248.
64. Quoted in Gilmour, *Curzon*, p. 345.
65. Ibid., p. 476.
66. Ibid., p. 481.
67. Ibid., p. 495.

Chapter 7: Edward Said and His Methodology

1. Edmund Leach, *Claude Lévi-Strauss* (New York: Viking, 1974), p. 13.
2. James Burnham, *Suicide of the West: An Essay on the Meaning and Destiny of Liberalism* (New York: John Day, 1964), p. 100.
3. Ibid., pp. 103–104.
4. Ibid., p. 123.
5. Jean-Paul Sartre, preface to Frantz Fanon, *The Wretched of the Earth* (New York: Grove Press, 1968).
6. I owe most of the observations in this paragraph to Fred Siegel, professor of history at the Cooper Union for Science and Art in New York.
7. Olivier Pétré-Grenouilleau, *Les Traites Négrières: Essai d'Histoire Globale* (Paris: Éditions Gallimard, 2004), pp. 287–93.
8. Ehud R. Toledano, *The Ottoman Slave Trade and Its Suppression, 1840–1890* (Princeton, NJ: Princeton University Press, 1982), pp. 91, 272, 273; quoted in Pétré-Grenouilleau, *Les Traites Négrières*, pp. 289–90.
9. Y. H. Erdem, *Slavery in the Ottoman Empire and Its Demise, 1800–1909* (New York: St. Martin's Press, 1996), p. xix; quoted in Pétré-Grenouilleau, *Les Traites Négrières*, p. 290.

10. Henry H. Gemery and Jan S. Hogendorn, "La traite des esclaves sur l'Atlantique: essai de modèle économique," in *Esclave facteur de production*, ed. Sidney Mintz (Paris: Dunod, 1981), pp. 18–45, quoted in Pétré-Grenouilleau, *Les Traites Négrières*, p. 74.

11. J. D. Fage, *A History of West Africa* (Cambridge: Cambridge University Press, 1959).

12. Pétré-Grenouilleau, *Les Traites Négrières*, p. 76. The entire chapter, with the significant title "Black Africa, Full Participant in the Slave Trade" (pp. 74–86), deals with this oft-neglected subject.

13. Patrick Manning, *Slavery and African Life: Occidental, Oriental and African Slave Trades* (Cambridge: Cambridge University Press, 1990), p. 93; quoted in Pétré-Grenouilleau, *Les Traites Négrières*, p. 288.

14. Basil Davidson, *The African Slave Trade* (Boston: Little, Brown, 1980), p. 255; L. H. Gann and Peter Duignan, *Africa South of the Sahara* (Stanford, CA: Hoover Institution Press, 1981), p. 4.

15. All the quotes in this paragraph are from Bernard Lewis, *Race and Slavery in the Middle East: An Historical Enquiry* (New York: Oxford University Press, 1990), pp. 50–53.

16. Paul Bairoch, *Mythes et paradoxes de l'histoire économique* (Paris: La Découverte, 1994), p. 203.

17. Pétré-Grenouilleau, *Les Traites Négrières*, p. 149.

18. Ibid., pp. 148–49.

19. J. Azumah, *Islam and Slavery* (London: Centre for Islamic Studies, London Bible College, 1999), p. 5; quoted in Caroline Cox and John Marks, *The 'West,' Islam and Islamism: Is Ideological Islam Compatible with Liberal Democracy?* (London: Civitas: Institute for the Study of Civil Society, 2003), p. 40.

20. Note presented by the secretary general to the fiftieth session of the United Nations General Assembly, October 16, 1995, quoted in Cox and Marks, *The 'West,' Islam and Islamism*, p. 40.

21. P. Lovejoy and J. Hogendorn, eds., *Slow Death for Slavery: The Course of Abolition in Northern Nigeria, 1897–1936* (Cambridge: Cambridge University Press, 1993), p. 30; quoted Cox and Marks, *The 'West,' Islam and Islamism*, p. 40.

22. John Eibner, "Eradicating Slavery in Sudan," *Boston Globe*, February 22, 2006, http://www.boston.com/news/globe/editorial_opinion/oped/articles/2006/02/22/eradicating_slavery_in_sudan/.

23. Jan Hogendorn, "The Hideous Trade: Economic Aspects of the 'Manufacture' and Sale of Eunuchs," *Paideuma* 45 (1999): 137.

24. Ibid., p. 146.

25. Robert C. Davis, *Christian Slaves, Muslim Masters: White Slavery in the Mediterranean, the Barbary Coast and Italy, 1500–1800* (New York: Palgrave Macmillan, 2003), p. 23.

26. Quoted in Giles Milton, *White Gold: The Extraordinary Story of Thomas Pellow and North Africa's One Million European Slaves* (London: Hodder & Stoughton, 2004), p. 67.

27. Ibid., p. 97.

28. Ibid., p. 68.

29. Ibid., p. 78.

30. Ibid., p. 107.

31. Ibid., p. 106.

32. Ibid., p. 105, quoting Germain Mouette.

33. B. Lewis, *Cultures in Conflict: Christians, Muslims, and Jews in the Age of Discovery* (Oxford: Oxford University Press, 1995), p. 72.

34. Kenneth R. Timmerman, *Preachers of Hate: Islam and the War on America* (New York: Three Rivers Press, 2004).

35. Kenneth R. Timmerman in Jamie Glazov, "Symposium: Islamic Anti-Semitism," FrontPageMagazine.com, October 31, 2003, http://www.frontpagemag.com/Articles/ReadArticle.asp?ID=10581.

36. Speech by Prime Minister Mahathir Mohamad of Malaysia to the Tenth Islamic Summit Conference, Putrajaya, Malaysia, October 16, 2003. Available online at http://www.adl.org/anti_semitism/Malaysia.asp (accessed June 1, 2007).

37. MEMRI (Middle East Media Research Institute), Special Dispatch Series, no. 375, May 3, 2002.

38. Amartya Sen, *Identity and Violence: The Illusion of Destiny* (New York: Norton, 2006), p. 66, and also at p. 16: ". . . distinguished Jewish philosopher fled an intolerant Europe."

39. Fouad Ajami, "Enemies, a Love Story: A Nobel Laureate Argues That Civilizations Are Not Clashing," *Washington Post*, April 2, 2006.

40. Moses Maimonides, *Moses Maimonides' Epistle to Yemen: The Arabic Original and the Three Hebrew Versions*, ed. Abraham S. Halkin, trans. by Boaz Cohen (New York: American Academy for Jewish Research, 1952).

41. Ibid., p. ii.

42. Ibid.

43. Ibid., p. iv.

44. Norman Stillman, *The Jews of Arab Lands: A History and Source Book* (Philadelphia: Jewish Publication Society of America, 1979), p. 236.

45. Maimonides, *Moses Maimonides' Epistle to Yemen*, p. viii.

46. Ibid., p. xviii.

47. A. Guillaume, *The Life of Muhammad, A Translation of Ibn Iṣhāq's Sīrat Rasūl Allāh* (1955; reprint, Oxford: Oxford University Press, 1987), p. 369.

48. Ibid., p. 368.

49. Ibid., pp. 482–83.

50. Ibid., pp. 364–69.

51. Ibid., pp. 665–66.

52. Ibid., pp. 461–69.

53. Ibid., pp. 437–45.

54. Ibn Sa'd, *Kitāb al-Ṭabaqāt al-Kabīrs*, trans. S. M. Haq (New Delhi: Kitab Bhavan, n.d.), vol. 1, p. 32.

55. *al-Bukharī*, *Ṣaḥīḥ*, trans. M. Muhsin Khan (New Delhi: Kitab Bhavan, 1987), vol. 5, book 59: Book of al-Maghazi (Raids), hadith no. 362, p. 241.

56. Guillaume, *The Life of Muhammad*, p. 689.

57. *Abū Dāwūd*, *Sunan* (New Delhi: Kitab Bhavan, 1997), vol. 2, hadith no. 3024, p. 861.

58. Jacob Neusner, trans., *Mishnah* (New Haven, CT: Yale University Press, 1988), p. 591: The Fourth Division: The Order of Damages, Sanhedrin 4:5.J.: "Therefore man was created alone, (1) to teach you that whoever destroys a single Israelite soul is deemed by Scripture as if he had destroyed a whole world."

59. Here are some more quotes from the Koran:

> **IX.29–31:** Fight against such of those who have been given the Scripture [Jews and Christians] as believe not in Allah nor the Last Day, and forbid not that which Allah has forbidden by His Messenger, and follow not the religion of truth, until they pay the tribute [poll-tax] readily, and are utterly subdued. The Jews say, "Ezra is the son of Allah," and the Christians say, "The Messiah is the son of Allah." Those are the words of their mouths, conforming to the words of the unbelievers before them. Allah attack them! How perverse they are!
>
> They have taken their rabbis and their monks as lords besides Allah, and so too the Messiah son of Mary, though they were commanded to serve but one God. There is no God but He. Allah is exalted above that which they deify beside Him.
>
> **IX.34:** O you who believe! Lo! many of the [Jewish] rabbis and the [Christian] monks devour the wealth of mankind wantonly and debar [men] from the way of Allah. They who hoard up gold and silver and spend it not in the way of Allah, unto them give tidings of a painful doom.
>
> **V.63–64**: Why do not the rabbis and the priests forbid their evil-speaking and devouring of illicit gain? Verily evil is their handiwork.
>
> The Jews say, "Allah's hands are fettered." Their hands are fettered, and they are cursed for what they have said! On the contrary, His hands are spread open. He bestows as He wills. That which has been revealed to you from your Lord will surely increase the arrogance and unbelief of many among them. We have cast enmity and hatred among them until the Day of Resurrection. Every time they light the fire of war, Allah extinguishes it. They hasten to spread corruption throughout the earth, but Allah does not love corrupters!
>
> **V.70–71:** We made a covenant with the Israelites and sent forth apostles among them. But whenever an apostle came to them with a message that did not suit their fancies, some they accused of lying and others they put to death. They thought no harm would follow: they were blind and deaf. God is ever watching their actions.

V.82: Indeed, you will surely find that the most vehement of men in enmity to those who believe are the Jews and the polytheists.

V.51: O you who believe! Take not the Jews and the Christians for friends. They are friends one to another. He among you who takes them for friends is one of them.

V.57: O you who believe! Choose not for friends such of those who received the Scripture [Jews and Christians] before you, and of the disbelievers, as make jest and sport of your religion. But keep your duty to Allah if you are true believers.

V.59: Say: O, People of the Scripture [Jews and Christians]! Do you blame us for aught else than that we believe in Allah and that which is revealed unto us and that which was revealed aforetime, and because most of you are evil-doers?

V.66: Among them [Jews and Christians] there are people who are moderate, but many of them are of evil conduct.

XXXIII.26: He brought down from their strongholds those who had supported them from among the People of the Book [Jews of Bani Qurayza] and cast terror into their hearts, so that some you killed and others you took captive.

V.60: Say: 'Shall I tell you who will receive a worse reward from God? Those whom [i.e., Jews] God has cursed and with whom He has been angry, transforming them into apes and swine, and those who serve the devil. Worse is the plight of these, and they have strayed farther from the right path.'

60. Baydawi, *Commentarius in Coranum. Anwaar al-Tanziil Wa-Asraar al-Ta'wiil*, ed. H. O. Fleischer (1846–48; reprint Osnabrück: Biblio, 1968), p. 63; English translation by Michael Schub.

More quotes from Baydawi:

. . . "because they disbelieved and killed the prophets unjustly" by reason of their disbelief in miracles, e.g. the splitting of the sea, the clouds giving shade, and the sending of the manna and quails, and splitting of the rock into twelve fountains/or, disbelief in the revealed books, e.g. the Gospel, Qur'an, the verse of stoning, and the Torah verse in which Muhammad is depicted; and their killing of the prophets like Shay'aa [Isaiah], Zakariyyaa, Yahyaa, et al., all killed unjustly because they considered that of these prophets nothing was to be believed and thus they deserved to be killed.

In addition [God] accuses them of following fantasy and love of this world, as he demonstrates in His saying [line 14] "this if for their transgression and sin" i.e. rebelliousness, contrariness, and hostility brought them into disbelief in the signs, and killing the prophets. Venal sins lead to serious sins, just as small bits of obedience lead to larger ones. . . . God repeated this proof of what is *inveterate* [in the Jews], which is the reason for their unbelief and murder, and which is the cause of their committing sins and transgressing the bounds God set.

61. From Ibn Kathir, *Tafsir Ibn Kathir* (Riyadh: 2000), vol. 1, pp. 245–46.

Al-Hassan commented, "Allah humiliated them under the feet of the Muslims, who appeared at a time when the Majus (Zoroastrians) were taking the jizya from the Jews. Also, Abu Al-'Aliyah, Ar-Rabi bin Anas and As-Suddi said that 'misery' used in that ayah means 'poverty.' 'Atiyah Al-'Awfi said that 'misery' means, 'paying the tilth (tax).' In addition, Ad-Dahhak commented on Allah's statement, "and they drew on themselves the wrath of Allah," 'They deserved Allah's anger.' Also, Ibn Jarir said that, "and they drew on themselves the wrath of Allah" means, 'They went back with the wrath. Similarly, Allah said, "Verily, I intend to let you draw my sin on yourself as well as yours" (Qur'an 5:29) meaning, 'You will end up carrying my and your mistakes instead of me.' Thus the meaning of the ayah becomes, "They went back carrying Allah's anger: Allah's wrath descended upon them; they deserved Allah's anger.' Allah's statement, "That was because they used to disbelieve in the Ayat (proofs, evidence, etc.) of Allah and killed the Prophets wrongfully," means 'This is what We rewarded the Children of Israel with: humiliation and misery.' Allah's anger that descended on the Children of Israel was a part of the humiliation they earned, because of their defiance of the truth, disbelief in Allah's Law, i.e., the Prophets and their following. The Children of Israel rejected the Messengers even killing them. Surely there is no form of disbelief worse than disbelieving in Allah's ayat and murdering the Prophets of Allah.

62. Robert Wistrich, *Antisemitism: The Longest Hatred* (New York: Schocken Books, 1991), p. 196.

63. Martin Jacques, "The Middle Kingdom Mentality," *Guardian*, April 16, 2005.

64. Frank Dikötter, ed., *The Construction of Racial Identities in China and Japan: Historical and Contemporary Perspectives* (Honolulu: University of Hawai'i Press, 1997), pp. 1–11.

65. Ibid., p. 2.

66. Ibid., p. 6.

67. Ibid., p. 7.

68. Ibid., p. 9.

69. Ibid., p. 10.

70. Ibid., p. 11.

71. Aparna Pallavi, "Racism in North India," Boloji.com, October 6, 2006, http://www.boloji.com/wfs5/wfs677.htm.

72. National Campaign on Dalit Human Rights Web site, http://dalits.org/default.htm.

73. "Dalit Houses Burnt Down at Gohana in Haryana," NCDHR Web site, http://dalits.org/Gohana1.htm.

74. "Delhi Declaration of National Summit on Reservation in Private Sector," NCDHR Web site, August 9, 2005, http://dalits.org/delhideclaration.htm.

75. G. B. Singh, *Gandhi: Behind the Mask of Divinity* (Amherst, NY: Prometheus Books, 2004), p. 102.

76. Ibid., p. 103.

77. Richard Grenier, "The Gandhi Nobody Knows," *Commentary* 75, no. 3 (March 1983): 64.

78. Iris Chang, *The Rape of Nanking: The Forgotten Holocaust* (New York: Basic Books, 1997); see also W. G. Beasley, *Japanese Imperialism, 1894–1945* (New York: Oxford University Press, 1987).

79. Michael Cook, *Muhammad* (Oxford: Oxford University Press, 1996), p. 86.

80. Michael Cook and Patricia Crone, *Hagarism: The Making of the Muslim World* (Cambridge: Cambridge University Press, 1977), p. viii.

81. Speros Vryonis Jr., *The Decline of Medieval Hellenism in Asia Minor and the Process of Islamization from the Eleventh through the Fifteenth Century* (Berkeley and Los Angeles: University of California Press, 1986), p. 164.

82. Quoted in ibid., p. 286.

83. Ibid., p. 402.

84. Ibid., p. 500.

85. Bernard Williams, *Morality: An Introduction to Ethics* (New York: Harper & Row, 1972), pp. 24–25.

86. Javed Majeed, *Ungoverned Imaginings: James Mill's* The History of British India *and Orientalism* (Oxford: Clarendon, 1992).

87. W. Empson, *Argufying: Essays on Literature & Culture*, ed. John Haffenden (London: Hogarth Press, 1988), p. 578.

88. Here are all the German colonies, with the dates when they were lost in square brackets:

> **Africa:** Cameroons (*Kamerun*), nowadays Cameroon and parts of the Central African Republic, Congo, Gabon and Nigeria [1916]; German East Africa (*Deutsch Ostafrika*), nowadays Tanganyika (continental part of Tanzania), Burundi, Rwanda and the Ruvuma triangle (nowadays part of Mozambique) [1919]; German Southwest Africa (*Deutsch Sudwestafrika*), nowadays Namibia [1915]; Gross-Friedrichsburg, nowadays in southern Ghana [1717] Togoland, nowadays Togo and the eastern part of Ghana [1914]
>
> **Asia:** Kiaochao/Tsingtao (*Pachtgebiet Kiautschou/Tsingtau*), nowadays Qingdao, part of China [1914]

Oceania: Carolinas Islands (*Karolinen-Inseln*), nowadays the Federated States of Micronesia [1914]; German New Guinea (*Deutsch-Neu-Guinea*), nowadays the northern half of Papua New Guinea [1919]; Marianas Islands (*Marianen Inseln*), nowadays Northern Marianas [1914]; Nauru [1914]; Palaos Islands (*Palau-Inseln*), nowadays Palau [1914]; Ralik Islands (*Ralik-Inseln*), nowadays Marshall Islands [1914]; Samoa, nowadays Samoa [1914]

89. Martin Kramer, ed., *The Jewish Discovery of Islam* (Tel Aviv: Moshe Dayan Center, 1999), p. vii.

90. Bernard Lewis, "The Pro-Islamic Jews," in *Islam in History: Ideas, People, and Events in the Middle East* (Chicago: Open Court, 1993), pp. 142, 144.

91. *Orientalism*, pp. 33, 57.

92. Christopher Hitchens, letter to the editor, *Atlantic Monthly*, November 2003.

93. Susan Bayly, "Colonial Cultures: Asia," in *The Oxford History of the British Empire: The Nineteenth Century*, ed. Andrew Porter (Oxford: Oxford University Press, 1999), p. 469.

94. C. A. Bayly, "The Second British Empire," in *The Oxford History of the British Empire: Historiography*, ed. Robin W. Winks (Oxford: Oxford University Press, 1999), p. 70.

95. Edward Said's words are in italics throughout this paragraph.

96. Khawaja's own summary—personal communication. His paper will appear in the collected papers of the conference: Irfan Khawaja, "Essentialism, Consistency and Islam: A Critique of Edward Said's *Orientalism*," in *Postcolonial Theory and the Arab-Israeli Conflict*, ed. Efraim Karsh (New York: Routledge, forthcoming, 2007).

97. David Armitage, "Literature and Empire," in *The Origins of Empire: British Overseas Enterprise to the Close of the Seventeenth Century*, ed. Nicholas Canny and Alaine Low (Oxford: Oxford University Press, 1998), pp. 101–102; emphasis mine.

98. Ibid., p. 110.

99. Ibid., p. 120.

100. David Fitzpatrick, "Ireland and the Empire," in *The Oxford History of the British Empire: The Nineteenth Century*, ed. Andrew Porter (Oxford: Oxford University Press, 1999), p. 504.

101. Robert E. Frykenberg, "India to 1858," in *The Oxford History of the British Empire: Historiography*, vol. 5, ed. Robin W. Winks (Oxford: Oxford University Press, 1999), p. 197.

102. Ibid., p. 207.

103. Ibid., p. 212.

104. Ibid.

105. D. A. Washbrook, "Colonial Discourse Theory," in *The Oxford History of the British Empire: Historiography*, ed. Robin W. Winks (Oxford: Oxford University Press, 1999), p. 607.

106. Bassam Tibi, *Islam between Culture and Politics* (New York: Palgrave Macmillan, 2005), pp. 236–37.

107. Robert Irwin, *For Lust of Knowing: The Orientalists and Their Enemies* (London: Allen Lane, 2006), p. 4.

Chapter 8: The Pathological Niceness of Liberals, Antimonies, Paradoxes, and Western Values

1. G. K. Chesterton, *The Napoleon of Notting Hill* (1904; reprint, Ware, UK: Wordsworth Editions, 1996), p. 17.

2. James Burnham, *Suicide of the West: An Essay on the Meaning and Destiny of Liberalism* (1964; reprint, New York: Regnery, 1985).

3. Winston Churchill, speech given at Royal Society of St. George, April 24, 1933, quoted in Richard M. Langworth, "'Our Qualities and Deeds Must Burn and Glow': Churchill's Wisdom Calls to Us across the Years," *Finest Hour* 112 (Autumn 2001), http://www.winstonchurchill.org/i4a/pages/index.cfm?pageid=280.

4. The whole section on poverty and militant Islam leans heavily on the article by Daniel Pipes, "God and Mammon: Does Poverty Cause Militant Islam?" *National Interest* (Winter 2002), http://www.danielpipes.org/article/104.

5. Ibid.

6. This usually means a tendency "to belittle belief and strict adherence to principle as genuine and dismiss it as a cynical exploitation of the masses by politicians. As such, Western observers see material issues and leaders, not the spiritual state of the Arab world, as the heart of the problem." Quoted in ibid.

7. Daniel Pipes, *Militant Islam Reaches America* (New York: Norton, 2002), p. 62.

8. The Mau Mau Uprising (1952–1960): an insurgency by Kenyan rebels against the British colonial administration.

9. Burnham, *Suicide of the West*, pp. 70–71.

10. Ibid., p. 115.

11. Benjamin Netanyahu, "Today, We Are All Americans," *New York Post*, September 21, 2001.

12. Benjamin Netanyahu, *Fighting Terrorism: How Democracies Can Defeat Domestic and International Terrorism* (New York: Farrar, Straus and Giroux, 1995), p. 82; quoted in Douglas Murray, *Neoconservatism: Why We Need It* (New York: Encounter Books, 2006), pp. 118–19.

13. Steven Emerson, International Terrorism and Immigration Policy, US House of Representatives Judiciary Subcommittee on Immigration and Claims, Subcommittee on Immigration and Claims Hearing on International Terrorism and Immigration Policy, January 25, 2000.

14. Christopher Hitchens, "Against Rationalization," *Nation*, September 20, 2001.

15. Daniel Freedman, "Bernard Lewis: U.S. May Lose War on Terror," *New York Sun*, September 13, 2006.

16. At Daniel Pipes's Web log, http://www.danielpipes.org/blog/668.

17. See Niall Ferguson, *The Pity of War* (Harmondsworth, UK: Penguin, 2006).

18. J. Conrad, *Under Western Eyes* (Harmondsworth, UK: Penguin, 1957), p. 85.

19. Christian Godin, *La Fin de l'Humanité* (Seyssel, France: Éditions Champ Vallon, 2003), p. 71.

20. Sayeed Abdul A'la Maududi, *Jihad in Islam*, 7th ed. (Lahore, Pakistan: Islamic Publications, 2001), pp. 8, 9.

21. Quoted by Eliot A. Cohen, "World War IV: Let's Call This Conflict What It Is," *Wall Street Journal*, November 20, 2001.

22. Geoffrey K. Pullum, *The Great Eskimo Vocabulary Hoax and Other Irreverent Essays on the Study of Language* (Chicago: University of Chicago Press, 1991), pp. 159–71.

23. Nathaniel Philbrick has studied Polynesia. The present population of Polynesia orginally came from the islands of Southeast Asia, their outrigger canoes enabling them to sail farther east and south. "The Polynesians' oceangoing canoes became their arks, transporting dogs, pigs, breadfruit seedlings, taro, and inevitably, rats to islands that had never seen the like. Once on a new island, the Polynesians set to work re-creating an agricultural society similar to the one they had left behind, a process that led to the extinction of countless indigenous species of animals and plants." Archaeologists working on one such island, Upolu, have come to the conclusion that it "once contained betwen 100 and 242 people per square kilometer—a density that would have had a disastrous effect on the island's ecology. This fostered the development of culturally sanctioned methods of population control—from infanticide to ritual sacrifice to cannibalism, as well as additional voyages of discovery." Nathaniel Philbrick, *Sea of Glory: America's Voyage of Discovery, the U.S. Exploring Expedition, 1838–1842* (New York: Penguin, 2004), p. 143.

24. K. Marx and F. Engels. *Manifesto of the Communist Party* (London, 1848), chap. 1.

25. See Dale Riepe, *The Naturalistic Tradition in Indian Thought* (Seattle: University of Washington Press, 1961).

26. Ibid., p. 247.

27. R. A. Nicholson, *The Mystics of Islam* (1914; reprint, London: Routledge and Kegan Paul, 1975), pp. 10–27.

28. See E. Underhill, *Mysticism: A Study in the Nature and Development of Man's Spiritual Consciousness* (1911; reprint, New York: Dutton, 1961), and William James, *The Varieties of Religious Experience* (1902; reprint, New York: Modern Library, 1999), lectures XVI and XVII, Mysticism.

29. Luc Barbulesco and Philippe Cardinal, *L'Islam En Questions* (Paris: Grasset, 1986), pp. 203–14.

30. *The Chambers Dictionary* (Edinburgh: Chambers, 2003), p. 1461.

31. David Gilmour, *The Long Recessional: The Imperial Life of Rudyard Kipling* (New York: Farrar, Straus and Giroux, 2002), p. 69.

32. Denis Judd, *Empire* (London: Fontana Press, 1997), p. 16. To the uninitiated: "no ball" and "googly" are cricketing terms.

33. Such as Dinesh D'Souza, the conservative thinker and commentator at the Hoover Institute, Stanford University.

34. Translation available at the Human Rights Solidarity Web site: http://www.hrsolidarity.net/mainfile.php/2001vol11no67/148/. Other edicts translated in Vincent A. Smith and Percival Spear, eds., *The Oxford History of India* (1911; reprint, New Delhi: Oxford University Press, 1981), pp. 129–32.

35. Available at the Asian Human Rights Commission Web site: http://material.ahrchk.net/charter/mainfile.php/eng_charter.

36. Janadas Devan, "Singapore Way," *New York Review of Books*, June 6, 1996.

37. For instance, the Abdorrahman Boroumand Foundation for the Promotion of Human Rights and Democracy in Iran (ABF) "is a non-governmental non-profit organization dedicated to the promotion of human rights and democracy in Iran. The Foundation is an independent organization with no political affiliation. It is named in memory of Dr. Abdorrahman Boroumand, an Iranian lawyer and pro-democracy activist who was assassinated allegedly by the agents of the Islamic Republic of Iran in Paris on April 18, 1991." ABF Web site, http://www.abfiran.org/english/foundation.php. There is Iranian Action Committee, Inc., a nonprofit nongovernmental organization founded by twenty-seven artists, lawyers, scientists, and human rights activists that is working to bring the Islamic Republic of Iran in front of International Human Rights Tribunals to be tried for crimes against humanity. Islamic Republic of Iran Crimes Web site, http://www.iricrimes.org/mission.asp. Other organizations include Regime Change Iran (http://www.regimechangeiran.com) and the Alliance of Iranian Women (Aryamehr), which advocates "a free, democratic, secular, and nationalistic government in Iran," among others.

38. Hirad Abtahi, "Reflections on the Ambiguous Universality of Human Rights: Cyrus the Great's Proclamation as a Challenge to the Athenian Democracy's Perceived Monopoly on Human Rights," in *The Dynamics of International Criminal Justice*, ed. Hirad Abtahi and Gideon Boas (Leiden: Brill, 2006), p. 12.

39. Plato, *Laws*, III, 694a, 694b; quoted in ibid., p. 30.

40. Bernard Lewis, *Race and Slavery in the Middle East: An Historical Enquiry* (New York: Oxford University Press, 1990), p. 20.

41. Barry Rubin, *The Long War for Freedom: The Arab Struggle for Democracy in the Middle East* (Hoboken, NJ: Wiley, 2006), p. 30.

42. L. Carl Brown, *Religion and State: The Muslim Approach to Politics* (New York: Columbia University Press, 2000).

43. Agence France-Presse, June 26, 2000.

44. Golnaz Esfandiari, "Iran: Prize-Winning Documentary Exposes Hidden Side of Iranian Society," http://www.parstimes.com/achive/2005/rfe/prostitution_behind_veil.html (accessed June 1, 2007).

45. Karl Vick, "Opiates of the Iranian People: Despair Drives World's Highest Addiction Rate," *Washington Post*, September 23, 2005, p. A1.

46. Golnaz Esfandiari, "Iran: New Ways Considered for Tackling Growing Drug Use among Young People," Eurasianet.org, December 7, 2003, http://www.eurasianet.org/departments/insight/articles/pp120703.shtml.

47. “Child Protection,” UNICEF Pakistan Media Centre, http://www.unicef.org/pakistan/media_1775.htm.

48. “Official Laws against Women in Iran,” Women’s Forum Against Fundamentalism in Iran Web site, http://www.wfafi.org/laws.pdf#search=%22plight%20of%20women%20in%20Iran%20%22.

49. Recent violence includes:

> January 1—Iran’s notorious Islamic court in the city of Rasht, northern Iran, sentenced Delara Darabi to death by hanging charged with murder when she was 17 years old. Darabi has denied the charges but Iran’s Supreme Court upheld her sentencing. Darabi, who is now 19, is an artist and engaged to a man who is also sentenced to imprisonment for his involvement in the alleged crime.
>
> January 2—Ahmadinejad ordered the closure of a daily newspaper and banned a planned women’s publication. His Cultural Ministry issued the ban order stating: “The Supervisory Board on the Press agreed to the temporary closure of Asia newspaper and Nour-e Banovan and ordered their cases sent to court.”
>
> January 4—Iran’s Paramilitary forces (Basijis and Ansar-e Hezbollah) launched an “acid attack” on two female university students in the town of Shahroud, northeastern Iran, to intimidate women. Acid was splashed in the faces of the two female students, aged 21 and 22, because they were not observing the strict Islamic dress code in Ferdowsi Street, Shahroud. Islamic vigilantes on a motorbike threw acid on the two women as they were walking. Ahmadinejad regularly addresses meetings of these Islamic vigilantes and praises their efforts “to purify the Islamic Republic of the vestiges of corrupt Western culture” and urges them to step up the campaign against the “mal-veiling” of women and girls.
>
> January 7—Iran’s notorious Islamic court has sentenced an 18-year-old female rape victim to death by hanging after she weepingly confessed that she had unintentionally killed a man who had tried to rape both her and her niece, according to state-run daily Etemaad. Nazanin, 17 at the time of the incident, and her 16-year-old niece Somayeh, were attacked by three men and she killed one of the men in self-defense.
>
> January 7—Ahmadinejad plans to segregate Iran’s pedestrian walkways on gender basis, according to Fatemeh Alia, a deputy in Iran’s Majlis (Parliament) and one of Ahmadinejad’s closest allies. As part of the government plan called “Increase the hejab (veil) culture and female chastity,” the Ministry of Housing and Urban Development has received orders to construct separate pedestrian walkways for men and women, according to Alia.

"Ahmadinejad Begins 2006 with Escalated Violence against Women and New Gender Apartheid Policies in Iran," Women's Forum Against Fundamentalism in Iran Web site, http://www.wfafi.org/wfafistatement23.htm.

50. Arthur M. Schlesinger Jr., *The Disuniting of America: Reflections on a Multicultural Society* (New York: Norton, 1992), p. 128.

51. Marianne Talbot, "Relativism," *Sunday Times* (London), July 24, 1994; cited in Melanie Phillips, *All Must Have Prizes* (London: Little, Brown, 1996), p. 221, and also in Murray, *Neoconservatism*, pp. 102–103. See also Marianne Talbot, "Against Relativism," in *Education in Morality*, ed. J. M. Halstead and T. McLaughlin (London: Routledge, 1998).

52. Burnham, *Suicide of the West*, p. 179.

53. Ibid., p. 201. See also Arthur Farnsworth quoting a conversation with Robert Frost, October 22, 1977, in Eugene C. Gerhart, *Quote It Completely! World Reference Guide to More than 5,000 Memorable Quotations from Law and Literature* (Buffalo, NY: W. S. Hein, 1998), p. 658.

54. The phrase, of course, comes from John Keats's *Letters*. He was not referring to Western civilization.

55. Bertrand Russell, *The Problems of Philosophy* (London: Williams & Norgate, 1912), chap. 15.

56. Roger Scruton, "The Defense of the West," lecture given at the Columbia Political Union, New York, April 14, 2005.

57. Caroline Cox and John Marks, *The 'West,' Islam and Islamism: Is Ideological Islam Compatible with Liberal Democracy?* (London: Civitas: Institute for the Study of Civil Society, 2003), pp. 12–13.

58. G. W. F. Hegel, *Aesthetics: Lectures on Fine Art*, trans. T. M. Knox (Oxford: Clarendon, 1988), vol. 1, p. 464.

59. Sophocles, *Antigone*, trans. Robert Fagles (New York: Penguin, 1984), p. 37.

60. Ibid., p. 77.

61. Roger Scruton, *The West and the Rest* (New York: Continuum, ISI Books, 2002), pp. 2–3.

62. Ibid., p. 4.

63. M. Anastos, *Aspects of the Mind of Byzantium*, Political Theory, Theology, and Ecclesiastical Relations with the See of Rome, Variorum Collected Studies Series (Ashgate: Ashgate Publications, 2001), chap. 7, pp. 484–519. Part (b) "The doctrine of the two powers" is available at http://www.myriobiblos.gr/texts/english/milton1_7.html#b.

64. Lewis Vaughn and Austin Dacey, *The Case for Humanism: An Introduction* (Lanham, MD: Rowman & Littlefield, 2003). The entire section on church-state separation is heavily indebted to this work.

65. John Locke, *A Letter concerning Toleration* (Amherst, NY: Prometheus Books, 1990), p. 20.

66. Leonard Busher, *Religion's Peace or a Plea for Liberty of Conscience* (1614), cited in H. Leon McBeth, *A Sourcebook for Baptist Heritage* (Nashville, TN: Broadmen Press, 1990), p. 72; and Vaughn and Dacey, *The Case for Humanism.*

67. Scruton, *The West and the Rest*, p. 6.

68. Thomas Paine, *The Age of Reason* (Secaucus, NJ: Carol Publishing, 1974), p. 52.

69. Thomas Nagel, "Moral Conflict and Political Legitimacy," *Philosophy and Public Affairs* 16 (1987): 230–31; quoted in Vaughn and Dacey, *The Case for Humanism*, p. 211.

70. Ibid., quoted in Vaughn and Dacey.

71. Scruton, *The West and the Rest*, p. 6.

72. Ibid., p. 7.

73. C. Darwin, *The Origin of Species* (London, 1859).

74. Scruton, "The Defense of the West."

75. Ibid.

76. Thomas Jefferson, "Thomas Jefferson to James Madison, 1787," *The Writings of Thomas Jefferson*, ed. Andrew Adgate Lipscomb and Albert E. Bergh (Washington, DC: Thomas Jefferson Memorial Association, 1903–1904), vol. 6, p. 388; Thomas Jefferson, *The Papers of Thomas Jefferson*, ed. Julian P. Boyd (Princeton, NJ: Princeton University Press, 1950), vol. 12, p. 440.

77. F. A. von Hayek, *The Road to Serfdom* (London: Routledge, 1944; reprint, Chicago: University of Chicago Press, 1976), pp. 152–53.

78. Frederick Douglass, "My Bondage and My Freedom" (1885), in *Frederick Douglass Autobiographies*, ed. Henry Louis Gates (New York: Library of America, 1994), pp. 392–93; quoted in Vaughn and Dacey, *The Case for Humanism*, p. 193.

PART 3: ORIENTALISM IN PAINTING AND SCULPTURE, MUSIC AND LITERATURE

Introduction to Part 3

1. Roger Scruton, "What Ever Happened to Reason?" *City Journal* (Spring 1999).

2. Stephen Schwartz, "Islam's Wrong Turns: The Muslims Need a Bernard Lewis of Their Own," *National Review*, February 25, 2002.

3. Now in the Sterling and Francine Clark Art Institute in Williamstown, Massachusetts.

4. Assia Djebar, *Femmes d'Alger dans leur appartement* (Paris: Albin Michel, Le Livre de Poche, 2002).

5. Francis Steegmuller, *Flaubert in Egypt: A Sensibility on Tour* (Chicago: Academy Chicago Limited, 1979).

6. Sarga Moussa, *Le Voyage en Égypte* (Paris: Robert Laffont, Bouquins, 2004).

7. Here are some of the recently published works I have consulted: Gérard-Georges Lemaire, *L'Univers des Orientalistes* (Paris: Éditions Place des Victoires, 2000); Christine Peltre, *Les Orientalistes* (Paris: Éditions Hazan, 2003); Kristian Davies, *The Orientalists: Western Artists In Arabia, The Sahara, Persia & India* (New York: Antique Collectors Club, 2005). Earlier works consulted include: Lynne Thornton, *Les Orientalistes:*

Peintres Voyageurs (Paris: ACR Édition, Poche Couleur, 1993); Lynne Thornton, *La Femme Dans La Peinture Orientaliste* (Paris: ACR Édition, Poche Couleur, 1993); Caroline Juler, *Les Orientalistes de l'École Italienne* (Paris: ACR Édition, Poche Couleur, 1994); Gerald M. Ackerman, *Jean-Léon Gérôme: His Life, His Work* (Paris: ACR Édition, Poche Couleur, 1997); Gerald M. Ackerman, *Les Orientalistes de l'École Britannique* (Paris: ACR Édition, 1991); Gerald M. Ackerman, *Les Orientalistes de l'École Américaine* (Paris: ACR Édition, 1994); Philippe Julian, *The Orientalists: European Painters of Eastern Scenes* (Oxford: Phaidon, 1977).

Chapter 9: Orientals as Collectors

1. John Dorfman, "Trendspotting: Beyond the Harem," *Art+Auction*, Annual Investment Issue, A Special Collectors Guide (2006).

2. Keith Windschuttle, "The Cultural War on Western Civilization," in *The Survival of Culture: Permanent Values in a Virtual Age*, ed. Hilton Kramer and Roger Kimball (Chicago: Ivan R. Dee, 2002), p. 105.

3. Dorfman, "Trendspotting."

4. Ibid.

5. Francis Haskell, "A Turk and His Pictures in Nineteenth-Century Paris," *Oxford Art Journal* 5, no. 1 (1982): 40–47.

6. *Portraits from the Empire: The Ottoman World and the Ottomans from the 18th to 20th Century with Selected Works from the Suna and İnan Kiraç Foundation Collection* (Istanbul: Pera Museum, 2005), p. 9.

7. Philippe Julian, *The Orientalists: European Painters of Eastern Scenes* (Oxford: Phaidon, 1977), pp. 70, 74.

8. Michael Lewis, *John Frederick Lewis R.A. 1805–1876* (Leigh-on-Sea, UK: F. Lewis Publishers, 1978), p. 91.

9. Ibid., pp. 96, 98.

10. "Delacroix, Eugène," WebMuseum, Paris, Web site, http://www.ibiblio.org/wm/paint/auth/delacroix/.

11. "Chassériau, Théodore," WebMuseum, Paris, Web site, http://www.ibiblio.org/wm/paint/auth/chasseriau/.

12. Fausto Zonaro Web site, http://www.faustozonaro.it/.

13. Les peintres orientalistes Web site, http://orientaliste.free.fr/index.html.

14. Stéphane Guégan et al., *Théodore Chassériau (1819–1856): The Unknown Romantic* (New Haven, CT: Yale University Press/New York: Metropolitan Museum of Art, 2002).

Chapter 10: Painting and Sculpture

1. R. Wittkower, *Selected Lectures of Rudolf Wittkower: The Impact of Non-European Civilizations on the Art of the West*, comp. and ed. Donald Martin Reynolds (Cambridge:

Cambridge University Press, 1989); R. Wittkower, *Allegory and the Migration of Symbols* (Boulder, CO: Westview Press, 1977).

2. Wittkower, *Selected Lectures of Rudolf Wittkower*, p. 2.

3. Ibid., pp. 10–11.

4. Ibid., p. 14.

5. Ibid., pp. 14–17.

6. Ibid., p. 19.

7. Ibid.

8. Rosamond E. Mack, *Bazaar to Piazza: Islamic Trade and Italian Art, 1300–1600* (Berkeley and Los Angeles: University of California Press, 2002), p. 13.

9. Wittkower, *Selected Lectures of Rudolf Wittkower*, p. 33.

10. Ibid., pp. 4–6.

11. Grace Hadley Beardsley, *The Negro in Greek and Roman Civilization: A Study of the Ethiopian Type* (Baltimore: Johns Hopkins University Press, 1929), p. ix.

12. A. J. Evans, *The Palace of Minos, I* (London: Macmillan, 1921), pp. 302, 310, 312, and figs. 230 a, b, and c; and *The Palace of Minos, II* (London: Macmillan, 1928), pp. 45–46.

13. Beardsley, *The Negro in Greek and Roman Civilization*, pp. 97–98

> This is the best known and probably the finest statuette of an Ethiopian [Black]. It came to light in the year 1763 at Châlon-sur-Saône in a chest, together with some other bronzes of evident Roman origin. The condition of the chest showed that it had not been buried long, though the mystery of its burial was never solved. The grace of the figure and the skill of the work are the reasons for its assignment by all to the Hellenistic period, notwithstanding that the rest of the bronzes were Roman.
>
> The statuette portrays an Ethiopian [Black] boy standing with his slim body bent gracefully at the waist, his left arm held in front of him as if supporting some object on his shoulder and his mouth open as if singing. It seems reasonably certain that his left hand held in place a *trigonon* which rested against his shoulder, and from which he is drawing the notes with his right hand, which is placed as if about to pick the strings. The dreamy sadness of his expression and the "langueur" of his pose give . . . the illusion that he is actually singing some sad song of his homeland. . . . While the characteristic Ethiopian features are present, particularly in the profile, they are treated so that the effect is pleasing. The hair is arranged in formal stages of curls—the Alexandrian style—the forehead is wrinkled, the nose is not coarse, and the thickness of the lips is moderated. The upper row of teeth is indicated, and the eyes are inset in silver, with a hollow to indicate the pupil. The work is generally assigned to Alexandria. The height is only 0.20 m., but the work is so excellent that photographs give the illusion of a large statue.

14. Ibid., p. 113:

> It is in these figurines also that we first find in Greek art any sense of the pathos of the Ethiopian's lot, though compassion for the life of the slave is found in Greek tragedies. Heretofore the only emotional element present has been that of humor and caricature; but among these terra-cottas and bronzes are a few which seem to show a consciousness of another mood. The artists regarded for an instant, not the strangeness which made the Ethiopian an object of entertainment to them, but the pathos of an exile from his own land.

15. Hermann Goetz, "Oriental Types and Scenes in Renaissance and Baroque Painting—I," *Burlington Magazine for Connoisseurs* 73, no. 425 (August 1938): 55–56:

> Thus, in the painting of that time, we meet also carefully observed oriental types, which could only have been created from direct observation of representatives of these people, while sojourning in Italy. . . . [W]e find many types of men of the Near East and Far East in the painting of these Trecentists: Syrians, Egyptians and North Africans in the pictures by Cimabue, Giotto, Duccio, Simone Martini, Pietro Lorenzetti, Taddeo Gaddi, Buffalmacco, Andrea da Firenze, Nardo di Cione, Agnolo Gaddi, Niccolò di Pietro Gerini, Lorenzo Monaco, etc. There are peasants and Bedouins in short coats and small turbans, or in North African hooded mantles; Syrians and men from Iraq with strongly-marked, bearded faces, long-flowing garments, often with embroidered Tirāz bands on their upper arms, mighty turbans and large neck- or breast-cloths; stout, brown Egyptians and Nubians with small turbans (especially beautiful in Giotto's St. Francis before the Sultan in Santa Croce, Florence, or with the high, pointed qalansuwah hat (Lorenzo Monaco); negroes (Giotto, etc.); Chinese, Mongols and Eastern Turks (soldiers as well as civilians), as characteristic in anthropological type as in costume, in the *Martyrdom of the Franciscans at Ceuta*, by Ambrogio Lorenzetti in St. Francesco at Siena (1331), in the *Ecclesia militans*, by Andrea da Firenze in the Spanish Chapel in Santa Maria Novella at Florence (1355), in a drawing at Oxford by Simone Martini, and finally, considerably later in date, in the works of Antonio Pisano.

16. Mack, *Bazaar to Piazza*, p. 149.
17. Ibid., pp. 150–51.
18. Goetz, "Oriental Types and Scenes in Renaissance and Baroque Painting—I," p. 61.
19. Mack, *Bazaar to Piazza*, p. 153.
20. Ibid.
21. Goetz, "Oriental Types and Scenes in Renaissance and Baroque Painting—I," p. 62.
22. F. Gilles de la Tourette, *L'Orient et Les Peintres de Venise* (Paris: Librairie Ancienne Édouard Champion, 1923), p. 2:

> The canvases of Gentile Bellini and Carpaccio where one finds at the feet of slim minarets, mosques with blue cupolas and covered in marble, bathed in golden

> light, graced with some figures from a Gothic Book of Hours, animated, however, by expressions gathered on the spot, some orientals in costumes so picturesque, and of a colour so warm, that they revive in our imagination, by a natural association born simply of these painters, for they are the sole documents truly talking to our imagination, mercantile Venice of the fifteenth century.
>
> We see over again the Turks in their long red or blue robe, with their piercing eyes, and aquiline profiles sharp as the blade of a yataghan, the Turkish sword, under their enormous turban so white and pure; the noble lords of Cairo, grave patriarchs in long beards, with short sharp gests, splendidly clothed in a cymar brocaded with strangely stylised golden flowers; the Greeks a little ambiguous, draped rather pitiably not in a blue chlamys but in long brown mantle, wearing sandals and resembling some monk or dubious heretical philosophers. We witness these exotic beings rubbing shoulders with ephebes, companions of *the Calza*, with the long necks of birds under their hair cut in a circle, the grave magistrates in their scarlet or black cymar, jolly damsels, candid, pure as a rose in May, eyes chastely lowered under their limpid little veils, with slim delicate waists in a stiff robe brocaded with gold, set with pearls and fantasies.

23. Ibid., p. 23.

24. Ibid., p.84, n3, referring to *Historia Turchesca di Gio Maria Angiolello Schiavo dall 'anno 1429 sin al 1513*, Bibliothèque Nationale, Mss. fds. ital. No 1238, quoted in L. Thuasne, *Gentile Bellini et Sultan Mohammed II* (Paris, 1888).

25. De la Tourette, *L'Orient et les Peintres de Venise*, p. 85.

26. Ibid., pp. 90–91.

27. Wittkower, *Selected Lectures of Rudolf Wittkower*, p. 203.

28. "Bellini, Gentile," *Encyclopedia Britannica* Online, http://www.britannica.com/eb/article-9015282.

29. Mack, *Bazaar to Piazza*, p. 157.

30. "Carpaccio, Vittore," Louvre Catalog Online, http://www.louvre.fr/llv/oeuvres.

31. Goetz, "Oriental Types and Scenes in Renaissance and Baroque Painting—I," p. 62.

32. Wittkower, *Selected Lectures of Rudolf Wittkower*, p. 206.

33. Mack, *Bazaar to Piazza*, p. 158.

34. Description at "Adoration of the Magi," Getty Museum Web site, http://www.getty.edu/art/gettyguide/artObjectDetails?artobj=900.

35. Traci Timmons, "About This Site," Vecellio.net: The Works of Cesare Vecellio, http://www.vecellio.net/about.html. See also Traci Timmons, "Habiti Antichi et Moderni di Tutto il Mondo and the 'Myth of Venice,'" *Athanor* 15 (1997): 28–33.

36. Interviewed by Laura Wolff Scanlan in "Translating Fashion: Customs and Clothes in the Age of Exploration," *Humanities* 26, vol. 1 (January/February 2005):

> Vecellio [*c*1521–1601] is very proud of being a Venetian, and the world is coming to him because it is the trading point between east and west. But at the

same time he is never so arrogant that he cannot see when something is just that much more wonderful than what he has in Venice. When he talks about the Turkish court, he talks about their clothing, he talks of the sultan, he says he dresses in unimaginable splendor and does not liken it to anything he has seen before. You would think he would take a European attitude of superiority in looking at the new world, but quite the contrary. He says the finest materials have come from there and they are rare and delicate and probably the most sumptuous clothing found in the whole world.

37. Mack, *Bazaar to Piazza*, p. 161
38. Ibid., pp. 161–63.
39. Goetz, "Oriental Types and Scenes in Renaissance and Baroque Painting—I," p. 62:

By the sixteenth-century the Turk had become a common and extraordinarily correctly depicted figure in Italian art. There are magnificent types to be found in Titian's works (the Pesaro Madonna painted for Jacopo Pesaro, the conqueror of Santa Maura); in those by Veronese (especially the *Martyrdom of S. Justina* at Florence; in the background of the *Family of Darius* in the National Gallery; the Adoration of the magi at Dresden and Vienna, etc.; but everywhere also orientals in the fanciful tradition of the fifteenth century); Tintoretto (*The Finding of the Holy Cross by S. Helena* in Santa Maria Mater Domini, Venice; the St. Mark series in the Palazzo Reale; pictures in the Scuola di San Rocco; the *Golden Calf* in Santa Maria dell'Orto where a woman wearing the Turkish *turtūr* is represented, etc.), and Tiepolo (the *Banquet and Embarkation of Cleopatra*, in the Palazzo Labia, Venice; the *Four Quarters of the Earth* at Würzburg; the *Adoration of the Three Holy Magi* at Munich; the *Crucifixion* in S. Alvise at Venice), etc.

40. Georges Marlier, *La Renaissance flamande Pierre Coeck d'Alost* (Brussels: Editions Robert Finck, 1966).

41. Full title: *Ces Moeurs et fachons de faire de Turcq avecq' les Regions y appertenantes, ont este au vif contrefaictez par Pierre Coeck d"Alost, luy estant en Turquie, l'An de Iesuchrist M.D.33., Lequel aussy de sa main propre a pourtraict ces figures duysantes à l'impression d'ycelles*. See ibid., p. 55.

42. Marlier, *La Renaissance flamande Pierre Coeck d'Alost*, p. 59.

43. Hermann Goetz, "Oriental Types and Scenes in Renaissance and Baroque Painting—II," *Burlington Magazine for Connoisseurs* 73, no. 426 (September 1938): 106.

44. Marlier, *La Renaissance flamande Pierre Coeck d'Alost*, pp. 60–72.

45. Wittkower, *Selected Lectures of Rudolf Wittkower*, pp. 207–209.

46. Jan Lievens, *Esther Accusing Haman* (c. 1620–30), Museum of Art, Raleigh, NC; often attributed to Rembrandt.

47. Rembrandt van Rijn, *Abraham Entertaining Angels* (1656), Museum of Fine Arts, Boston.

48. Wittkower, *Selected Lectures of Rudolf Wittkower*, p. 211.

49. Goetz, "Oriental Types and Scenes in Renaissance and Baroque Painting—II," p. 111.

50. Moses Gans, *Memorbook: A History of Dutch Jewry from the Renaissance to 1940* (Baarn: Bosch and Keuning, 1971), pp. 70–71; quoted in Steven Nadler, *Rembrandt's Jews* (Chicago: University of Chicago Press, 2003), p. 45.

51. Nadler, *Rembrandt's Jews*, p. 57.

52. Ibid., p. 59.

53. Ibid., pp. 60–61.

54. Ibid., p. 63.

55. Ibid., p. 64.

56. Ibid.

57. Ibid., p. 65.

58. Ibid., pp. 181–82.

59. Goetz, "Oriental Types and Scenes in Renaissance and Baroque Painting—II," p. 112.

60. Ibid.

61. Eugène Fromentin, *Oeuvres Complètes*, ed. Guy Sagnes (Paris: Gallimard, 1984), p. 627.

62. Romare Bearden and Harry Henderson, *A History of African-American Artists: From 1792 to the Present* (New York: Pantheon, 1993), p. 329.

63. Kevin L. Justus, *The Abduction from the Seraglio, Nine Exotic Delights from the Versailles of Louis XV, or the Hunts the Thing in Which We Catch the Character of the King* (forthcoming, 2007), p. 3

64. Ibid.

65. Auguste Boppe, *Les Peintres du Bosphore au Dix-Huitième Siècle* (Paris, Librairie Hachette et Cie, 1911). Perhaps it was Boppe who coined the term "Bosphorus Painters"; I am not sure.

66. Charles de Ferriol, *Recueil de cent estampes representant differentes nations du Levant, gravees sur les tableaux peints d'apres nature en 1707 & 1708. Par les ordres de M. De Ferriol Ambassadeur du Roi a La Porte. Et gravées en 1712 et 1713*, bound with *Explication de cent estampes qui representant differentes nations du Levant avec de nouvelles estampes de ceremonies Turques qui ont aussi leurs explications* (Paris: [Le Hay], Colombat, 1714).

67. Provided by Bernard J. Shapero Rare Books at http://www.polybiblio.com/shapero/63585.html:

> The most luxurious edition of this book, with hand-coloured plates heightened with gold and mica. A particularly fine example of this important collection of costume plates. In addition to the sixty or so plates depicting Turkish Court, noble, military and other costume, the work illustrates the regional, religious or national costume of several other parts of the Turkish Empire. These include

Greeks (10); Albanians (2); Jews (3); Hungarians (2); Wallachians (3); Bulgarians (2); Crimean Tartars (1); Armenians (5); Persians (2); Indians (2); Arabs (1); Barbary Coast (4); and Moors (1). The illustration of the Whirling Dervishes is one of the double-page plates at the end of the volume as mentioned. The plates for this work were commissioned by Charles de Ferriol (1652–1722), the French ambassador to the Porte between 1699 and 1709. Ferriol's embassy was made memorable by the colourful farce surrounding his refusal to give up his sword when presenting his credentials. The plates were engraved after drawings by the Flemish artist J. B. Vanmour, who lived and worked in Constantinople for many years during the first part of the eighteenth century. It has been suggested that Vanmour came to Constantinople with the entourage of the Marquis de Ferriol in 1699. A large proportion of his work was commissioned by the then Dutch ambassador to the Porte, Cornelis Calkoen, much of which is now in the Rijksmuseum. [Sixty-one of Vanmour's paintings are to be found in the Rijksmuseum in Amsterdam.] This important work forms the "basic prototype for Levantine costume plates. (Atabey)

68. Philip Mansel, "Painter in the Palace," *Cornucopia* 30 (2003–2004):

Vanmour also painted other scenes whose details, and accompanying notes written in an anonymous hand, provide invaluable information about the Ottoman past: for example the picture in this exhibition of a woman taking her young daughter to embroidery school is a reminder of the role of women in this important Ottoman handicraft. If most women were not taught to read and write, they were at least taught to sew. The picture of Calkoen advancing towards the grand vizir's Divan shows janissaries, on their payday, rushing to eat their pilav. If they remained motionless, it was a sign that they were preparing another of their frequent rebellions. Vanmour's pictures of Patrona Halil and his close friend and fellow rebel, Muslu Beşe, who in 1730 led the first popular revolution in Ottoman history, are rare individual portraits of Turks not from the Ottoman elite indeed, described in the notes as of "very low birth." Probably painted in the few weeks in which Patrona Halil held power before his murder on the new sultan's orders, such a portrait suggests that Vanmour was familiar with the inner political life of the Ottoman capital, as well as the diplomatic ceremonial of the European embassies.

69. Boppe, *Les Peintres du Bosphore au Dix-Huitième Siècle*, p. 25.

70. "Jean-Etienne Liotard," Musée d'art et d'histoire, Geneva, Web site, http://www.ville-ge.ch/musinfo/mahg/musee/presse/liotard/liotard2.html.

71. Baron de Tott, *Memoirs of Baron de Tott* (London, 1785; reprint, New York: Arno, 1973).

72. Boppe, *Les Peintres du Bosphore au Dix-Huitième Siècle*, pp. 150–51.

73. Ibid., p. 165, quoting M. de Butet.

74. Ibid., p. 170.

75. Antoine Ignace Melling, *Voyage Pittoresque de Constantinople et des rives du Bosphore d'après les dessins de M. Melling* (Paris: Treuttel et Wurtz, 1819).

76. Orhan Pamuk, *Istanbul: Memories and the City* (New York: Vintage, 2006), pp. 62–75.

77. *Portraits from the Empire: The Ottoman World and the Ottomans from the 18th to 20th Century with Selected Works from the Suna and İnan Kiraç Foundation Collection* (Istanbul: Pera Museum, 2005). Available online at www.pm.org.tr/sergiler 2d_en .html.

78. Ibid.

79. Ibid.

80. Fani-Maria Tsigakou, "The Rediscovery of the Hope Drawings," *Cornucopia* 1, no. 5 (1993–94): 59. Tsigakou's short article gives 1977 as the date of the rediscovery, but on p. 52 the date given is 1983.

81. David Watkin, "A Case of Regency Exoticism," *Cornucopia* 1, no. 5 (1993–94): 54.

82. Ibid.

83. Ibid., p. 58.

84. Ibid.

85. Ibid.

Chapter 11: Occidental Influence on Eastern Art

1. K. A. C. Creswell, *Early Muslim Architecture* (Harmondsworth, UK: Penguin, 1958), p. 1.

2. Oleg Grabar and Richard Ettinghausen, *The Art and Architecture of Islam 650–1250* (London: Penguin, 1991), p. 25.

3. Creswell, *Early Muslim Architecture*, p. 111.

4. Richard Ettinghausen, *Arab Painting* (Geneva: Editions d'Art Albert Skira, 1977), p. 67.

5. Sibylla Schuster-Walser, *Das safawidische Persien im Spiegel europäischer Reiseberichte (1502–1722)* (Baden-Baden/Hamburg: Grimm, 1970), pp. 51–52.

6. Bernard Lewis, *The Muslim Discovery of Europe* (London: Phoenix, 1982), p. 245.

7. Ibid.

8. Ibid., p. 256.

9. Ibid., p. 244.

10. Ibid., p. 257.

11. Gregory Minissale, "The Synthesis of European and Mughal Art in the Emperor Akbar's Khamsa of Nizami," *Asian Art*, October 13, 2000, www.asianart.com/articles/minissale/index.html. Minissale gives a comprehensive bibliography on the subject of European influence on Persian, Turkish, Mughal, and Indian art.

12. Ibid.

13. Reproduced in Stuart Cary Welch, *Imperial Mughal Painting* (New York: George Braziller, 1978), p. 55, plate 8.

Chapter 12: Nineteenth-Century Orientalist Art

1. Linda Nochlin, "The Imaginary Orient," *Art in America* (May 1983): 118–31, 187–91.

2. Ibid., p. 119.

3. Ibid.

4. Ibid., p. 122.

5. Ibid.

6. Lisa Small, *Highlights from the Dahesh Museum Collection: Essay and Catalogue* (New York: Dahesh Museum, 1999), p. 64.

7. Philippe Julian, *The Orientalists: European Painters of Eastern Scenes* (Oxford: Phaidon, 1977), p. 28.

8. All magnificently illustrated in Gérard-Georges Lemaire, *L'Univers des Orientalistes* (Paris: Éditions Place des Victoires, 2000).

9. Nochlin, "The Imaginary Orient," p. 122.

10. Raghu Rai, *Calcutta* (New Delhi: Time Books International, 1989). They can be viewed at the Magnum Photos Web site, http://www.magnumphotos.com/c/htm/FramerT_MAG.aspx?Stat=Portfolio_DocThumb&V=CDocT&E=2K7O3RBQ95I8&DT=ALB.

11. Raghu Rai, *Taj Mahal* (Milan: Idealibri, 1995).

12. Raghubir Singh, *Rajasthan: India's Enchanted Land* (New York: Thames and Hudson, 1981).

13. French for "flashy foreigner."

14. Walter Pach, trans., *The Journal of Eugène Delacroix* (New York: Hacker Art Books, 1980), pp. 160–61.

15. Gerald Ackerman, *Jean-Léon Gérôme: His Life, His Work* (Paris: ACR Édition, Poche Couleur, 1997), p. 188.

16. Alan Cowell, "Exploring Islamic Cairo," *New York Times*, January 1, 1989.

17. Orhan Pamuk, *Istanbul: Memories and the City* (New York: Vintage, 2006), pp. 38–39, 42.

18. Michael Sprinker, ed., *Edward Said: A Critical Reader* (Oxford: Blackwell, 1993), pp. 223–25; accused by Valerie Kennedy, *Edward Said: A Critical Introduction* (Cambridge: Polity Press, 2000), pp. 129–31.

19. I owe this point to Dr. Elisabeth Puin.

20. Examples taken mainly from Caroline Juler, *Les Orientalistes de l'École Italienne* (Paris: ACT Édition, Poche Couleur, 1994).

21. Wayne Franits, *Dutch Seventeenth-Century Genre Painting: Its Stylistic and Thematic Evolution* (New Haven, CT: Yale University Press, 2004), p. 1.

22. Nochlin, "The Imaginary Orient," p. 189.

23. John M. MacKenzie, *Orientalism: History, Theory and the Arts* (Manchester: Manchester University Press, 2004), p. 47.

24. Ibid.

25. Rosamond E. Mack, *Bazzar to Piazza: Islamic Trade and Italian Art, 1300–1600* (Berkeley and Los Angeles: University of California Press, 2002), p. 51.

26. Ibid., p. 71.

27. Ibid.

28. "There is no compulsion in religion—the right way is indeed clearly distinct from error. So whoever disbelieves in the devil and believes in Allah, he indeed lays hold on the firmest handle which shall never break. And Allah is Hearing, Knowing."

29. I owe these observations to Dr. Elisabeth Puin, who also helped decipher verse 256.

30. One Internet site has listed 1,222 Orientalist artists working in the nineteenth and up to the beginning of the twentieth century: http://orientaliste.free.fr/biographies/index.html.

31. Julian, *The Orientalists*, p. 47.

32. Ibid.

33. Ibid., p. 48.

34. Hubert Wellington, ed., and Lucy Norton, trans., *The Journal of Eugène Delacroix* (1951; reprint, London: Phaidon, 2004), p. 56.

35. Ibid., pp. 52–55.

36. Lemaire, *L'Univers des Orientalistes*, p. 340.

37. Ibid., p. 214.

38. Ibid., pp. 211–12.

39. Julian, *The Orientalists*, p. 48.

40. Ibid.

41. Lemaire, *L'Univers des Orientalistes*, p. 214.

42. Ibid., p. 204.

43. In private collection; illustrated in Ulrich W. Hiesinger, *Edwin Lord Weeks: Visions of India* (New York: Vance Jordan Fine Art, 2002), p. 15.

44. Gerald Ackerman, *The Life and Work of Jean-Léon Gérôme* (Paris: ACR Éditions, 1986), pp. 50, 52, 99; quoted by MacKenzie, *Orientalism*, p. 63.

45. C. Baudelaire, "Salon de 1845," in *Baudelaire Critique d'Art*, vol. 1 (Paris: Gallimard, 1965, pp. 26–27; quoted in Mary Anne Stevens, ed., *The Orientalists: Delacroix to Matisse, European Painters in North Africa and the Near East* (London: Royal Academy of Arts, 1984), p. 127.

46. Franits, *Dutch Seventeenth-Century Genre Painting*, p. 43.

47. Julian, *The Orientalists*, p. 29.

Chapter 13: Painters as Writers

1. Jane Munro, "Pilgrims Going to Mecca, 1861," in *The Orientalists: Delacroix to Matisse, European Painters in North Africa and the Near East*, ed. Mary Anne Stevens (London: Royal Academy of Arts, 1984), p. 115.

2. Ibid., p. 116.

3. All quotes taken from Conrad de Mandach, "Artistes Contemporains, Léon Belly (1827–1877)," *Gazette des Beaux-Arts* (January 1913): 73–84, (February 1913): 143–57.

4. Gabriel Séailles, *Alfred Dehodencq: Histoire d'Un Coloriste* (Paris: Paul Ollendorf, Éditeur, 1885), p. 10.

5. Ibid., p. 125.

6. Christine Peltre, *L'Atelier du Voyage* (Paris: Gallimard, 1995), p. 106.

7. Séailles, *Alfred Dehodencq*, p. 137.

8. One of Dehodencq's most famous paintings is *Execution of a Jewish Girl* (1861), now in Musée d'Art et d'Histoire du Judaïsme, Paris. Several books on Orientalist art (e.g., Séailles, *Alfred Dehodencq*, p. 148; Christine Peltre, *L'Atelier du Voyage*, p. 107) add the detail that Dehodencq actually witnessed the execution. But this is an error. The date of the Jewish girl's execution is uncertain, but we know it must have been between 1830 and 1834, the latter date being asserted by James Edward B. Meakin in "The Jews of Morocco," *Jewish Quarterly Review* 4, no. 3 (1892): 376. The earliest known primary source is a small volume by Eugenio Maria Romero, *El martirio de joven Hachuel o la heroina Hebrea* (Gibraltar: Imprinta Militar, 1837), p. 8. This text appeared in English translation in London in 1839 as "Jewish Heroine of the Nineteenth Century: A Tale Founded on Fact." Dehodencq, born in 1822, would have been only twelve years old in 1834. We also know that he first went to Morocco in 1853. I owe all this research to Dr. Andrew Bostom.

9. Peltre, *L'Atelier du Voyage*, p. 108.

10. Ibid., p. 109.

11. James Thompson and Barbara Wright, *La Vie et L'Oeuvre d' Eugène Fromentin* (Paris: ACR Édition, 1987), p. 63; quoting Eugène Fromentin, *Lettres de jeunesse*, ed. Pierre Blanchon (Paris: Plon, 1909), p. 173.

12. Thompson and Wright, *La Vie et L'Oeuvre d' Eugène Fromentin*, p. 87.

13. Ibid., p. 63; quoting Fromentin, *Lettres de jeunesse*, p. 334.

14. Eugène Fromentin, *Oeuvres Complètes*, ed. Guy Sagnes (Paris: Gallimard, 1984), pp. 24–29.

15. Ibid., pp. 215–17.

16. Ibid., pp. 238.

17. Ibid., pp. 298–99.

18. Stéphane Guégan et al., *Théodore Chassériau (1819–1856): The Unknown Romantic* (New Haven, CT: Yale University Press/New York: Metropolitan Museum of Art, 2002), pp. 57, 192.

19. Ibid.

20. Ibid., pp. 193–94; quoting from Chassériau's letters to his brother.

21. Ibid., p. 284.

22. Ibid.

23. Guégan et al., *Théodore Chassériau*, pp. 283–84.

24. Edwin Lord Weeks, *From the Black Sea through Persia and India* (New York: Harper and Brothers, 1895). A very much abridged, poorly produced paperback edition appeared in 2005 as Edwin Lord Weeks, *Artist Explorer: A Ride through Persia to India in 1892* (N.p.: Long Riders' Guild Press, 2005).

25. Ulrich W. Hiesinger, *Edwin Lord Weeks: Visions of India* (New York: Vance Jordan Fine Art, 2002), p. 10.

26. Ibid., p. 15.

27. Hiesinger, *Edwin Lord Weeks*, p. 18.

28. Quoted in ibid.

29. Quoted in ibid., p. 20.

30. Hiesinger, *Edwin Lord Weeks*, p. 24.

31. Weeks, *From the Black Sea through Persia and India*, p. 12.

32. Ibid., p. 31.

33. Ibid., p. 39.

34. Ibid., pp. 72–73.

35. Ibid., p. 83.

36. Ibid., p. 116.

37. Ibid., p. 145.

38. Ibid., p. 164.

39. Ibid., p. 177.

40. Ibid., p. 180.

41. Ibid., pp. 180–81.

42. Ibid., p. 183.

43. Weeks, *From the Black Sea through Persia and India*, pp. 186–94.

44. Ibid., p. 190.

45. Ibid., p. 284.

46. Weeks, *From the Black Sea through Persia and India*, p. 302; quoting James Fergusson, *History of Indian and Eastern Architecture* (London, 1876).

47. Hiesinger, *Edwin Lord Weeks*, p. 12.

48. Ibid., pp. 12–13.

49. Ibid., p. 31.

Chapter 14: John Frederick Lewis

1. Hugh Stokes, "John Frederick Lewis R.A. (1805–1876)," *Walker's Quarterly* (1929): 9.

2. Michael Lewis, *John Frederick Lewis R.A. 1805–1876* (Leigh-on-Sea, UK: F. Lewis, Publishers, 1978), p. 36.

3. Ibid.

4. Ibid., p. 21.

5. Gerald M. Ackerman, *Les Orientalistes de L'École Britannique* (Paris: ACR Édition, 1991), p. 191.

6. Stokes, "John Frederick Lewis R.A. (1805–1876)," p. 32. Stokes is quoting a critic he does not name, but possibly J. L. Roget, *A History of the Old Watercolour Society* (London: Longmans Green, 1891).

7. Lewis, *John Frederick Lewis R.A. 1805–1876*, p. 39.

8. Ibid.

9. Yale Center for British Art, New Haven, CT.

10. Lawrence Gowing, *Vermeer* (1955; reprint, Berkeley and Los Angeles: University of California Press, 1998), p. 13.

11. Quoted in Stokes, "John Frederick Lewis R.A. (1805–1876)," p. 12.

12. All details derived from Caroline Bugler, "A Frank Encampment in the Desert of Mount Sinai, 1842—The Convent of St. Catherine in the Distance" (1856), in *The Orientalists: Delacroix to Matisse, European Painters in North Africa and the Near East*, ed. Mary Anne Stevens (London: Royal Academy of Arts, 1984), p. 202.

13. Ibid., p. 203.

14. Quoted in Stokes, "John Frederick Lewis R.A. (1805–1876)," p. 27.

Chapter 15: Hegel and the Meaning, Significance, and Influence of Dutch Genre Painting

1. Eugène Fromentin, *The Old Masters of Belgium and Holland*, trans. Mary C. Robbins (New York: Schocken, 1963), pp. 132–33.

2. Ibid., pp. 131–34.

3. Christopher Brown, *Dutch Genre Painting* (London: National Gallery Publications Department, 1976), p. 5.

4. Wayne Franits, *Dutch Seventeenth-Century Genre Painting: Its Stylistic and Thematic Evolution* (New Haven, CT: Yale University Press, 2004), p. 2.

5. Brown, *Dutch Genre Painting*, p. 20.

6. Lawrence Gowing, *Vermeer* (1955; reprint, Berkeley and Los Angeles: University of California Press, 1998), p. 30.

7. Quoted in Franits, *Dutch Seventeenth-Century Genre Painting*, p. 120.

8. Brown, *Dutch Genre Painting*, p. 39.

9. Gowing, *Vermeer*, p. 25.

10. G. W. F. Hegel, *Aesthetics: Lectures on Fine Art*, trans. T. M. Knox (Oxford: Clarendon, 1988), vol. 1, p. 162.

11. Ibid., pp. 162–63.

12. Ibid., vol. 2, p. 885.

Chapter 16: Charles Cordier: Orientalist Sculptor

1. Laure de Margerie et al., eds., *Facing the Other: Charles Cordier (1827–1905) Ethnographic Sculptor* (New York: Harry N. Abrams, 2004), p. 15.

2. Ibid., p. 28.

3. Ibid.

4. De Margerie et al., *Facing the Other*, p. 28.

5. Ibid., p. 70.

6. Ibid.

7. Quoted in de Margerie et al., *Facing the Other*, p. 71.

8. Serge Lemoine, John R. Porter, and Peter Trippi, foreword in *Facing the Other: Charles Cordier (1827–1905) Ethnographic Sculptor*, ed. Laure de Margerie et al. (New York: Harry N. Abrams, 2004), p. 11.

Chapter 17: Religion, Piety, and Portraits

1. In no particular order here are some Orientalists and their paintings of places of worship: Lord Frederic Leighton, *Star of Bethlehem, Portions of the Interior of the Grand Mosque of Damascus*; Holman Hunt, *The Shadow of Death*; Tissot, *The Journey of the Magi*; Gérôme, *Interior of Mosque, Prayer in the Mosque of Amr, 1872, Prayer on the Rooftops, 1865, Muezzin's Call to Prayer, Prayer in the House of an Arnaut Chief, Prayer in the Mosque of Qayt-bay*; Ludwig Deutsch, *The Prayer at the Tomb, At Prayer*; Guillaumet, *Arabs Praying in the Desert, 1863*; Belly, *Pilgrims to Mecca*; Bauernfeind, *Lament of the Faithful at the Wailing Wall, Jerusalem*; Rudolf Ernst, *Lessons of the Koran, In the Mosque*; John Farquharson, *Interior of the Mosque of Sultan Hassan*; Fredrick Goodall, *The Head of the House at Prayer*; Walter Horsley, *There Is No God but God, 1882*; Robert Talbot Kelly, *In the Mosque, Cairo*; Frederick Arthur Bridgman, *Worshippers in a Mosque*; Edwin Lord Weeks, *The Golden Temple, Amritsar, Temples at Banares*; Chassériau, *The Day of Sabbath in the Jewish Quarter in Constantinople*.

2. Frédéric Goupil-Fesquet, *Voyage en Orient fait avec Horce Vernet en 1839 et 1840* (Paris, 1843), p. 99, quoted in Mary Anne Stevens, ed., *The Orientalists: Delacroix to Matisse, European Painters in North Africa and the Near East* (London: Royal Academy of Arts, 1984), p. 39.

3. John M. MacKenzie, *Orientalism: History, Theory and the Arts* (Manchester: Manchester University Press, 2004), plate 3, facing p. 74.

4. Gerald Ackerman, "Orientalist Painters," in *Auction Catalogue of the Forbes Magazine Collection of Orientalist Paintings, Drawings, Watercolors and Sculpture* (New York: Christie's, 1993), p. 18.

5. MacKenzie, *Orientalism*, p. 58.

6. Martin Kramer, ed., *The Jewish Discovery of Islam* (Tel Aviv: Moshe Dayan Center, 1999), p. 6.

7. All illustrated in Lynne Thornton, *Les Orientalistes: Peintres Voyageurs* (Paris: ACR Édition, 1994).

Chapter 18: Oriental and African American Orientalists

1. Quoted in Gérard-Georges Lemaire, *L'Univers des Orientalistes* (Paris: Éditions Place des Victoires, 2000), p. 266.
2. Romare Bearden and Harry Henderson, *A History of African-American Artists: From 1792 to the Present* (New York: Pantheon, 1993), p. 86.
3. Ibid., p. 107.
4. Ibid., p. 91.
5. Ibid., p. 101.

Chapter 19: Orientalism and Music

1. Roger Scruton, "What Ever Happened to Reason?" *City Journal*, Spring 1999.
2. Brigid Brophy, *Mozart the Dramatist* (New York: Da Capo Press, 1988), pp. 211–12:

> Having drawn on all the world, the taste for the exotic spilled over from the decorative arts into literature, drama and opera—in all of which it might also serve the propaganda purposes of reason. China (Horace Walpole's *Letter from Xo Ho to His Friend Lien Chi at Peking*): Turkey (whose exoticism spiced Gluck's opera *Die Pilger von Mekka* as well as Mozart's own *Zaide*, where Mozart's Pasha Selim keeps his seraglio, where Don Giovanni has been in pursuit of his quest, and where Candide ends his and decides to cultivate his garden): Persia (Montesquieu's *Lettres Persanes*; the Zoroastrian touch in Sarastro [in *Die Zauberflöte*]): Babylon (Voltaire's *La Princesse de Babylone*): Egypt (*L'Oca del Cairo* [Mozart's unfinished opera buffa]; *Thamos, König in Ägypten* [play by Baron von Gebler for which Mozart wrote incidental music]; Handel's opera on the theme of Caesar and Cleopatra; Tiepolo's pictures of the meeting between Antony and Cleopatra and of the banquet at which Cleopatra dissolved a pearl and gave it to Antony to drink; *Sethos*, [French novel by abbé Jean Terrasson] which provided a gloze on the dissolved pearl; and *Die Zauberflöte* itself): South America (where Frederick the Great set his opera [*Montezuma*], and where Voltaire has Candide find El Dorado): Abyssinia (the original title of *Rasselas* being *The Prince of Abissinia, A Tale*): India (Bernardin de Saint-Pierre's *La Chaumière Indienne*): the Indies (it scarcely matters whether East or West, any more than it matters whether the hero of *Die Zauberflöte* is a Japanese or, as it is said he appears in some editions, a Javanese, prince): the civilisation of the Red Indians (who provided Voltaire with a hero [the Huron in *L'Ingénu*]): Mauritius (or, as it then was, under

French colonisation, the île de France, which Bernardin de Saint-Pierre, who had spent some years there himself, made the paradisal setting of *Paul et Virginie*): even outer space (Voltaire's *Micromégas*).

3. Ibid., p. 214.
4. Ibid., p. 226.
5. Ibid., p. 229. The passages in square brackets above are Brophy's own footnotes.
6. Brigid Brophy, "Introduction," in *Die Zauberflöte and Die Entführung aus dem Serail*, by W. A. Mozart (New York: Universe Books, 1971), p. 100.
7. Ibid., p. 15.
8. Brophy, *Mozart the Dramatist*, p. 187.
9. Maynard Solomon, *Mozart: A Life* (New York: Harper Perennial, 1996), p. 344.
10. Ibid., pp. 330–31.
11. Ibid., p. 335.
12. James Darmesteter, *Sacred Books of the East, The Zend-Avesta* (Oxford: Oxford University Press, 1880), pp. xvii–xviii.
13. Robert Anderson, "A Parisian Disco? Rameau's 'Les Indes galantes,'" *Music & Vision*, September 7, 2005, http://www.mvdaily.com/articles/2005/09/indes1.htm.
14. Bruce Alan Brown, notes to CD of Gluck's *La Rencontre imprévue, ou les Pèlerins de la Mecque* (Paris: Radio France/Erato Discs, 1991).
15. John M. MacKenzie, *Orientalism: History, Theory and the Arts* (Manchester: Manchester University Press, 2004), p. 149.

Chapter 20: Literature and Orientalism

1. Simon Hornblower and Antony Spawforth, eds., *The Oxford Classical Dictionary*, 3rd ed. (Oxford: Oxford University Press, 1999), p. 423.
2. Clarence Dana Rouillard, *The Turk in French History, Thought, and Literature (1520–1660)* (Paris: Boivin & Cie, 1940; reprint, New York: Ams Press, 1973), p. 546.
3. Ibid., p. 570.
4. Marie-Christine Pioffet, "Diversité et métissages culturels dans l'Ibrahim ou l'Illustre Bassa," *Littératures* 34 (1996): 43–55.
5. Ibid., p. 54.
6. Edward Said, *Culture and Imperialism* (London: Vintage, 1994), p. 112.
7. Alan Sokal and Jean Bricmont, *Fashionable Nonsense: Post-Modern Intellectuals' Abuse of Science* (New York: Picador USA, 1998), p. 189.
8. Said, *Culture and Imperialism*, p. 115.
9. Susan Fraiman, "Jane Austen and Edward Said: Gender, Culture and Imperialism" in *Janeites: Austen's Disciples and Devotees*, ed. Deidre Lynch (Princeton, NJ: Princeton University Press, 2000), p. 213; quoted in Gabrielle D. V. White, *Jane Austen in the Context of Abolition: 'a fling at the slave trade'* (New York: Palgrave Macmillan, 2006), p. 4.

10. White, *Jane Austen in the Context of Abolition*, p. 1.

11. Ibid., p. 2.

12. Brian Southam, "The Silence of the Bertrams," *Times Literary Supplement*, February 17, 1995, pp. 13–14; referred to by Claire Tomalin in *Jane Austen: A Life* (Harmondsworth, UK: Penguin, 1998), pp. 234, 333.

13. Jane Austen, *Mansfield Park* (Ware, UK: Wordsworth Classics, 1992), p. 290.

14. White, *Jane Austen in the Context of Abolition*, pp. 2–3.

15. Marilyn Butler, "Introduction," in *Jane Austen: Selected Letters 1796–1817*, ed. R. W. Chapman (Oxford: Oxford University Press, 1985), p. xviii.

16. Tomalin, *Jane Austen*, p. 332.

17. As reported by Capel Lofft and quoted in Jerome Nadelhaft, "Somersett Case and Slavery: Myth, Reality, and Repercussions," *Journal of Negro History* 51, no. 3 (July 1966): 200–201.

18. You-me Park and R. S. Rajan, eds., *The Postcolonial Jane Austen* (London: Routledge, 2000), p. 8; quoted in White, *Jane Austen in the Context of Abolition*, p. 4.

19. White, *Jane Austen in the Context of Abolition*, p. 172.

20. Said, *Culture and Imperialism*, p. 97.

21. I owe these points to Irfan Khawaja.

22. Christopher Hitchens, *For the Sake of Argument* (London: Verso, 1994), p. 337.

23. Edward Said, *The Question of Palestine* (New York: Vintage, 1980), p. 65.

24. Hitchens, *For the Sake of Argument*, p. 337.

25. Said, *The Question of Palestine*, p. 65.

26. Hitchens, *For the Sake of Argument*, p. 335. Emphasis is Hitchens's.

27. George Eliot, "The Modern Hep! Hep! Hep!" in *Impressions of Theophrastus Such* in *Theophrastus Such, Jubal, and Other Poems* and *The Spanish Gypsy* (Chicago: Donohue, Henneberry, 1900), p. 76.

28. Ibid., p. 148.

29. George Eliot, "A Half-Breed" in *Impressions of Theophrastus Such* in *Theophrastus Such, Jubal, and Other Poems* and *The Spanish Gypsy* (Chicago: Donohue, Henneberry, 1900), p. 76.

30. George Eliot, "The Modern Hep! Hep! Hep!" p. 144.

31. Hitchens, *For the Sake of Argument*, p. 338.

32. Quoted in Craig Raine, "Kipling: Controversial Questions," *Kipling Journal* (September 2002): 10.

33. Said, *Culture and Imperialism*, p. 162.

34. Ibid., p. 163.

35. Raine, "Kipling: Controversial Questions," pp. 13–14.

36. Ibid., pp. 15–16; the joining lines inbetween the quotes from Kipling's letter are Raine's as well.

37. Ibid., p. 8.

38. Quoted by Raine, "Kipling: Controversial Questions," pp. 17–18.

39. R. Kipling, *From Sea to Sea*, vol. 2 (London: Macmillan, 1914), p. 263; quoted by Raine, "Kipling: Controversial Questions," p. 18.

40. Kipling, *From Sea to Sea*, vol. 2, p. 131; quoted by Raine, "Kipling: Controversial Questions," p. 26.

41. David Gilmour, *The Long Recessional: The Imperial Life of Rudyard Kipling* (New York: Farrar, Straus and Giroux, 2002), p. 17.

42. All discussed in Craig Raine's very lucid and balanced exposition in "Kipling: Controversial Questions," pp. 10–29.

43. Mark Kinkead-Weekes, "Vision in Kipling's Novels," in *Kipling's Mind and Art*, ed. Andrew Rutherford (London: Oliver & Boyd, 1964), p. 233.

44. Said, *Culture and Imperialism*, p. 162.

45. Ibid., p. 167.

46. Lionel Trilling, "Kipling," in *The Moral Obligation to Be Intelligent: Selected Essays* (New York: Farrar, Straus and Giroux, 2000), p. 65.

47. Nirad Chaudhuri, "The Finest Story about India," in *The Age of Kipling*, ed. John Gross (New York: Simon and Schuster, 1972), p. 29.

48. R. Kipling, *Kim* (London: Macmillan, 1901), p. 11.

49. See Indian scholar and former editor of the *Kipling Journal* Sharad Keskar's "Introduction to *Kim*," *Kipling Journal*, http://www.kipling.org.uk/rg_kim_intro_p.htm.

50. Said, *Culture and Imperialism*, p. 178.

51. G. Moorhouse, *India Britannica* (London: Paladin, 1984), p. 85.

52. Ibid., p. 84.

53. Denis Judd, *Empire* (London: Fontana Press, 1997), p. 72.

54. Moorhouse, *India Britannica*, p. 85.

55. Ibid.

56. Said, *Culture and Imperialism*, p. 184.

57. Ibid., p. 185.

Conclusion

1. Walter Pach, in *The Journal of Eugène Delacroix*, trans. Walter Pach (New York: Hacker Art Books, 1980), p. 100.

2. Ibid., p. 700.

3. George Eliot, "The Natural History of German Life," *Westminster Review*, July 1856, p. 54.

BIBLIOGRAPHY

Books

Ackerman, Gerald M. *Jean-Léon Gérôme: His Life, His Work.* Paris: ACR Édition, Poche Couleur, 1997.

———. *Les Orientalistes de l'École Américaine.* Paris: ACR Édition, 1994.

———. *Les Orientalistes de l'École Britannique.* Paris: ACR Édition, 1991.

———. *The Life and Work of Jean-Léon Gérôme.* Paris: ACR Édition, 1986.

Adkins, Lesley. *Empires of the Plain: Henry Rawlinson and the Lost Languages of Babylon.* New York: St. Martin's Press, 2004.

Aeschylus. *The Persians.* Translated by G. Murray. Oxford: Oxford University Press, 1939.

———. *The Suppliant Maidens: The Persians.* Translated and with introduction by Seth G. Benardete. Chicago: University of Chicago Press, 1956.

Ahmed, Aijaz. *In Theory: Classes, Nations, Literatures.* London: Verso, 1992.

Alfred, David, ed. *The Norton Anthology of English Literature: The Middle Ages.* New York: Norton, 2000.

Al-Ghazali. *Deliverance from Error.* Translated and edited by R. J. McCarthy. Louisville, KY: Fons Vitae, 2004.

Allen, Charles. *The Buddha and the Sahibs: The Men Who Discovered India's Lost Religion.* London: John Murray, 2002.

Amnesty International. *Iran Violations of Human Rights: Documents Sent by Amnesty International to the Government of the Islamic Republic of Iran.* London: Amnesty International Publications, 1987.

Anastos, M. *Aspects of the Mind of Byzantium.* Political Theory, Theology, and Ecclesiastical Relations with the See of Rome, Variorum Collected Studies series. Ashgate: Ashgate Publications, 2001.

Arab Human Development Report 2003: Building a Knowledge Society. New York: United Nations Development Programme, Regional Bureau for Arab States, 2003.

Arberry, A. J. *The Cambridge School of Arabic.* Cambridge: Cambridge University Press, 1948.

———. *Oriental Essays: Portraits of Seven Scholars.* London: George Allen & Unwin, 1960.

Aristotle. *Complete Works.* Edited by Jonathan Barnes. Princeton, NJ: Princeton University Press, 1985.

Arnold, Matthew. *Culture and Anarchy: An Essay in Political and Social Criticism.* London, 1869.

———. *Culture and Anarchy.* 3rd ed. New York: Macmillan, 1882.

Arrian. *Anabasis Alexandri*. Translated by P. A. Brunt. 2 vols. Cambridge, MA: Harvard University Press, 1976.

Austen, Jane. *Mansfield Park*. Ware, UK: Wordsworth Classics, 1992.

Azumah, J. *Islam and Slavery*. London: London Bible College, Centre for Islamic Studies, 1999.

Bacon, Helen H. *Barbarians in Greek Tragedy*. New Haven, CT: Yale University Press, 1961.

Bairoch, Paul. *Mythes et paradoxes de l'histoire économique*. Paris: La Découverte, 1994.

Baldry, H. C. *The Unity of Mankind in Greek Thought*. Cambridge: Cambridge University Press, 1965.

Barbulesco, Luc, and Philippe Cardinal. *L'Islam En Questions*. Paris: Grasset, 1986.

Barnes, Jonathan, ed. *The Complete Works of Aristotle*. Vol. 2. Princeton, NJ: Princeton University Press, 1985.

Barter, James. *Idi Amin*. Chicago: Lucent, 2004.

Bartram, W. *Travels and Other Writings*. New York: Library of America, 1996.

Basham, A. L. *A Cultural History of India*. Oxford: Oxford University Press, 1975.

———. *The Wonder That Was India*. New York: Grove Press, 1964.

Baydawi. *Commentarius in Coranum. Anwaar al-Tanziill Wa-Asraar al-Ta'wiil*. Edited by H. O. Fleischer. 1846–48. Reprint, Osnabrück: Biblio, 1968.

Bayly, C. A., Gordon Johnson, and John F. Richards, eds. *Cambridge History of India*. Vol. 5. Cambridge: Cambridge University Press, 1929.

Bearden, Romare, and Harry Henderson. *A History of African-American Artists: From 1792 to the Present*. New York: Pantheon, 1993.

Beardsley, Grace Hadley. *The Negro in Greek and Roman Civilization: A Study of the Ethiopian Type*. Baltimore: Johns Hopkins University Press, 1929.

Beasley, W. G. *Japanese Imperialism, 1894–1945*. New York: Oxford University Press, 1987.

Bell, Richard, ed. and trans. *The Quran*. 2 vols. Edinburgh: T. & T. Clark, 1937–39.

Bernal, Martin. *Black Athena: The Afroasiatic Roots of Classical Civilization*. Vol. 1: *The Fabrication of Ancient Greece, 1785–1985*. New Brunswick, NJ: Rutgers University Press, 1987.

Bevan, E. R. *The House of Seleucus*. 2 vols. London: Edward Arnold, 1902.

Bhattacharyya, S. K. *Genocide in East Pakistan/Bangladesh: A Horror Story*. Houston, TX: A. Ghosh, 1988.

Bingham, Caleb, ed. *The Columbian Orator*. Revised by Val J. Halamandaris. 1797. Reprint, Washington, DC: Caring Publishing, 1997.

Bisaha, Nancy. *Creating East and West: Renaissance Humanists and the Ottoman Turks*. Philadelphia: University of Pennsylvania Press, 2004.

Bloom, Howard. *The Lucifer Principle: A Scientific Expedition into the Forces of History*. New York: Atlantic Monthly Press, 1995.

Bodin, Jean. *Colloquium of the Seven about Secrets of the Sublime* (Colloquium Heptaplomeres de Rerum Sublimium Arcanis Abditis). Translated and edited by Marion Leathers Daniels Kuntz. Princeton, NJ: Princeton University Press, 1976.

Boppe, Auguste. *Les Peintres du Bosphore au Dix-Huitième Siècle*. Paris: Librairie Hachette et Cie, 1911.

Boswell, James. *The Life of Johnson*. Edited by R. W. Chapman. 1904. Reprint, Oxford: Oxford University Press, 1983.

Bouwsma, William J. *Concordia Mundi: The Career and Thought of Guillaume Postel (1510–1581)*. Cambridge, MA: Harvard University Press, 1957.

Bowra, C. M. *Heroic Poetry*. London: Macmillan, 1952.

Brague, Remi. *Eccentric Culture: A Theory of Western Civilization*. South Bend, IN: St. Augustine's Press, 2002.

Braun, Martin. *History and Romance in Graeco-Oriental Literature*. Oxford: Oxford University Press, 1938.

Broadhead, H. D. *The Persae of Aeschylus: With Introduction, Critical Notes and Commentary*. Cambridge: Cambridge University Press, 1960.

Brophy, Brigid. *Mozart the Dramatist*. New York: Da Capo Press, 1988.

Brown, Bruce Alan. *Gluck and the French Theatre in Vienna*. Oxford: Clarendon, 1991.

Brown, Christopher. *Dutch Genre Painting*. London: National Gallery Publications Department, 1976.

Brown, Judith M., and W. Roger Louis, eds. *The Oxford History of the British Empire*. Vol. 4: *The Twentieth Century*. Oxford: Oxford University Press, 1999.

Brown, L. Carl. *Religion and State: The Muslim Approach to Politics*. New York: Columbia University Press, 2000.

Burich, Nancy J. *Alexander the Great: A Bibliography*. Kent, OH: Kent State University Press, 1970.

Burke, Edmund. *On Empire, Liberty, and Reform: Speeches and Letters*. Edited by David Bromwich. New Haven, CT: Yale University Press, 2000.

Burkert, Walter. *Babylon, Memphis, Persepolis: Eastern Contexts of Greek Culture*. Cambridge, MA: Harvard University Press, 2004.

———. *The Orientalizing Revolution: Near Eastern Influence on Greek Culture in the Early Archaic Age*. Cambridge, MA: Harvard University Press, 1992.

Burnham, James. *Suicide of the West: An Essay on the Meaning and Destiny of Liberalism*. 1964. Reprint, New York: Regnery, 1985.

Burr, Millard. *A Working Document: Quantifying Genocide in the Southern Sudan 1983–1993*. Washington, DC: US Committee for Refugees, 1993.

Busher, Leonard. *Religion's Peace: A Plea for Liberty of Conscience*. 1614.

Canny, Nicholas, ed. *The Oxford History of the British Empire*. Vol. 1: *The Origins of Empire*. Edited by William Roger Louis. Oxford: Oxford University Press, 1998.

Cardinalis, Gasparis Contarini. *Opera*. Paris, 1571.

Carretta, Vincent, ed. *Unchained Voices*. Lexington: University Press of Kentucky, 1996.

Cassirer, Ernst. *The Philosophy of the Enlightenment*. Boston: Beacon Press, 1960.

Cassirer, E., P. O. Kristeller, and H. H. Randall Jr., eds. *The Renaissance Philosophy of Man*. 1948. Reprint, Chicago: University of Chicago Press, 1971.

Chang, Iris. *The Rape of Nanking: The Forgotten Holocaust*. New York: Basic Books, 1997.

Chang, Jung, and Jon Halliday. *Mao: The Unknown Story*. New York: Knopf, 2005.
The Chambers Dictionary. Edinburgh: Chambers, 2003.
Chardin, Sir John. *Travels in Persia 1673–1677*. New York: Dover, 1988.
Chaudhuri, Nirad. *Clive of India: A Political and Psychological Essay*. London: Barrie & Jenkins, 1975.
———. *Scholar Extraordinary: The Life of Professor the Rt. Hon. Friedrich Max Müller, P.C.* Delhi: Oxford University Press, 1974.
Chesterton, G. K. *The Napoleon of Notting Hill*. 1904. Reprint, Ware, UK: Wordsworth Editions, 1996.
Chunder, Bholanauth. *The Travels of a Hindoo to Various Parts of Bengal and Upper India*. London: N. Trübner, 1869.
Cicero. *De Officiis*. Translated by Harry G. Edinger. Indianapolis: Bobbs-Merrill, 1974.
Colebrooke, H. T. *Miscellaneous Essays, with the Life of the Author by Sir T. E. Colebrooke*. 3 vols. London: Trübner & Co., 1873.
Conrad, J. *Under Western Eyes*. Harmondsworth, UK: Penguin, 1957.
Cook, Michael. *Muhammad*. Oxford: Oxford University Press, 1996.
Cook, Michael, and Patricia Crone. *Hagarism: The Making of the Muslim World*. Cambridge: Cambridge University Press, 1977.
Cox, Caroline, and John Marks. *The 'West,' Islam and Islamism: Is Ideological Islam Compatible with Liberal Democracy?* London: Civitas: Institute for the Study of Civil Society, 2003.
Craik, George Lillie. *The Pursuit of Knowledge under Difficulties*. 2 vols. London: Library of Entertaining Knowledge, 1830–31.
Creswell, K. A. C. *Early Muslim Architecture*. Harmondsworth, UK: Penguin, 1958.
Crombie, A. C. *Medieval and Early Modern Science: Augustine to Galileo: The History of Science A.D. 400–1650*. 1952. Reprint, New York: Doubleday Anchor, 1959.
———. *Robert Grosseteste and the Origins of Experimental Science, 1100–1700*. Oxford: Clarendon, 1953.
Dadrian, V. N. *The History of the Armenian Genocide: Ethnic Conflict from the Balkans to Anatolia to the Caucasus*. Oxford: Berghahn Books, 1995.
Daniel, Glyn. *A Hundred and Fifty Years of Archaeology*. Cambridge, MA: Harvard University Press, 1976.
Daniel, Norman. *Islam and the West: The Making of an Image*. Edinburgh: The University Press, 1962.
Darmesteter, James. *Sacred Books of the East: The Zend-Avesta*. Oxford: Oxford University Press, 1880.
Darwin, C. *The Origin of Species*. London, 1859.
Davidson, Basil. *The African Slave Trade*. Boston: Little, Brown, 1980.
Davies, Kristian. *The Orientalists: Western Artists in Arabia, the Sahara, Persia & India*. New York: Antique Collectors Club, 2005.
Davis, Robert C. *Christian Slaves, Muslim Masters: White Slavery in the Mediterranean, the Barbary Coast and Italy, 1500–1800*. New York: Palgrave Macmillan, 2003.

De, S. K. *Bengali Literature in the Nineteenth Century, 1757–1857*. Calcutta: Firma K. L. Mukhopadhay, 1962.

De Boer, T. J. *The History of Philosophy in Islam*. London, 1933. Reprint, New York: Dover, 1967.

Deeb, Marius. *Syria's Terrorist War on Lebanon and the Peace Process*. New York: Palgrave Macmillan, 2003.

de la Tourette, F. Gilles. *L'Orient et les Peintres de Venise*. Paris: Librairie Ancienne Édouard Champion, 1923.

Deleury, Guy. *Le Voyage en Inde. Anthologie Des Voyageurs Français (1750–1820)*. Paris: Robert Laffont, 1991.

de Margerie, Laure, Édouard Papet, Christine Barthe, Maria Vigli, Serge Lemoine, and John R. Porter, eds. *Facing the Other: Charles Cordier (1827–1905) Ethnographic Sculptor.* New York: Harry N. Abrams, 2004.

Destremau, C., and Jean Moncelon. *Louis Massignon*. Paris: Plon, 1994.

de Tott, Baron. *Memoirs of Baron de Tott*. London, 1785. Reprint, New York: Arno, 1973.

Diehl, Ernst. *Anthologia Lyrica Graeca*. Vols. 1 and 2. Leipzig: B. G. Teubner, 1925; 2nd. ed., 1942; 3rd ed., 1949–52.

Diels-Kranz. *Die Fragmente der Vorsokratiker*. 6th ed. 1951. Reprint, Zurich: Weidmann, 1985.

Dikötter, Frank, ed. *The Construction of Racial Identities in China and Japan: Historical and Contemporary Perspectives*. Honolulu: University of Hawai'i Press, 1997.

Djebar, Assia. *Femmes d'Alger dans leur appartement*. Paris: Albin Michel, Le Livre de Poche, 2002.

Dodds, E. R. *The Greeks and the Irrational*. Berkeley and Los Angeles: University of California Press, 1962.

Drews, Robert. *The Greek Accounts of Eastern History*. Cambridge, MA: Harvard University Press, 1973.

D'Souza, Dinesh. *What's So Great about America*. New York: Penguin, 2002.

Easterman, D. *New Jerusalems*. London: Grafton, 1992.

Eliade, Mircea. *Journal I, 1945–1955*. Translated by Mac Linscott Ricketts. Chicago: University of Chicago Press, 1990.

Empson, W. *Argufying: Essays on Literature & Culture*. Edited by John Haffenden. London: Hogarth Press, 1988.

Erdem, Y. H. *Slavery in the Ottoman Empire and Its Demise, 1800–1909*. New York: St. Martin's Press, 1996.

Ettinghausen, Richard. *Arab Painting*. Geneva: Editions d'Art Albert Skira, 1977.

Ettinghausen, Richard, and Oleg Grabar. *The Art and Architecture of Islam 650–1250*. London: Penguin, 1991.

Evans, A. J. *The Palace of Minos, I*. London: Macmillan, 1921.

———. *The Palace of Minos, II*. London: Macmillan, 1928.

Fage, J. D. *A History of West Africa*. Cambridge: Cambridge University Press, 1959.

Ferguson, Niall. *The Pity of War*. Harmondsworth, UK: Penguin, 2006.

Ferguson, W. *The Renaissance in Historical Thought.* New York: Houghton Mifflin, 1948.
Fergusson, James. *History of Indian and Eastern Architecture*. London, 1876.
Ferriol, Charles de. *Recueil de cent estampes representant differentes nations du Levant, gravees sur les tableaux peints d'apres nature en 1707 & 1708. Par les ordres de M. De Ferriol Ambassadeur du Roi a La Porte. Et gravées en 1712 et 1713*. Bound with *Explication de cent estampes qui representant differentes nations du Levant avec de nouvelles estampes de ceremonies Turques qui ont aussi leurs explications*. Paris: [Le Hay], Colombat, 1714.
Field, Michael. *Inside the Arab World*. Cambridge, MA: Harvard University Press, 1994.
Franits, Wyane. *Dutch Seventeenth-Century Genre Painting: Its Stylistic and Thematic Evolution*. New Haven, CT: Yale University Press, 2004.
Freeman, Charles. *The Closing of the Western Mind*. New York: Vintage, 2005.
Freeman, Kathleen. *Ancilla to the Pre-Socratic Philosophers. A Complete Translation of the Fragments* in Diels, *Die Fragmente der Vorsokratiker*. Oxford: Basil Blackwell & Mott/Cambridge, MA: Harvard University Press, 1948.
Fromentin, Eugène. *Lettres de jeunesse*. Edited by Pierre Blanchon. Paris: Plon, 1909.
———. *Oeuvres Complètes*. Edited by Guy Sagnes. Paris: Gallimard, 1984.
———. *The Old Masters of Belgium and Holland*. Translated by Mary C. Robbins. New York: Schocken, 1963.
Gann, L. H., and Peter Duignan. *Africa South of the Sahara*. Stanford, CA: Hoover Institution Press, 1981.
Gans, Moses. *Memorbook: A History of Dutch Jewry from the Renaissance to 1940*. Baarn: Bosch and Keuning, 1971.
Garrett, G. T., and E. Thompson. *Rise and Fulfillment of British Rule in India*. 1935. Reprint, Allahabad: Central Book Depot, 1962.
Gilmour, David. *Curzon*. New York: Farrar, Straus and Giroux, 2003.
———. *The Long Recessional: The Imperial Life of Rudyard Kipling*. New York: Farrar, Straus and Giroux, 2002.
———. *The Ruling Caste: Imperial Lives in the Victorian Raj*. New York: Farrar, Straus and Giroux, 2005.
Gleig, G. K., ed. *Memoirs of the Life of Right Honorable Warren Hastings*. 2 vols. London: Richard Bentley, 1841.
Godin, Christian. *La Fin de l'Humanité*. Seyssel, France: Éditions Champ Vallon, 2003.
Goel, Sita Ram. *Hindu Temples: What Happened to Them, Islamic Evidence*. New Delhi: Voice of India, 1993.
Goupil-Fesquet, Frédéric. *Voyage en Orient fait avec Horce Vernet en 1839 et 1840*. Paris, 1843.
Gowing, Lawrence. *Vermeer*. 1955. Reprint, Berkeley and Los Angeles: University of California Press, 1998.
Grotius, Hugo. *The Rights of War and Peace*. Natural Law and Enlightenment Classics. Indianapolis: Liberty Fund, 2005.
Guégan, Stéphane, Vincent Pomarède, Louis-Antoine Prat, Bruno Chenique, Christine Peltre, Peter Benson Miller, and Gary Tinterow. *Théodore Chassériau (1819–1856):*

The Unknown Romantic. New Haven, CT: Yale University Press/New York: Metropolitan Museum of Art, 2002.

Guillaume, A. *The Life of Muhammad, A Translation of* Isḥāq's Sīrat Rasūl Allāh. 1955. Reprint, Oxford: Oxford University Press, 1987.

Haarhoff, T. J. *The Stranger at the Gate*. Oxford: Basil Blackwell, 1948.

Hagemann, Ludwig, ed. *Nicolai de Cusa Opera Omnia, Vol. VIII: Cribratio Alkorani*. Hamburg: Felix Meiner Verlag, 1986.

Hammond, N. G. L. *The Genius of Alexander the Great*. Chapel Hill: University of North Carolina Press, 1997.

Hampshire, S. *Freedom of Mind and Other Essays*. Oxford: Clarendon, 1972.

Harle, J. C. *The Art and Architecture of the Indian Subcontinent*. London: Penguin, 1986.

Hayek, F. A. von. *The Road to Serfdom*. 1944. Reprint, Chicago: University of Chicago Press, 1976.

Hegel, G. W. F. *Aesthetics: Lectures on Fine Art*. Translated by T. M. Knox. 2 vols. Oxford: Clarendon Press, 1988.

Herman, Arthur. *How the Scots Invented the Modern World*. New York: Three Rivers Press, 2001.

Herodotus. *The Histories*. Translated by Robin Waterfield. Oxford: Oxford University Press, 1998.

Hiesinger, Ulrich W. *Edwin Lord Weeks: Visions of India*. New York: Vance Jordan Fine Art, 2002.

Hill, George Birkbeck. *Boswell's Life of Johnson*. Vol. 1. Oxford: Clarendon, 1934–50.

Hitchens, Christopher. *For the Sake of Argument*. London: Verso, 1994.

Holwell, John Z. *Interesting Historical Events, Relative to the Provinces of Bengal, and the Empire of Indostan With a seasonable hint and persuasive to the honourable the court of directors of the East India Company. As also the mythology and cosmogony, fasts and festivals of the Gentoo's, followers of the Shastah. And a dissertation on the metempsychosis, commonly, though erroneously, called the Pythagorean doctrine*. 3 vols. London, 1765–71.

Homer. *Odyssey*. Translated by Robert Fitzgerald. New York: Doubleday Anchor, 1963.

———. *Odyssey*. Translated by Stanley Lombardo. Indianapolis: Hackett, 2000.

Hornblower, Simon, and Antony Spawforth, eds. *The Oxford Classical Dictionary*. 3rd ed. Oxford: Oxford University Press, 1999.

How, W. W., and J. Wells. *A Commentary on Herodotus*. Vol. 1. 1912. Reprint, Oxford: Oxford University Press, 1964.

Huff, Toby. *The Rise of Early Modern Science: Islam, China, and the West*. Cambridge: Cambridge University Press, 1993.

Ibn Khaldūn. *The Muqaddimah*. Translated by Franz Rosenthal. 2nd ed. 1967. Reprint, Princeton, NJ: Princeton University Press, 1980.

———. *Tasfir Ibn Kathir*. Riyadh: Darussalam, 2000.

Irwin, Robert. *For Lust of Knowing: The Orientalists and Their Enemies*. London: Allen Lane, 2006.

Jacoby, F. *Fragmente der griechischen Historiker*. 15 vols. Berlin, 1923–50. Reprint, Leiden: Brill Academic, 2005.

James, Lawrence. *Raj: The Making and Unmaking of British India*. New York: St. Martin's Griffin, 1997.

James, William. *The Varieties of Religious Experience*. 1902. Reprint, New York: Modern Library, 1999.

Jefferson, Thomas. *The Papers of Thomas Jefferson*. Edited by Julian P. Boyd et al. 33 vols. Princeton, NJ: Princeton University Press, 1950.

———. *The Writings of Thomas Jefferson*. Edited by Andrew Adgate Lipscomb and Albert E. Bergh. 20 vols. Washington, DC: Thomas Jefferson Memorial Association, 1903–1904.

Jones, William. *A Grammar of the Persian Language*. 1771. Reprint, Menston, UK: Scholar Press, 1969.

———. *The Works of Sir William Jones*. Edited by A. M. Jones. 13 vols. London, 1807. Reprint, 1993 in Collected Works, edited by Garland Cannon (New York: New York University Press, 1993).

Judd, Denis. *Empire*. London: Fontana Press, 1997.

Juler, Caroline. *Les Orientalistes de l'École Italienne*. Paris: ACR Édition, Poche Couleur, 1994.

Julian, Philippe. *The Orientalists: European Painters of Eastern Scenes*. Oxford: Phaidon, 1977.

Jüthner, Julius. *Hellenen und Barbaren*. Leipzig: Dieterich, 1923.

Kahn, Charles H. *The Art and Thought of Heraclitus*. Cambridge: Cambridge University Press, 1979.

Karsh, Efraim, and Inari Karsh. *Empires of the Sand: The Struggle for Mastery in the Middle East, 1789–1923*. Cambridge, MA: Harvard University Press, 2001.

Kees, Hermann. *Kulturgeschichte des alten Orients: Agypten*. Munich: Beck, 1933.

Kejariwal, O. J. *The Asiatic Society of Bengal and the Discovery of India's Past, 1784–1838*. Delhi: Oxford University Press, 1988.

Kennedy, Valerie. *Edward Said: A Critical Introduction*. Cambridge: Polity Press, 2000.

Kiernan, Ben. *The Pol Pot Regime: Race, Power, and Genocide in Cambodia under the Khmer Rouge, 1975–79*. 2nd ed. New Haven, CT: Yale University Press, 2002.

Kipling, R. *From Sea to Sea*. Vol. 2. London: Macmillan, 1914.

Kopf, David. *British Orientalism and the Bengal Renaissance: The Dynamics of Indian Modernization 1773–1835*. Berkeley and Los Angeles: University of California Press, 1969.

Kramer, M. *Ivory Towers on Sand*. Washington, DC: Washington Institute for Near East Policy, 2001.

———, ed. *The Jewish Discovery of Islam*. Tel Aviv: Moshe Dayan Center, 1999.

Kuklick, Bruce. *Puritans in Babylon: The Ancient Near East and American Intellectual Life, 1880–1930*. Princeton, NJ: Princeton University Press, 1996.

Kulkarni, V. B. *British Statesmen in India*. Bombay: Orient Longmans, 1961.

Lal, K. S. *Growth of Muslim Population in Medieval India, A.D. 1000–1800*. Delhi: Research Publications in Social Sciences, 1973.

Lane Fox, Robin. *Alexander the Great*. 1973. New York: Penguin, 2004.

Layard, Austin Henry. *Autobiography and Letters*. 2 vols. New York: Charles Scribner's Sons, 1903.

———. *Nineveh and Its Remains*. 2 vols. New York: George Putnam, 1853.

Leach, Edmund. *Claude Lévi-Strauss*. New York: Viking, 1974.

Lefkowitz, Mary. *Not Out of Africa: How Afrocentrism Became an Excuse to Teach Myth as History.* New York: Basic Books, 1996.

Lemaire, Gérard-Georges. *L'Univers des Orientalistes*. Paris: Éditions Place des Victoires, 2000.

Lessing, Gotthold Ephraim. *Nathan the Wise*. Translated by William Taylor of Norwich. London, 1830.

Lewis, Bernard. *Cultures in Conflict: Christians, Muslims, and Jews in the Age of Discovery*. Oxford: Oxford University Press, 1995.

———. *Islam and the West*. New York: Oxford University Press, 1993.

———. *The Muslim Discovery of Europe*. London: Phoenix, 1994.

———. *Race and Slavery in the Middle East: An Historical Enquiry*. New York: Oxford University Press, 1990.

Lewis, Michael. *John Frederick Lewis R.A. 1805–1876*. Leigh-on-Sea, UK: F. Lewis Publishers, 1978.

Lloyd, Seton. *Foundations in the Dust*. Harmondsworth, UK: Pelican Books, 1955.

Locke, John. *A Letter concerning Toleration*. Amherst, NY: Prometheus Books, 1990.

Long, A. A., and D. Sedley. *The Hellenistic Philosophers*. Vol. 1. Cambridge: Cambridge University Press, 1987.

Lovejoy, P., and J. Hogendoorn, eds. *Slow Death for Slavery: The Course of Abolition in Northern Nigeria, 1897–1936*. Cambridge: Cambridge University Press, 1993.

Ludlow, John Malcolm. *British India, Its Races, and Its History, Considered with Reference to the Mutinies of 1857: A Series of Lectures Addressed to the Students of the Workingmen's College*. 2 vols. Cambridge: Macmillan, 1858.

Luther, Martin. *Verlegung des Alcoran*. Translated by Ricoldo da Montecroce. Wittenberg: H. Lufft, 1542.

Luxenberg, Christoph. *Die Syro-Aramäische Lesart des Koran: Ein Beitrage zur Entschlüsselung der Koransprache*. Berlin: Verlag Hans Schiler, 2004.

Mack, Rosamond E. *Bazaar to Piazza: Islamic Trade and Italian Art, 1300–1600*. Berkeley and Los Angeles: University of California Press, 2002.

MacKenzie, John M. *Orientalism: History, Theory and the Arts*. Manchester: Manchester University Press, 2004.

Mackintosh, Sir James. *Memoirs of the Life of the Right Honourable Sir James Mackintosh*. Edited by R. J. Mackintosh. 2 vols. Boston: W. D. Ticknor, 1835.

Maimonides, Moses. *Moses Maimonides' Epistle to Yemen: The Arabic Original and the Three Hebrew Versions*. Edited by Abraham S. Halkin, translated by Boaz Cohen. New York: American Academy for Jewish Research, 1952.

Majeed, Javed. *Ungoverned Imaginings: James Mill's* The History of British India *and Orientalism*. Oxford: Clarendon, 1992.

Majumdar, R. C., and A. D. Pusalkar, eds. *The History and Culture of the Indian People.* 10 vols. London: G. Allen & Unwin, 1951.

Makiya, Kanan. *Cruelty and Silence.* New York: Norton, 1993.

———. *The Republic of Fear.* Berkeley and Los Angeles: University of California Press, 1998.

Malik, Charles Habib. *A Christian Critique of the University.* 1982. Reprint, Waterloo, ON: North Waterloo Academic Press, 1990.

Manning, Patrick. *Slavery and African Life: Occidental, Oriental and African Slave Trades.* Cambridge: Cambridge University Press, 1990.

Marlier, Georges. *La Renaissance flamande Pierre Coeck d'Alost.* Brussels: Editions Robert Finck, 1966.

Marraccio, Ludovico. *Alcorani textus universus, ex correctioribus Arabum exemplaribus summa fide, atque pulcherrimis characteribus descriptus, eademque fide, ac pari diligentia ex Arabico idiomate in latinum translatus. Appositis unicuique capiti notis, atque refutatione: His omnibus praemissus est Prodromus Totum priorem Tomum implens, In quo contenta indicantur pagina sequenti. Ludovico Marraccio E Congregatione Clericorum Regularium Matris Dei, Innocentii XI. Gloriosissimae memoriae olim Confessario (Patavi, MDCXCVIII).* Padua: Typographia Seminarii, 1698.

———. *Refutatio Alcorani in qua ad Mahumetanicae superstitionis radicem securis apponitur; et Mahumetus ipse gladio suo jugulator* 2. Padua, 1698.

Marshall, P. J., and Alaine Low, eds. *The Oxford History of the British Empire.* Vol. 2: *The Eighteenth Century.* Oxford: Oxford University Press, 1998.

Marx, K., and F. Engels. *Manifesto of the Communist Party.* London, 1848.

Mascarenhas, Anthony. *The Rape of Bangladesh.* Delhi: Vikas, 1971.

Matthew, H. C. G., and Brian Harrison, eds. *The Oxford Dictionary of National Biography.* Oxford: Oxford University Press, 2004.

Maududi, Sayeed Abul A'ala. *Jihad in Islam.* 7th ed. Lahore, Pakistan: 2001.

McBeth, H. Leon. *A Sourcebook for Baptist Heritage.* Nashville, TN: Broadmen Press, 1990.

McCrindle, J. W. *McCrindle's Ancient India: As Described by Megasthenes and Arrian.* Edited by Ramchandra Jain. 1877. Reprint, New Delhi: Today and Tomorrow's Printers & Publishers, 1972.

McNeill, William H. *Rise of the West: A History of the Human Community.* Chicago: University of Chicago Press, 1963.

Melling, Antoine Ignance. *Voyage Pittoresque de Constantinople et des rives du Bosphore d'après les dessins de M. Melling.* Paris: Treuttel et Wurtz, 1819.

Milosz, Czeslaw. *The Captive Mind.* New York: Vintage, 1959.

Milton, Giles. *White Gold: The Extraordinary Story of Thomas Pellow and North Africa's One Million European Slaves.* London: Hodder & Stoughton, 2004.

Moorhouse, Geoffrey. *India Britannica.* London: Paladin, 1986.

Morris, James. *Venice.* London: Faber and Faber, 1978.

Moussa, Sarga. *Le Voyage en Égypte.* Paris: Robert Laffont, Bouquins, 2004.

Murray, Douglas. *Neoconservatism: Why We Need It*. New York: Encounter Books, 2006.
Nadler, Steven. *Rembrandt's Jews*. Chicago: University of Chicago Press, 2003.
Narain, A. K. *The Indo-Greeks: Revisited and Supplemented*. Delhi: B. R. Publishing, 2003.
Netanyahu, Benjamin. *Fighting Terrorism: How Democracies Can Defeat Domestic and International Terrorism*. New York: Farrar, Straus and Giroux, 1995.
Neusner, Jacob. *Mishnah*. New Haven, CT: Yale University Press, 1988.
Newman, Cardinal John Henry. *The Idea of a University*. San Francisco: Rinehart Press, 1960.
Nicholas of Cusa. *De Pace Fidei and Cribratio Alkorani*. Translated by Jasper Hopkins. Minneapolis: Arthur J. Banning Press, 1994.
Nicholson, R. A. *The Mystics of Islam*. 1914. Reprint, London: Routledge and Kegan Paul, 1975.
Novati, Francesco, ed. *Epistolario di Coluccio Salutati*. 3 vols. Rome: Forzani E. C. Tipografi del Senato, 1896.
Ockley, Simon. *The History of the Saracens*. 6th ed. London: Henry G. Bohn, 1857.
Pach, Walter, trans. *The Journal of Eugène Delacroix*. New York: Hacker Art Books, 1980.
Paine, Thomas. *The Age of Reason*. Secaucus, NJ: Carol Publishing, 1974.
Pamuk, Orhan. *Istanbul: Memories and the City*. New York: Vintage, 2006.
Park, You-me, and R. S. Rajan, eds. *The Postcolonial Jane Austen*. London: Routledge, 2000.
Patai, Raphael. *Ignaz Goldziher and His Oriental Diary*. Detroit: Wayne State University Press, 1987.
Pearson, Lionel. *The Lost Histories of Alexander the Great*. Oxford: Basil Blackwell, 1960.
Peltre, Christine. *L'Atelier du Voyage*. Paris: Éditions Gallimard, 1995.
———. *Les Orientalistes*. Paris: Éditions Hazan, 2003.
Peters, F. E. *The Hajj*. Princeton, NJ: Princeton University Press, 1994.
Pétré-Grenouilleau, Olivier. *Les Traites Négrières: Essai d'Histoire Globale*. Paris: Éditions Gallimard, 2004.
Philbrick, Nathaniel. *Sea of Glory: America's Voyage of Discovery, the U.S. Exploring Expedition, 1838–1842*. New York: Penguin, 2003.
Phillips, Melanie. *All Must Have Prizes*. London: Little, Brown, 1996.
Pipes, Daniel. *The Hidden Hand: Middle East Fears of Conspiracy*. New York: St. Martin's Griffin, 1998.
Pirenne, Henri. *Mohammed and Charlemagne*. 1939. Reprint, New York: Barnes & Noble Books, 1961.
Porter, Andrew, and Alaine Low, eds. *The Oxford History of the British Empire*. Vol 3: *The Nineteenth Century*. Oxford: Oxford University Press, 1999.
Porter, Roy. *Enlightenment: Britain and the Creation of the Modern World*. London: Penguin, 2001.
Portraits from the Empire: The Ottoman World and the Ottomans from the 18th to 20th Century with Selected Works from the Suna and İnan Kiraç Foundation Collection. Istanbul: Pera Museum, 2005.

Pryce-Jones, David. *The Closed Circle: An Interpretation of the Arabs*. London: Paladin Grafton, 1990.

Pullum, Geoffrey K. *The Great Eskimo Vocabulary Hoax and Other Irreverent Essays on the Study of Language*. Chicago: University of Chicago Press, 1991.

Questions of King Milinda. Translated by T. W. Rhys Davids. Vol. 35 of *The Sacred Books of the East*. Oxford: Clarendon, 1890.

Rai, Raghu. *Calcutta*. New Delhi: Time Books International, 1989.

———. *Taj Mahal*. Milan: Idealibri, 1995.

Raleigh, Sir Thomas, ed. *Lord Curzon in India, Being a Selection from His Speeches as Viceroy & Governor-General of India, 1895–1905*. London: Macmillan, 1906.

Riepe, Dale. *The Naturalistic Tradition in Indian Thought*. Seattle: University of Washington Press, 1961.

Roberts, J. M. *History of the World*. New York: Oxford University Press, 1993.

———. *The Triumph of the West*. London: B. B. C. Publications, 1985.

Rodinson, Maxime. *Europe and the Mystique of Islam*. Translated by Roger Veinus. Seattle: University of Washington Press, 1987.

———. *La Fascination de l'Islam*. Paris: Editions La Découverte, 1978.

Roget, J. L. *A History of the Old Watercolour Society*. London: Longmans Green, 1891.

Romero, Eugenio Maria. *El martirio de joven Hachuel o la heroina* Hebrea. Gibraltar: Imprinta Militar, 1837.

Rosenthal, F. R. *The Classical Heritage of Islam*. London: Routledge, 1975.

Rouillard, Clarence Dana. *The Turk in French History, Thought, and Literature (1520–1660)*. Paris: Boivin & Cie, 1940. Reprint, New York: Ams Press, 1973.

Rubin, Barry. *The Long War for Freedom: The Arab Struggle for Democracy in the Middle East*. Hoboken, NJ: Wiley, 2006.

Russell, Bertrand. *In Praise of Idleness*. London: Allen and Unwin, 1935.

———. *The Problems of Philosophy*. London: Williams & Norgate, 1912.

Sale, George, trans. *The Koran*. 1734. London: Frederick Warne, 1915.

Said, Edward. *Culture and Imperialism*. London: Vintage, 1994.

———. *Orientalism*. New York: Vintage, 1994.

———. *The Question of Palestine*. New York: Vintage, 1980.

Said, Edward, and Christopher Hitchens, eds. *Blaming the Victims: Spurious Scholarship and the Palestinian Questions*. London: Verso, 1988.

Sarafian, Ara, ed. *United States Official Documents on the Armenian Genocide*. 4 vols. Watertown, MA: Armenian Review, 1995.

Sarkar, Sir Jadunath. *History of Aurangzib*. 5 vols. Calcutta: Sarkar & Sons, 1912–24.

Sartre, Jean-Paul. *The Wretched of the Earth*. New York: Grove Press, 1968.

Schlereth, Thomas J. *The Cosmopolitan Ideal in Enlightenment Thought: Its Form and Function in the Ideas of Franklin, Hume, and Voltaire*. South Bend, IN: University of Notre Dame Press, 1977.

Schlesinger, Arthur M., Jr. *The Disuniting of America: Reflections on a Multicultural Society*. New York: Norton, 1992.

Schuster-Walser, Sibylla. *Das safawidische Persien im Spiegel europäischer Reiseberichte (1502–1722)*. Baden-Baden/Hamburg: Grimm, 1970.

Schwab, Raymond. *The Oriental Renaissance: Europe's Rediscovery of India and the East, 1680–1880*. Translated by G. Patterson-Black and Victor Reinking. New York: Columbia University Press, 1984.

Scruton, Roger. *The West and the Rest: Globalization and the Terrorist Threat*. New York: Continuum, ISI Books, 2002.

Séailles, Gabriel. *Alfred Dehodencq: Histoire d'Un Coloriste*. Paris: Paul Ollendorf, Éditeur, 1885.

Sen, Amartya. *Identity and Violence: The Illusion of Destiny*. New York: Norton, 2006.

Seneca, Lucius Annaeus. *Moral Essays*. Translated by John W. Basore. Loeb Classical Library. 3 vols. London: W. Heinemann, 1928–35.

Silverberg, Robert. *To the Rock of Darius: The Story of Henry Rawlinson*. New York: Holt, Rinehart and Winston, 1966.

Singh, G. B. *Gandhi: Behind the Mask of Divinity*. Amherst, NY: Prometheus Books, 2004.

Singh, Raghubir. *Rajasthan: India's Enchanted Land*. New York: Thames and Hudson, 1981.

Sivan, Emmanuel. *Interpretations of Islam: Past and Present*. Princeton, NJ: Darwin Press, 1985.

Small, Lisa. *Highlights from the Dahesh Museum Collection: Essay and Catalogue*. New York: Dahesh Museum, 1999.

Smith, Adam. *An Inquiry into the Nature and Causes of the Wealth of Nations*. Edited by Edwin Cannan. 5th ed. London: Methuen, 1904.

Smith, Vincent A., and Percival Spear, eds. *The Oxford History of India*. 1911. Reprint, Delhi: Oxford University Press, 1981.

Smyth, H. W. *Aeschylean Tragedy*. Berkeley and Los Angeles: University of California Press, 1924.

Snowden, Frank, Jr. *Before Color Prejudice: The Ancient View of Blacks*. Cambridge, MA: Harvard University Press, 1983.

———. *Blacks in Antiquity*. Cambridge, MA: Harvard University Press, 1970.

Sokal, Alan, and Jean Bricmont. *Fashionable Nonsense: Post-Modern Intellectuals' Abuse of Science*. New York: Picador USA, 1998.

Solomon, Maynard. *Mozart: A Life*. New York: Harper Perennial, 1996.

Sophocles. *Antigone*. Translated by Robert Fagles. New York: Penguin, 1984.

Southern, R. W. *Western Views of Islam in the Middle Ages*. Cambridge, MA: Harvard University Press, 1978.

Sprinker, Michael, ed. *Edward Said: A Critical Reader*. Oxford: Blackwell, 1993.

St. Clair-Tisdall, Rev. W. *The Original Sources of the Qur'an*. London: Society for Promoting Christian Knowledge, 1905.

———. *The Sources of Islam: A Persian Treatise*. Translated and abridged by Sir William Muir. Edinburgh: T. & T. Clark, 1901.

Steegmuller, Francis. *Flaubert in Egypt: A Sensibility on Tour*. Chicago: Academy Chicago Limited, 1979.

Stern, Menahem. *Greek and Latin Authors on Jews and Judaism*. 3 vols. Jerusalem: Israel Academy of Sciences and Humanities, 1974–84.

Stevens, Mary Anne, ed. *The Orientalists: Delacroix to Matisse, European Painters in North Africa and the Near East*. London: Royal Academy of Arts, 1984.

Stiefel, Tina. *The Intellectual Revolution in Twelfth-Century Europe*. New York: St. Martin's Press, 1985.

Stillman, Norman. *The Jews of Arab Lands: A History and Source Book*. Philadelphia: Jewish Publication Society of America, 1979.

Swift, Jonathan. *Gulliver's Travels*. London, 1726. Reprint, Harmondsworth, UK: Penguin, 1985.

Tarn, W. W. *Alexander the Great*. 1948. Reprint, Boston: Beacon Press, 1956.

———. *The Greeks in Bactria and India*. 2nd ed. Cambridge: Cambridge University Press, 1951.

Teignmouth, Lord. *Memoirs of Sir William Jones*. London, 1807.

Thompson, James, and Barbara Wright. *La Vie et L'Oeuvre d' Eugène Fromentin*. Paris: ACR Édition, 1987.

Thoreau, H. D. *The Writings of Henry David Thoreau*. New York: Houghton Mifflin, 1906.

Thornton, Bruce. *Greek Ways: How the Greeks Created Western Civilization*. San Francisco: Encounter Books, 2000.

Thornton, Lynne. *La Femme Dans La Peinture Orientaliste*. Paris: ACR Édition, Poche Couleur, 1993.

———. *Les Orientalistes: Peintres Voyageurs*. Paris: ACR Édition, Poche Couleur, 1993.

———. *Les Orientalistes: Peintres Voyageurs*. Paris: ACR Édition, 1994.

Thuasne, L. *Gentile Bellini et Sultan Mohammed II*. Paris, 1888.

Tibi, Bassam. *Islam between Culture and Politics*. New York: Palgrave Macmillan, 2005.

Timmerman, Kenneth R. *Preachers of Hate: Islam and the War on America*. New York: Three Rivers Press, 2004.

Tocqueville, Alexis de. *Oeuvres Complètes*. Edited by J. P. Mayer and André Jardin. Paris: Gallimard, 1962.

Toledano, Ehud R. *The Ottoman Slave Trade and Its Suppression, 1840–1890*. Princeton, NJ: Princeton University Press, 1982.

Tomalin, Claire. *Jane Austen: A Life*. Harmondsworth, UK: Penguin, 1998.

Trilling, Lionel. *The Liberal Imagination*. Garden City, NY: Doubleday, 1950.

Underhill, E. *Mysticism: A Study in the Nature and Development of Man's Spiritual Consciousness*. 1911. Reprint, New York: Dutton, 1961.

Vatikiotis, P. J. *Among Arabs and Jews: A Personal Experience, 1936–1990*. London: Weidenfeld and Nicolson, 1991.

Vaughn, Lewis, and Austin Dacey. *The Case for Humanism: An Introduction*. Lanham, MD: Rowman & Littlefield, 2003.

Virgil. *Aeneid*. Translated by W. F. Jackson Knight. Harmondsworth, UK: Penguin, 1958.

von Grunebaum, G. E. *Islam: Essays in the Nature and Growth of a Cultural Tradition*. London: Routledge & Kegan Paul, 1955.

Vryonis, Speros, Jr. *The Decline of Medieval Hellenism in Asia Minor and the Process of Islamization from the Eleventh through the Fifteenth Century*. Berkeley and Los Angeles: University of California Press, 1986.

Wallerstein, Immanuel. *Geopolitics and Geoculture: Essays on the Changing World-System*. Cambridge: Cambridge University Press, 1991.

Wardman, H. W. *Ernest Renan: A Critical Biography*. London: University of London Athlone Press, 1964.

Watt, William Montgomery. *Muslim-Christian Encounters*. London: Routledge, 1991.

Weeks, Lord Edwin. *Artist Explorer: A Ride through Persia to India in 1892*. N.p.: Long Riders' Guild Press, 2005.

———. *From the Black Sea through Persia and India*. New York: Harper and Brothers, 1895.

Welch, Stuart Cary. *Imperial Mughal Painting*. New York: George Braziller, 1978.

Wellington, Hubert, ed., and Lucy Norton, trans. *The Journal of Eugène Delacroix*. 1951. Reprint, London: Phaidon, 2004.

Wells, J. *Studies in Herodotus*. Oxford: Basil Blackwell, 1923.

West, M. L. *Early Greek Philosophy and the Orient*. Oxford: Clarendon, 1971.

White, Gabrielle D. V. *Jane Austen in the Context of Abolition: 'a fling at the slave trade.'* New York: Palgrave Macmillan, 2006.

Wickremeratne, Ananda. *The Genesis of an Orientalist: Thomas William Rhys Davids and Buddhism in Sri Lanka*. Columbia, MO: South Asia Books, 1985.

Williams, Bernard. *Morality: An Introduction to Ethics*. New York: Harper & Row, 1972.

Winks, Robin W., and Alaine Low, eds. *The Oxford History of the British Empire*. Vol 5: *Historiography*. Oxford: Oxford University Press, 1999.

Wistrich, Robert. *Antisemitism: The Longest Hatred*. New York: Schocken, 1991.

Wittkower, R. *Allegory and the Migration of Symbols*. Boulder, CO: Westview Press, 1977.

———. *Selected Lectures of Rudolf Wittkower: The Impact of Non-European Civilizations on the Art of the West*. Compiled and edited by Donald Martin Reynolds. Cambridge: Cambridge University Press, 1989.

Wood, William. *New England's Prospect*. Edited by Alden Vaughan. 1634. Reprint, Amherst: University of Massachusetts Press, 1977.

Articles, Essays, and Lectures

Abtahi, Hirad. "Reflections on the Ambiguous Universality of Human Rights: Cyrus the Great's Proclamation as a Challenge to the Athenian Democracy's Perceived Monopoly on Human Rights." In *The Dynamics of International Criminal Justice*, edited by Hirad Abtahi and Gideon Boas. Leiden: Brill, 2006.

Ackerman, Gerald M. "Orientalist Painters." In *Auction Catalogue of the Forbes Magazine Collection of Orientalist Paintings, Drawings, Watercolors and Sculpture*. New York: Christie's, 1993.

Ajami, Fouad. "Enemies, a Love Story: A Nobel Laureate Argues That Civilizations Are Not Clashing." *Washington Post*, April 2, 2003.

Almog, S. "The Racial Motif in Renan's Attitude to Jews and Judaism." In *Antisemitism through the Ages*, edited by Shmuel Almog. Oxford: Pergamon, 1988.

Annas, Julia. "Stoicism." In *The Oxford Classical Dictionary*. Oxford: Oxford University Press, 1999.

Armitage, David. "Literature and Empire." In *The Origins of Empire: British Overseas Enterprise to the Close of the Seventeenth Century*, edited by Nicholas Canny and Alaine Low. Oxford: Oxford University Press, 1998.

Arnold, Matthew. "The Function of Criticism at the Present Time." In *Essays in Criticism*. London and Cambridge: Macmillan, 1865.

Aurelius, Marcus. "Meditations." In *The Stoic and Epicurean Philosophers*, edited by Whitney J. Oates. Book IV. New York: Random House, 1940.

'Azm, Sadiq al-. "Orientalism and Orientalism in Reverse." In *Forbidden Agendas: Intolerance and Defiance in the Middle East*, edited by Jon Rothschild. London: Al Saqi Books, 1984.

Baudelaire, C. "Salon de 1845." In *Baudelaire Critique d'Art*, vol. 1. Paris: Gallimard, 1965.

Bayly, C. A. "The Second British Empire." In *The Oxford History of the British Empire*. Vol. 5: *Historiography*, edited by Robin W. Winks. Oxford: Oxford University Press, 1999.

Bayly, Susan. "Colonial Cultures: Asia." In *The Oxford History of the British Empire*. Vol. 3: *The Nineteenth Century*, edited by Andrew Porter and Alaine Low. Oxford: Oxford University Press, 1999.

Bentham, Jeremy. "Emancipate Your Colonies." In *The Works of Jeremy Bentham*, edited by John Bowring. Vol. 4. 1843. Reprint, Bristol: Thoemmes Press, 1995.

Berg, Herbert. "The Implications of, and Opposition to, the Methods of John Wansbrough." In *The Quest for the Historical Muhammad*, edited by Ibn Warraq. Amherst, NY: Prometheus Books, 2000.

Bernard, P. *Fouilles d'Aï Khanoum I*, Campagnes 1965, 1966, 1967, 1968. 2 vols. MDAFA [Mémoires de la Délégation Archéologique Française en Afghanistan (Official Bulletins of French Archaeological Mission in Afghanistan)] XXI. Paris, 1973.

Berque, Jacques. "Au-delà de l'Orientalisme; Entretien avec Jacques Berque." In *Qantara* 13 (October/November/December 1994).

Beyala, Calixthe. "Le Credo d'Une Afro-Française" (Credo of an Afro-French Woman). Interview in *Le Point*, December 22–29, 2005.

Borrmans, Maurice. "Ludovico Marracci et sa traduction latine du Coran." *Pontificio Istitutio di Studi Arabi e d'Islamistica: Islamochristiana* 28 (2002): 73–86.

Briant, P. "Colonization, Hellenistic." In *The Oxford Classical Dictionary*, 3rd. ed, edited by Simon Hornblower and Antony Spawforth. Oxford: Oxford University Press, 1999.

Brophy, Brigid. "Introduction." In *Die Zauberflöte: Die Entführung aus dem Serail*, by W. A. Mozart. New York: Universe Books, 1971.

Brown, Bruce Alan. Notes to CD of Gluck's *La Rencontre imprévue, ou les Pèlerins de la Mecque*. Paris: Radio France/Erato Discs, 1991.

Bugler, Caroline. "A Frank Encampment in the Desert of Mount Sinai, 1842—The Convent of St. Catherine in the Distance." 1856. In *The Orientalists: Delacroix to Matisse, European Painters in North Africa and the Near East*, edited by Mary Anne Stevens. London: Royal Academy of Arts, 1984.

Bull, Ludlow. "Ancient Egypt." In *The Idea of History in the Ancient Near East*, edited by R. Dentan. New Haven, CT: Yale University Press, 1955.

Burman, Thomas E. "Polemic, Philology, and Ambivalence: Reading the Quran in Latin Christendom." *Journal of Islamic Studies* 15 (2004): 181–209.

———. "Tafsir and Translation: Traditional Qur'an Exegesis and the Latin Qur'ans of Robert of Ketton and Mark of Toledo." *Speculum* 73 (1998): 703–32.

Buruma, Ian. Review of *Out of Place: A Memoir* by Edward Said. *New York Times Book Review*, October 3, 1999.

Butler, Marilyn. "Introduction." In *Jane Austen: Selected Letters 1796–1817*, edited by R. W. Chapman. Oxford: Oxford University Press, 1985.

Cabanelas. "Juan de Segovia." *Al-Andalus* 14 (1949): 131–36.

———. "Juan de Segovia y el primer Alcoran trilingue." *Al-Andalus* 14 (1949): 157–61.

Canny, Nicholas. "England's New World and the Old." In *The Oxford History of the British Empire*. Vol. 1: *The Origins of Empire*, edited by Nicholas Canny. Oxford: Oxford University Press, 1998.

"Carolingian Schools." In *The Oxford Dictionary of the Christian Church*, 3rd ed., edited by F. L. Cross and E. A. Livingstone. Oxford: Oxford University Press, 1997.

"The Challenge of 'Black Athena.'" *Journal Arethusa* (Special Issue/Fall 1989). Published by the Department of Classics, State University of New York at Buffalo.

Chaudhuri, Nirad. "The Finest Story about India." In *The Age of Kipling*, edited by John Gross. New York: Simon and Schuster, 1972.

Cohen, Eliot A. "World War IV: Let's Call This Conflict What It Is." *Wall Street Journal*, November 20, 2001.

Colledge, Malcolm. "Greek and Non-Greek Interaction in the Art and Architecture of the Hellenistic East." In *Hellenism in the East: The Interaction of Greek and non-Greek Civilizations from Syria to Central Asia after Alexander*, edited by Amélie Kuhrt and Susan Sherwin-White. London: Duckworth, 1987.

Conrad, Lawrence I. "Ignaz Goldziher on Ernest Renan: From Orientalist Philology to the Study of Islam." In *The Jewish Discovery of Islam*, edited by M. Kramer. Tel Aviv: Moshe Dayan Center for Middle Eastern and African Studies, 1999.

Cowell, Alan. "Exploring Islamic Cairo." *New York Times*, January 1, 1989.

de Mandach, Conrad. "Artistes Contemporains, Léon Belly (1827–1877)." *Gazette des Beaux-Arts* (January 1913): 73–84, (February 1913): 143–57.

Deutsch, Karl. "On Nationalism, World Regions, and the Nature of the West." In *Mobi-*

lization, Center-Periphery Structures and Nation-Building: A Volume in Commemoration of Stein Rokkan, edited by Per Torsvik. Bergen: Universitetsforlaget/Irvington-on-Hudson, NY: Columbia University Press, 1981.

Devan, Janadas. "Singapore Way." *New York Review of Books*, June 6, 1996.

Dewey, Clive. "How the Raj Played Kim's Game." *Times Literary Supplement*, April 17, 1998.

Dey, Shumbhoo Chander. "Sir Charles Wilkins." In *Eminent Orientalists: Indian, European American*. 1922. Reprint, Madras: Asian Educational Services, 1991.

Diderot. "Pensées Philosophiques." In *Oeuvres Philosophiques*, edited by Paul Vernière. Paris: Garnier Frères, 1964.

Dorfman, John. "Trendspotting: Beyond the Harem." *Art+Auction*, Annual Investment Issue, A Special Collectors Guide (2006).

Douglass, Frederick. "My Bondage and My Freedom" (1885). In *Frederick Douglass Autobiographies*, edited by Henry Louis Gates. New York: Library of America, 1994.

Epictetus. "Discourses." In *The Stoic and Epicurean Philosophers*, edited by Whitney J. Oates. New York: Random House, 1940.

Fitzpatrick, David. "Ireland and the Empire." In *The Oxford History of the British Empire*. Vol. 3: *The Nineteenth Century*, edited by Andrew Porter and Alaine Low. Oxford: Oxford University Press, 1999.

Fraiman, Susan. "Jane Austen and Edward Said: Gender, Culture and Imperialism." In *Janeites: Austen's Disciples and Devotees*, edited by Deidre Lynch. Princeton, NJ: Princeton University Press, 2000.

Francfort, H. P. Fouilles d'Aï Khanoum. MDAFA [Mémoires de la Délégation Archéologique Française en Afghanistan] XXVII, Paris, 1984.

Freedman, Daniel. "Bernard Lewis: U.S. May Lose War on Terror." *New York Sun*, September 13, 2006.

Frykenberg, Robert E. "India to 1858." In *The Oxford History of the British Empire*. Vol. 5: *Historiography*, edited by Robin W. Winks. Oxford: Oxford University Press, 1999.

Gabrieli, G. "Gli studi orientali e gli ordini religiosi in Italia." *Il pensiero missionario* 3 (1931).

Gay, P. "The Subversive Anthropologist." In *The Party of Humanity*. New York: Knopf, 1964.

Gemery, Henry H., and Jan S. Hogendorn. "La traite des esclaves sur l'Atlantique: essai de modèle économique." In *Esclave facteur de production*, edited by Sidney Mintz. Paris: Dunod, 1981.

Goetz, Hermann. "Oriental Types and Scenes in Renaissance and Baroque Painting—I." *Burlington Magazine for Connoisseurs* 73, no. 425 (August 1938): 50–62.

———. "Oriental Types and Scenes in Renaissance and Baroque Painting—II." *Burlington Magazine for Connoisseurs* 73, no. 426 (September 1938): 105–15.

Goldziher, I. "Islam et Parsisme." In *Actes du premier Congres International d'Histoire des religions*. Vol. 1. Paris, 1900.

Gombrich, E. "Eastern Inventions and Western Response." *Daedalus* 127 (Winter 1998): 193–205.

Grenier, Richard. "The Gandhi Nobody Knows." *Commentary* 75, no. 3 (March 1983).

Grimm, R. E. "The Autobiography of Leonardo Pisano." *Fibonacci Quarterly* 11, no. 1 (February 1973): 99–104.

Haskell, Francis. "A Turk and His Pictures in Nineteenth-Century Paris." *Oxford Art Journal* 5, no. 1 (1982).

Heggy, Tarek. "Comments on the Required Change in Egypt." *Watani*, December 22 and 29, 2002.

Hogendorn, Jan. "The Hideous Trade: Economic Aspects of the 'Manufacture' and Sale of Eunuchs." *Paideuma* 45 (1999): 137–60.

Holt, F. L. "Menander 'Soter.'" In *The Oxford Classical Dictionary*, 3rd ed., edited by Simon Hornblower and Antony Spawforth. Oxford: Oxford University Press, 1999.

Holt, P. M. "The Treatment of Arab History in Prideaux, Ockley and Sale." In *Historians of the Middle East*, edited by B. Lewis and P. M. Holt. London: Oxford University Press, 1962.

Hourani, Albert. Interview with editor. In *Approaches to the History of the Middle East*, edited by Nancy Elizabeth Gallagher. London: Ithaca Press, 1994.

Hume, David. "The Stoic." In *Essays, Moral, Political, Literary*, edited by T. H. Green and T. H. Grosse. 2 vols. London: Longmans, 1875.

Humphreys, R. Stephen. "Tradition and Innovation in the Study of Islamic History: The Evolution of North American Scholarship since 1960." Lecture presented at the Institute of Oriental Culture, University of Tokyo, October 21, 1997.

Iyengar, M. S. Ramaswami. "Henry T. Colebrooke." In *Eminent Orientalists, Indian, European American*. 1922. Reprint, Madras: Asian Educational Services, 1991.

Jacques, Martin. "The Middle Kingdom Mentality." *Guardian*, April 16, 2005.

Johnson, Lee. "Towards Delacroix's Oriental Sources." *Burlington* 120, no. 900 (March 1978).

Johnson, Samuel. "The Adventurer" and "The Idler." In *The Weeks of Samuel Johnson*, Vol. 2., edited by John M. Bullitt, W. J. Bate, and L. F. Powell. New Haven, CT: Yale University Press, 1963.

———. "Taxation No Tyranny." In *The Works of Samuel Johnson*. Vol. 14. Troy, NY: Pafraets & Company, 1913.

Jones, Alan. "Sir William Jones as an Arabist." In *Sir William Jones, 1746–1794: A Commemoration*, edited by Alexander Murray. Oxford: Oxford University Press, 1998.

Jones, William. "Dissertation Sur La Littérature Orientale." In *The Works of Sir William Jones*, edited by Burton Feldman and Robert D. Richardson Jr. New York: Garland, 1984.

———. "Preface to *A Grammar of the Persian Language*." Reprinted in *Sir William Jones: A Reader*, edited by Satya S. Pachori. Delhi: Oxford University Press, 1993.

Juan de Segovia. "Prefatio Johannis de Segobia . . . in translationem noviter ex Arabico in

Latinum vulgareque Hyspanum libri Alchorani . . ." In *Juan de Segovia y el problema islamico*, edited by D. Cabanelas Rodriguez. Madrid: University of Madrid, 1952.

Justus, Kevin L. *The Abduction from the Seraglio, Nine Exotic Delights from the Versailles of Louis XV, or the Hunts the Thing in Which We Catch the Character of the King*. Forthcoming, 2007.

Keating, P. J. "W. S. Blunt." In *The Penguin Companion to Literature*. Vol. 1. Harmondsworth, UK: Penguin, 1971.

Keddie, Nikki. Interview with editor. In *Approaches to the History of the Middle East*, edited by Nancy Elizabeth Gallagher. London: Ithaca Press, 1994.

Kirk, Russell, "Introduction." In Giovanni Pico della Mirandola, *Oration on the Dignity of Man*, translated by A. Robert Caponigri. Chicago: Regnery, 1967.

Khawaja, Irfan. "Essentialism, Consistency and Islam: A Critique of Edward Said's *Orientalism*." In *Postcolonial Theory and the Arab-Israeli Conflict*, edited by Efraim Karsh. New York: Routledge, forthcoming 2007.

Kinkead-Weekes, Mark. "Vision in Kipling's Novels." In *Kipling's Mind and Art*, edited by Andrew Rutherford. London: Oliver & Boyd, 1964.

Kritzeck, James. "Robert of Ketton's Translation of the Qur'an." *Islamic Quarterly* 2 (1955): 309–312.

Lewis, Bernard. "Islamic Concepts of Revolution." In *Revolution in the Middle East, and Other Case Studies: Proceedings of a Seminar*, edited by P. J. Vatikiotis. London: G. Allen & Unwin, 1972.

———. "La carte du Proche-Orient." In *Islam et Politique au Proche-Orient aujourd'hui.* Paris: Gallimard, 1991.

———. "The Pro-Islamic Jews." In *Islam in History: Ideas, People, and Events in the Middle East*. Chicago: Open Court, 1993.

Lindsey, Ursula. "Egypt's Grand Mufti Issues *Fatwa*: No Sculpture." *Christian Science Monitor*, April 18, 2006. http://www.csmonitor.com/2006/0418/p01s02-wome.html.

Lüling, Günter. "Preconditions for the Scholarly Criticism of the Koran and Islam." *Journal of Higher Criticism* 3 (Spring 1996).

Mansel, Philip. "Painter in the Palace." *Cornucopia* 30 (2003–2004).

Meakin, James Edward B. "The Jews of Morocco." *Jewish Quarterly Review* 4, no. 3 (1892).

"Mercenaries." In *The Oxford Classical Dictionary*, 3rd ed., edited by Simon Hornblower and Antony Spawforth. Oxford: Oxford University Press, 1999.

Moles, John. "Cynic Cosmopolitanism." In *The Cynics: The Cynic Movement in Antiquity and Its Legacy*, edited by R. Bracht Branham and Marie-Odile Goulet-Cazé. Berkeley and Los Angeles: University of California Press, 1996.

Montaigne. "On Vanity." In *The Complete Works of Montaigne*, edited by Donald Frame. Stanford, CA: Stanford University Press, 1948.

Munro, Jane. "Pilgrims Going to Mecca, 1861." In *The Orientalists: Delacroix to Matisse, European Painters in North Africa and the Near East*, edited by Mary Anne Stevens. London: Royal Academy of Arts, 1984.

Myers, J. L. "Herodotus." In *The Oxford Classical Dictionary*. Oxford: Oxford University Press, 1978.

Nagel, Thomas. "Moral Conflict and Political Legitimacy." *Philosophy and Public Affairs* 16 (1987).

Narain, A. K., and Romila Thapar. "Sandracottus." In *The Oxford Classical Dictionary*, 3rd ed., edited by Simon Hornblower and Antony Spawforth. Oxford: Oxford University Press, 1999.

Netanyahu, Benjamin. "Today, We Are All Americans." *New York Post*, September 21, 2001.

Nochlin, Linda. "The Imaginary Orient." *Art in America* (May 1983).

Nussbaum, Martha. "Heraclitus." In *The Oxford Classical Dictionary*, 3rd ed., edited by Simon Hornblower and Antony Spawforth. Oxford: Oxford University Press, 1999.

Paddaya, K. "Sir William Jones: An Appreciation." *Bulletin of the Deccan College Post-graduate Research Institute* 54, no. 55 (1994–1995). Special numbers devoted to Sir Williams Jones.

Parry, A. A. "Blameless Aegisthus: A Study of AMYMON and other Homeric Epithets." In *Mnemosyne*, supp. 26. Leiden: Brill, 1973.

Pioffet, Marie-Christine. "Diversité et métissages culturels dans l'Ibrahim ou l'Illustre Bassa." *Littératures* 34 (1996): 43–55.

Raine, Craig. "Kipling: Controversial Questions." *Kipling Journal* (September 2002): 10–29.

Rapin, C. *La Trésorie du Palais Hellenistique d'Aï Khanoum*. In MDAFA (Mémoires de la Délégation Archéologique Française en Afghanistan). Paris, 1992.

Renan, Ernest. "Islamisme et la science." Lecture presented at the Sorbonne, Basel, Bernheim, March 29, 1883.

———. "Muhammad and the Origins of Islam." In *The Quest for the Historical Muhammad*, edited by Ibn Warraq. Amherst, NY: Prometheus Books, 2000.

"Review of Seyyed Hossein Nasr, *A Young Muslim's Guide to the Modern World*." *Muslim World Book Review* 14, no. 4 (1994).

Rodinson, Maxime. "A Critical Survey of Modern Studies on Muhammad." In *Studies on Islam*, edited by Merlin L. Swartz. New York: Oxford University Press, 1981.

———. Interview with editor. In *Approaches to the History of the Middle East*, edited by Nancy Elizabeth Gallagher. London: Ithaca Press, 1994.

———. "The Western Image and Western Studies of Islam." In *The Legacy of Islam*, edited by Joseph Schacht and C. E. Bosworth. Oxford: Oxford University Press, 1974.

Said, Edward "Impossible Histories: Why the Many Islams Cannot Be Simplified, reviewing Bernard Lewis, *What Went Wrong? Western Impact and Middle Eastern Response*." *Harper's* (July 2002).

———. "Israel-Palestine: A Third Way." *Le Monde Diplomatique* (September 1998).

Sastri, K. S. Ramaswami. "Max Müller." In *Eminent Orientalists: Indian, European American*. 1922. Reprint, Madras: Asian Educational Services, 1991.

———. "Sir William Jones." In *Eminent Orientalists: Indian, European American*. 1922. Reprint, Madras: Asian Educational Services, 1991.

Scanlan, Laura Wolff. "Translating Fashion: Customs and Clothes in the Age of Exploration." *Humanities* 26, no. 1 (January/February 2005).

Schwabl, Hans. "Das Bild der fremden Welt bei den frühen Griechen." In *Grecs et Barbares*. Vandoeuvres: Fondation Hardt, 1962.

Schwartz, Stephen. "Islam's Wrong Turns: The Muslims Need a Bernard Lewis of Their Own." *National Review*, February 25, 2002.

Scruton, Roger. "The Defense of the West." Lecture presented at the Columbia Political Union, New York, April 14, 2005.

———. "What Ever Happened to Reason?" *City Journal* (Spring 1999).

Sheridan, R. B. "On the Abolition of Slavery: House of Commons, 17th March 1807." In *The Speeches of the Right Honourable Richard Brinsley Sheridan: With a Sketch of His Life. Edited by a Constitutional Friend*. 3 vols. London, 1842.

Sherwin-Wine, S., and G. T. Griffith. "Seleucus I." In *The Oxford Classical Dictionary*, 3rd ed., edited by Simon Hornblower and Antony Spawforth. Oxford: Oxford University Press, 1999.

Sophocles. *Ajax*. Translated by R. C. Trevelyan. In *Complete Greek Drama*, edited by W. J. Oates and Eugene O'Neill Jr. Vol. 1. New York: Random House, 1938.

Sordi, M. In *Aufsteig und Niedergang Der Römischen Welt*, edited by Hildegard Temporini and Wolfgang Haase. Berlin and New York: Walter De Gruyter, 1975–, 2.30.1, 1982.

Southam, Brian. "The Silence of the Bertrams." *Times Literary Supplement*, February 17, 1995.

Sterne, Laurence. "Reply to Sancho. July 27, 1766." In *The Norton Anthology of English Literature: The Restoration and the Eighteenth Century*. New York: Norton, 2000.

Stokes, Hugh. "John Frederick Lewis R. A. (1805–1876)." *Walker's Quarterly* (1929).

"Synteresis." In *The Oxford Dictionary of the Christian Church*, 3rd ed., edited by F. L. Cross and E. A. Livingstone. Oxford: Oxford University Press, 1997.

Talbot, Marianne. "Against Relativism." In *Education in Morality*, edited by J. M. Halstead and T. McLaughlin. London: Routledge, 1998.

———. "Relativism," *Sunday Times* (London), July 24, 1994.

"Theodulf." In *The Oxford Dictionary of the Christian Church*, 3rd ed., edited by F. L. Cross and E. A. Livingstone. Oxford: Oxford University Press, 1997.

Timmons, Traci. "Habiti Antichi et Moderni di Tutto il Mondo and the 'Myth of Venice.'" *Athanor* 15 (1997): 28–33.

Trautman, Thomas R. "The Lives of Sir William Jones." In *Sir William Jones, 1746–1794: A Commemoration*, edited by Alexander Murray. Oxford: Oxford University Press, 1998.

Trilling, Lionel. "Kipling." In *The Moral Obligation to Be Intelligent: Selected Essays*. New York: Farrar, Straus and Giroux, 2000.

Tsigakou, Fani-Maria. "The Rediscovery of the Hope Drawings." *Cornucopia* 1, no. 5

(1993–94).

Vick, Karl. "Opiates of the Iranian People: Despair Drives World's Highest Addiction Rate." *Washington Post*, September 23, 2005.

Voltaire. "Alexandre." In *Questions sur l'Encyclopédie, par des amateurs*. 1773.

Washbrook, D. A. "Colonial Discourse Theory." In *The Oxford History of the British Empire*. Vol. 5: *Historiography*, edited by Robin W. Winks. Oxford: Oxford University Press, 1999.

Watkin, David. "A Case of Regency Exoticism." *Cornucopia* 1, no. 5 (1993–94).

Weinberg, Steven. "A Deadly Certitude." *Times Literary Supplement*, January 17, 2007.

White, J. M. "Introduction." In Edward William Lane, *Modern Egyptians*. New York: Dover, 1973.

Wilkins, C. "Inscription on a Pillar near Buddal, Translated from the Sanskrit." *Asiatick Researches* 1 (1788).

———. "A Royal Charter of Land, Engraved on a Copper Plate." *Asiatick Researches* 1 (1788).

Windschuttle, Keith. "The Cultural War on Western Civilization." In *The Survival of Culture: Permanent Values in a Virtual Age*, edited by Hilton Kramer and Roger Kimball. Chicago: Ivan R. Dee, 2002.

———. "Edward Said's 'Orientalism' Revisited." *New Criterion* 17, no. 5 (January 1999).

———. "The Ethnocentrism of Clifford Geertz." *New Criterion* 21, no. 2 (October 2, 2002).

———. "Liberalism and Imperialism." In *The Betrayal of Liberalism*, edited by Hilton Kramer and Roger Kimball. Chicago: Ivan R. Dee, 1999.

Web Sources

Abdorrahman Boroumand Foundation. http://www.abfiran.org/english/foundation.php (accessed November 2006).

"Adoration of the Magi." Getty Museum Web site. http://www.getty.edu/art/gettyguide/artObjectDetails?artobj=900 (accessed October 2006).

"Ahemadinejad Begins 2006 with Escalated Violence against Women and New Gender Apartheid Policies in Iran." Women's Forum Against Fundamentalism in Iran Web site. http://www.wfafi.org/wfafistatement23.htm (accessed November 2006).

Al-Afif al-Akhdar: "How Our Narcissistic Wound and Religious Narcissism Combine to Destroy Our Future," "Why Religious Narcissism is the Golden Collar [Obstructing] Our Assimilation into the Modern Age," and "Irrational Religious Education is the Obstacle to the [Arabs'] Joining the Modern Age." *Elaph.com*, June 15, 16, and 23, 2003. Excerpted in *MEMRI*, no. 576, September 21, 2003, www.memri.org/bin/articles.cgi?Page=archives&ID=SP57603 (accessed October 2006).

"Alcuin." Catholic Encyclopedia Online. http://www.newadvent.org/cathen/01276a.htm (accessed October 2006).

Anderson, Robert. "A Parisian Disco? Rameua's 'Les Indes galantes.'" *Music & Vision*, September 7, 2005. http://www.mvdaily.com/articles/2005/09/indes1.htm (accessed October 2006).

Asian Human Rights Commission Web site. http://material.ahrchk.net/charter/mainfile.php/eng_charter/ (accessed October 2006).

"Bellini, Gentile." *Encyclopedia Britannica* Online. http://www.britannica.com/eb/article-9015282 (accessed October 17, 2006).

"Blessed Maurus Magentius Raubanus." Catholic Encyclopedia Online. http://www.newadvent.org/cathen/12617a.htm (accessed July 2006).

Brown, Eric. "Stoic Cosmopolitanism." Eric Brown Research List. http://www.artsci.wustl.edu/~eabrown/abstracts.html#cosmo (accessed March 2006).

Burman, Thomas E. "Juan de Segovia and Quran Reading in Europe, 1140–1560." http://www.cishsydney2005.org/images/Burman_paper.doc (accessed June 2006).

———. Web site at the University of Tennessee. http://web.utk.edu/~history/f-burman.htm (accessed June 2006).

"Carolingian Schools." Catholic Encyclopedia Online. http://www.newadvent.org/cathen/03349c.htm (accessed March 2006).

"Carpaccio, Vittore." Louvre Catalogue Online. http://www.louvre.fr/llv/oeuvres/ (accessed October 2006).

"Chassériau, Théodore." WebMuseum, Paris, Web site. http://www.ibiblio.org/wm/paint/auth/chasseriau/ (accessed November 2006).

"Child Protection." UNICEF Pakistan Media Centre. http://www.unicef.org/pakistan/media_1775.htm (accessed January 15, 2007).

"Delacroix, Eugène." WebMuseum, Paris, Web site. http://www.ibiblio.org/wm/paint/auth/delacroix/ (accessed November 2006).

Eibner, John. "Eradicating Slavery in Sudan." *Boston Globe*, February 22, 2006. http://www.boston.com/news/globe/editorial_opinion/oped/articles/2006/02/22/eradicating_slavery_in_sudan/ (accessed November 2006).

Esfandiari, Golnaz. "Iran: Prize-Winning Documentary Exposes Hidden Side of Society," http://www.rferl.org/featuresarticle/2005/3/D8E8A186-D2F9-4345-9554-E6AA22C9408.html (accessed June 2007).

———."Iran: New Ways Considered for Tackling Growing Drug Use among Young People." Eurasianet.org. http://www.eurasianet.org/departments/insight/articles/pp120703.shtml (accessed January 15, 2007).

Fausto Zonaro Web site. http://www.faustozonaro.it/ (accessed November 2006).

Feser, Edward. "We the Sheeple? Why Conspiracy Theories Persist." *Technology, Commerce, Society Daily*, September 20, 2006. http://www.tcsdaily.com/article.aspx?id=092006B (accessed January 12, 2007).

Glazov, Jamie. "Symposium: Islamic Anti-Semitism." FrontPageMagazine.com, October 31, 2003. http://www.frontpagemag.com/Articles/ReadArticle.asp?ID=10581 (accessed November 2006).

Harriot, T. *A briefe and true report of the new found land of Virginia*, part 3. 1588. http://xroads.virginia.edu/%7ehyper/hariot/1590–3.html (accessed October 2006).

"History: From 1784–1861." Archaeological Survey of India. http://asi.nic.in/index2.asp?sublinkid=28 (accessed January 12, 2007).

Human Rights Solidarity. http://www.hrsolidarity.net/mainfile.php/2001vol11no67/148/ (accessed January 12, 2007).

Islamic Republic of Iran Crimes. http://www.iricrimes.org/mission.asp (accessed November 2006).

Keskar, Sharad. "Introduction to *Kim*." *Kipling Journal*. http://www.kipling.org.uk/bookmart_fra.htm (accessed November 2006).

Langworth, Richard M. "'Our Qualities and Deeds Must Burn and Glow': Churchill's Wisdom Calls to Us across the Years." *Finest Hour* 112 (Autumn 2001). http://www.winstonchurchill.org/i4a/pages/index.cfm?pageid=280 (accessed December 2006).

Les Peintures Orientalistes Web site. http://orientaliste.free.fr/index.html (accessed November 2006).

Lindsey, Ursula. "Egypt's Grand Mufti Issues *Fatwa*: No Sculpture." *Christian Science Monitor*, April 18, 2006. http://www.csmonitor.com/2006/0418/p01s02-wome.html (accessed October 2006).

"Liotard, Jean-Etienne." Musée d'art et d'histoire, Geneva, Web site. http://www.villege.ch/musinfo/mahg/musee/presse/liotard/liotard2.html (accessed November 2006).

Mahmoud, Fatma Abdallah. "Accursed Forever and Ever." *MEMRI, The Middle East Media Research Institute*, Special Dispatch Series, no. 375, May 3, 2002, http://memri.org/bin/articles.cgi?Page=archives&area=sd&ID=SP37502 (accessed January 15, 2007).

Minissale, Gregory. "The Synthesis of European and Mughal Art in the Emperor Akbar's Khamsa of Nizami." *Asian Art*, October 13, 2000. www.asianart.com/articles/minissale/index.html (accessed January 12, 2007).

National Campaign on Dalit Human Rights (NCDHR). http://dalits.org/default.htm (accessed October 2006).

"Official Laws against Women in Iran." Women's Forum Against Fundamentalism in Iran. http://www.wfafi.org/laws.pdf#search=%22plight%20of%20women%20in%20Iran%20%22 (accessed October 2006).

Olearius, Adam. *The Voyages and Travels of the Ambassadors*. Translated by John Davies. 1662. http://depts.washington.edu/uwch/silkroad/texts/olearius/travels.html (accessed August 2006).

Orientalist Artists. http://orientaliste.free.fr/biographies/index.html (accessed October 2006).

Pallavi, Aparna. "Indian Racism." Bolloji.com, September 10, 2006. http://www.boloji.com/wfs5/wfs677.htm (accessed October 6, 2006).

Pipes, Daniel. "God and Mammon: Does Poverty Cause Militant Islam?" *National Interest* (Winter 2002). http://www.danielpipes.org/article/104 (accessed January 12, 2007).

Rai, Raghu. *Calcutta*. http://www.magnumphotos.com/c/htm/FramerT_MAG.aspx?Stat=Portfolio_DocThumb&V=CDocT&E=2K7O3RBQ95I8&DT=ALB (accessed November 2006).

———. "Regime Change Iran." http://www.regimechangeiran.com/ (accessed November 2006).

"St. Isidore of Seville." Catholic Encyclopedia Online. http://www.newadvent.org/cathen/08186a.htm (accessed March 2006).

Syrian Human Rights Committee. http://www.shrc.org.uk/data/aspx/d3/1813.aspx (accessed October 2006).

Talbi, Muhammad. *Dialogue interreligieux ou conflireligieux pour Dialogue de Témoignage, d'Emulation et de Convergence* (Interreligious Dialogue for Convergence). http://www.unesco.org/webworld/peace_library/tunisia/andalous/french1.htm (accessed January 9, 2007). Originally published in *Revue d'Etudes Anadalouses*, Tunisia.

Timmons, Traci. "About This Site." Vecellio.net: The Works of Cesare Vecellio. http://www.vecellio.net/about.html (accessed October 2006).

"Theodulf." Catholic Encyclopedia Online. http://www.newadvent.org/cathen/14579b.htm (accessed March 2006).

INDEX